AF652763

# MIZORAM: DIMENSIONS AND PERSPECTIVES

## ABOUT THE EDITOR

**Prof. Jagadish K. Patnaik** is currently the Dean of the School of Social Sciences, Mizoram University (A Central University). He has obtained his Ph.D. from the Queen's University, Kingston, under the prestigious Commonwealth Scholarship (1989-1993). A Gold Medallist in M.A., he was also the topper in B.A. (Hons.) with Distinction from Berhampur University, Orissa. Prof. Patnaik has a number of research publications to his credit besides a book titled India and the GATT: Origin, Growth and Development.

# MIZORAM: DIMENSIONS AND PERSPECTIVES

## Society, Economy and Polity

*Edited by*

**JAGADISH K. PATNAIK**
Professor and Dean, School of Social Sciences
Mizoram University (A Central University)
Aizawl, Mizoram, India

**CONCEPT PUBLISHING COMPANY, NEW DELHI-110059**

**Cataloging in Publication Data—DK**
*Courtesy:* D.K. Agencies (P) Ltd. <docinfo@dkagencies.com>

**Seminar on Peace and Development in the North East (2006 : Shillong, India)**
Mizoram : dimensions and perspectives : society, economy and polity/ edited by Jagadish K. Patnaik.
p. cm.
Papers presented at the Seminar on Peace and Development in the North East, held at Shillong during 25-26 September 2006.
Includes bibliographical references.
Includes index.
ISBN 13: 9788180695148
ISBN 10: 818069514X

1. Mizoram (India)—Politics and government—Congresses. 2. Mizoram (India)—Economic policy—Congresses. 3. Justice, Administration of—India—Mizoram—Congresses. 4. Local government—India—Mizoram—Congresses. 5. Mizoram (India)—Social conditions—Congresses. 6. Mizoram (India)—History—Congresses. 7. Peace-building—India, Northeastern —Congresses. I. Patnaik, Jagadish Kumar, 1959- II. Title.

DDC 954.166 22

All rights reserved. No part of this work may be reproduced, stored in a retrieval system, or transmitted in any form or by any means, electronic, mechanical, photocopying, micro-filming recording or otherwise, without the prior written permission of the copyright owner and the publisher.

ISBN 13-978-81-8069-514-8
ISBN 10-81-8069-514-X

First Published 2008

© Jagadish K. Patnaik

*Published and Printed by*
Ashok Kumar Mittal
**Concept Publishing Company**
A/15-16, Commercial Block, Mohan Garden
New Delhi-110059 (INDIA)

*Phones* : 25351460, 25351794
*Fax* : 091-11-25357103
*Email* : publishing@conceptpub.com

# Preface

*Mizoram: Dimensions and Perspectives* is intended to meet the long standing need of the students and scholars for a better understanding of the hill state in the North East India. So far there is hardly any good text book of this sort on Mizoram dealing specifically with the post-accord phase. The developments in the pre-insurgency and during the insurgency have been dealt with at length though, there is no systemic book worth the name has been written so far. There is no doubt that Mizoram as a state of the Indian Union is over two decades old. It was originally a district under the greater Assam state until 1972 when it became a Union territory. The two decades old insurgency movement that took place during 1966-86 had severely dampened the growth of the state. The peace accord of 1986, however, put a stop to the deceleration. Following the onset of peace the state gradually limped back to normalcy and development process is picking up. Interestingly enough, this is the only peace accord in the region which has survived the test of time without any single instance of violation. It is rather amazing that everybody is curious to know about the reason why and how this accord continues to hold good in sustaining peace. There are numerous factors that work in its favour though, now scholars working on peace and conflict resolution studies are really interested to understand the dynamics of Mizo society to relate it to the longish peace.

In fact, the idea of editing this volume was mooted by the editor after attending a seminar in Shillong on the theme titled "Peace and Development in North East" in September 2006, which was organized jointly by the North East Council, Institute for Defence Studies and Analysis and the North Eastern Hill University. The editor presented a paper titled 'Mizoram: A Model of Peace.' The discussions that followed in the seminar motivated for editing this volume. Most of the delegates were curious to know about the factors that contribute to peace in Mizoram. There were also even suggestions to replicate the Mizoram model in the context of other states which are turbulent ridden. In this context it is important to understand the various dimensions of the state which serve as the parameters of peace. Moreover, the process of signing the accord and the post-accord experience of the state and the civil society provide succour for understanding peace and development in the state. Mizoram has to go far ahead in the field of economic development; though, the trends in the direction indicate that peace can be sustained with development.

The contributors have been experts in their respective fields. It has been the intention to produce a compendium on Mizoram so that the various dimensions of the state would figure with diverse perspectives. The editor has been careful in not intruding into the freedom of the contributors. As the authors have been given the freedom to write about their perspectives, the editor does not bear any responsibility for the opinions expressed by the authors. In any case, we hope that this book will serve the purpose of catering to everybody's interest.

**JAGADISH K. PATNAIK**

## Contents

## List of the Contributors

**Mr. C. Lalhmanmawia**, Sr. Lecturer, Government Kolasib College, Kolasib.

**D. Zaitinvawra,** Research Scholar, Department of Social Work, Mizoram University, Azawl.

**Dr. E. Kanagraj**, Lecturer, Department of Social Work, Mizoram University, Aizawl.

**Mrs. Irene Colbert**, Lecturer in Political Science, Government Lunglei College, Lunglei.

**Dr. J. Doungel**, Lecturer in Political Science, Lawngtlai College, Lawngtlai.

**Dr. J.V. Nunchunga,** Lecturer in Economics, J. Thankima College, Aizawl.

**Mr. J. Zahluna**, Lecturer in Political Science, Johnson College, Aizawl.

**Dr. Jagadish Kumar Patnaik**, Professor and Dean, School of Social Sciences, Mizoram University, Aizawl.

**Dr. K. Robin**, Lecturer, Department of History and Ethnography, Mizoram University, Aizawl.

**Dr. L.H. Chuanawma**, Lecturer in Political Science, P.U.C. College, Aizawl.

**Mr. L.T. Pudaite**, Retired Indian Foreign Service Officer and Formerly Ambassador to Korea, Myanmar, Slovakia, Bosnia, Herzegovina.

**Mr. Lallianchhunga**, Lecturer, Department of Political Science, Mizoram University, Aizawl.

**Dr. (Mrs.) Lalhriatpuii**, Lecturer in Economics, Mizoram University, Aizawl.

**Mr. Lalthakima**, Lecturer in Political Science, Pachhunga University College, Aizawl.

**Dr. Lalrintluanga**, Lecturer (Sr. Gr.), Department of Public Administration, Mizoram University, Aizawl.

**Mrs. Lalsangliani**, Research Scholar, Department of Political Science, Mizoram University, Aizawl.

**Dr. Lianzela**, Professor and Head, Department of Economics, Mizoram University, Aizawl.

**Dr. NVR Jyoti Kumar**, Professor, Department of Commerce, Mizoram University, Aizawl.

**Mrs. Padmalaya Mahapatra**, Reader in Political Science, Mizoram University, Aizawl.

**Dr. Pravakar Rath**, Professor and Head, Department of Library and Information Science, Mizoram University, Aizawl.

**Mr. S. Nongpoknganba Meitei**, Advocate, and Part-time Lecturer, Mizoram Law College, Aizawl.

**Dr. Vanlalchhanwna**, Reader, Department of Economics, Mizoram University, Aizawl.

# Introduction

JAGADISH K. PATNAIK

Scholastic work on Mizoram has been very scant. There have been a very few doctoral dissertations done on Mizo society, culture, and polity, though there have been some independent works done on different aspects of Mizo society as well, but they are also dated. In fact, whatever little work that has been done so far relate to the history of insurgency and the formation of separate statehood. There are some works done on various aspects of Mizoram which are written by Mizo intellectuals in Mizo language. Interestingly, the post-accord phase of Mizoram has been witnessing some dramatic changes, though there is hardly any serious work worth mentioning about this phase. More so is the case by the local intellectuals. It is, of course, difficult on the part of a single author to address all the important issues and dimensions on Mizoram. This is mainly because the intellectual resources in the state have been limited and also the research materials are scattered in the sense that much of them have been available in the local language.

This edited volume is an attempt at filling the gap. *Mizoram: Dimensions and Perspectives* is an attempt to pull up some of the important dimensions and perspectives on Mizoram that would provide some basis for our understanding of this hill state of the North East. The chapters are written mostly by young Mizo scholars who have evinced keen interest in understanding and analyzing the Mizo society. There are also some chapters in this volume contributed by scholars, mainly from the academia, working in Mizoram. These scholars have tried to present their perspectives on the different dimensions of Mizoram. A brief discussion on these chapters is relevant here.

The first chapter provides a general profile of Mizoram. The authors, Patnaik and Thakima, have tried to basically present the important facts about Mizo history, culture, demography, society, and polity. Although mostly compilation of facts on Mizoram in general, the authors have attempted to provide a background about the various dimensions and perspectives of the state. There are also attempts to present the scenario for portraying the state as a 'model of peace'. It has been argued that following the signing of the 'peace accord' in 1986, the state has been marching ahead in its pursuit of economic development. There is no doubt that a lot has to be done for improving the living standards of the rural folks on the hills of Mizoram. Nevertheless, Mizoram is one of the smaller states in the North East region which is grappling with its post-accord syndrome in a most peaceful manner compared to other states.

The second chapter deals with one of the important aspects of Mizoram history. In hindsight, insurgency may seem to be one of the prime movers for the formation of Mizoram state of the Indian Union. The arduous journey of signing the peace accord may also seem as a matter of fact. In reality, however, there are numerous theories about the strengths and weaknesses of the insurgent movement. Pudaite, a retired Foreign Service officer, has made a meticulous effort to reinterpret the story of the negotiation for peace between the insurgent group, Mizo National Front, and the Government of India. He has identified three main factors which contributed to the peace process. First, it was due to the desire of the MNF leader, Mr. Laldenga, for an early solution that really vindicated the process. Second, the role of the establishment, that is the Congress (I) government in the Centre, was very crucial. The author is clear in lauding the contributions of Lal Thanhawla though, he mentions about Indira Gandhi's determination for having peace on the hills. Lal Thanhawla was magnanimous in sacrificing his office of chief minister to give way to Mr. Laldenga during the interim phase. It is contended, however, that had he declined to step down, things would definitely have been against him. Third, the civil society, especially the church, played a commendable role in bringing peace. The church leaders were fearless and acted as the spokespersons of the civil society. The common people were fed up with insurgency. They wanted peace as soon as possible. It is the will of the people, which has been responsible for the continuing peace in the state.

In the third chapter, Lalrintluanga has attempted to provide an historical overview of insurgency movement in Mizoram. The movement for separate identity of the Mizo dates back to the colonial times, though it turned out to be a violent insurgency movement due to the utter neglect by the then state of Assam during the 1959 famine in the Mizo hills. The author has made attempts to look into the circumstances in which the movement for statehood was initiated and sustained by some political parties within the constitutional framework of the Indian Union. Although the movement for separatism did paralyze the statehood movement for nearly two decades, peace in the state came into being because of the contribution of the mainstream political parties which were spearheading the statehood movement.

The chapter on the state and civil society in the post-accord phase deals with the discontentment in the state of Mizoram in the aftermath of the signing of the peace accord. Discontent is just short of conflict, though it may not conflagrate into a violent conflict situation eventually. In this chapter, Patnaik argues that despite the semblance of peace in the state there has been discontentment among the people due to the unresolved issue of ethnic identity of some smaller groups. These smaller groups need to have full scale integration in the larger space of the pluralist Mizo community. The author, in main, has dealt with the Bru, Chakma, and Hmar tribes and their problem in the state. Although these three tribes may have inter-state and international ramifications, the author has tried to focus the issue within the context of Mizoram. There is also the discontent among the common people regarding the growing corruption in the state. The mushrooming growth of numerous non-government organizations to fight out corruption in the state in the last couple of years testifies the extent of frustration among the common people. Many of these organizations have made use of the Right to Information Act to expose the corrupt practices of the government.

E. Kanagaraj in his empirical work "Changing Agrarian Structure and Livelihood Options in Mizoram" has attempted to address the issue of transformation in rural livelihood options in Mizoram. The socio-economic dimension of the transition from the shifting cultivation to semi-settled agriculture has been examined in the context of the agrarian structure. It has been noticed that there has been significant and substantial changes in the rural agriculture economy. The study, however. contrary to the general understanding, reveals that the change in the cultivation pattern hardly impacted on the income of the cultivators. This is owing to, of course, the decline in the actual operational holdings. The study also deals with the perception of the farmers on the social and ecological consequences of switch over from the shifting cultivation.

Vanlalchhawna discusses the challenges and opportunities for sustaining peace in Mizoram. According to him, the two decades insurgency movement had a devastating impact on the economy and social structure of the Mizo society. The first decade following the peace accord has brought about moderate rate of growth, though the state has been able to make commendable success in health and education which are the foundations of sustainable development. He argues that peace in Mizoram can be sustained and deepened by improving the quality of governance and expanding economic opportunities for all sections of Mizo society. The author has also outlined the strategy for sustaining peace and development in Mizoram.

Lianzela has attempted to study the political economy of Mizoram by examining one of the important programmes undertaken by the MNF ministry. MIP (Mizoram Intodelhna Project) has been launched for bringing about self-sufficiency of the rural poor in Mizoram. The purpose of the project is to minimize the undesirable consequences of shifting cultivation. The farmers are assisted in adopting a more profitable, sustainable permanent system of farming through agro-horticulture, soil conservation, and animal husbandry sectors. The author contends that MIP would bring about self-sufficiency in food grain supply. This can, however, be possible only with fuller participation and cooperation of the people at the grassroots level and with a high degree of decentralization.

There is a cataclysmic change taking place across the globe in the areas of trade and commerce. The world has flattened following the triple convergence, as Thomas Friedman has it saying.[1] There are new horizons, and trade is now conducted in a borderless world. NVR Jyoti Kumar has tried to capture the scenario in the context of the NER with a special reference to Mizoram. He contends that border trade between the NER and its neighbouring countries have a vast potential; and its benefits might also accrue to Mizoram. The government and politicians of Mizoram as well as of NER have to learn from the success stories of other states in the mainland. By having good infrastructure, both in terms of technology and logistics

---

1. Thomas Friedman, *The World is Flat: A brief History of the Globalized World in the 21st Century* (New Delhi: Penguin Books India Pvt. Ltd., 2005).

Mizoram can develop in a borderless environment for the conduct of trade with its neighbours.

In a more scientific study of the development dimension of Mizoram, Nunchunga examines the inter-district development disparities in the state by making use of some statistical tools like Indexing method, Deprivation method, and Principal component analysis. The study is unique in the sense that it is for the first time developmental disparities of Mizoram as well as the inter-district developmental disparities have been examined by any trained economist. He has tried to combine all the variables of economic development and run Principal component analysis using SPSS software to extract only few variables that are more important than others for economic development. "What emerges from the above analysis is that agriculture and allied sector backed by good road communication is of utmost importance for achieving accelerated rate of economic development, and education sector is equally important along with women participation in industry related management."

The organizational structure of the state is impinging upon the autonomy of the numerous independent ethnic communities living in the state. Since democracy and decentralization can afford the opportunity for the smaller communities to develop within the framework of the state, the Constitution of India in the sixth schedule provides for autonomous district councils. These autonomous district councils have provided the necessary space for the distinct ethnic communities to maintain their identity. Doungel studies the implications of the sixth schedule in Mizoram in the three autonomous district councils that are in existence now. He has attempted to highlight the conditions which necessitated the introduction of district councils in Mizoram. The change in the structure and functioning of the district councils have brought about not only transformation in the living standards of the people, it also provided voice to the smaller communities within a pluralist structure.

Freedom and democracy can find expression with the active performance of political parties in the state. National political party like the Congress party has been a key player in the politics of Mizoram state. Since the beginning of Mizoram as a Union Territory and then subsequently as a state, the Congress party has been an inseparable part of the political process. Chhuanawma studies the performance of the Congress party since the Union territory days.

While appreciating the commendable performance of the Congress party, the author also examines the negative aspects. During its almost 17 years of rule the Congress has been instrumental in bringing about change in the state.

Democracy at the grassroots is the essence of devolution of powers. Mizoram has a strong tradition of grassroots democracy before it became a Union territory. The real grassroots democracy finds its manifestation in the village council system that was introduced to replace the traditional chief system. Zahluna, who has made a study of the structure and function of the village council system, argues that there is hardly any evidence of political will to make radical changes in the village council system. There is no doubt that in its half a century of existence, the village councils in Mizoram have made grassroots democracy more vibrant. Even then, there is still the need to reform the decentralization mechanism by bringing in reforms at the village level. Lalsangliani has examined the working of the grassroots democracy in the village council level and concluded that village councils over the years have become mere 'figureheads'. During the District council time, grassroots democracy was very vibrant. Now, however, there is a total erosion of authority by the Local Administration Department under the state government. There is a need to restructure the village level democratic process in Mizoram.

Historically the institutions and structures of Mizoram have developed in the context of Christianity and the colonial administration. In fact, the structures and cultures in Mizoram impinge on the Christian and tribal religious institutions. K. Robin's study on the Lakhers in Mizoram brings in a new perspective on the impact of Christianity and the colonial administration. While there is a total transformation in the society and economy, the tribes in the North East face 'unprecedented ecological crisis'. The forest resources have turned into semi-deserts and eventually it has completely altered the sources of economy. With the introduction of market economy, there is over dependence on others for importation of commodities. Christianity and colonialism might have significant contribution towards improving the cultural lives of the Lakhers, these have worked negatively on the community development in many respects resulting in the erosion of their traditional cultures and practices.

Women's position in Mizo community is such an important dimension that can hardly be overlooked. Mizo community is predominantly, though, patriarchal in nature. Women are, however, conspicuous in almost all aspects of community life. Irene Colbert has attempted to study women and politics in Mizoram. In this chapter, she has argued that there are efforts by numerous organizations to raise the status of women, but it has failed to do so in the field of politics. This is due to the practice of minimal participation of women in the community in decision making since pre-Christian era. Although Christian education has contributed to the raising of the status of women, patriarchy still continues to be the cause for the subordinate position. On the other hand, Padmalaya Mahapatra in her "reflections" contends that democratization of the socio-economic and political structures can promote women's empowerment and emancipation. For this purpose, she argues that in the context of Mizoram there is the need to have increased proportional representation of women in all elected bodies and fixation of certain quota of 'offices' therein. This can be realized with the increased political activities by autonomous women's bodies. In a still more focused study, Lalhriatpuii argues that the best predictors of female labour force participation in Mizoram as a whole are female literacy, freedom to work for women, sex ratio, and attitude of males towards female work. In her empirical analysis she demonstrates that male literacy does not hold any significant role in predicting the behaviour of women work participation.

Human rights are part and parcel of any democratic society. The human rights situation in the North East states is still more an important aspect of study. The different tribes in the region have been undergoing transition from tradition to modernity. In the process there are issues of human rights violations. This is also owing to the traditional structures which inhibit the growth of democratic institutions. Lallianchhunga has studied the human rights situation in Mizoram from the perspective of judicial administration in the state. In this chapter, the author has attempted to trace the history of human rights and judiciary in Mizoram since the colonial times to the present. One thing notable about Mizoram is that the separation of judiciary and executive has yet to come about into reality. This indirectly affects the human rights situation. The important civil society groups are still inclined to follow the traditional power structure where there is diffusion of authority. This has really delayed the implementation of the separation of judiciary and executive in the state. Thereby the situation of human rights in the state has only worsened, the author contends. The challenge before the Mizo civil society is to sensitizing the people about human rights in a more effective manner.

Lalhmanmawia in the next chapter discusses about the community based organizations and human rights in Mizoram. Although this chapter is mainly concerned with the role of these non-government organizations operating in Mizoram, the author feels, it has to be understood with due care keeping in mind the complications and sensitivities involved in it. The writer insists for change in the attitude of the leaders of the NGOs in the direction of human rights awareness and sensitivity.

In a completely different perspective though, Pravakar Rath contends that information and communication technology (ICT) and its applications in higher education will bring about a sea change in the North East and especially in Mizoram. He suggests for developing ICT infrastructure in higher education in NER and Mizoram to bridge the "digital divide" between the states and nations. Rath argues that an ICT based higher education can lead to societal transformation in the shape of knowledge generation, exchange and utilization that can help India to become a knowledge superpower.

# Chapter 1

## Mizoram
## *A Profile*

JAGADISH K. PATNAIK and LALTHAKIMA

### I. GEOGRAPHY: TOPOGRAPHY AND DEMOGRAPHY

The present Mizoram state, being the 23rd state of the Indian Union attained its statehood in February 1987. Mizoram occupies an area of great strategic importance in the north-eastern corner of India having a total boundary length of 630 miles—with Bangladesh and Myanmar. It is geographically situated between 22°20′and 24°27′ (N) and 92°20′and 94°29′(E) latitudes. The tropic of cancer runs through the territory.[1] The state is divided into eight districts:

(i) Aizawl,
(ii) Champhai,
(iii) Kolasib,
(iv) Lawngtlai,
(v) Lunglei,
(vi) Mamit,
(vii) Chhimtuipui,
(viii) Serchhip.

*Note*: This chapter is intended to provide some basic information about Mizoram. The facts are compiled from various works done on the state, though a general overview of the state will enable the reader to get a background about the various dimensions and perspectives on Mizoram. The authors have tried to make it more general rather than being too detailed.—*Editor*

Mizoram is a mountainous region. The climate in Mizoram is pleasant to cool in the upper reaches and humid in the plains but still tolerable. The winter temperature varies from 11 degree Celsius to 24 degrees and in the summer the range is 18 to 29 degrees which makes the state fairly comfortable throughout the year. The average rainfall is 254 centimetres every year.[2] But in the southern part of the state it rains more. Mizoram has hill ranges running from north-south. They are higher in the middle and taper off at both ends. The average height of the hills is 900 metres (about 3,000 feet) but the highest peak, the Blue Mountain also known as Phawngpui tlang by the Mizo goes up to 2,165 metres and is located in the southern part of the territory. The hills are steep and are separated by rivers which flow either northwards or to the south, and create deep gorges between the hill ranges.

With an area of 20,987 sq. km, Mizoram has a population of 891,058 (Eight lakh ninety one thousand and fifty-eight) people according to the 2001 census. The density of population is 42 persons per sq. km. Out of 891,058 population 459,783 are males and 431,275 are females. Mizoram at present is a highly educated state with high literacy levels, and what is more, the level of literacy among the women is also high, which hardly obtains anywhere in India.[3] The main languages spoken are Mizo and English. According to the 2001 census, the percentage of literacy in Mizoram is 88.49. Due to the high literacy rate it attained second position in literacy rates in India next to the state of Kerala. It was already high in the decadal census when the literacy in the state was 81.23 per cent.[4] About 90.69 per cent of males are literate and 86.13 per cent of women can read and write. This extremely high level has been attained over the years during which the Christian missions, who were allowed in by the British played a notable role in the spread of education. They not only converted the people to Christianity—now 95 per cent of the Mizo being Christians[5]—they also set up schools in every village. Now there is a church and school in every village in Mizoram, and the people laid great deal of stress on education without which no real progress of any kind is possible.

Mizoram or Zoram as it is sometime called is unique in many ways. The dwellers of the state are known commonly as Mizo. The history of the origin and coming of the Mizo to their present habitat is shrouded in mystery.[6] No systematic research has been made so far. There is no recorded history. As per the oral tradition, the Mizo ancestors emerged from a cave or rock known as Chhinlung somewhere in China. They moved through Tibet into the Hukwang valley in Burma over time, following the Chindwin into the Kubaw valley to enter the Lushai Hills in the 18th century.[7] It is accepted that Mizo are of Mongoloid stock and are believed to have immigrated into their present habitat, possibly sometime between 1400 and 1700 or 1800 AD from the upper Burma. However, the Mizo historians such as K. Zawla and Rev. Liangkhaia, who wrote "Ancient History and Culture of the Mizo People" and "History of Lushai" have argued that the Mizo were in the Chin Hills in Burma from 1400AD to 1700AD and their gradual movements of migration started between 1700 and 1730 or 1740 AD. But in the absence of any written history, more accurate dates about the movement cannot be envisaged. The Mizo, however, migrated from Burma for mainly two reasons— pressure of the Chin or the stronger clans of Burma and the pressure of over population. Thus the Mizo are not only concentrated in the present state of Mizoram, but also in the states of Manipur, Cachar District of Assam, Chittagong hill tracts and Chin Hills (Burma).

The Mizo as a whole possess a unique social system,[8] which although patriarchal, yet the women play a key role in the social affairs and in the process of betterment of the society. But, when looking at the inheritance law of the society the Mizo women lived a lower status, especially in the inheritance of property rights, they have not much inheritance right. The Mizo law of inheritance is simple. As a rule, the property of a father goes to the youngest son. The father may, however, give shares to other sons also. If there is no male issue, the property goes to the next of kin on the male side. The Mizo society did not provide for inheriting any property by the women. In fact the women were confined to the kitchen and the field and had no voice in the day to day affairs of the village. But in the family, the women do exert a lot of influence on their men folk and Mizo men in general are very much attached to their women. Before the annexation of the Lushai hills, due to fear of attacks from enemies, Mizo selected village sites on top of the hills from where they could observe enemy movements. Stockades used to be constructed for the protection of their village. There are very few springs at higher altitudes and hill tops in Mizo Hills, and as such, Mizo have to depend on rain water for irrigation and drinking purposes.[9]

## II. HISTORICAL OVERVIEW OF TRADITIONAL INSTITUTIONS

In the administrative life of the past, each village was a unit of administration under a chief called Lal. The chiefs were the supreme ruler of each of their own jurisdiction. In the beginning the selection for a chief was based on the power and ability of a person who had a capacity to command a large number of people and to repeal any attack by other chiefs or enemies as the early Mizo society lived a life of inter-clan clashes. Safety was need of the common people from the invasion of the neighbouring villages. The chieftainship thus, originated in the physical and intellectual power of any person.[10] The strength of a person and his ability to protect the people from the dangerous threats of the opponents is a necessary criterion to become a chief of any village. It thus appears that the institution of chieftainship emerged out of the collective needs of group life which characterized tribal living. There is no definite record regarding when the institution took concrete shape. But it is asserted that it happened at an early stage of evolution in their group life. Most of the historians of Mizo origin traced back the origin of chieftainship to the days of Zahmuaka who had six well-built sons. One of his descendants was Sailova from whom the Sailos of today trace their descent. In the long run, the Sailos became the most powerful chiefs and they ruled practically over the entire Mizoram at the time of the advent of the British.

- *Chieftainship*: The institution of chieftainship in the Mizo society was autocratic. The ruler exercises all authority and people have no right of participation in the government. The chief who control and regulate all aspects of the village life in accordance with the customary laws of the land was helped by the elders; they assist and advise the chief in the discharge of his duties. The chief was the all in all ruler within his jurisdiction excluding the religious function which were entrusted to a priest who was subject to the control of the chief.

  The functions of the chief were precise and definite. He was the guardian of the people, Commander-in- chief of his army and the chief justice. He settled all disputes between the villagers, supplied the essential commodities and in times of need, provided shelter to the fugitives. He distributed land for cultivation among the villagers. The chief had the right to receive and protect the fugitives who sought refuge in his house, by accident or unintentionally one may kill another. To escape punishment such persons sought shelter in the chief's house. Again, the chief had the power to banish any subject from his village and confiscate all his property. But this power was seldom exercised due to the deterrence on the part of the chief that if he behaves rudely, the people of his village might migrate to the jurisdiction of other chiefs. After the British ruled over the country, the powers of the chief were greatly reduced. Originally, he had the power of life and death over his subjects. But the British curtailed his powers and he had no power to sentence anyone for death.[11] The chief was only an instrument at the hands of the British although they retained much of their powers. Under the British, he must carry out all the orders issued by the superintendent. He must maintain the inter-village paths. He must scrutinize and certify the House Tax Assessment Register prepared by the circle interpreter. He must report to the superintendent all epidemics, heinous crimes, violent deaths and serious accidents occurring within his jurisdiction and the presence of foreigners within his area. He must also see that the village writer maintained a list of those who obtained licence to keep a gun. He must also see that all the villagers contribute free labour for the construction works of public utility. He was also responsible for the construction and maintenance of zawlbuk (Bachelors' dormitory).

- *Other Important Functionaries*: Other important functionaries in Mizo society in the pre-British period were the *Lal upas*, the *Zalen,* the *Ramhual, tlangau, thirdeng, puithiam* and *sadawt. The Lal upas* (elders) were those who were selected by the chiefs in his individual choice, nominated without considering the option of the villagers. They were generally chosen from amongst those who were rich, well-informed, broad-minded and influential persons in the village. They performed a multifarious functions and their main function is to assist the chief. The council of the elders had the right to select suitable lands for cultivation and not to pay taxes. Next to the *Upas* were the *zalens* who were also selected by the chief from aristocracy. They were required to help the chief in times of distress. They were entitled to exemption from tax (*Fathang)* and selected a plot of land for cultivation and house construction. *Ramhual* was the next village officer. He was selected by the chief from certain well-known families. Their main function was the distribution of land among the villagers for cultivation and for the construction of houses by the villagers. They were allowed to select the best piece of land for cultivation. The fourth village officer was *Tlangau* (Village crier) who announced the orders of the chief to the villagers. He also was exempted from the tax of *Fathang*. Another important functionary was *Thirdeng* (Blacksmith) who made and repaired agricultural implements of the villagers. The village priest known as *Puithiam* was another village officer. He must be available at all times to perform all kinds of ceremonies and next to the *puithiam* was *sadawt* (A special priest) who performed all the ceremonies of national importance in the life of the early Mizo society. No village could ignore their importance and they kept the historical Mizo society having a well-defined social system. Though there were some clans who practiced a slightly different administrative system, most of the village administration systems in the pre-British era in Mizoram were same.

- *Zawlbulk*: In the traditional Mizo society, there was an institution known as "Zawlbuk. This institution provides us a great insight about the social life of the Mizo. "Zawlbuk" used to occupy a central position in the organization and administration of a Mizo village in earlier days, and had functioned as the most potent institutionalized mechanism of social control.[12] "Zawlbuk" is a Mizo word which means "Bachelors House". But it has much deeper significance than what can be understood from such a simple connotation. It was not only the physical abode of the youth of the Mizo village, they were also shaped into a responsible adult member of society. The Mizo society in those days was deeply static in its form and had no problem of social change in its outlook. So the main function of the zawlbuk which the Mizo elders wanted to project before the youth was the assimilation of their cherished traditional forms and social norms and values than anything else. As education and formal teaching had not yet been established, the family was responsible for the education of their young men. The weakness and inadequacies of such a training and education, to meet the real needs of the society were counted through the collective mechanism of the zawlbuk.

With the passage of time, the process of modernization enveloped almost all aspects of life in Mizo society. The remarkable feature of the Mizo society is that it has yet retained the character of a closely related society even after modernity has reached their society. The Mizo form a close-knit society; they are classless and casteless. The society is cohesive and in times of crisis they have the capacity to rise as one community to safeguard and protect their identity and their social and cultural life. The notable feature of the Mizo society is of the so-called 'tlawmngaihna' which means 'service above self' or 'to sacrifice oneself for the good of others'. It is a value system which is very old, yet promoted in such a way that the society absorbs within its fold the modern social impact without sacrificing the core value of the custom. P.R. Kyndiah, the ex-Governor of Mizoram state in his statement about this system observed that "the core element which constitute the base and thrust of the society lies in the observance of tlawmngaihna an ancient code of ethic and conduct in which even today the Mizo of the present generation are ardent believers".[13] One writer remarked, "All voluntary services are rendered by the Mizo people under this useful custom of tlawmngaihna, which is continuing till now in Mizo society."[14] This value system is one of the important factors which safeguarded Mizo society from class distinction.

## III. RELIGION

The social life of the Mizo since the advent of Christianity experienced a constructive changes. The society is decorated by the church which has an immanent influence on the life of the people. Before the advent of Christianity, the Mizo who then considered themselves as a powerful militant people took great pride in subduing their rival tribes and raiding their neighbours. Apart from the inter-clan clashes, raids were directed towards the people in the plains of Cachar, Manipur, Sylhet, Tripura and the Chittagong Hill Tracts. It was one of such attacks on 27th January 1871. The Mizo killed a British named James Winchester at Alexandrapore and abducted his daughter Mary. The abduction of Mary Winchester heralded a new era in the history of the Mizo people. A millionaire in London, Robert Arthington having heard about the incident organized a missionary society called 'Arthington Aborigines Mission'. On the 11 January 1894 two missionaries, F. W. Savidge and J.H. Lorraine sponsored by the society arrived at Sairang near Aizawl to start the work of spreading the gospel among the Mizo. Special revivals brought about phenomenal success of the gospel preaching in Mizoram and by the end of the Second World War in 1945, the whole land comprising Mizoram embraced Christianity and the percentage of Christian religion has come up to 95 per cent as of now.

Religion has affected the life of the Mizo in a comprehensive but amazing way. No fact of spiritual or social life escapes its attention. An individual, a family and the community becomes so involved in the activities that the church indeed occupies a pivotal role in the society. Church activities do not confine only to preaching the gospel. It puts into action the teaching of Christ to love and care for the less fortunate. There are many social services run by the church which offers shelter to orphans and a home to the poor and destitute.

However, Mizo society is now at the cross road, many changes in social practices, social and economic life have taken place. At present, experience shows, the classless society among the Mizo in the past is now being replaced by the emergence of the classes (Neo-middle rich class) and class distinctions.[15] Reason for classless society in the past was that the Mizo society was traditional, whose structure was confined to limited production based on the pre-Newtonian science and technology. The main occupation of the Mizo was a slash and burn method of cultivation and hunting. The land belonged to the community and everyone was self-sufficient in economy. As such there was no institution of private property. But after the independence of India, with the expansion of developmental activities in Mizoram, the tribal economy is experiencing the impact of a fast enlarging money economy. The bad effects of a capitalistic money-economy are pronouncedly evident in different spheres of Mizoram today, which have helped the growth of the institution of private property in the Mizo society[16] this leads to the emergence of classes such as Neo-Middle rich class and the poor. The stark reality of the present Mizo society is these classes sufficient in economy. As such, there was no institution of private property. But after India attained independence with the divisions are on constant increase in the present Mizo society, as these classes already exist in other areas of the country. Thus the Mizo society has suffered the class distinctions which rear its ugly head due to the capitalist economy during the last five decades.

## IV. POLITICAL PROFILE OF MIZORAM

The advent of the British into Mizoram brought about many changes into the political lives of the Mizo. As a result of the second military expedition of the government of British India by 1889-90, the whole Mizoram was annexed to British for administrative purpose. The Lushai (Mizo) Hills were formally included in British India under the proclamation by the Governor General of India-in-Council on September 6, 1895[17] divided into two parts, viz. North Lushai Hills as a part of Assam and South Lushai Hills as a part of Bengal for administrative purpose. A political officer was in-charge of North Lushai Hills District whereas the South Lushai Hills District was under the charge of the superintendent. The District administrators, therefore, carried out administrative work but did not interfere much in the internal affairs of the Lushai. The Lushai chiefs carried on their rule in their villages under the guidance and instruction of the District administrators. For more convenience the South and North Lushai Hills were amalgamated as one Lushai Hills District of Assam on 1 April, 1898.

The growth of political consciousness among the Mizo cannot be clearly stated as there can be some controversy regarding the growth of political consciousness in the society. It was said that the First World War was the first intervention of the Mizo in the international affairs and gained a broader outlook after their participation in the First World War. During the First World War a labour corps consisting of 2,100 Mizo men was raised and sent to France under Lt. Col. Playfair. This 27th Labour Corps under Col. Playfair and Rev. D.E. Jones of the Welsh Mission earned a good name for itself when on active service in France. They were back at Aizawl in June 1918, they were met with a welcome ringing with joy and emotion. Out of 2,100 men who originally set out, 2,029 men had come back to Aizawl.[18] The Labour Corps was disbanded in June 1918, immediately after their return to Lushai Hills. There was some growth of political consciousness with the return to the Lushai Hills of a batch of Labour Corps recruits sent to France during the First World War.[19] But no forum or party emerged to articulate political demands before the Simon Commission or subsequently, the district remained an 'excluded area' under the 1935 Act. Due to the absence of party or forum in pursuance of the political consciousness gained after the First World War it was also said that 'Till the end of the Second World War the Lushai had no political consciousness'.[20] These two ideas though seemingly inconsistent could be justified on ground of the absence of party or any political forum. Though there was a political consciousness after the First World War, there was no visible political awakening or political activities of any kind in the Lushai Hills District.

Before 1952, the Lushai Hills was a district of the province of Assam. It was not represented in any legislature, Central or provincial. Under the Government of India Act, 1919, the Lushai Hills was declared as a backward area and therefore not represented in the Assam Legislative Council.[21] Under the Government of India Act, 1935, the Hill areas of Assam were divided into two categories—excluded and partially excluded areas. Under this Act, the Lushai Hills district was declared as an excluded area.[22] The word "excluded" only implied that the Lushais are "Outside the direct control of the provincial legislature". It implied that Lushai Hills was outside the control of the provincial Legislature of Assam and the responsibility to parliament for its administration was vested in His Excellency the Viceroy as Crown representative; the Superintendent was to administer the Lushai Hills as representative. Until 1935 the areas were administered by the Governor of Assam-in-Council. The subject of backward areas was termed as a "reserved subject" for the Assam Governor's special interest. This procedure emanated from the reforms introduced under the Government of India Act of 1919.

The Mizo commoners in the long run, realized fully, that the autocratic chief's rule was oppressive and unbearable but they could do nothing because the position of the chiefs was fully safeguarded by the British Superintendent. Since 1940 the Mizo began to think for better status. They did not like to be labelled even as a backward people. At the same time, they did not like to be swamped by the plains people. So when Robert Reid, the Governor of Assam visited Lushai Hills in December 1940, the Lushai put one of the points to him that they would be better off if they were attached to the Hills of Burma. There was another reason for political consciousness that the provision regulating the election of the one chief and the commoner from each circle as representative to the circle representative's committee set up in 1946 caused a resentment and led them to protest on the ground that their representatives should be more because their population is more than the chiefs.

History has proved that the will of the people cannot be suppressed for long. The proud tribal who cherished their freedom felt suffocated under the repressive authority of the superintendent and the chiefs. The "Quit India Movement" and the political activities of the Congress and other political activities had greatly influenced the educated Lushai youth in the Lushai Hills. The Lushais who had joined the services and had the opportunity to mix with people of other nations and states of India during the war also played an important role in the political awakening of the Lushais. They did not like the idea of handing over power to the "chiefs councils" and wanted to be part and parcel of the Union of India and enjoy all the privilege enjoyed by the people of other provinces after independence. So Mizo youth wanted to organize themselves into a political party. As a result, a political party called Mizo Union, for the first time ever in the Mizo history was formed in 1946 by R. Vanlawma who organized the youth and educated people in Lushai Hills District on April 9, 1946. Initially, that new political party was named "The Mizo Common People's Union Party". Later the name of the party was simplified as the Mizo Union. Mr. Pachhunga was elected as the first president of the party. Mr. McDonald, the then superintendent in Lushai Hills was said to have blessed the creation of the party.[23] The basic objections of the party were to do away with the chieftainship, ensure better employment opportunities for Mizo in Mizoram and reunification of all Mizo under one administrative unit.[24]

The Lushai educated youth wanted to have their own elected representatives in the Government. The Mizo Union was originally constituted to check illegal extractions by the chiefs and protect the villagers from exploitation. The chief's council that consisted of the representatives of the chiefs and nominees of the Superintendent set in process measures to counter the activities of the Mizo Union. The party retaliated by launching a movement to boycott the chiefs altogether. It started as a peaceful non-violent movement in 1948. The villagers were instructed by the Mizo Union workers not to carry out the orders of the chiefs or pay them any taxes. But very soon, violence broke out and the government also got involved on the ground that it was supporting the authority of the chiefs. The people were urged to defy the authority of the government as well as the chiefs and join together in a full scale Civil Disobedience movement.

The formation of the "commoner" Mizo Union demanding the abolition of chieftainship alarmed the chiefs and traditional elites who banded together to form the United Mizo Freedom Organisation (UMFO) in July 1947. The formation of this political party was initiated by Pu Lalmawia with the support of the Mizo chiefs and blessings of the then Superintendent on July 5, 1947. The main factor for the formation of the party was to counter the activities of the Mizo Union party, which had already become popular among the Lushais. The Mizo chiefs supported UMFO only because of their enmity towards the Mizo Union. The UMFO party could not last long because it lacked any constructive programmes and economic policy. The main cause of its failure is poor financial backing. After few years, UMFO had merged with the East India Tribal Union (EITU) under the chairmanship of Capt. Williamson Sangma. While the Mizo Union Party which was a stronger party, it stood for autonomous status for Mizo within India, the UMFO had stood for sovereignty outside the Indian Union without much noticeable support from the people. But, the newly formed "United Mizo Freedom Organisation" (UMFO), which was opposing the Mizo Union and championing the cause of the chiefs, was not looked upon with much favour by the government, as there were indications that it was working for the break away of the Lushai Hills District from the Indian Union and for linking the district with the Chin hills of Burma. The move of the Mizo Union to get the hereditary chieftainship abolished and to have Village Councils with members elected by the people of Mizo Hills themselves were considered more important by the people than the merger with Chin hills of Burma. The problems of forming Village Councils had eclipsed all the enthusiasm for bringing about union with Burma. The Mizo Union decided to remain with India. They wanted the Mizo Hills to remain as part of the Assam province and sent its assent to Assam Government. The British Superintendent of the Lushai Hills took it upon himself to convene a joint meeting on August 14, 1947 of the UMFO and a faction of the MU named the Mizo Union Council which had developed certain differences with the parent body. The conference explored the political options available to it and, finding union with Burma and independence impracticable, demanded safeguards for Mizo customary law and land rights, continuance of inner line restriction and the option to secede from India after ten years. However, chieftainship was perceived as an imposition and an obstacle to rising Mizo aspirations and it was this factor that perhaps weighed most in popular support for autonomy and development within India.[25]

Meanwhile the other sub-tribes of Mizo such as Pawi and Lakher became politically awakened and put a demand for separate autonomy so that they could manage their own internal affairs themselves. In response to the pressing demand of the Mizo Union Party a political status called Lushai Hills District Council was set up in 1952 for Lushai. A year later, in 1953, Pawi, Lakher Regional Council also came into being for Pawi, Lakher and Chakma. This was the time when the Mizo Union and the Congress ministry in Assam had a friendly relationship between each other. In 1954, two important legislations were enacted, facilitated by the friendly atmosphere between the Mizo Union Party and the Congress ministry in Assam. The first was the acquisition of the chief's rights, which came into force on April 1, 1954. The second one was Lushai Hills District (Change of Name) Act of 1954.

By an Act of the parliament, called the "Lushai Hills Disrict (Change of Name) Act No.18 of 1954, the name of the "Lushai District" was changed to "Mizo District", with effect from April 29, 1954. The term "Lushai" gradually disappeared from Mizo District. The "Assam Lushai Hills District (Acquisition of Chief's Rights) Act, 1954, came into force from April 1, 1954 in the area under the jurisdiction of Lushai District Council and from April 15, 1954 in the Pawi-Lakher region. The political status deprived the chiefs and their ministers of all their privileges and thereby abolished the chieftainship in Mizoram. The rights and interest of 259 Lushai and 50 Pawi-Lakher chiefs were taken over by elected village councils.[26] The post of the superintendent had been abolished and the whole area placed under the Deputy Commissioner and the Chief Executive members of the District and regional council, as mentioned earlier, the Mizo Union, holding the reins of the District Council

Administration, abolished the special privileges of the Lushai chiefs and their elders. However, all the chiefs were compensated in cash for the loss of their power and tribute. Since the voice of the people was very strong, the chiefs had no choice but to accept their fate calmly and be content with the compensation given to them. Some of the chiefs utilized the money received wisely, but majority of them squandered it and left a trail of misery for their dependents. The acquisition of the chief's right was certainly a bold and socialistic step taken by the Mizo Union keeping with the provision of the Democratic Indian Constitution. The district administration was in the hand of the Mizo Union Party who got majority in the District Council election held on 5 April 1952.[27]

**Famine and Insurgency**

There was a popular famine known by the Mizo as "Mautam" in the year 1959. The Mautam famine used to occur in Mizoram with an interval of every 50 years. The word "Mautam" means death of the bamboo. When the bamboos of the hills were flowered, it produced seeds like grains of wheat, and that particular variety of bamboo, like ordinary grass dries up. The seeds fall to the ground and before they sprout are eaten up by the jungle birds and rats. With the abundant supply of protein rich bamboo seeds, the rat grows and matures faster and produces a bigger litter than during the normal period. Earlier, a famine of considerable magnitude had taken place in 1911-12. People saw the flowering of bamboos all along the hill sides and realized its significance. So as a precaution, extra strong storage bins for food stuff were arranged and everyone thought that the serious famine could be avoided. But, as the paddy started ripening in the "jhums", rats appeared in the field overnight. The havoc created by the rats was terrible and very little of the grains was harvested. There were no roads to facilitate supplies to the remote villages. There were no organized porters, animal transport or mule tracks to carry the air dropped food supplies.

As a result of the outbreak of "Mautam" famine in Mizo district during 1959 causing immense hardship to the people. A relief organization called the Mizo National Famine Front was formed in 1960 to mobilize assistance for the distressed. Mizo youth were voluntarily involved in relief works in town and the remote villages. The Mizo villagers only saw the Mizo National Famine Front volunteers delivering food stuff in their villages and gave all the credit to Laldenga and his band of volunteers. Being in close contact with the MNFF volunteers, the poor villagers were bound to believe the words of the MNFF and take it as a gospel truth that the Assam government had neglected the Mizo and had not taken any worthwhile remedial measures before and during the famine period. Somehow the famine months came to a close. The MNFF under the leadership of Pu Laldenga, Pu Lalnunmawia, Pu Sainghaka and Pu Vanlalhruaia got the praise and all the credit for the supply of food stuffs to the remote villages.[28] When in 1960, the Mizo Union parted company with the Congress following the sharp differences on the famine relief operations and the issue of the state language was finalized, Pu Laldenga found it as the opportune moment to drop the word "Famine" from its appellation and transform Mizo National Famine Front itself into a new political party.[29] The word 'Famine' was dropped on 22 October 1961 and the organization became a political party. The demand for "Sovereign Independence for greater Mizoram" was raised. In a speech delivered on August 6, 1961 as president of the MNFF, Pu Laldenga had openly declared that Mizo were "Mongolians" and not "Indians" and had appealed to the Mizo people to free themselves from "Indian colonialism and achieve complete Independence". He had argued that the Mizo had been given a separate administration by the British, and Mizo have the right to be separate from India, especially as they had been completely neglected after independence by the Government of India. In December 1965 and 1966 the MNF with its volunteers started their activities by collecting funds from the people. On the 28th February, 1966 the MNF volunteers started an open armed revolt against the Indian government demanding sovereign independence state for the Mizo.[30] Since then the Indian troop moved into the district and the MNF volunteers with their leaders went underground. In the wake of MNF insurgency, political parties including the Indian Nation Congress which was set up in 1961 and headed by A. Thanglura could not make much headway. On 1st March 1966, the government was in for the unkind surprise to find the MNF insurgents launching raids on almost all the Security Posts simultaneously all over the Mizo Hills. "That was the Operation Jericho in action."[31] And thus began one of the series of longest negotiations in the history of the country. They dragged on for more than ten years and witnessed a number of failures in between. The ban of MNF under the Unlawful Activities (Prevention) Act of 1967 came sooner than expected.

When the insurgency in Mizoram was brought under control by the Indian Security Forces, the Mizo Union and the Congress party in Mizoram formed a new political body known as United Mizo Parliamentary Party with a view of making the demand for statehood more effective which was already demanded by the Mizo Union Party in 1963. Owing to the united effort and political skill of the said parties, the Government of India in 1971 agreed the proposal to constitute the Mizo Hills District into a Union territory for the time being. The implementation of the North-East Area (Reorganization) Act, 1971 raised the status of Mizo Hills District into a Union Territory on the 21st January 1972 with a 33-member Legislative Assembly (30 elected and 3 nominated) and one Lok Sabha seat, administered by a Council of Ministers and Lt. Governor as the administrative head. Accordingly, the already existed three regional councils were elevated to the status of the district councils such as the Pawi District Council, Lakher District Council and Chakma District Council with a view to having more autonomy in their own affairs. This was enforced by the government of Mizoram *vide* Notification No. LDP 8/72/53, dated 29 April 1972.[32]

In the first general election to the 30-member assembly seats of Mizoram Union Territory held on 28th April 1972. The Mizo Union came to power with a thumping majority and Mr. Ch. Chhunga became the Chief Minister. In 1974 the Mizo Union was merged with the Congress heralded by Mr. Lalthanhawla and a coalition ministry was run by the two parties under the chief ministership of Mr. Ch. Chhunga. During this decade a new political party which was known as the Mizo People's Party (MPP) was formed at Aizawl on December 11, 1974 and was headed by Mrs. Sanglianchhungi (ex-MNF). Brig. T. Sailo supported Mrs. Sanglianchhungi and her party, while campaigning under the banner of 'Human Rights Committee' so as to garner public support to his cause. When he officially formed the People's Conference, the MPP leaders felt let down and renamed their party as 'Mizo Democratic Front' (MDF) and declared that their party would continue the fight for "total independence of Mizoram" from the point where the MNF left off. But after the leaders were detained, the party had resigned its stand for total independence for Mizoram and stood for a "Greater Mizoram" within the Indian Union.[33] With the victory of the Janata Party in the general elections of March 1977, Morarji Desai was elected leader of the Janata Party and became the Prime Minister of India. With the hope of getting some benefits from the new Janata Government which had come to power in Delhi; some of the dissident Congress leaders like Pu J. Thanghuama and Pu Hrangdawla, even though not recognized by the All India Janata Party, formed the Mizoram Janata Party (MJP).[34] Within a short period, the MJP was able to increase membership mainly by securing defections from the Congress and some other opportunists waiting to get a chance to attain power and prestige. In a memorandum submitted to the Prime Minister of India in December 1977, the MJP urged that it was indispensable to elevate the political status of Mizoram with sufficient autonomy and special safeguards within the framework of the Constitution of India.[35]

On the 28th April 1975 another political party called Peoples Conference was formed under the leadership of a retired Brigadier of Indian Army named Thenphunga Sailo, who rapidly gained popularity as he initially formed Human Rights committee to safeguard the rights of the Mizo people who suffered excesses, and atrocities committed by the operating armed forces in Mizoram. The declared objectives of the human rights committee were:

- To move the courts against the action of the Government and Security forces for groping of villages in Mizoram since 1967.
- To uphold the legal rights of the oppressed civil population in Mizoram.
- To institute suitable measures including filing court cases against individual army officers and jawans who had allegedly created atrocities against the Mizo.

In fact, the exit of Pu Laldenga to Pakistan impelled the Mizo people to be on the look out for a suitable leader capable of handling the Mizoram problems. People looked him as an answer to their hope. Then, the Peoples Conference party won the Assembly polls of 1978 and the mid-term of 1979 and Mr. Thenphunga Sailo became the Chief Minister. During his ministry there were very often negotiation between the hostile underground MNF leaders and the Government of India but no result came out. In the fourth election to the Mizoram Legislative Assembly held on 25th April 1984, the Congress (I) under the leadership of Mr. Lalthanhawla rose to power securing 20 out of 30 seats and Mr. T. Sailo and his party suffered a great set back securing only eight seats.

Then the ruling Congress party fervently processed negotiation for peace between the Central Government and MNF leaders. Subsequently peace accord was signed on 30 June 1986 by the MNF leaders, the Central Government, and the ruling Congress leaders of Mizoram. Consequent upon the passage of the Constitution (53rd) Amendment Bill and the State of Mizoram Bill (1986) by the Parliament on August 7, 1986, Mizoram has been elevated from the status of a Union territory to be the 23rd state in the 1st schedule of the Constitution.[36] The State of Mizoram Bill also provided for a 40 member single chamber Legislative Assembly, three Districts, nine sub-divisions, three Autonomous Hill District Councils, and 301 Village Councils. But now the number of the Districts has gone up to 8. The first election in the state of Mizoram held in 1987 was won by the MNF ministry led by Pu Laldenga. Though, they suffered a setback due to the strength regained by the Congress (I) between 1989-98, the MNF at present is ruling the state since 1998.

Apart from the appearance of the regional clan-based political parties, Mizoram is noticing the participation of the national parties like the Bharatiya Janata Party, the Janata Dal, Lok Shakti and other parties which were seen as an alien parties by the Mizo. The appearance of these parties clearly indicates that the Mizo people are politically awakened and their political consciousness not only concentrated to the region-based politics. While some political parties are severely disliked by most of the Mizo people on ground of religion, their identity as an Indian led them accept even those political parties and as such openly contested elections within the state. But, till now a rare chance has occurred for the national parties to get power except for the Congress (I) which was formed in 1961 in Mizoram felt by the people as the home party. The weak position of the national parties except the Congress (I) in the state can be taken as an indication of the isolationism that persisted in the minds of the Mizo.

Therefore, looking back at the history of the state, it is acceptable that the improvement in social conditions of the Mizo paved the way for their political consciousness. The working of the Mizo with the other nations through the World War made the people politically conscious. The discontentment among the educated class of the society urged the then educated generation to imitate the broader world that resulted in the formation of a political party in the district. Their demand became higher and higher upon the Central Government. The increasing demand of the Mizo politically could not be blamed because it was a time when the Union of India was in restructuring; many nationalities were in demand of a better status and in these hours Mizo were unexceptional. As such many states of the present India attained their statehood during these eras.

The political consciousness that noticed a steady progress resulted in unsatisfaction of the people. Coupled with regionalism and economic backwardness there was an insurgency movement threatening the peaceful life of the region, the present state was plagued by the insurgency for twenty years. The insurgents were at the initial stage aimed at fighting for an independent sovereign status, to secede from the Indian Union. Though they failed to fulfil their intention, they put a severe pressure on the Indian government and their insurgent activities were one of the most prolonged insurgency movements in the country. The heed from the Central Government had inclined towards placating the insurgents. Therefore, gave the status of statehood to the Mizo. Hence, the improvement in socio-political life of the Mizo which has started in the indefinite period and progressing slowly at last, led to the attainment of statehood to become one of the states of India as of now.

## MIZORAM: A MODEL OF PEACE!

Now, Mizoram has celebrated the "Peace Fest 2006" to mark the 20th anniversary of peace in the state on the 20th April last year. Mizoram is unique in several respects. It came into being as a separate state following the signing of the peace accord after an arduous struggle of insurgency of two decades.[37] This accord seems to be the longest peace accord that has stood the test of time in the North East India. Contrary to the popular belief in the mainland, Mizoram exudes a semblance of peace and amity in the region. The pace of development in the region is far better than other neighbouring states. Save for a few infinitesimally small segment of population, which is minor aberration, the Mizo Accord serves as a model of Peace in the region. Whatever little pockets of resistance that exist at the moment may be due to slow pace of integration of the people living in the hinterland

The important groups of the Mizo civil society such as the Church, the YMA and the MZP now play a crucial role in sustaining the peace process that heralded following the signing of the peace accord twenty years ago. It is observed that these organizations work in tandem without contradicting each other's objectives. The transition from tradition to modernity and the process of development have been in progress with minimal tension in the society. This is owing to the cohesive nature of the Mizo community. The homogeneity of Mizo community is also a contributing factor in sustaining peace. The impact of Christianity in providing an identity to the Mizos as an ethnic community provides a fillip to the peace process as well. There are other distinct minority tribes like the Bru, Chakma and Lai who have been living in the state. Their aspirations for separateness from time to time have been rearing the ugly head. This, however, has marginal impact on the larger fabric of the Mizo society. These distinct tribal communities have separate autonomous district councils. The process of integration of these tribal groups into the mainstream Mizo society has been slow due to historical reasons. The process of peace in Mizoram is, however, vindicated by the recent signing of an understanding between the Bru insurgents and the government of Mizoram. The Brus have agreed to surrender their arms, and the government of Mizoram is undertaking the process of rehabilitation. The process of economic development in the state in the last 15 years has been remarkable, despite the pockets of poverty in the rural areas. This has also contributed to the peace in the state.

The emergence of Mizoram as a peaceful state in the last two decades can serve as a model to the neighbouring states in the region. The crucial role of the civil society groups needs to be given due place in such peace process so that any peace effort would find succor from it.

## NOTES

1. R.B. Veghaiwall *Census*, 1951, Assam Lushai Hills District Census Hand Book, p. 1.
2. Shyam Nath, *Panorama of North East India*, p.135.
3. *Ibid.*, p. 146.
4. *Ibid.*
5. *Ibid.*
6. *Ibid.*, p. 3.
7. B.G. Verghese, *India's North-East Resurgent: Ethnicity, Insurgency, Governance, Development*, p. 135.
8. P.R. Kyndiah. *Pillars of Mizo Society and Thoughts to Share*, p. 5.
9. C.G. Verghese & R.L Thanzawna, *A History of the Mizo*, Vol. 1, p. 12.

10. R.N. Prasad, *Government and Politics in Mizoram* p. 49.
11. R.N. Prasad, *op. cit.*, p. 65.
12. C.G. Verghese, & R.L., Thanzawna, Vol. I *op cit.*, p. 18.
13. P.R. Kyndiah, *op. cit.*, p. 5.
14. R.N. Prasad, *op. cit.*, p. 5.
15. *Ibid.*
16. *Ibid.*
17. *The Tribes of Mizoram: A Dissertation op. cit.*, p. 10.
18. C.G. Verghese, & R.L Thanzawna, *A History of the Mizo,* Vol. II, p. 341.
19. *The Tribes of Mizoram:A Dissertation, op. cit.*, p. 10.
20. *Ibid.*, p. 11.
21. V. Venkata Rao & H. Thansanga & Niru Hazarika., *A Century of Government and Politics in North-East India,* Vol. III, Mizoram, p.100.
22. *Ibid.*
23. C.G. Verghese, & R.L Thanzawna, *op. cit.*, p. 354.
24. *Ibid.*
25. B.G. Verghese, *op. cit.*, p.138.
26. *Ibid.*, p. 139.
27. C. Chawngkunga, *Important Documents of Mizoram,* p. 322.
28. C.G Verghese & R.L Thanzawna., Vol. II, *op. cit.*, p.12.
29. *Ibid.*, p. 14.
30. *Tribes of Mizoram*: *A Dissertation, op. cit.*, p. 12.
31. N.C. Ashthana & Anjali Nirmal, *Terrorism, Insurgencies and Counter Insurgency Operations,* p.151.
32. *The Mizoram Gazette*, Aizawl, 5th May 1972.
33. C.G. Verghese & R.L. Thanzawna, *op. cit.*, p. 162.
34. *Ibid.*
35. *Ibid.*, p. 163.
36. Dr. Durga Das Basu, *An Introduction to the Constitution of India,* p. 252.
37. Consequent upon the signing of the "Memorandum of Settlement" between Laldenga, the President of Mizo National Front and the Union Home Secretary, R.K. Pradhan on the 30th June 1986, the two-decade-old insurgency problem in Mizoram was buried. See Mizoram Accord 1986 in Appendix 1.

## BIBLIOGRAPHY

Ashthana, N.C., & Anjali Nirmal, (2001). *Terrorism, Insurgencies and Counter Insurgency Operations* (Pointer Publishers, Jaipur).

B.G. Verghese, (1996). *India's North East resurgent Ethnicity, Insurgency, Governance, Development.* (Konark Publishers Pvt. Ltd., Delhi).

Basu, Dr. Durga Das, (2004). *An introduction to the Constitution of India* (Wadhwa and Company Law Publishers, New Delhi) 19th edition.

Chawngkunga, C., (1998). *Important Documents of Mizoram* (Published by Art & Culture Deptt., Aizawl).

Kyndiah, P. R., (1999). *Pillars of Mizo society and thoughts to share* (Published by Secretary, Law and Parliamentary Affairs Department, Government of Mizoram, Aizawl, Mizoram).

Prasad, R.N., (1973). "Evolution of party politics in Mizoram", *Political Science Review,* Jaipur Vol. 12 No. (3 + 4) 19.

Prasad, R.N., (1987). *Government and Politics in Mizoram* (Published by Northern Book Centre, New Delhi).

Rao, V. Venkata, H. Thansanga, Niru Hazarika (1987). *A Century of Government and Politics in North-East India,* Vol. III, Mizoram (S. Chand & Company Pvt. Ltd., Delhi).

Shyam Nath (2004). *Panorama of North East India* (Authors Press, Delhi).

The Mizoram Gazette, Aizawl, 5th May, 1972. *The Tribes of Mizoram: A Dissertation* (Published by Tribal Research Institute, Directorate of Art & Culture, Aizawl), 1994.

Veghaiwall, R.B., *Census 1951 Assam Lushai Hills District, Census Hand Book.*

Verghese, Brigadier C.G., V.S.M. (Rtd.) & R.L. Thanzawna M.C.S. (Rtd.) (1997). *A History of the Mizo,* Vol. I (Vikas Publishing House Pvt. Ltd., Delhi).

Verghese, Brigadier C.G., V.S.M. (Rtd.) & R.L. Thanzawna M.C.S. (Rtd.) (1997). *A History of the Mizo,* Vol. II (Vikas Publishing House Pvt. Ltd., Delhi).

# Chapter 2

## Negotiating with Insurgency and Holding on to Peace
### *The Mizoram Experience*

L.T. PUDAITE

---

### Introduction

Of the few detailed narrative available in English about the insurgency movement launched by the Mizo National Front on February 28, 1966, there is not one that has been written from experience by a prominent participant in the movement. A few books by such participants have recently been published in Mizo language. Even some of these books appear to have been written not entirely as objective records of events with some political points of view in mind. A reluctance to 'expose' former underground colleagues may also be inhibiting.

An attempt at a study of any aspect of the MNF insurgency movement, therefore, continues to face the problem of the lack of reliable and non-speculative materials. And the demanding exercise of personal interviews with original participants, in this case, in the peace initiatives in the early stages of the insurgency is necessary. I should mention here the illuminating discussions I had with R. Zamawia, MNF Defence Minister till mid-1971, who also allowed me to freely use his unpublished manuscript.[1]

#### THE GENETIC DICHOTOMY OF THE MNF

In order to understand the process of the negotiations that culminated in the signing of the Peace Accord on 30 June 1986 between the

MNF and the Government of India, it seems necessary to first delve into some aspects of the nature of the insurgency movement as well as the possible motivations of its prime initiators. In this process, the reasons why the Accord lasts in Mizoram may also become apparent, if not fully, at least partially.

There is a view rather prevalent in Mizoram today that the MNF leadership, particularly the late Laldenga had actually intended to lead the MNF party into insurgency whereas the bulk of the MNF cadres, especially the young intellectual elite and the less educated believed in the cause of 'independence' for Mizoram and were prepared for a protracted struggle for it.[2] Often quoted in support of this view is the statement of Laldenga made in what may be termed as the pre-insurgency peace talks with Mizo Union party leaders, Ch. Chhunga (L) and Pahlira in mid-December 1965. He was quoted to have said, "Even if we decide to change our plan (rebellion), our boys will kill us. You will have to understand our predicament." After explaining his views on the impossibility of secession from the Indian Union and the sufferings that rebellion would bring to the innocent people in Mizoram, Ch. Chhunga was said to have replied, "If Zoram (Mizoram) can be saved from trouble by the death of Laldenga and Chhunga, we should both be ready to make the sacrifice."[3]

The former Mizo Union leader, C. Pahlira's assessment was that the then Chief Minister of Assam, B.P. Chaliha was trying to use Laldenga and his party as an instrument to destroy Mizo Union, which was the ruling party then in the District Council of Mizoram.[4] In a memorandum submitted to Prime Minister Indira Gandhi on 22 June 1966, the Mizo Union leaders also openly accused Chaliha of having given "active and material support to MNF."[5] Apart from his political ambitions, Laldenga, of course, had his personal grouse against the District Council, from the services of which he had resigned as an accounts official upon being investigated on charges of embezzlement. The treatment meted out by the Assam Government to the secret visit to East Pakistan of Laldenga, MNF Vice President Lalnunmawia and Sainghaka, later MNF Home Minister, in early December 1963 was rather lenient. Laldenga and Lalnunmawia were arrested on their return on 24 December 1963. Despite the seditious implication of the visit they were released on 14 February 1964 on a written promise that they would confine their political activities within the bounds of the Constitution of India. Laldenga also claimed to have convinced Chaliha then that 'independence' was only his slogan and that his real aim was to capture power in the district council.[6] "Right from the start, the MNF made its military and secessionist intentions very clear. But the Assam Chief Minister wilfully chose to ignore it.[7] Mrs. Laldenga (Biakdiki) was also reported to have said in a speech at MNF party function commemorating Laldenga's birthday on 11 June 2003 that her husband had aimed to overthrow the District Council, not to plunge Mizoram into bloodshed.[8] The manner in which Chaliha reacted to have screamed, "Laldenga stabbed me on my back!" He also overturned his office desk and abruptly dismissed an ongoing meeting at the mention of Laldenga's 'duplicity'.[9]

On the other hand, as the result of his 1963-end visit to Dacca, by December 1965, the Inter Services Intelligence (ISI) in East Pakistan had already trained two batches of MNF Volunteers (MNV). With several hundred more locally trained volunteers, the stage had been set for the MNF rebellion. In other words, those who had joined MNF to 'fight for Mizoram independence' were now ready to strike. Yet, even at the last hours on the 28th February 1966, after the 'Zero' hour had been set and volunteers were positioning to strike their appointed targets, there appeared signs of wavering on the part of some leaders.

There were two meetings of the MNF leadership at different locations on that night, one for the top leadership and the other for civil leaders such as Senators and high officials, to whom the decision to strike was to be conveyed for the first time. The Senators group sent to the Cabinet group a last minute suggestion to postpone the strike on the ground of suspicion that there had appeared to be a leakage of information about their move. In the Cabinet Meeting, J.F. Manliana, Chief Justice, and Lallianzuala Sailo, Senate representative spoke at length in favour of postponement. Time was getting late, yet Laldenga would not speak. Defence Minister R. Zamawina finally had to explain the impossibility of postponement at that hour, upon which Laldenga simply said, "Yes."[10] In any case, having jumped into the clutches of the Pakistani ISI, Laldenga could not have avoided creating serious troubles against India at one time or other.

Laldenga left Aizawl on the night of 28 February 1966 and eventually arrived at Dacca with his family and personal staff and took shelter there. He was supported to camping from there to enlist support of foreign powers. He returned to Mizoram in December 1966 to attend a parliament session held at Sialsir village from 11 to

15 December and lingered in Mizoram for about a week and returned again to Dacca.[11] At the Sialsir meeting he was virtually 'forced'[12] to hand over the powers of the President to Vice President Lalnunmawia. Laldenga's long absence from the scene of action especially during the early stages of insurgency and his manoeuvres to have a grip over the MNF movement by remote control were also complicating factors behind 'the widening gap of understanding' between him and most of the educated MNF cadres.[13]

### The Seeds of Negotiations and the Role of Church/Civil Society

Apart from the probable attitude of the MNF leadership towards peace settlement that can be inferred from the foregoing, Laldenga's meeting with Rev. Zairema in mid-December 1965, a little over two months prior to the start of the rebellion, could be the first definite indication that some of the top leaders did not intend to prolong the insurgency. Laldenga was accompanied by Lalhmingthanga, Foreign Minsiter and C. Lalkhawliana, Finance Minsiter, when he personally requested Rev. Zairama to organize a 'Peace Mission', once the MNF rose in revolt, along the same line as that had been set up in Nagaland. At this meeting, Rev. Zairema suggested that the MNF might contest the then impending election to the District Council, instead of going underground. Laldenga stated that his party was not yet strong enough to win elections and that they were now not in a position to retreat from the underground.[14]

As a 'self-respecting' Mizo, Rev. Zairema could not bring himself to convey his conversations of December 1965 with Laldenga to the Government of India. Nevertheless, he pursued single-mindedly the idea of peace mission immediately upon the start of the MNF armed uprising. On March 12, 1966 the Standing Committee of the Presbyterian Church Synod held an emergency meeting, in which representatives of the Baptist Church of south Mizoram also participated. The meeting decided: (a) to issue a public declaration and an appeal; and (b) to constitute a Citizens Committee.[15] Thus, the important, perhaps crucial, role of the Church and the civil society behind the subsequent peace parleys had begun. Indeed, Church leaders like Rev. Zairema, Rev. Lasawma, Rev. L.N. Ralte and Rev. H.S. Luaia representing both the Presbyterian and the Baptist, the largest Christian denominations in Mizoram, had taken a stand against any attempt to seek help from China.[16]

The Public Declaration and Appeal issued by the Church amply demonstrated the views of the civil society in Mizoram for which the Church had in fact become the main rallying point. The Presbyterian Church issued a pamphlet stating that the Church condemned the violent activities of Mizoram, describing them as opposed to the teachings of the Gospel as also against the laws of human rights.[17] This was objected to by the MNF Government, which issued a counter order stipulating that those who violated any of their instructions would be brought to 'justice'.[18] At another meeting of Standing Committee of Presbyterian Synod on 14 March 1966, it was decided to form "Christian Peace Committee" with members drawn from both the Presbyterian and Baptist Churches. This committee issued another pamphlet on 8-9 September 1966 essentially reiterating the Church's stand against violence and appealing for peace. For the first time, Rev. Zairema, Rev. L.N. Ralte and Rev. H.S. Luaia, representing the Peace Committee secretly met Laldenga as Sabul village on 2 November 1966 where they unequivocally condemned the letters sent by MNF threatening the lives of many people and the force collection of funds by masked MNF men at gun point. On the peace initiatives, however, no advance was made, perhaps, because of the presence of R. Zamawia, the MNF Defence Minister, who reproached H.S. Luaia and L.N. Ralte "for being anti-MNF and not neutral, and thus unfit to act as peace feelers."[19]

In March 1967, the Peace Committee met Sainghaka, the MNF Home Minister, and wrote to him that in April that:

> You have taken up this course in the firm belief that by doing so you will create better conditions for our children and the future generations to come. We admire the courage of your conviction. However, we would like to remind you that India herself has never been one nation. The Telugus are as different from the Punjabis as the Bengalis are from Mizos, yet we together are determined to build one mighty nation. In this process, each of us has a right as well as responsibility, and the welfare of our children in future depends on how we discharge and exercise our respective rights and responsibilities. We would also like to point that any self-respecting government shouid have naturally adopted the same attitude as the Government of India has adopted towards you.

> It might also be realized that the Government of India, in trying to keep up this self-respect and integrity, have incurred a great loss and a number of her sons too have sacrificed their lives. We firmly believe that the Government would go a step further to meet the desires of the Mizo people.[20]

They also urged Laldenga in May 1967 to allow the insurgents to avail of the amnesty offer made by the Government of India and advised him that such gesture would open the possibility of negotiations.

The next move for talks was a secret meeting at Lengre village on 25 February 1969 arranged by Rev. Zairema and Rev. Lalsawma with C. Lalkhaliana, MNF Finance Minister, the only senior MNF official who had not taken shelter in East Pakistan by then. The meeting was set because B.C. Carriappa, the Commissioner of Cachar and Mizo Hills Division would be ready for talks. Lalkhawliana gave them the following note: *"Knowing full well the stand of the Indian Government from the Church leaders, I am prepared to work and do my utmost to help create conditions that would lead to peaceful solution of the present situation provided, of course, the Government of India is prepared to respond to my appeal.*" The Church leaders wrote to Cariappa in March 1969 and attached the note from Lalkahwliana.[21]

Lalkhawliana on his part moved to East Pakistan with the copy of the note he had issued and the message he had received from B.C. Carriappa. Soon after his arrival in East Pakistan, an MNF Cabinet Meeting was held at Rangmati on 17 April 1969, where he reported on his talks with the Church leaders. After a brief discussion, the Cabinet unanimously gave the MNF President, Laldenga full authority to explore the possibility of negotiations with the Indian authorities.[22]

As authorized by his Cabinet, Laldenga sent in late May 1969 Vanlalngaia, Director of MNF Intelligence Service and a ranking officer of the same directorate, Rozama, to meet B.C. Cariappa for making arrangements for negotiations. At the same time he was deputed to make contancts with Indian authorities. Vanlalngaia inquired from Laldenga as to what was his concept of political settlement for Mizoram. Laldenga said, "The Kashmiri parallel was already there. Settlement was made and Sheikh Abdullah was installed as Chief Minsiter," Vanlalganaia also insisted on a Cabinet authorization for his mission, which Laldenga had already obtained in April 1969.[23]

As B.C. Cariappa was away from his headquarters at Silchar, the MNF emissaries met M.V. Thomas, Assistant Joint Director of Subsidiary Intelligence Bureau, along with Rev. Zairma and Rev. Lalswama at Lailapur Forest Rest House on 12 June 1969. The message that Vanlangaia and his colleague were to convey to Laldenga was not put in writing and was in the form of "impression". The impressions they had are: (i) Any 'political settlement short of independence' could be discussed; (ii) The venue for negotiations could be in a neighbouring country; and (iii) In the mean time, the MNF forces should be allied with the Bengali freedom fighters in East Pakistan.[24]

Unfortunately, the Assam Police arrested the two emissaries near Karimganj on 15 June 1969 while on their way back to Dacca before they could convey to Laldenga the message they carried in their head.[25] As the news of their arrest and of the purpose of their mission came out in the press, Laldenga flatly denied any knowledge of their mission. At any rate, it could have been dangerous for him to own this up under the very noses of his Pakistani ISI minders. Instead, Laldenga deftly used this incident for managing a group of educated cadres who, he reckoned, had lost confidence in his leadership.

**The MNF Split and Escape to the Arakan**

He accused the group, sometimes referred to as "Dumpawl" or Blue, of backtracking from their original goals. "I led you out of India; but I may not be fit to lead you back to it,"[26] he said to the guerilla commanders, implying that there were other leaders who were plotting to compromise with the Indian authorities. In March 1970, substantiating what was often described at the time in Mizoram as the 'split in the MNF', he removed Lalnunmawia from the post of Vice President and installed S. Linazuala in his place. He also removed his Army Chief Sawmvela who was replaced by the MNF Defence Mininster, R. Zamawia. The leading members of the so-called moderate group of the Blue group, including R. Zamawia this time were arrested and put in prison in mid-1971 and were released on the eve of the MNF escape on 17 December 1971 from Bangladesh to Arakans in Myanmar. With the growth of Bengali freedom movement and with the future of Pakistan becoming increasingly uncertain, Laldenga had become evidently eager to come to a political settlement with India. After Vanlalngaia's aborted mission, in 1970 and 1971 he sent at least 6 groups of emissaries to make secret contacts with Indian

Government.[27] Initially, he used for these errands an elite group of his personal guards called 'State Security Agency (SSA)' like Capt. Sangliana, Capt. Lalhleia, Capt. Thanthuama, Capt. Vaninmawia and Police SP Langhenga. The message they carried with them was "If we have talks, we will be able to arrive at a peace settlement satisfactory to both parties." The standard reply from the Indian Intelligence was: "Government of India agrees to talk, provided the peace settlement is within the Indian Union." (R. Zamawia)

A group consisting of R. Liantluanga, MNF Deputy Commissioner of Bungkawn, Sailianpuia Sailo, an accounts officer and Lalruata, a ranking civilian official, seemed to have been taken seriously by the Indian authorities, perhaps, because they did not belong to Laldenga's personal staff. Except for the refusal by the Assam Chief Minister M.M. Chowdhury to meet them, (on the ground that he was "disgusted" at the duplicity of Laldenga), they met several high ranking intelligence and Army officials and were even taken to New Delhi. However, no real talks were arranged. This was in the months of June-July 1971. By then, New Delhi already had no other plans, and talking of peace with Laldenga was apparently not one of its priorities. In fact, by December, with the creation of Bangladesh, Lalkhawliana, MNF Finance Minister, Lalhmingthanga, Foreign Minister, Thangkima, Education Minister, and 14 other high ranking MNF personnel escaped from the MNF detention and came over to India to surrender. By now, several senior MNF cadres were available to help the Indian authorities glean the intentions of Laldenga.

Since late 1960, India had been preoccupied with the 'liberation movement' in Bangladesh, which was expected to simultaneously deprive the MNF of safe sanctuaries and of active Pakistan assistance. The passing of the North East Areas (Reorganization) Act, 1971 by the Parliament also raised the political status of Mizoram to that of Union Territory, giving hopes of better political deal in future. At the birth of Bangladesh, the MNF movement was, perhaps, at its lowest point. After warding off the pursuing Mukti Bahinis and Indian soldiers, Laldenga held a brief meeting of both civilian and military officers of the rank of Captains and Deputy Commissioners and above, where it was decided unanimously to depute one more mission to explore negotiations with the Indian Government as also for all 335 non-combat civilians to return to Mizoram.

Lalnunmawia, former MNF Vice President, and R. Zamawia, former Defence Minister were appointed Special Envoys of the

President and were also to escort the civilian group back to Mizoram. Their credential letter No. M-7/71/139, dated December reads simply: "The under-mentioned gentlemen are commissioned as Special Envoys of the President to act and speak on behalf of Government of Mizoram" and was signed by Laldenga. Laldenga's parting words with Zamawia clearly showed his desperation. He said, "Try your utmost if only to save our lives."[28] They interacted once again with Indian intelligence officers. The initial responses they received from their interlocutors were like "things were different 8 months ago…you are too late... Don't expect anything big." The two emissaries returned with a message to the effect that "talks are possible" but without specifying "when and where the talks should be held.

In the meantime, in February 1972 the Arakan MNF group was able to establish contact with the Pakistani Embassy in Rangoon. "Once Laldenga came to know that he would be able to travel safely to Karachi, he decided to cancel the mandate to negotiate he had given us," said R. Zamawia. This was done by letter No. M-1/72/5, dated June 12, 1972 signed by S. Lianzuala, Vice President and Chairman, National Emergency Council (NEC). Laldenga and his family and close aides flew with travel documents under assumed names to Karachi in the third week of March 1972 and were lodged in the suburb of Rawalpindi.

## AGREEMENT OF 1976

After the loss of East Pakistan, the Z.A. Bhutto Government had no use for Laldenga. "They reluctantly allowed him sanctuary in Rawalpindi out of sheer sense of obligation for his past deeds against India."[29] Laldenga's continued presence in Pakistan could have been an inconvenience at a time when government was beginning to mend fences with India. His alienation from the Church leaders in Mizoram and his overtures to the communist in China and Burma had also taken away whatever credibility he may have otherwise had with the Christian and other altruistic ogranzations in the West and "his opportunistic politics had shown through."[30] His efforts to find a sanctuary in Western countries had drawn blank. If he was going to be unwelcome in Pakistan before long, he seemed to have no option but to mend his fences with India. At any rate, reading from his past deeds, this seems to be what he had originally intended.

In November 1973, he sent his aides, Zoramthanga and Lalsangliana to contact the Indian mission in Kabul. This could not have been arranged without Pakistan's assistance, also implying that Pakistan was desirous of getting rid of Laldenga. Such a secret contact would be with the officers of the Research and Analysis Wing (RAW) in the Indian mission, who would pass on to New Delhi the news of their 'contact' with their comments and wait for instructions. Zoramthanga had been sent again to Kabul nearly a year later, as no response seemed to be forthcoming from India. He must have adequately impressed upon the Indian intelligence operatives this time that Laldenga was sincere in his bid for peace and was ready to return to India when necessary. It was now arranged that he should fly to Geneva to meet RAW officer, which he did on August 20, 1974 on a passport issued by Pakistan in the name of Pete Lee.[31]

At Geneva, he met Hassan Walia, Additional Secretary, RAW and confirmed his willingness to return to India for talks by a letter to Prime Minister Indira Gandhi. The operative portions of the letter are:

> "Since November 1973, my officials have been meeting your representatives. .... I have already written to you.... As I had mentioned, I have no doubt in my mind that the solution of the Mizoram political system will have to be achieved within the Constitution of India.... In order that I could contact my underground colleagues for injecting into them my belief and conviction so that they come round to my line of thinking, I would request for the facility of my coming over to India.... For obvious reasons, I cannot tell them straightaway that I have agreed to discuss the solution of the problem within the Constitution of India. Those people do not have the opportunity to appreciate the problem in the wider context of political development all over the world."[32]

For the Government of India, however, it was crucial that Laldenga should come for negotiations only if he commanded the confidence of the rank and file of the MNF, which he did not appear to do, judging from intelligence agencies and the Mizo Church leaders had to be made into the processes through which a compromise of sorts was worked out within MNF leadership. As Laldenga had requested in his letter, New Delhi made arrangements in November 1975 for three of the top MNF leadership, Tlangchhuaka, the MNF Vice President, Biakchhunga, Army Chief and K. Chawngzuala, MNF Party President, to join him in the talks he was having with Hassan Walia, the RAW officer. However, serious differences emerged between Laldenga and his colleagues, especially with Biakachhunga and Tlangchhunaka, during the nine days of discussion in Cologne. It was decided that the three MNF leaders should proceed to New Delhi and that Laldenga would join in the new year of 1976.[33]

Laldenga arrived in New Delhi on 24 January 1976 and soon he and his three colleagues went through days of secret talks with Home Secretary S.L. Khurana, Mizoram Lieutenant Governor S.K. Chibber and Joint Secretary (Home) M.L. Kampani. On 18 February 1976, the MNF leaders and the Indian officials issued a signed "Press Statement" in which the MNF leaders "acknowledged that Mizoram is an integral part of India and conveyed to the Government of India their decision to accept the settlement of the problem in Mizoram within the framework of the Constitution of India." The other passages of the statement were on the arrangements needed for the Calcutta MNF Convention to be held from 24 March to 1 April 1976 and for handing over of all MNF arms to the Central Government. The Convention was held at the "Meeting Hall" of SIB at Calcutta. The Indian Intelligence conducted the entire programme of the convention from behind the scene.[34] "Since the RAW- IB axis was organizing it all for the rebels, there seemed to be no hitches in the entire exercise."[35] At the Convention, the meeting was formally converted into an MNF Assembly and elected Laldenga as President and Tlangchhuaka as Vice President and elected Zoramthanga for the first time as General Secretary. It gave a mandate to the MNF delegation led by its President to negotiate peace settlement with India "within the Constitution of India." It also decided to convert MNF party into a legalized political party in India.[36]

After a "series of discussions" with the same three Indian officials, the following agreement was signed on July 1, 1976 by Laldenga on the MNF side and S.L. Khurana on the government side.

"1. The MNF delegation acknowledged that Mizoram is an integral part of India and conveyed to the Government of India their resolve to accept a settlement of all problems in Mizoram within the Constitution of India.

2. In order to bring about a climate of understanding and an atmosphere of peace tranquillity in Mizoram at the earliest, the delegation agreed to abjure violence and suspend all activities. In furtherance of the above objectives, the underground delegation agreed to collect all underground personnel with their arms and ammunition inside mutually agreed camps within one month of their establishment and also agreed to hand over arms and ammunitions to the Government of India.
3. The Government of India also decided to suspend all operations thereafter by the Security Forces. Such suspension, however, would not apply to operation against underground personnel attempting to cross international border and to the maintenance of law and order.

It was agreed to continue the talks further."

This understanding could not be implemented primarily because Laldenga could not fulfil his part of the deal. Doubts regarding the surrender of arms and certain opposition by some MNF leaders in Arakan continued. While the government insisted on the surrender of arms by the MNF should precede the political settlement, the MNF wanted it to be the other way round. Except for a brief interruption for the celebration of Christmas in December 1976, since October of that year, the Security Forces had already resumed operations, which had been suspended earlier in March. Peace talks also resumed but proceeded erratically.

**Peace Talks and the Morarji Desai Government**

In the general elections held in March 1977, the Janata Party came into power in Delhi. The new government resumed talks on May 18 with Laldenga to find ways to implement the July 1976 agreement signed by the previous government. Principled and rigid as Desai was, if he did anything, it was basically to alienate the rebels even more. The failure of these talks led the government to ask Laldenga to leave India by June 6, 1977. On June 9, a group of 62 MNF cadres, led by Sawmvela, ex-Chief of Army, surrendered their arms to the Lieutenant Governor of Mizoram and declared that it was immoral to continue the armed insurgency after the New Delhi accord of July 1976.[37] Laldenga tried to appear reasonable by pleading for resumption of talks with government, but he was again asked to leave the country by November 21. He somehow managed to stay on in Delhi and pursued further dialogue with the then Home Minister, Charan Singh.

However, these informal talks also down irretrievably in March 1978, because Laldenga refused to give up his demand for an interim government to be headed by him and his party colleagues. Even before the July 1976 agreement, he had repeatedly asked that a clause should be included whereby he should automatically head a provisional government before calling for fresh elections. His argument was that no real peace would come in Mizoram unless the terms of the agreement were implemented by both sides under his personal supervision. The government, however, had not accepted it. Perhaps, this was the reason why he had not made serious efforts to fulfil his obligation under the accord, despite the assistance of "RAW-IB axis" made available to him.[38]

Meanwhile in the Arakan Hills, in his absence, Laldenga was facing serious problems regarding the loyalty of some of the MNF leaders to him. A number of them were in no mood to follow his instructions blindly. Ignoring Laldenga, from June 1979, they even elected three different Presidents—Brig. General Biakchhunga (18 June—26 October 1979), Tlangchhuaka (26 October 1978—24 January 1979), and Malsawma Colney (24 January—11 March 1979). By this time, Zoramthanga, Secretary to Laldenga, and Major Tawnluia, ADC to Laldenga arrived from Delhi and, with the hardcore loyalists to Laldenga; they successfully plotted the arrest of Malsawma Colney and his followers on 11 March 1979. On April 19, 1979, they convened the MNF Assembly and elected Laldenga as President. Zoramthanga and Tawnluia became Vice President and Army Chief respectively, and those who had opposed the leadership of Laldenga were dismissed and allowed to return to Mizoram. Thus, the personal staff of Laldenga finally took over the MNF political organization, thereby providing him an 'unquestionable authority' to negotiate with the Indian Government.[39]

In Mizoram, Brig. T. Sailo and his People's Conference Party won the elections in May 1978 and formed the new government. As he was allied with Janata Party, which had dismissed the peace talks with Laldenga as meaningless, Sailo's detractors accused him of being an obstacle to peace talks. They also blamed his 'advice' for the arrest by New Delhi of Laldenga on 8 July 1979.[40]

## Return of Congress (I) to Power and Politics of 'Peace Talks'

Indira Gandhi returned to head the government in New Delhi in January 1980. The leaders of the Congress Party in Mizoram lost no time in pleading to her to resume talks with Laldenga. Laldenga was released from prison and all charges against him are withdrawn on 30 June 1980. Counter insurgency operations in Mizoram were also suspended. Laldenga first had talks with Home Minister Giani Zail Singh before the veteran diplomat, G. Parthasarathy, the then Chairman, Policy Planning Division, Ministry of External Affairs, was entrusted with the tasks of negotiating peace settlement with Laldenga. But the talks were doomed to fail again as the 26-point proposals made by the MNF Executive Committee included some demands, which the government regarded as totally unacceptable. Parthasarathy could have perhaps whittled down Laldenga's demands to two essential points—to elevate Mizoram to a full-fledged State and to make Laldenga the Chief Minister of the interim government. Full statehood for Mizoram had already been agreed to in principle, but removal of Chief Minister Brig. T. Sailo would have been constitutionally impossible, as he refused to vacate his office and insisted on a contest in an election.

In Mizoram, hardly anyone believed any more, by then that peace could come without prior assurance to Laldenga that he would head the interim government following the peace settlement. And people knew that the vital piece for the rebel leader was still missing in the MNF Government settlement arranged so far. They also knew that in the absence of settlement the MNF would resort to renewed violence and that the response to such a renewed violence by the government would be massive. By a notification date 20 January 1982, the government again banned the MNF. Laldenga was asked to leave the country and he left for London on 21 April 1982. By the middle of 1982, 26 battalions of various units of Security Forces were operating in the State.[41] With several rounds of ceasefire and suspension of operations since the first peace parley, people had become used to a relaxed tenor of life. The new restrictions on the movement and dusk to dawn curfew were bitter reminder of the early days of the MNF insurgency and had a great psychological impact on the people. Demand for peace and agreement with government began to proliferate. The Baptist and the Presbyterian churches had always stood firm for peace. They were now joined by the powerful students union (Mizo Zirali Pawl), opposition MLAs and leading members of the civil society. Very soon, for the politicians, clamour for peace talks became a powerful means of rallying support and an effective weapon against the Sailo government and his People's Conference party, who were held responsible for the failure of the MNF-Government talks and the current suffering of the people.

The People's Conference Party (PC), once considered sympathetic by the MNF, now became a target of covert threats of attack by the latter essentially because of Sailo's attitude towards peace settlement especially his refusal to step aside to give way for Laldenga.[42] The order issued on 10 August 1982 by MNF Vice President Zoramthanga, in fact, included order to assassinate several PC leaders.[43] The PC was thus no longer safe for surrendering MNF to join. The Congress Party led by Lal Thanhawala decided to camping for the ouster of the Sailo government on a platform of peace. The Congress Party attracted many ex-MNF cadres who felt safe being in it, which was now seen as the best bet for bringing about the next peace-talks. The underground elements of the MNF also were using selective violence in support of the Congress. The Congress Party in Mizoram had been informally in contact with Laldenga after the break down of the talks in 1982. They had been consulting with the central Congress leadership in Delhi as to how Laldenga should be dealt with. Finally from London, Laldenga decided to support the Congress in the elections due to be held in April 1984. Thanhawla had sent two emissaries to meet Laldenga in London, who managed to bring taped speeches of Laldenga in support of the Congress in Mizoram. One of the emmisseries, Lalduhoma, who had resigned from the Indian Police Service to join the Congress was "planted by Laldenga" (R. Lalawia) to ensure that the Mizoram Congress did not renege on its commitment to renew the peace talks.[44] With this background of preparations, the Congress Party won the 1984 Assembly elections easily, and on 5 May 1984, Lal Thanhawla became Chief Minister.

## THE FINAL ACCORD WITH LALDENGA

On 6 September 1984, Laldenga issued a statement in London that he was ready to issue 'orders' to his followers for an immediate ceasefire as a first step to a negotiated settlement of the Mizoram problem. He returned to Delhi on 29 October 1984. He said, "I have come back to India to solve our problem and take my place as an

Indian in Indian politics.[45] The talks got going immediately. Unfortunately, Indira Gandhi was assassinated on 31 October 1984. Laldenga had in fact been scheduled to meet her at 5 O'clock on that evening. And the Central Government became preoccupied with the problem of law and order following the assassination of Indira Gandhi.

Laldenga had to wait for a few months. On 15 February 1985, Laldenga met the new Prime Minister Rajiv Gandhi. The negotiations were now entrusted with Home Secretary D. Pradhan. The talks could not be concluded in 1985. Ladenga left for London on 24 December ostensibly to celebrate Christmas with his family. On 27 February 1986, an all party meeting in Mizoram along with the Student Action Committee issued a joint call for all concerned to solve the insurgency problem once for all. They also submitted a memorandum to the Prime Minister urging resumption of the peace talks.

On 15 June 1986, Laldenga returned to New Delhi to resume talks. As the result of intra-Congress Party consultations, an arrangement was devised for the Mizoram Chief Miniser Lal Thanhawla to resign to make way for Laldenga. A "Confidential" Agreement between the MNF Party and Congress Party was thus signed on 25 June 1986 by Laldenga and Arjun Singh, Vice President of the Indian National Congress. The crux of this accord was that it stipulated in its first article: "On a date agreed to between Shri Laldenga and the Government of India, Shri Lal Thanhawla, the present Congress(I) Chief Minister will submit his resignation and Shri Laldenga will be elected the leader of the Government of Mizoram and be sworn in as the Chief Minister there."[46] Finally, Laldenga was about to realize his longstanding and cherished ambition. The Peace Accord, technically titled, "Memorandum of Settlement," was signed on 30 June 1986.[47]

### Main Factors behind the Accord

There were three main factors interacting in the process of the peace negotiations. A brief recap and an appraisal of the roles played by these elements may help in determining the clinching factor.

1. *Laldenga and the MNF*: Laldenga was keen to arrive at an early solution, but it must be one in which he would be able to call the shots in Mizoram following the settlement. This insistence was of course due to his political ambition; it could

also be to ensure safety for his life as he was said to be extremely distrustful of others concerning his personal safety and position.[48] However, he needed time to convert to his "line of thinking" the fighting cadres, largely composed of ex-servicemen and uneducated and hot blooded young men, who blindly believed in the 'struggle for independence'. This change of course could have been accomplished sooner that it was, had he taken the educated leaders into confidence. Perhaps, there was the danger of being labelled a fraud and ousted by another artful leader. However, the knowledge by the Government since July 1969 that Laldenga was ever ready to negotiate was an essential input into the process of peace negotiation.

2. *The Establishment*: This consisted of the Congress (I) government at the Centre and the local administration in Mizoram. Most of the leading 'over ground' political leaders of then Mizoram were deeply saddened by the tragic turn of events that the MNF movement had triggered. The Mizo Union leader such as Ch. Chhunga and his colleagues were evidently willing to make necessary sacrifices for peace, but there was nothing that they could do to initiate peace moves as the 'MNF government' was bent on paralyzing their authorities. In April 1971, for instance, they offered in writing to concede to MNF 75 per cent of the legislative seats in the elections expected to be held upon the elevation of Mizo Hills to the status of Union Territory in early 1972.[49] But by then Laldenga was busy sorting out his alleged detractors within the MNF leadership. Ch. Chhunga also resigned in May 1977 from the Chief Ministership, hoping this would facilitate settlement with MNF.[50] As Brig. T. Sailo and PC Party took a principled stand and rejected the idea of making Laldenga the Chief Minister in the interim, they were accused of sabotaging the peace talks in 1982 and they were virtually 'at war' with MNF.[51]

   The contribution of the Mizoram Congress (I) under the leadership of Lal Thanhawla towards the peace settlement was difficult to differentiate from the efforts of the central leadership of the party. Much credit has been given to the integrative vision espoused by Indira Gandhi towards the separatists in the Northeast and her efforts to penetrate ethnic insularities and extend participative democracy by devolution of appropriate autonomies.[52] (Amidst the multiple ethnic communities in the Northeast, as the government must have realized by now, devolution of power on the basis of ethnic identities has at time led to fragmentation and tendency towards ethnic radicalism with violent consequence.) And this overall approach was said to be at the background of the Centre's handling of the Mizo problem. This strategy of 'peace making' also currently carries with it the policy of projecting the Congress (I) as the defender of the cause of peace in Mizoram, which indeed helped it to consolidate its mass support there. It is in the execution of this policy that Lal Thanhawla performed creditably. The fact that he was ready to vacate his office to make way for Laldenga was also creditable, but then, given the scheme of Indira Gandhi's strategy, a refusal could also have cost him his leadership.[53]

3. *The Civil Society*: Much has been written about the role of the civil society and the Churches in this paper. With their impeccable credentials as workers for the advancement of the society and their prestige as religious leaders, the Church leaders were fearless and naturally become the spokesmen for the civil society and the common people at large. They were firm in their conviction that the MNF had forced Mizo people to take a wrong turn.[54]

As for the common people, with the break down of yet another peace talk in the early 1980s, they had become literally 'fed up' with insurgency. They simply wished to be left alone to live their own lives. All they wanted was peace at any price. At any rate, the overwhelming majority of the Mizos had never been taken in by Laldenga's propaganda, in the first place. The Mizo Union, the largest political party then, was solidly against the idea of rebellion and, as a result, a number of its activist were victimized and killed by MNF soon after the outbreak of the insurgency. Apprehensive of the disastrous consequences a rebellion could bring to the people many educated Mizos openly countered and even ridiculed the MNF propaganda.[55] Once the real intention of Laldenga became publicly evident, the people clearly sensed the futility of prolonging the insurgency. It could thus be safely asserted that upon the assumption of power by the Congress (I) in early 1984, most Mizos simply expected the new State Government to be fully engrossed in peace making and in ending the insurgency. In other words, insurgency was no longer 'feasible' as a political strategy in Mizoram. It had to be ended by whatever means available. Fortunately for the remaining MNF cadres, the common people were now largely ready to forgive and forget. In the ultimate analysis, therefore, it was the will of the people that ended the insurgency.

By the same token, it is the will of this same people, which has sustained peace in Mizoram so far. This is, in spite of the inadequate and improper fulfilment by the government of the clauses in the Peace Accord concerning the rehabilitation of the reformed rebels and relief of the victimized innocents during the insurgency.[56] These (Article 13) were the only provisions that could have gone some way in healing the "wounds," no matter how differently the victims felt. Two decades are now abutting to pass after the Mizoram Peace Accord was concluded. How long the people will continue to preserve peace will ·largely depend on the performance of those gentlemen, who are managing the affairs of the people on the pretext of governing them.

## NOTES

1. This research work is soon to be published.
2. For instance, R. Zamawia believed that the "*Struggle for independence for Mizoram was assigned to him by God*". R. Zamawia, former Defense Minister, MNF at an interview on 18.11.2005.
3. Quoted by James Dokhum in Ch. Chhunga Cahnchin (Biography) reconfirmed by C. Pahlira in an interview on 20.11.2005.
4. C. Pahlira, *Ibid.*
5. Vergehese, C.G. & Thanzawna, R.L. *A History of Mizos*, Vol. II, pp. 79. "One of these authors, without identifying which one, claimed to have been told by an ex-MNF official that the latter had collected Rs. 40,000 from Chaliha in 1963 for passing on to Laldenga.
6. Verghese, C.G. and Thanzawna, *Ibid.*, Vol. II, p. 22. The visit was arranged by R. Zamawia through the then Assistant High Commissioner of Pakistan, Shillong.
7. Sajal Nag, Contesting Marginality, 2002, p. 218 quoted by C. Nunthara in a seminar paper "*Analysing the Mizo Peace Accord*".

8. Tawrhbawm Daily of 12.6.2003 and confirmed on 22.11.2005 in an interview by R. Lalawina, former speaker of Mizoram Assembly (1999-2003), who also said that Laldenga had discussed the same point with him on two occasions.
9. Witnessed and reported by Denghnuna, IAS (retd.), then District Information Officer, Mizor Hills.
10. The portion on the meetings on 28 February 1966 is from the interview with R. Zamawi held on 18.11.2005.
11. Verghese, C.G. & Thanzawna, R.L., *op. cit.* p. 77.
12. C. Lakhawliana, MNF Finance Minster, at interview on 22.11.2005.
13. *Ibid.*
14. Rev. Zairema, then i/c Presbyterian Mission in Cachar District, at an interview on 22.11.2005. Rev. Zairema told me that he had not revealed this conversation with Laldenga to anyone inending to put it on record. He now wanted that "the truth be told".
15. John Vanlal Hluna, Quoted by J.S. Jafa, in *Mizoram: Contours of Non-military Intervention, Fautlines*.
16. John Vanlal Hluna Church and Political Upheaval in Mizoram, (Aizawl, Mizor History Association, 1985) pp.11, 121.
17. Declaration of Appeal of the Church, dated 12.3.1966. quoted by John Vanlal Hluna, *Ibid.*
18. MNF Home Ministry's Letter dated 16.3.1966. Quoted by John Vanlal Hluna, *Ibid.*
19. R. Zamwain, *op. cit.* and John Vanlal Hluna, *ibid.*
20. R.N. Prasad, Government and Politics in Mizoram, pp. 209-10.
21. Rev. Zairema, *op. cit.* and C. Lakhawliana, *ibid.*
22. C. Lalkhawlian, *op.cit.* This should also put to rest the allegations often against Laldenga by ex-MNF cadres that he made peace overtures without consulting MNF leadership.
23. Vanlalngaia at an interview on 20.11.2005. He said that his mission was decided over a glass of beer at a restaurant in Dacca Inter-Continental Hotel. According to him, Laldenga opened up after he showed a letter he received from E.L. Mendus, a former Christian Missionary in Mizoram, who had advised him that he and his politician friends would be able to organize assistance for Mizoram if the MNF could arrive at a political settlement within the Indian Union.
24. Vanlalngaia, *op.cit.*
25. Nirmal Nibedon, *Mizoram: the Dagger Brigade*, Lancers Publishers, New Delhi, 1980, p. 146.
26. Quoted in *Ibid.*, p. 145.
27. R. Zamawia, then MNF Defence Minister and Army Chief, *Ibid.* These are with his personal knowledge. He believes that there were more messengers deputed to India.
28. R. Zamawia's Manuscript.

29. V.S. Jafa, *op. cit.*
30. Bualhranga, MNF Senator at an interview on 26.11.2005.
31. Nirmal Nibedon, *Ibid.* p. 208.
32. M.C. Lalrinthatnga, Mizoram Politik Aizawl, 1993, p. 4; and Biakchhunga, Hnam Kasiam, Aizawl, 1966, pp. 97-98.
33. Biakchhunga requested Laldenga to return to Arakan to sort out the issue with National Council but the later refused. Interview with Biakchhunga on 15.11.2005.
34. M.C. Lalrianthatnga, *Ibid.* pp. 17.
35. Nirmal Nebedon, *op. cit.* 211. 'Rebels' here means Laldenga and his confidents such as Zormathatnga, the present Chief Minister. Tawnluia, Home Minster and few others. Most of the participants in the Convention did not have idea of why the whole tamasha was done this way.
36. M.C. Lalrinthanga, *op.cit.* 18.
37. V.S. Jafa, *op. cit.* The sequence of events in this section is largely taken from his paper.
38. Nirmal Nibedon, *op. cit.* 211.
39. Lalringthanga later visited Delhi and personally reported the news of successful plot to Laldenga on 1 May 1979.
40. M.C. Lalrinthanga, *op. cit.* p. 109. He quoted then Home Minister H.M. Patel's statement on 10.7.1979 in the Lok Sabha. "As proposed by the Mizoram Chief Minister, Laldenga was arrested."
41. V.S. Jafa, *op. cit.*
42. *Ibid.* p. 138. He said that PM told Laldenga that the Sailo government did not belong to her party and therefore she could not ask them to step down.
43. Quoted in M.C. Lalrinthatna, *ibid.*, pp. 151-54.
44. R. Lalwina, *op. cit.* He claimed that he had given a rent free house for five years and a hundred thousand rupees to Lalduhoma so that he could be politically active and work for peace. Lalduhoma became the President of the Congress and MP eventually. He did leave the Congress late and joined MNF Party.
45. Ved Marwah, *Uncivil Wars*, Harper Collins, 1995, New Delhi, p. 266.
46. The Text of the Agreement is at Appendix 1.
47. The Text of the Peace Accord is at Appendix 2.
48. R. Zamawia, *op. cit.*
49. V. Laichnga, MNF Deputy Foreign Secretary, at an interview on 24.11.2005. He was deputed to urge the Mizo Union leaders not to accept the Union Territory status in April, 1971 but was told by Ch. Chhunga that it was too late to change he situation. Instead, the Mizo Union leaders made the proposal in writing. V. Laichhinga was arrested on his return to the MNF Hqrs. But he handed over the papers he was carrying to the arresting officers.
50. Animesh Ray, *op. cit.* p.176.
51. M.C. Lalrinthatna, *op. cit.* 154.
52. V.S. Jafa, *op. cit.* and Ved Marwah, *op. cit.* p. 269.

53. According to Lal Thanhawla's brother-in-law, R.Vanneia, the former had offered to vacate his office during the pre-election campaigns leading to the 1984 MLA elections. No record is available on this. On the other hand, soon after the take over of power by Lal Thanhawla, the then Congress (I) President, Lalduhoma complained in a letter to Lalsawma, that the ruling party was trying to avoid taking steps towards 'peace talks'. In protest, he resigned, and formed another party called Mizoram Peace Congress.
54. Rev. L.N. Ralte wrote on 7 March, 1966 in a Visitors' Book of a Rest House he had fled to at the outbreak of the insurgency, "*I prayed that the Indian forces may annihilate the MNF.*" Rev. H.S. Luaia and Rev. C.L. Hminaga drove to Aizawl to plead to the District Commissioner T.S. Gill and the Army Commanders not to burn villages on the way to Lunglei. They on their part persuaded the MNF not to attack the oncoming Security Forces. As the result, Lunglei was spared from the straffing and bombing that Aizawl had suffered. Rev. H.S. Luaia also gave a tip to the possible location of an arms cache hidden by MNF. See R. Zamina, *op. cit.*
55. A veteran politician who at one time was Minister in the Assam Government, A.Thanglura commented that fighting for independence was like trying to drive into a flat rock. He was also quoted to have said, "If the MNF attain independence, I offer myself to be slaughtered for the celebration." These quotations are spread all over Mizoram.
56. Lianzela, "*Mizoram Peace Accord*", Paper presented at the OKD Institute of Social Change and Development, Guwahati, February 2005.

# Chapter 3

## Separatism and Movement for Statehood in Mizoram
### *An Historical Overview*

LALRINTLUANGA

Movement literally means "a series of actions and endeavours of a body of persons for a specific object."[1] It connotes a form of collective action of an identifiable section of the population with a purpose of bringing about a change, either partial or total, in the existing socio-economic and political arrangement of the system. When the collective action is somewhat sustained as distinct from a sporadic occurrence, it takes the form of a movement.[2] Within this framework of conceptualisation of a movement, an attempt is made here to look into the circumstances in which the movement for Mizoram Statehood was initiated and sustained by some political parties within the constitutional framework of the Indian Union and how far the movement for Statehood was paralysed by the Separatist politics that ultimately led to the outbreak of Insurgency in Mizoram. Moreover, this essay attempts to study the impact of insurgency on the working of over ground political parties in Mizoram and how those political parties reacted and responded to the problem of insurgency in Mizoram.

I

The movement for the creation of Mizoram State within the Indian Union was an indirect offshoot of the British policy of *'divide et imperia'* in North East India. When their colonisation of the entire

North East India was completed, the British rulers wanted to separate the hill tribes from the plains people on the pretext of preserving their distinct tribal cultures, traditions and taboos, social and political systems. As a consequence, the British administration drew an imaginary line, called "Inner Line," to regulate the strained relations between the Mizo and the plainsmen. Shortly, this "Inner Line" created a psychological barrier between the plains people and the Mizo.

The British Government passed another Act, called the Scheduled District Act, 1874, which empowered the Provincial Government to declare enactments by notification which were and were not actually in force in any part of such district.[3] In the Mizo Hills, this Act came into force from the day of amalgamation of the Northern and Southern portions of the district to form the present Mizoram on 1st April 1898.[4] Further, the British Government reinforced the earlier restrictions of entry of the outsiders inside the Mizo Hills by extending the Chin Hills Regulation of 1896, in a modified form, with effect from October 9, 1911.[5] Even today, the "Inner Line Regulation" and the "Chin Hills Regulation" are in force in Mizoram.

Yet, the British Government was apprehensive of the possibility of the spread of freedom movement as far as the Mizo Hills which would be difficult to control. Again, the British Government passed the Act, called the Government of India Act, 1919, by which only those Acts suitable to the Mizo Hills would be applied with such date and with such exceptions and modifications, as the Governor General-in-Council considered necessary.[6] The Mizo Hills was declared to be one of such backward tracts on January 3, 1921.[7] Accordingly, the British Government did not allow the Mizo to express their political feelings or participate in the democratic election of the Provincial Legislature of Assam introduced by the Government of India Act, 1919. In spite of this discouragement from the British administration, a group of persons under the leadership of Mr. Telela Ralte contacted the Superintendent of the Mizo Hills, in 1925, to initiate changes in the administration so that they could freely participate in the Assam politics. The immediate effect of this concrete political activity was the change of place of enforcement of the 'Inner Line Regulation, 1873' by the British Government from Cachar district to the Mizo Hills. Accordingly, the British Government issued a Notification by which the Superintendent of the Mizo Hills should strictly control the mobility of both the Mizo and the plainsmen by enforcing the 'Inner Line Regulation' from within the Mizo District with effect from March 9, 1933.[8]

Over and above, the Government of India Act, 1935, declared the Mizo Hills an "Excluded Area."[9] The "Excluded Areas" were to be administered by regulations and orders of the Governor of Assam who "was unfettered in his discretion in the executive functions in these areas."[10] Under the prevailing situation, the educated Mizo felt deprived of any opportunity to participate in the national or provincial politics whereas other hill tribes in the "Partially Excluded Areas" could send their common representative to the Provincial Government of Assam. Apparently, there was "no scope of popular participation in the Provincial Government of Assam as there was no elected representative of the Excluded Areas."[11]

In the absence of any other way out, some of the educated Mizo, under the auspices of one civil society, called 'the Young Lushai Association (YLA), began to mobilise Mizo public opinion for representation to the Provincial Government of Assam. But, they were suppressed by the colonial rulers with a heavy hand within no time. Meanwhile, a large-scale exposure of the Mizo to the outside world as war personnel, during the Second World War, had broadened the Mizo Commoners' outlook. When they returned home, they could not accept the archaic rule of their traditional Chiefs as they found continuing unchanged in their homeland.

Meanwhile, the Chiefs' Conference *alias* the Chiefs' Council formed by the Superintendent, L.L. Peters, in 1939, had a negative impact on the relationship between the Chiefs and the Mizo commoners. All the meetings and conferences of the Chiefs under the sponsorship of the Superintendent created a feeling of unity and a sense of co-ordination of activities among the Chiefs. Being assured of protection by the British authority, most of the Chiefs became an instrument of exploitation on the labour of their subjects on very simple pretext and hence became more and more irresponsible and autocratic.[12]

When A.R. MacDonald became the next Superintendent, he lifted his predecessor's prohibit order by way of encouraging the Mizo to take greater interest in the administration. He constituted the "District Conference" with the provision of equal representation from both the Chiefs and the Commoners which would "advise the Superintendent on all matters concerned with the administration of the district."[13] In fact, the motive behind the formation of the District

Conference by McDonald was to effectively mobilise the people to support Prof. R. Coupland's proposal for the creation of "Crown Colony of Eastern Agency" consisting of the hill areas of Assam and Burma which would be an independent State between India and Burma. But, the Commoners insisted on democratic election to the District Conference based on proportional representation while the Chiefs wanted to maintain *status quo*. But, the District Conference could not serve the desired purpose as the two sets of representatives could not reconcile their points of disagreement regarding representation.

Ultimately, the feeling of resentment of the people against the ruling Chiefs resulted in the formation of the first political party, called the "Mizo Union Party," in the Mizo Hills with the official blessing of the Superintendent, A.R. McDonald. The real motive behind the formation of the Mizo Union was to fight against the rights, privileges and vested interests of the traditional Chiefs that stood on their way to democratic participation in the Provincial Government of Assam. In the meanwhile, a move for a possible independent status for the Mizo Hills was being canvassed all over the Mizo Hills under the active support of MacDonald, Superintendent of the Mizo Hills. This proposed State was to be a "protectorate" of the British Government.[14] The Mizo Chiefs strongly supported the plans drawn up by the Superintendent while some of the Mizo Union leaders supported the cause of integration with the Indian Union which was not liked by the District Superintendent.

In fact, the original leadership of the Mizo Union party was more inclined to Mizoram independence. By contrast, the new leadership of the party was of the opinion that the future of the Mizo—socially, economically and politically—lied with the Indian Union. In its first general Assembly held on September 24, 1946 at Kulikawn locality of Aizawl, the Mizo Union also resolved: "In the event of India attaining a complete and unqualified independence, the Mizo were to be included in it, within the Province of Assam, with a sufficient number of representatives who will represent them on concurrent subjects with the Provincial Government."[15] Against this background, many of the Unionists advocating the secessionist move left the party and organised themselves into the Mizo Union Council (MUC) to effectively support the 'Crown Colony' or Mizo Independence from India. Thus, they wanted to be left by the British just as they had been before the occupation of their land by the British.[16]

When the British transfer of power to India, Pakistan and Burma was imminent, Mizo public opinion was greatly divided over the future political status of their land. However, they talked about four choices among the Mizo themselves, such as, joining Burma, Independence, British Dominion or Colony as well as District Autonomy within the Indian Union. But, the Mizo Union, the largest political organisation in the Mizo Hills, favoured the autonomous district council status within the Assam Province of India whereas the Mizo National Council had talked of Independence in the beginning of April 1947.[17] Around this time, the Constituent Assembly of India set up an Advisory Committee on Tribal Areas to consider the problem of Assam as well as the Tribal people.[18] The Advisory Committee, further, constituted a Sub-Committee[19] under the Chairmanship of Gopinath Bordoloi, the then Chief Minister of Assam, "to assess and advise on the future administration of the tribal and Excluded Areas inhabited by the hill people of Assam."[20] The Mizo Union was formally represented to the Advisory Sub-Committee by two of its leaders, namely, Mr. Khawtinkhuma and Mr. Ch. Saprawnga who were co-opted as members whereas the District Conference was not represented to the Advisory Sub-Committee. The Superintendent, McDonald, was very much exasperated by the inclusion of the two Mizo Union leaders as co-option members of the Sub-Committee while he thought that the District Conference alone represented the popular will of the district.[21]

On April 17, 1947, the Bordoloi Sub-Committee arrived at Aizawl to assess the public opinion for the future political status of the Mizo Hills.[22] The Committee met different organisations, prominent leaders, representatives of the Chiefs' Council and the Mizo Union. Though the Bordoloi Sub-Committee did not have any intention to take evidences from the representatives of the District Conference, the Superintendent, an *ex-officio* President of the District Conference, strongly requested the Chairman of the Advisory Sub-Committee to hear evidences even from the representatives of the District Conference as well. Finally, the Bordoloi Sub-Committee acceded to McDonald's request and, on April 18, 1947, met the five English speaking representatives of the District Conference duly elected by the members of the constituents of the District Conference.

While giving evidence before the Sub-Committee, Rev. Zairema demanded for local autonomy with supreme powers to make laws and enforce them. The division of powers and functions between

Assam and Mizoram should be decided by negotiation between the parties concerned. No Central and State laws should be extended to the District without the approval of the Mizo National Council. Besides, the Pastor appealed for integration of all the contiguous Mizo inhabited areas and the retention of their complete proprietary rights over land.[23] Further, he pleaded for financial provision at the disposal of Mizoram Government until the Mizo people were able to maintain themselves without financial assistance from the Centre.[24] Another representative of the District Conference from the Chiefs' Council, Mr. Kailuia, demanded that the Mizo Chiefs should retain the status that they occupied before the coming of the British to their land.[25]

While giving his evidence before the Bordoloi Sub-Committee, the General Secretary of the Mizo Union proper, Mr. H. Vanthuama, agreed with Rev. Zairema in many respects but differed from him in regard to the future status of Mizoram. He, further, stated that the moment the Mizo became economically and financially sound, the Mizo Hills would opt out of India.[26] Mr. H. Vanthuama spoke of the right of secession after ten years of association with the Indian Union from the date of the commencement of the new Constitution. Apart from giving evidences, the representatives of the Mizo Union, namely, Mr. H. Vanthuama, Mr. Lalbuaia and Mr. Dengthuama also submitted a "Draft Constitution of Mizoram" to the Constituent Assembly of India through the Bordoloi Sub-Committee.[27]

Mr. R. Vanlawma and Mr. Pachhunga, as the representatives of the Mizo Union Right Wing or loosely called the Mizo Union Council, endorsed the decision previously made by the party to fight for Mizoram independence.[28] Even if their political movement could not yield the expected result, the Mizo Union Council would not like the Mizo to be under the Provincial Government of Assam though that was what they once fought for from the platform of Mizo Union Party. The President of the Mizo Union Right Wing, Mr. Pachhunga, vehemently opposed the idea of remaining the Mizo Hills under the Assam Province. He preferred the Mizo Hills to be under the direct control of the Government of India instead of the Government of Assam.

Mr. H.K. Bawichhuaka of Mizo Union, who appeared before the Bordoloi Sub-Committee in his individual capacity, pleaded for District autonomy within the Indian Union, right to self-determination for the Mizo Hills after ten years from the commencement of the Indian Constitution and amalgamation of all the Mizo inhabited areas contiguous to the Mizo Hills.[29] The Mizo Hills would be one of the Districts of Assam with adequate representation to the Assam Legislative Assembly. There should be division of powers and functions between the Assam Legislative Assembly and the Mizo National Council. Mr. R. Thanhlira of Mizo Union also demanded that maximum autonomy for Mizoram. He also suggested that Defence, Communications and Foreign Relations should remain with Government of India and the rest with Mizoram so that the Mizo would enjoy maximum autonomy.[30] Mr. L.B. Thanga also supported the evidences given by the two members of the Mizo Union.

As polarisation was not yet complete, there were supporters of independence in both groups. All of them wanted safeguards from exploitation by the plains people.[31] The Bordoloi Sub-Committee also found that, in the Mizo Hills, "there were reasonable sections of the population who were concerned mainly with the protection of their lands, social customs and interest."[32]

The Superintendent of the Mizo Hills, A.R. McDonald, was sympathetic to the cause of Mizo solidarity and separate existence outside the Indian Union. After looking into all these peculiar characteristics of the Mizo Society, the District Superintendent thought out that the Mizo would be better off if they were attached to the hill areas of Burma. Even the Bordoloi Sub-Committee could clearly notice that the British Superintendent, McDonald, had been doing his best to set up a separate land for the Mizo to be called 'Mizoram'. On the contrary, what the Mizo Union wanted to achieve was democratisation of the polity and, for that, abolition of the rights and privileges of the traditional Chiefs so that even the Mizo Commoners could freely participate in the Provincial Government of Assam.

Meanwhile, the Chiefs' Council had already joined McDonald's campaign for independent status. Under his protective authority, the traditional Chiefs became more and more arrogant in their dealings with their respective subjects. As many of the Mizo Chiefs misused their powers and ruled their subjects with an iron hand, they were no more looked upon as the protectors of their subjects but as "a symbol of exploitation and oppression."[33]

When Indian Independence Day was around the corner, Mr. Pachhunga, President of the Mizo Union Council, and his associates were launching political campaign for Mizo independence. In spite of a strong opposition from the Mizo Union proper, the movement for Mizoram independence could receive the support of a sizeable section of the Mizo Society which ultimately led to the birth of a new political party called the 'United Mizo Freedom Organisation' (UMFO) on July 5, 1947 "with the objective of the Mizo Hills joining Burma."[34] The Chiefs' Council automatically joined the new party and became restless to counter the activities of the Mizo Union that was virtually formed to check illegal exactions by the Chiefs and, at the same time, to protect the villagers from exploitation by the Chiefs.

However, an analysis of the resolutions passed by the leading figures of the Mizo Society has indicated that there was a confusion in the minds of Mizo politicians whether they could opt out of India or not. But, the consensus among them was that the majority of them wanted to opt out of India after ten years of association with India.

## II

The dawn of Indian independence was marked by the appearance of discord between two hostile groups "claiming loyalties to conflicting objectives."[35] On that Independence Day, the pro-integrationist group of the Mizo Union intended to celebrate the Independence Day by taking out a procession which the secessionist group did not like to take place at all. Fortunately, upon the request of some veteran politicians, "an armed showdown was avoided by cancelling the procession."[36] As requested by R. Vanlawma, the General Secretary of the Mizo Union Council, the Superintendent, L.L. Peters, also did not hoist the National Flag of India.

The immediate effect of Indian independence was the dissolution of the District Conference and, in its place, the formation of an Advisory Council without equal representation of the Chiefs and the Commoners. As the first of its kind, democratic election to the Advisory Council was held in April 1948. The Mizo Union fought this election mainly on the platform of abolition of chieftainship and the widest measure of local autonomy within Assam State of the Indian Union and won all the seats excepting two in Aijal town, which were won by the United Freedom Organisation (UMFO).[37] The Mizo Union leaders construed the outcome of this election as the people's support for their avowed objectives of democratisation and integration.

The keen desire of the Mizo Union to link up their political life with Assam on the one hand and the fear of being submerged by the plains people on the other were reconciled by providing for an autonomous existence under the Sixth Schedule to the Constitution of India. With the implementation of the Sixth Schedule in the beginning of 1952, the erstwhile Lushai Hills District was given the status of an autonomous District under the Province of Assam. The first democratic election was successfully held as per the schedule. The Mizo Union won the election with a thumping majority and the separatist UMFO was badly beaten by the former. Following their capture of the District Council, the Mizo Union demanded "the immediate introduction of the Village Councils all over the district in the wake of the elections, in place of the present autocratic regime of the Chiefs."[38] Meanwhile, the Chiefs decided to adopt an attitude of non-cooperation with the District Council, which was interpreted by the Government "as an act of defiance of lawful authority."[39] The Mizo Union was tremendously elated by the change of attitude by the government towards the Chiefs.

Village Councils were to be set up in each village within the jurisdiction of the Mizo District Council according to the famous Act passed by the District Council known as 'the Lushai Hills District (Village Council) Act, 1953.'[40] Similarly, Village Councillors were to be elected by the people to replace the traditional chiefs and their Elders functioning in all the villages within the Mizo District. On April 25, 1953, the District Council passed a Bill for the abolition of the institution of Chieftainship. But, the implementation of the law was kept in abeyance as some of the Mizo Union leaders were opposed to the immediate abolition of Chieftainship. Village Council elections were held for the first time in Mizoram on July 24, 1954.[41] In this election, the Mizo Unionists proved their sway all over the district by winning all the village council elections. Again, a landslide victory of the Mizo Union in the first village council elections was taken as an indication of people's approval of the Mizo Union's policy—first, to abolish Chieftainship and, secondly, to integrate the Mizo Hills with Assam State of the Indian Union but enjoying the highest possible measure of local autonomy.

While the Mizo Union leaders were leaving no stone unturned to get rid of the institutions of Chieftainship and to install democratic institutions at the grassroots level, the UMFO leaders also began to admit that the people did not want to give them political mandate to pursue their policy of the Mizo Hills joining Burma. Even then, the UMFO leaders felt it necessary to fight for something better than the District Council status for the Mizo Hills. On 1 October 1953, the UMFO dropped its original policy of joining Burma and passed a resolution that "the government be requested to form a new state comprising Manipur, Tripura, the autonomous districts of Assam and N.E.F.A."[42]

While the majority of politicians from the hill tribes were not having much problem to go along with the State government, some of them began to have fear-psychoses due to the Language Policy of the State government to introduce Assamese in the schools run by the District Councils. Some of them felt that the autonomy stipulated in the Constitution of India was not adequate enough to safeguard the interest of the hill people. The Mizo Union, an associate of the Congress Party that was running the State government, was also very much astonished at the State Language Policy. From January 31 to February 3, 1954, the Executive Committee of the Mizo Union was convened which "expressed their concern on the introduction of Assamese in the Schools situated in the hill districts of Assam."[43] However, all the members were unanimous that if the introduction of Assamese in schools in non-Assamese speaking areas was done with the intention of drawing the hill and the plains people closer to have better understanding of each other, there should be reciprocity. If not, the teaching of Assamese to non-speaking people would be interpreted as "aimed at influencing and dominating the hill people through Assamese language."[44] Besides, the Executive Committee of the Mizo Union deliberated on the creation of a separate Hill State which was viewed as an action to counter-balance UMFO's idea of a separate Hill State for the hill areas of Assam.

When the States Re-organisation Commission (SRC) visited Assam, the Mizo Union and the District Council submitted a joint Memorandum to that Commission suggesting that the Mizo-inhabited areas of Manipur and Tripura should be annexed to Assam and these areas along with the Mizo Hills District should form one Mizo District. The UMFO also submitted a Memorandum to the Commission that demanded a separate Hill State consisting of all the hill areas of Assam. The Commission recommended in their Report that no changes should be made in the present constitutional pattern.

In spite of discouragement from the Commission, the movement for a separate Hill State started gaining a fertile ground for its growth among the leaders of the different political parties in the hill districts of Assam. When Prime Minister, Nehru, visited Shillong on March 28, 1955, a delegation of hill leaders met him to stress that the formation of an Eastern Hill States was a crying need of the hill people if the Central or the State Government really liked to remove the fear complex and suspicion created in them by the socio-economic backwardness of the hill districts of Assam.[45] The hill leaders also brought to the notice of the Prime Minister their grievances relating to the proposal for the imposition of Assamese as the State language and the concentration of socio-economic development programmes only within the confine of the plains. In return, Nehru appealed to the delegation for calm and impartial considerations on the S.R.C. Report.

In the meantime, the denial of the Hill leaders' demand for a separate Hill State by the Commission generated *esprit de corps* among the hill leaders to pursue their demand for a separate Hill State with a stronger cohesive force. As a consequence, the Chief Executive Members and prominent political leaders of Khasi and Jaintia Hills, the Garo Hills, the Mikir Hills and the Mizo Hills had a conference in the District Council Hall at Aijawl from October 26 to 28, 1955 and "resolved to demand creation of a separate Hill State comprising the hill districts of Assam."[46] The delegates, therefore, proposed to form a joint political platform for all the districts through which they would effectively press their demand for a separate Hill State for the hill tribes. Accordingly, the delegates of the Conference transformed the Highlanders' Union into a new political party called the Eastern Indian Tribal Union (EITU) with the programme of creation of Hill State.

It is interesting to point out here that though the Mizo Union, which was a party in power in the Mizo District, hosted the Conference of the Hill leaders, it politely refused to merge itself to the EITU for fear of being exploited and dominated by other hill tribes after the creation of Hill State. While the Mizo Union was intending to keep itself aloof from the movement for the creation of Hill State, the UMFO quickly stepped forward to take full advantage of that opportunity for broad basing and intensifying its separatist tendency. Meanwhile, the Mizo Union was split due to leadership crises in the party and finally, one of the factions called the Mizo Union Right Wing walked out of the main party and joined the UMFO. With this added strength, the UMFO merged itself into EITU, a newly formed political party, whose avowed objective was "the carving out of a Separate Hill State comprising the Hill Districts of Assam."[47] In spite of the merger that had taken place, the UMFO was allowed to maintain its separate organisational entity and to contest both the District Council and the Legislative Assembly elections until such time as the branch of EITU was officially inaugurated in Mizoram.

Under the auspices of the EITU, the UMFO took no chances to spread the gospel of a Hill State far and wide which caught the imagination of a large section of the Mizo Society. Within a short span, the UMFO was able to draw commendable support of the people for its aim of a separate Hill State "because of the increasing antipathy of the people against the Government of Assam whom the people charged with discrimination against the hill men in favour of the plains people."[48] In July 1956, the UMFO also boycotted the District Council and the Village Councils run by the Mizo Union on charges of corruption and maladministration. Though the movement fizzled out before yielding the desired result, "the Mizo Union's image had been tarnished by the allegations of favouritism in the distribution of pattas... of land."[49] Meanwhile, the Mizo Union remained an associate of the Assam Congress that was running the State Government. However, the Mizo Union too was not pleased with the Assam Congress's policy of imposing Assamese as the State official language that was not liked by all the hill tribes. Hence, the UMFO could gain a fertile ground for its growth with the help of its stand against the inefficiency of the District Council in bringing about socio-economic development of the Mizo District.

In February 1957, general elections to the District Council and the Legislative Assembly of Assam were held simultaneously for the second time. In the District Council election,[50] the Mizo Union could win only 11 out of 22 elected seats whereas the UMFO and its ally, EITU of Pawi-Lakher Region, bagged 8 and 2 seats respectively. It was evident from the election result that the Mizo Union was not able to form a stable government of the District with only 11 elected members. It is, however, important to note that, during the Second District Council election, the Mizo Union did not have any substantial and tangible policy that made it less popular with the people. Moreover, the Mizo Union's loss of two seats against the UMFO candidates, sponsored by the EITU, in the election to the Legislative Assembly of Assam had created an impression that the Mizo supported the movement for the creation of a separate Hill State.

It will not be out of place to point out that the eroding confidence of the hill people in the Assamese leadership as reflected by the election results was the negative consequence of the language policy adopted by the Assam Pradesh Congress Committee from the Asom Jatiya Mahasobha to make Assamese as the State official language.[51] Meanwhile, the Chief Minister of Assam, Bishnuram Medhi, fully understood the sensitivity of the language issue and hence did not like to hurriedly materialise the policy unless the minorities in the hill areas preferred Assamese as the State official language. Even then, the Chief Minister was under constant language pressures and demands of the Assamese to introduce the Language Bill in the Assam Legislature Assembly which was undesirable for the hill people.

In view of the deteriorating relationship between the Assam Government run by the Congress Party and the hill tribes, the late Prime Minister of India, Pandit Jawaharlal Nehru, visited Shillong, the capital city of Assam, to persuade the EITU leaders to participate in the administrative arrangement of the Assam Government under the Chief Ministership of B.P. Chaliha. As a result of his visit, Capt. W.A. Sangma from Garo Hills was appointed a Cabinet Minister in charge of the Tribal Areas Development, Mr. Larsing Khyriem of Khasi and Jaintia became a Deputy Minister and Mr. Lalmawia from the Mizo Hills, a Parliamentary Secretary. Mr. A. Thanglura, who was a Parliamentary Secretary in the Ministry of Bishnuram Medhi, was elevated to the status of the Chief Parliamentary Secretary.[52] However, Chaliha's approach was generally a success except in the Mizo Hills where he committed a grave mistake by making an alliance with the EITU which "outraged the Mizo Union, the erstwhile friend of the Congress."[53]

## III

In 1959, a dreadful famine called 'Mautam Famine' swept the entire Mizo District of Assam. There was widespread hardship and discontent among the people due to acute shortage of food-stuff in the nook and corner of the District as a result of the initial indifference of the Assam Government to the distress of the people and the inordinate delay in initiating relief measures. The Mizo Union leaders who were at the beginning staunch supporters of the Assam Congress Government gradually drifted away and became more and more critical of the Assam Government in their utterances. Meanwhile, those who were running the District Council were not happy either. They felt that the Assam Government did not attach much importance to the Mizo District Council as expected before.

Against this background, the Assembly of the Mizo Union was convened at Aizawl Theatre Hall, on 10 March 1959, to discuss whether the Mizo Union should continue to support the Hill State

Movement or should it fight for a separate Mizoram State. This was the first time some concrete idea for the formation of their own state was mooted out by the Mizo. One EITU leader, Mr. A. Thanglura, was very much irritated by the resolution passed by the Mizo Union for the creation of a separate Mizoram State.

Meanwhile, the Assam Pradesh Congress Committee (APCC), on 22 April 1960, passed a resolution demanding immediate introduction of Assamese.[54] Under the circumstances, the Mizo Union leaders had parted with the EITU and become a constituent of a new political party called 'All Party Hill Leaders' Conference' (APHLC) that was formed to demand the dropping of the Language Bill. In short, the third Conference of the APHLC held on 18 November 1960, at Haflong, demanded, as the only solution to the Language problem, "the immediate creation of a separate Hill State."[55] The representatives of the hill parties unanimously elected Mr. A. Thanglura of the Mizo Union as the first President of the APHLC.

About this time, the Mizo National Famine Front (MNFF) formed by some disgruntled local politicians as a welfare organisation to alleviate the plight of the people caused by 'Mautam Famine', "earned a good name by the devoted work of the its young volunteers who collected house-to-house donations and helped the people in distress."[56] As the motive behind the formulation of the Famine Front was the preparation of the ground for the founding of a new political party, its leaders made themselves popular with the Mizo people. When the Famine was over in 1961, the Famine Front was, as visualised by its leaders, converted into a political party called the 'Mizo National Front' (MNF). While Mr. R. Vanlawma suggested independence of Mizoram from India to be the avowed policy of the party, Mr. Thangliana Sailo suggested statehood for Mizoram instead. Mr. Laldenga, in a bid to bring about a consensus, "put forward a policy of independence of Mizoram with statehood as the real objective."[57]

Within a short span, the MNF movement could gain unprecedented popularity under the charismatic leadership of its founding Father, Laldenga. Ex-servicemen of the Indian Army, educated people, students, professionals and members of the Mizoram Congress, who had strong dislike for the Mizo Union as well as the ex-members of the erstwhile UMFO, joined the MNF Party. The MNF leaders started double-talk and sought to exploit the differences between the ruling Congress in Assam and the Mizo Union, the constituent of the APHLC, which was running the District Council.

Meanwhile, the APHLC committed a major mistake by rejecting Nehru's offer of the Scottish pattern of government for the hills. Though the APHLC made an attempt to reverse its former decision, those political parties constituting the APHLC had lost faith in the party leadership and started keeping distance from the APHLC. The Mizo Union leadership also became disillusioned about the prospects of Mizoram in a Hill State within which Mizoram would not have any link with other constituents. About this time, the Mizo Union contested the two bye-elections held in 1963 on the basis of its old stand regarding formation of a Hill State. But, the MNF, which raised secessionist and communal demands, won both the seats by small margins and sent Mr. John F. Manliana from Aizawl West and Mr. Lalmawia from Lungleh to the Assam Assembly.

Meanwhile, the MNF movement was gaining a fertile ground for its growth whereas the APHLC's image before the Mizo public was tremendously damaged by leadership crises of the party. In view of the prevailing political situations, an influential section of the Mizo Union leadership came to the conclusion that a separate Mizoram State within the Indian Union would be more advantageous than the composite "Eastern Frontier State". Accordingly, the special session of the Mizo Union General Assembly was convened on 10 July 1962 at Aizawl Theatre Hall, which "officially resolved to demand a separate state for the Mizo."[58] In fact, this resolution was passed to officially reaffirm the previous resolution passed by the Mizo Union Assembly, on 10 March 1959, for the creation of a separate state for the Mizo. Simultaneously, the Mizo Union withdrew from the APHLC and gave a clarion call for a Mizoram State.

Although the MNF leaders at first professed "non-violence" as the means for achieving their avowed objectives, it was an open secret that they had already made elaborate preparations for an armed insurgent movement. However, the motive behind the constant use of the word 'non-violence' by the MNF leaders was to earn the confidence of the Assam Chief Minister, Shri B.P. Chaliha. While the Mizo Union was contented with a separate Mizo state within India, the MNF preached for "sovereign independence" and, in order to draw the supports of foreign countries, sent its leaders and followers to East Pakistan.[59] In the first week of December 1963, the top leaders of the MNF, namely, Laldenga, Lalnunmawia and Sainghaka, crossed the border to East Pakistan and were received by the top military functionaries of Pakistani government.[60] These MNF leaders were successful in their mission as Pakistani government promised them supply of military hardware and training of MNF volunteers. When they returned home, Laldenga and his lieutenant, Lalnunmawia, were arrested by the Assam Government on charge of conspiring with Pakistan against India. But, they were released in February 1964 after Laldenga gave a written undertaking to B.P. Chaliha, the then Chief Minister of Assam, that "he and his party would play a constructive role in the development of the Mizo Hills District."[61]

Shortly after the release of Mr. Laldenga upon his written undertaking of good conduct, the MNF intensified its activities and initiated a concerted drive to forcibly collect donations from towns and villages, recruit volunteers and give them training with sophisticated arms imported *via* East Pakistan. Thus, the MNF took up arms in an attempt to achieve its goals and declared Mizoram a "Sovereign Independent State" on 1 March 1966 which openly unleashed insurgent activities in the Mizo District. They first attacked Aizawl Treasury and looted a handsome amount of money along with rifles and ammunition. Within a few hours, the MNF captured all important centres of the Mizo District and the civil administration in the District was virtually paralysed following widespread subversion by the armed volunteers of the MNF. Newspapers also flashed the immediate impact of Mizo insurgency on the administration of the District: "Administration in Mizoram paralysed following widespread subversion by the armed volunteers of the MNF."[62] Evidently, the law and order situation became deteriorated beyond the control of the Police and the Assam Rifles posted in the Mizo District.

Immediately on receipt of telegraphic message about the trouble made by the MNF's insurgent activities under the supreme leadership of Laldenga, the Government of India decided to adopt military measures to firmly deal with insurgent activities. On 2 March 1966, the Government of Assam declared the whole District as a "disturbed area" under the Assam Disturbed Areas Act, 1955. It was also declared as a "disturbed area" under the Armed Forces (Assam and Manipur) Special Powers Act, 1958. This Act gave extensive powers to the army on duty in the notified "disturbed area" to arrest any person, without any warrant, who had committed or who was suspected to commit a cognizable offence.[63] Besides, this Act also empowered the armed forces to enter and search any premises, without any warrant, "to make an arrest or to recover any person wrongfully restrained or confined or any stolen property or any arms, ammunition or explosive substances unlawfully kept in such premises."[64]

The Indian Security Forces were dispatched to Mizoram, which consolidated themselves at Aizawl, on 6 March 1966 to aid and assist the civil administration in the maintenance of law and orders in the District. The Armed Police were placed under the operational control of the Army for delaying with the disturbances. In order to contain the free movement of the insurgents, curfew was imposed from dusks to dawn, which continued for so many years. After the improvement of law and order situation, those who took shelter in the nearby villages began to return home. The Army was ordered by the Government of India "to remain in charge of operation as long as necessary in support of the civil administration."[65] The Government of India declared the MNF and its subsidiary organizations unlawful under Rule 32 of Defence of India Rules, 1962 and banned them. This declaration was followed by the shifting of MNF Headquarters from Aizawl to a big cave near Reiek village and then to secret places in the jungles within and outside the Mizo Hills.

The Mizo Union leaders squarely blamed the then Chief Minister of Assam, B.P. Chaliha, for the sad development of insurgency in the Mizo Hills. On 22 June 1966, a three-member deputation of the Mizo Union met the Prime Minister, Mrs. Indira Gandhi in New Delhi and submitted a Memorandum to her. The Mizo Union reiterated its demand for statehood for the Mizo Hills, which tremendously displeased the MNF. Some of the Mizo Union leaders were arrested by the MNF as a sign of protest against their avowed objective, that is, to attain statehood within the Indian Union. In those days, the Mizo politicians, particularly from the Mizo Union Party, were practically between the hammer and the anvil. However, after three weeks the civil authority at the District Headquarters, Aizawl, was restored in order to enable the democratically elected District Councillors to carry out their responsibility for running the District Administration. Even after the revamping of the District Administration, the *de facto* authority of the District Administration remained in the hands of the Security Forces. The District Councillors and Government officials wherever found were forced by the MNF insurgents to resign their services or to stay away from their offices located here and there. Under such gloomy situation, most of the District Council Members and even Mizo officers in Aizawl and other important places had to take night shelter in the buildings or houses located adjacent to the security posts.

In order to isolate the MNF insurgents and cut off their supply-lines, groping of villages was considered necessary by the Government. Accordingly, the Central Government Liaison Officer for the Mizo Hills District, under 57 Rule of the Defence of India Rules (DIR) 1962, issued two orders for groping of the interior villages to some selected places on the main road of Silchar-Aizawl-Lunglei, starting from Vairengte, the first village in Mizoram from the Silchar side, and stretching over a length of 400 kilometres.[66] Thus, a population of fifty thousand from 106 villages was resettled in 18 grope centres at a very short notice under the strict supervision of the army authority. A grouped village was officially called "Protected and Progressive Village" or in short, PPV. The PPV groping scheme was completed in three phases. The first phase of groping started on 4th January 1967. Immediately after the residents vacated the villages, all the houses therein were set on fire by the security force. All the eighteen PPVs were taken over by the Civil Administration within a month but "the security measures remained with the Post Commander."[67]

While the Mizo Hills District was passing through the darkest period of insurgency, the Election Commission of India issued a Notification for elections to the Lok Sabha and the Assam Legislative Assembly and fixed 17 February 1967 date for the elections. While preparations for the elections were under way, the MNF issued a strong warning to the local politicians not to participate in any of the elections conducted by Government of India or the State Government.[68] Against this background, the Mizo Union boycotted elections to the three seats in the Assam Legislative Assembly on the plea that there was no peace and normalcy in the Mizo District in view of the insurgency. Meanwhile, some of the District Congress Committee leaders and individuals filed their nominations for the three seats in the Assam Assembly for the Mizo Hills. After scrutiny, the Deputy Commission, as the Returning Officer, accepted the nomination papers of A. Thanglura for the Aizawl East and the Aizawl West constituencies and another nomination paper filed by Lalchunga Chinzah for the South Mizo Hills and declared them elected uncontested.

Insurgency tremendously affected all aspects of Mizo life after groping of villages by the Indian Army. This groping of villages brought about untold sufferings and miseries to the general public resulting in total ruination of the village economy and, more important than anything else, in the alienation of the minds of the villagers. There was a general feeling that "they were treated as aliens and worse than enemies."[69] Public resentment against groping was mounting but the then political leaders, namely, those of the Mizo Union and the District Congress Committee could not resist the imposition of the dreadful order for groping. As the public in Mizoram did not approve of the idea of groping, they became quite fed up with this unholy action of herding the villagers into concentration camps. The matter was referred to the Gauhati High Court by some individual enterprising leaders who challenged it on the ground that it was *ultra varies* of the Fundamental Rights.[70] Under such situation, the Mizo could not enjoy their democratic rights to elect their representatives to the Mizo District Council as well. The election to the fourth term District Council had to be kept in abeyance by the State Government.

Although public opinion in general was against groping of villages by force, the Government took new steps to grope villages in the border areas of north, east and west sectors of northern Mizoram under the scheme of New Grope Centres (NGCs). New groping of villages in the further interiors of the District was felt necessary to prevent hostile activities of the MNF volunteers who took temporary shelters in these three areas where army operation could not be concentrated. In 1969, the Deputy Commissioner passed an order for groping of 182 villages into 40 group centres.[71] Groping of villages under the scheme of New Grope Centre affected the life of about 50,000 people and was completed by October 15, 1969. Thus, the Centres were handed over by the army to civil administration in December 1969.

About the same time, the Deputy Commissioner issued an order for groping of 110 villages into 26 centres, which were called "Voluntary Grope Centres" (VGCs). The process of grouping under this scheme started under the supervision of the security forces in 1968 and continued till the end of 1969. The army authorities handed over the administration of these centres to the civil administration in the middle of 1970.[72] Though the groping of this was said to be a groping on voluntary basis, what happened in reality was exactly the opposite. Besides, there was one strange experience and the Mizo public. Before the Governor's promulgation of the ordinance was in effect, all the work of groping was already completed under the supervision of the army operation. It is publicity known to the Mizo even today that shifting of the villages was not voluntary but was rather forcibly done.[73]

There was another type of groping that came to be known in the official parlance as the "Extended Loop Area (ELA)." Under this scheme, 63 villages with a population of 40,000 in the area bordering Manipur in the north and Burma (Mynanmar) in the east were groped in 17 centres. It is strange to point in this connection that the groping was actually undertaken by the 59 Mountain Brigade operating from Manipur. The end of 1969 completed the process of groping and the grope centres were handed over by the army authorities to the Deputy Commissioner in the middle of 1970.[74]

Groping of villages under different schemes affected about 80 per cent of the rural population and about 65 per cent of the total population of the District. The total expenditure of the Government for groping came to about two crores of rupees while the Government's expenditure for the supply of free ration to the PPVs only for one year alone amounted to Rs. 71 lakhs.[75]

All the groping centres were securely fenced with either bamboo or wooden spikes by the civilians to prevent the insurgents from entering into the villages for food. The villagers compulsorily under the strict supervision of the security forces carried these fencing works out without receiving even single paisa as remuneration. In addition to this, those who had shifted from their ancestral homes to the new centres had to build their temporary and permanent dwellings without any grant from the Government. Under such a critical situation, those new residents of the groping centres had passed through "economic hardships, psychological sufferings, physical and mental tortures and numerous difficulties just in the name of operation accomplishment."[76]

For quite some time, the political situation in the Mizo Hills improved as the MNF insurgents did not intensify their unrest. Even the Mizoram Congress, which was almost defunct due to the insurgency and the leadership crisis of the party, found a congenial political atmosphere for its growth among the Mizo public. The Mizoram Congress was by nature opposed to the Mizo Union and the MNF at the initial stage of its formation. But, the policy of the party, as clearly reflected in the Party Constitution, was to make all-out efforts for the peaceful settlement of the Mizo problem through political dialogue and this policy drew the attention of the Mizo public who found themselves very helpless before the security forces.

The Mizo who charged the Congress as a party of the outsiders had a new ray of hope that only the Mizoram Congress, being an affiliate of the Assam Congress that was in power in the States would be in a position to do something to relieve the untold psychological sufferings, physical and mental tortures inflicted on them by the Security forces. Shortly, the MNF returnees, the pro-MNF people and the dispossessed families of the Mizo traditional Chiefs joined the Mizoram Congress. The Mizoram Congress Party was, thus, looked upon by the people as "overground MNF" because of "its declared policy of peaceful settlement of Mizo problem" and "its attempt to act as a mediator between the Government of India and the underground MNF."[77] After successfully aggregating diverse interest of the people, the Mizoram Congress could revamp its organisation, which remained non-functional for the last six years.

Following the grouping of villages, there was a sign of slight improvement of law and order situation in the Mizo District. The Assam Government also decided to conduct elections to the fourth term District Council, on 24 April 1970, after extending the life of the third District Council almost by another three years. By this time, two well-organised political parties, namely, the Mizo Union Party and the Congress Party contested the election.[78] Unlike before, those parties contesting the election did not receive any prohibitory order from the MNF. Even the Mizo Union freely contested the election with its avowed objective of creating Mizoram State within the Indian Union by unifying all the Mizo inhabited areas of Manipur, Cachar and Tripura.

The Congress Party fought the election on the platform of the peaceful settlement of the Mizo problem and, for that, offered itself as the messenger of peace between the Government of India and the underground MNF.[79] In this election to the District Council, the Congress captured 10 seats while the Mizo Union and the independent candidates bagged 9 and 3 seats respectively. Thus, the Congress Party formed the last District Council "with the help of two nominated members."[80] But, there could be no stable government in the Mizo District Council due to the prevailing stiff competition for positions among the leaders of the Mizoram Pradesh Congress Committee. On April 14, 1971, the coalition government formed by the Mizo Union with the Dengthuama faction of the Congress under the leadership of Mr. Ch. Chhunga "passed a resolution demanding a Mizoram State within India", and "the unification of all the Mizo inhabited areas."[81]

Meanwhile, Mr. Ch. Chhunga, in his capacity as the leader of the United Mizo Parliamentary Party (UMPP) coalition, successfully negotiated with the Central Government in July 1971 for the separation of the Mizo District from the Assam State to become a Union Territory. But, some Congress leaders of Hrangchhuana faction expressed their unhappiness over the Union Territory status and "staged a demonstration in the capital under the banner of a Mizo Students' Convention in defence of democracy and in opposition to the Union Territory proposal."[82] They were of the opinion that the *status quo* should continue till peace was fully restored in the Mizo District.

Meanwhile, the majority of the unionists "agreed to accept the status of a Union Territory with a demand that the Union Territory should be made a state in due course of time."[83] With the exception of a small segment of the Mizo population, the bulk of the political leadership of the Mizo Hills agreed to the creation of a Union Territory to separate the Mizo from Assam. Thus, the Central Government promptly took the necessary steps to usher in the new system of administration and the Union Territory of Mizoram "came into existence on January 21, 1971."[84] Unfortunately, some Mizo Union elements led by the former CEM, Mr. H.K. Bawichhuaka and former General Secretary, Mr. C. Pahlira "resigned from the party to record their insistence on full statehood demand."[85]

The first general election to the 30-member Legislative Assembly of the Union Territory of Mizoram was held on 18 April 1972. In this election, the Mizoram Congress Committee suffered a serious setback as the Mizo Union returned with an absolute majority. Thus, the Mizo Union formed the first ministry and Mr. Ch. Chhunga was unanimously elected to be "the first Chief Minister of popular Ministry on 3 May 1972."[86] But, the inception of the Mizo Union government was followed by hostile incidents of varying intensity in and around the urban centres of Mizoram. However, it was not surprising for the MNF insurgents to indulge in some daring acts to increase the anxiety of the government administration and the people loyal to the government under the changing circumstances.

Consequent upon the liberation of Bangladesh to become a sovereign nation in 1971, the MNF lost their safe sanctuary in the

Chittagong Hill Tracts of Bangladesh that eventually led to the shifting of their tactical headquarters to the dense forests of Arakan.[87] There was shortage of food supply and other amenities whereas their supremo, Laldenga, and his family were taking shelter in Pakistan. Meanwhile, a few batches of the MNF insurgents had infiltrated into Mizoram to raise funds, collect rations and recruit young boys and girls to its ranks. The MNF infiltration was instantly followed by brutal killings and widespread looting of treasury money and grains in the government godowns. On 28 February 1973, the anniversary day of the insurgency, the MNF insurgents had blown up the Aizawl Power House, which injured five people. Mr. Ch. Chhunga, the Chief Minister of Mizoram, said in Calcutta that the Mizo rebels had blown up the Power House on the "anniversary" of their insurgency, which began on 28 February 1965, "perhaps to tell the people that they are still alive."[88]

It will not be out of place to point out that, immediately after the formation of the Ministry by Mr. Ch. Chhunga, the Mizo Union leaders were said to be courted and persuaded by Mrs. Indira Gandhi, the Prime Minister of India, to merge with the opposition Congress Party in the Legislative Assembly of Mizoram. By this time, it was an open secret among the Mizo public that the Mizoram Congress was eager to be actively involved in the administration of the Union Territory and simultaneously, the Mizo Union "wanted to belong to an All India Party which may bestow patronage from the Centre."[89] Ultimately, Mr. Ch. Chhunga and Mr. Lal Thanhawla, the President of the Mizoram Congress, agreed to an unconditional merger after having a series of meetings with Mrs. Indira Gandhi, the Prime Minister of India, in New Delhi, on 13 and 14 November 1973.

But, the merger of the two political parties made a poor performance. The Mizo Union's expectation that the social, economic and political conditions of the people would greatly improve if the Mizoram Government was run by the same party as that holds power at the Centre, could not come true. Hence, the Mizo Society began to have an impression that the merger Congress Ministry was no better than the earlier Mizo Union Ministry. In the meanwhile, the Mizo Union elements and the 'original' Congressmen continued to have different mentalities. Besides, there was "an internal power-struggle between the two groups."[90] The Mizo Unionists absorbed in the Congress also alleged that no Congress leaders, both local and national, had even uttered a single word of disapproval of the hostile activities of the MNF. In the absence of an emotional solidarity among party members, there was no *esprit de corps* in the Mizoram Congress. So, the merger was practically unworkable to yield the result as expected by the right-thinking members of the Congress and the Mizo Union Parties before the merger took place. However, the merger was necessary in view of the strained relationship between the MNF underground and the Mizo Union which was running the Union Territory Government of Mizoram.

While the Mizo Union elements within the Congress Party were making comprehensible efforts to reconcile with the erstwhile Congress attitude of negotiations with the MNF, the insurgents had become very active once again and could be spotted everywhere in the rural and urban areas of Mizoram. They were terrorising the people and nobody dare speak against them. They were also "building up their strength and re-grouping."[91] Though the Chief Minister, Ch. Chhunga and the Congress President, Lal Thanhawla, had already proposed to hold unofficial talks about peaceful settlement of insurgency problem, their dream for an early materialisation of their political demands for Mizoram Statehood could not be translated into a reality for the moment.

## IV

However, it is evident that the movement for Mizoram Statehood was the by-product of political movements taking place not only in the Mizo Hills but also in other hill areas of the composite state of Assam. In fact, no political parties in Mizoram ever spelt out any specific political demand for Mizoram Statehood in their written constitution when democratisation of their traditional polity was at its initial stage. When Mizo Union, the first political party, came into existence, its principal political objective, among others, was to launch a democratic movement for the attainment of the highest possible degree of autonomy within the Assam State of the Indian Union. The United Mizo Freedom Organisation (UMFO), on the other hand, set a gigantic political objective to launch a democratic movement for Mizoram Independence. But the UMFO utterly failed to mobilise the people's support for its declared political objective. The UMFO had to make a policy shift from Independence to the Hill State Movement to conform to the policy of the Eastern India Tribal Union (EITU) and then the All Party Hill Leaders Conference (APHLC). When the

MNF came into existence, it revived the old objective of the UMFO to fight for Mizoram Independence and faced stiff opposition from the State and the Central Governments. Under such circumstances, the Mizo Union revised its policy of fighting for a Hill State under the umbrella of the EITU and the APHLC, and thus disassociated itself with the APHLC to launch a separate political movement for Mizoram Statehood. The Mizo Union leaders were of the opinion that the Mizo would feel insecure—socially, economically and politically, if they remained the constituent of the Hill State. The Mizo Union's movement for Mizoram State touched the hearts of the common people who wanted to safeguard their customs and traditions against the plains people. When the new leadership of the Mizoram Congress revamped the party organisation, it came out with a clear policy of negotiating the MNF and the Union Government on the insurgent problems through peaceful means. The Mizoram Congress Committee declared itself as the messenger of peace and hence left no stones unturned to work for the peaceful settlement of insurgency problems in Mizoram. Laldenga had a series of meetings with Central Congress leaders and finally, with the Prime Minister, Rajiv Gandhi. Finally, this was followed by the signing of the Mizoram Peace Accord on June 30, 1986 between the Union Home Secretary, R.D. Pradhan, Laldenga and Lalkhama, Chief Secretary of Mizoram.

## NOTES

1. Paul, Wilkinson. *Social Movements*, (Pall Mall, London, 1971), p. 1.
2. M.S.A. Rao (Ed.) *Social Movements in India*, Vol. I (Manohar Publications, New Delhi, 1984), p. 2.
3. Chaube, S.K. *Hill Politics in North East India*, (Orient Longman Ltd., New Delhi, 1973), p. 16.
4. Also see, 'Government of India's Proclamation No. 591-EB,' Vide *Assam Secretariat, Foreign A, May 1898, Nos. 13-46.*
5. 'Notification No. 784 P, dated the 9th October 1911,' Vide *Eastern Bengal and Assam Gazette, October 11, 1911, Part II*, p. 1992.
6. "Section 52 A (2) of the Government of India Act, 1919." as quoted in Ray, A.C. *op. cit.* p. 45.
7. Singh, Chandrika. *Emergence of Arunachal Pradesh as a State*, (Mittal Publications, Delhi, 1989), p. 89.
8. "Notification No.2107 A.P. dated March 9, 1993, issued by the Governor-in-Council," vide McCall, A.G. *The Lushai Hills District Cover*, (The Tribal Research Institute, Aizawl, 1980), p. 66.

9. McCall, A.G. *Lushai Chrysalis*, (Luzac & Co., London, 1949), p. 65.
10. Bhuyan, B.C. *Political Development of the North East*, Vol.I, (Omsons Publications, Delhi, 1989), p. 139.
11. Ray, A.C. *op. cit.*, p. 47.
12. Chaube, S.K. *op cit.*, p. 230.
13. Rao, V.V. *A Century of Tribal Politics in North East India*, (S.Chand & Co. Ltd., New Delhi, 1976), p. 162.
14. Constituent Assembly of India. *North-East Frontier Tribal and Excluded Areas Sub-Committee*, Vol.11 (Evidence), Part I, (Delhi, G.L.Publications, 1947), p. 26.
15. "Resolution passed in the first General Assembly of the Mizo Union" held from 24 to 26 September 1946 as quoted in Ray, A.C. *op.cit.*, pp. 122-23.
16. Vanlawma, R. *Ka Ram leh Kei*, (My Country and I), (Zalen Printing House, Aizawl, 1972), pp. 133-34.
17. *Ibid.*, p. 129.
18. *Constituent Assembly Debates*, Vol.11, Nos.4 (Delhi, 1946-47), pp. 308-11.
19. This Advisory Sub-Committee was also popularly known as a Bordoloi Sub-Committee after the name of its Chairman, Gopinath Bordoloi.
20. *Ibid.*
21. Chaltuahkhuma. *Political History of Mizoram*, (L.B. Press, Aizawl, 1981), p. 42.
22. *Proceedings of the North-East Frontier (Assam) Tribal and Excluded Areas Sub-Committee*, Vol.11 (Evidence) Part 1, Constituent Assembly of India, New Delhi, 1949, p. 2.
23. Prasad, R.N. *Government and Politics in Mizoram*, (Northern Book Centre, New Delhi, 1987), p. 83.
24. Lalnithanga, P. 'Autonomy Movements in Mizoram After Independence', in Prasad, R.N. (ed.) *Autonomy Movements in Mizoram*, (Vikas Publishing House Pvt. Ltd., New Delhi; 1994), p. 92.
25. Vanthuama, H. *op.cit.*, p. 66.
26. Prasad, R.N. *Government and Politics in Mizoram*, (Northern Book Centre, New Delhi, 1987), pp. 83-84. Also see, Lalnithanga, P. "Autonomy Movements in Mizoram After Independence," in R.N. Prasad (Ed.). *Autonomy Movements in Mizoram*, (Vikas Publishing House Pvt. Ltd., New Delhi 1994), p. 92.
27. *Draft Constitution of Mizoram for the future Administration of the District within the Province of Assam in free India*, submitted to the Constituent Assembly of India through the Bordoloi Sub-Committee on 17th April, 1947 by the Mizo Union, signed by Khawtinkhuma and H.Vanthuama, the President and the General Secretary respectively.
28. Pachhunga, Dahrawka, P.S and Hmartawnphunga. *Mizoram Din Phal Tur Ngaituah Hona, Vantlang Inkhawm*, (A Public Meeting Dealing with the Future Political Status of Mizoram), February 21, 1947, p. 1 (Pamphlet).

One month before the arrival of the Bordoloi Sub-Committee, the M.U. (Right Wing) convened a public meeting in Bengali Theatre Hall in Aizawl under the Chairmanship of Mr. Sainghinga, Assistant Superintendent of the Mizo Hills. Many Church leaders, teachers and other people totalling about 200, attended this meeting. In this public meeting, it was unanimously agreed that Mizoram Independence should be fought for.

29. Prasad, R.N. *op. cit.*, p. 84.
30. Lalnithanga, P. *op. cit.*
31. Chaube, S.K. *op. cit.* p. 176.
32. Rao, V.V. *op. cit.* p. 40.
33. Laldena. *Christian Missions and Colonialism*, (Venframe Institute, Shillong, 1998), p. 110.
34. Vanlawma, R. *op. cit.* pp. 147-48. Also see, Chaltuahkhuma. *op. cit.* pp. 42-43.
35. Ray, A.C. *op. cit.* p.124.
36. *Ibid.*, p. 125.
37. Vanlawma, R. *op. cit.* pp. 155-56.
38. *Demi-Official letter* by R.Thanhlira to Subramanian, 18 September 1951.
39. *Confidential Note by Subramanian, 30 April, 1952*, preserved by Tribal Research Institute, Government of Mizoram, Aizawl.
40. Zoram Hriattirna, *Lushai Hills District Council,* (Village Council) Act, 1953, p.15.
41. Khuma, V.H. *Political History of Mizoram*, (3 J Publication, Aizawl, 1999), p. 87.
42. *Proceedings of the Seventh General Assembly of the United Mizo Freedom Organisation* held at Aijawl on October 1 and 2, 1953.
43. 'Proceedings of the Meeting of the Executive Committee of the Mizo Union held under the Chairmanship of R.Thanhlira from January 31 to February 3, 1954,' Vide *The Assam Tribune* of February 12, 1954.
44. Ray, A.C. *op. cit.* p. 127.
45. Chaube, S.K. *op. cit.* p. 124.
46. Ray, A.C. *op. cit.* p. 131.
47. *Ibid.*
48. *Ibid.*
49. Chaube, S.K. *op. cit.* p. 116.
50. The elective seats of the District Council had been raised from 18 to 22 seats.
51. Chaube, S.K. *op. cit.* p. 128.
52. Ray, A.C. *op. cit.* p. 132.
53. Chaube, S.K. *op. cit.* p. 127.
54. Chaube, S.K. *op. cit.* p. 128.
55. *Ibid.*, p.133.
56. Ray, A.C. *op. cit.* p. 133.
57. Lalthangliana, 'Mizo National Front Movement,' in Prasad, R.N. (ed.)

*Autonomy Movements in Mizoram*, (Vikas Publishing House Pvt. Ltd., New Delhi, 1994), p.175.

58. Ray, A.C. *op cit.*, p.135. Also see, Chaube, S.K. *op. cit.* p. 179.
59. *Ibid.*, p. 134.
60. Nibedon, N. *Mizoram: The Dagger Brigade*, (Lancers Publishers, New Delhi, 1982), p. 45.
61. Lalthangliana, "Mizo National Front Movement" in Prasad, R.N. (ed.) *Ibid.* p. 177.
62. Banner Headline of *The Assam Tribune*, Gauhati, March 3, 1966.
63. The Armed Forces (Assam and Manipur) Special Powers Act, 1958, Section 4, Sub-Section (c).
64. *Ibid.*, Section 4.
65. The Minister's Statement, *Lok Sabha Debates*, March 3, 1966, Columns 3585-86.
66. *Orders No.CLD 1/1/-67/1*, dated Silchar, the 2nd January 1967, and *No.CLD 1/1-67/1-80*, dated Silchar, the 27th February 1967 passed by the Central Government Liaison Officer for the Mizo District.
67. Prasad, R.N. *op. cit.*, p. 199.
68. Thanglura, A. *op. cit.*, p. 236.
69. Government of Mizoram. *Brig. T. Sailo's Speeches and Writings*, (I&PR Department, Aizawl, 1983), p. 15.
70. *Ibid.*, p. 14.
71. Deputy Commissioner's *Order No.APGC/28/69/196*, dated the 22nd September 1969, passed under Section 13D of the Assam Maintenance of Public Order Act 1953.
72. *Deputy Commissioner's Order No.ANG/2/70/11,* dated Aijawl, the 29th August 1970.
73. Prasad, R.N. *op. cit.*, p. 201.
74. Ray, A.C. *op. cit.*, p. 175.
75. *Ibid.*, p. 177.
76. Prasad, R.N. *op. cit.*, p. 201.
77. Lalchungnunga. *Mizoram: Politics of Regionalism and National Integration*, (Reliance Publishing House, New Delhi, 1994), p. 95.
78. Chaltuahkhuma. *op. cit.*, p. 4.
79. *Election Manifesto of the Mizo District Congress Committee No.1. 1970.* (A small leaflet).
80. Chaube, S.K. *op. cit.*, p. 100.
81. *Ibid.*, p. 182.
82. *Ibid.*, p. 183.
83. Ray, A.C. *op. cit.*, p. 141.
84. *Ibid.*, p. 141.
85. Sarin, V.I.K. *op. cit.*, p. 218.
86. Government of Mizoram, *Heralding Mizoram State*, (DIPR & T. Aizawl), p. 5.
87. Ray, A.C. *op. cit.*, p. 164.

88. *The Statesman*, Calcutta, February 21, 1973.
89. "Politics of Merger in Mizoram", *The Hindusthan Standard*, Calcutta, February 18, 1974.
90. Lalchungnunga. *op. cit.*, p. 87.
91. *The Hindustan Times*, New Delhi, April 11, 1974.

# Chapter 4

## The State and Civil Society in Mizoram
## *The Post-Accord Syndrome*

JAGADISH K. PATNAIK

---

Following an arduous journey of insurgency and endless conflict spanning two decades, Mizoram assumed an identity as the 23rd state of the Indian Union.[1] This could be possible owing to a well negotiated and well drafted accord that was signed between the Government of India and the Mizo National Front (MNF) which was engaged in the insurgency. The interesting fact about this peace accord is that it seems to have endured the test of time with a longish peace in the region in contrast to all other peace accords which were signed during the time. The reason for such peace is the growing activism of the civil society and its interface/synergy with the state. It necessarily, however, does not mean that there is a total absence of discontentment in the state. There are pockets of discontent pertaining to the post-accord developments.[2] The issues pertaining to the Brus, Chakmas, Hmars and other ramifications in the state cannot be pushed under the carpet. They may seem to be small in intensity and number. They may be confined to certain areas of the state. They need, however, to be attended to immediately without any rancour. The present paper is intended to examine the pockets of discontentment that are manifested in the state. The paper also attempts to analyse the emergence of numerous non-governmental organisations which help facilitate the ventilation of the grievances.

The paper is organised as follows: first, we will provide a brief history of the emergence of Mizoram as a separate state of the Indian

Union; second, an analysis of the present scenario, specifically the areas of discontentment prevailing presently in Mizoram will be made; in the third section we will deal with the various organisations engaged in the articulation of the grievances and discontentment among the various sections of the society. Finally, the paper will conclude by way of suggestion that unless effective steps to plug the spots of discontentment are taken with seriousness, the peace and development in the state of Mizoram will be at stake. For this, the civil society groups, the state and Central Government have to work in tandem so that things will be in order. The paper is impressionist in analysis and is just indicative of the trends rather than exhaustive.

## I. MIZORAM: AN OVERVIEW

The history of the emergence of the state of Mizoram as an entity is typical in its own way.[3] Unlike other states of the North-East India except Nagaland, Mizoram assumed statehood as result of protracted years of violent struggle. The state witnessed worst kind of insurgent movement spanning over two decades.[4] Yet after the formation of the state, there is hardly any eruption of political violence of substantial proportion. The state has witnessed relatively a longer peace compared to other states in the region. There are, however, numerous cases of discontentment and problems of integration within the state of the various minority groups. The reason for such occurrences is the nature of development ushered in, as well as due to the composition of the demography of the state.

The problems of the state are also to do with the geographical contiguity with two neighbours with whom it does share common colonial history. It would not be wrong rather to attribute the present state of conflict and cleavage in the North-East region to the colonial times when there was the gradual movement of peoples across the border. As one writer remarks:

> "Among the most successful was that of Mizo unification which, to some extent, unified various tribes and put them under a single umbrella, and also borne a state, but, in the pessimistic view, only created more disintegration. Not mistaking, Mizo recognise, among others, Hmar as its member-tribe which results in a split:

> Mizo-Hmar and Hmar (which opines that Hmar is a Mizo-independent tribe or that Mizo extends its realm up to the Mizoram state boundary only). It also built a greater wall between tribes under Mizo and those under Kuki and Chin, making each nation look like a separate entity when, however, they are, in general term, one."[5]

Being one of the frontier states of Union of India, Mizoram is unique in several respects. It attained statehood in February 1987. It came into being as a separate state following the signing of the peace accord after an arduous struggle of insurgency of two decades.[6] This accord seems to be the longest peace accord that has stood the test of time in the North East India. Consequent upon the 53rd Amendment of the Constitution of India, the state of Mizoram was formed as the 23rd state with three Autonomous District Councils and 301 village councils along with three districts.[7] Now, however, the number of the districts has gone up to 8. Contrary to the popular belief in the mainland, Mizoram exudes a semblance of peace and amity in the region. The pace of development in the region is far better than other neighbouring states. Save for a few infinitesimally small segment of population, which is minor aberration, the Mizo Accord serves as a model of Peace in the region.

The state of Mizoram is of great strategic importance, as it is situated in the northeast corner of India. It has a boundary length of 630 miles with Bangladesh and Myanmar. With an area of 20,987 sq. km, Mizoram has a population of 891,058, as per the 2001 census. The density of population is 42 per sq. km. The main spoken languages are Mizo and English. The percentage of literacy in the state is 81.23 per cent, second to Kerala. It is hoped that in the next census Mizoram will overtake Kerala in literacy. The credit for the rate of literacy, however, goes to the efforts of the church, which is one of the most important organizations of the civil society. With 95 per cent of population being Christian, the Church plays a crucial role in the socio-cultural up-lift of the Mizo society. In every village in Mizoram there is at least one church and a school; and the people of Mizoram give great importance to education. For they know that without education there can be no progress. Although the history of the Mizo is shrouded in mystery, it is accepted fact that Mizo are of

Mongoloid stock and are believed to have migrated from the upper Burma sometime between 1400 and 1800 A.D. The Mizo language (of which the largest is Lushai) belongs to the Tibeto-Burmese family and is closely related to those of the Chin in the adjacent Chin state of Mynamar, as well as those of the Nagas, Kukis and others.[8] One historian claims, "Mizoram is a multi-ethnic and pluralistic state comprising as many as 14 tribes with different languages and dialects."[9] There is no denying, however, that the Mizo are a distinct ethnic community in India.

Mizo society has evolved dramatically in its structures and culture over the roughly three centuries of its existence in the Indian political system. Although the Mizo seemed to be the last segment to be absorbed into this region of the Indian political system, there is a tremendous transformation in the political life in the later part of 20th century. The shift has been generic in the sense that the chieftainship system that was being practiced in the past got transformed into village council system. Now there are attempts to replace the councils by local-self government at the grassroots level. The classless Mizo community is now slowly getting stratified in line with the economic advancement of certain sections of the society. The post-independent and post-accord phase specifically, has witnessed the emergence of the propertied class displacing the earlier communal economy in which everything belonged to the community. The emergence of private property has definitely vitiated the sublime peace of the traditional tribal community though; the cleavages and tension arising out of it do not lead to any social conflict unlike in other parts of the mainland.

The homogeneity of the Mizo society serves as its pillar of strength. The traditional practices and values of community life still sustain in different ways in the culture and society of Mizo people. The church and Christianity have given them a separate sense of identity. The socio-cultural dynamics of traditional Mizo community has crept into the religious practices, thus providing a sense of belonging with Christianity. It has also served as an integrating element for the strengthening of the society. There are other religious communities though; they constitute a small per cent of the total population (see Table 4.1).

**Table 4.1:** Population by Religion in Mizoram (2001) Census

| Sl. No. | Name of District | Christian | Hindu | Muslim | Sikh | Buddhist | Jains | Religion not stated | Others |
|---|---|---|---|---|---|---|---|---|---|
| 1 | 2 | 3 | 4 | 5 | 6 | 7 | 8 | 9 | 10 |
| 1. | Aizawl | 303893 | 14508 | 5185 | 105 | 576 | 30 | 208 | 1170 |
| 2. | Mamit | 50563 | 2404 | 1096 | 24 | 8579 | 17 | 6 | 96 |
| 3. | Kolasib | 59098 | 4273 | 1995 | 31 | 177 | 2 | 114 | 306 |
| 4. | Champai | 105061 | 2248 | 432 | 24 | 163 | 6 | 209 | 249 |
| 5. | Serchip | 52495 | 531 | 177 | 2 | 87 | 6 | 39 | 524 |
| 6. | Lunglei | 109024 | 4612 | 775 | 63 | 22429 | 28 | 14 | 98 |
| 7. | Lawngtlai | 32877 | 1910 | 230 | 73 | 38410 | 88 | 32 | 0 |
| 8. | Saiha | 59618 | 1112 | 209 | 3 | 73 | 2 | 39 | 0 |
| | Mizoram | 772809 | 31562 | 10099 | 326 | 70494 | 179 | 661 | 2443 |

*Source*: Statistical Handbook Mizoram 2006 (Aizawl: Director of Economics and Statistics, 2006) p. 5.

***The Autonomous District Councils in Mizoram*:** Although there is a homogenous ethnic Mizo community in the state, there is also the presence of some minority groups representing other ethnic-religious and linguistic denominations. These are Hmar, Pawi, Lakher or Mara, Riang or Brue and Chakma. Besides the eight districts in the state there are three Autonomous District Councils which form part of Mizoram. They are Lai Autonomous District Council (LADC), Mara Autonomous District Council (MADC) and Chakma Autonomous District Council (CADC). These autonomous district councils came into being as a result of the Sixth Schedule of the Constitution of India. The LADC and CADC fall under the geographical jurisdiction of Lawngtlai district and MADC falls under Saiha district. There are two sets of governments that are running in these two districts: One being run by the state administration and the other by the Autonomous Council. The autonomous councils have funding from Government of India as well as the state government. A glance at the following table provides some insight about the autonomous district councils in Mizoram.

**Table 4.2:** Autonomous District Councils in Mizoram

| *Sl. No.* | *Particulars* | *LADC* | *MADC* | *CADC* |
|---|---|---|---|---|
| *1* | *2* | *3* | *4* | *5* |
| 1. | Area in sq. km | 1870.75 | 1445.00 | 1500 |
| 2. | Population | 58700 | 51073 | 34528 |
| 3. | No. of voters | 35808 | 31763 | 18062 |
| 4. | Villages | 77 | 70 | 64 |
| 5. | Sub-villages | Nil | Nil | Nil |
| 6. | MDC | 23(elected) 4(nominated) | 22(elected) 4(nominated) | 13(elected) 3(nominated) |
| 7. | Executive committee | 1-CEM 9-Ems | 1-CEM 7-Ems | 1-CEM 5-Ems |
| 8. | No. of employees | 422 1294 | 32 1147 | 295 180 |
| 9. | Percentage of ST | 98.70 | 97.78 | 100 |
| 10. | Year in which last elections held | 27-10-2005 | 19-5-2005 | 15-2-2005 |

LADC = Lai Autonomous District Council.
CEM = Chief Executive Member.
MADC = Mara Autonomous District Council.
CADC = Chakma Autonomous District Council.
*Source*: Statistical Handbook Mizoram 2006 (Aizawl: Director of Economics and Statistics, 2006) p.112.

Besides the autonomous district councils—that itself speaks about the pluralist nature of the state—there are numerous small groups who have been either displaced due to some reason or other from Mizoram and were engaged in insurgency. Those small groups were earlier engaged in large scale violence with the majority ethnic Mizo community. Now the situation has changed to a great extent so much so that there is hardly the possibility of large-scale violence erupting in the near future. Now, although those groups do not have any substantial violent impact on Mizoram due to the numerous efforts to bring about peace, the extent of discontentment still continues in large measure. There are around nine such groups which have been engaged in insurgent activities that have implications for the state of Mizoram.[10] We will deal with some of these groups in a separate section.

## II. AREAS OF DISCONTENTMENT IN MIZORAM

As mentioned earlier, beneath the sublime peace on the Mizo hills in the post-accord Mizoram there are sporadic presences of areas of discontentment among some people. These issues of discontentment emanate from within as well as without. In this section, we will discuss the cases of discontentment relating specifically to the Hmars and Brues whose problems date back prior to the formation of separate statehood of Mizoram. We will also attempt at analyzing some of the areas of discontentment among the Chakmas who have a separate autonomous political unit within Mizoram, as well as among the Mizo people pertaining to governance in the state.

***Hmars:*** The Hmar is a distinct ethno-linguist community which owes its origin to the Indo-Burmese race. In Mizoram, the Hmar community is completely adapted into the Mizo culture, although there is still a small segment of population which is partially assimilated into the culture. While there is no substantial complaint from the former, the latter group, which is in the region of few thousands, tries to maintain its distinct identity in terms of language, tradition, and customs. It is this group which has been at loggerheads with the Mizo community. The real problem started during the insurgency days when the Hmars joined the Mizo National Front for creation of "Greater Mizoram" integrating all areas inhabited by the Hmars in Assam, Manipur, and Mizoram. The peace accord that was signed between the Mizo National Front and the Government of India did not incorporate the hopes and aspirations of the Hmar people. This resulted in the disappointment among the Hmars, leading to armed violence which erupted in 1991. Hmar cadres abducted tea executives and triggered off a spate of extortions in the Hmar inhabited areas of the States of Mizoram, Assam, and Manipur.[11] However, following nine rounds of negotiations, the Government of Mizoram and the Hmar Peoples Convention signed an agreement on the 27th July 1994 for establishing the Singlung Development Council. After the agreement over 300 militants surrendered along with their arms.[12] Some of those who were not happy with the agreement formed another group called Hmar Peoples Convention-Democracy in 1995. This organization initially started demanding for creation of an autonomous district in the north and northeast region of Mizoram. Now it is demanding for an independent Hmar state consisting of the Hmar inhabited areas of Mizoram, Manipur, and Assam. Although the outfit has a small number of cadres which may be in the region of 200 to 300, it has links with other insurgent groups in the region. It has alleged links with Bru National Army which operates from Mizoram. It has also links with the Zo ethnic militant groups which operate outside Mizoram. Its presence is conspicuous due to its animosity against the Dimasas in the Cachar and North Cachar Hills District of Assam.[13] As matters stand now, the Chief Minister of Mizoram Mr. Zoramthang has initiated negotiations with the HPC-D with the help of Charlton Lien Amo, an MLA from Manipur. The demand of the outfit is to involve the Union Government so that the provisions of the 1994 Peace agreement can be implemented effectively.

The discontentment, however, continues with regard to the non-implementation of the agreement for preserving and protecting the Hmar culture. So far the Government of Mizoram has not been able to introduce Hmar language as a medium of instruction at the primary level in the Hmar villages. Despite the state assembly recommending for the inclusion of the non-schedule areas in the sixth schedule of the Constitution, it has not been passed in the Indian parliament. The Sinlung Hills Development Council (SHDC) was created for the purpose of promoting the social, cultural, economic, and educational development of the people of north and north-eastern Mizoram seemed to have lost its purpose for want of funds. Now it seems to be a defunct body. The Chairman of SHDC, Hmingchungnunga, has virtually no power to deliver the goods. His alleged proximity with the MNF is also not appreciated by the people.

The HPC-D which parted ways with HPC is intent upon spearheading the movement for separate state for the Hmar people in Mizoram. It is impossible to make conjectures about the realization of such objective, though. The fact, however, is that the Hmar people want "speedy resolution of all pending basic issues."[14]

***Brus***: The Bru tribal community, also known as Reang, constitutes one of the few minority communities settled in Mizoram. This community which belongs to the minority Hindu religion, inhabited in the Mamit sub-division of the state. There were violent clashes between the ethnic Mizo and Bru way back in 1996 which led to formation of the Bru National Liberation Front (BNLF), an armed outfit which has cadre strength of about a little over 100. The immediate fallout of the ethnic clash was the exodus of a large number of the Brus to the neighbouring states of Tripura and Assam and some of them have been staying in six refugee camps in North Tripura

District since then.[15] Since the Brus constituted a distinct community, there was discontentment with respect to the protection of the economic, political, and cultural rights of these people. As a result, in the year 1994 a political organization called Bru National Union (BNU) was formed. The objective of the organization was the demand for the creation of an Autonomous District Council.

The Mizoram Government initiated talks with the BNLF and held a series of talks with the outfit since September 2001. After thirteen rounds of talks, the BNLF signed a Memorandum of Understanding (MOU) with the Mizoram Government. With this, the eight year old insurgency came to an end. Following the signing of the MOU, 800 rebels belonging to the Bru Liberation Front of Mizoram (BLFM) laid down their arms before Mizoram Home Minister at a function held in Tuipuibari, about 200 km south of the state capital Aizawl.[16] The Minister declared that the government would provide free ration for one year and Rs.40,000 to each of the surrendered rebels, besides reimbursing for the weapons deposited.[17] Now the main problem is regarding the repatriation of the refugees living in camps. For this purpose a financial package of INR 286.5 million has been sanctioned by the Union government.[18]

The return of the Brus from the refugee camps to their original homes in Mizoram has not been possible. There has been lot of opposition by the NGOs like the MZP and YMA regarding the identification of the repatriates. These NGOs insist that the government allow the repatriation of the Bru refugees into Mizoram on the basis of the voter list of 1995. However, there is the problem of the authenticity of the electoral roll, as the Mizoram Bru Refugee Committee (MBRC) alleged that around 1000 eligible voters were being omitted in the enumeration process that was carried out following an earlier MBRC submission to the Chief Election Commissioner that the Bru refugees had been denied their franchise in the general election of 1998 and the Parliamentary election of 1999.[19] The YMA and MZP systematically used voter list to identify the Reangs as outsiders. However, only 1733 out of 2406 voters in Kawrthah and 971 out of the total 1240 voters in Phuldungsei constituencies could cast their votes through postal ballots in the bye-elections held on 10 December 2005 as the YMA and MZP members physically prevented them from exercising their constitutional rights.[20]

The situation now has taken a different turn. The aftermath of the MOU seems to have accentuated the discontent to the extent that the Reang refugees in Tripura have started demonstration and hunger strike threats for their early repatriation. Elvis Chorkhy, President of the Mizoram Bru Displaced People's Forum (MBDPF), has said they are on agitation to press 16-point charter, the crux of which was their repatriation to Mizoram. "The squatting stir would continue for a week and if the demands are still not conceded we would go for an indefinite hunger strike at same venue."[21] Mizoram Bru Displaced People's Forum (MBDPF) general secretary Laldawngliana was further quoted as saying that the Zoramthanga government never talked to the refugees directly and all it did was talk to rebel outfits. Quoting a Catch-22 situation, he said the Mizoram government had set out a rule where the repatriation would not take place as long as there are rebels but that rebel groups would spring up as long as repatriation did not take place.[22] Over 33,000 refugees have been living in the six camps in Tripura who want to return to Mizoram. The civil society groups in Mizoram insist that at the time when the Brus fled their homes in 1997 the number was not that big. According to the Home Secretary of Mizoram, Mr. Ropiang, the state government has requested the NGOs like the MZP and YMA to verify whether all the refugees were *bona fide* residents of Mizoram.[23] The interface between the state and civil society can be healthy when conflict situations are resolved without any discontentment. In the case of the Reang refugees it seems to be counter-productive due to the intransigence of majority community NGOs to accommodate the displaced minority community in the state.

***Chakmas:*** Although the Chakmas are spread across three countries, the Chakmas living in Mizoram are more secure than their counterparts elsewhere.[24] The Chakmas are relatively late entrants to Mizoram.[25] Unlike other tribes who migrated from the east of Burma to the west, the Chakmas migrated from the west of Bengal towards the east of Mizoram. As mentioned earlier, the Chakmas in Mizoram enjoy special status under the sixth schedule of Constitution of India. They have their autonomous district council that was constituted way back in 1972 before the state of Mizoram came into being. The presence of Chakmas in Mizoram is considered as a potential threat to the culture and demography of the Mizo. The majority Mizo community does not appreciate the granting of autonomous status to the Chakmas as it was not consulted during that time. Second, the increase in the number of Chakmas either naturally or through illegal migration is seen as threat to the majority Christian Mizo population.

There are sporadic cases of intimidation by the local NGOs who were allegedly engaged in assaulting and torching the houses of some Chakmas. Even it has been alleged that the names of some families have been struck off from the electoral rolls. Some local groups see the Chakmas as foreigners.[26] This kind of attitude brings an atmosphere of mistrust and discontentment among the Chakma population in the state. Even now Chakmas are demanding for the recognition of Chakma language in the 8th schedule of the Constitution of India because of the distinct nature of their language. "The attitude of Mizo people towards Chakma as an immigrant population feeds to the strong feeling of identity of the Chakma people in the western part of the state."[27]

## III. DISCONTENTMENT AMONG THE MIZO

Besides the three important visible minority ethnic communities there are numerous other civil society groups who are engaged in articulation of the discontent among the majority Mizo community. These groups may be small in terms of organizational network, though they carry out very important function of articulating the discontent among the people. These organizations are different from the formidable groups like MZP and YMA. Yet more often times they demonstrate a clear sense of independence *vis-à-vis* these NGOs. Even these organizations have lately mustered courage and support from the common people in opposing the frontal NGOs or even the Church. The Mizo society, however, has become alarmed at the way the numerous anti-corruption associations have sprung up during the last few months. Last year alone saw the formation of at least four groups determined to fight corruption of which two are made up of farmers. This year has seen another two organizations.[28] A brief discussion about some of these organizations is in order.

The Peoples Right to Information and Development Implementing Society of Mizoram has been working for rooting out corruption at higher places (PRISM). The objective of the group is to fight corruption through filing Public Interest Litigation in the Gauhati High Court taking the help of the RTI Act 2005. As the President, Mr. Vanlalruate opines, "We are very concerned about the rampant corruption that is taking place in the state and we have been gathering information through the RTI Act."[29] There is another group called The Society for Social Action (SOASA), which is also working for rooting out corruption by using the RTI Act has been established recently. The Zoram Kuthanathawktu Pawl was established in Saitual by a group of farmers last year to fight for their rights. Soon after this, another farmers' group called Mizoram Cultivation and Labours Union (MICLUN) came into being. These organisations may seem to look like interest groups; in reality they have emerged due to the increasing discontent among the Mizo people with regard to the administration of the state and government.

The Human Rights and Law Network (HR&LN) is an organisation which is exclusively devoted to the issues relating to human rights in the state of Mizoram. Founded in 2003 this organisation has been actively engaged in highlighting the cases of HR violations and bringing them to justice. It also has been responsible in bringing to light some of the human rights violation committed by the leading civil society organisation like the YMA in their drive against India made foreign Liquor and Drugs. In the year 2005 there was a kind of confrontation of sorts over these issues between these two organisations which could be sorted with the intervention of the Church and some leading intellectuals of the community. The organisation is also engaged in looking after the Prisoners' rights, women's rights and children's rights at different levels. In fact, this organisation has been articulating the discontent among the common people against the excesses committed by the state and other organisations.

There are many mainstream organisations that have been there since quite long time. They are also engaged in articulating the discontentment among the people. The general perception, however, has been that the organisations are sometimes acting as supra political bodies to the extent of making the state government superfluous. The role of political parties also has not been so notable with regard to attending to the general discontent of the common people either directly or indirectly. As one observer remarked,

> "Political parties which had been in government in the past as well as the present have never tried to address the real problem. They have been obsessed with only how the party can survive and win the next election. They accumulate wealth in order to win election with cash, leaving the people as poor as before, if not poorer. The present situation in Mizoram does not bode well for the future because the people could rise up in revolution. In

other words, militancy may not be far away if reforms, both in the government and the society do not take place."[30]

## IV. CONCLUSION

The discussion in the above sections indicates the following conclusions. Although Mizoram is relatively a young state, it has inherited many of the problems of the north-east region of India. The state came into being in the backdrop of turbulence, though it could contain insurgency immediately in the aftermath of the signing of the peace accord. In the post-accord phase the mainstream civil society groups like the YMA, MZP or even the Church did contribute immensely in integrating the people under a common bondage. Unlike other states in the region, the homogeneity of the majority Mizo community did work in its favour. The presence of other minority groups is definitely a challenge to the Mizo sense of accommodation and tolerance. In the beginning there were identity clash among the majority and minority ethnic communities leading to a number of crises though, the people of Mizoram have overcome that phase.

The areas of discontentment that we did discuss in the preceding sections are the consequence of earlier conflict situations which have now been smothered in the ongoing peace efforts by various agencies. The discontent is rather a continuum of the peace process which is in the pipeline. There are also some areas of discontentment among the minority communities of the state which have been the consequence of external factor. The problem of the Chakmas, for instance, which has international implications, has little bearing on the larger issue of discontentment in the state. With regard to the Hmar and Bru also, there are efforts to resettle them back in the state. The discontentment among these communities may be very high. They do not seem to erupt into a major conflagration as the federal government is trying to work out the peace package in collaboration with the state government. The state government is coxed and cajoled by sanctioning a huge sum of grant for the resettlement of the Bru refugees who fled their homes. The vexed issue of the 'original inhabitants' of the state raised by the YMA and MZP will have to be sorted out through some mechanism. The discontentment among the Hmar about the non-implementation of the peace agreement may go out of control. Unless the majority Mizo community does incorporate them into their fold by recognising their distinct cultural identity, it will be very difficult to sort out the problem.

Secondly, the discontentment emanating from the governance of the state has rather raised many eye brows among the larger Mizo community. The pace of development in the recent years in the state has been far better than many states in the region though, discontentment continues to be high due lack of equity and justice. Corruption at high places has been a cause of concern to the elite of Mizoram. As we did discuss in the third section, there were numerous organisations which sprang up recently to root out corruption by making use of the RTI Act. The mushrooming of such groups is indicative of the extent of discontentment of the larger Mizo community about the failure of the state in delivering the goods to the people. As one intellectual has cautioned, "What is very clear is that the Mizo people are fed up with established norms and the administration which they see as a total failure because it had not addressed their problems....We cannot dismiss out of hand the possibility of an uprising that can take the form of militancy."[31]

Thus the post-accord syndrome of the state of Mizoram is replete with discontentment and discord among the people. While peace is very much present after the signing of the accord, Mizo society is undergoing the pangs of growth and development that is manifested in the form of discontentment. The state and the civil society of Mizoram have to be alive to this syndrome in order to capitalise on the longest peace it has in the region.

## NOTES

1. During the British rule, Mizoram was known as the Lushai Hills District, which formed a part of Assam. In 1954, its name was changed to the Mizo Hill District. After the secessionist movement under the Mizo National Front (MNF) arose, it was upgraded to the status of a centrally administered Union territory. In 1987, it attained full statehood. See www.manipuronline.com.
2. Discontent here refers to a state of affair just short of conflict. It may or may not conflagrate into a violent conflict situation eventually. It is, however, a constant irritant in the governance of the state.
3. See http://mizoram.nic.in/about/history.htm.
4. For the early history of insurgent movement in Mizoram see, V. Venkat Rao, *A Century of Tribal Politics in North East India* (New Delhi: S. Chand

& Co. Ltd., 1995), pp. 494-516; *see also*, K.P. Nath, "The Genesis of MNF Movement: Its impact on Mizoram Politics," *The North Eastern Hill University Journal of Social Sciences and Humanities*, vol. x, no. 2, pp. 52-55.

5. J.L. Thiek, "The Big Platform: In the Interest of Kuki-Chin-Mizo Unity", www.Kukiforum.com
6. Consequent upon the signing of the "Memorandum of Settlement" between Laldenga, the President of Mizo National Front, and the Union Home Secretary, R.K. Pradhan on the 30th June 1986, the two-decade-old insurgency problem in Mizoram was buried. See Mizoram Accord 1986.
7. For the district councils, See Arvind K. Sharma "District Councils in the North-East" in T.N. Chaturvedi, ed., *Fifty Years of Indian Administration: Retrospect and Prospect.* New Delhi: Indian Institute of Public Administration, 1998.
8. http://www.wikipedia.org.
9. Lal Dena, The unresolved issues of the Hmar, *www.manipuronlime.com*, dt. June 11, 2006.
10. They are as follow: 1. Hmar People's Convention (HPC); 2. Hmar People's Convention—Democracy (HPC-D); 3.Hmar Revolutionary Front (HRF); 4. Zomi Revolutionary Army (ZRA); 5. Zomi Revolutionary Volunteers (ZRV); 6. Indigenous People's Revolutionary Alliance (IRPA); 7. Kom Rem People's Convention (KRPC); 8. Chin Kuki Revolutionary Front (CKRF); 9. Bru National Liberation Front.
11. www.satp.org/satporgtp/countries/india/states/mizoram/terrorist_outfits/HPC_D.htm - 40k.
12. *Ibid.*
13. See "Dimasa-Hmar Communal conflict in Assam", http://hvk. org/articles/0703/104.html, dt. 3/3/2007; also see "Hmar women submitted memorandum to Sonia," http://ww.uniindia.com, dt.3/3/2007.
14. Lal Dena, The unresolved issues of the Hmar, *op. cit.* n. 9.
15. There is no certainty about the exact number of people who fled their homes after the clashes. According to the Human Rights Commission Report of 1988, the number is in the region of 40,000. The Mizoram Government claims that it is only 1600, while according to Tripura Government the number is 37,000.
16. www.globalsecurity.org, dt. 26 October 2006.
17. According to a Government of India release, "The Ministry of Home Affairs has agreed to extend grants-in-aid of Rs.28.64 crores to the Government of Mizoram for rehabilitation and resettlement of Bru National Liberation Front (BNLF) returnees and Bru refugees on their repatriation from Tripura to Mizoram. The Scheme includes housing assistance, cash assistance to BNLF returnees, housing assistance to Bru refuges, free ration for a period of three months to BNLF returnees and Bru refugees, expenditure on construction of rehabilitation camps, etc. With a view to ensure that the

work relating to rehabilitation and resettlement of BNLF returnees and Bru refugees does not suffer because of constraints of funds, an advance of 4.89 crores out of total placed grants-in-aid of Rs. 28.64 crores has been released to Government of Mizoram in 2004-5. The implementation of the Scheme by the State Government is being closely monitored by Ministry of Home Affairs."

18. "Patil declares package for Bru refugees," *Deccan Herald*, Feberuary 02, 2005.
19. The Bru 'Refugees'/IDPs Tangle: Exploring Options Paolienlal Haokip, www.icps, dt.12 August 2003.
20. Despite in Bru IDP camps in India, *Refugee Watch online*, February 27, 2006.
21. Reang refugees launch stir in Agartala, *Indigenous Herald*, www.nepic.com 23 February, 2007 Chorkhy has in a letter faxed to union home minister Shivaraj Patil set an ultimatum to accept their demands by March 1 failing which they would commence an indefinite hunger strike agitation at same venue. "All displaced Brus are thirsty for normal life. We are also citizens of India, indigenous and sons of the soil," he remarked.
22. New Bru rebel outfit, *Newslink,* March 3, 2007.
23. "Brus stage sit-in demonstration", *The Mizoram Post*, 24/2/2007.
24. The Chakma, also known as the Changma, are a tribe inhabiting the Chittagong Hill Tracts of Bangladesh. "The Chakma population today is estimated to be around 550,000 people, but it is spread over 3 different countries. The majority (approx. 300,000 people) are located in the Chittagong Hill Tracts of Bangladesh. This population spills over into neighbouring areas of south-west Mizoram State in India, where another 80,000 Chakmas live, and Burma (Myanmar) has 20,000 Chakmas. In addition to the earlier 30,000, Tripura State in India has also some 50,000 Chakma refugees who fled Bangladeshi Army operations ... in 1988. Another group of Chakmas, now numbering around 100,000 people, is found in the foothills of the Himalayas in Arunachal Pradesh." "The Chakmas are Buddhists and officially follow... Theravada... Buddhism, as practiced by the Chakmas, is... a mixture of southern and northern (Mahayana) forms, with a touch of Hinduism and aspects of shamanism and animism thrown into the mix." See www.wikipedia.org/wiki/Chakma
25. www.webindia123.com/Mizoram
26. See Sanjoy Hazrika, "Refugees within, Refugee without," www.south-asia.com/himal/April/chakma.htm
27. Satarupa Datta Majumdar, "The socio-economics of linguistic identity a case study in the lushai hills," www.languageinindia.com/sep2005
28. "Certain sections aftraid Mizoram going Manipur way," *Newslink,* February 11, 2007.
29. See, "State Government Faces more trouble with PIL admission," *Newslink,* December 20, 2006. "The PIL that has been admitted is based on information

that we have received through the RTI Act on purchase made through funds for police modernization. We found that all the purchases had been without call for tender and that the purchases were regularized later through the state purchase and advisory board."

30. "Certain section afraid Mizoram going Manipur way," Newslinik, *op. cit.*
31. *Ibid.*

# Chapter 5

## Changing Agrarian Structure and Livelihood Options in Mizoram

D. ZAITINVAWRA and E. KANAGRAJ

Shifting cultivation (widely known as jhum) has been construed as a major challenge to tribal development in India over many decades. In fact, the Tenth Five Year Plan has recognised it as one of the unresolved issues of planning for tribal development in India[1] (Government of India, 2001). Shifting cultivation is an agricultural system characterised by rotation of field rather than of crops by short period of cropping alternating with long fallow periods and by means of slash and burn (Sachchidananda, 1989). Its other characteristics are clearing by means of fire, absence of drought animals and manuring; use of human labour only, employment of dibbling stick or hoe, short period of soil occupancy alternating with long fallow periods (Satapathy *et al*. 2003). The origin of shifting cultivation is often traced back to the Neolithic period dated to 7000 BC on the basis of archaeological data[2] (Sharma, 1976). Shifting cultivation is known by a variety of names in different areas[3]. It is widely practiced in the hill regions of North Eastern States of Arunachal Pradesh, Assam, Manipur, Meghalaya, Mizoram, Nagaland and Tripura. The practice is also prevalent in isolated pockets of Orissa, Andhra Pradesh, Karnataka, Madhya Pradesh, Kerala, Maharashtra, Sikkim and Chhattisgarh.

About 10 million hectare of tribal land stretched across 16 states is estimated to be under shifting cultivation in India (Eswaraiah, 2003). According to a recent estimate of Forest Survey of India based on recent satellite images 1.73 millions hectares of land is affected by shifting cultivation in North-east India, while an estimated 12 per cent of tribal population in India still practices shifting cultivation, the number of families involved in shifting cultivation in North-east India is estimated to be 4.5 lakhs (Cf Darlong, 2004).

Shifting cultivation is not only practiced in India, but it is widely persistent among the indigenous communities, particularly in Africa, Latin America and parts of Asia. Tribal communities and hill people from time immemorial have practiced shifting cultivation in India.[4]

Shifting cultivation has been a subject of major debate since colonial era and has often been a victim of public misconception and simplified stereotypes. The practice has been criticized by environmentalists, foresters, development practitioners and policy makers as being primitive backward destructive or wasteful. From the last few decades the practice of it has become a burning issue. Opinion of the academics and policy makers on shifting cultivation can be divided into two schools of thought. A number of them consider it as a wasteful land use with primitive technology and harmful to eco system. On the other many scholars (e.g. Elwin, 1959; Chaturvedi and Uppal, 1960) have considered jhuming as a most possible human response to fragile tropical hill eco system (Hussain, 1993). The later construe it as a way of life while the former think it as a wasteful method of Cultivation (Agarwal, 1998). The Government policy on shifting cultivation has been in tune with the former and systematic efforts are made to control and transform shifting cultivation into settled agriculture.[5]

Research and development organizations have been involved in developing alternative approaches to transform shifting cultivation system into most sustainable form of land use. Moreover, shifting cultivators are often blamed for environmental degradation and are under tremendous pressure from authorities to adopt more permanent form of agriculture. The matter of fact is that despite the varying pressures and policies to wean away the farmers from practicing shifting cultivation, not much has been achieved as most of those communities still continue to practice shifting cultivation (Darlong, 2004).

The literature on shifting cultivation is expanding since 1950s. These studies were conducted most of the states of North-east as well other parts of India. These studies provide solid bedrock on which fresh studies can be undertaken. Yet there are few research gaps that could be identified. Firstly, there are a few studies in the context of

Mizoram. Secondly, the studies based on field survey are a few. Thirdly, the perception of the farmers about the difficulties and problems in shifting cultivation has yet to be explored, as they would indicate policy options. Fourthly, the farmers' willingness and the constraints in switching over from shifting cultivation to settled agriculture were rarely focused in the literature.

The present study tries to fill these gaps by way of surveying shifting cultivators and semi-settled agriculturists in two villages of Aizawl district. The present study focuses on the demographic, social and economic structural factors prompting the switch over of the farmers from shifting cultivation to semi-settled agriculture, the transformations in the livelihood patterns, as well as the cultivators' willingness to switching over to settled agriculture. It tries to find out the major constraints in switching over to settled agriculture from the perspectives of the farmers.

The results of the present study will be beneficial to planners, policy makers as well as civil society organisations interested in the uplift of the tribal population in India. It will facilitate a better understanding of the problems of shifting cultivators from their own perspective.

The chapter has been presented in four major sections. The first presents an overview of jhum in Mizoram. In the second the methodology of the present study is presented. The third section is devoted to discuss the results of analysis of the primary data and in the last section the conclusions are presented.

## I. JHUM IN MIZORAM: AN OVERVIEW

Mizos have been agriculturists from the beginning of the 18th century when they made their western trek to the present Mizo hills. They know only the form of farming known as shifting cultivation which forms the major activity of the Mizo economic life even today, wet rice cultivation is reported to be first practices in the year 1921 by the Mizo residents of Burma which marked the recorded adoption of a new technology in the culture of rice farming among the ethnic group of Mizo (Thangchungnunga, 1997).

The culture of the Mizos is intrinsically woven with their practice of shifting cultivation. The important festivals of Mizos viz., Chapchar Kut[6], Pawl Kut[7], and Mim Kut[8], are in fact associated with the various stages of shifting cultivation (Sen, 1992:428).

In Mizoram the livelihood base of majority of the population is cultivation especially shifting cultivation. In Mizoram 61 per cent of the working population depends on agriculture of which nearly 55 per cent were cultivators and 6 per cent were agricultural labourers according to the 2001 census. Out of 738 villages and 1,54,643 households 89,454 (57.85%) are cultivator households in Mizoram. Among the cultivators 78,195 (87%) households are practicing jhum and wet rice cultivation is practiced by 11,301 households (13%) (*Source* Government of Mizoram 2004:17).

A predominant majority of the households are depending on shifting cultivation for their livelihood all over the districts of Mizoram excepting in the Aizawl. Of the 1,54,643 households in the state more than one-half are depending on shifting cultivation (60%). More than three-fourth of the households of the districts of two thirds of the households of the districts of Champhai (77%), Kolasib (77%) and Saiha (75%) are shifting cultivators. Likewise more than two-thirds of the households of Mamit (68%) and Serchip (68%) are practicing shifting cultivation and one-half of them in the districts of Lawngtlai (62%) and Lunglei (58%) are jhumias. On the other hand over one third of the households of the Aizawl (34%) district depend on shifting cultivation (*Source* GOM, 2004:17).

As regards the agrarian structure of Mizoram a predominant majority of the cultivators of marginal farmers cultivating less than one hectare of land. 70 per cent of the cultivators are marginal farmers (less than 1 Hectare), 20 per cent of them are small farmers, while medium and large farmers constitute 6 and 4 per cent respectively. The mean size of land holding was worked out to 1.6 hectares.

A notable feature of the agrarian structure in Mizoram is that inequality is emerging in otherwise known as egalitarian tribal society. 70 per cent of the marginal farmers are in possession of 21 per cent of land while 10 per cent of medium and large farmers control over 60 per cent of land (*Source* GOM 2004:17).

## II. METHODOLOGY

The present study is based on the primary data collected through field survey in the villages in Aizawl district. These villages were purposively selected as the researcher has been working with them for the last one year as a student social worker for his concurrent placement. Two types of cultivators were compared so as to assess the changing patterns of agricultural livelihood and options.

Data was collected based on disproportionate stratified sampling design. The base of stratification is being type of cultivation, viz. shifting cultivation and semi-settled agriculture. From each categories sub-samples of equal size (30 farmers) was drawn using simple random sampling technique of Tippet's table of random numbers from the list of cultivators prepared in consultation with the leaders of the communities.

The primary data was collected through field survey with structured interview schedule. Primary data was collected from 30 respondents each from both shifting cultivation and semi-settled agriculture. The interview scheduled was compiled in Mizo and was administered to 60 respondents.

The collected data was processed with the help of computer by using Microsoft Excel. For analysis apart from averages, percentages and cross tabulation, Karl Pearson's correlation of co-efficient was used to draw the inferences.

## III. RESULTS AND DISCUSSION

The present study attempts to understand the changing patterns of agricultural livelihood in Mizoram. This section has been structured into three major sub-sections, viz., structural bases of cultivators, livelihood patterns, willingness to switchover from shifting cultivation to settled agriculture.

### Structural Bases of Cultivators

In the course of the fieldwork it was observed that two types of cultivation practiced in the Mizo villages. One is the traditional, ancient jhum, i.e. shifting cultivation and the other semi-permanent settled cultivation. The second form has been called semi-settled because the cultivators have not acquired the permanent title for the land though they are not shifting the land from time to time as the former practice still. In this context, the first and foremost question that arose pertains to the demographic, social, economic, agrarian structural characteristics of the cultivators. The comparative picture of shifting cultivator respondents and semi settled cultivators would reveal the social structural factors that are prompting shift form jhum to semi-settled cultivators.

#### *Demographic Structural Characteristics*

The demographic characteristics of the respondents that are discussed as under are gender, age group, marital status, education, type and size of family (see Table 5.1).

**Table 5.1:** Demographic Characteristics of Respondents

| *Sl. No.* | *Characteristics* | *Shifting N = 30* | Semi-settled *N = 30* | *Total N = 60* |
|---|---|---|---|---|
| *1.* | *Sex* | | | |
| | Male | 23 (76.67) | 24 (80.00) | 47 (78.33) |
| | Female | 7 (23.33) | 6 (20.00) | 13 (21.67) |
| 2. | *Age Group* | | | |
| | Youth (Below 35) | 2 (6.67) | 2 (6.67) | 4 (6.67) |
| | Middle (35-60) | 21 (70.00) | 21 (70.00) | 42 (70.00) |
| | Old (Above 60) | 7 (23.33) | 7 (23.33) | 14 (23.33) |
| | Mean Years of Age | 51.90±13.23 | 52.80 ±12.19 | 52.35±12.62 |
| 3. | *Marital Status* | | | |
| | Married | 27 (90.00) | 27 (90.00) | 54 (90.00) |
| | Divorced/Separated | 2 (6.67) | 1 (3.33) | 3 (5.00) |
| | Widowed | 1 (3.33) | 2 (6.67) | 3 (5.00) |
| 4. | *Level of Education* | | | |
| | Primary (1-4) | 13 (43.33) | 12 (40.00) | 25 (41.67) |
| | Middle (5-7) | 9 (30.00) | 6 (20.00) | 15 (25.00) |
| | High School (8-0) | 8 (26.67) | 11 (36.67) | 19 (31.67) |
| | Higher Secondary and Above | 0 (0.00) | 1 (3.33) | 1 (1.67) |
| | Mean Years of Education | 5.67 ± 2.55 | 6.50 ± 3.25 | 6.08 ± 2.92 |
| 5. | *Type of Family* | | | |
| | Joint | 12 (40.00) | 12 (40.00) | 24 (40.00) |
| | Nuclear | 18 (60.00) | 18 (60.00) | 36 (60.00) |
| 6. | Size of Family | | | |
| | Small (3 and Below) | 5 (16.67) | 3 (10.00) | 8 (13.33) |
| | Medium (4 - 6) | 11 (36.67) | 18 (60.00) | 29 (48.33) |
| | Large (7 & Above) | 14 (46.67) | 9 (30.00) | 23 (38.33) |
| | Mean Size | 5.77 ± 2.33 | 5.77 ± 2.01 | 5.77 ±2.16 |

*Source*: Computed Figures in parentheses are percentages Mean ± SD

As regards gender majority of the respondents were male invariably among the shifting cultivators and semi-settled agriculturists. More than three-fourth (76.67%) of the shifting cultivators and four-fifth (80%) of the semi-settled agriculturists were male. On the whole 78.33 per cent of the respondents were male.

Age is an important demographic variable and the aged are very much respected and revered in Mizo society. Age has been divided into three age groups, viz., youth (below 35 yrs.), middle age (36-60 yrs.) and old age (above 60 yrs.). Middle age group was predominant in both the categories of respondents. In the sample, more than two-third of both shifting cultivators and semi-settled agriculturists was aged between 36-60 yrs. On a whole majority of the respondents 70 per cent of both shifting cultivators and semi-settled agriculturists were of middle-age group. On the other hand, the respondents of both shifting cultivators (23.33%) and semi-settled agriculturists (23.33%) were old.

As regards marital status majority of the respondents of both shifting cultivators (90%) and semi-settled agriculturists (90%) were married. On the whole 90 per cent of the respondents of both shifting cultivators and semi-settled agriculturists were married.

Education is one of the basic needs. In fact, education is both a determinant as well as a major component of development. As regards to level of education, a slight difference in the level of education could be observed between shifting cultivators and semi-settled agriculturists. One half of the shifting cultivators and more than two fifth of the semi-settled agriculturists (43.33%) had primary (I—IV) education. The mean years of education clearly shows that the semi-settled agriculturists had greater level of education as compared to the shifting cultivators. The mean years of education for shifting cultivators was worked out to 6 years while that of semi-settled agriculturists was 7 years.

Family is one of the basic institutions of a society. The type and size of the family are two important indicators of structure of family. Nuclear family was found to be prominent among both shifting cultivators as well as semi-settled agriculturists. More than one-half of shifting cultivators (60%) and semi-settled agriculturists (60%) belonged to nuclear families. On the whole, 60 per cent of the respondents belonged to nuclear families.

The size of the family also reveals the structure of family. It was classified into three categories, viz. small (1-3 members), medium (4-6 members) and large (7 and above). Most of the shifting cultivators were in large family while most of the semi-settled agriculturists were in medium family. More than one-half (60%) of the semi-settled agriculturists were living in medium size family while more than one-third of shifting cultivators (36%) belonged to medium size family. Nearly one-half (46%) of the shifting cultivators and less than one-third of the semi-settled agriculturists were living in large families. Yet, the average family size of the respondents of both shifting cultivators and semi-settled was same, i.e. 6 members.

## *Social and Economic Structural Characteristics*

The social characteristics of the respondents discussed as under are educational status, type and size of family, religion and denomination while the economic characteristics of the respondents include primary occupation, and secondary occupation (see Table 5.2).

**Table 5.2:** Social and Economic Characteristics of Respondents

| *Sl. No.* | *Characteristics* | *Shifting N = 30* | *Semi-settled N = 30* | *Total N = 60* |
|---|---|---|---|---|
| *1.* | *Religion/Denomination* | | | |
| | Presbyterian | 21 (70.00) | 25 (83.33) | 46 (76.67) |
| | Isua Krista Kohhran | 4 (13.33) | 2 (6.67) | 6 (10.00) |
| | Judaism | 3 (10.00) | 0 (0.00) | 3 (5.00) |
| | Church of God | 1 (3.33) | 1 (3.33) | 2 (3.33) |
| | Roman Catholic | 0 (0.00) | 1 (3.33) | 1 (1.67) |
| | Fundamental Baptist | 1 (3.33) | 0 (0.00) | 1 (1.67) |
| | United Pentecostal Church | 0 (0.00) | 1 (3.33) | 1 (1.67) |
| 2. | *Sub-tribe* | | | |
| | Lusei | 20 (66.67) | 15 (50.00) | 35 (58.33) |
| | Hmar | 4 (13.33) | 6 (20.00) | 10 (16.67) |
| | Ralte | 4 (13.33) | 5 (16.67) | 9 (15.00) |
| | Paihte | 1 (3.33) | 4 (13.33) | 5 (8.33) |
| | Pawih | 1 (3.33) | 00.00 | 1 (1.67) |
| *3.* | *Primary Occupation* | | | |
| | Cultivation | 25 (83.33) | 27 (90.00) | 52 (86.67) |
| | Government Service | 2 (6.67) | 2 (6.67) | 4 (6.67) |
| | Business | 2 (6.67) | 1 (3.33) | 3 (5.00) |
| | Artisan | 1 (3.33) | 00.00 | 1 (1.67) |
| *4.* | *Secondary Occupation* | | | |
| | None | 23 (76.67) | 26 (86.67) | 49 (81.67) |
| | Cultivation | 5 (16.67) | 3 (10.00) | 8 (13.33) |
| | Business | 2 (6.67) | 1 (3.33) | 3 (5.00) |

*(Contd.)*

*(Contd.)*

| *Sl. No.* | *Characteristics* | *Shifting* *N = 30* | *Semi-settled* *N = 30* | *Total* *N = 60* |
|---|---|---|---|---|
| 5. | Secondary Occupation | | | |
| | None | 23 (76.67) | 26 (86.67) | 49 (81.67) |
| | Cultivation | 5 (16.67) | 3 (10.00) | 8 (13.33) |
| | Business | 2 (6.67) | 1 (3.33) | 3 (5.00) |

*Source*: Computed Figures in parentheses are percentages.

Religion is one of the social structural factors playing significant role in any society. At present Christianity is the religion of the Mizo tribe but a number of the denominations operate in Mizo society. Frequent visits to the Church and involvement in the Church activities are considered as prestigious in the Mizo society. The denominations professed in the sample village are Presbyterian, Isua Krista Kohhran (IKK), Church of God, Roman Catholic, Fundamental Baptist and United Pentecostal Church. A vast majority of the respondents were Presbyterian. More than two-third (70%) of the shifting cultivators and more than four-fifth (83.33%) of semi-settled agriculturists were Presbyterians by faith. On the whole 76.67 per cent belonged to Presbyterian Church.

There are different sub-tribes that constitute Mizo tribe. The major sub-tribe that inhabits in the village is Lusei. The other sub-tribes found in the village include Hmar, Ralte, Paite and Pawi (Lai). More than two-thirds of shifting cultivators (66.67%) and one-half (50%) of semi-settled agriculturists were of Lusei sub-tribe.

Primary occupation of vast majority of the respondents was agriculture. More than four-fifth of shifting cultivators (83%) and semi-settled agriculturists (90%) were engaged in agriculture as their primary occupation. Further, it was observed that a majority of the shifting cultivators and semi-settled agriculturists had no secondary occupation. More than three-fourth of shifting cultivators (77%) and four-fifth of semi-settled agriculture (87%) had no secondary occupation.

### *Structural Bases of Transformation to Semi settled-cultivation*

To identify the demographic, social and economic structural factors prompting the transformation from shifting cultivation to semi-settled agriculture Karl Pearson's correlation coefficients were computed.

The correlation coefficients were computed between type of cultivation (shifting = 0 and semi-settled = 1), and structural variables, viz. gender (male = 1, female = 0), age group (young = 1; middle aged = 2; aged = 3), family size (small = 1; medium = 2; large = 3), level of education (primary = 1; middle = 2; HSLC and above = 3), sub-tribe (Lusei = 1; others = 0), and denomination (Presbyterian = 1; others = 0). The results are presented in Table 5.3.

**Table 5.3:** Structural Bases of Transformation from Shifting Cultivation to Semi-settled Agriculture: Pearson's Coefficients of Correlation

| *Sl. No.* | *Social Structural Factor* | *Pearson R N = 60* | *Sig. (2-tailed)* |
|---|---|---|---|
| 1. | Gender | –0.04 | 0.76 |
| 2. | Age Group | 0.00 | 1.00 |
| 3. | Level of Education | 0.10 | 0.44 |
| 4. | Family Size | –0.07 | 0.57 |
| 5. | Sub-Tribe | –0.17 | 0.20 |
| 6. | Denomination | 0.16 | 0.23 |

*Source*: Computed.

The results reveal that neither the demographic factors nor the social structural factors are responsible for the transformation from shifting cultivation to semi settled agriculture. The correlation coefficients of neither of the demographic variables, viz., gender (–0.4), age group (00), level of education (0.10) and family size (–0.17) nor those of social structural factors (–0.17) sub-tribe and denomination (0.16) was significant even at 5 per cent level.

## Livelihood Patters of Cultivators

To understand the livelihood of the shifting cultivators and semi-settled agriculturists a comprehensive discussion on the changing patterns of agrarian structure, technology, and cropping pattern and input use is attempted in the following sub-sections.

### *Agrarian Structure*

The agrarian structure in the context of shifting cultivation has some unique features like common ownership, jhum cycle etc. The agrarian structure can be better understood in terms of these features. Hence, hereunder the discussion on them follows (see Table 5.4).

**Table 5.4:** Agrarian Structural Characteristics

| Sl. No. | Characteristic | Shifting N = 30 | Semi-settled N = 30 | Total N = 60 |
|---|---|---|---|---|
| 1. | Jhum Cycle (Years) | 7 | 0.00 | |
| 2. | Type of Title | | | |
| | No Title/Common Land | 13 (43.33) | 0 (0.00) | 13 (21.67) |
| | Temporary Pass | 4 (13.33) | 2 (6.67) | 6 (10.00) |
| | Periodic Land Pass | 12 (40.00) | 27 (90.00) | 39 (65.00) |
| | Land Settlement Certificate | 1 (3.33) | 1(3.33) | 2 (3.33) |
| 3. | Area of Land Owned (Mean Acres) | 1.37 ±1.53 | 2.72 ± 1.85 | 2.04 ±1.81 |
| 4. | Area of Land Cultivated (Mean Acres) | 1.92 ± 1.18 | 1.98 ± 0.83 | 1.95 ±1.01 |

Figures in parentheses are percentages ± SD
** P<0.01 * P<0.05.
*Source*: Computed.

A notable feature of shifting cultivation is the rotation fields, known as jhum cycle. The jhum cycle refers to the period of rest allowed to jhum land for recoupment of fertility (Agarwal, 1998:133). The pressure of the population, biomass of the forest, slope of the field, quality and depth of soil, the quantity and distribution of rainfall in different months were supposed factors that determine the jhum cycle. Areas of sparse population generally have longer jhum cycles (15 to 20 years), while areas with high population pressure shorter cycle. Hence, the period of fallowing, i.e. the jhum cycle varies from village to village and slope to slope (Husain, 1993:382). It was reported in the earlier studies that the jhum cycle has narrowed down in the North-East India from 10-20 years to 5-10 years. The average of jhum cycle is about 6 years, which varies from state to state (Datta, 1992). Mizoram and Tripura were reported to have the longest cycles of over 9 years in the region, closely followed by Nagaland (8-9 years), the Mikir Hills and North-Cachar hills districts of Assam (7-8 years). The shortest jhum cycle was estimated for Meghalaya (5-6 years). And the shortest possible jhum cycle was found in the states of Arunachal Pradesh (2-3 years) and Manipur (1-2 Years) (Agarwal, 1985:118). According to an estimate by Guha (1973:1) the period of jhum cycle in Meghalaya was 4 to 5 years; it was 5 years in Mizoram while 10 years in the Mikir Hills of Assam (Cf Agarwal, 1985:118).

In the study village the jhum cycle found among the shifting cultivators was 7 years, while there was absence of jhum cycle among semi-settled cultivators. Thus it is lower than the jhum cycle reported by Agarwal (1985: 118) and greater than the estimates of Guha (1973). The shorter duration of jhum cycle could be attributed to the increased population pressure on land (Borthakur, 2002:125; Husain ,1993:382).

Common ownership of land is a distinct feature of Mizo society. Before the advent of the British, the village chief was the custodian of land within his jurisdiction and since the advent of the British; all land has been considered to be the government land. Landholding is considered as one of the major indicators of livelihood and development. The title indicates the nature of ownership of land possessed by the cultivator. There are different tittles of land found to exist in the village where the present study was conducted, viz., common land, temporary pass, periodic land pass, and land settlement certificate. Among the shifting cultivators mostly no title was found, i.e. they were reportedly cultivating common land while a significant proportion had acquired periodic land pass also. More than one-third of the shifting cultivators had no ownership title and cultivating common land. Also nearly one-third of them (40%) had periodic land pass also. On the other hand, more than four fifth (90%) of semi-settled agriculturists have got periodic land pass for their land cultivation.

As regards ownership (possession) a greater area of landholding was observed among the semi-settled agriculturists as compared to the shifting cultivators. The average area of land owned by the shifting cultivators was 1.37 while it was 3 acres for semi-settled agriculturists. Though there was marked difference in the size of landholding there was no difference in the area of land cultivated between the shifting cultivators and semi-settled agriculturists. The average land cultivated by the shifting cultivators and semi-settled agriculture was same at 2 acres. This is less than the mean size of land holding in Mizoram which was worked out to 1.6 hectares. The gap between land possessed and cultivated among both the type of cultivators could be attributed to inadequate labour supply and lack of capital for investment.

### *Tools and Implements used in Cultivation*

Tools and implements form the technology and part of the economic infrastructure, i.e. forces of production. The advancement in tools and implements use is necessitated for economic development in general and agricultural development in particular. In other words as economy progresses or modernises more and more advanced tools replace or substitute the primitive tools. The variety of tools and implements used by Mizo, shifting cultivators was reported by previous studies (for instance Thangchunnunga, 1997:88). In the present study a specific question was posed that how tools use changes when a typical jhumia becomes semi settled cultivator.

The results of survey indicate that altogether there are a variety of 13 tools and implements in use among both shifting cultivators and semi-settled agriculturists. These tools and implements were classified into four categories, i.e. forest clearance tools, land preparation tools, weeding tools, and harvesting tools. As the switch over occurs the number of tools used increases. On the whole 10 tools and implements were possessed and used by the shifting cultivators while semi-settled agriculturists possessed 12 tools. Of the 10 tools used by shifting cultivators 3 were forest clearance tools 4 were for harvesting, 2 were for weeding. On the other hand out of 12 tools and implements used by semi-settled cultivators, 3 were for forest clearance, 2 were for land preparation, 3 were for weeding and 4 were meant for harvesting. Thus except the tools meant for harvesting, use of all other tools increase with the switch over to semi-settled agriculture (see Table 5.5). Interestingly, though the number of tools used increases there is no shift in pattern of tools use.

**Table 5.5:** Tools and Implements used in Cultivation

| *Sl. No.* | *Tool/Implement* | *Shifting N = 30* | *Semi-settled N = 30* | *Total N = 60* |
|---|---|---|---|---|
| 1. | Forest Clearance Tools | 3.27 ± 2.30 | 3.37 ± 1.56 | 3.32 ± 1.95 |
| 2. | Land Preparation Tools | 0.30 ± 0.65 | 1.80 ± 0.41 | 1.05 ± 0.93 |
| 3. | Weeding Tools | 2.17 ± 0.53 | 2.87 ± 0.43 | 2.52 ± 0.60 |
| 4. | Harvesting Tools | 4.03 ± 1.30 | 3.77 ± 1.17 | 3.90 ± 1.23 |
| 5. | Number of Tools | 9.77 ± 3.00 | 11.80 ± 2.31 | 10.78 ± 2.85 |

*Source*: Computed (Figures in parentheses are percentages).

### *Cropping Pattern*

As regards cropping a remarkable feature of shifting cultivation is that almost all varieties of cereals and vegetables are grown in one field, which is rather impossible to have in wet plain land (Datta, 1992:32). This is mainly because most of the crops are grown for subsistence. The major crops that are cultivated by both shifting cultivators and semi-settled agriculturists are chilli, bean, mustard, pumpkin, bitter gourd, lady's finger and wild brinjal. There are some crops, which are cultivated mostly in semi-settled agriculture such as squash, cabbage cauliflower, pineapple, lemon, tomato, broccoli, carrot coriander, mutter chana and radish. While crops like rice, gourd, watermelon, cucumber, maize, sesamum are cultivated mainly by shifting cultivators.

The most important concern of us here is that of how cropping pattern changes when settlement takes place. To accomplish this crops cultivated are divided into four categories, viz., cereals, pulses and oilseeds, vegetable and fruits. It was not possible to measure actual area of cultivation of these crops because the farmers do not have such measurement perspective. So the number of crops cultivated per farm in each of this category was worked out to understand the cropping pattern changes.

**Table 5.6:** Cropping Pattern: Number of Crops Cultivated per Farm

| *Sl. No.* | *Crop* | *Shifting N = 30* | *Semi-settled N = 30* | *Total N = 60* |
|---|---|---|---|---|
| 1. | Cereals | 1.90 ± 0.31 | 0.37 ± 0.49 | 1.13 ± 0.87 |
| 2. | Pulses and Oil Seeds | 2.03 ± 0.18 | 1.47 ± 0.68 | 1.75 ± 0.57 |
| 3. | Vegetables | 8.57 ± 1.50 | 11.83 ±2.12 | 10.20 ± 2.46 |
| 4. | Fruits | 1.10 ± 0.31 | 0.73 ± 0.64 | 0.92 ± 0.53 |
| 5. | Number of Crops | 13.60 ± 1.61 | 14.40 ± 2.59 | 14.00 ± 2.18 |

Figures in Parentheses are Percentages to the total Mean ± SD.

*Source*: Computed.

Surprisingly, both the shifting cultivators and semi-settled agriculturists reportedly cultivated 14 crops. Of 14 crops cultivated by a typical shifting cultivator 9 were vegetables, 2 were either pulses or oil seeds, 2 were cereals and 1 was fruit. On the other hand of the 14 crops cultivated by a representative semi-settled agriculturist 12 were vegetables, 1 was pulse or oil seed and 1 was a fruit. It is clear there was a cropping pattern shift from food crop to vegetable crops. It can be seen as a shift from subsistence cultivation to commercial agriculture as the switch over takes place from shifting cultivation to settled agriculture. It is also an undeniable fact that among the shifting cultivators too the tendency to produce for the market rather than for household consumption is seen. It could be observed that the vegetable crops, which are mainly grown for Aizawl market, are predominant among both the type of farmers.

### *Pattern of Input use*

Pattern of input used in cultivation determines the level of productivity, production and income of the cultivator. Sachchidananda (1989) observed the changing patterns of input use as the switch over from shifting cultivation to settled agriculture takes place in Arunachal Pradesh. Generally increase in the use of chemical inputs; human labour and animal power are expected in the wake of switch over. Input use in cultivation was observed with interview schedule in terms of seed, labour, organic manure and chemical fertilizers (see Table 5.7).

As regards seeds between the shifting cultivators and settled agriculturists no difference in use was observed in the case of local seeds and HYV seeds. But it is interesting to note that still widely the local seeds are in use among both the type of cultivators. Mostly they reportedly use local seeds for cultivation. The mean use score of local seed for shifting cultivators as well as settled cultivators was worked out to 2. On the other hand it seems that both use rarely the HYV seeds. The mean use score of HYV seed for both was worked out to 0.2.

With regard to human labour use increase in male labour was observed as the switch over from shifting cultivation to semi-settlement takes place. The mean male labour use score of the shifting cultivators was 1 while that of semi settled agriculturists was worked out to 2. On the other hand no such change was observed in case of the female labour. It was one and the same use for the shifting cultivators and semi-settled cultivators. Further, no notable change in the use of family labour or hired labour was observed. The mean use score of hired labour was 2 for both the type of cultivators while that of family labour was 3. Interestingly, the pattern of labour use is similar among both the type of cultivators. Male labour was greater than the female labour use among both the type of cultivators. The application of family labour was observed to be greater than the hired labour in both the type of cultivation.

Chemical inputs use as well as organic inputs use have increased as the switch over from shifting cultivation to semi-settlement takes

**Table 5.7:** Pattern of Input Use in Cultivation: Mean Scores

| Sl. No. | Input | Shifting N = 30 | Semi-settled N = 30 | Total N = 60 |
|---|---|---|---|---|
| *I.* | *Seed* | | | |
| 1. | Local | 2.00 ± 0.00 | 2.00 ± 0.00 | 2.00 ± 0.00 |
| 2. | HYV | 0.20 ± 0.41 | 0.20 ± 0.41 | 0.20 ± 0.40 |
| *II.* | *Labour* | | | |
| 3. | Hired Male | 1.03 ± 0.96 | 1.37 ± 0.72 | 1.20 ± 0.86 |
| 4. | Hired Female | 0.73 ± 0.69 | 0.93 ± 0.52 | 0.83 ± 0.62 |
| 5. | Family Male Labour | 1.60 ± 0.77 | 1.87 ± 0.43 | 1.73 ± 0.63 |
| 6. | Family Female Labour | 1.50 ± 0.68 | 1.43 ± 0.50 | 1.47 ± 0.60 |
| 7. | Male Labour (3+5) | 1.32 ± 0.69 | 1.62 ± 0.45 | 1.47 ± 0.60 |
| 8. | Female Labour (4+6) | 1.12 ± 0.49 | 1.18 ± 0.31 | 1.15 ± 0.40 |
| 9. | Hired Labour (3+4) | 1.77 ± 1.43 | 2.30 ± 1.06 | 2.03 ± 1.28 |
| 10. | Family Labour (5+6) | 3.10 ± 1.03 | 3.30 ± 0.60 | 3.20 ± 0.84 |
| *III.* | *Organic Manure* | | | |
| 11. | Pig Manure | 0.60 ± 0.81 | 0.50 ± 0.73 | 0.55 ± 0.77 |
| 12. | Cow Dung Manure | 0.43 ± 0.73 | 1.20 ± 0.81 | 0.82 ± 0.85 |
| 13. | Poultry Manure | 0.37 ± 0.67 | 0.93 ± 0.74 | 0.65 ± 0.76 |
| 14. | Domestic Waste | 0.00 ± 0.00 | 0.07 ± 0.25 | 0.03 ± 0.18 |
| 15. | Neem Cake | 0.03 ± 0.18 | 0.63 ± 0.61 | 0.33 ± 0.54 |
| *IV.* | *Chemical Fertilizer* | | | |
| 16. | Nitrogen (Urea) | 0.97 ± 0.89 | 1.80 ± 0.41 | 1.38 ± 0.80 |
| 17. | Phosphate | 1.13 ± 0.86 | 1.83 ± 0.38 | 1.48 ± 0.75 |
| 18. | Potash | 0.47 ± 0.73 | 1.60 ± 0.56 | 1.03 ± 0.86 |
| 19. | Micro Nutrients | 0.07 ± 0.25 | 0.40 ± 0.50 | 0.23 ± 0.43 |
| *V.* | *Organic Pesticide* | *0.00 ± 0.00* | *0.03 ± 0.18* | *0.02 ± 0.13* |
| *VI.* | *Inorganic Inputs Use* | *0.67 ± 0.54* | *1.43 ± 0.25* | *1.05 ± 0.57* |
| *VII.* | *Organic Input Use* | *0.24 ± 0.30* | *0.56 ± 0.27* | *0.40 ± 0.33* |

Mean ± S.D.

*Source*: Computed.

place. The mean score of inorganic input use for the shifting cultivators was 0.67 while it was 1.43 for semi-settled agriculturists. Similarly, the mean score of organic input use for shifting cultivators was 0.24 while that of semi settled cultivators was worked out to 0.56. In spite of these both cultivators reportedly had used greater frequency of inorganic chemical inputs as compared to the organic ones. It is note worthy to mention here that the legislature of Mizoram has passed legislation for adopting organic farming over chemical agriculture.

## *Household Income*

Household Income indicates the standard of living of the respondents. How far the semi-settled cultivators are better off than the shifting cultivators is the question that arose in the context of structural transformation. The composition of household income has been analysed on the basis of its sources, i.e. government service, agriculture, livestock and business (see Table 5.8). The predominant source of income of the households of shifting cultivators and semi-settled an agriculturists was cultivation invariably. More than two third (72.31%) of the respondent of both shifting cultivation and semi-settled agriculture (72.23%) had earned their income from Agriculture. Interestingly, the annual household income of both the respondents of shifting cultivation and semi-settled agriculture is almost same. The mean annual household income of shifting cultivators was worked out to Rs. 36,414.13 while it was Rs. 32,708.27 for semi-settled agriculturists. Similar level of income between the settled and shifting cultivators was reported in the earlier studies too. This was attributed to the similar level of production and productivity in spite of settlement in permanent cultivation (Ninan, 1992).

**Table 5.8:** Composition of Household Income

(*Values in Rupees*)

| *Sl. No.* | *Source* | *Shifting N = 30* | *Semisettled N = 30* | *Total N = 60* |
|---|---|---|---|---|
| 1. | Agriculture | 36414.13 ±12769.92 (72.39) | 32708.27 ± 17407.72 (72.23) | 34561.20 ± 15250.95 (72.31) |
| 2. | Livestock | 6583.33 ± 3779.25 (13.09) | 9213.33 ± 11216.67 (20.34) | 7898.33 ± 12526.93 (16.53) |
| 3. | Business | 4966.67±11686.96 (9.87) | 1148.80±4766.60 (2.54) | 3057.73±9055.86 (6.40) |
| 4. | Government Service | 2339.20±11047.54 (4.65) | 2215.47±10977.30 (4.89) | 2277.33±10918.93 (4.76) |
| 5. | Total | 50303.33 ± 23551.43 (100) | 45285.87 ± 22294.09 (100) | 47794.60 ± 22876.53 (100) |

Figures in parentheses are percentages. Mean ± SD.

*Source*: Computed.

### *Perceived Personal Difficulties in Shifting Cultivation*

Finding out the difficulties and problems in shifting cultivation as perceived by the farmers is one of the objectives of the present study. The respondents were asked to report their agreement in a four point scale strongly agree, agree, disagree and strongly disagree. The mean score of each of this problem for both the type of farmers is presented in Table 5.9. The simple average of the four difficulties was considered as the personal difficulties score.

In the study, the respondents reported that clearance of forest; sowing of seeds, weeding, and low yield were the prominent personal difficulties. Interestingly, there is no noticeable difference between the shifting cultivators and semi settled agriculturists in their perception on the personal difficulties in shifting cultivation. On all the four difficulties in shifting cultivation, viz., clearance of forest, sowing of seeds, weeding and low yield there was a complete agreement between the shifting cultivators and semi-settled cultivators. The mean score of overall personal difficulties for the shifting cultivators as well as settled cultivators was worked out to 2.58.

**Table 5.9:** Perceived Difficulties and Problems in Shifting Cultivation: Mean Score

| *Sl. No.* | *Difficulty/Problem* | *Shifting N = 30* | *Semi-settled N = 30* | *Total N = 60* |
|---|---|---|---|---|
| *I.* | *Personal Difficulties* | | | |
| 1. | Clearance of Forest | 2.73 ± 0.74 | 2.77 ± 0.43 | 2.75 ± 0.60 |
| 2. | Weeding | 2.60 ± 0.50 | 2.50 ± 0.51 | 2.55 ± 0.50 |
| 3. | Low Yield | 2.43 ± 0.50 | 2.60 ± 0.50 | 2.52 ± 0.50 |
| 4. | Sowing of Seeds | 2.53 ± 0.51 | 2.43 ± 0.50 | 2.48 ± 0.50 |
| 5. | Perceived Difficulties in Shifting Cultivation (1:4) | 2.58 ± 0.36 | 2.58 ± 0.37 | 2.58 ± 0.36 |
| *II.* | *Socio-Ecological Consequences* | | | |
| 6. | Loss of Wild Animals Birds and Insects | 2.73 ± 0.45 | 2.90 ± 0.31 | 2.82 ± 0.39 |
| 7. | Soil Erosion | 2.67 ± 0.48 | 2.87 ± 0.35 | 2.77 ± 0.43 |
| 8. | Loss of Forest Cover | 2.70 ± 0.47 | 2.83 ± 0.38 | 2.77 ± 0.43 |
| 9. | Reduction of Water Retention Capacity of Soil | 2.50 ± 0.51 | 2.80 ± 0.41 | 2.65 ± 0.48 |
| 10. | Reduced Rainfall | 2.50 ± 0.51 | 2.70 ± 0.47 | 2.60 ± 0.49 |
| 11. | Fire Accidents due to Jhum | 2.20 ± 0.41 | 2.07 ± 0.25 | 2.13 ± 0.34 |
| 12. | Perceived Social Ecological Consequences (6:12) | 2.55 ± 0.26 | 2.69 ± 0.23 | 2.62 ± 0.25 |

Mean ± S.D.

*Source*: Computed.

Further, it was observed that clearance of forest was perceived by both the type of cultivators as the most difficult one with shifting cultivation. The second most perceived problem of shifting cultivators was that of weeding for the shifting cultivators while the second most difficulty from the perception of the semi-settled cultivators was that of low yield which had fourth rank by the former. Sowing of seeds ranked third with regard to the former but ranked third by the latter.

### *Social Ecological Consequences of Shifting Cultivation*

The question here is that how far the farmers perceive the social ecological consequences of the shifting cultivation reported by natural and social scientists alike such as loss of wild animals birds and insects (Buchi, 1997), soil erosion (Singh *et al.,* 2000; Agarwal, 1985; Patnaik, 1982; Majumdar, 1947), loss of forest cover (Chatterjee, 1993), reduction of water retention capacity of soil, reduced, rainfall (Buchi, 1997), fire accidents due to jhum (Jha, 1997). A four-point scale (Strongly agree to strongly disagree) was used to measure the perception of the farmers on these problems. The simple average of all these item scores was considered as the perceived social ecological consequences. The mean scores are presented in Table 5.9.

Both the types of cultivators perceived all the social ecological problems except fire accidents due to jhum. The mean perception scores on loss of wild animals, birds and insects, soil erosion, loss of forest cover, reduction of water retention capacity of soil, reduced rain fall of both the type of cultivators were approximately 3. The mean perceived social ecological consequence score is slightly greater for semi-settled cultivators as compared to the shifting cultivators. Similarly, excepting the fire accident due to jhum the mean scores of the semi-settled cultivators are observed to be greater than the shifting cultivators.

### *Transformation from Shifting Cultivation to Semi-Settled Agriculture*

In the previous sub-sections the patterns of the agricultural livelihood across the two types of cultivators, viz. shifting and semi-settled cultivators was discussed in terms of agrarian structural characteristics, tools use, cropping pattern, input use and income. Also the farmers' perception on the problems of shifting cultivation from the personal and social ecological points of view was analyzed.

The question that arises in this context is that how far the changes are substantial and significant. To answer this question, Karl Pearson's coefficients of correlation were worked out. The independent variable was type of cultivator (shifting cultivator = 0; semi-settled cultivators = 1). The dependent variables were those related to agrarian structure, tools and implements use, cropping pattern, input use, agricultural income, perceived personal difficulties, and perceived social consequences (these are explicated in the previous sub-sections). Table 5.10 presents the results of correlation analyses of the transformations in the wake of switch over from shifting cultivation to settled agriculture.

As a result of switch over from shifting cultivation to semi-settled agriculture significant and substantial changes were observed in the agrarian structure, tools and implement use, cropping pattern, input use, and perception of the farmers on the social ecological consequences. Yet no significant change in the income of the cultivators was noticed due the switch over.

In the agrarian structure, the size of landholding had observed to have increased significantly but there was no change in the actual size of the land being cultivated (operational holding). The correlation coefficient between the type of cultivator and the size of landholding (0.38) was positive and significant at 1 per cent level. On the other hand the correlation coefficient between the type of cultivator and the size of operational landholding (area of the land cultivated) (0.03) was not even significant at 5 per cent level.

In tools and implements used significant increase in the total number was observed in contrary to the reduction in the use expected. The correlation coefficient between the number of tools used by the farmer and the type of farmer (0.36) was positive and significant at 1 per cent level. The number of forest clearance tools and harvesting tools did not significantly decrease as expected. The correlation coefficient of type cultivator with forest clearance (0.03) and that of harvesting tools (-0.11) were not even significant at 5 per cent level. On the other hand the number of weeding tools and land preparation tools seem to have increased significantly. The correlation coefficients of type of cultivator with the weeding tools (0.59), and land preparation tools (0.81) were positive and significant at five per cent level.

As switch over from shifting cultivation to semi-settled agriculture occurs the cropping pattern also undergoes significant and substantial

**Table 5.10:** Transformation from Shifting Cultivation to Semi-settled Agriculture: Zero Order Correlation Coefficients

| *Sl. No.* | *Factor* | *Pearson's R N = 60* | *Sig. (2-tailed)* |
|---|---|---|---|
| *I.* | *Agrarian Structure* | | |
| | Size of Landholding | 0.38** | 0.00 |
| | Size of Operational Landholding | 0.03 | 0.80 |
| *II.* | *Tools and Implements Use* | | |
| | Number of Tools | 0.36** | 0.00 |
| | Forest Clearance Tools | 0.03 | 0.84 |
| | Weeding Tools | 0.59** | 0.00 |
| | Land Preparation Tools | 0.81** | 0.00 |
| | Harvesting Tools | -0.11 | 0.41 |
| *III.* | *Cropping Pattern* | | |
| | Number of Crops Cultivated | 0.19 | 0.16 |
| | Number of Cereals | -0.89** | 0.00 |
| | Pulses and Oil Seeds | -0.50** | 0.00 |
| | Vegetables | 0.67** | 0.00 |
| | Fruits | -0.35** | 0.01 |
| *IV.* | *Input Use* | | |
| | Local Seed | NA | NA |
| | HYV Seed | 0.00 | 1.00 |
| | Inorganic Inputs Use | 0.68** | 0.00 |
| | Organic Input Use | 0.50** | 0.00 |
| | Male Labour | 0.25* | 0.05 |
| | Female Labour | 0.08 | 0.53 |
| | Hired Labour | 0.21 | 0.11 |
| | Family Labour | 0.12 | 0.36 |
| *V.* | *Agricultural Income* | *-0.12* | *0.35* |
| *VI.* | *Perceived Problems in Shifting Cultivation* | | |
| | Perceived Personal Difficulties | 0.00 | 1.00 |
| | Perceived Social Ecological Consequences | 0.29* | 0.03 |

** P<0.01 * P<0.05.

*Source*: Computed.

change. Though the number of crops did not change significantly as excepted there is a qualitative transformation from subsistence to commercialization takes place. The correlation coefficient of type of cultivator with the number of crops (0.19) was not significant at 5 per cent level. The number of subsistence, i.e. food crops meant for household consumption decreased significantly while that of commercial crops, i.e. vegetables and fruits increased significantly. The correlation coefficient of the type of cultivators with number of cereals (-0.89), pulses and oil seeds (-0.5) and fruits (-0.35) were negative and significant at 1 per cent level while that of vegetables (0.67) was positive and significant at 1 per cent level.

As regards input use in cultivation no significant changes were observed in the seeds use, while there were significant changes observed in the case of organic and inorganic input use and labour use. The frequency of use of local seed as well as HYV seed did not change significantly. The correlation coefficients of type of farmer with the local seed as well as HYV (0.00) were not even significant at 5 per cent level. Unexpectedly, use of both organic and inorganic inputs has increased significantly. The correlation coefficient of the type of farmer with the frequency of inorganic inputs use (0.68) and organic inputs use (0.50) were both positive and significant at 5 per cent level. As regards labour the frequency of use of both family labour as well as hired labour did not significantly change. The correlation coefficients of type of cultivator with the frequency of family labour (0.12) and hired labour (0.21) were not even significant at five per cent level though positive. But in the labour use the frequency of use of male labour did increase though the female labour use frequency did not change significantly. The correlation coefficient of the type of cultivator with the frequency of male labour (0.25) was positive and significant at 5 per cent level, while that of female labour (0.08) was not even significant at 5 per cent level.

The most important question from a rural development perspective is that what happens to the standard of living of the cultivators. In other words how does the income from agriculture change as the shift from shifting cultivation to semi-settled agriculture takes place? The statistical analysis indicate no change in the income of cultivators as result of the switch over to semi-settled cultivation though cropping pattern, tools use, inputs use and labour use have changed significantly. The correlation coefficient of the type of the farmer with the agricultural income (-0.12) was not even significant at 5 per cent level.

The last question with regard to transformation is the change in the farmers' perception on the problems of shifting cultivation. The perception of the farmers does change significantly with regard to the social ecological consequences but not with regard to the personal difficulties. Interestingly, an increased realisation of the social ecological consequences of shifting cultivation was observed due to the switch over to semi-settled agriculture. The correlation coefficient of type of farmer with the perceived personal difficulties (0.00) was not significant at 5 per cent level while that of perceived socio-ecological consequences (0.29) was significant at 5 per cent level.

## Willingness to Switch over from Jhum to Settled Agriculture

Shifting cultivation is considered as an integral component of tribal culture wherever it is practiced (Majumdar, 1976). Hence, the reluctance of the cultivators owing to its cultural base is considered as a major stumbling block towards weaning away the practice of shifting cultivation. In spite of this a number of authors report the willingness of the jhumias to practice settled agriculture (Dasgupta and Banerjee, 1992; Bose *et al.,* 1982; Majumdar, 1976). Malabika Dasgupta and Ashis Banerjee (1992:35) observed that the farmers chosen settled agriculture as primary alternative over the shifting cultivation in their Tripura study. Bose, Ghatak and Bera (1982: 224) in their Orissa study noted the willingness of the shifting cultivators to practice settled agriculture. D.N. Majumdar (1976) also reported willingness in the case of Garo jhumias in spite of its harmonious linkage with their culture.

These studies conceive willing to settle in permanent cultivation as a unidimensional phenomenon. But in fact willingness to switch over from jhum to settled agriculture involves a number of shifts, viz., from jhum to settled agriculture, common ownership of land to private ownership, right to transfer or sale, right to lease or contract. Hence, to operationally measure willingness to switch over from shifting cultivation to settled agriculture a four-point agreement scale (strongly agree to strongly disagree) was used including these four shifts. The simple average of all the four items was considered as the willingness to switch over from shifting cultivation to settled agriculture. The mean scores are presented in Table 5.11.

Both the types of cultivators were willing to switch over to the practice of settled agriculture. The mean score of the respondents of shifting cultivation was 2.73 while that of semi-settled agriculture was 2.86. Interestingly, both were willing to practice settled agriculture, acquire private ownership of their land and right to lease, contract and sell the same. The willingness to settle in permanent land was the first and foremost shift readily accepted by both the shifting cultivators and semi settled agriculturists. The mean score of willingness of the shifting cultivator to switch over to settled-agriculture was 2.90 while it was 2.97 for semi-settled cultivators. The willingness for shifting from common ownership of land to private ownership was second in the order. The mean score of the shifting cultivators was worked out to 2.90 and that of semi-settled agriculturists was 2.87. Both the types of farmers were reportedly willing to have right to transfer, sale, and lease or contract the land. The overall mean score was 2.68.

**Table 5.11:** Respondents' Willingness to Switch over from Jhum to Settled Agriculture: Mean Scores

| *Sl. No.* | *Type of Shift* | *Shifting N = 30* | *Semi-settled N = 30* | *Total N = 60* |
|---|---|---|---|---|
| 1. | Shift from Jhum to Settled Agriculture | 2.90 ± 0.40 | 2.97 ± 0.18 | 2.93 ± 0.31 |
| 2. | Common Ownership of Land to Private Ownership | 2.90 ± 0.31 | 2.87 ± 0.35 | 2.88 ± 0.32 |
| 3. | Have Right to Transfer or Sale | 2.53 ± 0.51 | 2.83 ± 0.38 | 2.68 ± 0.47 |
| 4. | Right to Lease or Contract | 2.60 ± 0.50 | 2.77 ± 0.43 | 2.68 ± 0.47 |
| 5. | Willingness to Switch over (1:4) | 2.73 ± 0.29 | 2.86 ± 0.22 | 2.80 ± 0.26 |

Figure in Parentheses are percentages Mean ± S.D.

*Source*: Computed.

Though there were some studies reporting the willingness of the jhumias to settle in permanent cultivation, there were no studies indicating the factors affecting such willingness. In the present study it was attempted to identify the factors affecting the willingness of the jhumias with the help of Karl Pearson's correlation coefficient. Pearson's correlation coefficients were worked out for the willingness score with type of cultivators (shifting cultivator = 0; Semi-settled agriculturists = 1), sub tribe (Lusei = 1; otherwise = 0), denomination (Presbyterian = 1; otherwise = 0), family size (number of members), age group (young = 1; middle = 2; aged = 3), gender (male =1; female = 0), level of education (primary = 1, middle = 2, HSLC and above = 3), area of land owned (acres), area of land cultivated (acres), number of crops, cereals, pulses and oil seeds, vegetables, fruits, perceived difficulties in shifting cultivation (score), and perceived social ecological consequences (score). The correlation matrix is presented in Table 5.12.

**Table 5.12:** Correlates of Willingness to Switch Over to Settled Agriculture: Zero Order Correlation Matrix

| *Sl. No.* | *Factor* | *Pearson's R N = 60* | *Sig. (2-tailed)* |
|---|---|---|---|
| 1. | Age Group | -0.33** | 0.01 |
| 2. | Gender | -0.01 | 0.91 |
| 3. | Family Size | -0.28 | 0.03 |
| 4. | Level of Education | 0.26* | 0.04 |
| 5. | Sub-Tribe | 0.05 | 0.70 |
| 6. | Denomination | -0.05 | 0.68 |
| 7. | Type of Cultivators | 0.24 | 0.06 |
| 8. | Area of Land Owned | -0.16 | 0.21 |
| 9. | Area of Land Cultivated | -0.16 | 0.22 |
| 10. | Number of Crops | -0.01 | 0.91 |
| 11. | Cereals | -0.30* | 0.02 |
| 12. | Pulses and Oil Seeds | -0.09 | 0.49 |
| 13. | Vegetables | 0.18 | 0.18 |
| 14. | Fruits | -0.28* | 0.03 |
| 15. | Perceived Personal Difficulties | 0.13 | 0.32 |
| 16. | Perceived Social Ecological Consequences | 0.30* | 0.02 |

** P<0.01 * P<0.05.

*Source*: Computed.

Among the demographic structural factors, viz., age group, gender, family size and level of education, willingness to switch over had significant association with age group and level of education. The correlation coefficients of gender (-0.01) and family size (-0.28) were not significant at 5 per cent level while that of age group (-0.33) was negative and significant at 1 per cent level. It implies that as age of the cultivator increases the willingness to switch over declines. On the other hand the correlation coefficient of willingness to switch over of level of education (0.26) was positive and significant at 5 per cent level. It means that the willingness to switch over to settled agriculture increases with the level of the education of the cultivator.

Of the social structural factors, viz., sub-tribe and denomination none had any significant association with the willingness to switch over to settled agriculture. The correlation coefficient between willingness and social structural factors such as sub-tribe (0.05), denomination (-0.05), were not even significant at 5 per cent level.

Among the agrarian structural factors, viz., type of cultivators, area of land owned, area of land cultivated none had significant association with the willingness to switch over to settled agriculture. The correlation coefficients of type of cultivators (0.24), area of land owned (-0.16), area of land cultivated (-0.16) were not even significant at 5 per cent level.

Cropping pattern seems to have associated with the willingness to switch over to settled agriculture. Though the number of crops cultivated, number of pulses and oil seeds and vegetables cultivated had not significantly associated with willingness the number of cereals and fruits cultivated had negative association. The correlation coefficients of number of crops (-0.01), pulses and oil seeds (-0.09), vegetables (0.18) were not significant at 5 per cent level. On the other hand the coefficients of correlation of cereals (-0.30) and fruits (-0.28) were significant at 5 per cent level. It is clear that those who have been primarily cultivating cereals and fruit crops for their subsistence (household consumption) have lower level of willingness to switch over as compared to those who cultivate commercial crops for the market.

Perception of the social ecological consequences rather personal difficulties in shifting cultivation were found to be significantly associated with the cultivators' willingness to switch over to settled agriculture. The correlation coefficient of perceived personal difficulties (0.13) was not even significant at 5 per cent level while that of perceived social ecological consequences (0.30) was positive and significant at 5 per cent level. It implies that as the social ecological awareness increases the farmer's willingness to switch over to settled agriculture also increases.

### *Constraints to Switch over to Settled Agriculture*

The farmers may have a number of constraints, problems or obstacles in switching over from jhum to settled agriculture (Datta, 1992;

Ramakrishnan, 1992; Ninan, 1992; Dasgupta and Banerjee, 1984; Hungyo, 1982). To identify and prioritise them the practitioners of both shifting cultivation and semi-settled agriculture were asked to rank eight constraints, which were identified in the course of pilot study and pre-testing in switching over from shifting cultivation to settled agriculture. To obtain a comprehensive picture transmutation of ranks into scores Garrett's procedure was used with an appropriate modification (Garrett, 1966:328-332)[9]. Table 5.13 presents the number of persons, mean transmuted scores and the ranking of the various constraints for the switch over from shifting cultivation to settled agriculture.

Among these eight constraints lack of adequate capital for investment lack of irrigational facilities and non-suitability of land for settlement are the top three constraints in switching over from jhum to settled agriculture by both the shifting cultivators and semi-settled agriculturists. Interestingly, all the respondents had ranked these three constraints though their ranking varies. Same order of preference was observed among the shifting cultivators as well as semi-settled agriculturists. Both the type of respondents ranked lack of adequate capital for investment, lack of irrigational facilities and non-suitability of land for settlement in the same order.

Lack of technical know how obtained the fourth rank followed by inadequate labour supply in the fifth position in the overall ranking. Lack of technical know how was ranked by 90 per cent of the shifting cultivators with fourth rank while it obtained fifth position and ranked by 80 per cent of the semi-settled agriculturists.

Inadequate labour supply was ranked by more than fourth-fifth of the respondents to fifth rank by the shifting cultivators and ranked by more than three-fourths of the semi-settled cultivators to 4th position.

Lack of marketing facilities, lack of transport and non-remunerative prices for the agricultural produce were ranked as the last three constraints in switching over from shifting cultivation to settled agriculture. It does not mean that they are not at all problematic. Interestingly, these were also ranked by a vast majority of the respondents invariably, which implies the realisation of the constraints. Lack of marketing facilities obtained sixth and seventh ranks from the shifting cultivators and semi settled cultivators. Yet more than two-thirds of the former and three fourth of the later had ranked this constraint. Lack of transport facilities acquired eighth rank from the shifting cultivators and sixth rank from semi-settled cultivators though

**Table 5.13:** Constraints in Switch over from Shifting Cultivation to Settled Agriculture: Mean Transmuted Scores and Ranks

| *Sl. No.* | *Constraint* | *Shifting N = 30* | | | *Semi-settled N = 30* | | | *Total N = 60* | | |
|---|---|---|---|---|---|---|---|---|---|---|
| | | *Number* | *Mean* | *Rank* | *Number* | *Mean* | *Rank* | *Number* | *Mean* | *Rank* |
| 1. | Inadequate Capital for Investment | 30 (100) | 7.25 | 1 | 30 (100) | 7.38 | 1 | 60 (100) | 7.32 | 1 |
| 2. | Lack of Irrigation Facilities | 30 (100) | 6.97 | 2 | 30 (100) | 6.75 | 2 | 60 (100) | 6.86 | 2 |
| 3. | Non-Suitability of Land for Settlement | 30 (100) | 6.46 | 3 | 30 (100) | 5.92 | 3 | 60 (100) | 6.19 | 3 |
| 4. | Lack of Technical Know How | 27 (90.00) | 4.60 | 4 | 24 (80.00) | 3.41 | 5 | 51 (85.00) | 4.01 | 4 |
| 5. | Inadequate Labour Supply | 25 (83.33) | 3.72 | 5 | 23 (76.67) | 3.51 | 4 | 48 (80.00) | 3.62 | 5 |
| 6. | Lack of Marketing Facilities | 20 (66.67) | 2.35 | 6 | 23 (76.67) | 2.88 | 7 | 43 (71.67) | 2.62 | 6 |
| 7. | Lack of Transport Facilities | 18 (60.00) | 2.24 | 8 | 20 (66.67) | 2.91 | 6 | 38 (63.33) | 2.58 | 7 |
| 8. | Non-remunerative Price | 19 (63.33) | 2.12 | 7 | 21 (70.00) | 2.57 | 8 | 40 (66.67) | 2.35 | 8 |

Figures in Parentheses are percentages.

*Source*: Computed.

more than two-thirds of the latter and one-half of the former ranked them. Non-remunerative price for agricultural produce was ranked to seventh position among the constraints by the shifting cultivators and to eighth position by the semi settled cultivators in spite of being ranked by more than two-thirds of the respondents.

## IV. CONCLUSIONS

As a result of switch over from shifting cultivation to semi-settled agriculture significant and substantial changes were observed in the agrarian structure, tools and implement use, cropping pattern, input use, and perception of the farmers on the social ecological consequences. Yet no significant difference in the income of the cultivators was observed. In the agrarian structure, the size of land holding had increased significantly but there was no change in the actual size of the land being cultivated (operational holding). On contrast to our expectation of reduction in the tools use significant increase in the total number tools and implements used was observed. The number of forest clearance tools and harvesting tools did not significantly decrease as expected. On the other hand the number of weeding tools and land preparation tools has increased significantly. As switch over from shifting cultivation to semi settled agriculture occurs the cropping pattern also undergoes significant and substantial change. Though the number of crops did not change significantly as excepted there is a qualitative transformation from subsistence to commercialization takes place. The number of subsistence, i.e. food crops meant for household consumption decreased significantly while that of commercial crops, i.e. vegetables and fruits increased significantly. As regards input use in cultivation no significant changes were observed in the seeds use, while there were significant changes observed in the case of organic and inorganic input use and labour use. The frequency of use of local seed as well as HYV seed did not change significantly. Unexpectedly use of both organic and in organic input use have increased significantly. As regards labour the frequency of use of both family labour as well as hired labour did not significantly change. But in the labour use the frequency of use of male labour did increase though the female labour use frequency did not change significantly. As regard standard of living of the cultivators the statistical analysis indicated no change in the income of cultivators as result of the switch over to semi-settled cultivation though cropping pattern, tools use, inputs use and labour use have changed significantly. The farmer's perception on the problems of shifting cultivation seem to have changed due to the switch over significantly with regard to the social ecological consequence but not with regard to the personal difficulties. Interestingly, a greater realisation of the social ecological consequences of shifting cultivation was observed due to the switch over to semi-settled agriculture.

Willingness to switch over from jhum to settled agriculture involves a number of shifts, viz., from jhum to settled agriculture, common ownership of land to private ownership, right to transfer or sale, right to lease or contract. Both the types of cultivators were willing to practice settled agriculture. Interestingly, both were willing to practice settled agriculture, acquire private ownership of their land and right to lease, contract and sell the same. The willingness for shifting from common ownership of land to private ownership was second in the order. Both the types of farmers were reportedly willing to have right to transfer, sale, lease or contract the land.

The analysis of factors affecting the willingness of the cultivators to switch over to settled cultivation revealed that among the demographic structural factors, viz., age and gender, family size and level of education, willingness to switch over had significant association with age group and level of education. As age of the cultivator increases the willingness to switch over declines while it increases with the level of the education of the cultivator. Of the social structural factors, viz., sub-tribe and denomination none had any significant association with the willingness to switch over to settled agriculture. Among the land tenure or agrarian structural factors, viz., type of cultivators, area of land owned, area of land cultivated none had significant association with the willingness to switch over to settled agriculture. Cropping pattern seems to have associated with the willingness to switch over to settled agriculture. Though the number of crops cultivated, number of pulses and oil seeds and vegetables cultivated had not significantly associated with willingness the number of cereals and fruits cultivated had negative association. It was found that those who have been primarily cultivating cereals and fruit crops for their subsistence (household consumption) have lower level of willingness to switch over as compared to those who cultivate commercial crops for the market. Perception of the social ecological consequences rather than that of personal difficulties of shifting cultivation is found to be significantly associated with the cultivators' willingness to switch over to settled agriculture. It was observed that with the increase in social ecological awareness the farmer's willingness to switch over to settled agriculture also increases.

The farmers have a number of constraints, problems or obstacles to switching over from jhum to settled agriculture. Lack of adequate capital for investment, lack of irrigational facilities and non-suitability of land for settlement were the most important three constraints to switching over to settled agriculture according to both shifting cultivators and semi-settled agriculturists.

The Mizo cultivators, whether practicing shifting cultivation or semi-settled agriculture they are willing to switch over to settled agriculture. Hence, it is no longer a matter of willingness or awareness of the problems. The most crucial issue is that whether settled agriculture is a viable alternative to shifting cultivation. In other words, will it improve the living standards of poor tribal jhumias? The results of the present study unfortunately support the doubts of the previous studies over the improved production, productivity and returns and hence income of the tribal cultivators practicing settled agriculture in the North east India (Ninan, 1992). In the light of the results of the present study, it can be argued that jhum provides food security to the poor as they cultivate more than 14 crops. The crop diversification sustains the household and reduces the simple jhumias vulnerability to destitution. Will the settled agriculture ensure such sustainability against all sorts of shocks and risks of market economy? The scientists of all sorts both natural and social need to deliberate on these issues. Unless the viability of the settled agriculture in providing better standard of life and immunity against poverty, settled agriculture should not be imposed on the tribal people from above. The present study throws the challenge to the advocates of settled agriculture to demonstrate empirically (intensive large scale field experiments) the economic and social viability of their system they presume at the outset of advocating it.

## NOTES

1. According to the tenth plan document the unresolved issues are displacement of tribals, tribal land alienation, indebtedness, shifting cultivation and deprivation of forest rights while the persisting problems include low literacy and high drop out rates, inadequate and inaccessible health services,

nutritional deficiencies and diseases, lack of adequate irrigation facilities, extreme/abject poverty, endangering of intellectual rights crimes/atrocities against STs, neglect of forest villages, extinction of primitive tribal groups, ineffective Implementation of PESA, 1996 and routinised mechanism of TSP.

2. This marked a revolutionary change in human societies from food gathering to food production. In fact its origin is traced to as far back as the Neolithic period between the years 1300 to 3000 B.C (Ninan, 1992). Gordon Childe (1986) identified the Neolithic farmers of Danube Valley as nomadic cultivators. Chang (1970) also showed that the Neolithic farmers of Formosa were shifting cultivators. It is therefore clear that we can trace back the history of shifting cultivation to about 9000 years from the presents.
3. In the larger part of North Eastern India, the term frequently used for shifting cultivation is '*jhum*' and in Mizoram the natives call it '*Lo*' (Thangchungnunga, 1997). It bears different names in other communities. In Meghalaya it is known as '*Bogma*' among the Garos. '*Lyngkhalum*' or '*Shyrti*' among the Khasis, '*Rit*' among the Mikirs of Assam, '*Tekonglu*' among the Ao Nagas of Manipur, Gudia, Bagda, Sarban Donger Chara, Podu in Southern Orissa and *Peuda* in Madhya Pradesh and as '*Podu*' among the Hill Reddies of Andhra Pradesh.
4. *Chitememe* in Zambia and '*Chinampa*' in Tropical America. '*Chena*' in Sri Lanka, '*Karen*' in Japan, '*Ladang*' in Indonesia, '*Humoh*' in Java, '*Cagin*' in Phillipines, '*Milpa*' in Central America '*Roco*' in Brazil, '*Caomib*' in Mexico, and '*Sartage*' in Ardennes.
5. The official view of the Government of India on shifting cultivation could be understood from the following extract from Tenth Five Year Plan document. "Shifting cultivation, which is not ecologically sound, is still being practiced by the tribals living on the higher slopes of hilly areas of the country. As estimated, more than 6 lakh tribal families in the North Eastern states, Orissa, Andhra Pradesh and Himachal Pradesh practice shifting cultivation on a continuous basis. This shifting cultivation is integrally linked to the tribal economy in the areas where it is practiced and their social and economic activities and rituals are also centred around this practice. The problem of shifting cultivation is a very complex one, involving economic, social and psychological aspects of the tribal communities. Although shifting cultivation is one of the prime sources of living for the tribals, yet the same has been severely restricted. The Ministry of Agriculture has been implementing a scheme for control and transformation of shifting cultivation in the North Eastern states, but the pace of its implementation has been very slow."
6. *Chapchar Kut* is the most important festival held in between the cutting of jungle and jhum land usually in the last part of February and first part of March every year. The word *Chapchar* is the combination of two words Chap and char. Chap means strewn trees, bamboos and bushes over the

vast jhum fields while char refers to the process of their being dried up. *Kut* means festival. *Mizos* believe that Festival would ensure a good harvest in their jhum field.

7. *Pawl Kut* is celebrated when rice harvest is almost reaped. This festival of mainly for the children who are dressed on their best attire and are fed with rice, meat and boiled eggs.
8. *Mim Kut* is observed during August and September when Maize harvest is reaped. This Festival is celebrated with feasting, singing and dancing.
9. Henry E. Garrett (1966) had suggested a procedure for transmuting the ranks into interval scores so that they can be further subjected to analysis. According to his procedure the ranks are first converted into per cent position by means off the following formula:

$$\text{Per cent position} = 100(R - 0.5)/N$$

where R is the rank of the individual or item in the series and N is the number of individuals or items ranked. Secondly, with the help of Garrett's table the corresponding scores of the ranks are obtained. The scores are used for further analysis. In the case situations like the present one where a number of respondents were asked to rank a number of items (constraints/ suggestions) all are not ranking all items. To obtain aggregate comprehensive mean score Garrett suggests computation of average only by including the number of persons who ranked the particular item. This is suitable to the situations like that of Garrett gives whereby the judges are always do not aware of all the persons whom they are supposed to rank. In the present context both the number of persons ranking as well as their ranking need to be given weightage so as to obtain priorities. Giving weightage to only the ranks neglecting the number of persons who chose the particular item will mislead the policy maker. Hence, instead of obtaining mean transmuted score by dividing the sum of transmuted scores by the number of persons ranked the particular item, the average was obtained by dividing the number of persons.

## REFERENCES

Agarwal, A.K. (1985). North East India: *An Economic Perspective*. Allahabad: Chugh Publications.

Agarwal, A.K. (1998). North Eastern Economy: Problems and Prospects. Delhi: Mittal Publications.

Borthakur, D.N. (2002). "Shifting Cultivation in North East India: An Approach towards Control". In Bimal, J. Deb (ed.) *Development Priorities in North East India*. New Delhi: Concept Publishing Company.

Bose, Saradendu, S. Gothak, and R.K. Bera (1982). "Shifting Cultivation in India". In Singh K.S. (Ed.) *Economic of the Tribes and their Transformation.* New Delhi: Concept Publishing Company.

Buchi, Nana K. (1997). "Shifting Cultivation and its Impact on Forest Ecosystem". In P.M. Mohapatra and P.C. Mohapatra (eds.) *Forest Management in Tribal Areas: Forest Policy and people's participation.* New Delhi: Concept Publishing Company.

Chaterjee, N.S. (1993). "Shifting Cultivation in Tripura—Some Strategies for Development". In K. Alam (ed.) *Agricultural Development in North India—Constraints and Prospects.* New Delhi: Deep and Deep Publications.

Chaturvedi, M.D. and B.N. Uppal (1960). *A Study of Shifting Cultivation.* New Delhi: Indian Council of Agricultural Research.

Darlong, Vincent T. (2004). *To Jhum or not to Jhum—Policy Perspective on Shifting Cultivation.* Guwahati: The Missing Link.

Das Gupta, Malabika (1994). "Continuity and Change in Tribal Society: *A Study of the Economic Aspects of Tribal Jhumia Society in Tripura*". In Milton A. Sangma (ed.), *Essays on North East India.* New Delhi: Indus Publishing Company.

Das Gupta, Malabika and Asis Banerjee (1992). "Jhuming as the Way of Life of the Jhumias: An Analysis of Data from Tripura." In Budhadeb Chowdhuri (Ed.), *Tribal Transformation in India: Economy and Agrarian Issues*, New Delhi: Inter India Publication.

Datta, P.S. (1992). *India's North East: A Study in Transition.* New Delhi: Har Anand Publications and Vikas Publishing House.

Elwin, V. (1959). A Philosophy for NEFA. Shillong: North East Frontier Agency.

Eswaraiah, G. (2003). "Challenges of Rural Eco System in India". *Employment News*, 27(50). 1-3.

Government of Mizoram (2004). *Statistical Abstract: Department of Agriculture and Minor Irrigation 2003-2004.* Aizawl: Directorate of Agriculture and Minor Irrigation, Government of Mizoram.

Husain, Majid (1993). "Shifting Cultivation and Sustainable development in Nagaland". In Amitava Mukherjee, and V.K. Agnihotri (eds.) *Environment and Development.* New Delhi: Concept Publishing Company.

Husain, Zabid (1993). Is Shifting Cultivation a Stumbling Block in Eco-Development? *Journal of the North Eastern Council*, 14(1), 14-16.

Jha, L.K. (1997). *Shifting Cultivation.* New Delhi: A.P.H. Publishing Corporations.

Majumdar, D.N. (1976). "Shifting Cultivation: Is it a way of Life? An Analysis of Garo Data". In B. Pakem, J.B. Bhattacharjee, B.B. Dutta, and B. Datta Ray (eds.) *Shifting Cultivation in North East India*, Shillong: North East India Council for Social Science Research (NEICSSR).

Ninan, K.N. (1992). Economics of Shifting Cultivation in India, *Economic and Political Weekly*, 27(13), 67-91.

Patnaik, N. (1982). "Shifting Cultivation in Orissa". In K.S. Singh (ed.) *Economics of the Tribes and their Transformation*, New Delhi: Concept Publishing Company.

Ramakrishnan, P.S. (1992). "Jhum: Is there a Way Out." In Budhadeb Chowdhuri (ed.) *Tribal Transformation in India: Economy and Agrarian Issues*, New Delhi: Inter India Publication.

Sachchidananda (1989). *Shifting Cultivation in India.* New Delhi: Concept Publishing Company.

Satapathy, K.K., B.K. Sharma, S.N. Goswami, and N.D. Verma (2003). *Developing Lands Affected by Shifting Cultivation.* New Delhi: Department of Land Resources, Ministry of Rural Development, Government of India.

Sen, S. (1992). *Tribes of Mizoram: Description Ethnology and Bibliography.* New Delhi: Gyan Publishing House.

Sharma, Tarun C. (1976). "The Prehistoric Background of Shifting Cultivation". In B. Pakem, J.B. Bhattacharjee, B.B. Dutta, and B. Datta Ray (eds.) *Shifting Cultivation in North East India.* Shillong: North East India Council for Social Science Research (NEICSSR).

Singh, N.P., Pramod Kumar, and N.D. Verma (2000). "Agro-based Industries—A Boon for the Shifting Cultivation". *Journal of the North Eastern Council* 20 (4). 38-46.

Thangchungnunga (1997). "Shifting Cultivation and Emerging Pattern of Change in Land Relation". In L.K. Jha (ed.) *Natural Resource Management, Mizoram.* New Delhi: APH Publishing Corporation.

# Chapter 6

# Challenges and Opportunities for Sustaining Peace and Development in Mizoram

VANLALCHHAWNA

## Introduction

Civil war, ethnic conflict, terrorism, communal violence and insurgency have become common across the world especially in the underdeveloped regions during the last four decades. During 1990-2002 alone, there were 56 major armed conflicts in 44 different locations in the world. Amongst the continents, Africa has experienced a high prevalence of civil wars. Over the last 40 years, nearly 20 African countries have experienced at least one period of civil war.

Conflict is a major constraint to development with critical impact on physical, economic and social capital, as well as the social fabric of the countries involved. Social scientists have attempted to explore the causes of conflicts/civil wars and also quantify their economic consequences. Civil conflict stemmed from a complex interaction of economic, social, historical and political factor. However, a consensus is emerging among scholars that, contrary to popular belief, civil wars and ethnic conflicts in several parts of the world are not due, primarily, to ethnic and religious diversity, but rather to high levels of poverty, failed political institutions and economic dependence on natural resources (Elbadwai & Sambanis, 2000). Deep political and economic development failures, not tribalism, ethnic hatred and linguistic fragmentation, are the root causes of the problem. The implication of these findings is significant. Something can be done to reduce the prevalence of violent conflicts in the affected countries and prevent their recurrence. Democratic reform improved political governance and institutions for economic management are needed in conflict-torn societies to manage effectively the challenges facing them, to maintain political stability and also to diversify their economies.

Conflict has a devastating impact on the economy and society. It undermines economic performance, exacerbates poverty and disrupts development efforts. The destruction of physical infrastructure, interruption of education and health services, and indirect effects on trade, tourism and business confidence, all weaken a country's fiscal position and hurt economic growth. During conflict, per capita income declines partly because it directly reduces production and partly because it causes a gradual loss of capital stock like skilled manpower, infrastructure facilities etc. The breakdown of social orders increases the cost of economic transactions, further decelerating real income of the people. Civil war and violent armed conflicts inflicted heavy sufferings in terms of displacement, mortality and poverty to non-combatant within the country. Neighbouring countries are also instantly affected with refugees flooding them. Besides, conflict regions are used not only for production and transportation of hard drugs but provide safe haven for several terrorist organisations as well.

The Mizo insurgency movement during 1966-1986 gave rise to intense armed conflict between Mizo National Front who spearheaded the movement and the security forces. This conflict gave rise to untold miseries to the Mizo people—valuable human lives were lost and property worth millions of rupees were destroyed—and perpetrated a crippling blow to the then administrative machinery of the district council. This paper briefly examines some of the consequences the MNF insurgency movement had on the socio-economic structure of Mizo society and highlights the development performances of Mizoram economy during the post-conflict period. Finally, it also underlines the strategy for sustaining peace and sustainable economic development of the state.

## Impacts of Mizo Insurgency Movement on Economy and Society

The two-decade old political conflict in Mizoram inflicted heavy damage to the self-sufficient tribal economy and social structure. Physical and social infrastructures like bridges, educational institutions, dispensaries etc. were destroyed. Many primary and middle schools and dispensaries were destroyed and set ablaze by the security forces while others had been simply abandoned following village groupings. For instance, primary schools decreased by nearly 30 per cent from 602 in 1960-61 to 425 in 1971-72. Though physical and social infrastructure that existed under the Mizo District Council in the mid-1960s was insufficient, they were an important structure of the economy. Their destruction further retarded physical and human capital formation which formed the very foundation of the development of the state.

The underground movement badly disrupted economic activities. It paralysed the operation of traditional agricultural system, i.e. jhum cultivation, adversely affecting the production of rice and other crops. The breakdown of physical and social infrastructure further hindered the supply of foodstuffs, medicines and other medical emergencies to the people who remained on the brink of starvation death and poor health condition. Many people suffered and died of diseases like malaria, cholera etc. in the absence of proper medical care and health facilities. Agriculture produces like ginger, sesame, chillies etc. remained rotten in open yards, as commercial activities were hampered for several years. As a result, agricultural income of the rural people was significantly reduced. Business and other development activities were arrested due mainly to absence of infrastructure facilities, lack of capital and business opportunities. Entrepreneurship development was also virtually impossible. Banking facilities could not be expanded; till today, the banking habit of the Mizo people, compared with other tribals in the North-eastern region, is still very low both in rural and urban areas.

The village groping scheme, implemented forcibly by the security forces during 1967-70 to counter the activities of MNF underground and also to speed up development works in rural areas had shaken adversely the social and economic foundation of Mizo society. The scheme affected more than 80 per cent of the total population in 1971. Some of the negative impacts highlighted by a noted Mizo sociologist C. Nunthara (1989), may be summarised as follows:

- Widespread famine condition prevailed in groping centres due primarily to dislocation of jhum cultivation;

- Low productivity of agriculture as jhum cycle had been shortened following the concentration of agriculture workers in the groping centres;
- Village groping had loosened the traditional village solidarity based on tribal setting and also village sub-groups rivalry emerged in the groping centres. As people felt less attached to the village new environment, they migrated to towns in search of commercial opportunities;
- Village gropings scheme had, instead of eliminating MNF influences on the people, only strengthened the support base of the MNF movement. Military atrocities like burning of houses, forcible taking of properties, large-scale killings and rapes in the groping centres and elsewhere in the villages gave Mizo people negative attitude towards security forces;
- Groping of villages resulted in a change-over from relatively undifferentiated, homogeneous village communities to relatively differentiated, heterogeneous village communities in terms of wealth and prestige.
- Groping of villages resulted to greater emphasis on the value of cash money which had given rise to immediate emphasis on monetary profits resulting in widespread misappropriation of development funds at all levels. Crimes had tremendously increased in the groping centres.

## Overview of Development Performance of Mizoram Economy in the Post-Accord Period

The development performance of Mizoram economy could broadly be divided into three distinct phases—the district council period covering the insurgency period (1952-1971), the Union Territories period (1972-1985) and the post-statehood period. During the entire district council period, the total planned expenditure amounted to Rs. 11 crore. Besides strengthening district administration, the emphasis of economic activities with whatever resource available during this period was education and health development. The process of planned economic development began to take shape only under Union Territory (1972-1986), during which planned expenditure grew rapidly. It rose from Rs. 4.37 crores in 1972 to Rs. 60.12 crores in

1986-87. However, security operations and insurgency-related activities often disturbed normal life, adversely affecting the implementation of several development schemes. Under this situation, apart from delay of project works, diversion of planned funds under dubious heads of account become routine norms and practices for government functionaries. Not only did development works slow down, there were several instances of leakage and misuse of plan fund.

The restoration of peace in Mizoram, following the peace agreement between the Government of India and Mizo National Front signed on the 30th June 1986, provided both a unique development opportunities and challenges in Mizoram. Peace and development are closely interrelated. Peace improves the environment for development and economic development can help secure and deepen the peace. Since 1986, planned expenditure increased rapidly and several new development initiatives were started. The state economy also recorded a steady growth during the 1990s. Some of the important initiatives were introduction of New Land Use Policy (NLUP), formulation of Mizoram Industrial Policy in 1989, expansion of education and health facilities, farm mechanisation, creation of new Government departments, establishment of state enterprises etc. The main features of the state economy are given in Table 6.1.

The State has 8.9 lakh people with a density of 42 per sq. km as against the national average of 324 in 2001. There were 22 statutory towns, classified as 'urban' in 2001 census, accounting for 50 per cent of the total population. Infant mortality rate was 23 per thousand persons in 2001 as against the all-India average rate of 71 persons per thousand. It has the third lowest infant mortality rate in the country after Kerala and Pondicherry. The economy is mainly of agricultural, with small secondary sector and an expanding tertiary sector, mainly dominated by public administration. In 1999-2000, the Gross State Domestic Product (GSDP) at current prices was Rs.1409 crores. However, the per capita income, estimated at Rs.14,909, is lower than the national average of Rs.15,626. Primary sector contributed 23 per cent of Net State Domestic Product (NSDP) while secondary and service sector accounted for 15 and 62 per cent respectively. In 1991, about 66 per cent of the working population were engaged in agriculture, 5 per cent in industry and 29 per cent in service sector.

**Table 6.1:** Basic Socio-Economic Indicators of Mizoram

| *Sl. No.* | *Particulars* | *Units* | *Mizoram* | *All India* |
|---|---|---|---|---|
| 1. | Area | Sq. km | 21081 | 166285 |
| 2. | Population (2001) | lakh | 8.9 | 10264.43 |
| | Population density | Per sq. km | 42 | 324 |
| | Sex ratio | Persons | 938 | 933 |
| | Infant Mortality Rate (2001) | Persons | 23 | 71 |
| 3. | Gross SDP in current prices 1999-2000 | Rs. crores | 1409 | 17,46,501 |
| 4 | Per capita NSDP in current prices 1999-2000 | Rs. | 14,909 | 15,626 |
| 5. | Distribution of NSDP 1999-2000 | | Per cent | |
| | (i) Primary sector | - do - | 23 | 24 |
| | (ii) Secondary sector | - do - | 15 | 27 |
| | (iii) Tertiary sector | - do - | 62 | 48 |
| 6. | Occupational Structure 1991 | | per cent | |
| | (i) Primary sector | - do - | 66 | 67 |
| | (ii) Secondary sector | - do - | 5 | 13 |
| | (iii) Tertiary sector | - do - | 30 | 20 |
| 7. | Human Development Index 1991 | Rank | 7 | — |
| 8. | Infrastructure Index | | Points | |
| | (i) CMIE Index 1992-93 | - do - | 63 | 100 |
| | (ii) 11th Finance Commission | - do - | 82 | 100 |
| 9. | Poverty ratio | | Per cent | |
| | (i) Planning Commission 1993-94 | - do - | 26 | 36 |
| | 1999-2000 | - do - | 19 | 26 |
| | (ii) State Government 1993-94 | - do - | 53 | na |
| | 1999-2000 | - do - | 36 | na |

*Sources*: (i) Government of India, Economic Survey 2002-2003, Ministry of Finance and Company Affairs.
(ii) Eleventh Finance Commission.
(iii) Statistical Handbook, Mizoram, various years.

Agriculture, the backbone of the economy, is still based on shifting cultivation. As local food production is inadequate, the state is compelled to import substantial quantities of foodstuffs and other essential items from other states. Moreover, the state has hardly any flat lands suitable for settled agriculture operations. According to the State's Directorate of Agriculture, the estimated potential area for agriculture like wet rice cultivation, terracing, horticulture and forestry in 1991 were as follows:

1. 0-8% slope suited for Wet Rice Cultivation (WRC) is 50,021 hectares;
2. 8-20 per cent slopes suited for terracing, plantation etc. are 87,824 hectares;
3. 20-50 per cent slope suited for horticulture etc. is 9,33,168 hectares; and
4. Above 50 per cent slope suited for forestry is 9,88,369 hectares.

Mizoram has the second highest literacy rate in the country. The human development index, prepared by the Planning Commission in 1991, has ranked Mizoram at 7th position out of 32 states and Union territories. Amongst the north-eastern states, it has the highest human development index in 1991. Mizoram has made rapid progress in developing infrastructure facilities, particularly power, roads, education and health during the last three decades. Telecommunication facilities are also fast coming up in recent years. However, the levels of these facilities are still inadequate and remain to be low as compare to other states. As given in Table 6.1, Centre for Monitoring Indian Economy (CMIE) Infrastructure Index (1992-93) gave Mizoram 63 points as against national average of 100. Meanwhile, the Index of Social and Economic Infrastructure, prepared by the Eleventh Finance Commission, accorded 82 points. Poverty ratio is a good indicator of the level of development in the state. The Planning Commission estimated that, taking Assam figure as the average for North East, about 19 per cent of the population in Mizoram were below poverty line in 1999-2000. However, the estimates of poverty ratio, as given by state government, were 36 per cent. These estimates showed that there are no reliable estimates of poverty level in Mizoram.

Government is the most important sector of the state economy. In fact, public expenditure is the main driving force of the economy. About 23 per cent of the total work force is employed in public administration, generating 16 per cent of state income in 1991. Some of the key fiscal indicators of state, as given in Table 6.2. have, however, shown a deteriorating trend. As the revenue sources were weak and inadequate, the state is heavily dependent on fiscal transfers from Central Government. States own revenue contributes less than 7 per cent of the total receipts of the state during 1998-2002. As observed in the table, fiscal transfers as a proportion to total disbursement of the state have declined gradually. From 55 per cent to total disbursement in 1998-99, gross fiscal transfers fell down to 45 per cent in 2002-03. It may be noted that state's plan outlay has been financed mainly from Central assistance as state's own resources are negligible and sometimes even less than zero. The budgetary policy of the state has focused consistently on achieving rapid economic development of the state. So far, the major share had been given to development expenditure such as education, health, water supply, agriculture, road and bridges etc. but their share as a proportion to aggregate disbursement, have diminished gradually from 73 per cent in 1998-99 to 69 per cent in 2002-03. The state government failed desperately to increase the rate of investment in social and economic services and also to check the growth of unproductive expenditure. Recent pay revision has considerably worsened the already deteriorating fiscal condition of the state.

**Table 6.2:** Fiscal indicators of State Government, Mizoram

| *Sl. No.* | *Particulars* | *Units* | *1998-99* | *2002-03* |
|---|---|---|---|---|
| 1. | State's own revenue/total receipt | per cent | 4.40 | 6.18 |
| 2. | Gross transfers/total disbursement | per cent | 55.00 | 45.45 |
| 3. | Revenue surplus/deficit | Rs. in crores | 78.03 | (-)109.35 |
| 4. | Revenue surplus/deficit/GSDP | per cent | 6.26 | (-)4.97 |
| 5. | Fiscal deficit | Rs in crores | 98.81 | 315.12 |
| 6. | Fiscal deficit/GSDP | per cent | 7.93 | 14.33 |
| 7. | Plan expenditure/total expenditure | per cent | 40.31 | 0.86 |
| 8. | Capital expenditure/total expenditure | per cent | 17.33 | 14.25 |
| 9. | Development expenditure/total expenditure | per cent | 72.74 | 68.60 |
| 10. | Interest payment/revenue expenditure | per cent | 10.67 | 11.77 |
| 11. | Outstanding debts | Rs. in crores | 860 | 1832 |
| 12. | Debt/GSDP | per cent | 69.03 | 83.31 |

*Source*: Extracted from Report of the Comptroller and Auditor General of India, for the year ended 31 March, 2003, Government of Mizoram.

Revenue deficit, which is the excess of revenue expenditure over revenue receipt, has been continuously rising in recent years. Except in 1998-99, the state has experienced revenue deficits consecutively for four years during the period between 1998-99 and 2002-03. The revenue deficit was more than Rs.109 crore in 2002-03, showing that revenue expenditure has been met from borrowed funds. The state's fiscal deficit, which represents the total borrowing requirements of the state, has been rising steadily over the years. It increased from Rs. 99 crore in 1998-99 to Rs. 315 crore in 2002-03. Since the state government resorted to large public borrowings to meet its shortfall in plan and non-plan expenditure, the total debt liability of the state increased significantly. In fact, Mizoram is now one of the highest indebted states in India. The total outstanding liabilities of the state, which stood at Rs. 1832 crore in 2002-03, is well above 80 per cent of Gross State Domestic Product. The debt profile also reflects a significant growth in the share of internal debt and provident fund and a reduction in loans and advances from Central Government. Interest payment has grown rapidly from 10.67 per cent of revenue expenditure in 1998-99 to 11.77 per cent in 2002-03. Since the state suffers persistent shortfall of budgetary receipts over expenditure, it frequently resorted to short term borrowings from Reserve Bank of India.

The economic performance of the State, though quite encouraging in certain aspects, is far from satisfactory. The fruits of economic development have been confined to a few sections of society. Educated unemployed population has been soaring high in the urban areas and the rural populace remained largely untouched by development process. Absence of economic opportunities trigger greater competition for scarce resources, jobs, contract works etc. while local elite groups easily bypassed or ignored normal legal and social constraints for acquiring economic benefits. This situation has already yielded to social tension and may easily explode into violent civil conflict.

## Strategy for Sustaining Peace and Development

Implementing the peace accord is the first step towards peacekeeping. In order to sustain peace and promote development, a wide range of confidence-building measures must be put into effect. Since, underdevelopment and political alienation had been deeply embedded in the Mizo insurgency movement, institution buildings and economic development are keys to conflict prevention and sustaining peace in

Mizoram. Violent conflict is commonly associated with poor governance and weak public institution. Good governance promotes social cohesion, stability and economic development. Institution building includes structural reform as well as capacity building and more strengthening of existing institutions. In other words, institution building is the creation of governance capacities. It entails the dismantling and reformation of old organisations and institution—legal, administrative, economic as well as social—the improvement of efficiency and effectiveness of existing institutions, restoration of destroyed institutions and enhancement of authorities' professionalism. Several key elements are involved to the promotion of good governance and institution building which may be enumerated as follows:

(i) Disclosing budgets, debts, expenditures and revenues so that payments and beneficiaries are known to all. A transparent government is the need of the hour.
(ii) The legal system must be free from political forces or any other organisation, to ensure that its decisions are independent and impartial.
(iii) Involving and empowering the citizens to participate in government. Decentralisation can help increase civil participation and promote local capacity-building and sustainable community-centred development.
(iv) Civil service reform is a crucial dimension of strengthening public institutions. A capable and efficient civil service is the main ingredient of sound public administration. Limited skill, overstaffing and indiscipline contributed to low morale, weak incentives to improve performance, and illicit activities in the civil service.
(v) Mizoram has more than 40 government departments and some state enterprises. These public institutions including the civil services are the bridge between the state and society, enabling citizens to communicate their interests and needs to the government. They are the means through which government implements policies. The improvement of the efficiency and effectiveness of these institutions are crucial in restoring people's confidence in development efforts, social healing and reconstruction of conflict-torned society.

(vi) Enhancing public security is another crucial dimension for strengthening public institution. For peace building to succeed, citizens must feel secure and have some freedom of movements. Reform of public service including the security sector—their efficiency, equity and accountability—should be a priority. Citizens must feel that their lives and property are made safer by the works of the security services.

(vii) Corruption may be regarded as the single greatest obstacle to economic and social development. Corruption is usually defined as the abuse of public office for private gain through bribery, patronage, nepotism or theft of assets. It undermines development by distorting the rule of law and weakening the institutional foundation on which economic growth depends. Strengthening judicial system and increasing transparency in government processes are key aspects of anti-corruption strategy.

(viii) Government needs to actively encourage the participation of all segment of civil society in economic policy debates and explaining the short-term costs, as well as the medium and long-term benefits of policy options.

Economic development is paramount for the prevention of future conflict, and for post-conflict societies to avoid relapse into violence. The higher is the level of per capita income, lower is the risk of conflict. If a country or a particular region suffers economic stagnation, is highly dependent on primary commodities export, and has low per capita income and that income is unequally distributed, it is at high risk of civil war or violent conflicts. Economic stagnation and low income, and badly distributed, create a pool of impoverished and disaffected young men who can be cheaply recruited by the "entrepreneurs of violence". In the context of Mizoram, the following steps may be suggested to the rapid economic development on a sustainable basis:

(a) Health and education are the key elements in human resource development. Though Mizoram had made significant progress in literacy level and improving health facilities since 1970s, their services are far from satisfactory; their delivery system remain virtually inefficient and inadequate. Steps must be taken to increase the involvement of communities in the planning, monitoring and financing of health and education and make effort to upgrade private education and health services.

(b) The crucial issue of fiscal imbalance needs to be addressed with some urgency in order to improve the overall health of the economy. The state's fiscal condition requires strong measures to arrest the ever-expanding non-plan expenditure, avoid wasteful expenditure and generate additional resources. The steps needed to achieve this goal include improving the tax system and widening of tax base, reforming public enterprises, increased social sector and infrastructure spending, better targeting of social subsidies, downsizing and upgrading the civil service and improving cost recovery in power and other economic services.

(c) Self-sufficiency in food and provision of gainful employment in agriculture and industry are the two prerequisites for development and prosperity of the state on a sustainable basis. Mizoram enjoys favourable agro-climatic condition for horticulture, spices cultivation and plantation crops such as tea, coffee, etc. but these sectors remain largely unexplored till today due to non-availability of institutional support, inadequate infrastructure facilities and absence of clear-cut policy guidelines. Provision of necessary infrastructure and appropriate institutional support are needed for the development of these sectors.

(d) Mizoram has potentials for development in sector like natural resources, horticulture, tourism etc. Private sector development through a better investment climate is the key to development of the state. Over time, it will be the private sector, not the state government that creates jobs and promotes economic growth. Private sector needs skilled manpower and also the support of infrastructure facilities like sound credit institution, good road, adequate power supply etc. Modification of existing land and labour policy along with improvement in infrastructure facilities are some of the critical measures for attracting private capital both national and foreign. The existing business associations like chamber of commerce, industrial and traders association need to be strengthened by the state government. They should be encouraged to interact with national level business associations. Entrepreneurship development should be another key component for private sector development.

## Conclusion

Mizoram has become the most peaceful state in the North Eastern Region following the peace agreement between the MNF and Government of India. Though, the end of armed conflict brought peaceful atmosphere for development, the state has been able to record only moderate growth in income and output. Even the benefits of growth have not trickled down to the people at large. This shows that sustainable economic development can only be achieved in the long run. Peace is the first essential condition for development and prosperity; and only sustainable development will bring enduring peace in the state. Successful development intervention requires two conditions—firstly, a participatory planning process that involve all segments of the society which will give people a solid stake in decision making and in how their resources are spent; second, restoring people's trust in development requires major changes to the quality of governance, particularly with respect to public transparency, anti-corruption measures and the administration of justice. Unless appropriate policy frameworks which addressed the root causes of the conflict were constituted, the hard won peace in Mizoram may not be sustained and the prospects of a prosperous Mizoram and its sustainable development would vanish the dreams.

## REFERENCES

Breaking the Conflict Trap: Civil War and Development Policy accessed from www.worldbank.org.

Comptroller and Auditor General of India (2004) Report of the Comptroller and Auditor General of India—for the year ended 31 March, 2003, Government of Mizoram.

Elbadawi, Ibrahim and Nicholas Sambanis, (2000) "Why Are There So Many Wars in Africa? Understanding and Preventing Violent Conflict" in *Journal of African Economies*, December, accessed from www.worldbank.org

Government of India, (2004) *Economic Survey 2002-2003*, Ministry of Finance, Economic Division.

Government of Mizoram Statistical Handbook, Mizoram, (various years), Department of Economic and Statistics.

Nunthara, C., (1989): *Impacts of the introduction of Groupings of Villages in Mizoram*, Omsons Publications, New Delhi.

Report of the Eleventh Finance Commission, Ministry of Finance.

# Chapter 7

## Political Economy of Mizoram
## *A Study of MIP*

LIANZELA

---

### Introduction

A project for self-sufficiency of the Rural Poor in Mizoram called MIP (Mizoram Intodelhna Project changed into Mizoram Intodelhna Programme) was launched by the Mizo National Front (MNF) Ministry. The main purpose of the programme is upliftment of the rural poor especially the shifting cultivators. Its main concern is attainment of self-sufficiency, food security and better livelihood for the cultivators. This programme, if implemented will minimize the undesirable consequences of shifting cultivation such as destruction of forest, removal of top soils, landslides and degradation of land. The farmers will be assisted in adopting a more profitable, sustainable permanent system of farming through agro-horticulture, soil conservation, animal husbandry sectors etc.

### Method of Cultivation

The main method of cultivation in Mizoram is shifting cultivation or jhuming. The mountainous country with its steep slopes and narrow valleys and a few level areas led to the tradition of felling of forests on the steep slopes, burning the remains of the forest and growing crops without terraces and without contour cultivation. The total area of land having slope from 0 to 10 per cent where there may be a possibility of Wet Rice Cultivation (WRC) is 59,197 hectares which is merely 2.8 per cent of Mizoram and the total area of land having slope of 10 to 33 per cent is only 5,09,365 hectares. It is obvious that only a portion of these areas of comparatively gentle slope will be suitable for preparation of WRC. Till today, total command area of 3,358 hectares had been completed for irrigation. The number of households having WRC are between 9,000 to 10,000. Many of them have only small plots which have been properly cultivated. More than 90 per cent are having no proper irrigation system. Therefore, even though shifting cultivation is destructive for environment, back breaking and unremunerative for the cultivators, the vast majority of rural and semi-urban householders have to resort to this primitive method of cultivation for want of any alternative farming system or occupation. Rice is the staple food of the people and paddy harvested from jhums is still much more than that harvested from WRC.

Out of six agro-climatic zones, i.e. alpine, temperate sub-alpine, sub-tropical hills, sub-tropical valleys, mild tropical hills and mild tropical plain zones for the entire North Eastern Region four agro-climatic zones have been identified in Mizoram as follow: Temperate sub-alpine zone, sub-tropical hill zone, mild tropical hill zone and mild tropical zone.

In the economic classification of workers as per Population Census 2001, out of the total 888,573 persons, 35 per cent are engaged in agricultural activities of which 12 per cent are cultivators and 13 per cent are agricultural labourers. Time series data from 1993-94 to 2001-02 exhibits that agricultural sector (Animal and Crop husbandry) contribute about 26 per cent of the total Net State Domestic Product (NSDP) of Mizoram and has the highest share in comparison to other sectors. Hence it has a paramount importance in the State economy. In the neighbouring north eastern states, the contributions of agriculture sector to total NSDP are 35.09 per cent in Assam, 30 per cent in Nagaland, 34 per cent in Tripura, 30 per cent in Meghalaya and 33 per cent in Manipur (Data Quarterly Bank NEDFI vol-3 Issue 1 January 2004).

**Previous Schemes in Mizoram**

Prior to the launching of MIP in Mizoram, there were schemes similar to MIP launched by different ministries in the State Government in Mizoram in their respective term. During Peoples Conference (PC) Ministry headed by Brig. T. Sailo in the late 1970s, a scheme called

Garden colony was launched to do away with shifting cultivation. The scheme well fitted itself under the broad scheme of IRDP newly introduced at that time. But before any significant result was made there was a change in the State Government. The new ministry headed by Congress (I) introduced Land Use Policy in 1980s. The objective of the said Land Use Policy was basically same with the previous schemes since the new government just did not like to continue with the old one it was then changed. It is something like putting old wine in the new bottle. Again, before any substantial result could be made there was a new government in the State headed by the Mizo National Front (MNF) Party. The new name opted for the project was Jhum Control, the basic idea still remained more or less same. In 1987-88 annual plan period the state government singled out Aibawk Community Development Block for intensive operation of the jhum control programme under the caption "Aibawk Jhum Control Project". In the first year of operation, the cost of the project came to Rs. 5.86 lakhs. In view of the problem faced in the different stages of the implementation of the programme, the state government agreed to form a state level Co-ordination Committee. Under the chairmanship of the Chief Secretary, Government of Mizoram, ten members are nominated to the committee for a term of two years.

There was yet another change in the state government. This time, it was headed by the Congress (I) Party. The scheme got its new name called New Land Use Policy (NLUP).

The main objective of the NLUP is to ensure rapid socio-economic development in harmony with ecological balance. Although self-sufficiency in food grains production is one of the objectives, it should be understood that the flat land available for Wet Rice Cultivation (WRC) is very limited. Stress has to be laid on horticultural plantation, forestry, livestock rearing and small scale and cottage industries as alternative means of livelihood for rural households. To supplement the family income and to meet a tribal family needs during the gestation period of the main occupation, subsidiary schemes like vegetable gardening, rearing of pigs and poultry will also be introduced.

The following strategy which is more or less the same, recommended by the National Commission on Agriculture is adopted—

1. Reclaiming land having potential for wet rice cultivation and

providing minor irrigation so as to encourage settled cultivation in valleys and on terraced slopes.

2. Identifying areas suitable for horticulture plantation at the rate of at least 2 hectares of plantation per family.
3. Developing suitable areas for agricultural operations, commercial forest plantations, which would give full occupation to jhumia families.
4. Identifying jhumia families on the basis of their individual aptitude and capability to take up livestock rearing or small and cottage industry on full time basis.

Under the NLUP land will be temporarily allotted to the selected families by the village council at the size of two hectares per family. These selected families will be issued Land Settlement Certificate (LSC) later on, on merit basis (how they actually utilize the land allotted to them temporarily by the Village Council Court). In this way, on a more permanent basis land will be allotted to the selected people.

For the smooth and better functioning of administrative works, the Rural Development Department was entrusted to take up and to supervise all the activities of NLUP operation from the end of 1989-90. All the required funds had been put to a common pool under the charge of the department from the Annual Plan 1990-91. With a view to assess the overall impact of the scheme, the Rural Development Department conducted a survey of beneficiaries during the period 1990-91. The sector-wise distribution of beneficiaries is as follow:

**Table 7.1:** Sector-wise Distribution of NLUP Beneficiaries in Mizoram

| *Sl. No.* | *Sector* | *Number of Beneficiaries* |
|---|---|---|
| 1. | Agriculture | 5439 families |
| 2. | Animal Husbandry and Veterinary | 6358 families |
| 3. | Industries | 998 families |
| 4. | Soil and Water Conservation | 225 families |
| 5. | Sericulture | 95 families |
| 6. | Fisheries | 317 families |
| 7. | Forest | 839 families |
| | *Total* | *14271 families* |

*Source*: Department of Rural Development, Annual Plan 1990-91.

From Table 7.1, it can be seen that the largest number of beneficiaries under the NLUP were from Agriculture and allied sectors.

A principle of mono scheme was adopted first when the scheme was introduced in Aibawk Block. It was soon found inadequate to meet the diversified need of occupational choice. As per the advice of the Government of India, a composite scheme has been drawn up for enabling the selected families to choose alternative occupation in other sectors. Besides, the beneficiaries who had opted for one main occupation will be required to take up subsidiary occupation of kindred activities. For example, if the individual has opted for wet rice cultivation as his main occupation, his subsidiary occupation is specified to consist of vegetable growing, piggery, poultry and so on.

The NLUP intended to cover the entire state. It was implemented in Agriculture and allied sectors, animal husbandry sector and industry sector in 13 Rural Development Blocks. Assistance to the beneficiaries was given in phases (two to three years) with a ceiling of Rs. 30,000 per family. But, this ambitious NLUP could achieve only limited success. The practice of primitive jhuming cultivation remained unabated resulting in degradation of land and large scale deforestation. It was terminated in 2000-01.

The probable causes of failures of this NLUP can be summarized as follow:

1. Lack of clear guidelines for the programme. There was no guidelines prepared for the first two programmes. The third programme has brief and sketchy programme.
2. Too much political interference in the selection of the beneficiaries.
3. Awareness building among the selected beneficiaries was inadequate.
4. Lack of community mobilization. No grassroots organization was set up at the village level.
5. Inadequate extension services and technical support resulting in inefficient utilization of inputs.
6. Lack of monitoring and weak follow-up action on implementation of the programme.
7. Lack of Participatory Rural Appraisals.

## Mizoram Intodelhna Project/Programme

The new ministry voted to power in 2000, after their assumption of office has given a serious thought on the critical issues of backwardness, unemployment particularly in rural areas, harnessing available local resources and generating income and employment amongst the rural poor. Thus, the government of Mizoram in their endeavour for a major breakthrough in the development process considered it necessary to workout a development strategy aiming at efficient exploitation of local resources, increasing productivity and generating employment. Accordingly, a Task Force was constituted to study the whole gamut of the causes of the rural poverty, the short-comings of the previous schemes, and to formulate a scheme for the development of the rural poor. The said Task Force consists of experts from different disciplines, progressive farmers, experts and prominent citizens. Original Members of the Task Force are: Rev. Liandawla (Convener), Mr. Rualzakhuma (IAS retd.), Prof. Lianzela, Lalnghinglova (Wing Commander retd.), Dr. H. Saithantluanga. The said Task Force was reconstituted on 15th March 2005 to revise the existing MIP Guidelines and to formulate policies on implementation of the MIP. The members are Rev. Liandawla (Convener), Prof. Lianzela, Wg.Cdr. Lalnghinglova, Shri C. Lalzarliana, Shri K. Vanlalauva (sitting MLA), Shri Lalthlengliana (sitting MLA) and Dr. H. Saithantluanga.

They then prepared a scheme called "Mizoram Intodelhna Project—a project for self-sufficiency of the Rural Poor in Mizoram. The concept employed in Watershed Project Management has been adopted for MIP. The main target groups are shifting cultivators. The implementation will be monitored at every level including at the state level. The MIP would develop some new procedures while discarding some old practices. Power under MIP would highly be decentralized to effect higher degree of implementation.

## Aims and Objectives of MIP

The main purpose of MIP (as put in the original guideline) is the upliftment of the rural poor specially the shifting cultivators. Its main concern is creation of self-sufficiency, food security and better livelihood for them. The aims and objectives are as follows:

1. To assist and guide the shifting cultivators so that they may adopt a more profitable, better and more permanent system of cultivation, and to give them essential resources needed for achieving self-sufficiency and food security.
2. To help the rural cultivators to produce cash crops and to develop a profitable market for agricultural produce to raise their economic status.
3. To stop or minimize the undesirable consequences of shifting cultivation, such as destruction of forests, removal of top soils, landslides, degradation of land, climatic change etc.
4. To rehabilitate steep hill sides and to transform them into orchards of various fruits and cash crops or useful forest of trees and bamboos so as to yield good income and to also beautify the landscape.
5. To liberate the jhumias from their drudgery so that they may have more dignified standard of life, and provide them with opportunity of higher income generating employment.

The revised/modified guidelines of MIP stated the aims and objectives in the following:

1. To conserve, upgrade and utilize land, water, plants, animals and human resources in an integrated manner to meet the growing demands of cereals, pulses, oilseeds, fruits, meat and vegetables.
2. To generate massive employment during project period and regular employment after project period for small and marginal farmers.
3. To improve environment, restore ecological balance and promote agricultural production through scientific on farm Land Development and Terraces.
4. To promote development of Water Resources for domestic use as well as small scale irrigation by constructing Rain Water Harvesting Dams.
5. To promote quality planting materials in community Nursery for development of rain-fed horticulture.
6. To promote livestock production to meet the growing demand of meat and manures.

## Prioritization of Crops

There are some crops which can be grown easily in Mizoram but are being imported at huge costs. These crops are being given priority in the MIP for immediate production in the state. They include potato, onion, garlic, pulses, edible oil (mustard oil), soyabean and maize. In the revised guidelines modifications were made to include items such as passion fruits, red oil palm, grapes, papaya and some medicinal plants. Instead of cultivating them in each and everywhere, cluster approach would be made. To link these items with market is one of the important steps taken by the new guideline. In fact memorandum of understanding had already been signed with some firms/ organizations for marketing of selected products.

Stipulations for the cultivators under MIP and their responsibilities are worked out in the following:

1. Farmers' Association will take responsibilities for implementation of the project.
2. Villagers are expected to make every effort for successful implementation of the project and the village council agreed to extend all possible co-operation.

Families to be covered under MIP are: *bona fide* Indian citizens who are permanent residents of the villages of Mizoram, and

1. Families who earn their livelihood from Agriculture and allied activities including Animal Husbandry.
2. Families whose members do not have regular works or employment even if they are not cultivators.

Responsibilities of the farmers are enunciated in the following:

Beneficiary of the MIP should abide by the following clauses and should give in writing his agreement to do so.

1. He should not utilise any part or portion of the assistance for anything other than for the purpose for which it is given.
2. Any kind of the assistance should not be handed over to

another person except with the written permission of the appropriate authority.

3. Any asset, movable or immovable, created or procured through the assistance should not be sold or given to others without the permission of the appropriate authority.
4. Before the completion of the scheme under the MIP, the beneficiary should not migrate from the village without prior permission of the government.

Under MIP due importance is given to monitoring aspect. As such there would be village level, district level and state level monitoring of the scheme. This system is expected to yield good result.

The MIP guideline has also clearly specified how community organization and institutional arrangement should be made. For example, a team of officers is selected to look after and supervise technically and administratively the implementation of the scheme at the Block level. The team is called Project Implementing Agency (PIA). There will also be the District Project Committee at each district headquarters. Besides there will be the Mizoram Intodelhna Project Executive Authority (MIPEA) under the chairmanship of Ministry of Agriculture. Under the MIP the State Level Project Committee (SLPC) is the Apex Body of the Project. Finally, there will be High Level Project Committee (HLPC) under the chairmanship of Chief Minister of Mizoram. The HLPC is to deal with issues relating to the policy, finance and other important matters.

**Assistance Under MIP**

Originally, the quantum of assistance proposed to the beneficiary was Rs. 50,000. Each beneficiary, before getting the assistance is required to prepare a project with the help of an expert in the field. The project may cost well above Rs. 50,000. The assistance to be received would not exceed Rs. 50,000. Any amount above the said quantum would be met by the beneficiary himself. The fund is to be released in a phase manner. In the first year an amount of Rs. 7500 will be released. And in the second and third year Rs. 15,000 each will be released. In the final year, the remaining Rs. 12,500 will be released.

According to the guideline, the fund for the whole village (say for 100 farmers) would be given (in each phase) to the Farmers

Association of that village. The Association will deposit the Fund in the nearby Bank. The Fund will then be released at the right time. In this way the grassroots people are involved in the programme. This is never done in the previous schemes like NLUP etc.

**Release of Fund**

Fund for phase 1 and 2 had been released as follows:

| *District* | *No. of Families* | *Total Amount (In rupees)* |
|---|---|---|
| | **Phase I (2003-03)** | |
| Aizawl | 7943 | 5,95,72,500.00 |
| Lunglei | 4509 | 3,38,17,500.00 |
| Saiha | 1564 | 1,17,30,000.00 |
| Kolasib | 3025 | 2,26,87,500.00 |
| Champhai | 5664 | 4,24,80,000.00 |
| Lawngtlai | 727 | 54,52,500.00 |
| Mamit | 3112 | 2,33,40,000.00 |
| Serchhip | 3849 | 2,88,67,500.00 |
| *Total* | *30,393* | *22,79,47,500.00* |
| | **Phase II (2003-2004) at the rate of Rs. 4,000 per family** | |
| *Aizawl* | *4,571* | *1,82,84,000.00* |
| Lunglei | 2,076 | 83,04,000.00 |
| Saiha | 440 | 17,60,000.00 |
| Kolasib | 4,254 | 1,70,16,000.00 |
| Champhai | 4,028 | 1,61,12,000.00 |
| Lawngtlai | 623 | 24,92,000.00 |
| Mamit | 1,329 | 53,16,000.00 |
| Serchhip | 1,993 | 79,72,000.00 |
| *Total* | *19,314* | *7,72,56,000.00* |
| *Phase I & II Total* | *49,707* | *30,52,03,500.00* |

As mentioned earlier beneficiaries are to get Fund under MIP in four installments. For the second installment, fund disbursed is at the rate of Rs. 3500 per family. Following is the quantum of Fund released for the eight districts.

| *District* | *No. of beneficiaries (family)* | *Amount (in rupees)* |
|---|---|---|
| Aizawl | 3670 | 1,28,45,000.00 |
| Lunglei | 2448 | 85,68,000.00 |
| Saiha | 174 | 6,09,000.00 |
| Kolasib | 299 | 10,46,500.00 |
| Champhai | 1533 | 53,65,500.00 |
| Lawngtlai | 325 | 11,37,500.00 |
| Mamit | 1418 | 49,63,000.00 |
| Serchhip | 864 | 30,24,000.00 |
| *Grand Total* | *10,731* | *3,75,58,500.00* |

**Marketing Plan**

Normally a project of this kind should not include marketing plan. However, as a well organized marketing system is vital to the success of agricultural development, a marketing plan is included in MIP without earmarking funds for its execution. It is expected that the funds earmarked by the Government of India for development of Agricultural Marketing Infrastructure will be made available for such development in Mizoram. Moreover, "Technology Mission for Integrated Development of Horticulture in the North Eastern States" also envisaged appropriate steps for promotion of marketing including export as would ensure remunerative prices of Agri-horticultural produces. Marketing Plan of MIP is so designed as would enable MIP Marketing Board to avail of all in structural technical and financial assistance available under the scheme of NHB, DMI, APEDA etc. As such this marketing plan may be implemented side by side along with the MIP.

Mizoram is suitable for cultivation and production of various kinds of crops, fruits, spices and cereals. But lack of marketing opportunity and proper system of marketing outside Mizoram has hindered the growth of agriculture. Some preliminary steps had been taken for the development of marketing by the state government. Trade and Commerce Department was created in 1987. The Mizoram State Agricultural Produce Marketing (Regulation) Act, 1996, and the Mizoram State Agricultural Produce Marketing Regulation (General) Rules, 1996 are also in place and these statutory provisions will further lend support for building up viable marketing system for Agri-horticultural produces.

MIP Marketing Board will act as the pioneering agency in the marketing and progressively take up action institutionalizing the whole market system by creating market committees, market areas, market yards, sub-market yards etc. Infrastructures such as warehouses, cold storages, buildings and other structures for post-harvest processes in the market yards/sub-market yards are to be constructed. Apart from agricultural produce, inputs required by the farmers will be made available in these markets. There should be one or more terminal/ wholesale market for the whole of Mizoram at the most convenient place. This will be a market centre where commodities from other markets will flow in to be redistributed elsewhere including places outside Mizoram.

While actual marketing should be done by private individuals or organizations, Government will create favourable atmosphere and provide facilities. Government of Mizoram through Trade and Commerce Department may help in creation of marketing networks, establishment of Distributors and Agencies or retail outlets in co-ordination with the efforts of the private traders.

**Conclusion**

As MIP is a new scheme introduced lately by the MNF ministry, it is still too early to make judgement about the success or failure of the scheme. The original scheme of assisting farmers for four consecutive years had not yet been done (computed) due to late introduction. Any way there is a good prospect of its success as the scheme is addressing itself to various vital issues like contract farming, making link road, constructing cold storage, providing infrastructure facilities for marketing etc. Monitoring and evaluation aspect of the scheme is also to be done at various stages. For cultivating horticultural and other crops, cluster approach would be used. Processing, wherever possible would also be given due emphasis. Funding pattern has also undergone a slight change and this is expected to bring better result. Additional Central Assistance Fund would be utilized at its full. The line departments are instructed to implement the MIP schemes that fall under their jurisdiction. With full co-operation of the grassroots people and with a high degree of decentralization MIP would bring self-sufficiency in food grain supply and would lead the economy in to the path of sustainable development.

## REFERENCES

Damain Singh, *The Last Frontier People and Forests in Mizoram*, Tata Energy Research Institute, 1996.

Guidelines for *Mizoram Intodelhna Projects* (MIP) Government.

Lianzela, *Economic Development of Mizoram*, Spectrum Publications, Guwahati: Delhi, 1994.

Project Report on *Mizoram Intodelhna Project* (MIP), A Project for self-sufficiency of the Rural Poor in Mizoram 2003-04 prepared by the Office of the Mizoram Intodelhna Project Executive Authority, Government of Mizoram, Aizawl.

Revised Guidelines of Mizoram Intodelhna Programme (MIP), (Mizo-2004).

# Chapter 8

## India's North-East Region and Border Trade in the Context of Emerging Borderless World
### *The Mizoram Experience*

NVR JYOTI KUMAR

---

**Introduction**

The North-East region (NER) of India which comprises eight states, namely Arunachal Pradesh, Assam, Manipur, Meghalaya, Mizoram, Nagaland, Sikkim and Tripura shares most of its boundary with China, Bangladesh, Bhutan and Myanmar. The NER shares only about two per cent of its border with the mainland of the country and the remaining 98 per cent is connected with the neighbouring countries. This paper is designed to examine some issues of border trade pertaining to India's North-East region. To be more specific, the objectives of the paper are three-fold: (i) to examine the magnitude of illegal border trade which is taking place between the NER and the neighbouring countries, and the implications involved in the liberalisation of border trade; (ii) to present a bird's eyeview of the NER's resources and export potential with special reference to Mizoram's border trade practices with Myanmar and Bangladesh; and (iii) to highlight the need to evolve a strategy with a view to integrate the NER with the global economy in the context of emerging borderless world.

**Dominance of Illegal Trade**

Border trade may be referred as the exchange of goods and services among different countries in border areas. The trade between the NER and the neighbouring countries may be classified into legal and illegal trade. One can estimate the extent of official trade, its volume and value through the land custom stations which are located along the international borders between the NER and the neighbouring countries. But there is a dearth of information with regard to the quantity of illegal or unofficial border trade. Many researchers found it extremely difficult to quantify the volume of such illegal unofficial trade. Moreover, many studies estimated that the official trade account for only an insignificant proportion in the total volume of border trade in North-East region. For example, the IIFT study (1995) estimated the annual volume of trade that took place at Moreh, Champhai and Lungwa (NER-Myanmar border) at around Rs. 2200 crores. Moreh contributes the larger share of Rs.1600 crores followed by Champhai Rs.500 crores, and Lungwa contributes around Rs.100 crores. It was estimated that the extent of unofficial trade may be more than 44 times compared to official trade,[1] and the volume of trade through NER-Myanmar border is at least five times higher than the NER-Bangladesh trade.[2]

The NCAER conducted a study (1995) to examine many issues of the unofficial trade between the NER and Bangladesh.[3] It covered nine districts of West Bengal, three each of Assam and Tripura which were known as the most active centers of unofficial trade. The study identified the principal goods smuggled to Bangladesh through Assam and Tripura include: food/edible goods, live animals, wood/timber, cotton, printed saris, bicycle/bicycle parts, cosmetics, bidies, baby food, cement, coal and kerosene. The volume of such unofficial exports to Bangladesh through three Border States was estimated at Rs.1165 crores per annum. West Bengal accounted for about 96 per cent, followed by Assam (three per cent) and Tripura (one per cent). The two main smuggled-out items from Karimganj district were: sugar and printed cotton *saris* in that order. Wood and timber constituted the single most important smuggled-out item from Dhubri district of Assam and the three select districts of Tripura.

The illegal imports to the NER were, however, restricted to mainly synthetic fabrics, hilsa fish, and electronic goods. The NCAER study estimated the volume of illegal imports to Assam and Tripura at Rs.1.8 crores each.

The North East India Council for Social Science Research (NEICSSR) organised a seminar on "Border Trade in North-East India: Perspective, Issues and Problems," in 1998 in Shillong with an objective to look into the various facets of the border trade between the NER and the neighbouring countries.[4] The scholars who participated in the seminar made an attempt to understand as to whether there exists any basis for trade in terms of compatibility between the resource or production structure of the NER and the demand structure of the neighbouring countries, particularly Bangladesh and Myanmar, with whom India is having significant trade relations. Some of the observations made on the basis of the study on the structure of NER's border trade are: [5]

1. NER is having significant trade with two of the four neighbouring countries that is, Bangladesh and Myanmar.
2. Much of the NER-Bangladesh trade flows through legal channels. But it is just reverse in case of NER-Myanmar trade.
3. While the NER-Bangladesh is characterised by unidirectional flow of goods from the NER to Bangladesh, the direction is reverse in case of NER-Myanmar trade.
4. The NER-Bangladesh trade basically involves flow of mineral products/raw materials from the NER-Bangladesh, much of the NER-Myanmar trade involves exchange of consumer goods mostly originated outside both the areas.
5. The total volume of NER-Myanmar trade is likely to be four times more than that of the NER-Bangladesh trade.

Although there are several arguments in favour of liberalisation of border trade in NER, an examination of the existing pattern of informal border trade, as revealed by certain studies,[6] suggest that such liberalisation may have some negative implications also. For instance, narcotic drugs and alcoholic beverages constitute one of the major groups of illegal imports to NER from some neighbouring countries. The other group of smuggled goods into the region includes items such as ready-made garments, electrical and electronic goods and cosmetics. Interestingly, such goods are not produced from the neighbouring countries but mainly in East and South-east Asian nations. It is to be noted that most of such products are, at present, in the negative list of imports of the Government of India.

On the other hand, the illegal exports from India through NER consist mainly of certain goods such as food grains, fertilizers, cement and medicines. The NER is excessively dependent on the other parts of the country for many consumer and capital goods. The NER is a net importer of oil seeds, sugar, meat, fish, and eggs and so on. The Shukla Commission estimated the import bill on this count at Rs. 2,500 crores per annum. Therefore, freer export of consumer and capital goods may lead to their shortage and price hike in NER.[7]

**Export Potential of NER**

The North-East region accounts for about eight per cent of the country's geographical area and about four per cent of population. Tribal population accounts for more than 30 per cent of the total population of NER. Inadequate and poor infrastructure, inhospitable terrain and a comparatively late start in the development process are some of the reasons for economic backwardness of the region. However, the NER has certain strengths.[8] For example, the NER has following resources:

1. Hydro-electric potential, estimated at the minimum of 40,000 mW.
2. Assam alone has an estimated 1,300 million tonnes of oil and 156 billion cubic metres (BCM) of natural gas. Not even 40 per cent area has been explored. Assam, Mizoram, Tripura, Nagaland, Arunachal Pradesh and even Brahmaputra basin have a number of oil bearing strata, still to be explored. Other mineral resources such as thorium and limestone are available in huge quantities.
3. A gas pipeline can be created linking Tripura (and probably Mizoram) gas and Assam's Barak Valley gas with the Duliajan-Numaligarh-Guwahati gas pipeline. This can be extended all the way up to Siliguri and Barauni. Since an oil pipeline already exists till Barauni and a product pipeline is being laid from Numaligarh to Siliguri, right of way is not a problem. In fact, laying down of the gas pipeline will be much less costly.

   Further, this pipeline could be linked with Myanmar's gas field. India will have a safe pipeline system through India's land all the way up to Delhi, instead of going through Bangladesh.
4. The NER is one of the few bio-diversity zones in the world.

It has immense flora and fauna. The world's annual trade on medicinal and aromatic oil/plants amounts to over $60 billion. North-East only supplies, mostly taken clandestinely, the raw materials for many of the industries inside and outside the country.

5. The climate of NER is suitable for wide range of agro-horticultural as well as exotic floricultural products. With support services like training, tissue culture labs, production, finance, marketing tie-ups and farm to market roads, the region can produce both for domestic market and international market.
6. The multi-ethnic culture coupled with snow capped mountains and mighty Brahmaputra provides ideal setting for development of tourism.
7. Guwahati, the premier city in the North-East, can really become a centre for higher learning and superior medical facilities. It cannot only cater to the entire region, but also the neighbouring countries.
8. The NER has a large pool of literates. With training, these talents can be utilised, amongst others, in IT sector, paramedical, biotech, aviation, entertainment and hospitality industries.

Therefore, a number of resource based products of NER, viz., mineral resources (coal, limestone, sillimanite, gypsum, china clay, oil and natural gas), agricultural resources (rice, pulses, oilseeds, maize, jute, potato, mesta), horticultural products (pineapple, banana, orange, papaya, lemon, arecanut, pears, plum, passion-fruit, ginger, turmeric, chilies, cardamom, bay-leaf, tomato, squash), forest resources (wood, cane, bamboo, medicinal herbs and plants), sericulture (eri, muga and mulberry silk), floriculture (orchids and other flowers), plantation products (tea and rubber) may be exported provided proper infrastructural facilities and industrial environment are created. Further, there has been enough scope to develop export-oriented industries based on coal and limestone, petrochemicals, medicinal plants, sericulture, jute, floriculture, horticulture and handlooms and handicrafts.[9]

North-East region contributes five per cent of fruits and 4.2 per cent vegetables to the country's horticulture production. Although not a major producing region, the region has a lot of potential to be exploited as some of the best and rare quality fruits and vegetables are produced in the NER. For example, pineapples produced in the region are considered to be of the highest quality. The importance of North-East region in the horticultural sector of the country can be understood from the following[10]:

1. North-East region accounts for around 45 per cent of the total pineapple production in the country.
2. NER produces 22 per cent of the total honey produced in the country, which is worth Rs. 537 lakh.
3. North Eastern states including Sikkim produced 1000 mt of Agaricus/Lentinus type of mushrooms in 1996-97.
4. Assam produced 109.8('000 mt) of citrus fruit during 1999-2000.
5. North-East region produced 65,700 mt of sweet potato, which is 6.5 per cent of the country's production in 1999-2000.
6. The states of Assam, Meghalaya, Mizoram, Nagaland and Sikkim produced 53,900 mt of tapioca in 1999-2000.

Exports from the NER mainly consist of agricultural products. During 2000-01, exports took place from the NER mainly to bordering countries of Bangladesh and Myanmar. Large quantity of cardamoms from Sikkim are exported to Pakistan, Afghanistan and Middle East. Most of the exported items from the NER are in the raw form without any value addition leading to low price realisation. It was estimated that the processed food and vegetable sector will grow to the tune of Rs. 2000 crore by 2005 in India. The total exports of processed products from India were to the tune of Rs.1000 crore during 1999-2000. Although India produced a wide variety of food products, utilisation of raw material for production of processed products is not high. Less than two per cent of the fruits and vegetables grown in the country are processed.

At the initiative of the Minister of State for Commerce, Jairam Ramesh, a high level delegation held the third sectoral summit of the North Eastern Council (NEC) at Guwahati on 9th March, 2007. For the first time, there was an interaction in this summit in a systematic way between the North-East State governments and the Commodity Boards—comprising tea, coffee, spices and rubber—and the

Agricultural and Processed Food Products Export Development Authority (APEDA).[11] Many of these boards (such as spices and rubber boards) tend to be Kerala-centric, while the Coffee Board is rather Karnataka-centric. A feeling has gained ground over the years in Assam and other north-eastern States that though this geography accounts for 55 per cent of India's tea production, the Tea Board has not really looked after the region's interests.

With regard to rubber production, only nine per cent of the country's rubber production comes from the North-East and above 82 per cent from Kerala, where the limits of area expansion have been reached and further expansion has to come from productivity enhancement. India is one of the fastest growing consumer markets for natural rubber and if India doesn't increase domestic production the country will end up being a major importer of the commodity. The only place where natural rubber expansion can take place in terms of cultivation is the NER. Rubber has huge potential to transform the region economically. Against a potential of 4.5 lakh in the NER, the present area under rubber plantations is just 13 per cent. Rubber is a major thrust area for the geographical belt in the 11th Plan (2007-12). With immense possibilities to increase the area under rubber in Tripura and Assam, the States could also benefit greatly from setting up downstream (processing) industries.

Spices hold immense potential, particularly organic ginger, chili and black pepper, both for expansion of production and marketing. ITC has identified Sikkim, Nagaland and Meghalya for undertaking cultivation, processing and marketing of cardamom, naga chilies, ginger and turmeric. A tripartite agreement involving ITC, Spices Board and the respective State governments is to be concluded shortly. In the export of tea, the share of the NER is lower, as South India accounts for over 50 per cent of Indian tea, though the former accounts for 55 per cent of the country's tea production. In 2006, there was breakthrough and over two million kg of tea from Assam was exported to Pakistan. The Tea Board has assured that in three months time, a logo for Assam orthodox tea and a Geographical Indication (GI) would be announced.

APEDA is in the process of establishing cold storages at the airports in Guwahati, Aizawl, Imphal, Dimapur, Agartala and Bagdogra. The process can be expedited with the active involvement of the respective State governments. To complete the cold chain from the field to the point of export, APEDA is working with a logistics firm through Concor. The four Agricultural Export Zones (AEZs) in the NER prioritized on the basis of their potential and stage of implementation include pineapples (Tripura), ginger (Sikkim), orchids and cherry pepper (Sikkim) and fresh and processed ginger (Assam). These four AEZs are expected to be operationalised by December 2007.

## The Mizoram Experience

### *Economy: A SWOT Analysis*

SWOT is the acronym used in the Management discipline dealing with the strengths, weaknesses, opportunities, and threats of an organization or economy. An attempt is made here to understand the features of Mizoram economy with the help of SWOT analysis. The picturesque State of Mizoram, perched on the high hills of north-eastern corner of India, is flanked by Bangladesh on the west with an international border to 318 km and Myanmar on the east and south with an international border of 404 km. It has an area of 21,087 sq km with the Tropic of Cancer running right through the heart of Mizoram. Two sister states of Manipur and Assam border it on the north while Tripura lies in the north-west. The State of Mizoram is the smallest of the North Eastern States in terms of population, i.e. 8.9 lakh as per 2001 Census.[12]

- *Strengths*: Out of 12 States that comprise India's east and north east, Mizoram achieved second position in overall ranking, according to the fourth annual *India Today* rankings of India's Best and Worst States.[13] The State is showing remarkable improvements in infrastructure, consumer market and budget and prosperity. Mizoram has about 2,60,000 hectares of cultivable barren land. It is a potential state for certain cash crops. Its climate is very suitable for cultivation of cut flowers. Women in Mizoram play a key role in socio-economic life. The State has strength in nursing, because of its cultural environment. Specifically, the Mizo sense of selfless service coupled with Christianity also contribute in promoting hospitality management.
- *Weaknesses*: Severe soil erosion and land slides are quite common in the State due to loose soil formation and heavy

rainfall. The State also lacks mineral resources. The future of a state depends upon the availability of infrastructure network, which can stimulate new investment in other sectors. Mizoram is suffering from severe shortage of water and electricity. Investors feel discouraged for the setting up of heavy industries in Mizoram due to these factors. Mizoram's ranking is comparatively very low in terms of investment environment even among North Eastern States. The consumption rate in Mizoram is quite high; and people spent about 180 and 182 per cent national average on consumption (inflation and inequality adjusted) during 1993-94 and 1999-2000, respectively. In other words, the State was spending about 75 per cent of its income on consumer goods, keeping an insignificant portion for investment. This unprecedented level of consumption in a State like Mizoram puts a serious question mark on the consumption sustainability.

- *Opportunities*:[14] In Mizoram, certain multi-purpose bio-fuel plants can grow well in about 50 per cent of uncultivated land, that is, 1,30,000 hectares. This mission, if implemented successfully, would generate employment for more than one lakh people and yield revenue of Rs. 325 crores a year. Bamboo mission envisages an integrated programme of expansion of plantation of bamboo, spices, the scientific management, and promotion of community level value addition and entrepreneurship. It involves cultivation of bamboo in more than 10,000 hectares, in addition to the existing bamboo cultivation. This will ultimately lead to the creation of 40,000 jobs and the market opportunities worth over than Rs.32 crores with an investment of Rs.13 crore.

  Mizoram is a potential state for cultivation of certain cash crops such as ginger and tapioca and fruits like kiwi, orange, hatkora, banana, grapes and passion fruits. The first shipment of 1000 cut flowers from Mizoram and Meghalaya was exported to United Arab Emirates in August 2006. According to an estimate, the demand for cut flowers of anthurium grew by about 38 per cent between 1999 and 2002.

  At present, Mizoram is attracting only one lakh tourists every year. The President of India, Abdul Kalam, in his vision statement has set the target of attracting five lakh tourists. It was estimated that every tourist, whether national or international, would generate at least four jobs. Mizoram has the potential of creating a Rs.50 crore tourism industry.

- *Threats*: The industrial sector in Mizoram is not in a position to attract the required private investment either from outside of the State or from within. The decline in share of primary sector relative to income and corresponding rise in labour force result in slowdown of productivity, negative growth in manufacturing since 1990s has its far-reaching consequences on the economy. Much of income in secondary sector arises from construction which is unplanned and thereby causes a serious threat to the environment. The expansion of tertiary sector, particularly in public administration and not by a market economy, benefits only small section of the people resulting in growing unemployment and social unrest. According to an estimate, Mizoram has the highest number of government employees per one lakh population.

***Border Trade with Myanmar***

Union of Myanmar (Burma till May 1989) is located between South and South-east Asia, on Bay of Bengal. Myanmar joined the regional group BISTEC (Bangladesh, India, Sri Lanka, Thailand Economic Cooperation) in 1997, which then became BIMSTEC. In 1997, the Association of South-East Asian Nations (ASEAN) admitted Myanmar as a member. Known as the "rice bowl of the far East" Myanmar also grows sugarcane, peanuts and beans. The chief minerals are petroleum, lead, tin, zinc, tungsten, copper, antimony, silver and gems. The rubies, sapphires and jade found in Myanmar are especially famous. Teakwood is exported.

Development of border trade is one of the clauses enshrined in the Mizoram Peace Accord of 1986. But there was considerable delay in initiating proactive measures to encourage official border trade. Border trade between India and Myanmar was formalised through signing of India-Myanmar Border Trade Agreement in 1994.

The two designated Border Trade Points were established at Moreh (Manipur) and at Champhai (Mizoram) borders, respectively. Accordingly, one Land Customs Station (LCS) was established at

Zokhawthar, near Champhai on the eastern side border of Mizoram. The State government has further acquired about 125 acres of land at Khawnuam which is eight km away from Zokhawthar for establishment of Indo-Myanmar Border Trade Township. This township has been planned for accommodating office buildings and staff quarters. The secretary of NEC along with the chief secretary of Mizoram visited the township and LCS site at Zokhawthar on 28th April, 2001. They were fully satisfied with the facilities available there. The NEC sanctioned Rs.9.31 crores for setting up of Special Economic Zone (SEZ) at Khawnuam during 10th Plan period. Meanwhile, the state government has completed the construction of the Bailey bridge between India and Myanmar in 2002 at Zokhawthar. The second Border Trade Point was opened on 31st January, 2004 by the Minister of Commerce of Myanmar at Zokhawthar-Rih sector (The first Border Trade Point was opened in 1994 at Moreh in Manipur). In the year 2004, the existing condition that imports from Myanmar into India should precede exports from India was deleted. It has also been decided to permit rising of invoices in other convertible currencies in addition to US dollars. Accordingly, the guidelines for the border trade have been revised as follows:

(a) The barter trade shall be restricted to land route as per the Border Trade Agreement between the two countries. Such border trade transactions shall take place only by way of head load or non-motorized transport system.

(b) There will be no monetary transaction under the barter trade arrangement.

(c) The consignments of imports and exports should be invoiced in US dollars or any convertible currency (i.e. Euro, Japanese Yen and Sterling Pound).

(d) The value of goods exported under barter trade should not exceed US$ 20,000 or Euro/Japanese Yen/Sterling Pound equivalent to US$ 20,000 per transaction.

Traditional free exchange or barter trade has been restricted to 22 items agreed upon by the two countries since 1994. They are: mustard/rape seed; pulses and beans; fresh vegetables; fruits; garlic; onions/chilies; spices (excluding nutmeg, mace, cloves, cassia); bamboo; minor forest products (excluding teak); betal nuts and leaves;

food items for local consumption; tobacco, tomato, red broom; sesame; reain; coriander seeds; soybean; roasted sunflower seeds; katha; and ginger. However, the Indo-Myanmar border trade has been suffering from certain problems. They include:

(a) Sometimes both Indian and Myanmar authorities unilaterally and abruptly banned trading of certain items listed in the Agreement in gross violation of the Agreement. For example, previously India stopped import of onion and export of wheat flour. Myanmar also banned export of onion, garlic, groundnut, rice, etc. for some period. In such occasions the traders of both the countries should be informed in advance to avoid financial loss due to breach of contract.[15]

(b) The Indian traders feel that Myanmar is not in a position to supply the required items at competitive price. High rate of customs duty on some items such as resin, katha and soybean acted as disincentive for Indian importers.

(c) Indian traders favour the inclusion of some more items in the list shown in Annexure-I of the Border Trade Agreement. The local businessmen on both sides should be consulted while revising the list.

(d) Official trade between India and Myanmar was stopped way back during 1960s. Since then, the traders belonging to both the countries have been indulging in illegal trade. The customs personnel are not well-equipped to guard the entire 1640 km Indo-Myanmar border. Though it is illegal, people residing in the border areas, find it quite convenient to involve in trading activities with Myanmar's traders without following the 'cumbersome' procedures of international trade. In fact, most of the traders are ignorant of such procedures.

(e) Improper infrastructural facilities such as warehousing, efficient and cost effective transportation system, and the absence of EXIM Bank branch, Directorate General of Foreign Trade (DGFT) branch, lack of coordination among various government departments etc. are posing serious problems to the business community.

(f) Problem of exchange of documents, poor telecommunications and postal facilities on the Myanmar side and inadequate banking system have hindered full-fledged trade, which has been mostly of the barter variety.

(g) Non-applicability of the Asian Currency Union (ACU) dollar mechanism in Myanmar, because of the sanctions by US government against that country, has prevented emergence of a proper LC system of trade.

Though the trade between two countries was officially open a few years back, the full swing of trade is yet to take off owing to a variety of problems mentioned above. Unfortunately, the LCS border point with Myanmar at Champhai (Mizoram) has to become fully operational. Rites, a research organisation, has conducted a study on how Moreh LCS can be improved to increase trade volumes. Informal trade with Myanmar at Moreh was estimated close to Rs.2,000 crore, against the Rs.10 crore of formal trade. The Government of India has asked the State government of Manipur to speed up the land acquisition process for complete modernisation of the Moreh LCS, turning it into an integrated customs check-post with all amenities, including food testing facilities. Although there is no formal study undertaken with respect to Mizoram, the same trends seem to be present here also.

### *Border Trade with Bangladesh*

Bangladesh is surrounded by India, Myanmar and the Bay of Bengal. Although half of Bangladesh's GDP is generated through the service sector, nearly two-thirds of the people are employed in the agriculture sector, with rice as the single most important product.

The official border trade between Mizoram and Bangladesh is almost non-existent. The government of Mizoram is, however, strongly favouring the operationalisation of border trade in this sector. The Ministry of Commerce, Government of India has agreed to develop a border township having all infrastructure near Tlabung. The project has been in the process of execution.

The Trade and Commerce Department of Mizoram has sent a trade delegation to Bangladesh in June 2001 to explore the possibility of marketing of agricultural commodities such as ginger and chilies. Although different chambers of commerce and industries of Dhaka, Chittagong, Sylhet, etc., responded positively for opening up of border trade between Bangladesh and Mizoram, the traders of both the sides have yet to achieve headway in this regard.

Mizoram since long time has been requesting the governments of India and Bangladesh to open up traditional river route from Tlabung to Chittagong port. This suggestion had received positive response from the then Prime Minister of Bangladesh, when the Mizoram chief minister met her in 1999. As this route is considered the vital economic line for the land locked State of Mizoram, the Government of India has initiated fresh attempts to get this route opened up early. There has been a continuous dialogue between different chambers of commerce and industry between both the sides of the countries.[16]

It is to be noted that one LCS at Thegamukh had been active till 1965 and became dormant since then. The Mizoram government wants it to be responded on the following considerations:

(a) Mizoram is keen to export its bamboo (either in raw form or in semi-processed form) to Karnaphuli Paper Mill of Bangladesh on sustainable basis on the long term agreement.
(b) Mizoram can export stone metal and stone chips to Bangladesh for infrastructural development like road construction and buildings.
(c) Mizoram can supply its surplus produce such as ginger, hatkora, oranges, sesame and papaya to Bangladesh.
(d) Mizoram can import crockery, cement, iron and steel, garments, cosmetics and toiletries and so on from Bangladesh.

Bangladesh has not accepted the proposal of opening of LCS at Thegamukh due to its remoteness from the district headquarters of Rangamati. Similarly, the issue of opening of Karnaphuli river line route between south Mizoram and Rangamati-Kaptai-Chittagong (Bangladesh) is pending for long time. The Government of India has been making efforts to impress upon Bangladesh for necessity of opening this traditional river line route between India (Mizoram sector) and Bangladesh, and for the inclusion of this route in the Chapter-VIII of the Protocol for Trade and Transit between the two countries and for the approval of Chittagong (Bangladesh), Kaptai, Rangamati and Tlabung (India) as ports-of-call under the said Chapter.

## Beyond Border Trade: Integrating with the Global Economy

### *Regional Cooperation with Myanmar*

Myanmar plays a crucial role in India's quest for strategic convergence with its South-East Asian partners. Attempting to isolate Myanmar, as observed by G. Parthasarathy, had disastrous consequences for internal security in the North-East States between 1988 and 1993. Smuggling of narcotics and cross-border insurgencies increased sharply. However, India undertook a process of extensive economic and regional cooperation with Myanmar. India has provided assistance to Myanmar in areas such as information technology, telecommunications, and higher education.

Myanmar considers India as its largest export market mainly because of its potential to meet the India's ever growing requirements for pulses and beans. Myanmar's border trade with India is, however, lagging far behind compared to its border trade with China. In this context, the bureaucracy in New Delhi has to understand the ground realities of the border trade and evolve a better border trade policy in consultation with the main stakeholders. More creative border trade practices would enable the NER to satisfy its requirements for agricultural commodities such as rice by imports from Myanmar. With Myanmar joining ASEAN as a member, the country is, in fact, set to become the "land bridge" linking India with the globally dynamic economies of its ASEAN partners. India is taking keen interest in developing transport corridors to Thailand through Myanmar with the twin objectives of giving Indian exports and tourists access by land to South-East Asia and helps the NER in its economic development. India has provided financial assistance to modernise the Myanmar Railways and supplied rails and rolling stock. India is now envisaging a trans-Asian rail network that would link Hanoi with New Delhi.

India's efforts to make Myanmar a key hub for its Look East policy has been strengthened with the formation of the BIMSTEC Grouping, which brings together Bangladesh, India, Sri Lanka, Bhutan and Nepal, from SAARC, and Myanmar and Thailand, from ASEAN, in a common endeavour to establish a free trade area by 2016. When A.P.J. Abdul Kalam, the President of India visited Myanmar in April 2006, Myanmar expressed its readiness to consider alternative Indian proposals for transportation and utilisation of the off-shore gas to

India. Experts are advising the Indian government to transport this gas to Tripura through a Myanmar-India corridor that bypasses Bangladesh. By expeditiously implementing the proposal for the Tamanthi hydro-electric project on the Chindwin river in Myanmar (about 40 km from the Nagaland border) the Indian government can help the NER by providing 1200 mw of power.[17]

Myanmar has been so far the safe heaven for the North-East insurgency. Recently, however, Myanmar has assured to flush out North-East rebels from the country. This might result in a better environment for the conduct of trade in the region. Businessmen in the region are now looking forward to the Indo-Myanmar rail link for increasing volume of bilateral trade. Regional traders hope that the proposed India-Myanmar rail connection will take bilateral trade to a new level. A feasibility study report for the India-Myanmar rail link carried out by the Ministry of External Affairs is currently under consultation. On the traders' level, effort is being made to increase the volume of business after the India-Myanmar trade began in 1995 through Manipur's Moreh border.

Traders from the NER and Myanmar are planning to meet in Moreh sometime in 2007 to find out ways for strengthening and increasing bilateral trade. The forthcoming meeting is assuming importance in the wake of trilateral Memorandum of Understanding signed between the Union of Myanmar Border Trade Chamber of Commerce, Indo-Myanmar Border Traders' Union of Manipur, and Industries of Trade Fair Association of Assam in Guwahati in March 2007 when a 31-member trade delegation from the neighbouring country visited the city. The region can capitalise on the growing demand in Thailand and other South East Asian countries for agricultural produce such as bamboo shoots, mushrooms, capsicum and different kinds of chilies grown in the NER.[18]

### *Integration with East Asia*

India's economic integration with East Asia in the emerging East Asian community would fit the Look East Policy pursued by India since 1991 as a part of which India became a dialogue partner of ASEAN. India has been stitching together a series of agreements to create a framework within which Indian business can work with their East Asian counterparts. The Indian industry is rapidly integrating with the East Asian production networks especially in critical knowledge-based parts of the value chain. The Indian firms are also developing their own production networks incorporating East Asian nations. With rapid growth of intra-regional trade, East Asia has emerged India's largest trade partner surpassing the US accounting for nearly 40 per cent of her global trade. India is virtually integrated with East Asian economy. With age-old civilisational links with East Asian countries, India feels much more integrated with the region besides the geographical contiguity with China, Myanmar, Thailand and Indonesia. Its well-developed transport and trading linkages with West, Central and South Asia could make India act as a bridge between these regions and East Asia.[19] Over the past few years, Asian nations have recognised the importance of regional economic integration and have initiated a series of steps to benefit from it. In addition to sub-regional attempts in the framework of ASEAN, SAARC and BIMSTEC groupings, a number of initiatives of broader economic integration are underway to push the agenda of regional economic integration. Besides deepening the sub-regional cooperation between its 10-member states, ASEAN has also served to bring major Asian countries, namely, Japan, China, India and South Korea together as summit-level dialogue partners who meet at the Asian summits annually. Therefore, a complex web of the FTAs connecting Asian countries and all these countries is in progress and a virtual Asian or East Asian economic community is emerging. Many experts believe that JACIK (Japan, China, India and Korea) approach to East Asian integration is catching a popular imagination and is a preferred option over the ASEAN +3 approach.

Major investments in development of regional public goods and regional infrastructural projects such as Asian railway, Asian highway, Asian satellites and Asian information infrastructure would facilitate trade and other economic exchanges within Asia. It is to be noted that 32 Asian countries have endorsed the Asian highway project which would cover a network of 1,41,000 km of standard roadway, crisscrossing all these countries with linkages to Europe. When completed, it will be the largest road network in the world. The proposed highway will pass through four states of NER of India. It will enter Meghalaya after crossing Bangladesh, then enter Assam and pass through two more states, Nagaland and Manipur, before entering Myanmar. The project will provide a critical linkage between the NER of India and the other Asian countries and is expected to promote trade, commerce and tourism in the region.

The reopening of the Nathu La (which means "the pass of the listening ear"), the land route *via* the Himalayas that had once linked Sikkim with Lhasa in China's Tibet Autonomous Region, was an event of strategic and economic importance. The pass was sealed after the 1962 war. It was in 2003 that negotiations to open the Nathu La route began, prompted in large part by initiatives taken by the Sikkim government. According to a study by the Nathu La trade study group, besides the direct gains to India, the reopening of this trade route could generate a whole range of benefits to the otherwise landlocked state of Sikkim and neighbouring states. It is expected that India could well emerge as a major supplier of intermediate products for the manufacturing units in China. Trade through the Nathu La will initially be restricted to border trade. Only 15 specified items can be imported into India such as wool, animal skins, salt and silk. The list of permissible exports contains 25 items including farm implements, food products and textiles. Indo-China trade is now growing by 40 per cent more a year and two-way trade stood at Rs. 79,000 crore in 2005-06. A recent study sponsored by Asian Development Bank concludes that after the reopening of the trade route through Nathu La trade with countries of South and South-east Asia was expected to improve the economy of the entire region with the trade turnover increasing by at least five times. Similarly, the restoration of the Stilwel road between the NER and Myanmar could re-establish vital linkages between the regions.[20]

In pursuance of India's Look East Policy since 1991, trade between India and South-east and East Asia has significantly improved. India has operational bilateral trade agreements with Sri Lanka and Thailand, and has negotiated a comprehensive pact with the ASEAN. If the creation of a larger Asian Economic Community (AEC) extending from India in the West to Japan in the north-east comes about, it would be the second largest group in the world next to the North American Free Trade Agreement (NAFTA) bloc, and even larger than the European Union (EU). Between 1999-2000 and 2003-04, India's total merchandise exports rose from $ 36.8 bn to $ 63.6 bn (73 per cent increase). However, the pace of growth was much more impressive in exports to China (a six fold rise) and ASEAN (a two and a-half time increase). Undoubtedly, India's trade with countries to the east has been growing phenomenally.[21]

Mutually beneficial legal trade across the border will certainly bring development and prosperity to the border regions. However, there is a growing suspicion about India rushing into a series of relationships without adequate stakeholder consultation. A calibrated approach to opening up the market which aims at protecting the domestic producers' interests is required. Some experts advocate the need for economic integration of eight States of the North-East region. The eight States of the region have their own strengths and weaknesses in terms of resources. Each depends on the other in various ways. This mutual economic dependence should be converted into a positive synergy through the creation of a common market in the region. For instance, the abundant water resources available in the region primarily imposed costs on the region because of the recurring floods. In fact, there are conflicting objectives of States like Arunachal Pradesh and Assam in harnessing of the water resources. Assam is having a significant interest in flood management while Arunachal Pradesh wants to develop its hydropower primarily for income and job generation. In order to ensure optimal use of the scarce resources of the region for development, certain institutional framework where the stakeholders could have free exchange of ideas need to be developed.[22] The NER, being closer to the South East Asian nations rather than to the mainland in terms of culture and geographical contiguity, is supposed to gain in large measure. It could serve as a corridor for the ASEAN nations. So far, however, there has been no substantial or tangible gain for the region. In any case, although common market *per se* is between two or more countries for the conduct of free trade without any barriers, the NER can be considered as a common market without any trade barriers among the eight States of the region.[23]

## Towards Borderless Economy

By 2040, Asian's share of world's Gross Domestic Product (GDP) will be 42 per cent, while that of North America will reduce to 23 per cent[24]. China is expected to overtake the US as the world's largest economy by 2040. Since the 1980s the average Asian GDP growth has been double the world average. Asian's share of world's GDP has been raising from 12 per cent in 1960 to 14.5 per cent in 1970 to 17 per cent in 1980, and to 23 per cent in 2003. It is expected that in another 30 years Asia will overtake North America as the continent with the world's largest economy. India, with its large economy, a thriving private sector, a large pool of manpower, and a diversified industrial base, could gain from the rise of Asia.

All these years borders have been viewed as liabilities. In the era of global economy, these are in fact our assets. As Kenichi Ohmae argued, national borders are far less constructive than they once were. This is because of technology, and international and bilateral agreements in the area of trade. Despite the importance of protecting the borders of nation-states, the world has already attained the position of being effectively without borders, in terms of four key business factors. Ohmae labelled these business factors the four C's: Communications, Capital, Corporations (i.e., companies) and Consumers. The surplus capital in advanced countries is looking for opportunities to invest. The logic of the global economy is to attract companies, customers, and capital to a specific region or a company from the rest of the world.[25]

It no longer matters if a country or region-state does not have its own well-established domestic industry or home markets. What is important is to have an educated and motivated workforce. A region must also have good infrastructure, in both technology and logistics. It has traditionally been the role of government to provide physical infrastructure. In the last two decades, there has been a rise in public-private partnerships (PPPs) as a means of injecting efficiency into their provision. In particular, they must facilitate inward access to the region and outward access from the region to the markets by land, sea, and air. In India, there are regions such as Andhra Pradesh, Maharashtra, Kerala, Tamil Nadu and the vicinities of Mumbai and Bangaluru, which are eagerly embracing the global economy and are looking outward to the rest of the world for investment and prosperity. They are truly behaving like city-states like Singapore without depending much on central government.[26] Japan has few minerals and it had to import natural resources and add value and then export. The difference lies in the "value-addition". Those who do not add value do not eat. Japan's "economic miracle" after the Second World War was the result of a vision called Value-added trade. The governments and politicians of the North-East states of India, including Mizoram, have to learn lessons from such success stories. Mizoram can achieve a standard of living that is both rising and sustainable. This can be achieved if it can produce goods and services that meet the test of national and international competitiveness.

## NOTES

1. IIFT (1995). *Study on Promotion of Border Trade between India and Myanmar,* New Delhi.
2. Das, Gurudas (2000). 'Trade between the North-Eastern Region and Neighboring Countries: Structures and Implications for Development' in Gurudas Das and R.K. Purkayastha (eds,) *Border Trade: North-East India and Neighboring Countries,* Akansha, New Delhi, p. 43.
3. Sudhakar, Chaudhuri K. (1995). *Cross Border Trade between India and Bangladesh,* Working Paper No.58, NCAER, New Delhi.
4. Gurudas Das and R.K. Purkaytastha (eds.) (2000). *Border Trade: North-East India and Neighboring Countries,* Akansha, New Delhi, is the outcome of the seminar.
5. Das, Gurudas (2000). *op cit*, pp. 42-43.
6. For example, a survey on 'Informal Border Trade in the North-Eastern Region' was carried out for a UN-ESCAP sponsored study by Research and Information System for Non-aligned and Developing Countries, New Delhi in 1996.
7. Bezbaruah, M.P. (2000). 'Liberalisation of Border Trade: Prospects and Impediments' in Gurudas Das and R.K. Phurkayastha (eds.), *Border Trade: North-East India and Neighboring Countries,* Akansha, New Delhi, p. 88.
8. Madhab, Jatyanta (2005). 'Enabling the North-East,' *Yojana,* December, pp. 10-11. Das, Gurudas (2000). *op cit*, p. 45.
9. Sarma, B.K. and S.N. Goswami (2000). 'Border Trade in North-East India: An overview', in Gurudas Das and R.K. Phurkayastha (eds), *Border Trade: North-East India and Neighboring Countries,* Akansha, New Delhi. p.101.
10. Das, Gangadhar (2004). 'Fruits and Vegetables Production in North-Eastern Region: Export Potential', *The Indian Journal of Commerce,* Vol. 57, No. 3, July-September, pp. 42-51.
11. Srinivasan, G. (2007). 'North-East: Meet Readies Roadmap for Development', *The Hindu Business Line,* March 20, p. 7.
12. Lakhera, M.M. (2006). 'Development and Investment Potential', *Yojana,* December, p. 58.
13. Saran, Rohit, and Choudhury, Sushmita, (2006). ' The Leader, Last Hurrah', *India Today*, September 11.
14. Based on the speech delivered by A.P.J. Abdul Kalam, the President of India in a special session of Mizoram State Legislature Assembly in 2005. The visionary President of India proposed seven missions for Mizoram (see Kalam, A.P.J. Abdul 'Missions for Mizoram Prosperity', *Yojana,* December 2006).
15. Thomas, C. Joshua (2000). 'Indo-Myanmar, Border Trade: An Assessment on the Moreh-Tamu Sector' in Gurudas Das and R.K. Phurkayastha (eds.), *Border Trade: North-East India and Neighboring Countries,* Akansha, New Delhi, p. 158.

16. Based on information provided by the Department of Trade and Commerce, government of Mizoram in a Workshop-*cum*-Awareness programme held in Aizawl during November 9-11, 2005.
17. Parthasarathy, G., (2006). 'Myanmar—Gateway to S-E Asia', *The Hindu Business Line,* April 25, p. 8.
18. 'Regions Traders Eye Moolah in Myanmar', *Times of India,* April 30, 2007. p. 3.
19. Kumar, Nagesh, (2005). 'A Broader Asian Community and a Possible Roadmap', *Economic and Political Weekly,* September 3-9. Vol. XL, No. 36, pp. 3926-31.
20. "Indo-China Relations: A Historic Reopening' (2006*). Economic and Political Weekly*, July 22-28, Vol. XLI. No.29, p. 3132.
21. 'India and ASEAN: Getting Closer' (2004). *Economic and Political Weekly*, December 4-10, Vol. XXXIX No. 49, p. 5189.
22. Vanlalchhawna (2006). 'India's Look East Policy: Challenges and Opportunities for North East India', Eighth Annual Conference of North Eastern Economic Association, *Souvenir*, Department of Economics, Mizoram University, Aizawl, pp. 20-21.
23. Patnaik, Jagadish K. (2006). 'India's Look East Policy and the North-East. A Study of the Implication of a Common Market in the Region', Eighth Annual Conference of North Eastern Economic Association, *Souvenir,* Department of Economics, Mizoram University, Aizawl, p. 23.
24. Mukherjea, D.N. (2005). 'Engaging Asia', *Businessworld*, 12 December, pp. 36-41.
25. Ohmae, Kenichi (2005). *The Next Global Stage: Challenges and Opportunities in Our Borderless World,* Wharton School, New Delhi, pp. 20-22.
26. *Ibid.*, p. 200.

# Chapter 9

## Inter District Developmental Disparities of Mizoram

J.V. NUNCHUNGA

This chapter categorized all the 8 districts of Mizoram State; on the basis of primary, secondary, and tertiary sector; into highly developed, relatively developed, less developed and least developed district using certain statistical tools like Indexing method, Deprivation method, and Principal component analysis. This is the first and the only study regarding developmental disparity of Mizoram as well as inter-district developmental disparities. This chapter is divided into 3 sections: Section 1 deals with the introduction of the topic, the tools of analysis, and the rationale of the study; Section 2 deals with calculation of developmental score of agriculture and allied sector, industry and allied sector and basic and infrastructure services using the statistical tools; and the last section deals with the findings and conclusion of the study.

Mizoram has a per capita income of Rs. 26,673 during 2006-07 at current prices with a Gross State Domestic Product of Rs. 2,96,549 lakh at current prices (1999-2000) series during 2006-07. The Plan outlay during 11th Five-Year Plan stood at Rs. 2,500 crore.[1]

Regarding the income share, the poorest 40 per cent of the population earned only 8.54 per cent of the total income while the richest 10 per cent earned 41.22 per cent of the total state's income during 2006. In the mean time the Gini coefficient (which measure the income gap between the rich and the poor) was increasing at an alarming pace of 10.11 in 1981 to 31.27 in 2006.[2]

SECTION 1

## Introduction and the Meaning of Development

According to Charles P. Kindle Berger and Bruce Herrick "*Economic development is generally defined to include the acceleration of economic growth, improvement in material welfare, especially for persons with the lowest incomes, the eradication of poverty with its correlates of illiteracy, disease, and early death.*"[3] It also includes changes in the composition of inputs and outputs that generally include shift in the underlying structure of production away from agriculture towards industrial activities, the organization of the economy in such a way that productive employment is generally among the working age population rather than the situation of privilege minority; and the correspondingly greater participation of broadly based groups in making decision about the directions, economic and otherwise, in which they should move to improve their welfare.

The aim of Developmental Planning is to accelerate economic growth with attainment of egalitarian socio-economic order with balanced development of the region. The fast growing information technology in an unequal socio-economic condition set forth a sense of relative deprivation between the people of various communities which results in various political demands and violence. Violence and terror cannot be solved unless the root cause is dismantled politically and economically. Otherwise there would be a political and social turmoil that, in turn, retard the overall economic progress of the whole region and hence having balanced regional growth is of paramount importance for the overall development of a region.

The study of developmental disparity has great importance as well as relevance in the economy, especially in developing economies like ours. Developmental disparity is used by Economists to answer a wide range of questions concerning political, social, and economic problems. The study of inter-district developmental disparity is important to find out and identify economically backward areas in order to enable the government to formulate suitable schemes to be implemented in an integrated manner by various departments for the benefit and upliftment of such areas in the state. For these reasons, a study of the developmental disparity is highly relevant and very important.

Regarding the nomenclature of developmental stage of the district, the choice depends largely on sensitivity of the audience and the sensitivity of the analyst.[4] As such the term backward, underdeveloped, etc., should be avoided in this chapter.

This finding would be helpful for framing developmental planning for the state of Mizoram to reduce intra-state developmental disparities. This could also be the guiding principle for budget allocation to different departments and some districts of Mizoram wherein less developed region may be given due importance and attention to reduce regional imbalances.

**Tools of Analysis**

This study is based on Indexing method, Deprivation method, and Principal component analysis using SPSS package, which are defined as—

*Indexing*: Let $I_{ij}$ be the value of the *i*th variable for *j*th district;

where $i = 1, 2....m$, and $j = 1, 2....n$. First obtain $I_i = \frac{\sum_{j=1}^{n} I_{ij}}{n}$ for *j*th district. Secondly, obtain $I_j = \frac{I_{ij}}{I_i} \times 100$ for district, then, finally, obtain

'Index value' = $\frac{1}{n}\sum_{i=1}^{n} I_j$ ,

If the 'Index value' of *j*th district $\geq 100$ termed the district as 'Relatively Developed', otherwise, 'Less developed'.

1. *Deprivation*: is the deprivation indicator for *j*th district with respect to *i*th variable. Then it is defined as—

$$I_{ij} = \frac{(\underset{j}{Max}\ X_{ij} - X_{ij})}{(\underset{j}{Max}\ X_{ij} - \underset{j}{Min}\ X_{ij})}$$

where $X_{ij}$ indicates the value of *i*th variable with respect to *j*th district. Obviously, $I_{ij}$ range from 0 and 1. Secondly,

calculate 'total deprivation value' = $\frac{\sum_{i=1}^{n} I_{ij}}{n}$ , thirdly, obtain 'deprivation value (DI)' = (1 – average deprivation value) If 'deprivation value' is 0.8 and above, lies between 0.8 and 0.5, and less than 0.5, the districts are respectively termed as 'Highly developed', 'Relatively developed' and 'Less developed'.

2. *Principal Component Analysis*: Principal component analysis is a special case of factor analysis. Using SPSS software Principal component, factor loadings and factor scores are obtained which are used for determining overall developmental score (ODC). If the ODC is greater than 1, between 1 and 0, and less than 0, they are respectively termed as 'Highly developed', 'Relatively developed' and 'Less developed'.

## Variables/Indicator of Development

The working group (1969) appointed by Planning Commission had recommended 15 indicators of development (or backwardness) for backward areas like Mizoram which were accepted by the Planning Commission[5]. These indicators are total population and density, cultivable area per cultivator, net area sown per agriculture worker, workers engaged in agriculture sector as a percentage of total workers, percentage of gross irrigated area to net sown area, intensity of cropping, per capita (rural) gross value of agricultural production, establishment (manufacturing and repairs) using electricity, No. of workers per lakh population employed in manufacturing sector, mileage of surface road per 100 sq. km of area and per lakh population, No. of commercial vehicle registered in a district, male and female literacy rate, No. of seats per million population for technical training, percentage of male and female school going children to the population in the age group of 6-11 and 11-14 years and hospital beds per lakh population.

Due to non-availability of statistical data regarding certain indicators listed above, the suitability of some of these indicators to reflect the backwardness of Mizoram economy, the very ground reality of Mizoram economy and the availability of data, 35 developmental variables/indicators are selected of which 9 are from primary/agricultural and allied sector, 8 from secondary/industrial sector and the remaining 18 from service/basic and infrastructure services.

**Limitation of the Study**

Since this study relies solely on secondary information, all types of its disadvantages will be applicable here:

1. Data for Mizoram are not necessarily of the same year. There may be 3 or 4 years gap between them; however, some data cannot change within a span of just 3/4 years. Even if there were a difference, it would not be significant meaningfully.
2. Most of the figures are for the year 2003, 2004, and 2005. However, few data are also for 2006 figure. The sources of information are secondary in nature.[6]

SECTION 2

**Agriculture and Allied Sector**

One of the foremost important ingredients for economic development is a sustained growth in agricultural production. If we look back at the economic development of our global history, the role of agriculture was empirically established. As the tenth five-year plan has rightly said, "Agriculture development is central to economic development of the country". Any change in agriculture sector-positive or negative has a multiplier effect on the entire economy. The agricultural sector acts as a bulwark in maintaining food security and in the process, national security as well. To maintain ecological balance, there is a need for sustainable and balanced development of agriculture and allied sectors.[7]

Agriculture forms the backbone and strength of Mizoram economy; it occupies a place of pride in a less developed region like Mizoram. There is 6,31,000Ha of estimated area available for horticultural crops, of which 35,984 hectares are actually utilized by 2000-01. Mizoram as a whole has a total gross cropped area of about 1,04,689 hectares; against this the gross irrigated area was 11,629 hectares only. Fisheries in Mizoram are only fresh water fisheries including both culture and capture fisheries. The forest cover is Reserved-7909 sq. km; Protected-3568 sq. km and Unclassified-5240 sq. km.[8] The Primary sector contributes 18.52 per cent of total production in Mizoram during 2006[9]. The sectoral contribution is given in the Table 9.1.

**Table 9.1:** Table Showing the Percentage Contribution of Agriculture and Allied Sector

*(in per cent)*

| *Primary Sector* | *2000-01* | *2001-02* | *2002-03* | *2003-04* |
|---|---|---|---|---|
| 1. Agriculture | 20.35 | 21.32 | 19.92 | 19.23 |
| 2. Forestry | 0.71 | 0.72 | 0.71 | 0.55 |
| 3. Fishing | 1.05 | 1.39 | 1.28 | 1.34 |
| 4. Mining & Quarrying | 0.13 | 0.22 | 0.10 | 0.45 |
| Total | 22.24 | 23.65 | 22.01 | 21.57 |

*Source*: Statistical handbook of Mizoram 2003.

***Developmental Score of the Sector***

These variables/indicators are being selected for measuring level of agriculture and allied sectoral development subject to the availability of reliable data.

1. Percentage of cultivable land to total geographical area.[10]
2. Combine productivity of paddy, oilseeds and pulse in terms of metric tonne per hectares for the year.
3. Percentage of sown area to total geographical area.
4. Productivity of Jhum in terms of metric tonne per hectares.
5. Productivity of wet rice cultivation in terms of metric tonne per hectares.
6. Percentage of area under high yield variety and wet rice cultivation to total geographical area.
7. Food availability in terms of metric tonne per person.[11]
8. Productivity of fish (in terms of quintal per fishpond).
9. No. of livestock per person.[12]

Based on these indicators, the developmental score of all districts in respect of agriculture and allied sector are determined. The outcome of the determination is present in the tables. From the Appendix Table 9.1 (i.e. using Indexing method) it can be concluded that (in descending order) Kolasib, Champhai, Serchhip and Saiha district are 'Relatively developed' whereas Mamit, Lunglei, Lawngtlai and Aizawl district are 'Less developed'.

A slightly different result emerged from deprivation method (i.e. the Appendix Table 9.2) which categorize Kolasib as 'Highly developed', Champhai as 'Relatively developed' and all other districts as (in ascending order) Mamit, Serchhip, Lunglei, Saiha, Lawngtlai and Aizawl as 'Less developed'.

From the Appendix Table 9.3, factor component analysis suggests to retain only three principal components that explain 88.699 per cent of the total variation. From the Appendix Table 9.4, we know that Indicator 6th, 7th and 1st are the most important indicators that explain 95.5 per cent, 92.2 per cent and 91.2 per cent respectively of the total variables variance. As can be seen from Appendix Table 9.5, this approach categorizes Kolasib as 'Highly developed'. Lawngtlai, Aizawl and Lunglei district as 'Relatively developed' whereas Mamit, Champhai, Serchhip and Saiha district as 'Less developed'.

The conclusion that can be made regarding the level of agriculture and allied sector development is that Kolasib district is undisputedly the most developed district and Champhai, the next. Aizawl, the state capital and Lunglei, the second most important town of the state, and Mamit district may be describe as 'less developed' in respect of agriculture and allied sector.

## Industry and Allied Sector Profile of Mizoram

Industrialization has a major role to play in the development of the underdevelopment countries. The level of its industrialization largely influences the gap in per capita income between developed and underdeveloped region. Mizoram till today is one of the most backward states in India due to many pertaining inhibiting factors among which, lack of basic infrastructure, shyness of capital and unregulated market facilities are prominent.[13]

There are as many as 2,718 registered small-scale industries in Mizoram of which 2632, 48 and 38 are perennial, seasonal, and casual in nature of operation respectively. These small scale industries generates an employment opportunities for 2176 females and 6837 males. By 2005-06, the total installed and generated electric power in the state is 47.07 MW and 400.315 MW respectively. There are 1,61,247 LPG subscribers up to March 2006 and 84.94 per cent of villages are electrified as well as given safe drinking water facilities.[14]

Industrial and Allied sector contributes 19.01 per cent of total production in 2006.[15] A more detailed information is available in Table 9.2.

**Table 9.2:** Table showing the percentage contribution of Industry and Allied Sector to NSDP

*(in per cent)*

| *Sl. No.* | *Industry and allied sector* | *2000-01* | *2001-02* | *2002-03* | *2003-04* |
|---|---|---|---|---|---|
| 1. | Manufacturing | 1.11 | 0.99 | 0.91 | 0.94 |
| 2. | Construction | 10.05 | 11.28 | 11.72 | 12.23 |
| 3. | Electricity, Gas and Water Supply | 3.53 | 2.42 | 2.24 | 2.12 |
| | Total | 14.69 | 14.69 | 14.87 | 15.29 |

*Source*: Statistical Handbook of Mizoram 2003.

## *Developmental Score of the Sector*

These indicators are selected for measuring level of Industry and allied sectoral development subject to the availability of reliable data.

1. Percentage of secondary workers to the total workforce.
2. No. of registered small scale industry per 1,000 population.
3. Women manage percentage of small scale industry.
4. Percentage of female to the total employment.
5. Percentage of small scale industry unit that used electricity.
6. Percentage of electrified houses.
7. No. of water point per 1000 population.
8. No. of LPG connection per house.

Based on these indicators, the developmental score of all districts in respect of industry and allied sectors are determined. The outcome of the determination is present in the tables. From the Appendix Table 9.6 (i.e. using Indexing method) it can be concluded that Aizawl district alone is 'Relatively developed' and all other districts like (in descending order) Saiha, Lunglei, Kolasib, Champhai, Serchhip, Lawngtlai and Mamit district are 'Less developed'.

The same result emerges from deprivation method (i.e. Appendix Table 9.7) which also categorizes Aizawl district alone as 'Highly developed' and all other districts like (in ascending order) Saiha, Lunglei, Kolasib, Champhai, Serchhip, Lawngtlai and Mamit district as 'Less developed'.

In Appendix Table 9.8, principal component analysis suggests retaining of only two principal components that explain 91.646 per cent of the total variation. From Appendix Table 9.9, we know that variables 1st, 8th and 2nd are the most important variables that explain 98.1 per cent, 97.7 per cent and 96.2 per cent respectively of the total variable's variance. As can be seen from Appendix Table 9.10, this approach categorize Aizawl district alone as 'Highly Developed'. Lunglei, Kolasib, Champhai, and Serchhip as 'Relatively developed' while Mamit, Saiha and Lawngtlai district as 'Less developed'.

If we compare the result of indexing method and deprivation method, they give unanimous result, i.e. the ranking is the same in both methods, but it is slightly different in principal component analysis.

The conclusion we can make regarding the level of secondary/ Industrial and allied sector development is that Aizawl district is 'Highly developed' and Lunglei district, Champhai district, Kolasib district and Serchhip district are the leading 'Relatively developed' district. Since all the three methods place Lawngtlai, Saiha and Mamit district under 'Less developed category' they may be described as 'less developed district'.

## SECTION 3

### Basic Infrastructure and Services

Infrastructure has played a key role in the developmental process of any country. The three layers of communication (viz. physical communication, electronic communication and knowledge communication), good banking services, quality education, better health services, etc are the key ingredients for a healthy and sustained economic growth. The absence of these services quickly and radically reduces quality of human life and their productivity.

In certain area, Mizoram occupied a place of pride at national level. These areas are literacy, village electrification, provision of safe drinking water and infant mortality rate. However, in other areas Mizoram is still lacking behind as compared to other states.

Since there is a causal relationship between the services sector and basic infrastructure and services, it is worthwhile to look at the sectoral contribution of service sector at factor cost at current prices (in 1999-2000 series) in Table 9.3. The service sector contributes 62.47 per cent of states product in 2006[16]. The sectoral contribution is given in Table 9.3.

There is one Central University, 26 Colleges, 76 Higher Secondary schools, 484 High schools, 1121 Middle schools and 1688 Primary schools with student enrollment of 414, 7140, 10,555, 41,610, 88,044 and 1,32,046 respectively in 2005-06. There are 43277 telephone connections with 10 Hospitals, 9 Community Health Centres, 57 Primary Health Centres and 351 Sub-Centres look after by 155 doctors, 393 Nurses, 88 pharmacists, 656 health workers and 38 Lab. Technicians. During—2005-06, there is 84,225 and 617 domestic and foreign tourists arrived at Aizawl.[17]

**Table 9.3:** Table Showing the Percentage Contribution of Service Sector

| *Sl. No.* | | *2000-01* | *2001-02* | *2002-03* | *2003-04* |
|---|---|---|---|---|---|
| 1. | Transport, storage and communication | 1.04 | 1.06 | 1.21 | 0.75 |
| 2. | Trade, hotel and restaurants | 9.11 | 9.5 | 8.68 | 8.77 |
| 3. | Banking and insurance | 2.86 | 2.54 | 3.76 | 3.92 |
| 4. | Real estate, ownership of dwelling and business services | 17.73 | 17.78 | 18.36 | 20.19 |
| 5. | Public administration | 16.15 | 16.18 | 17.97 | 16.48 |
| 6. | Other services | 16.18 | 14.6 | 13.14 | 13.03 |
| | | 63.07% | 61.66% | 63.12% | 63.14% |

*Source*: Statistical handbook of Mizoram 2003.

### *Developmental Score of the Sector*

These indicators are selected for measuring level of basic and infrastructure service development subject to the availability of reliable data.

1. Literacy rate (2001).
2. Percentage of urban population.
3. No. of Primary and Middle schools per 10,000 population.
4. No. of High schools and Higher Secondary schools per 10,000 population.
5. No. of Colleges per one lakh population.
6. Infant survival per 1,000 (= 1—Infant mortality rate).
7. No. of Hospitals/Dispensaries per 10,000 population.
8. No. of medical beds per 10,000 population.

9. Percentage of above poverty line families.
10. No. Telephone connection per population 100 population.
11. No. of Tourist accommodation like departmental rest house, I.B. hotel and tourist lodge/spot per 100 sq. km.
12. No. of Post offices per 10,000 population.
13. No. of Police stations (and Outpost) per 1000 sq. km.
14. Road length per 100 sq. km.
15. Road length per lakh population.
16. Credit-Deposit Ratio.
17. No. of bank (i.e. Branchs) for one lakh population.
18. No. of libraries per 10,000 population.

Based on these indicators, the developmental score of all districts in respect of basic and infrastructure services are determined. The outcome of the determination is present in the tables. From the Appendix Table 9.11 it can be concluded that, indexing method classified (in descending order) Kolasib, Saiha, Serchhip, Champhai, Mamit and Aizawl districts as relatively developed whereas Lunglei and Lawngtlai districts are less developed districts. A slightly different result emerges from deprivation method (from Appendix Table 9.12), which categorize (in ascending order) Champhai, Serchhip, Kolasib, and Mamit and Aizawl district as relatively developed and Saiha district, Lunglei district and Lawngtlai as less developed.

In Appendix Table 9.13, Principal component analysis suggests to retain only five principal components that explain 96.484 per cent of the total variation. From Appendix Table 9.14, we know that variable 1st, 8th, and 2nd are the most important than other that explain 98.1 per cent, 97.7 per cent, and 96.2 per cent respectively of the total variable's variance. As can be seen from Appendix Table 9.15, this approach categorize Aizawl district alone as 'Highly developed'. Lunglei, Kolasib, Champhai, and Serchhip as 'Relatively developed' while Mamit, Saiha and Lawngtlai district as 'Less developed'.

The conclusion that can be made regarding the level of basic and infrastructure service sector development is that Aizawl, Champhai, Kolasib and Serchhip districts are the leading districts since all methods place them under Highly/Relatively developed category. Lunglei district is placed under less developed by two methods and hence may be categorized as 'less developed district' while Lawngtlai district is categorized as 'less developed' by all three methods, hence the district may be described as 'Less developed district'.

SECTION 4

## Conclusion

If we combine all the variables of economic development and run Principal component analysis using SPSS software to extract only few important variables that are more important than others for economic development, we arrived to the following observations:

In Appendix Table 9.16 there are six components whose initial Eigenvalue is greater than unity and this suggestion retain only six indicators/variables to represent the original indicators/variables. These six components explain up to 97.89 per cent of the total variation and the last 29 components explain only 2.11 per cent of the total variation.

Within the first Principal component (i.e. from Appendix Table 9.17), there are nine variables whose factor loadings is relatively high; namely percentage of secondary workers to the total workforce, No. of Registered SSIs per 1,000 population, No. of LPG connection per house, percentage of urban population, No. of Primary and Middle school per 10,000 population, Infant survival rate, percentage of Above Poverty Line family, No. of phone per 100 population, Road length per 100 sq. km. Within the second Principal Component, there are two variables whose factor loadings are relatively high, namely women manage percentage of small-scale industry and percentage of female to the total employment. Within the third Principal Component, there are two indicators/factors whose factor loadings are relatively high; namely Productivity of Jhum in terms of metric tone per hectares and No. of Post offices per 10,000 persons. Within the fourth Principal Component, there are two variables whose factor loadings are relatively high; namely percentage of shown area to total geographical area and percentage of area under high yield variety and wet rice cultivation to total geographical area. Within the fifth Principal Component, there is one indicator/factor whose factor loadings is relatively high, i.e. Productivity of fish (in quintal) per fishpond and within the sixth Principal Component, there is one indicator/factor whose factor loadings is relatively high, i.e. No. of colleges per lakh population.

Among the above 17(seventeen) variables, some are merely the indicator of development and hence they have nothing to do with the process of economic development. There are 9(nine) variables that are important in bringing about economic development. From primary/agriculture and allied sector we have (1) Productivity of Jhum in terms of metric tone, (2) Sown area to total geographical area,

(3) Percentage of area under high yield variety and wet rice cultivation to total geographical area, (4) Productivity of fish in terms of quintal per fishpond. From Secondary/Industrial sector, we have (1) Women manage percentage of Small Scale Industry (2) Percentage of female to the total employment. From Tertiary/Basic and infrastructure service sector, we have (1) No. of Primary and Middle schools per 10,000 population, (2) No. of colleges per lakh population and (3) Road length per 100 sq. km.

What emerges from the above analysis is that agriculture and allied sector backed by good road communication is of utmost importance for achieving accelerated rate of economic development, and education sector is equally important along with women participation in industry related management.

Now, we have gone through all the analysis and categorization of districts according to their developmental score in Indexing, Deprivation and Principal component analysis. The next task is to make a comparison and concluding part in so far as the developmental status of all districts of Mizoram is concerned.

Now, to arrive at an ordinal conclusion, numerical value is arbitrarily assigned for various developmental statuses as less developed—0, Relatively Developed—1 and Highly Developed—2[18]. From Appendix Table 9.18, we have seen that Aizawl, the state capital of Mizoram stood at the top scoring point 9 in the ordinal scale, it is categorized as 'Highly Developed District'. Kolasib is at the second position scoring point 8 in the ordinal scale, Champhai at the third position scoring point 7 in the same scale; followed by Serchhip scoring 6 in the scale. These three districts may be called be categorized 'Relatively developed district'. Lunglei district score point 3 and may be categorized 'Less developed district' whereas Mamit, Saiha, and Lawngtlai district respectively score point 2, 2 and 1 so that they may be categorized as 'Least developed district' within the state of Mizoram.

While formulating budget Government of Mizoram must give top priority on those important factors of development (viz. agriculture, elementary and college education, road connectivity and women empowerment) which play a major role for economic growth to achieve a sustained and higher economic growth, and also give special consideration to those district which are lacking behind in respect of economic development to reduce regional economic imbalances. So that Mizoram will enjoy accelerated economic growth with the egalitarian socio-economic order as well as balanced development of the region simultaneously.

**NOTES**

1. Economic cell, Planning & Programme Implementation Department, *Economic Survey 2006-07* (Aizawl: Govt. of Mizoram, 2007) p. 1, 10.
2. J.V. Nunchunga, *A mathematical study on the income distribution and estimation of inequality with special reference to Mizoram*, (unpublished Ph.D. thesis, Mizoram University, 2007).
3. Charles P. Kindleberger and Bruce Herrick, *Economic Development* (New York: McGraw-Hill, 1977) p. 1.
4. Jagdish Bhagwati, *The Economics of Underdeveloped Countries* (London: World University Library, Weidenfield and Nicolson. 1971) p. 9.
5. A.K. Agarwala and P. Hazarika, *Developmental disparities, A Quantitative insight* (New Delhi: Akansha Publishing House, India. 2004), p.16.
6. The sources are *NE newsletter*, N.E. Division, Ministry of Home Affairs, New Delhi; *Village Level statistics of Mizoram*: 2003; Economics & Statistics Department, Aizawl; *State Domestic Product of Mizoram* (1993-94 to 2001-02; New series), Directorate of by Economics & Statistics, Government of Mizoram, *On all India third census of small-scale industries in respect of Mizoram*; Compiled and issued by Directorate of Industries Mizoram, Aizawl, Statistical Abstract; *Department of Agriculture & Minor Irrigation* Mizoram, Published by Directorate of Agriculture & Minor Irrigation, Mizoram, Aizawl, *Socio-Economic Review, Mizoram 2000-01*, Issued by Economics & Statistics, Government of Mizoram, Many more leaflets, Brochures and in formations obtain from various departments.
7. Rudder Datt and K.P.M. Sundharam, *Indian economy* (New Delhi: S. Chand & Company Ltd. 40th Revised Edition, 1999), p. 448.
8. Economic cell, Planning & Programme Implementation Department, *op. cit.* pp. 20, 21, 24, 25.
9. J.V. Nunchunga, *op. cit.*
10. A land whose slope less is than 100 per cent is suitable and termed as cultivable land.
11. The total Paddy/Rice production within the district is assumed to be consumed up in the district itself.
12. The total no. of cattle, Buffaloes, Mithun, Sheep, Goats, Mules, Horses, Pigs, Fowl, Ducks, Turkey, others are taken as total Livestock of the state.
13. Directorate of Economics & Statistics; *Socio-economics Review Mizoram 2000-01* (Aizawl: Govt. of Mizoram, 2002), p.11.
14. Economic Survey 2006-07, *op. cit.*, p. 35, 36.
15. J.V. Nunchunga, *op. cit.*
16. J.V. Nunchunga, *op. cit.*
17. Economic Survey 2006-07, *op. cit.* pp.9, 28, 29.
18. J.V. Nunchunga, *op. cit.*

# Appendices

**Table 9.1:** Level of Agricultural and Allied Sector Development (Using Indexing Method)

| *Name of Districts* | *Area (in Sq.Km)* | *% of cultivable land to total area* | *Combine Productivity of Paddy, Oil-seeds & Pulse* | *% of Shown area to total area* | *Productivity of Jhum (MT/Ha)* | *Productivity of WRC (MT/Ha)* | *% of area under HYV and WRC to total area* | *Productivity of WRC (MT/Ha)* | *% of area under HYV and WRC to total area* | *Food availability (MT per person)* | *Production of fish(in qlts) per Ha* | *No. of livestock per person* | *Total Index* | *Average index Value* | *Status* |
|---|---|---|---|---|---|---|---|---|---|---|---|---|---|---|---|
| Aizawl | 3576.31 | 51.38 | 1.472 | 3.41 | 0.76 | 1.94 | 0.61 | 1.94 | 0.61 | 0.05 | 9.09 | 1.1 | 69.80 | | |
| | | ***104.44*** | ***97.42*** | ***107.30*** | ***121.6*** | ***87.99*** | ***38.28*** | ***87.99*** | ***38.28*** | ***38.55*** | ***62.56*** | ***70.06*** | ***728.21*** | ***80.91*** | ***D*** |
| Champhai | 3185.83 | 50.73 | 1.366 | 3.76 | 0.59 | 2.22 | 3.35 | 2.22 | 3.35 | 0.22 | 75.42 | 2.37 | 140.04 | | |
| | | ***103.12*** | ***90.40*** | ***118.59*** | ***94.40*** | ***100.94*** | ***211.88*** | ***100.9*** | ***211.88*** | ***173.9*** | ***519.06*** | ***150.9*** | ***1563.2*** | ***173.7*** | ***RD*** |
| Serchhip | 1421.6 | 49.54 | 1.06 | 3.59 | 0.59 | 1.80 | 1.52 | 1.80 | 1.52 | 0.13 | 79.98 | 1.78 | 140.00 | | |
| | | ***100.70*** | ***70.15*** | ***113.20*** | ***94.61*** | ***81.78*** | ***95.96*** | ***81.78*** | ***95.96*** | ***104.5*** | ***550.45*** | ***113.3*** | ***1324.7*** | ***147.1*** | ***RD*** |
| Kolasib | 1382.51 | 56.25 | 2.065 | 7.46 | 0.88 | 2.45 | 8.31 | 2.45 | 8.31 | 0.32 | 2.8 | 1.95 | 82.48 | | |
| | | ***114.34*** | ***136.66*** | ***235.09*** | ***139.8*** | ***111.29*** | ***524.95*** | ***111.2*** | ***524.95*** | ***253.9*** | ***19.27*** | ***124.2*** | ***1659.5*** | ***184.4*** | ***RD*** |
| Mamit | 3025.75 | 50.85 | 1.451 | 2.36 | 0.55 | 2.29 | 0.94 | 2.29 | 0.94 | 0.19 | 4.22 | 2.2 | 65.06 | | |
| | | ***103.36*** | ***96.03*** | ***74.50*** | ***87.60*** | ***104.03*** | ***59.32*** | ***104.0*** | ***59.32*** | ***154.9*** | ***29.04*** | ***140.1*** | ***848.94*** | ***94.33*** | ***D*** |
| Lunglei | 4538 | 56.02 | 1.534 | 2.06 | 0.59 | 2.20 | 0.29 | 2.20 | 0.29 | 0.11 | 14.53 | 1.52 | 78.86 | | |
| | | ***113.87*** | ***101.52*** | ***64.91*** | ***94.06*** | ***99.98*** | ***18.19*** | ***99.98*** | ***18.19*** | ***89.98*** | ***100.00*** | ***96.82*** | ***779.35*** | ***86.59*** | ***D*** |
| Lawngtlai | 2557.1 | 50.93 | 1.131 | 2.40 | 0.83 | 2.17 | 0.84 | 2.17 | 0.84 | 0.11 | 5.76 | 1.02 | 65.20 | | |
| | | ***103.52*** | ***74.85*** | ***75.69*** | ***132.7*** | ***98.79*** | ***53.32*** | ***98.79*** | ***53.32*** | ***87.60*** | ***39.64*** | ***64.97*** | ***731.17*** | ***81.24*** | ***D*** |
| Saiha | 1399.9 | 27.87 | 1.477 | 3.35 | 0.40 | 2.06 | 0.41 | 2.06 | 0.41 | 0.18 | 36.65 | 2.45 | 74.85 | | |
| | | ***56.65*** | ***97.75*** | ***105.49*** | ***63.51*** | ***93.78*** | ***26.15*** | ***93.78*** | ***26.15*** | ***143.1*** | ***252.24*** | ***156.0*** | ***994.77*** | ***110.5*** | ***RD*** |
| Mizoram | 21087 | 49.20 | 1.511 | 3.174 | 0.626 | 2.2011 | 1.583 | 2.201 | 1.583 | 0.125 | 14.53 | 1.57 | 74.52 | | RD |

(Figure in **Bold** *Italics* indicates Index value for a particular indicator.)

**Table 9.2:** Level of Agricultural and Allied Sector Development (Using Deprivation Method)

| Sl.No. | Name of Districts | Area (in sq. km) | Percentage of shown area to total area | % of cultivable land to total area | Combine Productivity of Paddy, Oilseeds & Pulse | Productivity of Jhum (MT/Ha) | Productivity of WRCs(MT/Ha) | % of area under HYV and WRC to total area | Food availability (MT per person) | Productivity of fish(in Qlts) per Ha | No. of livestock per person | Total index | EDI (=1- Average index) | Status |
|---|---|---|---|---|---|---|---|---|---|---|---|---|---|---|
| 1. | Aizawl | 3576.3 | 3.406 | 51.38 | 1.472 | 0.762 | 1.937 | 0.606 | 0.049 | 9.09 | 1.1 | | | |
| | | | ***0.751*** | ***0.17*** | ***0.55*** | ***0.238*** | ***0.789*** | ***0.960*** | ***1.000*** | ***0.92*** | ***0.94*** | ***6.323*** | ***0.30*** | ***LD*** |
| 2. | Champhai | 3185.8 | 3.764 | 50.73 | 1.366 | 0.592 | 2.222 | 3.354 | 0.219 | 75.42 | 2.37 | | | |
| | | | ***0.685*** | ***0.19*** | ***0.599*** | ***0.595*** | ***0.351*** | ***0.618*** | ***0.372*** | ***0.06*** | ***0.05*** | ***3.528*** | ***0.61*** | ***RD*** |
| 3. | Serchhip | 1421.6 | 3.593 | 49.54 | 1.06 | 0.593 | 1.800 | 1.519 | 0.132 | 79.98 | 1.78 | | | |
| | | | ***0.716*** | ***0.24*** | ***0.964*** | ***0.592*** | ***1.000*** | ***0.847*** | ***0.694*** | ***0.00*** | ***0.46*** | ***5.518*** | ***0.39*** | ***LD*** |
| 4. | Kolasib | 1382.5 | 7.462 | 56.25 | 2.065 | 0.876 | 2.450 | 8.310 | 0.320 | 2.8 | 1.95 | | | |
| | | | ***0.000*** | ***0.00*** | ***0*** | ***0.000*** | ***0.000*** | ***0.000*** | ***0.000*** | ***1.00*** | ***0.3*** | ***1.350*** | ***0.85*** | ***HD*** |
| 5. | Mamit | 3025.7 | 2.365 | 50.85 | 1.451 | 0.549 | 2.290 | 0.939 | 0.195 | 4.22 | 2.2 | | | |
| | | | ***0.944*** | ***0.19*** | ***0.532*** | ***0.684*** | ***0.246*** | ***0.919*** | ***0.460*** | ***0.98*** | ***0.17*** | ***5.131*** | ***0.43*** | ***LD*** |
| 6. | Lunglei | 4538 | 2.060 | 56.02 | 1.534 | 0.590 | 2.201 | 0.288 | 0.113 | 14.53 | 1.52 | | | |
| | | | ***1.000*** | ***0.01*** | ***0.463*** | ***0.599*** | ***0.383*** | ***1.000*** | ***0.761*** | ***0.85*** | ***0.65*** | ***5.713*** | ***0.37*** | ***LD*** |
| 7. | Lawngtlai | 2557.1 | 2.402 | 50.93 | 1.131 | 0.832 | 2.174 | 0.844 | 0.110 | 5.76 | 1.02 | | | |
| | | | ***0.937*** | ***0.19*** | ***0.801*** | ***0.092*** | ***0.424*** | ***0.931*** | ***0.772*** | ***0.96*** | ***1*** | ***6.105*** | ***0.32*** | ***LD*** |
| 8. | Saiha | 1399.9 | 3.348 | 27.87 | 1.477 | 0.398 | 2.064 | 0.414 | 0.180 | 36.65 | 2.45 | | | |
| | | | ***0.762*** | ***1.00*** | ***0.563*** | ***1.000*** | ***0.593*** | ***0.984*** | ***0.514*** | ***0.56*** | ***0*** | ***5.978*** | ***0.34*** | ***LD*** |
| | Mizoram | 21087 | 3.174 | 49.20 | 1.511 | 0.627 | 2.201 | 1.583 | 0.126 | 14.53 | 1.57 | | | |
| | | | ***0.794*** | ***0.25*** | ***0.47*** | ***0.522*** | ***0.383*** | ***0.839*** | ***0.715*** | ***0.848*** | ***0.61*** | ***5.433*** | ***0.40*** | ***LD*** |

(Figure in **Bold** *Italics* indicates Deprivation value for a particular indicator.)

**Table 9.3:** Level of Agricultural and Allied Sector Development using Principal Component Analysis

| Component | Initial Eigen values | | | Extraction Sums of Squared Loadings | | | Rotation Sums of Squared Loadings | | |
|---|---|---|---|---|---|---|---|---|---|
| | Total | % of Variance | Cumulative % | Total | % of Variance | Cumulative % | Total | % of Variance | Cumulative % |
| 1. | 4.246 | 47.172 | 47.172 | 4.246 | 47.172 | 47.172 | 3.705 | 41.171 | 41.171 |
| 2. | 2.538 | 28.196 | 75.369 | 2.538 | 28.196 | 75.369 | 2.411 | 26.790 | 67.961 |
| 3. | 1.200 | 13.330 | 88.699 | 1.200 | 13.330 | 88.699 | 1.866 | 20.738 | 88.699 |
| 4. | .647 | 7.189 | 95.888 | | | | | | |
| 5. | .278 | 3.094 | 98.982 | | | | | | |
| 6. | .069 | .766 | 99.748 | | | | | | |
| 7. | .017 | .194 | 99.942 | | | | | | |
| 8. | .005 | .058 | 100.000 | | | | | | |
| 9. | .000 | .000 | 100.000 | | | | | | |

**Table 9.4:** Level of Agricultural and Allied Sector Development Using Principal Component Analysis

*Rotated Component Matrix (A)*

| | Component | | |
|---|---|---|---|
| | *1* | 2 | *3* |
| Shown sq.km | .912 | .215 | .025 |
| Cultivable | .178 | .786 | .110 |
| Productivity | .654 | .044 | .637 |
| Jhum | .272 | .911 | .177 |
| WRC | .533 | .014 | .740 |
| WRCHYV | .955 | .266 | .107 |
| Food | .922 | -.239 | .190 |
| Fish | .152 | -.327 | -.902 |
| Livestock | .520 | -.824 | -.079 |

**Table 9.5:** Level of Agricultural and Allied Sector Development using Principal Component Analysis

*Factor Score*

| *Sl. No.* | *Districts* | *Fac1_1* | *Fac2_1* | *Fac3_1* | *Total* | *Status* |
|---|---|---|---|---|---|---|
| 1. | Aizawl | -0.81903 | 1.0483 | -0.07906 | 0.15021 | RD |
| 2. | Champhai | 0.86083 | -0.49482 | -0.97696 | -0.61095 | LD |
| 3. | Serchhip | -0.00014 | 0.19584 | -2.17397 | -1.97827 | LD |
| 4. | Kolasib | 2.26742 | 0.80534 | 0.80948 | 3.88224 | HD |
| 5. | Mamit | -0.24612 | -0.745 | 0.96414 | -0.02698 | LD |
| 6. | Lunglei | -0.71353 | 0.13515 | 0.6618 | 0.08342 | RD |
| 7. | Lawngtlai | -0.85947 | 1.06842 | 0.19323 | 0.40218 | RD |
| 8. | Saiha | -0.14866 | -2.06206 | 0.1107 | -2.10002 | LD |
| | Mizoram | -0.34131 | 0.04882 | 0.49065 | 0.19816 | RD |

**Table 9.6:** Level of Industry and Allied Sector Development (Using Indexing Method)

| *Sl. No.* | *Name of Districts* | *% of secondary workers to the total workforce* | *No. of Registered SSI's per 1,000 population* | *Women manage % of SSI* | *% of female to the total employment* | *% of SSI's unit that used electricity* | *% of electrified houses* | *No. of Water point per 1000 population* | *No. of LPG connection per house* | *Index total* | *Index average Value* | *Category* |
|---|---|---|---|---|---|---|---|---|---|---|---|---|
| 1. | Aizawl | 4.04 | 5.97 | 26.39 | 24.83 | 56.52 | 93.96 | 60.60 | 1.8 | 274.11 | | |
| | | ***210.42*** | ***195.74*** | ***98.80*** | ***102.86*** | ***104.5*** | ***125.13*** | ***171.14*** | ***189.47*** | ***1198.15*** | ***149.77*** | ***RD*** |
| 2. | Champhai | 0.74 | 1.78 | 24.44 | 18.32 | 56.38 | 72.23 | 15.94 | 0.45 | 190.28 | | |
| | | ***38.54*** | ***58.36*** | ***91.50*** | ***75.89*** | ***104.3*** | ***96.19*** | ***45.02*** | ***47.37*** | ***557.20*** | ***69.65*** | ***LD*** |
| 3. | Serchhip | 0.49 | 1.31 | 20.55 | 18.93 | 43.08 | 74.23 | 19.27 | 0.59 | 178.45 | | |
| | | ***25.52*** | ***42.95*** | ***76.94*** | ***78.42*** | ***79.72*** | ***98.85*** | ***54.42*** | ***62.11*** | ***518.93*** | ***64.87*** | ***LD*** |
| 4. | Kolasib | 1.11 | 1.85 | 25.66 | 23.67 | 61.96 | 81.32 | 3.51 | 0.56 | 199.64 | | |
| | | ***57.81*** | ***60.66*** | ***96.07*** | ***98.05*** | ***114.6*** | ***108.30*** | ***9.91*** | ***58.95*** | ***604.40*** | ***75.55*** | ***LD*** |
| 5. | Mamit | 0.29 | 0.58 | 27.78 | 17.48 | 58.36 | 64.27 | 6.90 | 0.08 | 175.74 | | |
| | | ***15.10*** | ***19.02*** | ***104.01*** | ***72.41*** | ***107.9*** | ***85.59*** | ***19.49*** | ***8.42*** | ***432.03*** | ***54.00*** | ***LD*** |
| 6. | Lunglei | 0.76 | 1.18 | 26.54 | 17.80 | 46.95 | 73.26 | 36.89 | 0.73 | 204.11 | | |
| | | ***39.58*** | ***38.69*** | ***99.36*** | ***73.74*** | ***86.88*** | ***97.56*** | ***104.18*** | ***76.84*** | ***616.84*** | ***77.10*** | ***LD*** |
| 7. | Lawngtlai | 0.38 | 0.53 | 38.46 | 37.05 | 10.25 | 31.22 | 16.55 | 0.18 | 134.62 | | |
| | | ***19.79*** | ***17.38*** | ***143.99*** | ***153.48*** | ***18.97*** | ***41.58*** | ***46.74*** | ***18.95*** | ***460.87*** | ***57.61*** | ***LD*** |
| 8. | Saiha | 1.09 | 1.45 | 39.77 | 28.91 | 21.59 | 52.13 | 22.39 | 0.75 | 168.08 | | |
| | | ***56.77*** | ***47.54*** | ***148.90*** | ***119.76*** | ***39.95*** | ***69.42*** | ***63.23*** | ***78.95*** | ***624.52*** | ***78.07*** | ***LD*** |
| | Mizoram | 1.92 | 3.05 | 26.71 | 24.14 | 54.04 | 75.09 | 35.41 | 0.95 | 221.31 | | RD |

(Letters in the **Bold** *Italics* indicates Index value.)

**Table 9.7:** Level of Industry and Allied Sector Development (Using Deprivation Method)

| *Sl. No.* | *Name of Districts* | *% of secondary workers to the total workforce* | *No. of registered SSI's per 1,000 population* | *Women manage % of SSI* | *% of female to the total employment* | *% of SSI's unit that used electricity* | *% of Electrified houses* | *No. of Water point per 1000 population* | *No. of LPG connection per house* | *Total Index* | *EDI* | *Category* |
|---|---|---|---|---|---|---|---|---|---|---|---|---|
| 1. | Aizawl | 4.04<br>***0*** | 5.97<br>***0*** | 26.39<br>***0.70*** | 24.83<br>***0.62*** | 56.52<br>***0.11*** | 93.96<br>***0.00*** | 60.60<br>***0.00*** | 1.8<br>***0.00*** | 274.11<br>***1.43*** | ***0.82*** | ***HD*** |
| 2. | Champhai | 0.74<br>***0.00*** | 1.78<br>***0.77*** | 24.44<br>***0.80*** | 18.32<br>***0.96*** | 56.38<br>***0.11*** | 72.23<br>***0.35*** | 15.94<br>***0.78*** | 0.45<br>***0.78*** | 190.28<br>***4.55*** | ***0.43*** | ***LD*** |
| 3. | Serchhip | 0.49<br>***0.95*** | 1.31<br>***0.86*** | 20.55<br>***1.00*** | 18.93<br>***0.93*** | 43.08<br>***0.37*** | 74.23<br>***0.31*** | 19.27<br>***0.72*** | 0.59<br>***0.70*** | 178.45<br>***5.84*** | ***0.27*** | ***LD*** |
| 4. | Kolasib | 1.11<br>***0.78*** | 1.85<br>***0.76*** | 25.66<br>***0.73*** | 23.67<br>***0.68*** | 61.96<br>***0.00*** | 81.32<br>***0.20*** | 3.51<br>***1.00*** | 0.56<br>***0.72*** | 199.64<br>***4.88*** | ***0.39*** | ***LD*** |
| 5. | Mamit | 0.29<br>***1.00*** | 0.58<br>***0.99*** | 27.78<br>***0.62*** | 17.48<br>***1.00*** | 58.36<br>***0.07*** | 64.27<br>***0.47*** | 6.90<br>***0.94*** | 0.08<br>***1.00*** | 175.74<br>***6.10*** | ***0.24*** | ***LD*** |
| 6. | Lunglei | 0.76<br>***0.87*** | 1.18<br>***0.88*** | 26.54<br>***0.69*** | 17.80<br>***0.98*** | 46.95<br>***0.29*** | 73.26<br>***0.33*** | 36.89<br>***0.42*** | 0.73<br>***0.62*** | 204.11<br>***5.08*** | ***0.36*** | ***LD*** |
| 7. | Lawngtlai | 0.38<br>***0.98*** | 0.53<br>***1.00*** | 38.46<br>***0.07*** | 37.05<br>***0.00*** | 10.25<br>***1.00*** | 31.22<br>***1.00*** | 16.55<br>***0.77*** | 0.18<br>***0.94*** | 134.62<br>***5.76*** | ***0.28*** | ***LD*** |
| 8. | Saiha | 1.09<br>***0.79*** | 1.45<br>***0.83*** | 39.77<br>***0.00*** | 28.91<br>***0.42*** | 21.59<br>***0.78*** | 52.13<br>***0.67*** | 22.39<br>***0.67*** | 0.75<br>***0.61*** | 168.08<br>***4.76*** | ***0.40*** | ***LD*** |
| | Mizoram | 1.92<br>***3.75*** | 3.05<br>***5.44*** | 26.71<br>***19.22*** | 24.14<br>***19.57*** | 54.04<br>***51.71*** | 75.09<br>***0.30*** | 35.41<br>***0.44*** | 0.95<br>***0.49*** | 221.31<br>***100.93*** | ***0.46*** | ***LD*** |

(Letters in the **Bold** *Italics* indicates Deprivation value.)

**Table 9.8:** Level of Secondary/Industry and allied Sector development (Using Principal Component Analysis)

*Total Variance Explained*

| Component | Initial Eigen values | | | Extraction Sums of Squared Loadings | | | Rotation Sums of Squared Loadings | | |
|---|---|---|---|---|---|---|---|---|---|
| | *Total* | *% of Variance* | *Cumulative %* | *Total* | *% of Variance* | *Cumulative %* | *Total* | *% of Variance* | *Cumulative %* |
| 1. | 4.664 | 58.301 | 58.301 | 4.664 | 58.301 | 58.301 | 4.032 | 50.402 | 50.402 |
| 2. | 2.668 | 33.345 | 91.646 | 2.668 | 33.345 | 91.646 | 3.300 | 41.244 | 91.646 |
| 3. | .373 | 4.659 | 96.305 | | | | | | |
| 4. | .181 | 2.258 | 98.563 | | | | | | |
| 5. | .083 | 1.040 | 99.603 | | | | | | |
| 6. | .028 | .354 | 99.957 | | | | | | |
| 7. | .003 | .035 | 99.992 | | | | | | |
| 8. | .001 | .008 | 100.000 | | | | | | |

*Extraction Method*: Principal Component Analysis.

**Table 9.9:** Level of Secondary/Industry and allied Sector Development (Using Principal Component Analysis)

*Rotated Component Matris (A)*

| | Component | |
|---|---|---|
| | *1* | 2 |
| Secondary | .981 | .082 |
| SSI | .962 | .194 |
| Women | -.074 | -.933 |
| Female | .145 | -.922 |
| Electric | .187 | .927 |
| Electrified | .554 | .814 |
| Water | .906 | -.018 |
| LPG | .977 | .121 |

**Table 9.10:** Level of Secondary/Industry and allied Sector Development (Using Principal Component Analysis)

| *Districts* | *Fac1_1* | *Fac2_1* | *Total* | *Status* |
|---|---|---|---|---|
| Aizawl | 2.361 | 0.158 | 2.52 | HD |
| Champhai | -0.46 | 0.722 | 0.25 | RD |
| Serchhip | -0.466 | 0.675 | 0.20 | RD |
| Kolasib | -0.353 | 0.638 | 0.285 | RD |
| Mamit | -1.069 | 0.62 | -0.44 | LD |
| Lunglei | -0.096 | 0.40 | 0.311 | RD |
| Lawngtlai | -0.57 | -2.03 | -2.60 | LD |
| Saiha | 0.040 | -1.36 | -1.321 | LD |
| Mizoram | 0.619 | 0.16665 | 0.78 | RD |

**Table 9.11:** Level of Basic and Infrastucture Sector Development (Using Indexing Method)

| Sl. No. | Name of Districts | X1<br>Literacy rate('01) | X2<br>% of urban population | X3<br>No. of Primary and M/s per 10,000 population | X4<br>No. of H/S and HSS per 10,000 population | X5<br>No. of colleges per lakh population | X6<br>Infant survival per 1,000 (=1-IMR) | X7<br>No. of Hospital/ Dispensary per 10,000 population | X8<br>No. of medical beds per 10,000 population. | X9<br>% of APL family (=100-BPL) | X10<br>No. of phone per 100 population | X11<br>No. of tourist accommodation per 100sq. km |
|---|---|---|---|---|---|---|---|---|---|---|---|---|
| 1. | Aizawl | 96.64 | 73.23 | 253.67 | 66.21 | 3.24 | 0.49 | 37.67 | 148.61 | 67.09 | 14.94 | 2.91 |
| | | ***109.21*** | ***148.09*** | ***80.47*** | ***105.55*** | ***115.30*** | ***79.52*** | ***72.34*** | ***84.67*** | ***134.02*** | ***158.43*** | ***117.81*** |
| 2. | Champhai | 91.88 | 28.03 | 353.1 | 68.05 | 2.96 | 0.71 | 60.16 | 226.85 | 49.02 | 4.67 | 2.13 |
| | | ***103.83*** | ***56.68*** | ***112.01*** | ***108.48*** | ***105.34*** | ***115.22*** | ***115.54*** | ***129.24*** | ***97.92*** | ***49.52*** | ***86.23*** |
| 3. | Serchhip | 96.16 | 52.59 | 340.3 | 68.42 | 1.8 | 0.77 | 66.62 | 183.65 | 37.09 | 7.77 | 3.31 |
| | | ***108.67*** | ***106.35*** | ***107.95*** | ***109.07*** | ***64.06*** | ***124.96*** | ***127.94*** | ***104.63*** | ***74.09*** | ***82.40*** | ***134.01*** |
| 4. | Kolasib | 90.45 | 59.32 | 283.71 | 42.64 | 3.28 | 0.62 | 36.08 | 190.24 | 48.40 | 8.9 | 5.64 |
| | | ***102.21*** | ***119.96*** | ***90.00*** | ***67.97*** | ***116.73*** | ***100.62*** | ***69.29*** | ***108.39*** | ***96.68*** | ***94.38*** | ***228.34*** |
| 5. | Mamit | 80.09 | 17.34 | 385.15 | 51.35 | 3.21 | 0.78 | 85.05 | 240.72 | 37.11 | 5.14 | 2.08 |
| | | ***90.51*** | ***35.07*** | ***122.18*** | ***81.86*** | ***114.23*** | ***126.58*** | ***163.34*** | ***137.15*** | ***74.13*** | ***54.51*** | ***84.21*** |
| 6. | Lunglei | 84.20 | 42.40 | 336.85 | 69.26 | 2.19 | 0.64 | 67.08 | 189.57 | 34.94 | 7.37 | 2.07 |
| | | ***95.15*** | ***85.74*** | ***106.86*** | ***110.41*** | ***77.94*** | ***103.86*** | ***128.83*** | ***108.00*** | ***69.80*** | ***78.15*** | ***83.81*** |
| 7. | Lawngtlai | 56.46 | 12.71 | 468.17 | 43.81 | 2.74 | 0.82 | 38.33 | 82.14 | 28.96 | 2.79 | 1.37 |
| | | ***63.80*** | ***25.70*** | ***148.51*** | ***69.84*** | ***97.51*** | ***133.08*** | ***73.61*** | ***46.80*** | ***57.85*** | ***29.59*** | ***55.47*** |
| 8. | Saiha | 82.43 | 32.44 | 300.87 | 69.05 | 1.64 | 0.57 | 70.70 | 231.82 | 40.42 | 5.6 | 2.21 |
| | | ***93.15*** | ***65.60*** | ***95.44*** | ***110.07*** | ***58.36*** | ***92.50*** | ***135.78*** | ***132.08*** | ***80.74*** | ***59.38*** | ***89.47*** |
| | Mizoram | 88.49 | 49.45 | 315.24 | 62.73 | 2.81 | 0.62 | 52.07 | 175.52 | 50.06 | 9.43 | 2.47 |
| | | 100 | 100 | 100 | 100 | 100 | 100 | 100 | 100 | 100 | 100 | 100 |

*(Contd.)*

**Table 9.11** (*Contd.*)

| | X12 | X13 | X14 | X15 | x16 | x17 | X18 | | | |
|---|---|---|---|---|---|---|---|---|---|---|
| | *No. of Post office per 10,000 population* | *No. of PS+ Outpost per 1000Sq.km* | *Road length per 100Sq. km* | *Road length per lakh population* | *Credit-Deposit Ratio* | *No. of banks for 1 lakh population* | *No. of Lib. for 10,000 population.* | *Total Index* | *Average Index* | *Category* |
| 1. Aizawl | 3.18 | 2.8 | 35.03 | 368.65 | 21.00 | 9.42 | 4.89 | | | |
| | ***64.50*** | ***128.44*** | ***166.10*** | ***73.86*** | ***76.98*** | ***91.28*** | ***102.95*** | **1909.52** | ***106.08*** | ***RD Aizawl*** |
| 2. Champhai | 6.02 | 1.26 | 26.9 | 845.38 | 33.88 | 9.86 | 8.48 | | | |
| | ***122.11*** | ***57.80*** | ***127.55*** | ***169.36*** | ***124.19*** | ***95.54*** | ***178.53*** | **1955.11** | ***108.62*** | ***RD Champhai*** |
| 3. Serchhip | 4.86 | 2.11 | 20.55 | 526.01 | 45.46 | 16.2 | 7.74 | | | |
| | ***98.58*** | ***96.79*** | ***97.44*** | ***105.38*** | ***166.64*** | ***156.98*** | ***162.95*** | **2028.88** | ***112.72*** | ***RD Serchhip*** |
| 4. Kolosib | 3.61 | 3.62 | 26.78 | 607.08 | 30.43 | 16.4 | 4.59 | | | |
| | ***73.23*** | ***166.06*** | ***126.98*** | ***121.62*** | ***111.55*** | ***158.91*** | ***96.63*** | **2049.55** | ***113.86*** | ***RD Kolasib*** |
| 5. Mamit | 6.26 | 1.98 | 17.12 | 831.29 | 37.88 | 14.44 | 5.3 | | | |
| | ***126.98*** | ***90.83*** | ***81.18*** | ***166.54*** | ***138.86*** | ***139.92*** | ***111.58*** | **1939.64** | ***107.76*** | ***RD Mamit*** |
| 6. Lunglei | 5.25 | 1.76 | 13.96 | 462.03 | 40.14 | 9.48 | 3.94 | | | |
| | ***106.49*** | ***80.73*** | ***66.19*** | ***92.56*** | ***147.14*** | ***91.86*** | ***82.95*** | **1716.48** | ***95.36*** | ***D Lunglei*** |
| 7. Lawngtlai | 3.15 | 1.56 | 10.44 | 365.6 | 42.91 | 5.48 | 0.82 | | | |
| | ***63.89*** | ***71.56*** | ***49.50*** | ***73.24*** | ***157.29*** | ***53.10*** | ***17.26*** | **1287.62** | ***71.53*** | ***D Lawngtlai*** |
| 8. Saiha | 14.30 | 4.29 | 18.34 | 422.21 | 71.70 | 8.22 | 1.15 | | | |
| | ***290.06*** | ***196.79*** | ***86.96*** | ***84.59*** | ***262.83*** | ***79.65*** | ***24.21*** | **2037.68** | ***113.20*** | ***RD Saiha*** |
| Mizoram | 4.93 | 2.18 | 21.09 | 499.15 | 27.28 | 10.32 | 4.75 | | | |
| | 100 | 100 | 100 | 100 | 100.00 | 100 | 100 | 1800.00 | 100.00 | Mizoram |

(Letters in the **Bold *Italics*** indicates Index value.)

**Table 9.12:** Level of Basic and Infrastructure Service Sector Development (Using Deprivation Method)

| Sl. No. | Name of Districts | X1 Literacy rate('01) | X2 % of urban population | X3 No. of Elementary School per 10,000 population | X4 No. of H/S and HSS per 10,000 population | X5 No. of colleges per lakh population | X6 Infant survival per 1,000 (=1-IMR) | X7 No. of Hospital/Dispensary per 10,000 population | X8 No. of medical beds per 10,000 population | X9 % of APL family (= 100-BPL) | X10 No. of phone per 100 population | X11 No. of tourist accommodation per 100sq. km |
|---|---|---|---|---|---|---|---|---|---|---|---|---|
| 1. | Aizawl | 96.6 | 73.2 | 253.7 | 66.2 | 3.2 | 0.5 | 37.7 | 148.6 | 67.1 | 14.9 | 2.9 |
| | | ***0.0*** | ***0.0*** | ***1.0*** | ***0.1*** | ***0.0*** | ***1.0*** | ***1.0*** | ***0.6*** | ***0.0*** | ***0.0*** | ***0.6*** |
| 2. | Champhai | 91.9 | 28.0 | 353.1 | 68.1 | 3.0 | 0.7 | 60.2 | 226.9 | 49.0 | 4.7 | 2.1 |
| | | ***0.1*** | ***0.7*** | ***0.5*** | ***0.0*** | ***0.2*** | ***0.3*** | ***0.5*** | ***0.1*** | ***0.5*** | ***0.8*** | ***0.8*** |
| 3. | Serchhip | 96.2 | 52.6 | 340.3 | 68.4 | 1.8 | 0.8 | 66.6 | 183.7 | 37.1 | 7.8 | 3.3 |
| | | ***0.0*** | ***0.3*** | ***0.6*** | ***0.0*** | ***0.9*** | ***0.2*** | ***0.4*** | ***0.4*** | ***0.8*** | ***0.6*** | ***0.5*** |
| 4. | Kolasib | 90.5 | 59.3 | 283.7 | 42.6 | 3.3 | 0.6 | 36.1 | 190.2 | 48.4 | 8.9 | 5.6 |
| | | ***0.2*** | ***0.2*** | ***0.9*** | ***1.0*** | ***0.0*** | ***0.6*** | ***1.0*** | ***0.3*** | ***0.5*** | ***0.5*** | ***0.0*** |
| 5. | Mamit | 80.1 | 17.3 | 385.2 | 51.4 | 3.2 | 0.8 | 85.1 | 240.7 | 37.1 | 5.1 | 2.1 |
| | | ***0.4*** | ***0.9*** | ***0.4*** | ***0.7*** | ***0.0*** | ***0.1*** | ***0.0*** | ***0.0*** | ***0.8*** | ***0.8*** | ***0.8*** |
| 6. | Lunglei | 84.2 | 42.4 | 336.9 | 69.3 | 2.2 | 0.6 | 67.1 | 189.6 | 34.9 | 7.4 | 2.1 |
| | | ***0.3*** | ***0.5*** | ***0.6*** | ***0.0*** | ***0.7*** | ***0.5*** | ***0.4*** | ***0.3*** | ***0.8*** | ***0.6*** | ***0.8*** |
| 7. | Lawngtlai | 56.5 | 12.7 | 468.2 | 43.8 | 2.7 | 0.8 | 38.3 | 82.1 | 29.0 | 2.8 | 1.4 |
| | | ***1.0*** | ***1.0*** | ***0.0*** | ***1.0*** | ***0.3*** | ***0.0*** | ***1.0*** | ***1.0*** | ***1.0*** | ***1.0*** | ***1.0*** |
| 8. | Saiha | 82.4 | 32.4 | 300.9 | 69.1 | 1.6 | 0.6 | 70.7 | 231.8 | 40.4 | 5.6 | 2.2 |
| | | ***0.4*** | ***0.7*** | ***0.8*** | ***0.0*** | ***1.0*** | ***0.8*** | ***0.3*** | ***0.1*** | ***0.7*** | ***0.8*** | ***0.8*** |
| | Mizoram | 88.5 | 49.5 | 315.2 | 62.7 | 2.8 | 0.6 | 52.1 | 175.5 | 50.1 | 9.4 | 2.5 |
| | | 0.2 | 0.4 | 0.7 | 0.2 | 0.3 | 0.6 | 0.7 | 0.4 | 0.4 | 0.5 | 0.7 |

*(Contd.)*

Table 9.12 (*Contd.*)

| Sl. No. | Name of Districts | X12 No. of Post office per 10,000 population. | X13 No. of P.S + Outpost per 1000Sq.km | X14 Road length per 100Sq.Km. | X15 Road length per lakh population | x16 Credit-Deposit Ratio | x17 No. of banks for 1 lakh population | X18 No. of Lib. for 10,000 population | Overall EDI | EDI | |
|---|---|---|---|---|---|---|---|---|---|---|---|
| 1. | Aizawl | 3.2 | 2.8 | 35.0 | 368.7 | 21.0 | 9.7 | 4.9 | | | |
| | | 1.0 | 0.5 | 0.0 | 1.0 | 1.0 | 0.5 | 0.5 | ***9.2*** | **0.51** | **RD** |
| 2. | Champhai | 6.0 | 1.3 | 26.9 | 845.4 | 33.9 | 9.9 | 8.5 | | | |
| | | 0.7 | 1.0 | 0.3 | 0.0 | 0.7 | 0.5 | 0.0 | ***9.9*** | **0.55** | **RD** |
| 3. | Serchhip | 4.9 | 2.1 | 20.6 | 526.0 | 45.5 | 16.2 | 7.7 | | | |
| | | 0.8 | 0.7 | 0.6 | 0.7 | 0.5 | 0.0 | 0.1 | ***9.9*** | **0.55** | **RD** |
| 4. | Kolasib | 3.6 | 3.6 | 26.8 | 607.1 | 30.4 | 16.4 | 4.6 | | | |
| | | 1.0 | 0.2 | 0.3 | 0.5 | 0.8 | 0.0 | 0.5 | ***9.5*** | **0.53** | **RD** |
| 5. | Mamit | 6.3 | 2.0 | 17.1 | 831.3 | 37.9 | 14.4 | 5.3 | | | |
| | | 0.7 | 0.8 | 0.7 | 0.0 | 0.7 | 0.2 | 0.4 | ***9.5*** | **0.53** | **RD** |
| 6. | Lunglei | 5.3 | 1.8 | 14.0 | 462.0 | 40.1 | 9.5 | 3.9 | | | |
| | | 0.8 | 0.8 | 0.9 | 0.8 | 0.6 | 0.6 | 0.6 | ***7.3*** | **0.40** | **LD** |
| 7. | Lawngtlai | 3.2 | 1.6 | 10.4 | 365.6 | 42.9 | 4.1 | 0.8 | | | |
| | | 1.0 | 0.9 | 1.0 | 1.0 | 0.6 | 0.0 | 1.0 | ***4.3*** | **0.24** | **LD** |
| 8. | Saiha | 14.3 | 4.3 | 18.3 | 422.2 | 71.7 | 8.2 | 1.2 | | | |
| | | 0.0 | 0.0 | 0.7 | 0.9 | 0.0 | 0.7 | 1.0 | ***8.6*** | **0.48** | **LD** |
| | Mizoram | 4.9 | 2.2 | 21.1 | 499.2 | 27.3 | 10.3 | 4.8 | | | |
| | | 0.8 | 0.7 | 0.6 | 0.7 | 0.9 | 0.5 | 0.5 | ***8.1*** | **0.45** | **LD** |

(Letters in the **Bold *Italics*** indicates deprivation value.)

**Table 9.13:** Level of basic and Infrastructure Service Sector Development (Using Principal Component Analysis)

*Total Variance Explained*

| Component | *Initial Eigen values* | | | *Extraction Sums of Squared Loadings* | | | *Rotation Sums of Squared Loadings* | | |
|---|---|---|---|---|---|---|---|---|---|
| | *Total* | *% of Variance* | *Cumulative %* | *Total* | *% of Variance* | *Cumulative %* | *Total* | *% of Variance* | *Cumulative %* |
| 1. | 7.040 | 39.111 | 39.111 | 7.040 | 39.111 | 39.111 | 6.408 | 35.602 | 35.602 |
| 2. | 3.878 | 21.542 | 60.653 | 3.878 | 21.542 | 60.653 | 3.181 | 17.674 | 53.276 |
| 3. | 3.394 | 18.854 | 79.508 | 3.394 | 18.854 | 79.508 | 2.771 | 15.394 | 68.670 |
| 4. | 1.852 | 10.292 | 89.799 | 1.852 | 10.292 | 89.799 | 2.623 | 14.574 | 83.244 |
| 5. | 1.203 | 6.685 | 96.484 | 1.203 | 6.685 | 96.484 | 2.383 | 13.240 | 96.484 |
| 6. | .430 | 2.388 | 98.872 | | | | | | |
| 7. | .178 | .990 | 99.863 | | | | | | |
| 8. | .025 | .137 | 100.000 | | | | | | |
| 9. | .000 | .000 | 100.000 | | | | | | |
| 10. | .000 | .000 | 100.000 | | | | | | |
| 11. | .000 | .000 | 100.000 | | | | | | |
| 12. | .000 | .000 | 100.000 | | | | | | |
| 13. | .000 | .000 | 100.000 | | | | | | |
| 14. | .000 | .000 | 100.000 | | | | | | |
| 15. | .000 | .000 | 100.000 | | | | | | |
| 16. | .000 | .000 | 100.000 | | | | | | |
| 17. | .000 | .000 | 100.000 | | | | | | |
| 18. | .000 | .000 | 100.000 | | | | | | |

**Table 9.14:** Level of Basic and Infrastructure Service Sector Development (Using Principal Component Analysis)

*Rotated Component Matrix(A)*

| | *Component* | | | | |
|---|---|---|---|---|---|
| | *1* | *2* | *3* | *4* | *5* |
| Literacy | .789 | .357 | .216 | .235 | .379 |
| Urban | .852 | -.291 | .090 | .099 | .409 |
| Elementary | -.914 | -.094 | .241 | -.114 | -.266 |
| Higher Sec. | .471 | .269 | .145 | .761 | -.316 |
| Colleges | .206 | .054 | .282 | -.926 | .003 |
| ISR | -.886 | .117 | .384 | -.030 | .113 |
| Hospital | -.310 | .735 | -.049 | .475 | -.064 |
| Beds | .157 | .920 | -.229 | .177 | .151 |
| APL | .938 | .023 | .080 | -.295 | -.059 |
| Telephone | .896 | -.266 | .116 | -.027 | .174 |
| Tourist | .386 | -.059 | -.147 | -.252 | .852 |
| Post | -.037 | .443 | -.731 | .443 | -.234 |
| Police | .378 | -.058 | -.865 | .047 | .305 |
| Road density | .880 | .132 | .126 | -.274 | .149 |
| Road | -.168 | .869 | .278 | -.321 | .163 |
| CDR | -.423 | .146 | -.653 | .564 | -.090 |
| Bank | .098 | .369 | .156 | -.031 | .893 |
| Library | .295 | .529 | .698 | .066 | .316 |

**Table 9.15:** Level of Basic and Infrastructure Service Sector Development (Using Principal Component Analysis)

| *Sl. No.* | *Districts* | *Fac1_1* | *Fac2_1* | *Fac3_1* | *Fac4_1* | *Fac5_1* | *Total* | *Status* |
|---|---|---|---|---|---|---|---|---|
| 1. | Aizawl | 1.957 | -0.798 | 0.306 | -0.446 | -0.611 | 0.406 | **RD** |
| 2. | Champhai | 0.165 | 1.430 | 0.944 | -0.370 | -0.813 | 1.356 | **HD** |
| 3. | Serchhip | -0.267 | -0.128 | 0.955 | 1.640 | 1.445 | 3.64 | **HD** |
| 4. | Kolasib | 0.308 | -0.267 | -0.763 | -1.321 | 1.917 | -0.126 | **LD** |
| 5. | Mamit | -0.895 | 1.503 | 0.059 | -0.816 | 0.087 | -0.062 | **LD** |
| 6. | Lunglei | -0.159 | -0.2 | 0.376 | 1.019 | -0.307 | 0.643 | **RD** |
| 7. | Lawngtlai | -1.699 | -1.625 | 0.069 | -0.675 | -0.808 | -4.747 | **LD** |
| 8. | Saiha | 0.09 | 0.42 | -2.29 | 1.029 | -0.576 | -1.324 | **LD** |
| | Mizoram | 0.500 | -0.251 | 0.342 | -0.058 | -0.331 | 0.202 | **RD** |

**Table 9.16:** Overall Development Indicators using Principal Component Analysis (Total Variance Explained)

*(Extraction Method: Principal Component Analysis)*

| Component | Initial Eigen values | | | Extraction Sums of Squared Loadings | | | Rotation Sums of Squared Loadings | | |
|---|---|---|---|---|---|---|---|---|---|
| | Total | % of Variance | Cumulative % | Total | % of Variance | Cumulative % | Total | % of Variance | Cumulative % |
| 1. | 11.981 | 34.233 | 34.233 | 11.98 | 34.23 | 34.233 | 10.42 | 29.795 | 29.795 |
| 2. | 7.664 | 21.897 | 56.130 | 7.664 | 21.89 | 56.130 | 6.792 | 19.407 | 49.202 |
| 3. | 6.464 | 18.468 | 74.598 | 6.464 | 18.46 | 74.598 | 6.233 | 17.809 | 67.011 |
| 4. | 4.732 | 13.521 | 88.119 | 4.732 | 13.52 | 88.119 | 6.047 | 17.279 | 84.290 |
| 5. | 2.109 | 6.026 | 94.145 | 2.109 | 6.026 | 94.145 | 2.694 | 7.698 | 91.987 |
| 6. | 1.313 | 3.751 | 97.895 | 1.313 | 3.751 | 97.895 | 2.068 | 5.908 | 97.895 |
| 7. | .651 | 1.859 | 99.754 | | | | | | |
| 8. | .086 | .246 | 100.000 | | | | | | |
| 9. | .000 | .000 | 100.000 | | | | | | |
| 10. | .000 | .000 | 100.000 | | | | | | |
| 11. | .000 | .000 | 100.000 | | | | | | |
| 12. | .000 | .000 | 100.000 | | | | | | |
| 13. | .000 | .000 | 100.000 | | | | | | |
| 14. | .000 | .000 | 100.000 | | | | | | |
| 15. | .000 | .000 | 100.000 | | | | | | |
| 16. | .000 | .000 | 100.000 | | | | | | |
| 17. | .000 | .000 | 100.000 | | | | | | |
| 18. | .000 | .000 | 100.000 | | | | | | |
| 19. | .000 | .000 | 100.000 | | | | | | |
| 20. | .000 | .000 | 100.000 | | | | | | |
| 21. | .000 | .000 | 100.000 | | | | | | |
| 22. | .000 | .000 | 100.000 | | | | | | |
| 23. | .000 | .000 | 100.000 | | | | | | |
| 24. | .000 | .000 | 100.000 | | | | | | |
| 25. | .000 | .000 | 100.000 | | | | | | |
| 26. | .000 | .000 | 100.000 | | | | | | |
| 27. | .000 | .000 | 100.000 | | | | | | |
| 28. | .000 | .000 | 100.000 | | | | | | |
| 29. | .000 | .000 | 100.000 | | | | | | |
| 30. | .000 | .000 | 100.000 | | | | | | |
| 31. | .000 | .000 | 100.000 | | | | | | |
| 32. | .000 | .000 | 100.000 | | | | | | |
| 33. | .000 | .000 | 100.000 | | | | | | |
| 34. | .000 | .000 | 100.000 | | | | | | |
| 35. | .000 | .000 | 100.000 | | | | | | |

**Table 9.17:** Component Matrix (*A*) Rotation Converged in 9 Iterations

| *Variables* | *Principal Components* | | | | | |
|---|---|---|---|---|---|---|
| *Indicators* | *1* | 2 | *3* | *4* | *5* | *6* |
| *Shown Sq. km* | .209 | .068 | -.099 | **.968** | -.001 | .048 |
| Cultivable(V-1) | -.077 | .501 | -.808 | .059 | .206 | .046 |
| Productivity(V-2) | .312 | .121 | .075 | .648 | .646 | .064 |
| **Jhum**(V-3) | .097 | -.184 | **-.881** | .387 | .128 | .063 |
| WRC(V-4) | -.314 | .036 | -.065 | .417 | .701 | .397 |
| **WRCHYV**(V-5) | -.014 | .173 | -.207 | **.926** | .087 | .189 |
| Food(V-6) | -.327 | .187 | .243 | .831 | .174 | .265 |
| **Fish**(V-7) | -.111 | .305 | .308 | .003 | **-.876** | .065 |
| livestock(V-8) | -.236 | .300 | .804 | .346 | -.062 | .289 |
| **Secondary**(V-9) | **.959** | -.104 | -.187 | -.111 | .058 | .072 |
| **SSI**(V-10) | **.959** | .003 | -.215 | -.084 | -.041 | .121 |
| **Women**(V-11) | -.205 | **-.896** | .292 | -.131 | .215 | .037 |
| **Female**(V-12) | -.044 | **-.968** | -.211 | .034 | -.018 | -.016 |
| Electric(V-13) | .380 | .814 | -.107 | .243 | .237 | .252 |
| Electrified(V-14) | .719 | .659 | -.103 | .186 | .028 | -.024 |
| Water(V-15) | .791 | -.072 | -.149 | -.553 | -.017 | -.162 |
| **LPG**(V-16) | **.973** | -.041 | -.075 | -.145 | -.055 | -.139 |
| Literacy(V-17) | .636 | .657 | .191 | .237 | -.258 | -.049 |
| **Urban**(V-18) | **.829** | .255 | -.203 | .289 | -.081 | -.339 |
| **Elementary**(V-19) | **-.851** | -.250 | -.276 | -.327 | -.061 | .152 |
| Higher Sec.(V-20) | .420 | .285 | .490 | -.466 | -.422 | -.144 |
| **Colleges**(V-21) | .180 | .166 | -.541 | .193 | .425 | **.623** |
| **ISR**(V-22) | **-.912** | .101 | -.244 | -.108 | -.223 | .070 |
| Hospital(V-23) | -.401 | .450 | .683 | -.357 | .041 | -.079 |
| Beds(V-24) | -.025 | .555 | .785 | .162 | .107 | .189 |
| **APL**(V-25) | **.912** | .146 | -.096 | .139 | -.020 | .336 |
| **Telephone**(V-26) | **.914** | .219 | -.228 | .050 | .074 | -.201 |
| Tourist(V-27) | .285 | .260 | -.154 | .881 | .062 | -.211 |
| **Post**(V-28) | -.041 | -.260 | **.963** | -.021 | -.033 | -.040 |
| Police(V-29) | .415 | -.353 | .499 | .544 | .182 | -.292 |
| **Road density**(V-30) | **.803** | .263 | -.083 | .324 | -.187 | .335 |
| Road(V-31) | -.372 | .644 | .201 | .194 | .037 | .599 |
| CDR(V-32) | -.383 | -.413 | .731 | -.013 | -.188 | -.315 |
| Bank(V-34) | -.066 | .707 | -.001 | .569 | -.022 | -.225 |
| Library(V-35) | .094 | .844 | -.092 | .088 | -.438 | .265 |

*Extraction Method*: Principal Component Analysis.
*Rotation Method*: Varimax with Kaiser Normalization.

**Table 9.18:**

| Name of district | Primary/Agri-culture & allied sector | | | Secondary/In-dustrial & allied sector | | | Tertiary/Basic & Infrastructure Services | | | Total score |
|---|---|---|---|---|---|---|---|---|---|---|
| | *M-1* | *M-2* | *M-3* | *M-1* | *M-2* | *M-3* | *M-1* | *M-2* | *M-3* | |
| Aizawl | 0 | 0 | 1 | 1 | 2 | 2 | 1 | 1 | 1 | **9** |
| Champhai | 1 | 1 | 0 | 0 | 0 | 1 | 1 | 1 | 2 | **7** |
| Serchhip | 1 | 0 | 0 | 0 | 0 | 1 | 1 | 1 | 2 | **6** |
| Kolasib | 1 | 2 | 2 | 0 | 0 | 1 | 1 | 1 | 0 | **8** |
| Mamit | 0 | 0 | 0 | 0 | 0 | 0 | 1 | 1 | 0 | **2** |
| Lunglei | 0 | 0 | 1 | 0 | 0 | 1 | 0 | 0 | 1 | **3** |
| Lawngtlai | 0 | 0 | 1 | 0 | 0 | 0 | 0 | 0 | 0 | **1** |
| Saiha | 1 | 0 | 0 | 0 | 0 | 0 | 1 | 0 | 0 | **2** |
| Mizoram | 1 | 0 | 1 | 1 | 0 | 1 | 1 | 0 | 1 | **6** |

[*Criteria*: Score > 8.5 = HD, 5.5 – 8.5 = RD, 2.5-5.5 = LD and < 2.5 = Least Developed][1].

1. This criterion has a reference to JV. Nunchunga, *op cit*.

# Chapter 10

## Autonomous District Councils

## *A Study of the Implications of the Sixth Schedule in Mizoram*

JANGKHONGAM DOUNGEL

---

### Introduction

The District Council, enshrined in Sixth Schedule to the Constitution of India is unique in various aspects and its uniqueness can be unequivocally verified by analyzing its functioning. An in-depth study of the District Council functioning cannot be undertaken without tracing the genesis of the Sixth Schedule to the Constitution of India in the state since the Lushai Hills era. Prior to that, the Status of Mizoram in pre-independence era ought to be briefly traced so as to highlight the condition which necessitated its transformation to the present Political Status. Hence, the chapter aims at tracing the historical root of the introduction of District Council in Mizoram with the objective to analyzing the present Autonomous District Councils of the State.

### Changing Status of Mizoram Since Pre-Independence Era

Mizoram which was earlier known as the Lushai Hills had no regular Administrative set-up till 1891. In 1891, the territory was divided into two Administrative Sub-Divisions such as North Lushai Hills under the Government of Assam and South Lushai Hills under the Government of Bengal. As a result of the Chin-Lushai Conference, held at Calcutta in 1898, the two Lushai Hills were amalgamated into one and named as the Lushai Hills and was subsequently brought under the administrative control of Assam with effect from 1st April, 1898.[1] And, as per the Government of India Act of 1919, the Governor General-in-Council declared the Lushai Hills as backward area on 3rd January, 1921. Further, in pursuance to the provision of the Government of India Act, 1935, the Lushai Hills District was declared as an excluded area in 1936. Prior to that, the Inner Line Regulation had been already enforced in the Lushai Hills with effect from 28th August, 1930.[2]

The name of the District changed into Mizo Hills District from Lushai Hills District with effect from 1st September, 1954 as per the Lushai Hills District (Change of Name) Act, 1954 (Act XVIII of 1954) which was enacted by the Indian Parliament[3]. The then Mizo Hills District continued to be part of Assam till it was declared as Union Territory with the name "MIZORAM" on 21st January, 1972, under the provision of the North Eastern Areas (Recognition Act of 1972). Ultimately, Mizoram becomes the 23rd State of the Indian Union from 14 July, 1986 as a result of assent given by the President of India to the Constitution Fifty-Third Amendment Act, 1986.[4]

## Genesis of the Sixth Schedule to the Constitution of India and District Council Set up in Mizoram

The Tribal Areas had drawn special attention of the administration since pre-independence era. Therefore, the Cabinet Mission under Sir Stafford Cripps also had suggested the formation of an Advisory Committee, to study on the rights of minorities and tribes of excluded area. Accordingly, an Advisory Committee was set up by the Constituent Assembly on 24th January, 1947 and the Advisory Committee further appointed a Sub-Committee known as the North Eastern Frontier (Assam) Tribal and Excluded Area Committee with Gopinath Bordoloi as Chairman. The Bordoloi Committee, consisting of Rupnath Brahma, A.V. Thakkur, B.N. Rau and Rev. J.J.M. Nichols Roy visited Aizawl in April 1947, to study the mind of the Mizo people, their administrative problems and the desire to have autonomy for their area. As Mizos were not represented in the Committee, the Committee co-opted Saprawnga and Khawtinkhuma from the Mizo Union Party to represent the Mizos.[5]

The Sub-Committee in Aizawl asked the Mizo representatives belonging to various interests, such as, Political Leaders, Church Leaders, Chief Representatives, Ex-Servicemen and Government

Officials whether they wanted to remain with Central Legislature or Provincial Legislature. Further, the Committee also wanted to know the extent to which people of Lushai Hills desire to have autonomy.[6] However, the Pawis and the Lakhers were not aware of the visit of the Bordoloi Committee and their case was also not represented by any Political Leaders, Political Parties or groups.[7] Besides visiting the Lushai Hills, the Bordoloi Committee also extensively toured the North Cachar Sub-Division, Mikir Hills, and the Naga Hills District and submitted its report to Ballabhbhai Patel, Chairman, and Advisory Committee on Fundamental Rights etc. The report dealt with various aspects relating to administration of the tribal areas such as thoughts on development, special features of these areas, Land, Forest, Jhuming, Courts, Finance, Control of Immigration, Service etc. After discussing the matter, the Advisory Committee forwarded it to the Constituent Assembly on 4th March, 1948.[8]

The Constituent Assembly finally considered the matter on 5th, 6th, 7th September, 1949 and there was animated discussion on the Bordoloi Committee Report. After a long and heated debate in the Constituent Assembly, certain Amendments were made, the Sixth Schedule finally emerged and found place in the Constitution in Articles 244(2) and 275(1)[9]

After the Indian Constitution was brought into force, the immediate formation of the District Council in the Hill Districts was not possible. The government initiated move to set up an interim Advisory Council in the Hill District of Assam. As such, an Advisory Council election was held for the Chief for electing the Chief Representatives on 23rd March, 1948 and for the Commoners for electing the Commoners representatives on the basis of Adult Franchise on 15th April, 1948. The Advisory Council comprised 35 members, out of which 10 were Chief Representatives and 25 were Commoner representatives and LL. Peter, Superintendent of the Lushai Hills was Chairman of Advisory Council[10]. From the Pawi-Lakher Region, Z. Hengmang and Vako were the commoner representatives and Chhummunga was the Chief Representative. At this juncture, the representatives from the Pawi-Lakher region had reached the acme of Political limelight because they were aware of the fact that the Pawis and the Lakhers could be facilitated with Regional Council under the provision of the then proposed Sixth Schedule to the Constitution of India. Therefore, they vigorously pursued their demand for establishment of Regional Council by obtaining permission for formation of Political Party. Subsequently, a Political Party known as the Pawi-Lakher Tribal Union (PLTU) was formed at Lawngtlai on 25th October, 1949 with Z. Hengmang as the President[11]. In the meantime, the Lushai Hills Advisory Council was changed into Advisory Committee in 1949 which function till 1951. It is a notable feature that Z. Hengmang and Vako were still accommodated in the downsized Lushai Hills Advisory Committee and they steadfastly utilized their status by vigorously pursuing the demand for formation of a viable Regional Council for the Pawis and the Lakhers[12]. The First General Election of the Lushai Hills District Council was held on 4th January, 1952 and the Mizo Union won 15 seats, out of 18 seats for which election was held. Therefore, the Mizo Union formed the First Executive/Government with Lalsawia as the Chief Executive Member and Dr. Rosiama as the Chairman. Finally, the Lushai Hills District Council was inaugurated on 26th April, 1952 at Aizawl by Bishnuram Medhi, the then Chief Minister of Assam.[13] Further, the Lushai Hills District came to be known as Mizo District as per the Lushai Hills District (Change of Name) Act, 1954 (Act XVIII of 1954) of the Indian Parliament. Consequently, the Lushai Hills District Council also came to be known as Mizo District Council since 1954. And to accomplish the relentless Political demand of the Pawi-Lakher region, a Regional Council called the Pawi-Lakher Regional Council was inaugurated with Headquarters at Saiha, by Ch. Saprawnga, Parliamentary Secretary to the Government of Assam at Lunglei on 23rd April, 1953.[14]

## Emergence of the Present Autonomous District Councils of Mizoram

The process for abolition of the Mizo District Council began with formation of Union Territory of Mizoram. As such, the Mizo District Council was deleted from Part III of the Sixth Schedule to the Constitution of India with effect from15th February, 1972[15]. However, the ruling Party of the then Mizo District Council was scheduled to continue as the caretaker government till the formation of the Legislature of the Union Territory of Mizoram. Contented not only with the dissolution of the Mizo District Council, leaders of the erstwhile Mizo District Council, namely Ch. Chhunga, Dengthuama and other leaders even persuaded leaders of the Pawi-Lakher Regional Council (PLRC) for abolition of the PLRC as well as to halt the demand for District Council for better integration of the people of Mizoram. However, the leader of the PLRC undauntedly adhered to their demand for higher Political status in the form of District Council. Finally, the Pawi-Lakher Regional Council was trifurcated into three Regional Councils, namely Pawi Regional Council (PRC), the Lakher Regional Council (LRC), and the Chakma Regional Council (CRC) on 2nd April, 1972 as per the Administration of Mizoram Notification No. CCMP/3/72-77 of 1.4.1972. The Headquarters of PRC was located at Lawngtlai, LRC at Saiha and CRC at Borapansuri which later shifted to Chawngte 'C' (Kamalanagar)[16]. Administrative arrangement was also made in such away that the existing member of the PLRC would automatically be Members of their respective Regional Councils. Likewise, employees of the PLRC were also given direction to serve under their respective Regional Council on the basis of ethnicity.[17] The Mizo District Council Executive/Government under the Leadership of Zalawma as the Chief Executive Member acted as the caretaker government of Mizoram till the formation of the legislature of Mizoram. In the meantime, S.J. Das was appointed as the Chief Commissioner of Mizoram.[18] Certain administrative changes took place at this critical juncture and Mizoram was divided into three new revenue districts. The North Mizo District came to be known as Aizawl District, the South Mizo District came to be known as Lunglei District and the erstwhile Pawi-Lakher Regional Council area came to be known as Chhimtuipui District.[19] The Chief Commissioner also had appointed interim Chief Executive Member (CEM) for the three Regional Councils, namely L. Chinzah for the Pawi Regional Council, Zakhu Hlychho for the Lakher regional Council and Atul Chandro Chakma for the Chakma Regional Council. After constituting the Legislative Assembly of Mizoram, the dissolution of the Mizo District Council was officially proclaimed by the newly appointed Lieutenant Governor of Mizoram, S.P. Mukherjee and Mizo District Council ceased to exist.[20]

On the same day when the dissolution of the Mizo District Council was promulgated on 29th April, 1972, the three Regional Councils were upgraded to the status of full-fledged Autonomous District Council, but they (District Council) were continued to be governed by their respective interim Government till the conduct of District Council Election in June 1973. As a result, the Pawi Regional Council came to be known as Pawi Autonomous District Council, the Lakher Regional Council as Lakher Autonomous District Council and

Chakma Regional Council as the Chakma Autonomous District Council with effect from 29th April, 1972.[21] Despite the identification of Lai as "Pawi" and Mara as "Lakher" in Mizoram, the Lais and the Maras regarded the popular terms "Pawi" and "Lakher" as derogatory terms. They demanded for change of their District Council name after their ethnic original name. Thus under the Sixth Schedule to the Constitution (Amendment) Act, 1988 of Indian Parliament (No.67 of 1988), the Pawi Autonomous District Council was changed into Lai Autonomous District Council.[22] However, the name of the tribes is still listed as Pawi and Lakher in Scheduled Tribe List of the State.[23]

## Functioning of the Present Autonomous District Councils of Mizoram

As provided in sub-paragraph 6, paragraph 2 of the Sixth Schedule to the Constitution of India, the Government of Mizoram had enacted the Mizoram Autonomous District Council (Constitution and Conduct of Business of the District Councils) Rules, 1974 which then become the guiding principle of governance for the three Autonomous District Councils of Mizoram. The Government of Mizoram also created a separate Department in Secretariat known as "District Council Affairs (DCA) Department", to look after the affairs of the three Autonomous District Councils of Mizoram, and funds for the District Councils are channelised through this department with the approval of the state finance department. Thus, the DCA department becomes the main controlling authority concerning the affairs of the District Councils of the State.[24] District Council as governmental set up at the local level with three organs of government signifies certain resembling trait with the State Government and Central Government in its functioning. As a matter of fact, the Governor is the executive head of the various district councils within the state as he is also the head of the state. The law enacted by the District Council cannot come into force till the Governor gives his assent. In the like manner, the Chairman and the Deputy Chairman are elected from amongst the Member's of District Council (MDC) themselves and they are similar to the Speaker and the Deputy Speaker of the Legislative Assembly of the State. The District Council also has an Executive Committee which function is similar to Cabinet of the State Government. The Chief Executive Member (CEM) is the Head of the Executive Committee and he is elected by the MDC from amongst themselves as Leader of the House. The CEM also recommends certain MDCs for appointment as Executive Members (EMs) to the Governor of Mizoram for his approval.[25] The post of CEM and EMs are similar respectively to Chief Minister and Cabinet Ministers of State. Each Autonomous District Council has also two Secretaries, one for the Executive Committee who is designated as the Executive Secretary and the other for the Legislative who is designated as the Legislative Secretary. The post of Executive Secretary is a replica of Chief Secretary of State Government or Cabinet Secretary of the Union Government whereas the Legislative Secretary can be compared to Secretary, Assembly Secretariat of the Legislative Assembly of State and Secretary General of the Lok Sabha or Rajya Sabha. Over and above these, each District Council also has the Court President and Recorder who is a replica of the Chief Justice of the High Court or the Supreme Court.

The three Autonomous District Councils of Mizoram were previously under the administrative jurisdiction of Chhimtuipui Revenue District. However, as a result of the bifurcation of Chhimtuipui District into Lawngtlai District and Saiha District in 1998, Lawngtlai District covers the geographical area of the Lai Autonomous District Council and Chakma Autonomous District Council with Headquarters at Lawngtlai whereas; the Mara Autonomous District Council alone remains in Saiha District. Analyzing in the strict sense of the term, Lawngtlai District and Saiha District are the only Tribal Area among the districts of Mizoram in accordance with the Provisions of the Sixth Schedule to the Constitution of India.[27] Some of the functioning of the three Autonomous District Councils shall be briefly analyzed as given below.

### *Administrative Set-up*

The Chakma Autonomous District Council (CADC) is the smallest in area among the District Councils of Mizoram and its geographical area is 686.35 sq. km.[28] The Headquarters of the CADC is located at Kamalanagar (Chawngte 'C') and CADC also has 37,630 populations and there are 69 Village Councils under CADC administered area.[29] The structural organization of the CADC is broadly categorized into three main organs such as legislative, executive, and judiciary on the pattern of separation of powers. Further, it (CADC) also has 23 departments and 1003 employees till 2001.[30]

The Mara Autonomous District Council (MADC) has a geographical area of 1399.90 sq. km[31] and its Headquarters is located at Saiha. Tuipang is the Sub-Headquarters of the MADC. There are 62 Village Councils and 37,500 population in the MADC administered area. Like the CADC, the MADC is also broadly categorized into three main structural organs such as legislative, executive and judiciary. It also has 23 departments and 1246 employees till 2001.[32]

The Lai Autonomous District Council (LADC) is the largest in geographical area among the three Autonomous District Councils of Mizoram and its area is 1870.75 sq. km. The Headquarters of the LADC is located at Lawngtlai, Sub-Headquarters at Bualpui 'NG' and Divisional Headquarters at Diltlang, Sangau, Vathuampui, Chawngte 'P' and Lungtian. As per the 2005 Statistical and Population Report of the Local Administration Department of the LADC, there are 84 villages, 2 sub-villages, 84 Village Councils, and 60,149 population in the whole LADC area. The structural set-up of the LADC is also categorized into three broad organs such as legislative, executive, and judiciary. Further, it has 25 functioning departments and some other minor departments with more than 1,500 employees.[33]

## *Legislative Function*

The Legislative Department in each Autonomous District Council is administratively headed by the Legislative Secretary and the department has to make necessary arrangement for convening Session and receive questions from MDC's which should be submitted to the Chairman for scrutiny. The Chairman has to see whether the questions are concern of the District Council and questions should be submitted 15 days before the Session. The Legislative Department also makes arrangement for election of Chairman, Deputy Chairman, and the Chief Executive Member under the supervision of the concerned Presiding Officer. Further, it also has to record and publish the proceedings of the District Council Session and it should also send Bill for approval of the Governor after being authenticated by the Chairman. However, the real legislative function or law-making power is exercised by the legislature of the District Council which comprises of Members of the District Council (MDCs). At present, the CADC has 17 members (13 Elected and 4 Nominated), the MADC has 26 members (22 Elected and 4 Nominated) and the LADC has 27 members (23 Elected and 4 Nominated)[34].

On the basis of power conferred by paragraph 3 of the Sixth Schedule to the Constitution of India and as per the provision laid down in Rule 73 of the Mizoram Autonomous District Council (Constitution and Conduct of Business of the District Council) Rules, 1974, the Autonomous District Council has certain legislative powers. Accordingly, the MADC has enacted 28 Legislations and passed 29 resolutions, the CADC has enacted 14 legislations and passed 41 resolutions whereas the LADC has enacted 30 legislations and passed 167 resolutions.[35]

The speciality of the District Council lies in its law-making power as enshrined in paragraph 3 and, other powers enumerated in paragraphs 4-10 of the Sixth Schedule to the Constitution of India can also be effectively exercised only if appropriate laws are made by it (District Council).[36] However, law-making power is not yet effectively utilized by the District Council till now. It is an undeniable fact that huge amount of taxes and revenue is lost annually due to absence of appropriate laws and rules. It is indeed paradoxical to mention that some of the laws enacted by the erstwhile Pawi-Lakher Regional Council are still enforced in some of the District Councils particularly in the LADC. Therefore, laws should periodically be reviewed and necessary amendment be made so as to meet the requirement of the changing time.[37] It is indeed the often complain of the District Council authority that the State Government has delayed fund and also has encroached upon the powers of the District Council. But, it is a fact that State Government can encroach upon the powers of District Council in certain instances due to absence of appropriate law. As enshrined in paragraph 9 of the Sixth Schedule, share of royalties accruing from extraction of minerals within District Council can be undertaken only by the agreement of State Government and concerned District Council. Further, any dispute in this regard between the State and District Council should be decided by the Governor in his discretion.[38] A notification had been issued by the State Government in November 2005 that, anything concerning quarry or extraction of stones, boulders etc. from quarry should be reported to District Industry Officer or Sub-Divisional Industry Officer of the concerned district even in the District Council area.[39] It is an interesting feature that the MADC has recently enacted the Motor Vehicle Act which enabled it to collect entry fee from each vehicle entering the MADC area but the other two District Councils have not yet enacted it.[40] Therefore, awareness should be created in such a way that the District Council should effectively utilize the legislative function for ethnic preservation and socio-economic development of the area.

### *Executive Function*

As stated earlier, the Executive functions of the District Council are vested in the Executive Committee. The Executive Committee is headed by the Chief Executive Member (CEM) but the administrative responsibility of the Executive Committee lies with the Executive Secretary. It is evident that all departments of the District Council other than the legislative and judiciary are under the direct supervision of the Executive. The executive comprises the political executive (Executive Members) and their bureaucrats (Officers), and the main work of the executive is to execute the plans of the District Council as well as to enforce and implement the laws and legislations, enacted by the legislature. In fact, the Executive Secretary and his team of officers under his supervision are expected to provide flesh and blood to the skeleton like legislation which is provided by the Legislature. As provided in paragraph 6(2) of the Sixth Schedule to the Constitution of India, certain departments are created in District Council with the approval of the Governor of Mizoram.[41] At present, the executive department of both the CADC and MADC have 21 departments under their control whereas the executive in LADC has 23 departments under its control along with some minor departments.[42] Yet, the normal official process of file or official matter is often neglected in the District Council functioning. The reason being, officers of different departments are hardly utilized by the political executive and it is observed that the works of the bureaucrats are often performed by the Executive Members for their political advantage against the norms of decency. Further, official advertisement and notifications are often issued by the Executive Members rather than by the concerned officer who is the Administrative Head of the Department. Moreover, politicization of recruitment, and appointment of less qualified candidate, in certain posts have been the feature of appointment in the District Council as it can be seen in the LADC. Therefore, merit should be emphasized in recruitment and adequate training should also be provided to the bureaucracy of the District Council for effective performance of official function.

As provided in paragraph 6(1) of the Sixth Schedule to the Constitution of India, Primary School was entrusted to the District Council in 1975 and Middle School (Upper Primary School) was further entrusted to the District Council in 1994. For effective implementation of the development schemes, District Councils have certain development departments such as Rural Development, Public Health Engineering Department (PHED), Public Works Department (PWD), Agriculture, Industry, Veterinary, Soil and Water Conservation, Local Administration, Fishery etc. However, the performance of such departments is not up to the mark due to misuse of funds and over politicization. In fact, the development works are not qualitative enough for bringing real development.[43] Moreover, Land Revenue, Environment and Forest, and Art & Culture Departments are also required to further intensify their works for development of the area as well as for fulfilment of the provisions which are laid down in the Sixth Schedule to the Constitution of India.

### *Judicial Function*

As provided in sub-paragraph (4) of paragraph 4 of the Sixth Schedule to the Constitution of India, the District Council may constitute the District Council Court with the approval of the Governor of Mizoram. Over and above that, provision for establishment of Village Council Court was also enshrined in sub-paragraph (1) of the same paragraph.[44] Accordingly, three tier court, namely, Village Council Court, Intermediate District Council Court and District Council Court are subsequently established by each of the Autonomous District Council under the provision of the Pawi-Lakher Autonomous Region (Administration of Justice) Rules, 1954 which was adopted by each of the District Council. Later, the LADC and MADC have made their own Rules for this purpose in 1974 and 1981 respectively and courts under the two District Councils are now looked after under the provision of these Rules.[45] Further, the CADC also has taken steps in this regard and Chakma Law Code was enacted in 1997.[46] Even then, the District Council Court can litigate only if both Parties in the case are Tribals. Therefore, if non-tribals are involved in the case, it cannot be litigated by the District Council Court. The Lai Autonomous

District Council Court is located at Lawngtlai and Intermediate District Council Courts are two in number in LADC which are located in Lawngtlai and Bualpui 'NG' respectively. The Mara Autonomous District Council Court is located at Saiha and the Intermediate District Council Court is located at Tuipang. Likewise in the CADC, both the District Council Court (CADC Court) and Intermediate District Council Court are located in Kamalanagar.[47] At present, the CADC has 69 Village Council Courts, LADC has 84 Village Council Courts and MADC has 62 Village Council Courts.[48]

Village Council Court is the hierarchical judicial set-up at the village level which comprises of 3 to 11 members. It can impose fine up to the limit of Rs. 60 and any appeal to judgement of the Village Council Court shall lie to the Intermediate District Council Court. Likewise, an appeal against the judgement of the Intermediate District Council Court shall lie to the District Council Court. In fact, Judicial Officer of Intermediate District Court and Court President and Recorder of the District Council Court are equivalent to First Class Magistrate of the State Government. As such, they can impose fine and pass sentence to the extent which First Class Magistrate can litigate. Any appeal of the Intermediate District Council Court is to be accompanied by a copy of the order appeal against and a clear statement of the ground of appeal are to be filled within sixty days of the date of order, excluding the time required for obtaining a copy of the order appealed against. Likewise, any appeal against the judgement of the District Council Court should also be laid only in the Guwahati High Court and the limit for filing an appeal should be ninety days from the date of order or decision.[49] The District Council Court mainly deals with customary law but the performance of the court is not satisfactory. As a measure for qualitative improvement of the District Council Court, it is high time that law graduates are appointed in important judicial post, along with that, codification of customary law should also be fulfilled by the District Council without delay.

## Limitation in the Functioning of the District Council

District Council as a governmental set-up at the local level is inflicted with certain inherent contradiction and criticisms. Some of the factors which disturb the effective functioning of the District Council are groupism, clanism, political instability, small constituency, defection and unprincipled politics,[50] negligence by State Government, inadequate efforts in law-making, extreme politicization of official works and recruitment, dependency syndrome,[51] nepotism, lack of technically qualified personnel in specialized post, frequent reshuffle of officers and norms of promotion against the recruitment rules, lack of adequate training to officers and lack of far-sighted policy etc. The above cited factors are present in one way or the other in each of the District Council. Indeed, rules and impartiality are often sidelined to the corner in functioning of the District Council system in Mizoram.

In it is evident that groupism, clannism and unprincipled politics are unavoidable feature of the District Council functioning. Till now, general election for electing Member of the District Council (MDC) had been conducted 8 times in LADC and 7 times in both MADC and CADC. As most of the constituencies are small, candidates can risk their electoral fortune with the support of family or clan related votes which resulted in clannism feeling. It should be recollected that political controversy in LADC was adjudged as Chinzah-Hnialum rivalry which genesis could be traced to erstwhile Pawi-Lakher Regional Council (PLRC) era, and later on mushroom into psychological clannish rivalry in the form of Chinzah-Fanchun rivalry and the likes. Likewise, similar trend may also be witnessed in the other two District Councils, though it may be of lesser intensification. It should also be highlighted that, Vawmbuk, a village with just 830 votes in LADC area is a MDC constituency. Therefore, groupism and clannism intensified unprincipled politics which automatically lead to political instability. Further, defection is an inherent political problem in each of the Autonomous District Council. It is a notable feature that most of the prominent politicians in LADC with the exception of few (just one or two) have defected a minimum of three times till now. It should also be highlighted that complete five years rule of a particular party under the leadership of a particular person was witnessed four times in MADC, thrice in CADC and only once in LADC till now.[52] Moreover, change of government was witnessed 17 times in LADC, 13 times in MADC and 11 times in CADC. It is evident that long term and far-sighted policies are unlikely to be adopted in the midst of such chronic political instability. The problem of defection the District Council area is that many politicians regard defection as political statesmanship.[53]

It is often alleged by District Council Authority that District Council is neglected by the State Government. Indeed, the State

Government also acts in a prejudicial and unfair manner in many instances. The latest case in point, being, victimization of the Indian National Congress (INC)—Maraland Democratic Front (MDF) coalition government and installation of the Mizo National Front (MNF) government by manipulating the nominated seats through Machiavellian tactics in MADC. When the same Party is in power in both the District Council and State, there is cordial working relation and the issue of non-cooperation was seldom heard. However, complaint of negligence, non-release of fund, encroachment of District Council power and non-cooperation are the normal grievances raised by the District Council whenever different Parties are in power in the two governmental set-up.[54] In fact, there are certain truths of negligence to the District Council by the State Government in many respects. Yet, the District Councils are also themselves responsible for problems and shortcomings due to their dubious role. Thus, inadequate efforts in law-making, extreme politicization of official works and recruitment, nepotism, lack or absence of technically qualified personnel, posting, and promotion of officers against proper norms, lack of adequate training to officers, and lack of far-sighted policy are the inherent contradiction of the District Councils which are their own making. In fact, extreme politicization of all functioning is the special characteristic with which the District Councils of Mizoram can be identified. Thus, even developments works are politicized which led supporters of different elected members to depend on District Council fund without working, which only increase dependency syndrome among the people. Remedial measures to many of the problems faced by the District Council can be effectively solved by the District Council themselves but adequate steps should also be taken to ameliorate the victimizing tendency of the State Government.

**Issue of the Sixth Schedule to the Constitution (Amendment) Bill, 2006**

The issue of the Sixth Schedule to the Constitution (Amendment) Bill, 2006 is the most talk about political issue in the Sixth Schedule area of Mizoram at this juncture. As such, different Political Parties such as Indian National Congress (INC), Bharatiya Janata Party (BJP), Mizo National Front (MNF), Maraland Democratic Front (MDF) and Lairam People's Party (LPP) of the region are struggling to take political advantage out of this contentious issue. The Bill is expected to be tabled in the Parliament in the near future and it concerns about the up gradation of the Status of the Autonomous District Council of Mizoram to the Status of Autonomous Council and Territorial Council of Assam under the provision of the Sixth Schedule to the Constitution of India. It was also highlighted in 1st September 2006 issue of the *Shillong Times* that the Central Government is considering the issue earnestly for implementation.[55] Therefore, it should tactfully analyzed whether the enactment of this bill be a boon or bane?

The said bill provided for up graduation of the present three Autonomous District Councils of Mizoram to the Status of Autonomous Territorial Council. Different subjects which are allocated to Autonomous Council and Territorial Council under the provision of paragraph 3 of the Sixth Schedule to the Constitution of India are also proposed to be assigned to the proposed Autonomous Territorial Council. It also laid down that over 30 departments are to be handed over to the proposed Autonomous Council, even to the extent of looking after to College Education. Likewise the power of Autonomous Territorial Council is also to be enhanced to all the departments. It is also further laid down that the Chief Executive Member and Executive Member will be equal to the status of the Cabinet Minister and Minister of State of the State Government for protocol purposes in the Autonomous Territorial area.[56]

Taking the pros and cons of the issue into consideration, it is indeed thought provoking to state whether the higher political status will be beneficial for the area or not? In fact, it is really doubtful whether the so-called higher political status or power enhancement would do justice for the area in the absence of adequate implementation of the provision provided to the present Autonomous District Council. The issue needs the tactful dealing of the situation by the District Council Authority. It is an undeniable fact that the quality of learning in the District Council area degraded since the handling over of Primary Education to District Council in 1975, and further wrong was committed with the handling over of middle school (Upper Primary School) education in 1994. In fact, politicization of recruitment even to the extent of recruiting unqualified and less competent people in teacher post and appointment of less qualified candidate in the Officer post are the consequential effect of District Council's control over education. As a matter of fact, had college education been handed over to the Autonomous Territorial Council as stated in the proposed bill, the educational system would have gone through extreme-politicization. Similarly same impact may also have be seen in all other departments.

**Conclusion**

In conclusion from the study of the genesis and functioning of the Sixth Schedule provision to the Constitution of India in Mizoram since the era of the Mizo District Council and the erstwhile Pawi-Lakher Regional Council (PLRC) it can be objectively inferred that many changes had taken place in the functioning. It was the evident that the enormous contribution of the Mizo District Council and the erstwhile PLRC had tremendously excelled the functioning of the present Autonomous District Council. It is noticed that there is a substantial increase of Grand-in-aid witnessed in the three autonomous district councils. However, the achievement of the District Council with respect to development works, creation of durable assets and long term beneficial policy for people of the area was not satisfactory. Despite certain limitations, it is evident that the three Autonomous District Councils enable the ethnic tribes of the region to preserve and protect their land, ethnic identity, custom, culture, and tradition. Over and above these, sense of participation in the Local Self-Government and democratic spirit are also inculcated in the mind of the people. It is highly required that the District Council should take adequate step in law-making so as to effectively utilize its legislative, executive and judicial functions for preservation and development of their respective area.

The Autonomous District Councils also provided employment to many educated and less educated people of the area. So it (District Council) is good machinery for solving unemployment problem of the area. There are charges and counter charges about political interference in recruitment and appointment. Therefore, it is imperative that qualified and qualitative personnel are recruited even if political interference is there. Moreover, the administrative structure of the District Council also should be properly streamlined so as to give more responsibility to the bureaucracy. Further, training opportunity should also be arranged for officers. It should also be suggested that the number of seats in the legislature of the District Council should be arranged in such away that, each constituency should have average of 1,500 voters so that dummy candidates and history setters may not be unknowingly elected on clan-related votes.

Besides these, prestige and efficiency of judiciary should be protected by making provision for appointment of law graduates in judicial post.

The issue of the Sixth Schedule to the Constitution of India is the most talked about issue among the different tribes of the North-East India. Those tribes who are not facilitated with the Sixth Schedule provision are also clamouring for it because they are aware of the benefits of the Sixth Schedule. In fact, tribals of the Hill Areas of Manipur, Paite, Hmar, Brus etc. of Mizoram and some tribes from Assam are still demanding for facilitating them with Sixth Schedule provision. So far as the functioning of the District Councils of Mizoram is concerned, it can be impartially stated that both the State Government and District Council are equally responsible for certain loopholes in the functioning of the District Council System. Therefore, it is high time that the State Government allocate all those funds and facilities which are due to the District Council. Likewise, the District Council should also properly do their home-work without putting all the blames on the State Government. However, with respect to enhancement of power, which bill is yet to be tabled in parliament, it would be a healthy development if decision is not taken in haste. Thus, adequate steps should be taken up without delay, so that District Councils may be better equipped for effectively meeting any challenge and to utilize it even if higher political status is accorded.

## REFERENCES

1. Singh, S.N., (1994) Mizoram, Mittal Publication, New Delhi, p.113.
2. Doungel, Jangkhongam, (2003) The Role and working of the Lai Autonomous District Council, Mizoram, Ph.D. thesis, Manipur University, unpublished, pp. 52-53.
3. Hansaria, B.L., (1983) Sixth Schedule to the Constitution of India—A Study, Jyoti Printers, Guwahati, pp. A 279-A 280.
4. *Op. cit.*, p.1.
5. Prasad, R.N., (1987) Government and Politics in Mizoram (1947-1986), Nothern Book Centre, New Delhi, p. 76.
6. Rao, Venkata, V., Thansanga, H., Hazarika, Niru, (1987) A Century of Government and olitics in North East India, Volume III, Mizoram, S. Chand & Company, Pvt. Ltd. New Delhi, p.10.
7. Doungel, Jangkhongam, *op. cit.*, p. 26.
8. Hansaria, B.L., *op. cit.*, p. 10.

9. *Ibid.*
10. Lalbiaknema, C., (1998) Mizote Leh Politics (The Mizo's and Politics) R.T.M. Press & Computer, Aizawl, p. 76.
11. Interview with Hengmang Z., Lawngtlai, 15th December 2000.
12. Hengmang Z., (1988) Ka vahvaihpui ram leh hnam (The Land and the Nation, I wanderd with), Pawi District Council, Lawngtlai, pp. 32-34.
13. Lalsawia, (1994) Zoram Hming-mel (Zoram at at a glance), Lalsawia, Aizawl, pp. 63-65.
14. Doungel, Jangkhongam, *op. cit.*, pp. 6-7.
15. Chakraborty, P., (2005) Fifth and Sixth Schedule to the Constitution of India, updated and annoted, Capital Publishing House, Delhi, pp. 272.
16. *Op. cit.*, pp. 58-59.
17. Hengmang Z., *op. cit.*, pp. 76-77.
18. *Op. cit.*
19. "The Uniqueness of the erstwhile Pawi-Lakher Regional Council", a research paper, contributed by Dr. Jangkhongam Doungel in Journal of the North East India Council for Social Science Research (NEICSSR), October, 2005, p. 32.
20. *Op. cit.*
21. Hnialum, R.T., (1988) Road to Pawi Autonomous District Council, Lai Autonomous District Council, p. 8.
22. Chakraborty, P., *op. cit.*, pp. 283.
23. Government of Mizoram, (2000) Statistical Hand Book of Mizoram, Directorate of Economics & Statistics, Aizawl, p. XI.
24. A memoradum submitted to the Honourable Prime Minister of India in 2000 for creation of the Union Territory of the Lai, the Mara and the Chakma tribes of Mizoram by the Lai, Mara and Chakma UT Demand Committee.
25. Government of Mizoram, (1989) Mizoram Autonomous District Council (Costitution and Conduct of Business of the District Council) Rules, 1974, Mizoram Gazette Extraordinary, issue No. 72(A), 18.9.1989, Controller of Printing and Stationery, Aizawl, pp. 4, 9 & 13-15.
26. Doungel, Jangkhongam, The Role and Working of the Lai Autonomous District Council, Mizoram, *op. cit.*, pp. 64-65.
27. Local Self Government in Automous District Council Area of Mizoram with Special Reference to the Lai Autonomous District Council, Seminar Paper, presented on XV North East India Political Science Association (NEIPSA) Conference by Dr. Jangkhongam Doungel at Silchar on 22nd January 2006, p. 5.
28. Government of Mizoram, Statistical Hand Book of Mizoram, 2000. *op. cit.*, p. XI.
29. I. Sources from Inglon Chakma, Under Secretary, Legislative Department, Chakma Autonomous District Council, Kamalanagar, November, 2005.
    II. Silver Jubilee Souvenir of the Chakma Autonomous District Council (1972-1997), Edited by L.B. Chakma, Kamalanagar, 1997, pp. 82-101.

30. Chakma Autonomous District Council (Legislative Department, Records and Documents, Kamlanagar, 17th August, 2001.
31. Government of Mizoram, (2000) Statistical Hand Book of Mizoram, *op. cit.*, p. XI.
32. Mara Autonomous District Council (Legislative Department, Records and Documents), Saiha, 14th December, 2001.
33. Local Self Government in Autonomous District Council Area of Mizoram with Special Reference to the Lai Autonomous District Council, *op. cit.*, pp. 5-6.
34. Doungel, Jangkhongam, The Role and Working of the Lai Autonomous District Council, Mizoram, *op. cit.* pp. 93-95.
35. *op. cit.*
36. Government of India, (1996) Constitution of India (As on 1st June, 1996), Department of Publication, New Delhi, pp. 153-158.
37. Ram rorelna tha (Good Government), Paper presented by Dr. Jangkhongam Doungel in Political Education Seminar, organised by Lairam Jesus Christ Baptist Church (LJCBC) Assembly at Lawngtlai on 1st October, 2005 and at Bualpui 'NG'on 10th October, 2005.
38. "Discretionary Powers of the Governor with Special Reference to the Sixth Schedule Area of Mizoram" in Mizoram College Teachers' Association (MCTA) Silver Jubilee Souvenir, contributed by Jangkhonagm Doungel, Aizawl, 2003.
39. Government of Mizoram, Notification No. A. 46011/1/2001-GAD of 23rd November, 2004, Aizawl.
40. Governmet of Mizoram, Mizoram Gazettee Extra-ordinary, Vol. XXXIV, 16th November, 2005, Issue No. 314, Director of Printing & Stationery, Aizawl, 2005.
41. Government of India, Constitution of India (As on 1st June, 1996), *op. cit.*, p. 156.
42. Local Self Government in Autonomous District Council Area of Mizoram with Special Reference to the Lai Autonomous District Council, *op. cit.*, p. 5.
43. Doungel, Jangkhongam, The Role and Working of the Lai Autonomous District, Mizoram, *op. cit.*, pp. 127-128.
44. Bakshi, P.M., (2006) the Costitution of India, Universal Law Publishing Co. Pvt. Ltd, Delhi, pp. 345-347.
45. Thanhranga, Dr. H.C., (1994) Administration of Justice in Mizoram, Lengchhawn Press, Chuauhrangi. P.C., Aizawl, pp. 13-14.
46. Government of Mizoram, Mizoram Gazette Extraordinary, 15th December, 1987, issue No. 409, Vol. XXVI, Director of Printing & Stationery.
47. *Op cit.*
48. Local Self Government in Autonomous District Council Area of Mizoram with Special Reference to Lai Autonomous District Council, *op. cit.*, p. 6
49. Doungel, Jangkhongam, The Role and Working of the Lai Autonomous District Council, Mizoram, *op. cit.*, pp. 118-124.

50. "Political Awareness—Problem and Prospect of the Functioning of the Lai Autonomous District Council with Objective Analysis of the Electoral Politics" by Jangkhongam Doungel in *Hmasawnna Kailawn II*, edited by Dr. R. Ramthara and published by Lai Reformation Forum (LRF), Aizawl, 2003, pp. 13-17.
51. Resource mobilization through Local Institution: A case Study of the Autonomous District Councils of Mizoram, paper, presented at training/ off Campus Course on Role and Responsibilities of the officials and elected Representatives of the District Council, organised by the National Institute of Rural Development (NIRD) at Lawngtlai on 4th April, 2006.
52. *Op. cit.*, pp. 13-17.
53. *Op. cit.*, p. 7.
54. *Ibid.*, p. 6.
55. 4th September, 2006 issue of *Ram Eng*, Local Daily News Paper, Edited by Lalrinmawia, H., Lawngtlai, Mizoram.
56. The Sixth Schedule to the Constitution (Amendment) Bill, 2006.

# Chapter 11

## The Congress Party in Mizoram
### *An Analysis of Its Performance*

L.H. CHHUANAWMA

---

Of all the existing parties in Mizoram, the Congress party had held the reigns of power for the longest period. Since 1966 when the MNF launched an independent movement, Mizoram today became arguably the most peaceful state in India. The Congress's role in the peace process, namely in the signing of the Mizo Accord (1986), is equally important as is that of the MNF.

The Congress party was in power in Mizoram altogether for 16 years, including its rule in the Mizo District Council for about 10 months. These 16 years exclude 1 year of Congress-MU coalition Executive Committee in the Mizo District Council headed by MU and 5 months of Interim Congress-MNF coalition government headed by the MNF. Of all the existing political parties in the state, the Congress ruled in Mizoram for the longest period. Only the erstwhile Mizo Union party, with an unparalleled 18 years of rule, surpassed the period of reign by the Congress. The MPC was in power for 5 years and 6 months. Assuming the present Zoramthanga-led government completes its 5-year tenure, the MNF would have been in power for 12 years. The following table makes this clear even after assuming that the present MNF government lasts its full term with Zoramthanga as Chief Minister.

Besides, the Congress leader Lal Thanhawla had occupied the top seat of power for the longest period among all the leaders, past and present, in Mizoram. He was Chief Minister for 12 years and 2 months, while T. Sailo (PC/MPC) held the post for 5 and a half year, the late Laldenga (MNF) 2 years and Zoramthanga (MNF) 10 years (assuming he completes his current term).

**Table 11.1:** Parties and duration of their rule in Mizoram

| *Party* | *Duration of Rule* | *Periods of Rule* |
|---|---|---|
| MU | 21 years | 18 years in 1952-1970, 1 year in 1971-1972, 2 years in 1972-1974. |
| INC | 16 years | 10 months in 1970-1972, 3 years in 1974-1977, 2 years and 2 months in 1984-1986, 10 years in 1989-1998. |
| MPC | 5½ years | 6 months in 1978, 5 years in 1979-1984. |
| MNF | 12 years | 6 months of 'Interim Rule' in 1986-1987, 1 year and 6 months in 1987-1988, 10 years in 1998-2008. |

During its long years of rule in Mizoram, the Congress party has done many things. The party's performance may be analyzed under the following heads:

## Political

### *Establishment of Peace*

The role played by the Congress party in facilitating MNF-Government of India peace negotiations culminating in the signing of the Mizo Peace accord in 1986 has become too familiar a story. As such, only significant points relating to the Congress's role in the peace process are mentioned here.

The Mizo District Congress Committee that was 'revived' on 20th December 1967 had as its policy number one restoration of peace in the then Mizo District. The Mizo Union that was in power in the District Council in the 1960s could not embark on peace initiative though it very much wanted because the MNF suspected the dormer's credentials to be 'an ambassador of peace'. Therefore, the Congress was the only political party that could effectively put on the mantle of a peace negotiator at that time. The Congress immediately seized the moment and in January 1968, it sent a memorandum to the Assam Government urging the latter to look for a political and not a military solution to the Mizo problem. The party also appealed to the MNF leaders and the Central leaders likewise. It sent 'peace delegations' four times to Delhi in 1968 alone. Further, on 11th November 1970, a resolution that reads: "Let the MNF and the Union Government start a dialogue" ("MNF leh Sawrkar laipui inbe rawh se", in Mizo) was adopted in the Mizo District Council.[1] This was to show that peace agenda had the popular mandate and that the party was serious about it. Because of the party's efforts, there began to be a fundamental shift of policy with regard to the Indian government *vis-à-vis* the Mizo problem. In his speech in the Parliament on 19th November 1970, Union Home Minister Y.B. Chavan said that 'Mizoram problem was a political problem'.[2] Hitherto this, the Indian government viewed the MNF insurgency purely as a law and order problem calling for a military solution. The 'merger Congress' UT government (1974-1977) continued to pursue the peace policy leading to the signing of the MNF-government of India agreement commonly referred to as the July Agreement or the First July Agreement.

The road to openly and officially start the MNF-Government of India peace dialogue was ultimately paved by the *1st July Agreement* signed by the MNF delegation led by its President Laldenga that included the present MNF President and Chief Minister of Mizoram Zoramthanga and S.L. Khurana, Home Secretary to the Indian Government, in New Delhi on 1st July 1976. Point number one of the agreement reads—*The MNF delegation acknowledged that Mizoram is an integral part of India and conveyed to the Government of India their resolve to accept a settlement of all problems in Mizoram within the framework of the Constitution of India.*

That T. Sailo-led PC Governments, which was in power in the Union Territory of Mizoram (June 1978-November 1978; May 1979-May 1984), launched a bloody and costly operation to eliminate the MNF by using the Indian army as well as a special unit of the Mizoram Police called 'Special Force' is common knowledge. The MNF countered by killing some of the PC MLA candidates during the 1979 and 1984 assembly elections. During the PC reign of power in Mizoram and that of the Janata Party in Delhi, Laldenga and his son Danmawia were arrested in Delhi on charges of waging war against the Indian state and passport forgery, the two were jailed in the famous Tihar Jail in Delhi on 8th July 1978. When no one including the PC leaders came forth to help them, Congress leaders Lal Thanhawla and Sainghaka bailed the two out of jail with great difficulty on 29th October 1979. The main reason of peace settlement was impossible because T. Sailo did not accede to the demands of Ladenga which were, among others, dismissal of T. Sailo's Ministry in Mizoram to be followed by formation of an interim Government in Mizoram headed by the MNF till a fresh election was held. In short, T. Sailo's refusal to step down as Chief Minister prevented peace settlement.[3]

The Congress party that had peace as its main poll plank in all its election manifestoes of 1970, 1972, 1978, 1979 and 1984, won the 1984 Assembly election largely because of its peace initiatives and the support extended to it by the underground MNF. In his taped message from London, Laldenga asked the people of Mizoram to vote for the Congress in the election. When the Congress party staged a comeback at the Centre in 1980 and in Mizoram in 1984, negotiations for peace in Mizoram resumed earnestly. As a result, the *Memorandum of Settlement* also commonly referred to as the *Mizo Accord*, was signed at 7:00 pm (IST) on 30th June 1986, at the chamber of Union Home Minister in New Delhi. On behalf of the MNF Laldenga signed on the Accord while RD Pradhan, Home Secretary to the Government of India, and Lalkhama, Chief Secretary to the Government of Mizoram, were the other signatories to the Accord.

As per the Accord, the MNF agreed to surrender all its personnel including arms, ammunitions and equipment apart from resolving to abide by the law. The Indian Government agreed to confer statehood on the Union Territory of Mizoram. In order to felicitate signing of the Accord, the MNF and the Indian National Congress had earlier reached an agreement in New Delhi on 25th June 1986 whereby the MNF and Congress would form an Interim Coalition Government in Mizoram. Though MPCC leaders were not signatories they were consulted and had agreed on the MNF-INC agreement.

As per the Agreement, Lal Thanhawla and his Council of Ministers relinquished their office on 20th May 1986 and the new Congress-MNF coalition government was sworn in on 21st August 1986. The MNF President Laldenga as Chief Minister headed the MNF-Congress government while the Congress President Lal Thanhawla became a Deputy CM. By the State of Mizoram Act, 1986 (34 of 1986), enacted by the Parliament, Mizoram became the 23rd State of the Union of India on 20th February 1987.

### *Lessening People's Sufferings during the Insurgency*

The Mizo Independent Movement launched by the MNF since 1966 was followed by a massive retaliation from the Indian Government.

Torture, rape, killing, detention, imprisonment, destruction of properties, forcible groping of villages, etc. were orders of the day. Almost every person, including members of the then ruling party in the Mizo District Council, the MU, were suspected by the Indian security forces to be either a member of the MNF or an MNF sympathizer. The Congress party, the first and the only national party to have been established in the then Mizo District, which was openly opposed to the MNF's separatist policy was in power both in Assam state and at the Centre during the 1960s and the 1970s. The Indian security forces seemed to have acknowledged and accepted interventions, on behalf of the suffering masses, from the Congress leaders during the period immediately following the outbreak of insurgency. The Congress leaders would carry cards in their shirt pockets bearing personal and party identifications. The cards were literally tickets to personal security and freedom apart from being symbols of power and authority in those days.

The Congress leaders freed many innocent people detained in Assam Rifles Quarter Guard, Brigade Quarter Guard and Police Lock up besides freeing those in various jails in Mizoram and Assam. The party was also able to stop the Indian army's attempt to forcibly grope villages like a historic place Biate. An attempt to forcibly grope villages along the Sialsuk ridge (now Sateek Assembly Constituency) and other villages such as Lungpho into Keitum and N. Hlimem into Kawnpui was also prevented when the move was successfully challenged in the Gauhati High Court in 1970-71. There were several other instances of the Congress leaders coming to the aid of people denied of their rights by the Indian security forces. Those human rights violations involved rape and molestations, torture, forced labour, burning of houses, destruction of properties and so on.[4] The words 'human rights' were unheard of then in the District, but the Congress acted as a champion of human rights in those darkest days in the history of Mizoram, the post-1966 period lasting for about a decade. That the party did all those mostly while out of power may be noted.

The first newspaper published by the Congress called *Hruaitu* (which means *Leader*), *a* Mizo weekly, and later replaced by another one called *Remna Palai* (which means *Ambassador for Peace*), a Mizo daily, were used to launch both the campaigns against the abuse of human rights and for establishment of peace. Although the party continued to work for lessening the burden of the people till the final settlement of peace in 1986, the emergence of T. Sailo, a retired

Brigadier of the Indian Army who launched a full-fledged human rights movement by forming the Human Rights Committee in 1974, somewhat eclipsed the Congress's efforts in this regard.

### *The HPC Accord (1994)*

The post-Accord peace in the state was very soon disturbed by violent activities of the Hmar People's Convention that demanded, since its formation on 18th December 1986, an Autonomous District Council for the Hmars living in the north eastern parts of Mizoram under the 6th Schedule to the Constitution of India. To end this, the Congress government signed an accord with the HPC called *Memorandum of Settlement between the Government of Mizoram and the Hmar People's Convention* on 27th July 1994 at Aizawl. Accordingly, the Government of Mizoram constituted Sinlung Hills Development Council, with its headquarters at Sakawrdai, in 1997. The HPC accord was the first political settlement the government of Mizoram has ever reached with a group demanding autonomy within Mizoram.

### Administrative

(a) *Policy towards statehood*: To start with, the first administrative demand made by the Congress was the *Scottish Pattern of Administration*, also known as *Nehru Pattern of Administration* or simply as *Nehru Plan*, adopted by the party as its main electoral plank in the 1962 District Council election. Proposed by Prime Minister Jawaharlal Nehru, *The Nehru Plan* intended "to give the largest measure of autonomy within the framework of maintaining connection with Assam" to the hill areas of Assam.[5] But details of the scheme were never clearly spelt out. Since they did not want to antagonize Assam Congress leaders, the Congress leaders chose *Nehru Plan* as this would not entail the Mizo District leaving Assam. The party never pursued this policy, quite unpopular among the people, beyond the 1962 election.
On April 14, 1971, the coalition Executive Committee (INC-MU-Independents) under the leadership of Ch. Chhunga passed a resolution demanding a *Mizoram State* within India, and "the unification of all the Mizo inhabited areas.[6]

Meanwhile, the Central Government was considering elevation of the Mizo District to a Union Territory status. The Congress-MU joint letter, submitted to the Indian Prime Minister Indira Gandhi on 5th September 1971, read: "To us peace and prosperity is most important and in this context granting of Statehood to Mizoram is considered imperative. The status of Union Territory for Mizoram can only be a transitional measure.... The interest of Pawi and Lakher region shall be safeguarded by granting a District Council, as provided in the 6th schedule to the Constitution".[7]

Dengthuama's group (Congress 'O') of the District Congress and its coalition partner in the District Council the MU reluctantly accepted a UT status for Mizoram. But Hrangchhuana's faction (Congress 'R') submitted a separate memorandum to the Prime Minster of India on 1st September 1971 rejecting the UT proposal and demanded that "the future administrative set up of the Mizos be considered only after, and in the light of recommendation of a proposed convention called 'Mizo People's Convention' to be "immediately convened by the Government".[8]

Despite this, Prime Minister Indira Gandhi announced the elevation of the Mizo District into a Union Territory at Aizawl on 21st January 1972. On hearing this, Congress MLA A. Thanglura, who had earlier conveyed his objections to the Prime Minster on the proposed UT and instead demanded creation of "United Mizo-Manipur State" comprising Mizo-inhabited areas of Assam, Manipur and Mizoram, resigned as Assam Cabinet Minister in protest.[9]

Apart from the demand for statehood jointly pursued with the MU in 1971, the Congress that was dissatisfied with the UT had formed a State Sub-Committee with Lal Thanhawla as its Convener in 1975. Moreover, its Assembly election manifestoes of 1978 and 1979 clearly contained the demand for statehood. However, the party never earnestly pursued the demand for Mizoram state because it feared that the same would derail the peace process. It was only in 1978 that the Congress for the first time included the demand for statehood in its election manifesto. A claim by some that the 1972

Congress election manifesto contained 'Promise to have statehood' is incorrect as the original copy of the said manifesto available with this researcher clearly reveals that no such demand was made by the party in 1972.

In the words of Lal Thanhawla, the Congress had accepted, albeit reluctantly, a UT status for Mizoram for three reasons: (a) The desire for Mizoram to be out of Assam was so great that the party considered a UT more acceptable than continuing under Assam as a mere District. The party therefore accepted 'UT with Legislature'. (b) The Union Government seemed to be well bent on conferring a UT status to Mizoram despite the wish of the people to the contrary. (c) If statehood were granted to Mizoram, the MNF would not have any face saving 'trophy' to bring home.[10] So the party did not consider it wise to wholeheartedly follow its statehood policy to its logical conclusion. For this very reason, the party claimed that even when the Central Congress Government was open to the idea of granting statehood to Mizoram in the early 1980s, the then Mizoram Congress UT Government and the party leaders ruled out the option (of statehood).[11] Thus, the Congress had shown great foresight in deftly handling the issue of statehood.

(b) *Creation of Administrative Districts*: Upon the attainment of the status of Union Territory, and on 1st September 1972 Mizoram was divided into three administrative districts: Aizawl, Lunglei and Chhimtuipui with their respective headquarters at Aizawl, Lunglei and Saiha. Aizawl was made the capital of the new Union Territory. On 29th July 1998, the Congress government created eight new Administrative Districts by demarcating the existing three Districts of Aizawl, Lunglei and Chhimtuipui. The new Districts were: Aizawl, Champhai, Kolasib, Mamit, Serchhip, Lunglei, Lawngtlai and Saiha.

## Infrastructure

*Infrastructure* is defined as *the basic systems and services or the basic physical and organizational structures that are necessary for a country, a government, a society, an enterprise or an organization to run or operate smoothly, for example buildings, transport, water and power supplies*. The Congress governments have built a vast array of infrastructure for Mizoram.

1. *Buildings*: Between 1989 and 1998 alone, about a hundred RCC buildings for offices of the state government, educational institutions, hospitals and other public health centres, tourist lodges, guest houses, jails, etc. were constructed (and a few purchased). Some of these were:[12] 300-bedded Civil Hospital, Mizoram Legislative Assembly, State Guest House, Tourist Lodges (one each at Chaltlang, Aizawl, Kolasib, Champhai, and Lunglei), State Museum, Youth Hostel, Yatri Niwas (Tourist Home), High Court complex, Legislators' Home, SCERT and DIET complexes, Mizoram Houses (one each at Salt Lake, Kolkata, and Guwahati), Circuit House at Lunglei. (Otherwise indicated, the buildings are located at Aizawl).
   The Congress governments also started constructions of what today have become the best of buildings in Mizoram: Chief Minister's bungalow at MacDonald Hill, Aizawl (commenced 1995); Saikuti Hall at Lunglei (commenced in May 1996, completed on 30th August 2003); Millennium Centre at Dawrpui, Aizawl (commenced in 1995-96, completed on 15th August 17, 2006). Initially this landmark Centre was called Aizawl Auditorium, also informally known as 'Hawla Auditorium' after Lal Thanhawla, but it was renamed Millennium Centre by the MNF government in 2003.
2. *Communications*: (i) Bridges—Between 1989 and 1998, the Congress governments have constructed numerous bridges, such as, nineteen (19) Bailey bridges, four (4) Suspension bridges, five (5) STP bridges, six (6) RCC Slab Minor bridges, two (2) Stiffened Girder Suspension bridges, one (1) Girder bridge, four (4) RCC bridges, three (3) RCC T. Beams, Jeep-able Suspension bridge and Built-up Girder bridge-one each.[13] The Congress government (1993-1998) had also initiated works on

what has now become the longest bridge in the state, the Kolodyne Bridge on R Kolodyne at Kawlchaw.

(ii) *Roads*: [14] The Congress governments have completed four (4) NEC (North Eastern Council)-funded black topped road projects and sixteen (16) state 'all-weather' road projects during its tenure.

By far the largest development project in Mizoram, the Rs. 350.00 cr. (US $ 70.00 million Mizoram World Bank Funded State Roads Project locally known as World Bank Roads, such as Aizawl-Thenzawl-Lunglei Road, Aizawl Bypass Road, etc. was actually initiated by the Congress government. The Congress government and the funding agency, the International Development Association, a subsidiary of the Word Bank (officially known as International Bank for Reconstruction and Development), had signed Project Coordinating Consultancy Service Agreement on 22nd August 1998.

Besides this, the Congress governments either undertook several other road projects afresh or continued ongoing projects such as Lawngtlai-Nalkawn-Chamdur Road, Champhai-Tiau-Falam-Tidim Road (completed up to Tiau), etc. Moreover, construction of several roads was completed when the party was in power even prior to 1989.

(iii) *Lengpui Airport*: Commenced in December 1996 and completed in December 1998 in a record time, the lone airport in the state-Lengpui airport, located at 44 kms away from Aizawl, is the second largest airport after Guwahati airport of Assam in the North East India. Capable of accommodating a Boeing 737 aircraft, it is also the only airport in the entire country purely under the state government control.

(iv) *Computerization of Railway Out Agency*: The only train booking counter in Mizoram, the Railway Out Agency at Aizawl, was computerized in 1997 when the Congress was in its last leg of power.

3. *Water supply*: [15] During the Congress rule between 1989 and 1998, the party claims to have supplied water to 1341 villages

through different methods such as gravity (piped water), hand pumps (tube well), rainwater harvesting, and IVSS (improvement of village spring sources). Urban water supply projects were started and completed by the Congress governments in Lunglei, Saiha, Serchhip, Kolasib, Hnahthial and Zawlnuam. Started by the PC government in 1983, Greater Aizawl Water Supply Scheme (GAWSS) Phase-I was continued by the Congress government since the party came to power in May 1984. It was commissioned in December 1988. The Congress government also initiated GAWSS Phase-II and got the Central Government sanction for the Scheme in 1997. Work on Phase-II commenced in March 2000 during the MNF rule.

**Power**

Various steps taken by the Congress governments in augmenting power supply in the state may be enumerated as under:

(i) *Micro, Mini and Small Hydroelectric Projects*: The Congress governments have either completed hydroelectric projects such as Khawiva-110 kW, near Lunglei; Tuirivang-300 kW, near Muallungthu; Maicham Phase 1: 2 mw, near N Vanlaiphai; Vawralui-100 kW, near Khawlian; Ramrilui-300 kW, near Chawngte; Teirei-3 mW, near W Phaileng; Leiva-100 kW, near Kawlbem. Works on Tuipanglui-3 mW, near Tuipang was commenced in 1992 and completed in 2005; Kau-Tlabung-3 mW, near Thenhlum in 1994 and completed in 2005).[16] (Tuila-30 kW, Tuipui-50 kW, Lau-30 kW, Tuisumpui-450 kW, Tuidum-30 kW and Laililui-30 kW projects thought commissioned during the Congress rule were later closed or damaged because of flood, high maintenance costs, damaged machineries, etc.).

(ii) *Thermal and Diesel Power Projects*: The Congress government initiated 8 mW Rokhia (Tripura) Gas Thermal Project for Mizoram that was commissioned in 1998. It also started 5 mW Diesel Power Plant at Zuangtui, Aizawl, was commissioned in 1997. It also laid necessary groundwork for both 20 mW HFO-Based Diesel Generating Power Plant at Bairabi, and 1.5 mW Diesel Power Plant at Champhai, commissioned during the MNF rule respectively on 7th May 2004 and in December 1998.[17]

(iii) *Major Hydroelectric Projects*: The Congress governments had also undertaken investigations and other necessary works on major projects such as Bairabi, Tuirial, Tuivai, Kolodyne: Phase-I and Phase-II, Tuivawl and Tuirini hydroelectric projects. Since these are all major projects in which investigations alone take a long time, work could not commence during the Congress rule.

(iv) *Transmission Lines and Sub-Stations*: The Congress governments had put in place nine 132 kv Transmission Lines, two 33 kv Transmission Lines and twelve Sub-Stations (nine 132 kv; one 66 kv and two 33 kv) during 1990-1998.[18]

**Education**

Various achievements of the ruling Congress party in the field of education noted in the following manner:

(i) *Establishment of the MBSE*: The Congress government under Ch Chhunga's leadership took a landmark step by passing The Mizoram Board of School Education Act, 1975 on 24th September 1975. Under the Act, the Mizoram Board of School Education was established at Aizawl in November 1976. Creation of MBSE not only ended Mizoram's association with the Secondary Education Board of Assam that had hitherto exercised control on the education system in Miozram but also marked a new era in the history of the development of education in Mizoram. The entire school education system of Mizoram including Higher Secondary Education has been under the jurisdiction of MBSE since then.

(ii) *Institutions*: It was during the Congress rule that the erstwhile Mizoram Institute of Education was established in 1975 at Aizawl for teachers' training in Bachelor of Education. Again during the party's rule the MIE was upgraded into college on 26th March 1997 and the same was renamed College of Teachers' Education at the same time. This centrally recognized institute, affiliated to the Mizoram University, is the only one for B. Ed. training in the state. Besides, Teachers' Training Institute at Lunglei was upgraded to District Institute of Education and Training by the Congress government in 1993. On 16th October 1975, Mizoram Hindi Training College was opened at Durtlang in Aizawl. Though maintained by the state government, the MHTC is affiliated to Central Institute of Hindi, Agra. In 2006, the MHTC offers four courses: M.Ed., B.Ed., D.E.D. (Diploma in Education), and J.T.T.C. (Junior Teachers' Training Certificate in Hindi). The Congress government also opened Women Polytechnic at Durtlang in Aizawl in September 1998. It now offers Diploma courses in four Departments. Two very important educational institutions established during the Congress rule, College of Veterinary Science and Animal Husbandry and RIPANS are mentioned under a different head.

(iii) *Upgradations*: In 1992, the Congress government upgraded three Deficit Colleges to Government Colleges, viz. Kolasib College, Saiha College and Zirtiri Women College at Aizawl. Besides, seven Aided Colleges were upgraded to Deficit status. They were: J Buana College at Lunglei and Aizawl North College in 1991; Mamit College and Saitual College in 1993; Khawzawl College and Zawlnuam College in 1994; and Aizawl West College in 1995. The Congress governments also upgraded many schools (Primary, Middle and High schools) to Deficit and Government status. On 26th September 1975 the Congress government adopted an Independent MLA Sapliana-sponsored resolution for the establishment of a University College at Aizawl under the North Eastern Hills University (Shillong). In pursuance of this resolution, on 19th April 1979 the PC government upgraded the then Pachhunga Memorial Government as University College and simultaneously renamed the same as Pachhunga University College. Today, PUC has become arguably the best college in the state.

(iv) *Policy decisions*: An important development took place in the management of education in the state in 1989-91 when the Congress government took certain crucial policy decisions. The single Directorate of School Education was trifurcated into Directorate of Higher and Technical Education (college and university), Directorate of School Education (schools including Plus 2) and Directorate of Art and Culture in order to facilitate better management of the system in 1989. Further, to improve the functionality of educational institutions, a 'Comprehensive School Scheme' was introduced in a phased manner from 1991. In the same year, 1490 out of 1823 schools were organized into 199 'School Complexes' with the main aim of decentralizing management. Two more important decisions were: to delegate the power of drawing and disbursing money to all Headmasters of new Government schools, and to upgrade the existing Sub-Divisions into Educational Districts as well as to create two more Educational Districts.[19]

In 1995 during the Congress rule, Plus 2 stage was de-linked from colleges and selected schools were upgraded to Higher Secondary Schools. From 1997, Central Board of Secondary Education course was introduced in the Higher Secondary Schools of the state replacing the MBSE course.[20]

Largely because of the efforts by the Congress governments, Mizoram improved its literacy ranking in the country from the third (74.26 per cent) in 1981 to the second (82.27 per cent) in 1991 position.

(v) *University*: Contrary to the general perception that the Congress party always wanted a state University, the party had always been committed to establishment of a Central University in Mizoram. Way back in 1992, the Congress government passed a resolution in the Assembly for establishment of a Central University in the state. The 1993 MPCC (I)-MJD joint election manifesto also contained a promise to establish a Central University in Mizoram. But owing to serious financial crunch in the country at that time, the Union Government did not allow setting up of Central Universities across the country. Under this circumstance, an informal Cabinet Meeting held on 10th August 1995 accepted a state University offered by the Union government. Chief Minister Lal Thanhawla announced this in his Independence Day speech on 15th August 1995 at Aizawl. However, because of serious opposition to this from various quarters, the government at its formal Cabinet Meeting held on 6th May 1997 decided to "revive the earlier demand for establishment of a Central University in Mizoram". When Prime Minister I.K. Gujral visited Aizawl on 22nd May 1997, the Congress government reiterated its demand for a Central University. On that very day, the PM announced that a Central University would be established in Mizoram (A one time grant of Rs. 4 crores sanctioned by the Planning Commission of India for 'Mizoram State University' in 1995-96 was utilized for laying of water pipelines, construction of internal and approach roads, etc. at the then Tanhril NEHU campus, now Mizoram University). An Act of Parliament finally established Mizoram University (a Central University) established on 2nd July 2001 at Aizawl.

**Socio-Economic**

Besid what have already been discussed, various other socio-economic programmes implemented by the ruling Congress may be further analyzed under the following heads:

(i) *Health and family welfare*: It was during the Congress rule that the first World Bank project in Mizoram, a Rs. 67.00 crore RCH (Reproductive and Child Health) Project was implemented in the state during 1997-2002. This money, purely grant, was utilized for infrastructural developments: purchase of vehicles, furniture and equipments, and construction of buildings, operation theatres and labour rooms. Hundreds of contract workers were employed for 5 years: 15 doctors, 60 health workers, 170 staff nurses and 16 lab technicians. The RCH Project was so successful that the Department was awarded Rs. 25 lakhs by the Central Government.

A 300-bedded Civil Hospital, Administrative Building of

Civil Hospital, Cobalt Therapy Unit, Central Medical Store, all at Aizawl, have been put in place during the Congress rule. Between 1988-89 and 1998, hospitals has increased from 11 to 13, Primary Health Centres from 33 to 43, Sub-Health Centres from 314 to 336; however, during the same period, Subsidiary Health Centres has decreased from 22 to 13 on account of up gradations of several SHCs to PHCs. A Post-Partum Unit was established for delivery and post-delivery care at Kulikawn, Aizawl, on 20th August 1993. The Congress government also passed a resolution, interestingly sponsored by an opposition MLA Dr. R. Lalthangliana, in the State Assembly in 1996 for the creation of 'Mizoram State Hospital' as a 'special project'. This was the origin of the State Referral Hospital at Falkawn, near Aizawl, conceived and planned by the Congress government. A scheme approval for starting the NEC-funded RIPANS (Regional Institute of Para Medical and Nursing Sciences), at Aizawl, the only nursing and medical science institute in the state also was obtained by the Congress government on 30th March 1995. RIPANS started functioning from January 1996 with the first batch of students. Construction of RIPANS complex at Zemabawk, Aizawl, was begun in 1998. In 2006, RIPANS offers three Degree courses (affiliated to Mizoram University), three Diploma courses, and one Certificate course (both recognized by All India Council for Technical Education, New Delhi).

(ii) *Animal Husbandry and Veterinary*: Some of the main achievements of the AH&V Department during the Congress's tenure may be briefly noted.

(a) *Farms*: Various farms were established such as seven Piggery Farms, four Rabbit Production Base Farms, four Fodder Demonstration Farms; Cattle Breeding, Pig Multiplication, Buffalo Breeding, Mithun Breeding, Goat Demonstration Farms—one each; two Poultry Demonstration Farms.

(b) *Institutions*: Construction of buildings for College of Veterinary Science and Animal Husbandry at Selesih in Aizawl was started on 30th October 1995 and the College started functioning on 23rd February 1998. The College is under Central Agriculture University, Jorhat (Assam). In 2006, it offers a 5-year plus 6-month internship degree courses BVSc&AH (Bachelor of Veterinary Science & AH) in 17 Departments.

Other small institutions established when the Congress was in power include School of Veterinary Science at Lungpher near Lunglei, National Demonstration-*cum*-Training Centre at Selesih, Aizawl, Artificial Insemination Centre at Sihphir near Aizawl, National Demonstration-*cum*-training Centre for farmers' training at Champhai, and National Demonstration-*cum*-Training Centre for Department Officers at Champhai.

(c) *Introduction of exotic breed in pigs*: Introduction of exotic breed in pigs, bigger and fast growth type was first begun in Mizoram in 1974 during the tenure of 'merger Congress' Ministry (UT). Then in 1998, Large White Yorkshire and Landrace breeding stock, lean meat type was imported from the USA and Australia by the Congress government (Shortly after this, the same stock was imported from the same sources during the MNF's rule in 1999).

(d) *MULCO*: Mizoram Milk Producers' Cooperative Union Ltd. (MMPCUL) was started in 1984 with the government as a shareholder. In 1991, the Congress government initiated Aizawl Dairy Project 10,000 litres capacity. In 1994, the Project began production and MMPCUL was renamed MULCO (Mizoram Multi-Commodity Producers' Cooperative Union Ltd.). Apart from its main produce milk, MULCO also produces *ghee, paneer, dahi, rasgula, rosmalai and gulab jamun.* MULCO has become a very successful society today.

(iii) *Industry*: Some of the prominent measures taken by the Congress when in power for development and promotion of industry in the state are listed below:

(a) *Industrial Training Institute*: Aizawl Industrial Training Institute that had been functioning at Silchar (Assam) since its inception in 1964 was shifted to Aizawl in March 1975 by while Ch Chhunga was the Chief Minister. The only industrial training institute in the state, the ITI is maintained by the state but is affiliated to Director-General of Employment and Training, Government of India, New Delhi. In 2006, the Institute offers one-year and two-year Certificate Courses in 22 different trades.

(b) *Machineries*: Between 1989 and 1993, machineries such as Maize Milling Plant at Khawzawl, Ginger Oil & Oleoresin Plant at Sairang, Fruit Juice Concentrate Plant at Chhingchhip, Tung Oil Extraction Unit at Zemabawk in Aizawl, Gur & Khandsari Plant at Saitual, Flour Mill at Zuangtui were installed.

(c) *The Industrial Policy of 1989*: The first Industrial Policy in Mizoram was adopted when, on 15th March 1989, the Congress government notified *The Industrial Policy of Mizoram, 1989*. With a view to gradually abandoning the practice of shifting cultivation, a shift from primary to secondary sectors was attempted by encouraging development of rural industries like handloom, handicraft, village and cottage industries. Institutional, marketing etc. supports and incentives like subsidies, grant-in-aid, etc. were announced to enable industrial development in the state. Domestic market and local entrepreneurs were sought to be protected by prohibiting people from outside the state to set up small scale industries. However, investment from outside was allowed in medium and large scale industries in through joint ventures.

Any approach to industrial development in the state since then had been guided by this Policy until *The New Industrial Policy of Mizoram, 2000* was announced by the MNF's government in 2000. Without entirely replacing the 1989 Policy, the 2000 Policy supplements the former. However, in matters of granting incentives/subsidies to industries, industries set up before 24th December 1997 shall be governed by the old Policy whereas all those set up after this shall be governed by the new Policy.

(d) *Corporations*: The 1989 Industrial Policy envisaged setting up of industrial projects considered viable in large and medium sectors through state-owned corporations. Accordingly, Mizoram Food and Allied Industries Corporation Limited (MIFCO) was set up in 1989, Zoram

Electronics Development Corporation (ZENICS) in 1991 and Mizoram Agricultural Marketing Development Corporation Limited (MAMCO) in 1993—all at Aizawl. The first two are under Industries Department while MAMCO is under Trade and Commerce Department.

(d) *MKVI Board*: The Congress government had established Mizoram Khadi and Village Industries Board on 1st March 1986 with a view to promote Khadi and Village industries. The MKVIB is both a statutory and a promotional body.

(iv) *The New Land Use Policy*: The Congress government in 1984-86 launched a massive economic development project known as Land Use Policy (LUP). In its new form as NLUP since 1989, this became the Congress party's flagship development programme and the most visible image of the party till this day. The MNF's government replaced the LUP with a Centrally Sponsored Scheme called Jhum Control Project in 1987. The Congress government revived the LUP in 1989 with a new name, New Land Use Policy ('New' was added). While the implementing agency of the LUP was Forest Department, a newly created Rural Development Department was made the implementing agency of the NLUP. The NLUP basically intended to draw farmers away from the traditional occupation of shifting cultivation to permanent occupation. Every farming household was offered to choose anyone of the forty-six (46) trades broadly classified under three sectors: Agriculture and Allied sector, Animal Husbandry and Industries. The government directly gave cash purely as grant ranging from Rs. 20,000.00 to Rs. 58,000.00 to beneficiaries of the NLUP.[21]

The NLUP covered 15 out of the total 22 RD blocks in Mizoram. Though stress was given to rural areas, poor urban families were also covered by the scheme. The MNF government continued it between 1998 and 2001 before terminating the same and implementing its own version called MIP (Mizoram Intodelhna Programme or Mizoram Self-Sufficiency Project) since 26th March 2002. Between 1990 and 2001, a total of Rs. 1,58,76,84,839.00 (Congress's period: Rs. 1,51,44,02,538.00 and 65445 families; MNF's period: Rs. 7,32,82,301.00 and 13034 families) was given to 78479 families of beneficiaries. With another 4628 beneficiary families in 1984-87, altogether 83107 household families benefited from the NLUP.[22]

(v) *Agriculture and Allied Sectors*: A brief account of the main activities and achievements of various Congress governments under Agriculture and Allied Departments, viz. Agriculture and Minor Irrigation, Horticulture, Sericulture, and Fisheries Departments is given below:

(a) *Agriculture and Minor Irrigation*: During the Congress regime, some laboratories, research centres, etc. were set up, viz. Soil Testing Laboratory at Aizawl, Krishi Vigyan Kendra (English: 'Farm Science Centre') at Kolasib in association with the Indian Council of Agricultural Research, Seed Testing Laboratory at Aizawl, State Bio-Fertilizer Production Unit at Neihbawi near Aizawl, Biological Control Laboratory at Aizawl. These provide institutional and R&D support to develop agriculture in the state. A beginning in organic farming was made by implementing Organic Farming Programme in 1994.

A very significant decision was taken when in August 1984 Minor Irrigation Wing of PWD was transferred to the Agriculture Department thereby giving a much-needed technical support to the latter. Minor Irrigation Wing then began to have a separate Annual Plan from 1985-86 onwards. Above all, irrigation projects began to be departmentally executed, as poor farmers were unable to execute works that required huge financial investment and technical expertise. This enabled, for the first time, irrigation projects to start earnestly in Mizoram.[23] Several minor irrigation projects were completed between 1989 and 1998—48 River Diversion Schemes and two River Lift Schemes, bringing a substantial agricultural land under irrigation. Water and Power Consultancy Services, a Government of India undertaking, prepared Master Plan for development of Irrigation-1995. The Master Plan estimates that irrigation potential of the state is 100000 ha. Out of this 96000 ha is Surface Water Potential and 4,000 ha is Ground Water Potential.[24]

Former Director of Agriculture R Thansanga told this researcher that agriculture mechanization was modestly implemented by the Congress governments through introduction of bulldozers that levelled land for cultivation entirely free of cost; giving machineries and agriculture implements such as tractors, power tillers, water pump sets, oil expellers, sugarcane crushers, paddy harvesters etc. to farmers subsidized at 50 per cent of the cost. Besides, several kilometres of Agriculture Link Roads were constructed. Massive support to farmers by way of supplying, free or at 50 per cent subsidy, fertilizers and manures, hybrid and quality seeds for French beans, squash and other commercial crops were also given to farmers.

(b) *Horticulture*: A separate Directorate of Horticulture was carved out of its parent body Agriculture Department in 1993. Farmers were supported by way of supplying, free or at 50 per cent subsidy, fertilizers and manures, Mandarin orange and hatkora seedlings, banana and pineapple suckers, Assam lemon cuttings. Plantation of Mizoram banana variety (known locally as *khumtung balhla* or *lawng balhla*), perhaps the best variety of banana in the country, was massively and successfully promoted. 'Green House' concept in horticulture and agriculture was also introduced in the state in 1994. Most successful in kitchen gardens, vegetables and crops are grown under controlled temperature and climate using ultraviolet stabilized films as roofs.[25]

(c) *Sericulture and Fisheries*: Horticulture Department was carved out as full-fledged Directorate from the Industry Department in 1985. Silkworm rearing was encouraged by organizing cooperative societies and farmers' groups that were in turn given institutional supports and various incentives like loans, grants, mulberry cuttings, etc. Silk Reeling and Twisting Plant was installed at Zemabawk, Aizawl on 18th September 1992. In 1993, Fisheries Department was separated from the Agriculture Department and was made a full-fledged Directorate.

(vi) *Legislation*: Many laws were passed by the Congress governments over the years that have transformed socio-economic life of the people one way or the other. Some of them are: The Mizoram Iskuts (Restriction on movement beyond Inner Line) Order, 1991; The Mizoram Agricultural Produces (Restriction on Movement) Order, 1994; The Mizoram State Agricultural Produces Marketing Regulation Act, 1996. These laws have been invoked several times whereby import of items like cabbages, brinjals, fish etc. into Mizoram was either stopped or restricted in order to protect domestic market and to promote local produces.

There are many more achievements of the Congress party while in power. In passing, several laws it enacted, the groundwork it laid for shifting the 1st Assam Rifles of the Indian Army out of the centre of Aizawl, and the 39,214 families it had given Galvanized Iron sheets for roofs free of cost may be mentioned. On 1st May 1991, the Congress government created Mizoram Public Service Commission on the lines of the Union Public Service Commission. The MPSC is responsible, among others, for recruitment and promotion of top administrative officials of the state including Mizoram Civil Service and Mizoram Police Service.

**Role in Socio-Economic Transformation of Mizoram**

The role of Congress party in bringing about socio-economic transformation in Mizoram may be briefly examined under the following heads:

(i) *Impact of the NLUP*: In spite of many criticisms like faulty implementation of the scheme, absence of monitoring and evaluation of the scheme etc., the NLUP has tremendous economic impact on hundreds of families in particular and on the economy of Mizoram in general. Lalsiama Fambawl, who was in charge of the Publicity Wing of the NLUP from 1994 to 1998, told the researcher that the success rate of the NLUP in terms of its lasting economic impact on the beneficiaries would be around 30 per cent. According to him, the NLUP has sustained the livelihood of hundreds of families till today in several areas of trade, notably in AH&V, Industry, Agriculture and Allied sectors. His account of the success of NLUP is given below (The researcher's interviews with other government officials, academics etc. and a few "Success Stories of the NLUP" published by the government have largely corroborated Fambawl's accounts)[26]:

(a) *Animal Husbandry and Veterinary sector*: Mithun rearing (for meat and plowing fields) in areas such as Farkawn, Vaphai, Lungpho and Hmawngkawn. Hill cattle rearing (for meat and milk) in areas like Rulchawm, Saitual, Tualvung and Farkawn. The present members of a very successful cooperative society in and around Aizawl, the MULCO are beneficiaries of the NLUP.

(b) *Industry sector*: Furniture workshops, tailoring, black smithy, shoe repairing, weaving and knitting. These successful cottage industries could be found in most parts of the state, especially in urban areas. Baktawng village is the best example of the success of NLUP-generated economy from where wooden furniture is today being supplied in large quantities to all parts of Mizoram.

(c) *Agriculture and Allied sectors*: *Mandarin Orange* (local name: *Serthlum)* in Thingsulthliah, Tlungvel, Seling, Bunghmun and Baktawng areas under Thingsulthliah RD block; West Phaileng, Serhmun, Kawrthah, Bunghmun, Rengdil, Zawlnuam, Kawrtethawveng and Tuidam areas under W Phaileng and Zawlnuam RD blocks; Ropuichhip, Reiek and Mamit in Reiek RD block; and Kawnpui in Thingdwal RD block. *Areca nut* (Betel nut, local name: *Kuhva*) in Zamuang, Zawlnuam, Bunghmun (Borai), Kanhmun, Bilkhawthlir and Vairengte areas. *Banana* in Thingsulthliah, Tlungvel, Seling, Khumtung and Baktawng areas. *Hatkora* in areas within Thingdawl RD block, Aizawl and the surrounding areas. *Assam Lemon* (local name: *Limbu*) in areas under Thingsulthliah and Reiek RD blocks. *Pineapple* (local name: *Lakhuihthei*) in areas under Serchhip and Thingsulthliah RD blocks. *Passion Fruit* (local name: *Sapthei*), in several parts of the state, Fisheries in Zawlnuam and Thingdawl RD blocks.

(ii) *Increase in cropped area and production*: As a result of various measures taken by the Congress governments over the years, areas under irrigation and crop cultivation has increased besides an increase in production of rice and other crops as indicated by some available data. Net irrigated area in the state has increased from 6.105 thousand ha (1992-93) to 8.517 thousand ha (1998-99), areas sown more than twice has increased from 2.281 thousand ha (1990-91) to 131.546 thousand ha (1998-99), and total cropped area has increased from 104.879 thousand ha (1990-91) to 128.806 thousand ha (1998-99).[27]

From a mere 40,700 MT (Metric Tonnes) in 1974-75, total rice production has jumped to 1,10,189 MT in 1998-99. High Yielding Variety (rice) production has tremendously increased from only 60 MT in 1988-89 to 13,008 MT in 1998-99. Increase in production of some commercial crops, measured in MT, is especially illustrative of the success in Horticulture. Production of chilies grew from 227 in 1974-75 to 3,132 in 1993-94; ginger from 7,055 in 1980-81 to 10,495 in 1990-91; turmeric from 181 in 1975-76 to 1,731 in 1993-94; horticulture vegetables from 8,661 in 1987-88 to 26,827 in 1998-99; sugarcane from 2,956 in 1987-88 to 7,863 in 1998-99.[28]

The following table tells a further success story.

**Table 11.2:** Export of Various Crops to Outside Mizoram (*1995-1998 & 1998-1999*)[29]

| *Sl. No.* | *Name crops* | *1995-1998* | *1998-1999* |
|---|---|---|---|
| 1. | Ginger | 2,48,836 qt | 1,53,840s qt |
| 2. | Chilies | 28,406 qt | 7,866 qt |
| 3. | Sesamum | 3,318 qt | 1,024 qt |
| 4. | Squash | 49,940 qt | 20,528 qt |
| 5. | Ram Cotton | 254 qt | 15 qt |
| 6. | Turmeric | 360 qt | 30 qt |
| 7. | Orange | 86,23,034 no | 2,79,570 no |
| 9. | Pineapple | 46,962 qt | 3,109 qt |

As a result of the steps taken by the Congress while in power, Mizoram today becomes largely self-sufficient in vegetables such as cabbages, French beans, brinjals and bitter gourd (*charratis*). Since the introduction of *Lakadong* (*Shillong*) variety of turmeric during the Congress rule, Mizoram is now able to meet its substantial domestic demand in this essential curry powder. Moreover, the state is now exporting large quantities of squash, ginger and chili (Officials of the Horticulture Department, Government of Mizoram, claim that Mizoram is the world's native of a *bird eye* chili variety known locally as *hmarchate*. Commercial cultivation of this uniquely aromatic chili, highly demanded outside the state, was initiated and promoted during the Congress rule).[30]

(iii) *Rising income level and decreasing incidence of poverty*: People's income level has also steadily risen. The per capita income of Mizoram has risen from Rs. 1,289.00 in 1980-81 to Rs. 4,026.00 in 1988-89 and from Rs. 4,135.00 in 1989-90 to Rs. 13,479.00 in 1998-99.[31]

(iv) *Rural housing*: Apart from the other rural housing schemes implemented by the Congress governments, the significance of providing GI sheet for housing to thousands of families is particularly noteworthy. Domestic electrification is impossible in most traditional Mizo thatched houses because it is illegal to electrify thatched houses. Provision of GI sheets therefore enabled electrification of thousands of rural houses. In deed an electrifying effect! With the GI sheets, villagers began to build timber houses (that last for ten to twenty years) replacing traditional rural thatched houses that normally last two or three years only. Apart from providing save and secure shelters (thatched roofs are unsafe from the hazards of hails and storms), the new houses now enabled rural folks to actively pursue meaningful economic activities which they were hitherto hindered from doing so since house building previously took much of their time. This has a tremendous impact on the rural economy and society.

(v) *Peace dividends*: People like the former senior Congress leader CL Ruala listed establishment of peace in Mizoram as the greatest and the single most important contribution of the Congress in Mizoram. He told the researcher that all that has been achieved, including socio-economic developments, in the post-1986 Mizoram are, in his opinion, due all to this. It is, in deed, true that Mizoram has been able to embark on development Programmes only after the MNF insurgency ended in 1986. The very 'Peace Bonus' (Central grants to Mizoram given ostensibly for being a model of a 'peaceful state') the MNF Chief Minister Zoramthanga is now fond of talking about is a classic case of the peace dividend. Proper investigations on major hydroelectric projects, for example, could only begin after the MNF's menace ended. Engineers and surveyors could never venture into deep forests and river valleys for fear of the MNF prior to 1986.

As noted before, peace and security, albeit on a small scale, had been provided to the people by the Congress even while out of power during the 1960 and the 1970s. Considering the prevailing turmoil and warlike conditions in those days, this was no insignificant accomplishment either.

(vi) *Socio-economic mobility*: Because of the various communication networks put i`n place during the Congress rule, there has been a greater degree of mobility in labour, goods, services and tourists from within and from outside Mizoram especially since the late 1990s. The number of private vehicles increased from 4,750 in 1989 to 19,648 in 1998-99,[33] a 24.18 per cent increase during a decade of the Congress rule. Today Mizoram is able to export outside the state highly perishable yet profitable commodities such as flowers through the Lengpui airport. It has also started playing a role in the process of national integration by enabling people-to-people contact along with exchange of ideas and cultures *vis-à-vis* the 'mainstream' on a much larger scale than was previously possible.

(vii) *Improvement in public health and family welfare*: There had been a marked improvement on public health and family welfare because of the Congress governments' efforts on this front. In 1995, there were 250 hospital beds per lakh persons in Mizoram as against an all-India figure of 93 beds per lakh persons. From 22.00 and 0.80 in 1991, Infant Mortality Rate and Maternal Mortality Rate in the state respectively have come down to 17.33 and 0.6 in 2002,[34] perhaps the lowest in the country. In its August 2005 issue, a weekly magazine *India Today* rated Mizoram as No. 1 on Primary Health Care among ten small states in India. The previous Congress rule has laid a foundation for this.

(viii) *Education and human resource development*: In literacy, Mizoram has jumped from the third position in India in 1981 (59.88 %) to the second position in 1991 (82.26 %). Though still behind Kerala with 90.92 per cent in 2001, Mizoram has further improved its literacy percentage to 88.49 per cent in 2001. The credit for making this great literacy strides must go to the Congress rule.

Mizoram has also made progress towards human resource development. The state government has reserved seats in the various medical and engineering colleges in the country where students from Mizoram are admitted and given stipends. By the end of Congress rule (in 2000), there seems to be a 'surplus' of trained manpower as far as the number of educated unemployed persons suggest (though lack of employment opportunities in the private sector could be another reason as well). As on 1st April 2000, the number of registered unemployed skilled labour in Mizoram was: B.A.: 6335; B.Sc.: 507; B.Com.: 315; B.Ed.: 134; B.Sc. (Agri.): 129; M.B.B.S.: 47; B.D.S.: 20; B.E.: 188; B.V.Sc.: 22; LL.B.: 14; M.A.: 530; M.Sc.: 108; M.Com.: 25; M.Ed.: 15; M.Sc. (Agri.): 14; M.B.A.: 7.[35] Today, Mizoram stands perhaps first among the NE states in India in terms of being the state with the highest percentage of skilled local labor force.

(ix) *Milk and meat productions*: By the end of the Congress rule in 1997-98, what many claim is the only wholly profit venture cooperative society in the state MULCO (that produces milk and milk products) had an annual business turnover of 1.4 crore rupees. With an annual business turnover of 10 crore rupees and an annual profit of Rs. 1,66,062.00 in 2003-04, MULCO has provided livelihood to many people in and around Aizawl. Again primarily on account of efforts made by the Congress government (viz. setting up institutions,

> providing supports and incentives, etc.), the AH&V sector has made significant contributions to the economy of the state. It was estimated that Mizoram produced eggs, milk, and meat worth Rs. 227.412 crores in 2003-04.[36] Thanks mainly to the introductions exotic breed in pigs in Mizoram during the Congress, the state is today self-sufficient in pork (though not in piglets), perhaps the only meat item in which the state is self-sufficient, thereby providing livelihood to large numbers of people.

One very significant, and yet controversial, policy decision taken by the Congress government that hugely impacted both the society and the economy was the enforcement of The Mizoram Excise Act, 1973 and The Mizoram Excise Rules, 1983 on 10th October 1984. Because of this Indian Made Foreign Liquor was imported and sold through licences thereby earning huge revenues to the exchequer. Saying that this was destructive to society, the church demanded introduction of total prohibition in the state. Therefore, the Congress government passed The Mizoram Liquor Total Prohibition Act, 1995 on 14th December 1995 that repealed the ME Act of 1973 and the ME Rules of 1983. It also passed The Mizoram Liquor Total Prohibition Rules, 1996 on 16th September 1996. A blanket ban on manufacturing, sale or consumption of liquor has been imposed in Mizoram (except the three Autonomous District Councils) since then. While some say this has robbed the state a chance to earn badly needed money, some say it has cleansed Mizo society of hordes of social evils allegedly associated with liquor. Public debate on the issue still rages on even after a decade of total prohibition.

## Critical Appraisal

The Congress performance during its long years of rule in Mizoram has been severely criticized. Barring the construction of Lengpui airport and facilitating establishment of peace, many people in Mizoram feel that the Congress governments did not have any lasting achievement.

The most fundamental argument of critics has been that despite the long Congress rule, major development projects failed to take off and that there has been no significant socio-economic transformation in the state during its rule. This, it is said, is because of two main reasons: alleged large-scale corruptions involving politicians (MLAs, Ministers, etc.), bureaucrats and contractors that wrongly and disastrously diverted development funds and an alleged absence of any long-term vision or plan on the part of the Congress leaders.

The party's flagship, the NLUP, was also severely criticized for faulty policies like allowing indiscriminate selection of trades by farmers resulting into uneconomic and haphazard cultivation and plantation of plants and crops in certain areas, alleged large-scale corruption, total absence of monitoring and evaluation, etc.

The Congress governments' two major failures have been on industry and power sectors. Excepting the Flour Mill at Zuangtui, handed over to private an entrepreneur that is operating till today, all the costly machineries installed during the Congress rule all lay idle for some time to ultimately rust and rod away. Moreover, in the absence of power, no major industry can be set up. In stead of focusing on one or two major hydroelectric projects which would have been a better option, small projects have been developed some of which had to be closed down owing to their uneconomic viability. The mini projects like the ones at Tuipang and Thenhlum ran into serious problems such as delayed execution that skyrocketed cost of projects, problems with turbines and generators, and alleged corruption.

In spite of a measure of socio-economic transformation brought about by the Congress rule, surprisingly many people in the state today generally feel that the Congress governments 'had done nothing', or that the 'achievements' of the Congress was not commensurate to its long rule and its money was not well spent. This was because the perceived negative image of the Congress among the public at large seemed to have negated whatever it might have had actually achieved. P Lalnithanga, for instance, writes that during the long years of the Congress rule in Mizoram, "there is practically no achievement worth the name which could be considered real and tangible."[37]

Above all, the rich-poor gap that has steadily grown ever since the District became a Union Teritorry in 1972 was sharpened during the Congress rule. What was worse for the party was that many felt it deliberately encouraged the divide so that it would remain in power: by making the rich, seen as the party's traditional supporters, richer while making sure the poor remain poor, if not poorer!

The party that took some steps in tackling corruption seemed to have practically gave up any serious attempt at it from about, say,

1993 when the party captured power for the second time in a row. Barring a few leaders such as J Lalsangzuala, its leaders seemed to begin indulging in large-scale corruptions especially during 1993-98. Literature abounds on cases of alleged financial misappropriations by Congress leaders.[38] People such as Ch Saprawnga, however, held that Congress leaders were corrupt by nature who had began corrupt practices as early as 1970 when, during their rule in the District Council, they unscrupulously grabbed lands on a large scale.[39]

During its long reign, the party developed an unsavory image. Its image among the people on the whole had become so bad, especially during its last tenure of 1993-98, that all kinds of ills such as AIDS, liquor and drug addictions, debauchery, hedonism, disdain for dignity of labour, irresponsible exercise of power, willful bad governance, unabashed and illegal amassing of wealth, etc. was all attributed to the Congress misrule. Its pet NLUP project that the party claimed would provide 'Chatuan Lo' (Literally 'Eternal Jhum or Paddy Filed') had even been accused of "ruining the Mizos" allegedly for offering easy money while Lengpui airport was allegedly constructed merely "to felicitate pleasure trips" of the Congress leaders to places like Delhi and Calcutta.[40]

The public perception of Congress record of governance and achievements was equally bad. Especially towards the end of its rule in the 1990s, the party, in short, was largely seen as incapable of doing any good. When, for instance, the Congress government began construction of Lengpui airport in 1996, it was joked that the airport would be so badly constructed it would be only fit for raven landing! Moreover, many people actually believed the joke to be a practical one at the time. A series of the Congress government's bungling on major projects had emboldened the then opposition parties to say, on the day of commencement of work on Lengpui airport, things, like "Congress workers gathered at Lengpui on April Fool's Day!" ("Congress hovin April Fool an hmang!")-MNF; and "Congress workers make a fool of themselves!" ("Congress hovin at an so!")-PC.

However, contrary to the prevailing perception in Mizoram that the Congress has done 'nothing worthwhile', a close look at of the accounts of its performance reveals that it is rather quite commendable. It has done particularly well in building a vast network of roads including construction of an airport, establishing educational institutions and improving literacy, improving health care and medical facilities, constructing several notable buildings, improving the lot of a section of the population, and in bringing about peace in Mizoram.

## NOTES AND REFERENCES

1. Mizoram Congress (I) Committee: *Politik Thu Thlung Thar-Remna athleng ta* (*A New Political Agenda-Peace has been established*-in Mizo). Thunder Press, Aizawl, 20 January 1987, p. 5.
2. Ibid., p. 5; MPCC (I): *Indian National Congress Kum 100-na: 1885-1985* (*Centenary of the INC: 1885-1985 in Mizo)*. Bethesda Printing Press, Aizawl, 1985, pp. 29-32.
3. Chawngsailova, *Mizo National Front and its Role in Mizoram Politics*, Unpublished Ph.D. Thesis submitted to the Department of Political Science, NEHU, 1997, pp. 122, 164, 200; Saprawnga, Ch. *Ka Zin Kawng* (*My Journey*—in Mizo). Synod Press, Aizawl, 1990, p. 273.
4. Vanlawma, R., *Ka ram leh Kei (My Country and I) Political History of Modern Mizoram (in Mizo)*. Lengchhawn Press, Aizawl, 1989, pp. 343-344; see also Dokhuma, James: *Mizoram Chief Minister hmasaber Ch. Chhunga chanchin (The story of the first Chief Minister of Mizoram: Ch. Chhunga*-in Mizo*)*. The Gilzom Offset Press, Aizawl, 1999, pp. 117-118; MCC (I): *Indian National Congress Kum 100-na: 1885-1985* (*Centenary of the INC: 1885-1985 in Mizo)*. Bethesda Printing Press, Aizawl, 1985; ZV Lalmawia, Ex-EM: 'Buaina hnua Mizorama Congress Party lo din tan dan leh Mizo District Council hnuhnung ber', in MPCC: *Remna Lamtluang (The Road to Peace*-in Mizo), pp. 25-27. (A 'documentary souvenir' published 'In commemoration of 20 years of peace'). Synod Press, Aizawl, 2006
5. V. Venkata Rao, *A Century of Tribal Politics in North East India: 1874-1974*. S. Chand & Company Ltd., New Delhi; 1976, V. Venkata Rao (1976), pp. 382-389.
6. S.K. Chaube, *Hill Politics in North East India,* Orient Longman Ltd., New Delhi, 1973, p.182.
7. *MU-INC letter to Indira Gandhi, Prime Minister of India*, New Delhi, 5th September 1971, signed by Ch. Chhunga, CEM of Mizo District Council and R. Dengthuama, President of MDCC, on behalf of the 'Eight Member Mizo Delegation'.
8. *A Memorandum to the Prime Minister of India submitted by the Mizo District Congress Committee (Ruling),* Aijal, 1st September 1971. The signatories were: Hrangchhuana, President of MDCC; V Lalthanzauva, Vice President of MDCC; Pachhunga, MDCC Treasurer; Lalsangzuala, GS of MDCC; H. Hrangdawla, Jt. Secretary of MDCC; and 5 MDCs such as P.C. Saprema, Ṭhangchungnunga, R. Lalhuzauva, F.C. Nghina, B. Sangchema.
   *Note*: It is curious that an Independent MDC B. Sangchema was a signatory among the MDCC (R).

9. Thanglura, A., *Zoram Politic Lumlet Dan* (*The Dynamics of Politics in Zoram*—in Mizo). Lengchhawn Press, Aizawl, 1999, p. 289; see also *Letter to the Prime Minister of India: Proposal of Converting the Mizo Hill into Union Territory*, submitted by A Thanglura, John F. Manliana and L. Chinzah, 8th June 1971, quoted in A Thanglura (1999), pp. 285-287.
10. Lal Thanhawla, Convener of State Sub-Committee of the Mizoram PCC: *Proposed Special Provisions for Mizoram laid for discussion before State Sub-Committee of the Mizoram PCC*, Aizawl, 12th November 1975; Lal Thanhawla, President of Mizoram Congress: *Minutes of the State Sub-Committee of the MPCC*, Aizawl, 30th June 1979.
11. Mizoram Congress (I) Committee (1987) cited above in Notes & References at sl. no. pp. 10-11; Mizoram Congress (I) Committee: *Mizoram Congress (I) leh Inbiakna (Mizoram Congres (I) and Peace Dialogue*—in Mizo), Aizawl, 1981, pp. 4-5.
12. R.L. Valla, ex-PWD Minister: '*Kum 1988-1998 Inkara PWD Hnathawh te*' ('*Achievements of PWD between 1988 and 1998*'—in Mizo), in MPCC: *Congress Ministry khan eng nge a thawh?* (*What Congress Ministries had done?*—in Mizo). Aizawl, 2000, pp. 37-41. *Note: There seems to be a mistake in the period of Congress tenure among the contributors of articles in this Congress booklet. The period covered should have been 1989-1998, and not 1988-1998. Necessary corrections have been affected in analyzing the party's achievement accordingly.*
13. *Ibid.*, pp. 42-45.
14. *Ibid.*, pp. 46-47.
15. Lalhuthanga, '*PHE Kum 10 chhung (1988-98) Congress sorkar hnathawhleh hmachhawp te*' ('*10 years of PHE achievements and initiatives during Congress rule*'—in Mizo), in MPCC (2000) cited above in Notes & References at sl. no. 12, pp. 15-19; *Salient Features of Urban Water Supply in Mizoram*, PHE Department, Government of Mizoram, Aizawl, 2005.
16. *Status of Hydel Projects in Mizoram*, Office of the Chief Engineer, Power & Electricity, Government of Mizoram, Aizawl, February 2006; C.L. Ruala: '*Mizoram Power a kan intodelh nan a Congress sorkar hnathawh leh hmachhawp tlangpui*' ('*Congress main achievements and initiatives for making Mizoram self-sufficient in power*'—in Mizo) in MPCC (2000) cited above in Notes & References at sl. no. 12, pp. 24-36.
17. C.L. Ruala, *op. cit.*
18. *Ibid.*
19. S. Homchaudhuri, *'Educational Policy of Mizoram—An Analysis'*, in RN Prasad & A.K. Agarwal (Ed): *Modernisation of The Mizo Society*, Mittal Publication, New Delhi, 2003, p. 62.
20. *Ibid.*
21. Liansuama Ex-RD Minister, 'Mizoram thingtlang leh khawpuia mirethei chhan chhuah nana Congress sawrkar (RD Deptt.) hnathawh leh hmachhawp tlangpui' ('Performane of the Congress government in the attempts to

remove poverty'—in Mizo) in MPCC (2000) cited above in Notes & References at sl. no. 12, pp. 7-8; Mizoram Congress (I): *Hmasawnna Programmeme* (*Development Programmeme*—in Mizo). Exodus Press, Aizawl, 1986, p. 6.

22. *Ibid.*

    *Notes*: Details on the NLUP and its critique are available in Lianzela: 'Implementation of New Land Use Policy in Mizoram' in R.N. Prasad & A.K. Agarwal (Ed) (2003), p. 145.
23. *Statistical Abstract, Department of Agriculture & Minor Irrigation, Mizoram*: (2002-2003), pp. 76-77.
24. *Ibid.*, pp. 85-90.
25. Interviews with officials (who wanted to remain anonymous) of Agriculture and Horticulture Departments, Aizawl, February 2006.
26. Interview with Lalsiama Fambawl, the State's Information & Public Relations Officer i/c Publicity Wing of the NLUP from 1990 to 1998, conducted at Aizawl on 5.3.06.
27. Directorate of Economics & Statistics, Government of Mizoram (GOM), Aizawl: *Statistical Handbook: Mizoram 1989*, DM Press, Aizawl, 1989, p.84; Directorate of Economics & Statistics, GOM, Aizawl: *Statistical Handbook: Mizoram 2000*, Milan Press, Aizawl, 2000, p.132.
28. *Statistical Abstract, Department of Agriculture & Minor Irrigation, Mizoram*: *(2002-2003)*, pp. 20, 28.
29. *Statistical Handbook of Mizoram*, Directorate of Economics & Statistics, GOM, Aizawl; Milan Press, Aizawl, 2000, p.143.
30. Interviews with officials (who wanted to remain anonymous) of Agriculture and Horticulture Departments, Aizawl, February 2006.
31. Directorate of Economics & Statistics, GOM, Aizawl: *Statistical Handbook: Mizoram 2000*, Milan Press, Aizawl, 2000, p.29; Directorate of Economics & Statistics, GOM, Aizawl: *Statistical Handbook: Mizoram 2002*, Everly Press, Aizawl, 2002, p.45.
32. Directorate of Economics & Statistics, GOM, Aizawl: *Statistical Handbook: Mizoram 2002*, Everly Press, Aizawl, 2002, p.9.
33. Directorate of Economics & Statistics, GOM, Aizawl: *Statistical Handbook: Mizoram 1989*, DM Press, Aizawl, 1989, p.84; Directorate of Economics & Statistics, GOM, Aizawl: *Statistical Handbook: Mizoram 2000*, Milan Press, Aizawl, 2000, p.132.
34. Directorate of Economics & Statistics, GOM, Aizawl: *Statistical Handbook: Mizoram 2002*, Everly Press, Aizawl, 2002, p.47; *Hand Book of Health & Family Welfare Department (Institutions): 1998,* Directorate of Health Services, GOM, Aizawl, 1998, p. 5.
35. Directorate of Economics & Statistics, GOM, Aizawl: *Statistical Handbook: Mizoram 2000*, Milan Press, Aizawl, 2000, p.96.
36. *AH & V Department abstract* by the Directorate of Animal Husbandry & Veterinary Department, GOM, Aizawl, 2006.

37. P. Lalnithanga: *Emergence of Mizoram* (Second Edition). Lengchhawn Press, Aizawl, 2005, p. 256.
38. Alleged indulgences of Congress leaders in corruption have been documented in various literature, e.g. MC Lalrinthanga: *Thudik Hailanna: Zoram* Politik) (*Unravelling the Truth*: *Zoram Politics*-in Mizo). __, Aizawl, 2001; F. Hmingthanga: *Mizoram Politic Thlirletna* (*A Review of Mizoram Politics*—in Mizo). The Zo-Awm Press, Aizawl, 2003; PC Gen. Hqrs: *Pu Hawla Ministry: Sualna Khurpui* (*Mr Hawla's Ministry: A Den of Evils*—in Mizo). Aizawl, 1995; Mizo National Youth Front, Hqrs. Aizawl: *Corruption Sorkar nge Kristian Sorkar* (*Whether Corrupt Government or Christian Government*—in Mizo). RD Press, Aizawl, ___.
39. Ch. Saprawnga, (1990). p. 255.
40. F. Hmingthanga, (2003). pp. 12-18, 76-78; PC Gen. Hqrs (1995) cited in Notes & References at sl. no. 39; P. Lalnithanga (2005), pp. 288-289.

# Chapter 12

## Village Councils in Mizoram
### *The Structure and Function*

J. ZAHLUNA

---

The success of democratic system involves the extent of the participation of the citizens. No democratic system can flourish unless it appreciates the needs and aspirations of the community. Decentralization is inherent in the application of the democratic ideals to the administrative organisation. Democratic decentralization aims at widening the area of people's participation, autonomy, and authority through dispersion of powers from the top to the bottom. As Harold Laski puts, "Unless we begin by the admission that all problems not central problems, and that the results of problems not central in their incidence require decision at the place, and by the persons, where and by whom the incidence is most deeply felt".[1]

It is now widely accepted that grassroots democratic institutions at the local levels are essential for national growth and development and for effective participation of the people and they are integral and indispensable part of the democratic process. Grassroots democracy based on small unit of government enables the people to feel a sense of responsibility and to inculcate the values of democracy. These institutions strengthen the roots of democracy and the strength of a democratic government lies in the democratic consciousness of its people and their active participation in the affairs of the government. People's participation is *sine qua non* for development and it has been realized through the creation of various local bodies at the local levels.

## I

Before the advent of the British in Mizoram, administration of village was centred on the hereditary Chief. The Chief was assisted by the council of elders called Upas, who were appointed and dismissed by him. The Chief was a benevolent ruler, guardian, leader and defender of the people. The Chief was the supreme authority over the villagers whose word was law within the limits of his jurisdiction. The recognition and honour given to the position of a Chief enabled him to enjoy certain privileges.

Although all power was theoretically in the hands of the Chief, practically speaking, he would never try a case without consulting his Upas. In dealing with cases, the Chief and the Upas were guided by the established customs. The way the Chief ran his administration certainly contained some elements of democracy and social justice for all the members of the village community.

The village occupied the most important place in the traditional administrative system. Every village was autonomous and led a community life. The people of the village lived on the basis of self-sufficiency in matters of food, cloth, and shelter. As far as possible, the villagers avoided any dependence on outside assistance. People belonging to different clans mutually help each other in their day to day life. The village had a close knit village community, well organised and ordered life which contributed to their tranquillity and happiness. The main source of strength of the village community was derived from the strong social and economic bases developed by them with their own efforts, manpower, resources, and commitments.

When Mizoram came under the British administration in 1890, it did not bring any drastic change in the administration of the Chiefs. The village administration under the Chief was carried on under the overall supervision of the Superintendent or the Sub-Division Officer (S.D.O.). The Chiefs continued to carry on all internal and local administration in their respective villages with hardly any interference from either the Superintendent or S.D.O., unless a certain matter was specifically brought to their notice. But the annexation of the British resulted in certain changes in the liberties of the Chiefs. The Chiefs were divested of some of their autocratic powers including right to impose capital punishment, seize food stores and properties of the villagers, to tax traders doing business in their jurisdictions, right to freedom to make their sons Chiefs under their own jurisdiction etc.[2]

In 1898 the Superintendent issued order which laid down certain duties of the Chiefs. In 1937, the Government modified the powers and duties of the Chiefs and issued fresh order.[3]

The steps taken by the Government resulted in the gradual increase of the Chiefs' duties and decline of their powers and positions. As Parry puts it, "British rule, therefore, has led inevitably to a diminution in the importance of the Chiefs".[4] The British followed the policy of the internal control of the villages by their own leaders, the Chiefs. The aim was to interfere as little as possible between the Chiefs and their people and to impress upon the Chiefs their responsibilities for the maintenance of order in their villages.[5]

After India's Independence, the Constituent Assembly set up a Sub-Committee, known as the North East Frontier (Assam) Tribal and Excluded Areas Committee, to recommend an institutional framework for governance of the hill areas of Assam. The Sub-Committee was headed by Gopinath Bordoloi, the Chief Minister of Assam and popularly known as the Bordoloi Committee. The Bordoloi Committee recommended that in each of the Hill District, a District Council should be formed to promote and regulate the tribal way of life according to their own genius. The recommendations were accepted and incorporated into Article 244(2) and included in Part A of the Table appended to paragraph 20 of the Sixth Schedule to the Constitution of India.

Under the Sixth Schedule, the Lushai Hills District Council and the Pawi-Lakher Regional Council (PLRC) were inaugurated on 25th April, 1952 and 23rd April, 1953 respectively. The Lushai Hill District (Chiefship Abolition) Act, 1952 was passed by the Assam Legislative Assembly with effect from 1st January, 1953. According to the Act, all the existing Chiefs as on 25th April, 1952 within the Lushai Hill District were to be abolished. However, the Chiefs were allowed to function according to the instructions given by the District Council until another alternative was formed.[6] Armed with the Sixth Schedule, the District Council enacted certain legislations which abolished and reduced the special privileges enjoyed by the Chiefs. The Lushai Hills District (Reduction of Fathang) Act, 1953 reduced the amount of Fathang (Fathang is the due payable to a Chief by villagers which amounted to six tins of paddy or Rs. 2 per household per year) from six tins to three tins of paddy if paid in kind or from rupees two to rupees one per year if paid in cash.[7] The Lushai Hills District (Social Customs) Act, 1953 abolished the traditional dues payable to the Chief like Sa Chhiah (flesh tax), Chi Chhiah (salt tax) and Khuai Chhiah (bee tax) with effect from 1st June, 1953.[8] Similarly, the PLRC passed the Pawi-Lakher Autonomous Region (Social Customs and Practices) Act, 1953 and the Pawi-Lakher Autonomous Region (Reduction of Fathang) Act, 1953 which abolished and reduced the traditional dues payable to the Chief within its jurisdiction.

The District Council in its meeting on 15th April, 1953 adopted the list of villages as being declared to have Village Councils which was published in the Assam Gazette on 27th May, 1953.[9] The District Council prepared the groundwork for the introduction of modern representative democratic institutions by passing the Lushai Hills District (Village Councils) Act, 1953 on the 13th July, 1953, which received the assent of the Governor of Assam on 29th November, 1953 and published in the Assam Gazette on 9th December, 1953.[10] The first Village Council election was held during 21st April—6th July, 1954,[11] which was the biggest ever democratic exercise in electing the largest number of candidates through secret ballot. A high degree of political activity was noticed in the Village Council elections. Almost in every village, it was an intensely contested elections and there were very few cases of political somnolence leading to candidates being returned uncontested. The PLRC also enacted the Pawi-Lakher Autonomous Region (Village Councils) Act, 1954 on 24th September, 1954. The Village Council was introduced with a belief that people would participate actively in various political processes and establish a genuine political control over them. By doing so, they will have a voice in the all-round development of the village. Most importantly, Village Council was aimed at democratizing the system by decentralizing the power structure.

## II

The Village Councils were officially inaugurated with great fanfare during the 22nd July—12th August 1954 and started functioning from the 16th August 1954. The introduction of Village Council brought about a significant change in the traditional village administration. It brought modern participatory political process in Mizoram and replaced the traditional political institutions. It gave a new orientation to politics and changed the outlook of the people. It widened the political horizon of the people by making them to look beyond their communities instead of fragmented villages or communities. The new concept of election, representation, and majority decisions slowly started creeping into these bodies. A new set of leadership having wider political perspective and modern outlook emerged through the Village Council. The leadership of these bodies was also undergoing a slow change and newly emerging leadership started gaining influence in the institutions. Thus, the introduction of Village Council system brought about a total and far reaching change in the entire socio-political ethos of Mizoram.

The Government of Assam passed the Lushai Hills District (Acquisition of Chiefs' Rights) Act, 1954, which received the assent of the President of India on 26th June, 1954 and published in the Assam Gazette on 30th June, 1954. The traditional Chiefship was abolished and the rights and interests of 259 Chiefs in Mizo District and 50 Chiefs in Pawi-Lakher Regional Council were acquired with effect from 1st April, 1955 and 15th April, 1956 respectively. The Chiefs were paid compensation of Rs.14 lakhs.[12] Thus the oldest institution of traditional hereditary Chieftainship has come to an end.

The following table shows the number of clan-wise Chiefs whose rights and interests were abolished:[13]

**Table 12.1:** Number of clan-wise Chiefs whose rights and interests abolished

| *Name of Clans* | *Number of Chiefs* |
|---|---|
| Sailo | 169 |
| Pawi | 27 |
| Fanai | 19 |
| Lakher | 15 |
| Hmar | 12 |
| Hualngo | 10 |
| Zadeng | 8 |
| Ralte | 7 |
| Chawngthu | 6 |
| Thangluah | 6 |
| Zahau | 6 |
| Paihte | 4 |
| Chenkual | 3 |
| Khiangte | 3 |
| Palian | 3 |
| Tlanglau | 2 |
| Tuikuk | 2 |
| Pachuau | 1 |
| Hauhnar | 1 |

*(Contd.)*

**Table 12.1:** (*Contd.*)

| *Name of Clans* | *Number of Chiefs* |
|---|---|
| Tlau | 1 |
| Hnamte | 1 |
| Gurkha | 1 |
| Pang | 1 |
| Chakma | 1 |
| Total | 309 |

The reasons for the abolition of Chieftainship were:

1. The people were disgusted with the system of autocratic rule of the Chiefs. Some Chiefs abused their powers by ruling excessively and this has been an intolerable burden of the villagers.
2. The different kinds of taxes levied by the Chiefs had been too heavy for the poor villagers to bear. There was nothing that the Chief could not snatch from the citizens by any means. People were properties of the Chiefs.
3. Free services rendered to the Chiefs by each family of the villagers have affected the family economy as a result that a single-man family could never produce enough food for his family.
4. The new system of administration based on the democratic principles had been infused in the minds of some of the local leaders. People, therefore, wanted to have their leaders elected on this principle. They wanted to have a voice in the administration of their own affairs and for the welfare of the public.
5. The principle of equality of men in the eye of God enshrined in the Christian doctrine and the equality of men before law induced people to rebel against the Chiefs.[14]

The administration of the village by a hereditary Chief was replaced by a democratic system of village administration through Village Council. As was in the past, village administration remained autonomous and was carried on by the Village Council under the overall supervision of the District Council.

III

When Mizoram attained the Union Territory status on 21st January, 1972, the Mizo District Council was abolished on 29th April, 1972. The PLRC was trifurcated into three Regional Councils, viz., Pawi, Lakher and Chakma on 2nd April, 1972. The Lushai Hills District (Village Councils) Act, 1953 and the Pawi-Lakher Autonomous Region (Village Councils) Act, 1954 have been adapted by the Government of Mizoram and the three Autonomous District Councils respectively for the administration of the villages in their respective areas. A Department called Local Administration, Town Planning and Housing was set up to take over, *inter alia*, the village administrations through Village Councils. When Mizoram was elevated to a full-fledged State on 20th February, 1987, the existing laws which were applicable in the Union Territory of Mizoram continue to be applicable to the State of Mizoram by the State of Mizoram Adaptation of Laws Order (No. 2) 1987.

*Composition*: The Village Council is the lowest administrative unit in Mizoram. The State Government may, by notification, propose any village to have a Village Council and define its territorial limits. A Village Council may comprise one or more villages and the number of members is determined by the number of houses it contains:

(a) For village not exceeding 200 houses, there shall be 3 members;
(b) For village with more than 200 houses, but not exceeding 400 houses, there shall be 5 members;
(c) For village with more than 400 houses, but not exceeding 700 houses, there shall be 7 members;
(d) For village with more than 700 houses, but not exceeding 1500 houses, there shall be 9 members;
(e) For village with more than 1500 houses, there shall be 11 members.[15]

*Qualification of Members*: A Village Council is a lawfully constituted body. To be qualified for election to the Village Council, a person must (a) be a member of Scheduled Tribe; (b) attained the age of 25 years; (c) be a voter where he seeks election; (d) not be a member of any other Village Council; (e) have a sound mind and stands so declared by a competent Court of Authority; and (f) not have been convicted by an offence under the Lushai Hills Autonomous District (Administration of Justice) Rules, 1953 before and after the commencement of the Act.[16]

*Term of Office*: The normal term of a Village Council is 3 years, but it can be extended or shortened for a period not exceeding 18 months in aggregate.[17] All members of the Village Council shall hold office during the life of the Village Council. A member elected to fill a vacancy shall hold office for the remaining term of office of the member whose seat falls vacant.

*Renumeration*: Members of the Village Council, Secretary and Tlangau (village crier) are entitled to receive remunerations as follows:

| | | |
|---|---|---|
| (a) President | : | Rs.300 per month |
| (b) Vice-President | : | Rs.250 per month |
| (c) Secretary | : | Rs.200 per month |
| (d) Member | : | Rs.150 per month |
| (e) Tlangau | : | Rs.125 per month.[18] |

*President*: The President is elected by and from among the elected members of the Village Council. The President occupies a pivotal position in Village Council administration and enjoys considerable authority and powers. He must ensure that the meetings of the Village Council are conducted with proper order, decorum, and decency and have the power of enforcing his decision as follows:

(a) He may direct any member whose conduct is disorderly to withdraw immediately from the day's meeting.
(b) If any member is ordered to withdraw for a second time from a meeting of the same session, the President may suspend him for the remaining period of the same session.
(c) If any member fails to comply with the order given to him under the above reasons, the President shall report, in writing the conduct of the member, to the State Government. On receipt of such report, the State Government may, if it thinks necessary, suspend the member for any period considered reasonable.

The President shall issue notices and instructions to prevent the outbreak of fire, epidemic, etc. in the village. Whenever notices, orders, circulars, or letters received from the State Government to be re-distributed to other villages, he shall send through the Secretary. The President is responsible for the compliance of all orders and notifications issued by the authority. He shall cause all orders and notifications to be read out by the Secretary in the meeting of the Village Council and, if necessary, to brought to the knowledge of the public. He shall examine the books kept by the Secretary from time to time.

- *Vice-president*: The Vice-President is elected by the elected members from among themselves. During the vacancy in the office of the President or the incapacity or absence of the President, the Vice-President shall perform the duties and exercise the powers of the President.
- *Secretary*: The Secretary, who is a village writer, is appointed and dismissed by the State Government on the recommendation of the President. The Secretary shall not be a member of the Village Council but may take part in the Village Council deliberations with no vote.[19] The Secretary shall record all the proceedings of the Village Council and Village Council Court under the signature of the President. All the orders, notifications and records, signed by the President, shall be published by him. All the books and records of the Village Council and Village Council Court shall be keep by him and send to the State Government when asked for.
- *Tlangau*: Normally, there shall be only one Tlangau (village crier) for each Village Council. If it is found necessary to have more than one Tlangau, prior approval of the State Government should be obtained. Tlangau is appointed by the Village Council through selection from the applicants. Tlangau shall bring to the notice of the public all orders and notifications as directed by the Village Council. He shall summon all parties and persons required by the Village Council or Village Council Court to attend its meetings. Any member of the Village Council may order the Tlangau to summon all the villagers in case of emergency. The Tlangau

has to inform all the members for the meetings of the Village Council summoned by the President. The Tlangau shall be exempted from Hnatlang* enforced by the Village Council and Zoram Chhiah (zoram tax).

- *Executive*: The Executive body of a Village Council consists of the President, Vice-President, and the Secretary. Neither the President nor the Vice-President shall hold the office of the Secretary.
- *Meeting*: The President shall preside over all the meetings of the Village Council. He shall summon the meeting whenever necessity arises. A meeting of the Village Council can be called on a requisition made in writing by at least two-thirds of the members. No person other than a member of the Village Council shall vote or speak or take part in its deliberation and any person contravening shall be punishable with a fine not exceeding Rs.50 by the Village Council.[20] Normally, all the decisions are taken by a majority of votes of the members present and voting, but in case of equality of votes, the President has a casting vote.

The President or Vice-President can be removed by the State Government on the grounds of losing the support of the majority of members but refuses to tender resignation or is too inefficient or too corrupt to carry on the village administration or is acting in a manner prejudicial to the interest of the State.[21]

If a member absents himself continuously in ten consecutive

---

* Hnatlang means common service rendered by the people for common good.

*Resignation, Removal And Dissolution*: The President may resign before the expiration of his term of office by giving notice in writing to the State Government. It becomes effective from the date of the information to the President that it has been accepted by the State Government. The Vice-President may also resign his office address to the President who shall, without delay, forward to the State Government for acceptance. Any member may at any time resign his office in writing under his hand address to the President or Vice-President, in the absence of the President, who shall, without delay, forward it to the State Government for acceptance. Until his resignation is accepted, he shall continue to function as such.

meetings without permission, the Village Council may convene a special meeting and declared his seat vacant after giving him an opportunity for a hearing. In such case, the Village Council shall inform the State Government.[22]

If, in the opinion of the State Government, a Village Council is too inefficient or is not able to carry on the village administration or is acting in the manner prejudicial to the interest of the State or any other reasons considered sufficient for dissolution, it can dissolve such Village Council. During the period of such dissolution, the State Government can appoint any person or persons to assume charges of the village administration and also act as a Village Council Court for the remaining period of the term.[23]

- *Village Council Fund*: Every Village Council shall constitute a Village Council Fund. Except district revenue and taxes, all collections by or on behalf of the Village Council, authorized by law, shall be paid into the Village Council Fund. The President shall be the Treasurer and the Secretary shall keep the list of the collections. The account should be open for examination by any subscriber of the collection.
  The Village Council may appoint a Treasurer from among the members who shall keep development grants and other funds exclusive of a collection authorized by law. The Treasurer shall maintain the account which the Village Council may conduct inspection in its sitting and by any official authorized by the State Government.[24]
- *Power, Function and Responsibilities*: The Village Council has the power to allot land within its boundaries for jhum cultivation each year through a draw of lots. It also has the power to enforce Hnatlang in the interest of the public whenever occasion demands. Any person who does not comply with the order of Hnatlang shall be liable to run either in kind or cash which may not exceed Rs.50 per Hnatlang day unless he has been exempted from Hnatlang.[25] The Village Council has the power to exempt any person from Hnatlang at its own discretion. No person who is 60 years or above shall be compelled to do any Hnatlang. Any person below 15 years shall not be allowed to represent in the Hnatlang. Every person shall have the option of payment of

cash compensation in lieu of Hnatlang at the rate of not exceeding Rs.25 per Hnatlang day.[26]

The Village Council can allot sites within its jurisdiction for residential and non-agricultural purposes with the exception of shops, stalls, hotels and other business houses of the same nature and issue Pass and may incorporate such conditions in the Pass.[27] In case of violation of any such conditions, the Village Council may either cancel the Pass or impose a fine of Rs.50. A Village Council can evict person having unauthorized occupation of land and may order for vacation within 7 days. In case the unauthorized person persists beyond 7 days, the Village Council may order demolition of the building or impose a fine of Rs.5 per day so long as the unauthorized occupant persists.

In the village where Master Plan and detail plan or site plan have been done, house site may be allotted by the Village Council by giving a Pass where survey and settlement operation has not been done. In the village where jhumming cultivation is practised, the Village Council shall be the competent authority to allot land for jhumming cultivation for a period of one year, subject to any rules or regulations in force in this respect.[28]

Every year each Village Council shall specify a period for cutting a jungle and for doing all preparatory activities for the purpose of jhum, during which all villagers having jhum must start and finish the same. The Village Council shall specify a date for burning of jhum-land which shall inform all villagers at least three days ahead of the fixed date. In a place where there is a danger of spreading of fire beyond the jhum area, the Village Council may enforce Hnatlang to clear the jungle to prevent spreading of fire, in which all persons having jhum had to participate.[29]

The Village Council shall keep registers for the animals seized and feed them properly. The feeding charge must be collected from the owner. If the animal be not claimed within 7 days, the Village Council shall cause them to be sold by public auction and the sale proceeds shall be deposited into the local fund. Animal tax shall be collected by the Village Council within its jurisdiction and fifty per cent shall be credited to the local fund and the remaining fifty per cent shall be credited to the Consolidated Fund of Mizoram. The Village Council shall maintain registers for animals within its jurisdiction and keep accounts of registration fee.[30]

The Village Council may dispose of dead trees in the manner it considers most beneficial for the village within the Village Safety Reserve. It may also distribute land within the Village Supply Reserve.[31] Each Village Council shall constitute Village Forest Fire Prevention Committee to prevent the outbreak of fire. The Village Council shall take appropriate measures towards desired compliance by all villagers or households in this regard.[32] Each Village Council shall be responsible for the sanitation of the village. A Sanitation Committee may be appointed by the Village Council.

- *Village Council Court*: It was under the Lushai Hills Autonomous District (Administration of Justice) Rules, 1953 that judicial powers were entrusted to the Village Council. The Rules provided for the establishment of Village Council Court—the judicial wing of the Village Council. The Village Council Court was established with the objective of providing speedy and inexpensive system of justice to the villagers. The members of the Village Council or not less than three members of the Village Council elected by the members among themselves shall constitute the Village Council Court. The quorum of the Court shall be three members or half of the total number of the Village Council. The jurisdiction of the Court extends to the territorial limits of the village. The Court was given the power to try suits and cases, both civil and criminal, in which both the parties belong to Scheduled Tribes.

  In civil matters, the Court had jurisdiction to try cases which fall within the purview of village or tribal laws and customs. The Court has the power to award all costs and compensation to those against whom unfounded or vexatious suits and cases have been instituted before the Court. The fines and payment imposed and ordered may be enforced by distraint of the property of the offender. In criminal cases, the Court was given the power to try cases which fall within the purview of tribal laws and customs and offences of petty nature, simple assault and hurt, affront and affray of whatever kind, drunken or disorderly brawling, public nuisance and simple cases of wrongful restraint. However, the Court is not competent to try offences of which the punishment is obligatory under the

Indian Penal Code.[33] The Court has the power to impose a fine for any offence it is competent to try, up to the limit of Rs.500.[34] The Court may award payment in restitute or compensation to the aggrieved or injured party in accordance with the tribal laws. The Court has the power to order attendance of the accused and witnessed to be examined and to imposed a fine not exceeding Rs.100 on any person willfully fail to attend when so ordered. An appeal against the judgements or decisions of the Village Council Court lies with the Subordinate or Additional District Council Court, which must be preferred within 60 days of the decisions. However, the Village Council Court could not try cases of heinous crimes like murder, rape, sexual intercourse with minor and sodomy.[35]

- *Election to Village Councils*: Up to 1971, Village Council elections were conducted in accordance with the provisions of the Lushai Hills District (Election to Village Councils) Rules, 1954. At present, all elections to Village Council shall be held under the provisions of the Mizoram (Election to Village Councils) Rules, 1974 as amended from time to time. The Governor shall, by notification, called upon the constituency concerned to elect the number of members to be returned and shall appoint the date or dates for such elections. A candidate must furnish a security deposit of Rs.25 to the Returning Officer along with his application for candidature within the time prescribed.

Voting at elections shall be conducted by symbol system. Candidates shall elect symbols on the approved list, according to their preferences. If more than one candidate selected the same symbol, the Returning Officer shall decide by drawing lots. The number of election symbols at present is 60.[36] Each candidate shall have his own ballot box at his own expense. The ballot box should be one foot square box made of sawn timber having a hole in one and half inches long and half inch wide on the top side for casting votes. One or more Polling Stations shall be set up for the same constituency depending upon the number of voters in the concerned constituency. For Village Council election, universal adult suffrage with 18 years is the qualifying age of the voter. Each voter shall be given as many ballot papers as there are seats to be elected. In case of equality of votes, the Returning Officer shall decide membership between those candidates by drawing lots.

A candidate shall forfeit his deposit if the number of valid votes polled by him does not exceed one-sixth of the total number of valid votes polled. The elections of the members are subject to the approval of the State Government and requires a formal Government notification.[37]

The Governor shall constitute an Election Tribunal to hear and dispose of all election petitions arising out of the general elections to Village Councils. The election of a member can be challenged through a petition signed by a person, who was a candidate at the election, to the Governor or any Officer appointed by him, within 30 days of the declaration of the election results. A petition shall be accompanied by a Treasury Challan showing a deposit of Rs.35. Such deposit shall be forfeited to the Government in case the petition fails. If, however, the petition succeeds, the deposit shall be refunded. An election petition may be withdrawn within 14 days from the date of filing with a refund of the security deposit.

## IV

*Village Council Politics*: Since its inception in 1954, Mizoram witnessed 14 general elections to Village Council. The elections were contested entirely on party lines. Every time these elections have produced great enthusiasm among the people and elections have been keenly contested by political parties and independents. The electoral politics at Village Council level is found to be working slightly different from the State level. Each of the political parties harbours its desire to expand its sphere of influence, strengthen the local units of party organisation, build up its local base of political power and try to gain maximum number of seats. Therefore, political parties are engaging in amazing political feat. Sometimes political parties contested the elections on an electoral adjustment with other political parties in selected villages and at the same time put up candidates against the same parties in other villages. In Mizoram, Village Council elections witnessed little political violence mainly because of the administrative skill of the State Government, political parties' commitment to democratic norms and above all people's cooperation.

The usual common techniques of electioneering were canvassing by the candidates and their supporters from house to house, exchanging solutions, handshaking to create emotional impact partisan appeals. Written impressive slogans and posters showing the names of the candidates and their election symbols were littering every available space of the walls. Appeals were made in the name of the political parties and contained references to past performances, qualifications, biographical sketches, the candidates' love for the village etc. Some candidates issued printed personal appeals to voters. Leaflets and pamphlets have been distributed and urged voters to support.

## V

*Reorganisation of Village Council*: To make it more effective, the role, and functions of the Village Council need to be reviewed. Over the years, several attempts have been made to reform the Village Council institutions. The first major move was made in 1979 when the Government of Mizoram appointed a Special Study Team, consisting of 9 members under the Chairmanship of the Minister, L.A.T.P.&H. The terms of reference of the Study Team were:

(a) To make an in-depth study of the Ashok Mehta Committee Report and to examine its applications for Mizoram in the light of the minutes of the meeting of the Council of Ministers held on the 14th May, 1979.

(b) To examine the position of the existing Village Council system in Mizoram in the light of the report of the Ashok Mehta Committee and to make recommendations to the Government of Mizoram on the improvement of the existing Village Council as to the size, composition, remunerations and powers including the question of transfer of more administrative, development and financial powers from the Government.[38]

The Study Team made an exhaustive study of administrative problems partaining to the Village Council institutions and submitted its report called the Mizoram Panchyati Raj Bill, 1981. The Bill envisaged a two-tier systems—a federation of villages having a population between 15,000-20,000 to form the lower-tier and Development Councils covering the area of revenue sub-divisions to form the upper-tier. But the Bill was never introduced in the Mizoram Legislative Assembly.[39]

The Mizoram Legislative Assembly unanimously passed a resolution tabled by its member, Pu Lalnghenga, on 9th September, 1983. The resolution said, "This Assembly is of the opinion that it is a high time to increase the remuneration and facilities of the Village Councils, and, therefore, resolves that (a) Remuneration of the Village Council Members, Secretaries and Tlangau be enhenced, (b) Recurring grant be given to them in proportion to the size of the villages".[40]

On 18th March, 1994, the Mizoram Legislative Assembly unanimously passed a non-official resolution tabled by Pu Lalrinchhana, which read, "This House is of the opinion that the rules, remunerations, powers and functions of the Village Council need ratification and the Committee be formed immediately to pursue this".[41] In pursuance of the above resolution, the Government of Mizoram constituted a Committee, consisting of 12 members, to determine the existing laws relating to Mizoram Village Councils; remuneration of the Village Council members and their powers and responsibilities and to recommend changes to suit the present days conditions.[42] But nothing tangible came out of the above committee.

The Government of Mizoram appointed an Administrative Reforms Commission on 29th September, 1995, to review the existing administrative arrangements and to recommend appropriate structural mechanism and to study the implications of the 73rd and 74th Constitutional Amendments and to explore the possibility of harmonious implementation in Mizoram. The Commission submitted its Interim Report in 1998 and recommended structural modification of the administrative machinery which involved a three-tier system of local government institutions in rural areas—Village Council at the village level, Area Development Council at intermediate level and District Development Council at district level and Municipalities at the urban areas.[43] The Report was placed before the Departmental Committee as well as Consultative Committee. The Consultative Committee decided that the Report be processed for Cabinet approval with a view to introducing a Bill in the Mizoram Legislative Assembly.[44] However, nothing has been done even to implement some of the most rational and concrete recommendations of the Commission.

In 1999, the Mizoram Panchayats Bill, 1999 was prepared. The Bill provided for a two-tier system of administration—Gram Panchayat at the village level with five years term and Zilla Parishad in every district level with five years term.[45] But there was hardly any steps taken towards its enactment.

When the Draft Mizoram Village Councils Bill was constituted in 2003, it was hailed as a breakthrough in bringing about a vibrant system of participatory democracy at the grassroots level and to provide democratic decentralization in the true sense of the term. The Bill, which contained guidelines for the State to put in place the Village Council institutions, was exhaustive and comprehensive covering all aspects of the Village Council system.[46] The Bill generated a lot of hope about devolution of powers and expectations ran high. Two years have passed since then and there is hardly any evidence of sincerity to the implementation of the Bill.

## VI

*Conclusion*: Generally speaking, all the attempts were praiseworthy so far as they go. But there is hardly any evidence of "political will" to make radical changes in the concept of the Village Council institutions. The political parties in Mizoram have yet to develop definite programmes and policies in regard to Village Council institutions. The political leadership has stressed only the "emotional aspects" of Village Council institutions without attempting any genuine devolution of administrative and financial powers to these bodies. It remained a "mere slogan", "oral announcement" and "paper declaration" and left the system in a moribund condition. "Political neglect" is considered to be an important reason for the dormancy of these bodies.

Under the existing framework, the Village Councils remain only field agencies for the development and maintenance of civic services and for the execution of State programmes in their respective areas. At present, more development schemes and programmes are chalked out at the State level and pushed through the Village Councils. The Village Councils are assigned by the State Government a large number of responsibilities in respect of implementation, execution and monitoring of development programmes rather than endowed them with greater powers and resources. Finance occupies a very important place and it has been the life blood of the Village Councils. The ability of the Village Councils to discharge their functions depend to a large extent on the availability of funds. Lack of resources and almost total dependence on State administrative machinery resulted in the ineffective functioning of the Village Councils. The Village Councils have no independent sources of revenue. It is very necessary that specific mention may be made in the Act in clear terms as to which of the taxes the Village Councils can levy. The present financial resources of the Village Councils are absolutely inadequate to meet the expenditure of their expanding activities.

The Village Councils are not merely to carry out schemes evolved by the State Government with resources allocated to them. They have more responsibilities than the assigned and imposed functions and they are to be involved in preparing the village plans, prioritising the people's needs at the village levels. They have to chalk out various programmes based on local needs peculiar to the local areas, mobilising resources and integrating the village plans into State Plan. Logically speaking, more number of development programmes and schemes are to be evolved from below. If the Village Councils are to functions as instrument of social transformation, they should be given more powers to deal with subjects that had a bearing on the people's actual needs. They can serve their purposes only through devolution of powers, authorities and resources.

The Village Council institutions in Mizoram completed 50 years in 2004. Five decades are a reasonable period for the institution to demonstrate its utility. The importance and role of Village Council has substantially increased with the increase in population, civic amenities, and its area. Since Village Councils are largely managed by people who are not adequately educated and are not well-versed in administration, it is most essential that proper and regular training, guidance, and supervision of these bodies should be made. The successful functioning of Village Councils would depend upon the extent of powers delegated to them, upon the availability of resources, upon the understanding between them and the State Government as well as administrative assistance made available to them.

## NOTES

1. Harold J. Laski, *A Grammar of Politics*, George Allen & Unwin, London, 1960, p. 411.
2. A.G. McCall, *Lushai Chrysalis*, Tribal Reserch Institute, Government of Mizoram, Reprint 2003, p. 202.

3. Sangkima Mizos, *Society and Change*, Spectrum Publications, Guwahati, 1992, pp. 119-120.
4. N.E. Parry, *The Lakhers*, Firma KLM Pvt. Ltd., Calcutta, Reprint 1976, p. 14.
5. Sir Robert Reid, *The Lushai Hills*, Firma KLM Pvt. Ltd., Calcutta, Reprint 1978, p. 60.
6. The Lushai Hills (Chiefship Abolition) Act, 1952, Chapter II, Sec. 5.
7. Notification No. TAD/R/3/53, the 25th May, 1953.
8. Zoram Hriattirna, 15th May, 1953, p. 1.
9. Notification No. E.749/C-11, the 5th June, 1953.
10. Notification No. TAD/R/61/52, the 1st December, 1953.
11. Notification No. E. 489/T-3, the 12th April, 1954.
12. J.V. Hluna, Political Development in Mizoram Since Independence, *Historical Journal Mizoram*, Vol. II, Mizo History Association, Aizawl, 1997, p. 13.
13. Zatluanga, Mizo Chanchin I, Royal Press, Aizawl, Reprint 1997, pp. 137-143.
14. H.L. Malsawma, *Sociology of the Mizos*, Spectrum Publications, Guwahati, 2002, pp. 23-24.
15. The Lushai Hills District (Village Councils) (Amendment) Act, 1999, Sec.2. The Lushai Hills District (Village Councils) (Amendment) Act, 1999 abolished the nominated members.
16. The Lushai Hills District (Village Councils) Act, 1953, Chapter II, Sec.4.
17. The Lushai Hills District (Village Councils) (Amendment) Act, 1975, Sec.5.
18. No. LAD/VC-83/94(A), the 7th October, 1996.
19. The Lushai Hills District (Village Councils) (Amendment) Act, 1985, Chapter III, Sec.13.
20. The Lushai Hills District (Village Councils) Act, 1985, Chapter III, Sec.13(3).
21. The Lushai Hills District (Village Councils) (Amendment) Act, 1986, Chapter II, Sec.7(10).
22. The Lushai Hills District (Village Councils) Act, 1953, Chapter II, Sec.6(3).
23. *Ibid.* Chapter V, Sec. 25(1).
24. *Ibid.* Chapter III, Sec.15.
25. The Mizoram (Village Councils) (Amendment) Act, 1996, Chapter II, Sec. 8(3).
26. *Ibid.* Chapter II, Sec. 9(3).
27. The Lushai Hills District (House Site) Act, 1953, Sec. 3.
28. The Mizoram (Land Holding and Settlement) Act, 2000, Chapter IV, Sec.12 and 19.
29. The Mizoram (Prevention and Control of Fire in the Village Ram) Rules, 2001, Rule 4(3).
30. The Mizoram Animal (Control and Taxation) Act, 1980, Sec. 21(2).
31. The Mizo District (Forest) Act, 1955, Sec. 3(a) and (b).

32. No. B.11011/19/91-FST, the 8th February, 2000.
33. The Lushai Hills Autonomous District (Administration of Justice) Rules, 1953, Rule 14.
34. The Mizoram (Administration and Justice) (Amendment) Rules, 1996, Rule 15.
35. Mizo Hnam Dan, 1956 as amended in 1960, Sec.4.
36. The Mizoram (Election to Village Councils) Rules, 1990, Rule 14.
37. The Mizoram (Election to Village Councils) (Amendment) Rules, 1974, Rule 32.
38. No. LAD/VC-13/78/200, the 21st July, 1979.
39. C. Nunthara, "Mizoram" in George Mathew (ed) *Status of Panchayati Raj in the States and Union Territories of India*, Institute of Social Sciences, New Delhi, 2000, p. 219.
40. Proceedings of the Twelfth Session of the Third Mizoram Union Territory Legislative Assembly, 12th Session from 8 to 13 September, 1983, p. 103.
41. Proceedings of the Second Session of the Third Mizoram State Legislative Assembly from 8-29 March, 1994, p. 165.
42. No. LAD/VC-83/94/14, the 24th August, 1994.
43. Interim Report on Administrative Reforms, 1998, pp. 48-68.
44. C. Nunthara, *op. cit.* p. 219.
45. The Mizoram Panchayats Bill, 1999.
46. The Draft Mizoram Village Councils Bill, 2003.

# Chapter 13

## Grassroots Democracy
## *The Working of Village Council System in Mizoram*

LALSANGLIANI

### Introduction

Democracy has been practiced and experienced by the people of Mizoram only few years before India got her independence. The then Superintendent A. McDonald had organized a District Conference to aid and advice him in managing the affairs. The Lushai Hills which was divided into 20 circles would send two representatives each in the District Conference, one representing the commoners and the other representing the chiefs. The first election to the members of the District Conference was held on 16th January, 1946 at Aizawl. After the formation of the District Conference the Mizos got the permission for organizing into a political party by the Superintendent which was granted on 9th April 1946.[1] Consequently, the Mizo middle class had started forming the first Political party in the Lushai Hills which was known as Mizo Union. The Mizo Union, since its formation had started taking all necessary steps in order to have better political and administrative set-up in the Lushai Hills looking ahead for certain reforms for their future political set-up. The desire for enjoying political rights by the leader of the Lushai Hills has been fulfilled and the Mizos were awakened from their deep slumber of "Backward-Track" or "Excluded Area".

On the eve of the Indian independence an Advisory Committee on minorities, tribals, etc. was formed under the chairmanship of Sardar

Vallabhbhai Patel by the Constituent Assembly of India on 25th January 1947. The advisory Committee has appointed a Sub-Committee called the Bordoloi Sub-committee after the name of its Chairman Gopinath Bordoloi, the Premier of Assam, to aid and advice the Advisory Committee on the affairs of the North Eastern tribal areas. Being an excluded area the Lushai Hills had no representatives in the Constituent Assembly. So, the Sub-Committee of the Constituent Assembly invited the Mizo Union (the only political party in the Lushai Hills) to send their representatives for serving the co-opted members. Accordingly, the Mizo Union after a meeting had nominated Pu. Saprawnga and Pu. Khawtinkhuma, the then President and Vice-President of the Mizo Union to join the Sub-Committee as co-opted members.[2]

The Bordoloi Sub-Committee was to make a spot visit of the hill areas and make a study of the hopes and aspirations of the hill people in the "Excluded Areas" and "Partially Excluded Areas" when the British Government decided to transfer power to the people of India. The Sub-Committee had visited the hill areas and reached Aizawl on 17th April 1947, there they have a long discussion on how the Lushai Hills would be governed when the British had left India with the leaders of the Mizo Union and the representatives of the District Conference. The most important points which they have discussed were that there should be a District Council elected by the people, the Mizos should have at least 3 representatives in the Assam Legislative Assembly, there should be one minister in charge of the tribal areas and that the District Council should look after the primary education, Inner Line Regulation and all civil and criminal cases should be taken care by the District Council according to the Customary law of the tribals. Further, the Mizo Union in its memorandum submitted to the Bordoloi Sub-Committee, demanded the following: (i) The Mizo inhabited areas of the neighbouring districts should be included in the Lushai Hills District, (2) Lushai should be called Mizos, (3) Internal administration should be left to the Mizos and (4) Liberal financial assistance should be given.[3] There was a sharp difference of popular opinion among the Mizos regarding the future of the Lushai Hills.

## Recommendations of the Bordoloi Committee

The Bordoloi Sub-Committee noted the anxiety of the hill people about their land and their fear of exploitation by the economically advanced people, especially the money lenders. The Committee recommended for the Autonomous District Council to be constituted democratically with the power of legislations over the occupation and use of land other than reserved forest and the cultivation of jhum. The District Council should have the power to make law on the use of land, village forest, and agriculture. The District Council should be entrusted to provide administration of justice. The Committee also recommended for the Provision of Regional Council in the District to protect the distinct culture and dialect of smaller tribes. The Committee was not keen to allow the Lushai Hills District to enjoy the status of being "Excluded Area" as it felt that there was a much advancement of the area.[4] It also suggested that the tribal of the region should enjoy uninterrupted freedom in the practice of their respective customs, inheritance, social organizations and way of life.[5]

**Formation of the District Council**

The report of the Bordoloi Committee was placed before the Constituent Assembly for discussion. There was a criticism against the recommendations for creation of the District Council and Regional Council in the hill districts of Assam on the ground that it might sow the seed of separatist tendency among the Indians. Such a vast power in the hands of the tribes should lead to chaos, anarchy and disorder throughout the country and the creation of such council would jeopardize the interest of the whole country. Dr. Ambedkar had defended the creation of the District Council in the Constituent Assembly. He pointed out the differences between the tribes in Assam and other parts of the country, who have been Hinduised and assimilated into the Hindu society among whom they lived. But the tribes of Assam developed their own culture and language or dialect and their own religion. Their internal organization, laws of inheritance and marriage, fundamentally differ not only from those of the plains but also from their own immediate neighbouring tribes.[6] Moreover, the hill areas are the frontier of the country which should be well protected and the political aspirations of the people in these areas should be satisfied.

After a long deliberation, the committee submitted its report to the Chairman Advisory Committee on Fundamental Rights and Minorities Sardar Vallabhbhai Patel for approval; it was later on forwarded to the President of the Constituent Assembly with some amendments. The Constituent Assembly after much debate and deliberation finally approved the provisions of District Council and Regional Council, which were inserted in the Sixth Schedule of the Constitution. The District Council had been given wide and extensive law making power with respect to the administration of their areas under the provision of paragraph 3 of the Sixth Schedule of the Constitution. The District Council is also empowered to regulate trading and money lending by non-tribals in the district. The Inner Line Regulation introduced by the colonial power was also upheld. A regional autonomy had thus emerged to enable the hill people to safeguard their way of life, to participate in the political life of the country and the administration of their own area, and to develop themselves according to their own genius and tradition.

Mizoram, the then Lushai Hills was incorporated into the state of Assam in 1947 when India Independent Act came into force. The Central Government immediately informed the matter to the Mizo Union which accepted the incorporation of the district into Assam state in accordance with the provision of the Sixth Schedule. The Government of Assam enacted the Assam Autonomous (Constitution of the District Council) Act, in 1951.[7] The Central Government under the provision contained in the Sixth Schedule to the Constitution, Articles 244(2) and 275(1) has created six autonomous districts in Assam: United Khasi and Jaintia Hills, Garo Hills, Lushai Hills, Naga Hills, North Cachar Hills and Mikir Hills.[8] There was to be a District Council for each autonomous district, the Governor would divide the areas divided by them into an autonomous region. On the basis of this provision an autonomous region, the Pawi-Lakher Regional Council was created in Mizoram. In this way, the Mizo District Council for the Mizos and Pawi-Lakher Regional Council for the Pawi and Chakma tribes were set up in 1952 and 1953 respectively.[9] The member of the District Council and the Regional Council were to be elected for a term of five years. The entire Mizo District administration including the District Council was controlled and looked after by a department known as Tribal Areas Department (TAD) under Government of Assam headed by a Tribal Minister.[10]

The Strength of the Mizo (Lushai) Hills District Council at the beginning of its inception was 24 which consist of 18 elected members and 6 nominated members to ensure the participantion of every section of people in the society. The nominated members of the Lushai Hills District Council consists of one representative of the government, women's representatives, two representatives from the chiefs, one representative from the commoners and another representative from the smaller tribes.[11] The newly created Pawi-Lakher Regional Council also consists of 12 members including 2 nominated seats.[12] The creation of the Autonomous District Council within the state of Assam fulfilled the aspirations of the Lushai, now called the Mizos to a great extent. With the introduction of these Councils, the post of Superintendent was abolished and the whole area of Lushai Hills was placed under a "Deputy Commissioner", with much curtail powers, and the Chief Executive Members of the District and Regional Councils.

**Legislative Power of the District Council**

Under the Sixth Schedule to the Constitution, the District Council has been vested with the power to make laws with respect to—

1. the allotment, occupation or use, or setting apart, of land which is a reserved forest, for the purpose of agriculture or grazing or for any other purposes likely to promote the interests of the inhabitants of any village or town, subject to the power of compulsory acquisition of any land for public purposes by the Government of Assam;
2. the management of any forest not being reserved forest;
3. the use of any canal or water-course for the purpose of Agriculture;
4. the regulation of the practice of jhum or other forms of shifting cultivation;
5. the establishment of village or town committees or councils and their powers;
6. any other matter relating to village or town administration, including village or town police and public health and sanitation;
7. the appointment or succession of chiefs or headman;
8. the inheritance of property;
9. marriage; and
10. social customs.

The District Council or Regional Council is also empowered by the Constitution to establish Village Councils for the village administration; make appointment of members and presiding officers of the Village Councils and courts and to appoint officers for the administration of laws made under paragraph 3 of the Sixth Schedule. The Council may also appoint officers, if necessary, to administer the law made by the Councils.

**Abolition of Chieftainships**

The supremacy of the chiefs was a great nuisance to the commoners because some of the chiefs had utilized their power arbitrarily. The traditional tax and privileges given to the traditional chiefs was a great burden to the commoners. As Christianity and mission activities were opposed to the interest of the traditional elites, the new privileged class became wholly dominated by the commoners and posed a challenge to the traditional elites. In this way the British rule gradually loosened the traditional holds resulting in a declining tendency of chief's traditional powers. A new set of rules based on democratic principle was envisaged by the people. Later on, the refusal of the chiefs to join the Mizo Union party had created a bitter atmosphere of political rivalry causing a strained relation between the traditional elites and the new privileged class.

In the first election of the Lushai Hills District Council, out of 18 elected members the Mizo Union, greatly supported by the commoners had got 17 seats and only 1 seat was won by the UMFO, supported by the traditional elites. The District Council, soon after its formation, began to make laws on various subjects aimed at bringing about the development of Mizoram. It passed several laws on different subjects within a short period and made commendable work in matters of legislation. The first session of the District Council was convened on 23rd June, 1952 and the session continued till 10th July, 1952.[13] Armed by the Sixth Schedule to the Constitution which had empowered them to pass law, majority of the members entertained a revengeful attitude towards the chiefs and expressed their views in favour of the abolition of chieftainship in the Lushai Hills. Accordingly, its first piece of legislation called the Lushai Hills (Chiefs Abolition) Act, 1952, was passed by the District Council with effect from January 1, 1953.[14] Accordingly, the entire existing chiefs within the District Council were to be abolished and all their powers and their rights to receive customary gifts were automatically abrogated. The chiefs were, however, allowed to function as rightful chiefs until another body was formed as substitute.

The chiefs were now reduced to mere figure heads in the Mizo society. They were no more looked upon as absolute ruler by the people. The District Council enjoyed the right to exercise overall powers on the chiefs. The District Council in its memorandum of April 3, 1953 justified the abolition of chiefship and accused the chief of exercising their power arbitrarily and blamed them as the cause of formation of the political party in 1946.[15] Accordingly the Government of Assam Legislative Assembly passed a bill which became an Act known as, The Assam (Lushai Hills Acquisition of Chief's Rights) Bill, 1954.[16] The Act mainly deals with the compensation to be given to the chiefs and the settlement of their land. It further empowered the District Council to administer all the chiefs' land. With these as many as 255 chiefs in the Lushai Hills and 50 chiefs in the Pawi-Lakher Regional Council were abolished on April 1, 1956 respectively.[17] In this way the oldest institution of the Mizo Society came to an end, the system of chiefship so long in vogue was done away with and the right and interest of the Chiefs were taken over by the District Council. This paved the way for the creation of a democratically set up institution at the grassroots level.

## Formation of the Village Council

With the formation of the District Council the whole administrative set up of the Lushai Hills was changed enabling the people to participate in the formation of the Government through adult franchise. Now with the extinction of the Chieftainship, the Village Council elected through franchise was to be formed in order to substitute the hereditary chiefs, who had all the administrative powers and responsibility for managing the affairs of the villages in the Mizo traditional society. The proposed new system of forming the Village Council was discussed at length in the District Council's sessions. The first was the enactment of the Lushai Hills District (Village Council) Act, 1953 (The Lushai Hills Act No. V of 1953). The Governor of Assam gave his assent to the Act on November 29, 1953 and the same was published in the Assam Gazette, dated 9th December, 1953.[18] The Act empowered the District Council to form a Village Council in every village within the jurisdiction of the Lushai Hills District Council. Accordingly, the District Council had started taking all necessary steps for the formation of the Village Council. It also provided that the number of the Village Councils would vary from village to village depending upon the number of houses. The Village Councils were divided into various groups in accordance with the Constituency of the District Council. Mr. Hrangaia, an Executive Member of the Lushai (Mizo) Hills District Council was appointed as a member in-charge of the Village Council.

The first election to the Village Council was held from April 23 to July 7, 1954 with the polling party moving from one village to another conducting the election.[19] In the election the Mizo Union captured most of the interior villages while the United Mizo Freedom Organization (UMFO), another political party largely supported by the chiefs and their followers, won only few seats in the interior villages. After the election of the Village Council the date for the inauguration of the Village Council in each circle was appointed by the District Council, the Chief Executive Member—Mr. Lalsawia, Executive Members—Mr. Hrangaia and F. Sangkunga, Mr. Thanhlira MP were appointed to inaugurate various Village Councils of different Circles where the newly elected members were to be present.[20] According to the notification served by the Lushai Hills District Council the first sitting of the Village Council of all the villages was held on August 16,1954, where the President and Vice President were elected. The elected President had to select a person from amongst the villagers, who will act as a Secretary during the tenure of the term, on the basis of personal qualification.[21] The Act, further provides that, of the total number of members of the Village Council one-third or nearest shall be nominated by the executive committee and the rest elected by the adult of the village in accordance with the rules made by the District Council under the Act. After completing all formalities the Village level administration which so long rest with the chiefs began to be performed by the Village Councils in Lushai Hills from 1954. Thus the villages in the Lushai Hills became a village republic where the head of the village or President was elected by the villager for a fixed period. The dream of having democratically set up villages where people would become their own masters had been for the first time fulfilled in the Lushai Hills and democracy had started finding its place at the grassroots level under the District Council.

As stated under Section 3, sub-section (4) of the Lushai Hills District (Village Councils) Act, 1953, all the villages did not have Village Council. In order that a village should have a Village Council, there must be first of all a village establishment by a District Council having an area demarcating its boundaries. Number of members of the Village Council shall be decided in accordance with the number of houses in the village as specified below:

- For villages not exceeding 60 houses, there shall be 5 members;
- For villages between 61 and 100 houses, there shall be 6 members;
- For villages between 101 and 140 houses, there shall be 7 members;
- For villages between 141 and 180 houses, there shall be 8 members;
- For villages between 181 and 220 houses, there shall be 9 members;
- For villages between 221 and 260 houses, there shall be 10 members;
- For villages between 261 and above, there shall be 11 members.

However, the prescribed number of Village Council members was modified in March 1970, after the system of compulsory grouping of villages was introduced. The change in the composition of the ratio of the Village Council membership with the number of households was revised due to the proportionate increase of village population after the introduction of grouping scheme which reads:

- For villages not exceeding 100 houses, there shall be 4 members;
- For villages between 101 and 200 houses, there shall be 5 members;
- For villages between 201 and 300 houses, there shall be 6 members;
- For villages between 301 and 400 houses, there shall be 7 members;
- For villages between 401 and 500 houses, there shall be 8 members;
- For villages between 501 and 600 houses, there shall be 9 members;

- For villages exceeding 600 houses, there shall be 10 members.

Again in 1991, an Amendment was made in order to change the criteria for the ratio of the number of seats in the Village Council and number of its nominated elements. It received the assent of the Governor of Mizoram on 3rd April, 1991 stating that one-fourth or nearest to its members shall be nominated and the rest shall be elected on the basis of adult-franchise. The criteria for the number of members were as determined below:

- For villages not exceeding 100 houses, there shall be 4 members;
- For villages with more than 100 houses, but not exceeding 200 houses there shall be 5 members;
- For villages with more than 200 houses, but not exceeding 300 houses there shall be 6 members;
- For villages with more than 300 houses, but not exceeding 400 houses there shall be 7 members;
- For villages with more than 400 houses, but not exceeding 500 houses there shall be 8 members;
- For villages with more than 500 houses, but not exceeding 600 houses there shall be 9 members;
- For villages with more than 600 houses, but not exceeding 900 houses there shall be 10 members;
- For villages with more than 900 houses, but not exceeding 1200 houses there shall be 11 members;
- For villages with more than 1200 houses, but not exceeding 1500 houses there shall be 12 members;
- For villages with more than 1500 houses, but not exceeding 1800 houses there shall be 13 members;
- For villages with more than 1800 houses, but not exceeding 2100 houses there shall be 14 members;
- For villages with more than 2100 houses there shall be 15 members.

Later on, in 2006 the criterion for the number of members of the Village Council was again changed. Under the ordinance of the Lushai Hills District (Village Council) (Amendment) Ordinance, 2006

(Ordinance No. 1 of 2006, Dated 10.2.2006) the composition of the Village Council with the number of households are as under:

(i) For village not exceeding 200 houses, there shall be 3 (three) members;
(ii) For village with more than 200 houses, but not exceeding 500 houses there shall be 4 (four) members;
(iii) For village with more than 500 houses, but not exceeding 800 houses, there shall be 5 (five) members;
(iv) For village with more than 800 houses, there shall be 6 (six) members.

At its inception out of 410 villages only 288 Village Councils were constituted in the Lushai Hills District. In the Pawi-Lakher Regional Council there were 72 Village Councils out of 123 villages.[22] The number of Villages having Village Council in Mizoram keeps on increasing with the passage of time and more villages has been recognized by the District Council. The latest record maintained by the state government had shown that there are 556 Village Council looked after by the state government with 2036 members. The following table may indicate the number of Village Council and its member in each district looked after by the state government.

**Table 13.1:** The number of Village Councils and its members in the 16th General Election held on 24th and 25th February 2006

| *Sl. No.* | *Name of the Districts* | *Number of Village Councils* | *Number of members of of the Village Councils* |
|---|---|---|---|
| *1* | *2* | *3* | *4* |
| 1. | Aizawl District | 166 | 664 |
| 2. | Lunglei District | 132 | 457 |
| 3. | Champhai District | 100 | 350 |
| 4. | Mamit District | 72 | 244 |
| 5. | Kolasib District | 44 | 168 |
| 6. | Serchhip District | 42 | 153 |
| 7. | Total | 556 | 2036 |

*Source*: Results of General Election to Village Council 2006, issued and published by Directorate of Local Administration.

Besides, the above mentioned number of Village Councils and its members there are other Village Councils which were look after by the District Council which got the right to make their own laws as empowered by the Sixth Schedule to the Constitution. Though nominated seats have been abolished under the state government in 1999 the three Autonomous District Councils still continue to have nominated seats within their jurisdictions which indicates that the District Council have got enormous power in looking after the Village Council. The nominated members are usually appointed from those persons capturing majority seats and in the drawn Village Council nominated seats usually goes to those persons who belongs to the majority party in the District Council. The following table may indicate the number of Village Councils and number of its elected members in each Autonomous District Council within the state of Mizoram.

**Table 13.2:** The Number of Village Councils and Number of Its Members under the Autonomous District Councils

| *Sl. No.* | *Name of the District Council* | *No. of Village Council* | *No. of member of the Village Councils* |
|---|---|---|---|
| *1* | *2* | *3* | *4* |
| 1. | Lai (Pawi) Autonomous District Council | 77 | 209 |
| 2. | Mara (Lakher) Autonomous District Council | 70 | 240 |
| 3. | Chakma Autonomous District Council | 65 | 305 |
| 4. | Total | 212 | 754 |

*Source*: Secretariat of the District Council Affairs.

From Tables 13.1 and 13.2 we have come to know that in the whole state of Mizoram there are 768 Village Councils and 2790 elected members.

The Administrator or the District Council has got the power to abolish a Village Council if the number of households of the village has, in his opinion, too small to have a Village Council of its own. In such a situation the villages shall be comprised the nearest village having a Village Council.

## Composition of the Village Council

The composition of the Village Council consists of all the elected members who were elected by the villagers on the basis of adult franchise; nominated members in case there are nominated members, Secretary and Tlangau or Village Crier. The President and Vice President of the Village Council are elected by the member of the Village Council from amongst the elected members of the Council.[23] The Secretary is appointed by the Government on the recommendation of the President from amongst the villagers. The appointment of Tlangau is made by the Village Council's full sitting from among the applicants through an advertisement.

- *The Executive*: The executive body of the Village Council consists of the President, the Vice-President, and the Secretary. While the President and Vice-President were elected from among the members, Secretary is appointed and dismissed by the government on the recommendation of the President. The secretary is not a member of the Village Council. He participates in the meetings of the Village Council but does not enjoy the right to vote. The Secretary keeps all records and had taken the charge of the Village Writer and had no right to cast his vote when decisions are taken. He records the proceedings of the meetings and published notices, orders and proceedings. Similarly, either the President or the Vice-President should not be eligible to hold the office of the Secretary of the Village Council. They are considered as public servants.
- *The President*: The President is the Executive head of the Village Council and all executive functions are carried out in his name. He shall cause notices and instructions for prevention of dangers such as outbreak of fire, epidemics, etc. He shall be responsible for the compliance of all orders and notifications issued by the administrator or the District Council. He shall cause all such orders and notifications to be read by the Secretary in the meetings of the Village Council and shall examine the books kept by the Secretary from time to time as he may deem necessary. The President also act as a Treasurer of the Village Council and all local funds and development fund were taken care by him, he should see that the cash book of the Village Council is maintained properly.

- *The Vice-President*: The Vice-President shall have position next to the President and in the absence of the President he shall perform the duties of that office and during such period the power of the President shall be vested in him.
- *The Secretary*: The Secretary of the Village Council was substitute of the Khawchhiar or Village Writer in Mizoram since October 15, 1954; they were in charge of all the responsibilities of the Village Writer during the colonial period.[24] He shall record all the proceedings of the Village Council as well as the Village Courts and such records shall be signed by the President. He shall publish orders and notifications and records as may be necessary, such orders, notifications, and records shall be signed by the President. On receipt of any order, notice, or circular or letters from higher authority, the Secretary shall cause it to be served as may be directed and shall be responsible to carry such directions. He shall keep all the books and records of the Village Council and of the Village Court. He also acts as a Financial Secretary of the Village Council and is expected to maintain a good record of the receipt and expenditure of the Village Council on the advice of the President who act as a Treasurer of the Village Council. All the books and records shall be kept ready to be examined at any time by the Officers of the concerned department, or any members of the Village Council in this behalf.
- *The Tlangau*: The Tlangau or Village Crier always holds an important position in the Mizo villages from time immemorial. The Tlangau shall bring to the notice for the public all orders and notifications the Village Council may direct to be notified. He shall summon all parties and other persons required by the Village Council or Village Court to attend its meetings. He shall carry notice to all members of the Village Council for all meetings of the Village Council recommended by the President. If any emergency occurs requiring the gathering of public in the interest of the village any member of the village may, without the previous approval of the President, order the Tlangau to summon all the villagers.

## Qualification to be a Member of the Village Council

A member of the Village Council should be a member of a Scheduled Tribe, he must have attained the age of 25 years on the qualifying date, he must be a voter in the village where he desires to contest, he must not be a member of any other Village Council, he must be of sound mind and he must not be convicted by any court or imprisoned three years before.[25] A person who has been employed as a government servant on regular basis cannot be elected as a member of the Village Council.

### *Terms of Office*

The normal term of the Village Council is three years from the date of its first meeting, unless dissolved sooner. However, the life of the Village Council may be extended or shortened for a period not exceeding 18 months.[26] Although, the term of the office of a Village Council is three years normally, if the government finds that the Village Council is too week, inefficient and is not able to carry on the village administration, it can dissolve such Village Council and during the period of such dissolution the government can appoint its Circle Assistant or some other officers to look after the administration of the dissolved Village Council. The government, if necessary, may conduct an election of the dissolved Village Council for the remaining period of the term.[27] However, under the District Council whenever the Village Councils are dissolved, the Executives of the District Council in its first session have to lay down the reason for discussion by the members in the meeting and all necessary actions may be taken. But under the government of Mizoram discussion about the Village Council were never made in the Assemblies as the provision for it has been deleted when Mizoram was upgraded into a Union Territory.

It may be interesting to note that the first four general elections of the Village Council was conducted smoothly in 1954, 1957, 1960 and 1963. However with the outbreak of violence and insurgency, the 1966 Village Council election was suspended for several years. During this period all political activities were suspended, the term of the existing District Council and Village Council were extended. After the returning of normalcy in political situation, political leaders reactivated political parties and the District Council resumed its normal functions. The fifth Village Council election was thus held in 1971 after a lapse of eight years.

However, under the District Council whenever the Village Councils were dissolved, the Executives of the District Council in its first session have to lay down the reason for discussion by the members in the meeting and all necessary actions may be taken.

In case, the President of the Village Council wants to resign before the expiry of his term he has to give his resignation to the government with his own handwriting but resume his duties till his resignation has been accepted. The Vice-President will give his resignation to the President who will forward it to the government for acceptance.[28] The President also has to forward the resignations of other members of the Village Council to the government, and whenever any post in the Village Council remains vacant it is the duty of the President to inform the government or an officer in-charge of it for necessary action. The government may remove the President and the Vice-President on grounds of inefficiency, corruption, loss of majority support of members or "acting in a manner prejudicial to the interest of the state."[29] But the Village Council has no power to impeach President and Vice-President. If a member remains absent in ten consecutive meetings without proper information, the Village Council can dismiss him in a specially convened meeting for the purpose and communicate the decision to the Government.

### *Election to the Village Council*

Election to Village Council is conducted by the District Council under the Autonomous District Councils and the Government of Mizoram under the state government. The administrator shall, by notification in Gazette fix the number of seats for each constituency to form a Village Council. Every Village has got their own electoral rolls which shall include the names of all persons who are *bona fide* residents and entitled to vote in the election to Village Council, in accordance with clause (g) of Rule 2 of the Mizoram (Election to Village Councils) Rules, 1974 as amended. The administrator shall appoint a Registration Officer for each district for the Village Council and may appoint one or more persons as Assistant Registration Officer to assist the Registration Officer in the performance of his function.[30] The Registration Officer shall appoint a Returning Officer, who will also function as Presiding Officer, and also Polling Officers, to conduct the election of each Village Council constituency.[31] The Registration Officer, Assistant Registration Officers and Polling Officers are usually appointed from among the teachers of the concerned village. The Retuning Officer has been empowered to appoint a substitute to a Polling Officer in case of illness or any unavoidable circumstances and inform the Registration Officer accordingly. No Civil Courts shall have jurisdiction to question the legality of any action taken or any decision given by the Returning Officer or by any other person appointed under these Rules in connection with the election.[32] The Administrator shall, by notification in the Gazette shall appoint the date or dates for such election in each constituency simultaneously or consecutively according to convenience.

Any person whose name is included in the electoral roll of the constituency and who is not otherwise disqualified under section 4 of the Lushai Hills District (Village Council) Act, 1953 may offer himself or herself as a candidate for election to a Village Council and shall inform the Returning Officer, in writing of his intention to do so by a particular date to be notified in this behalf by the Returning Officer in the respective constituency on a date and time to be notified by him. The scrutiny of candidature shall be taken up by the Returning Officer in the respective constituency on a date and time to be notified by him. A candidate shall furnish a security deposit of Rs.25 to the Returning Officer along with his application for his candidature which will be refunded in the event of the withdrawal of candidature or at the earliest date after the conclusion of the Election.[33]

Election to the Village Council is conducted by symbol system. Each candidate should select a symbol out of those prescribed by rules. They are chicken, cock, cage, lantern, hen, house, horse, axe, spade, pen, kettle, sickle, men's smoking pipe, Mizo hat, umbrella, etc. The number of election symbols is 60 in accordance with the notification served by the Local Administrative Department before the Village Council election of 2006.[34] If more than one candidate selected same symbol, the Returning Officer shall decide by lot to whom of those the symbol shall be assigned.

As regards arrangement of voting there should be one or more polling stations for the same constituency depending upon the number of voters.[35] One election agent of the candidate appointed in writing and submitted to the Returning Officer shall be admissible into the Polling Booth in the case of candidate absenting himself from the Polling Station. The Returning Officer shall fix the hours of polling votes. Each voter should be given as many ballot papers as equal to the number of seats to be filled up. Each voter shall record his vote/

votes by dropping only one ballot paper in each box containing the symbol assigned to the candidate of his choice. After the closing of the poll, the Presiding Officer shall, in the presence of the candidates or their agents, close the ballot boxes in safe custody until the commencement of counting of votes, which shall be as soon as possible carried out by the Returning Officer and those persons whom he had appointed to assist him in counting of votes. In case of equality of votes the Returning Officer shall decide membership between those candidates by drawing lots. The list of elected shall be published in the Gazette.

In case, election of a member to constitute a Village Council cannot be held due to any reason considered unavoidable by the administrator or the District Council but the circumstances demand immediate constitution of such Village Councils, the administrator may also nominate the remaining number of members who shall hold office for a period not exceeding one year from the date of the first meeting of the Council.

### *Powers and Functions of the Village Council*

The Mizo Chiefs from time immemorial had governed their villages with unwritten laws with the advice of the Upas and elders, which they think is most suitable for the villagers. Later on, these unwritten laws developed into a tradition and culture of the people occupying the Lushai Hills. N.E. Parry, the Superintendent of the Lushai Hills from 1924 to 1928 collected the custom which have been practiced by various chiefs and prepared a book which was published in 1928; the book was greatly utilized by the chiefs and elders in giving judgements to the villagers.[36] Later on, when the Lushai Hills was placed under the Sixth Schedule of the Constitution having its own District Council, N.E. Parry's book with certain modification was developed into a Mizo Customary Law and was published in 1957. The book was legally utilized by the District Council Court and Village Council Court till recently in Mizoram.

The Village Council since inception has got certain functions and responsibilities being substitute of the Village Chiefs who enjoyed enormous power and had taken up the responsibilities of legislating, executing and protecting the village and the villagers. It is the duty of the Village Council to see that the villagers have enjoyed enough liberty in every sphere of life. The powers and functions of the Village

Council may be broadly divided into two groups, which are the executive and judicial functions which has been discussed below:

**(A) The Executive Powers and Functions of the Village Council**

The Executive powers and functions of the Village Council may be discussed under the following:

(i) *Distribution of Jhum land for the Purpose of Shifting Cultivation*: The first important executive function of the Village Council is the distribution of Jhum land within its jurisdiction. Jhumming or Shifting Cultivation being the most important source of livelihood for the villagers in Mizoram and administering the jhum land always play an important role in administration of the villages. The Lushai hills District (Jhumming) Regulation, 1954 had empowered the Village Council to distribute jhum land each year to the villagers on the appointed time. The law has been adapted by the Dissolution of Mizo District Council (Miscellaneous Provision) Order, 1972 when the Mizo District Council was dissolved. The law has been again adapted by the State of Mizoram under The State of Mizoram Adaptation of Laws Order (No.2) of 1987.[37] The Village Council has got the responsibility of reporting the place and area to be cultivated or distributed every year in the month of September, in written to the Government. The jhumland was distributed by means of lots. The privileges given to the President, Vice-President, and members of the Village Council to select the jhum site were suspended since 1958.[38] This may be due to the remuneration of the members in terms of money since August 16, 1957.

Disobedience of the Village Council or Government's Order on the distribution of Jhum land is punishable with a fine of Rs.500 and failure of cultivating the selected site is punishable with a fine of Rs.100.[39] The Village Council therefore needs to be very careful while fixing the area to be cultivated each year. The Village Council was given the responsibility of preventing the outbreak of fire while burning the trees for clearing the jungles. If there is any dispute concerning the distribution of jhum land, the final decision will be made by the Government or officer in charge of it.[40]

(ii) *Enforcement of Hnatlang or Collective Labour*: The next important function of the Village Council is the enforcement of "Hnatlang", which means common service for the common good of the villagers which the residents of the village are to render whenever the need for it arises in the village. The Lushai Hills District (Village Council) Act, 1953, section 9 had empowered the Village Council to call for Hnatlang whenever the need for it was felt by the members of the Village Council. All developmental works, cleanliness or sanitation, helping out the poor and needy, etc. cannot be carried out by the government alone but can be carried out by the collective labour under the supervision of the Village Council.

The Village Council was also empowered to exempt anyone from Hnatlang but the reason for it must be carefully recorded. People above the age of 60 years were also exempted from Hnatlang and children below the age of 15 years cannot be accepted as a representative of a household. Absentees from hnatlang without any reason thereof, are punishable with a fine of Rs.50.[41]

(iii) *The Control of Animal and Taxation of Animal*: The third executive power and function of the Village Council is controlling of the animals within their village. The Mizo Animals (Control and Taxation) Act, 1980 (as amended in 1991) had empowered the Village Council to control and tax the animals within their jurisdiction. The task of collecting animal tax was given to the Village Council. The Village Council get 50 per cent of the tax collected and another 50 per cent will be given to the Government as a consolidated fund of Mizoram. All the people having animal should get them register and the registration fee of an animal is 50 paisa and that of a young animal is 25 paisa.[42] The Village Council was to maintain the registration fee and accounts of the register that may be checked by the officer in charge from time to time.[43]

The Village Council should see that no animal in the village was a nuisance to the neighbours or villagers and every animal should have their own homes. The owner of any animal caught in the street may be fined with a sum of Rs. 50 and if any animal destroyed somebody's property, the owner of the animal had to compensate the victim.[44] The Village Council has got the right to auction any animal caught, if it was not claimed by the owner within a period of seven days, subject to proper notification.[45]

(iv) *Allotment of House Sites for the Villagers*: The fourth important executive function of the Village Council is the allotment of house sites in the village for the villagers to live in. The Lushai Hills District (House Sites) Act, 1953 had empowered the Village Council to distribute land within its jurisdiction for the construction of houses for homes. But the Village Council was not authorized to distribute land for the purpose of agriculture, shops, hotels and any other forms of business.

(v) *Prevention and Control of the Outbreak of Fire*: The fifth important executive function of the Village Council is the Prevention and Control of Fire within its jurisdiction as given in "The Mizoram (Prevention and Control of Fire in the Village Ram) Rules, 1983. The Village Council was given the responsibility of preventing the outbreak of fire within its jurisdiction. In accordance with the office memorandum No. B11011/19/91-F51 dated the 8th February, 2000, Aizawl; all the villages were to set up a Village Forest Fire Prevention Committee in which the President of the Village Council was to be the appointed chairman of the committee. The committee was to appoint Fire Watcher for a period of two months, i.e. 15th February to 15th April which would be a voluntary work. In case there is an outbreak of fire the villagers were expected to stop the fire on the basis of hnatlang under the supervision of the Village Council. Moreover, the Village Council was assigned to give information or report to the Deputy Commissioner/SDO (Civil) for necessary action.

The responsibility of the Village Council in order to prevent the outbreak of fire is given under the Mizoram (Prevention and Control of Fire in the Village Ram) Rules, 2001.

(a) The Village Council has to fix the period for clearing the jungles and cutting down tree for the purpose of jhumming every year.
(b) The Village Council should fix the date for burning down the jhum sites and the notice should be served three days before the fixed date.
(c) The Village Council should see that all preventive measures have been taken for the prevention of the outbreak of fire.
(d) Subsidiary shifting jhum cultivators should inform the Village Council seven days before they were going to burn their subsidiary jhum. The Village Council will then fix the date for burning down the subsidiary jhum.
(e) The Village Council will take all preventive measures for the outbreak of fire before the proposed subsidiary jhums were burnt down.

(vi) *Control and Protection of Forest*: The sixth important function of the Village Council is the control and protection of safety, supply and Protected Forest Reserve under the Mizo District (Forest) Act, 1955 (Act No. IV of 1955). There are three types of forest reserve, they are:

- *Village Safety Reserve*: This reserve have been protected to prevent the village from the outbreak of fire, to maintain the health of the villagers and to maintain the purity of springs and streams from which the villagers fetch water for domestic purposes. These reserves should not be used for any other purpose and cutting down of trees within this area is strictly prohibited.
- *Village Supply Reserve*: These reserves have been protected so that the trees and bamboos within this area may be utilized only for domestic purposes. All the villagers are allowed to cut down trees and bamboos within the village supply reserves.
- *Protected Forest Reserve*: This reserve area should not be

utilized for any other purposes unless permission has been obtained from the government.

The Village Council is given the responsibility of protecting this reserved forest and maintain the records of its boundaries.

(vii) *Sanitation of the Village*: Chapter II of the Lushai Hills District (Village Council) Act, 1954 had clearly indicated that the Village Council is responsible for the sanitation of the village. The Village Council has been empowered to establish a Sanitation Committee and make certain law which would regulate the functioning of the Committee. The member of the Village Council being very small in number may not be able to maintain the sanitation of the whole town or village. With the help of this committee that may be grouped into various sections, the Village Council has to carry out this important function and prevent the spread of various diseases.

In addition to the above, the normal functioning of Village Council covers a variety of items. It has to handle all the developmental programms, with the help of the administrative officials, within their respective jurisdiction. The President is to report the harvest of rice of his village to the Government so that the Government will be able to take remedial measures if the harvest is very poor. In any severe incidence takes place in the village, the Village Council is responsible to inform the Government. The Village Council is to carry all the duties assigned to it by the Government. Also it is to consider the welfare of the villagers, in bringing their felt needs to the notice of the Government such as for opening of school, post office, construction of inter-village path and construction of roads and approach foot-path to jhum, etc. The Village Council is also expected to take various steps in order to prevent the spread of communicable diseases or epidemics, etc. The President also acts as a communicating link between the villagers and the Government.

**(B) The Judicial Functions of the Village Council**

The most important function of the Village Council is the Administration of Justice in the village. For this purpose the Village

Council is empowered to organize the Village Court constituted under the administration of Justice Rule, 1953 and the member of the Village Council Court as a bench. The Village Court is the lowest court of the District Council and later on the state. The Village Council has to appoint three of its members or up to half of its members to be members of the Village Court.[46] The normal term of its member is of three years. The Village Court can give judgments only in the presence of at least three of its members. Therefore, in a Village Council where there are only three members, court judgments can be given only in the presence of all the members.

A Village Court can try suits and petty cases in which both the parties belong to Scheduled Tribes or Tribes resident within its jurisdiction in accordance with the customary laws of the village, but the court should not try offences in respect of which the punishment is obligatory under Indian Penal Code. A Village Court shall try all cases in open Durbar in the presence of the complainant and the accused and their witnesses, if any, it shall decide the issue by a simple majority of votes and pronounce decision as soon as possible. Registers of all suits and cases disposed of by a Village Court shall be kept by the Court.

The Village Court, which was given the responsibility of maintaining law and order in the village, has been empowered to try the following cases:

1. Civil cases if both the parties were tribal and the nature falling within the purview of village or tribal laws and customs.
2. Criminal cases falling within the purview of tribal laws and customs and offences of petty nature, such as petty theft and pilfering, mischief and trespass of petty nature, simple assaults and hurt, affront and affray of whatever kind, drunken or disorderly brawling, public nuisance and simple cases of wrongful restraint.
3. The Village Court can decide cases which are concerned with the following:

    (a) The Lushai Hills District (Village Council) Act, 1953 as amended from time to time;
    (b) The Lushai Hills District (House Site) Act, 1953 and the Mizoram Land Holding and Settlement Act, 2000;
    (c) Administration of Justice Rules, 1953;

(d) The Lushai Hills (Jhumming) Regulation, 1954;
(e) The Mizo District (Forest) Act, 1955;
(f) The Mizoram Animal (Control and Taxation) Act, 1980 and the Mizoram (Control and Taxation) Rules, 1982.
(g) The Mizoram (Prevention and Control of Village Fire in the Village Ram) Rules, 2001.

4. The Village Court has got the power to fine an accused up to a sum of Rs.500 depending upon the crime he has committed.[47] If the accused person fails to pay the amount, the Village Council has the power to confiscate his property.
5. The Village Court has the power to summon a witness but if the witness failed to appear in the court he can be fined a sum of Rs.100.[48]
6. The Village Court has an enormous power of deciding cases concerning the inheritance of property in accordance with the customary law.

It might be important to note that those persons convicted by the Civil Court cannot be given a punishment more than a fine of Rs.500. Moreover the person convicted by the Village Court cannot be sent to a Jail and no legal practitioner is permitted to plead on behalf of his client in the Village Council Court. The Village Court has the right to send an accused person to higher court. An appeal against the decision or orders of the Village Council Court can be made in the Subordinate District Council Court or Additional Subordinate District Council Court within a period of 60 days after the judgement has been given.[49]

The Village Council, although it is the lowest political institution, is very important in view of the fact that it is constituted in pursuance of the provisions of valid law. Under Section 43 of the State of Mizoram Act, 1986, all laws in force during the Union Territory of Mizoram, should continue to be in force in Mizoram until alter, repeal or amended and this includes the Village Council Act by which the Village Council was constituted. The President, Vice-President and members of a Village Council including the secretary are deemed to be public servants under Section 21 of the Indian Penal Code. As such obstructing their performance of duties in the discharge of administration of the village will be an offence as is the case with other public servants.

### *Conduct of Business*

The Lushai Hills District (Village Council) Act, 1953 early describes how the meeting of the Village Council has been carried out. The President presides the meeting of the Village Council, in the absence of the President, the Vice-President will be in charge of the duties of the President. The President can summon the meeting of the Village Council whenever necessity arises and if or when two-thirds of the member in writing made a request to the President to call for a meeting.[50]

The resolution in the meeting of the Village Council is taken by the majority of votes. The President at the initial stage does not caste his vote but acts as a tie breaker when there is equality of votes. The meeting of the Village Council may be conducted in the presence of non-members but no person other than a member of the Village Council shall vote nor shall speak or take part in its deliberation and any person contravening this provision shall be punishable with a fine not exceeding Rs.50.[51] The President shall preserve order and have all powers necessary for the purpose of enforcing his decision during the meeting. For this purpose he may direct any member whose conduct in his opinion, is disorderly to withdraw immediately from the day's meeting, if any person is ordered to withdraw for the second time from a meeting of the same session of the Council, the President may suspend the member for the remaining period. If any member fails to carry out the direction given to him, the President shall report in writing, the conduct of the member to the Administrator which may lead to suspension of the member for any period considered reasonable by the Administrator.

The Secretary of the Village Council has no right to cast his vote when decisions are taken but may share his views on certain topics with the permission of the President. The Secretary shall record all the proceedings of the Village Council and such record shall be signed by the President. He shall publish all orders, notifications and records as may be necessary and such orders, notifications and records shall be signed by the President. All the resolutions passed by the Village Councils were informed to the villagers through the village Crier or Tlangau. All decisions in the meeting of the Village Council are carried out in the name of the President who can greatly influence the decisions of the meeting through his criticism and advice.

Therefore, the working of the Village Council to a large extent depends upon the personality of its President.

***Financial Resources of the Village Council***

The most important financial resources of the Village Council are as follows:

- The Village Council was entrusted to collect Ranchhiah or Animal Tax of which fifty per cent of the tax goes to the Village Council and the other fifty per cent was given to the Government. This tax became the most important financial resources of the Village Council;
- Another important financial resource of the Village Council was those fines which were collected by the Village Courts from the Villagers as a penalty for the crimes they have committed or for breaking certain laws;
- While discussing the financial resources of the Village Council we may also mention that sometimes the government had entrusted the Village Council for certain development works, such as construction and maintenance of roads, and footpaths, sanitation works etc. Therefore various development funds and local funds were given into the hands of the Village Council which were utilized according to the necessity felt by the Village Council. For this reason, people often think that the Village Council is merely a development unit. The Village Council was also often entrusted by the state government to utilize various sanctions which were meant to uplift or help the poor and the needy under various schemes.
- The Village Council was not given the post of a Treasurer but the President of the Village Councils act as a Treasurer, managing the financial affairs of the Council. The Secretary of the Village Council was to act as a Financial Secretary of the Village Council. All the Village Council were given a cash/account book by the government in which the Financial resources and expenditure of the Village Council is to be recorded properly. These cash books may be checked by those persons appointed by the District Local Administrative

Officer at any time and failure of maintaining cash book may lead to dissolution of the Village Council.

The Village Council though embodied with various powers and functions has to suffer a serious setback owing to its scarce financial resources. All developmental functions which were to be carried out in the name of the Village Council could not reach up to the expectation of the masses due to the paucity of funds which paved a way for the loss of confidence of the masses.

***The Working of the Village Councils under the District Council***

The Village Council at the initial stage of its formation was looked after by the District Council. The people had rightfully accepted the Village Council as their real representative and the feeling that they are being governed by their own representatives at the village level creates great enthusiasm to the people. The peoples have been well aware of the political changes and welcome the new system of administration. Moreover, the people became more aware of the happenings around them and the existence of democracy at the grassroots level became an important means of educating the people in the field of politics. Besides, in the absence of traditional propriety and sanctions, the Village Council has no arbitrary power beyond those sanctioned by the Rules.

The formation of the Village Council brought in it vast changes regarding the administration of justice which was taken up by the representatives of the people, all cases relating to the native Mizo were taken care of by the District Council Courts and the Village Council Courts. While only those cases involving non-tribal were taken up in the courts of the Deputy Commissioner and his assistance.

However, in the Pawi-Lakher regions, there has not been strong and antagonistic forces operating against the traditional elites; and the traditional rulers, to a large extent, continue to dominate the new councils. It was only after 1966 that political pressure began to take the shape and form of groupings based on clan membership in this region. Among the Chakmas, there has been little evidence of institutional changes in their political organization as a result of new political set up brought about in Mizoram. Thus, in the areas inhabited by the Pawis, the Lakhers and the Chakmas, there has been little change in the distribution of powers even though the institutional form of legitimate power became shifted from chiefship to the new Councils.

The Sixth Schedule to the Constitution had given enormous power to the Autonomous District Councils for the Administration of its own territories, therefore, the State Government of Assam had little or no involvement in the village administration which was kept in the hands of the Mizo District Council. The District Council had made all laws and regulation for the administration of the Village Council. All elections to the Village Council at the beginning were conducted by the District Council. It prepared the Electoral Roll and declared the Constituency of each Village Council. The District Council would fix all the necessary and important dates for the conduct of election; it also appoints the Presiding Officers, Returning Officers, Registration Officers and all other important persons for the conduct of Election; it announced the election results and appointed the President, Vice-President and Secretary of the newly elected members of the Village Council. The District Council has got the power to dissolve the Village Council and announce bye-elections according to its own law. Therefore, the Village Council has worked according to the laws which were made by the District Council and disobedience of law may lead to suspension or dissolution of the Village Council. Under the District Council, the state government of Assam or the bureaucrats had little or no involvement in the village administration or working of the Village Council. The District Council was greatly responsible for the smooth functioning of the Village Councils.

### *The First Term of the Village Councils under the District Council*

The First General Election to the Village Councils within the Lushai Hills District Council was held in 1954 in which only the two existing political parties in the Lushai Hills, Mizo Union and United Mizo Freedom Organization (UMFO) have contested the election. In this election most of the interior villages were captured by the Mizo Union and a few Villages by the United Mizo Freedom Organization. The Notification served by the District Council on 1st October, 1954 had revealed that there were 360 Village Councils in the whole District.[52]

### *The Second Term of the Village Council under the District Council*

The second General Election to the Village Council under the District Council was held in 1957. As with the first election the Mizo Union won thumping majority and only few Councils were captured by the UMFO. The result of the Village Council as given by the District Council Notification on June 10, 1957 had revealed that there were 384 Village Councils in the District Council.[53]

### *The Third Term of the Village Council under the District Council*

The Third General Election to the Village Council was held in 1960, in which the loyalty of the UMFO had contested in the name of a new political party known as Eastern Indian Tribal Union, designed to fight for a hill state. As in the previous elections, the Mizo Union had captured most of the seats in this election too.[54]

### *The Fourth Term of the Village Council under the District Council*

The Fourth General Election to the Village Council under the District Council was held in 1963, more political parties have started finding their place in the hill areas of the Mizo Hills for contesting the election. The new regional political party called the Mizo National Front (MNF), which was set up by the newly educated Mizos in order to show their grievances against the State and Union Governments held an important position in this election. The Indian National Congress had also formed various Councils in this election. In the fourth election of the Village Council, the political situation in the Mizo Hills had experienced great changes. The Mizo Union had suffered a great set-back in this election in comparison with the previous elections.

The administration went on smoothly until the outbreak of the political uprising and unrest caused by the MNF's arm revolt in 1966. The administration in the Mizo Hills District faced a serious threat. Due to the MNF launching of the armed revolt; the entire Mizo District (Mizoram) was declared "Disturbed Area" under the Assam Disturbed Area Act, 1955 and the Assam and Manipur Arm Forces Special Power Act.[55] In order to check the atrocities of the MNF in the District on the one hand and to assure safety and security of the loyalists as also for the development of the district on the other, the grouping of villages' scheme was carried out. Under the scheme villagers in the far-flung and isolated places were brought to different places mainly along the roadsides. The bigger villages with bigger number of population came under the name "Protected and Progressive Villages" commonly known as PPVs. In Aizawl Sub-Division there are 79 group centres and in Lunglei Sub-Division there are 29 group centres.[56] The normal political activities were suspended for over three years and the terms of the existing District Council and the Village Councils had been extended. However, during this period many members of the Village Council have resigned themselves and many new members were also appointed by the District Council as the prevailing situation of the Mizo Hills was not favourable for conducting election. There were also some Villages who appointed their own members of Village Council without the knowledge of the District Council.[57]

When normalcy has return back into the Mizo Hills, the fifth election to the District Council was held on 23rd April, 1970 in which Mizo Union was defeated for the first time by the Congress, which became the main rival of the Mizo Union. The newly elected District Council, soon after its formation began to take steps in order to conduct the election of the Village Council in which there was a great tussle between the Mizo Union and the Congress.

### *The Fifth Term of the Village Council Under the District Council*

In 1971 the last and fifth election to the Village Council under the Autonomous District Council was held which experienced great changes. The electoral roll were revised thoroughly, those villages which were used as PPV centres were the only villages which were allowed to have Village Council though some of the villagers had returned back to occupy their own villages. The people were allowed to cast their vote in the grouping centres and those people who are willing to be member of the Village Council were also given the opportunity of contesting the election and be elected as a member of the Village Council. The number of Village Council which was 422 in the 1963 election decreased to 158 in this election. Out of 158 Village Councils, Mizo Union could form only 65 Village Councils though it was still the single largest political party in the district. Many political leaders had shifted their loyalty to the Indian National Congress, which formed 40 Village Councils, followed by UMPP which captured 27 Village Councils.[58]

During this period villages the Lushai Hills were characterize by great famine as it was impossible for them to continue their daily works of Jhum cultivation on which the economy of the villagers totally depends. The government had supplied rations but those were not sufficient to meet the crisis. In order to solve the problem villagers were allowed to move back to their own villages and resume their works but they were not given the permission to settle there permanently. They were allowed to go back to their villages only for economic purposes because the economy of the people greatly depended upon jhum cultivation and forming of big villages would give them great problem as they had to walk long distance for their daily works. These reoccupied villages were not given the status of a village but they were known as "Thlawhbawk" which means a temporary sub-village created for the sole purpose of jhumming in a certain area for a specified period. They were allowed to stay there only few seasons to resume their cultivation and later on move back to their grouping centres. Though, many of the Thlawhbawks have large population yet they still remained under the Administrative Control of the Grouping Centres.

The main reason why the people had greatly supported the Indian National Congress in this election was poverty of the people brought about by the MNF uprisings and its after effect. The people believed that being a Congress member, which was the dominant all India party, could perhaps save them from economic hardship and atrocities of the security forces, which had brought great sufferings to the people. They thought that better relationship with the central government was the only means of bringing peace and prosperity in the Mizo Hills. Moreover, the increasing aversion to the Mizo Union as a result of the party's failure to achieve results, also helped the Congress in gaining support, apart from the fact that the Mizo Union was an anti-MNF party.

### *The Working of the Village Councils under the Government of Mizoram*

*Administrative Set-up after the Formation of the Government of Mizoram*: Following the turning of Mizo District Council into Union Territory of Mizoram, the Mizo District Council and Pawi-Lakher Regional Council were abolished in accordance with the provision of the North-Eastern Areas (Reorganization) Act, 1971 and simultaneously three other Autonomous District Councils were created on April 2, 1972 to safeguard the interests of minority tribes which were Pawis, Lakhers and Chakmas. These newly created Autonomous District Councils were named after the three minority tribes which were: the Pawi (Lai) District Council, the Lakher (Mara)

District Council, and the Chakma District Council with their headquarters located at Lawngtlai, Saiha and Chawngte (Kamalanager) respectively. The three newly formed District Councils enjoyed the same powers and functions as provided in the Sixth Schedule to the Constitution of India. Further, for the convenience of administration, the Government of Mizoram had also divided the Union Territory into three districts—Aizawl District with its headquarters at Aizawl, Lunglei District with its headquarters at Lunglei and Chhimtuipui District with its headquarters at Saiha.

The Village Councils under the erstwhile Regional Council became the Village Councils of the Pawi, Lakher and Chakma District Council in the manner that such village as would fall under each of the Pawi, the Lakher and the Chakma District Councils till new Village Councils for each of three District Councils were elected. The first Village Council election under the Pawi District Council was held in 1974 and 41 were constituted. After this, the number of Village Councils increased and in 1976 the Pawi District Council held 54 Village Councils. The total Village Councils under the Lakher District Council in 1974 was 43. Similarly, the number of the Village Councils under the Chakma District Council was 24.[59] These District Councils were given full autonomy within their own jurisdictions to manage the affairs of the Village Councils. The government of Mizoram has little or no control over the management of the Village Councils which falls within the jurisdiction of the three autonomous District Councils.

After attaining the status of Union Territory in Mizoram, the structure of local administration did not change. The Lushai Hills District (Village Council) Act of 1953 was adopted in the area specified by the Act, under the Dissolution of Mizo District Council (Miscellaneous Provisions) Order, 1972. The adaptatation has made certain changes, such as: the term "District Council" and "Executive Committee" has been replaced by "Administrator". The newly created three District Councils also adopted the Pawi-Lakher Autonomous Region (Village Councils) Act, in their respective areas over which the Government of Mizoram has no control. In short, there are two sets of Village Councils in Mizoram now, one administered by the government of Mizoram and another by the three District Councils of Pawis, Lakhers and Chakmas. We shall make a study of those Village Councils which were administered by the state government.

### *Formation of the Local Administrative Department*

The new Government then started organizing different departments, creating new directorates and inducting Directors to manage them. Plans for smooth functioning of various departments were made with the abolition of the District Council after the inauguration of Union Territory; there was a particular department to look after the Village Council in place of the former District Council. A new department to look after the Village Councils was made by the Government of India, known as Local Administrative Department (LAD). To head the new Local Administration Directorate, the Additional Deputy Commissioner was given an ex-officio designation of Joint Secretary, Local Administrative Department. In that capacity, for all practical purposes he functions as Director.[60]

The Village Councils Affairs being replete with politics and the Local Administrative Department being for all practical purposes the successor of the District Council, problem faced by various Village Councils, like boundary disputes between villagers and demarcation of village boundary all went to the Joint Secretary, Local Administrative Department for solutions. The task of looking after the Village Council was a challenging one. A Minister in-charge of the Village Council and the Department of Local Administration was given an independent charge in the Union Territory of Mizoram.

### *The Village Council under the Local Administrative Department*

The working of the Village Councils under the Government of Mizoram has been greatly influenced by the bureaucrats and officers who were looking after the department. However, it has been slowly characterized by inadequacies of being a local self-government because it is now the bureaucrats of the state government and not the representatives of the people, who decide the number of members of the Village Council. They reorganize by abolishing, amalgamating, or bifurcating the village councils without their consent. The concerned department now decides the date for the election of the Village Council, and makes all important appointments. The bureaucrats and officers decide the dissolutions and make all the arrangements for the conduct of election and appointing all important officers in charge of the election. In these way grassroots democracy in Mizoram has been greatly influenced by the bureaucrat and the spirit of the founding fathers of the local-self government has been gradually declining.

*The First Term of the Village Council under the Government of Mizoram*

The First General Election to the Village Councils under the Union Territory of Mizoram was held on 7th and 5th May, 1975, which was conducted for the first time by the Local Administrative Department. In these elections there were 163 Village Councils exceeding the previous number only by 5. Among the 163 Village Councils 50 of them have got 3 members, 37 of them have got 4 members, 24 of them have got 5 members, 37 of them have got 6 members and 14 of them have got 7 members. Altogether there were 738 elected members in the whole Village Councils look after by the Government of Mizoram.

*The Second Term of the Village Council under the Government of Mizoram*

The Second General Election to the Village Councils under the Government of Mizoram could not be conducted in 1979, owing to the tension between the underground militants and the Central Government. For the first time all the Village Councils within the two districts of Aizawl and Lunglei, looked after by the Government of Mizoram were dissolved by the Lt. Governor of the Union Territory of Mizoram, with effect from November 19, 1979.[61] The dissolved Village Councils were placed under the charge of their respective Sub-Divisional Officers, Block Development Officers, and Administrative Officers including Circle Assistants. The termination of the members of the Village Councils before conducting fresh election was severely criticized by those political parties in opposition.

In 1982 the second election of the Village Councils was conducted on 15th February in Lunglei District and on 24th February in Aizawl District.[62] In this election, there were 141 Village Councils in Aizawl District and 41 Village Councils in Lunglei District. In this election, People's Conference Party has got majority seats in 63 Village Councils and Congress (I) Party has got majority seats in 59 villages, the rest were won by Independent and *there were few councils where no single party had the majority*. The People's Conference Party earned great support from the people in the Assembly as well as local politics from the beginning of its formation in 1975. It was formed under the leadership of a retired army officer popularly known as Brig. T. Sailo, who had founded the Human Rights Committee in Mizoram, lessening the confrontational activities of the armies in Mizoram.

A remarkable incidence in the history of the Village Council had taken place in 1982. On 1st March, 1982, the Central Government had granted permission to the villagers to move back and settle permanently in their original villages. They were also permitted to reorganize the Village Councils which was celebrated with great joy on 11th March, 1982. After making all necessary arrangements, by-election of Village Councils to these villages were held on 24th February, 1983.[63] The villages which were recognized only as tlawhbawk were once again given the right to form their own Village Council. In this election, out of 191 Village Councils People's Conference Party had formed 136 Village Councils which was more than seventy per cent of the total number of Village Councils.[64] The Congress had captured the second largest number of the Village Councils getting majority seats in 30 villages and the few remaining were divided among independents and other small political parties. It may be interesting to note that the number of Village Councils having other than three seats in this election were only 5, which clearly indicates that the reoccupied villages were very thinly populated and moreover all the villagers did not return back to their villages after the groping of villages. The villages which have got only three members were those villages which have got only less than one hundred households and that two or more villages may form one Village Council. Therefore, it may indicate that Villages in Mizoram during this period were very thinly populated.

### *The Third Term of the Village Council under the Government of Mizoram*

The Third General Election of the Village Council under the Government of Mizoram was announced to be held on 1st and 2nd November, 1984 and its result was declared on 14th December, 1984. In this election the number of Village Councils had increased in great number because of the reorganization of the Village Councils. Altogether, 306 Village Councils have been elected in Aizawl District and 112 Village Councils have been elected in Lunglei District. In this election most of the Village Councils were captured by the Congress (I) which shows that the election of the Village Councils are greatly influenced by state politics. Those political parties which have got the largest number of seats in the Assembly of the Union Territory are likely to get the largest number of seats in the Village Council election. Moreover, the capabilities of the Village Council to a great extent depend upon the relation between the members of the Village Councils and those parties in power in the Assembly of which the people were very much aware of.

*The Fourth Term of the Village Council under the Government of Mizoram*

The Fourth General Election of the Village Councils under the Government of Mizoram was held on 5th November, 1987, this was the first Village Council General Election since Mizoram became a full-fledged state. Elections were held for 340 Village Councils in Aizawl District and 112 Village Councils in Lunglei District. The result of this election reveals that Mizo National Front, which was reestablished as a political party in 1986, won great support from the people because many new leaders joined the party finding new places because of their achievement in bringing peace in Mizoram. Later on, the Administrator of the Village Council had to conduct bye-election to 16 Village Councils on 15th July, 1988 because these Village Councils were dissolved by the Department due to failure of administration.

*The Fifth Term of the Village Council under the Government of Mizoram*

The Fifth General Election of the Village Councils under the Government of Mizoram was held on 25th October, 1990 in which there was a great tussle between the Congress (I) and the MNF. In this election, there were 14 villages of which the result were withheld because election materials were stolen by anti-social elements in 14 villages and election for those villages were again held on 30th November. The Congress (I) has got 151 Village Councils among 349 Village Councils in Aizawl District and the MNF has got 110 Village Councils. There were 29 Villager Councils where no single party had the majority to from the Executive Body; and the rest were divided among other political parties and independent candidates. In Lunglei District elections were held for 116 Village Councils.

During this tenure bye-elections to some of the Village Councils were held on 7th May 1992. The department had conducted bye-election because some of the Village Councils were newly created, some of them dissolved and some of them could not conduct election in 1990 because they were within the demand area of Hmar People Conference, who had demanded the creation of their own District Council causing great disturbances in the demand area.

### *The Sixth Term of the Village Councils under the Government of Mizoram*

The Sixth General Election of the Village Councils under the Government of Mizoram was held from 1st May to 4th May, 1994 and its result was declared on 3rd June, 1994. In this election, elections to 358 Village Councils were held in Aizawl District and 121 Village Councils in Lunglei District.

### *The Seventh Term of the Village Council under the Government of Mizoram*

The Seventh General Election of the Village Councils under the Government of Mizoram was held in 1997 in which elections were held in 393 villages in Aizawl District and in 127 villages in Lunglei District. The election results were declared on 26th May, 1997, which shows that the Indian National Congress earned the greatest support in local politics followed by its main rival MNF. After the expiry of the term of the existing Village Councils, the first meetings of the newly elected Village Councils were held on 6th May, 1997.

### *The Eighth Term of the Village Councils under the Government of Mizoram*

The Eighth General Election of the Village Councils in Aizawl and Lunglei Districts was held on 16th December, 1999 under the Government of Mizoram. Elections were held for 504 Village Councils, 378 Village Councils in Aizawl District and 126 Village Councils in Lunglei District. Due to the elimination of the nominated seats the numbers of elected members increased in great number in this election.

*The Ninth Term of the Village Councils under the Government of Mizoram*

The Ninth General Election of the Village Councils under the Government of Mizoram was held in 2002 on the 30th and 31st October. In Aizawl District elections were held in 164 villages, in Mamit District elections were held in 67 villages and in Serchhip District election were held in 40 villages. The election in Aizawl, Mamit and Serchhip Districts were conducted by District Local Administration Officer, Local Administrative Department, Aizawl and his staffs with the help of those persons appointed for the purpose. In Lunglei District election were held in 129 villages, in Champhai District elections were held in 92 villages and in Kolasib District election were held in 39 villages. The elections in Lunglei Champhai and Kolasib were conducted by the District Officers and those persons appointed for the purpose. Many political parties such as: Mizo National Front, Indian National Congress, Mizo Peoples Conference, Zoram Nationalist Party, etc. had participated in this election. The overall result of this election had revealed that there was a great struggle for power between the Congress and MNF in this election.

*The Tenth Term of the Village Councils under the Government of Mizoram*

The Tenth General Election of the Village Councils in Mizoram was conducted by the concerned department on 24th and 25th February 2006. Out of 556 Village Councils elections were held in 553 villages, in which there were 2036 seats. The District Local administrative Officers, Local Administrative Department of the concerned district conducted the elections. The MNF party was greatly supported by the people in this election, out of 553 Village Councils MNF has formed 337 Village Councils which is more than 60 per cent of the total Village Councils. It may also be noted that out of 2036 seats only 33 Female candidates were elected.

## Conclusion

From the above discussion it may be said that the working of grassroots democracy at the Village Council level has undergone great changes during five decades of its existence. Originally embodied with great powers and authority under valid laws, now the Village

Council has been transformed into a mere figurehead. The District Council had made great achievement in establishing the Village Council, in the form of Local self-government penetrating the spirit of democracy at the grassroots level. The District Council in its meetings made long discussion for the welfare of the Village Councils and took great responsibility in looking after the Village Councils. The dissolution and bye-elections, creation of new Village Councils and solutions of its problems were discussed in its meetings.

Since Mizoram got its own government as a union territory and later as a state, the responsibility of looking after the Village Councils had been taken up by the Local Administrative Department. The problems of the Village Councils and its solution were never discussed in the Assemblies. The destinies of the Village Council are in the hands of the bureaucrats and government officials, who are embodied with great powers in looking after the functioning of the Village Council. The Village Councils were to carry out the Notification and Orders which were frequently served by the Government or higher authorities, failing which might lead to inefficiency of the Village Council calling for serious actions, even to the extent of dissolution of the Councils without the consent of the Council. In fact, the state government controls the activities of the Village Councils that makes the later enjoy minimum autonomy.

It may also be important to note that in order to look into the welfare of the Mizoram Village Councils "Mizoram Village Welfare Committee" was set up on 26th February, 1992. Later on the Committee was transformed into "Mizoram Village Council Association" on 22nd August, 1997. The most important objectives of the Association were to uphold the dignity of the Village Councils and that Mizo Culture and way of life may be well protected. All the Village Councils under the Government of Mizoram were expected to affiliate themselves in the Association. Till recently no remarkable achievement was made by the Mizoram Village Council Association which may be due to the lack of support from the government, in whose hands all powers of local administration were vested.

## NOTES

1. Chaltuahkhuma, *Political History of Mizoram,* (David Memorial Press, Aizawl, 2001) p. 53.

2. Brigadier C.G. Verghese, V.S.M (Rtd.) and R. L. Thanzawna, M.C.S. (Rtd.), *A History of the Mizos, Volume-I,* (Vikas Publishing House, Pvt. Ltd., New Delhi-110014, 1997) p.356.
3. Animesh Ray, *India—The Land and the People, Mizoram*, (National Book Trust, India, New Delhi, 1993) P. 152.
4. S.N. Singh, *Mizoram: Historical, Georaphical, Social, Economic, Political and Administrative* (Mittal Publications, New Delhi-110059, 1994) p.132
5. Chitta Ranjan Nag, *Post-Colonial Mizo Politics, 1947-1999*, (Vikas Publishing House, New Delhi-110014, 1999) p.35.
6. V. Venkata Rao, *A Century of Tribal Poitics in Noeth-East India, 1874 1974*, (S.Chand & Company Ltd., New Delhi, 1976) p.184.
7. S.N. Singh, *op cit.,* p.145.
8. K.M. Zakhuma, *Political Development in Mizoram from 1946 to 1989*, (Offset printers and paper works, 2001) p.137.
9. S.N., Singh, *op. cit.* p.145.
10. P. Lalnithanga IAS (Retd.) *Emergence of Mizoram,* (Lengchhawn Press, Aizawl, 2005) p. 28.
11. K. Lawmzuala, *Mizo District Council Kha,* (Lengchhawn Press, Aizawl, 2002) p. 22.
12. Lalrinmawia, *Mizoram History and Cultural Identity,(1890-1947),* (Spectrum Publication, New Delhi) p. 110.
13. Dr. Sangkima, *Mizos: Society and social Change*, (Spectrum Publications, Guwahati: Delhi, 1992) p. 175.
14. *Ibid.*, p. 175.
15. *Ibid.*, p. 177.
16. R.Vanlawma, *Ka Ram leh Kei, (My Country and I)*, (Lengchhawn Press, Aizawl-796001, 1989) p. 231.
17. V.H. Khuma, *Political History of Mizoram,* (Omnipresent Offset, Ramhlun North, Aizawl), p. 89.
18. Dr. Sangkima, *Mizos: Society and Social Change*, (Spectrum Publications Guwahati: Delhi, 1992) p. 177.
19. K. Lalrinzuali, DLAO, *Paper presented on 27th Oct., 2004 at the 4th Mizoram Village Council Association General Conference.*
20. Notification No. E 4290 V-3 Dated 7th May 1954 of the Lushai Hills District Council.
21. Zoram Hriatirna, August 15, 1954.
22. Dr. H.C. Hrangthanga, *Village Councils in Mizoram,* (Lengchhawn Press, Aizawl, 1994) p. 3.
23. Sub-Section (1) of Section 7 of the Lushai Hills District (Village Council) Act, 1953
24. Executive Department Order No.EV.202/v-4, Dt: 28th Sept., 1954. of The District Council, Mizo District.
25. Section 4 of the Lushai Hills District (Village Council) Act, 1953.

26. Section 5 of the Lushai Hills District (Village Council) Act, 1953.
27. Section 25 of the Lushai Hill District (Village Council) Act, 1953.
28. Sub-Section (4) & (5) of Section 7 of Lushai Hills District (Village Council) Act, 1953.
29. Sub-Section (10) of *Ibid.*
30. Sub-Rule (1) of Rule 4 of The Mizoram (Election to Village Councils) Rule, 1974 as Amended.
31. Sub-Rule (4) of *Ibid.*
32. Rule 37, *Ibid.*
33. Rule 13 of The Mizoram (Election to Village Council) Rules, 1974 as amended in 1990.
34. DLAO, Local Administrative Department, Aizawl; District, *Notification No-B-12020/11/2005-DLAO(A).*
35. Rule 17 of The Mizoram (Election to Village Council) Rules, 1974 as amended in 1990.
36. Mizo Customary Law, 2006, Introduction.
37. Directorate of Local Administration Department, Government of Mizoram, *Village Council Kaihhruaina.* p. 12.
38. Mizo District Council, Executive Order No.12 of 1957.
39. Section 10 of the Lushai Hills District (Jhumming) Regulation, 1954, (as amended in 1996).
40. *Ibid.*
41. Section 9 of The Lushai Hills Disrict (Village Council) Act, 1953. (As amended in 1996).
42. Sub-Section (1) of Section 21 of The Mizoram Animal (Control & Taxation) Act, 1980 (as amended in 1991).
43. Sub-Section (3), *Ibid.*
44. Sub-Rule (2) of Rule 21 *Ibid.*
45. Rule 23, *Ibid.*
46. Sub-Rule (1) of Rule 6 of the Lushai Hills Autonomous District Administration of Justice Rules, 1953.
47. Rule 15 Sub-Section 1 of The Lushai Hills Autonomous District (Administration of Justice) Rule, 15.
48. Sub-Section (3) of Section 15, *Ibid.*
49. Rule 16. *Ibid.*
50. Section 12 of The Mizoram (Village Council) Act, 1953.
51. Section 13 of *Ibid.*
52. *Zoram Hriattirna*, 15th October 1954.
53. *Ibid.*, 15th June, 1957.
54. R.Vanlawma, *Ka Ram leh Kei (My Country and I)*, (Lengchhawn Press, Aizawl, Third Edition 1989) p. 267.
55. Chitta Ranjan Nag, *Post Colonial Mizo Politics,1947-1998,* (Vikas Publishing House, New Delhi-110002) p. 80.
56. *Mizoram District Gazetteers, 1999*. p. 232.

57. R.Vanlawma, *Ka Ram leh Kei*, (Lengchhawn Press, Aizawl-796 001).
58. District Local Administration Officer, LAD, Aizawl, *Village Council Election Result (1954-2006).*
59. Dr. HC.Thanhranga, *Village Councils in Mizoram,* (Lengchhawn Press, Aizawl, 1994) p. 4.
60. P. Lalnithanga, IAS (Retd.), Former Director of LAD, *an Article in Local Administrative Department's Magazine,* 1991-92. p. 15.
61. The Mizoram Gazette, *Notification No. LAD/VC-1/78/Vol. II/121, the 19th Nov., 1979.*
62. Chaltuahkhuma, *Political History of Mizoram,* (David Memorial Press, Aizawl, 2001) p. 289.
63. *Ibid.*, p. 293.
64. Calculated from, *Village Council Election Result, (1954-2006),* DLAO, LAD, Aizawl.

## REFERENCES

Chaltuahkhuma, (2001). *Political History of Mizoram*, David Memorial Press.

Dirctorate of Economics and Statistics, (2004 & 2006). *Aizawl, Mizoram, Statistical Handbook of Mizoram.*

Director of Art and Culture, Mizoram, (1989). *Mizoram District Gazetteers*, M/s Eastern Press & Publications, Guwahati-781001.

Directorate of Local Administration Department, Aizawl, Mizoram, *Compilation of Acts, Rules & Regulations.*

Directorate of Local Administration, (2004). *Government of Mizoram, Village Council Kaihruaina*, Hauhlira Offset Press, Aizawl.

Directorate of Local Adminitration, LAD, Village Council Election Result, 2002 and 2006.

District Local Administrative Officer, LAD, (1954-2006). Aizawl, Village Council Election Result Bureau.

Hermana, C., (1999). *Zoram Politics Thli Tleh Dan*, Vol-II, (1972-1979), Preston Production, Aizawl-796001.

Lalbiaknema, C., (1995). *Kan Chenna Mizoram*, Synod Press, Aizawl.

Lalchungnunga, (1994). *Mizoram:Politics of Regionalism and National Integration*, Reliance Publishing House, New Delhi.

Lalmanzuala, (2003). *Zoram Kalsiam* 3, Lengchhawn Press, Aizawl.

Lalnithanga, P., (2005). *Emergence of Mizoram*, Lengchhawn Press, Aizawl.

Lawmzuala, K., (2002). *Mizo District Council Kha (1952-1962)*, Lengchhawn Press, Aizawl-796001.

Local Administrative Department, Government of Mizoram, *Magazine 1991-1992.*

Local Administrative Department, Secretariat (Village Council Wing), Record Files.

*Mizoram Gazette*, Regular and Extra ordinaries.

Nag, Chitta Ranjan, (1999). *Post-Colonial Mizo Politics 1947-1998*, Vikas Publishing House, New Delhi-110014.

Nunthara, C., (1996). *Mizoram: Society and Polity*, Indus Publishing Company, New Delhi, 110027.

Prasad, R.N., and A.K. Agarwal, (1995). *Study of Public Administration in Mizoram*, Lengchhawn Press, Aizawl.

Prasad, R.N., (1987). *Government and Politics in Mizoram*, Northern Book Centre, New Delhi.

Rao, Venkata V., (1976). *A Century of Tribal Politics in North-East India, 1874-1974*, S. Chand & Company Ltd., New Delhi-110055.

Ray, Animesh, (1993). *Indian—The Land and the People, MIZORAM*, National Book Trust, New Delhi-110016.

Sangkima, Dr., (1992). *Mizos: Society and Social Change*, Spectrum Publications Guwahati, Delhi.

Singh, S.N., (1994). *Mizoram: Historical, Geographical, Economic, Political* and Administrative, Mittal Publications, New Delhi.

Thanhranga, H.C. (1994). *Village Councils in Mizoram*, Lengchhawn Press, Aizawl-796 001.

The Lushai Hills District (Village Council) Act, 1953.

Vanlawma, R., (1989). *Ka Ram Leh Kei* (My Country and I), Lengchhawn Press, Aizawl-796001.

Vanthuama, H., (2001). *Mizoram Politics Chanchin* (1952 Hmalam).

Verghese, C.G., and R.L Thanzawna, (1997). *A History of the Mizos volume-II*, Vikas Publishing House, New Delhi-110014.

Zakhuma, K.M., (2001). *Historical Development in Mizoram From 1946-1989: A Study with Special Reference to Mizoram*, J.R. Bros. Offset Printers and Paper Works, Aizawl.

Zoram Hriattirna Mizo Hills District Council Notifications.

*Zoram Hriattirna*, A fortnightly Information Magazine of Mizo District Council.

# Chapter 14

## The Lakhers in Mizoram

### *The Impact of Christianity and Colonial Administration*

K. ROBIN

Assam, the eastern most frontier province of the British Indian Empire, consisted of the great Brahmaputra valley in the north, and the Surma valley in the south, together with the hills forming the watershed between them, and parts of the mountainous tracts which separate India from Tibet and Burma (now Myanmar).[1] The religious and spiritual interests of the inhabitants of the valleys and of the hills forming the watershed were being cared for by two missionary societies. The tribes living in the un-surveyed forests and mountains of the border for the most part, however, were wholly un-evangelized, especially those living in the extreme south eastern corner inhabiting the North Arakan Yoma Mountains lying between the sea coast of the Bay of Bengal and Burma.[2] These hill people offered a most encouraging field of labour for the Christian missionaries as they thought them to be unprejudiced, and apparently to have no real religion of their own and that they were willing to accept whatever was first brought to them.[3] It was in this background that the Gospel was presented to them while they were yet in their traditional state of condition. Where this had already been done large numbers of these tribesmen have embraced and became ardent followers of the new faith.

The advent of Christianity in Mizoram was the consequence of gradual extension of the work that had been carried on for some decades in the region by the Welsh Calvinistic Methodist Mission (later Welsh Presbyterian Mission) in the Khasi and the Jaintia Hills of the then Assam, and by the British Baptist Missionary Society (BMS) in the Chittagong Division of the then Eastern Bengal (now Bangladesh).[4] In the meantime a small area in the southernmost corner of Mizoram inhabited by the Lakhers (Mara) was assigned to a third mission, the Independent Lakher Pioneer Mission.[5]

The colonial officials' interests in the Lakher 'country' can be traced back to the last decade of the 19th century. In fact, this interest was governed again by the twin motives of protecting their subjects under their jurisdiction and their larger interest of safeguarding their Eastern frontiers, but the policy of annexing the Lakher land could not materialize as a result of their hesitation in investing their capital without the expectation of fruitful revenue returns. Their designs of controlling the tribes without investing any resources got materialized when the Lakher Pioneer Mission established its mission station in 1907 at Sherkor (Saikao). The colonial officials left the task of 'civilizing' the so-called 'savages' in the hands of the Christian missionaries. Therefore, the 'imperial forces' and the missionaries were in close collaboration in their bid to exercise their hegemony.

It was evident that there existed difference of opinion between the Government and the Mission in numerous respects. The Authorities were in favour of retaining many practices such as drinking, dancing, *Laipho* culture,[6] etc., while the missionaries forbid the converts and insisted to abstain from all such kind of habits and completely dissociate themselves from it. Moreover, consciously or unconsciously, the missionaries also promoted the ideas of liberalism, democracy, and freedom for women in their educational institutions. What seemed quite evident was that as Herbert Kane aptly remarked 'education has always been an integral part of the Missionary movement',[7] while the Government remained completely indifferent.[8] L.L. Peters, the sub-divisional officer of Lunglei made the following remarks on the Mission education[9]:

> "We have arrived at that stage in the progress of education, where a little learning is a dangerous thing. It follows therefore that the Mission should realise the need for closer co-operation with Government in all their activities as any such cleavage is obvious; it means that one day, sooner or later as education spreads and political self-consciousness forms, the natives will begin to ask us, their white trustees, why between equal Christian groups there

exist such divorce between precept and practice and we should not be able to give any satisfactory answer without mutual recrimination."

Peters was of the view that this kind of perceptions brought about a situation where at least to the local people a gulf seems to yawn between the two kinds of white men, i.e. the missionary and the administrative officer. 'Most men in the Government services had the standard ideas of the middle class English men and did their jobs to the best of their abilities and devoted a good deal of their attention to sports, recreations, dancing whenever they could find an opportunity. They regarded alcoholic refreshment as almost essential part of the day's routine.' In the missionary circles, however, it was astonishing to find how many people still regarded playing cards as the 'Devil's Bible', trace of alcoholic as a deadly sin. It is, therefore, surprising the amount of hostility veiled or open between the official representatives and different Christian sects.[10]

For Peters, 'he thought that the time had come when the hair spitting ingenuities in defence of dogmas should give way to more practical needs of the people. In support of the Government he said that the mission should take the courage in both hands and refrain from too strictly enforcing many senseless taboos.'[11]

The district authorities were of the opinion that moderation and balance were essential factors in life. The more practical approach would have been to reform their indigenous practices than prohibiting them from performing their age-old practices side by side with the new religion. In the meanwhile the missionaries claimed that they were also determined to preserve all the good things of the indigenous cultures and at the same time adding new and better things and thereby transforming it into a new Christian culture.[12]

The teachings of the missionaries took a deep root in the minds of the early converts and its influence is still felt among many of the Christians. On the other hand, the educated people now imbued with political self-consciousness were determined to revive some of the indigenous cultural practices that had already been abandoned. The result was that a sort of ill-feelings and misunderstanding developed not only within the society in general but also within the church itself that had a weakening effect on the church organisation.[13]

The advent of the missionaries and the consequent introduction of the British rule brought about drastic and significant changes in the social, cultural, political, economic and religious life of the Lakhers. In fact as in the words of Mangkhosat Kipgen, 'the advent of outside elements was indeed an epoch making development in the history of the people of Mizoram. It marked the end of the long period in which they had lived in isolation and the beginning of a new world.'[14] In this regard the Lakhers were no exception in tasting the wind of change that was fast enveloping the entire country. They could not remain in isolation for long as the spread of Christianity, introduction of British rule, western education had all together set the process of modernization.

Prior to the introduction of the British rule, the Lakhers had enjoyed considerable supremacy within their own entity. It was a known fact that they practiced frequent raids and fought numerous wars especially when they thought that their resources were being threatened. It was in this background that they proved to be a constant source of terror to their neighbours and to the people of the plains of Eastern Bengal.

A.G. McCall was of the opinion that the reasons for raiding and 'head-hunting' were perhaps to propitiate evil spirits and a passport to *Athikhi* (paradise) after death, and also to exhibit their might and prowess over their foes and also to gain the respect of a prospective bride.[15] Moreover, what seemed to be quiet evident was that slaying an enemy especially a non-Lakher was accorded an overwhelming regard and respect by the community. Therefore, when a man killed a person, he brought home the head to justify his claim with true courage and valour.

Whatever may have been the case, however, with the spread of Christianity, 'headhunting' was gradually stopped. The missionaries taught the people that killing of human beings was an act against God who was the creator of all living and non-living things in the universe. The missionaries were trying hard to sensitize the people morally conscious of the abominable practice, for they knew unless this was done, the practice would remain alive and continued. Thus they began to preach the gospel, which was against killing of human beings. In this way the missionaries indirectly inculcated the idea that headhunting was sin.[16] Accordingly, in 1918, the British government took direct action against the people of Zyhno when they last carried out their raid. Eventually the Hawthai and Tlosai tribes also gave up their habit of 'headhunting'.[17] Thus, both the Government and the missionaries were responsible for bringing to an end the age-old practices of the Lakher within a short span of time.

Another area of change that was immediately witnessed was the abolition of slavery. The British found this institution abhorrent and therefore, freed slaves that appealed to them in accordance to the Slavery Abolition Act of 1833, which terminated slavery throughout the British Empire.[18] Slavery (*Sei*) among the Lakhers undoubtedly approximated more closely to what is generally connoted by the word slavery than did the Lushei *bawi* system.[19] The Lushei *bawi* was never seemed to be a slave, he was only a chief's dependent, he was never sold and the relationship between him and his chief was one of mutual help. Among the Lusheis only chiefs could have *bawis*, while among the Lakhers, chiefs, nobles and anyone who made captives in war could own slaves.[20] The Lakher Slaves (*Sei)* was the counterpart of the Lushei *Sal,*[21] a captive made in war who was the personal property of his captor, but even these *Sal* seem to have been much better treated than the *Sei* (slaves) were treated by the Lakhers, whose behaviour to their slaves resembled that of the Chins rather than that of the Lusheis.[22]

The liberation of *Sei* or the chief's dependents undoubtedly diminished his wealth and importance. As soon as the area was taken over by the British, large numbers of *sei* came forward to pay the forty rupees ransom, which frees them from their obligations to the chief. Some of these freed men remained in the village, but many migrated elsewhere.

As has already been noted in the preceding chapters, the Lakhers were worshippers of nature and believed in a variety of gods and spirits. The superstitious beliefs and its associated cultures were soon done away with particularly as a result of the spread of Christianity and with the introduction of education among the people. Fertile lands, which once were avoided for cultivation for fear of spirits, began to bloom into fertile farms. Rivers and streams, which were once forbidden for use because of fear of spirits, now are used for wet cultivations. Thus, people were freed from bondage of spirits in their everyday lives.[23] Charles L. Allen stated that, "Religious faith is the best preventive measure against the maladies of the soul, mind and body, and it is the most powerful medicine we have ever discovered for carrying them."[24]

R.R. Shimray, when he described about the Nagas asserted that, "the love of Christ was implanted in the hearts of the Head-hunters and their entire lifestyle and social fabric was affected and reversed and that from head-hunters they have become heart-hunters".[25] The same is true to the case of the Lakhers that with the advent of Christianity, the entire social fabric got affected one way or the other.

Offerings and sacrifices that were being made to the spirits and gods gradually disappeared.[26] Now that instead of offering sacrifices to the unknown, they decided to give tithes and other offerings of thanks givings to their newly accepted God. The indigenous ways of celebrating festivals was now replaced by the Christian festivals in which Christmas took a primary status. In course of time, the importance of the customary festivals like *Sahria Ku, Lyuvah Ku, Chithieh Ku* etc., and other social gatherings and amusements were abandoned and memories of such are now almost forgotten.[27] New festivals like Easter Sunday, Good Friday and the like now bear significance in their lives.

The most remarkable result following the introduction of the British administration was the gradual weakening of the positions and powers of the chiefs, though however, the Government allowed the chiefs to continue their rule in accordance with the orders which they issued from time to time. A number of rights and privileges that had been enjoyed and exercised by the chiefs were allowed to retain unaltered. But the British Government had exercised certain powers over the chiefs thus affecting some of their traditional rights and status.[28] For example, any succession was subject to the approval of the Superintendent of the then Lushai hills,[29] who was also authorized to regulate the succession.

The chief, hitherto, who was the owner of the land under his jurisdictions, was no longer absolute over his hold. The government reserved the right to take away any or whole of the land under his possession whenever required for Governmental purposes. The land could also be taken away from the chiefs as a measure of punishment whenever they violated or in anyway disobeyed Government order.[30] Moreover, the chiefs were provided with a document that clearly demarcated the boundaries of their respective lands.

Besides, large number of rights enjoyed by the traditional chiefs had been arbitrarily taken away.[31] Some of these rights were,

1. Right to order capital punishment.

2. Right to seize food stores and property of villagers who wish to transfer their allegiance.
3. Right over the land.
4. Right to tax traders doing business within the chief's jurisdiction.
5. Right to freedom of action in relation to making their sons chiefs under their own jurisdiction.
6. Right to attach the property of the villagers when they wished or deemed fit with or without fault on the part of the villagers, and many more rights were taken away from them.

In the light of these developments, it appears that the chiefs turned out to be merely agents of the larger imperial interests and became puppets in the hands of the British.

Through education, large number of Lakhers were imbibed with the ideas of liberty, equality and democratic values. It also brought about significant changes in their outlook and perceptions and now that significant number of efficient and competent leaders was produced through the new learning who could assume leadership at all levels. At least one person from almost every family was employed either in the government services or in the church. Hygiene and health care has considerably improved their quality of life than ever before. Holy Bible, hymnbooks, and other literatures relating to various subjects have been published in the Lakher language, which immensely helped in preserving their cultures and identity. Another outstanding consequence was the fact that the status of women has been greatly strengthened and improved.[32]

As the Lakher society is patriarchal by nature, perhaps women in the society received the worst treatment. Women had no right either in the family or in the society. In body, mind and spirit, she belonged to her father, brother or husband. Her men folk would treat her as they liked and his friends scorned a man who did not beat his wife as a coward.[33] A woman possessed virtually nothing though she did most of the works beginning from dawn and continued it unceasingly till late at night. She might not go to sleep till her men folk retired, who generally sit late enjoying tobacco pipe. She would cook pig's food for the next day, and then spun cotton for clothes and above all bears the arduous task of child rearing.[34] In complete contrast, men always occupied a high and respected position not only in the family but also in the social life as a whole. They were solely responsible for their family affairs. Men did hard works like clearing of the jungles for jhum, building houses, hunting, and fishing. In their spare time those elderly and bachelors stays at *Laipho* courting girls, and sometimes they also accompanied them in collecting firewood.[35]

It was in this state of affairs where women were faring quite poorly that Christianity and education brought solace to them. Very soon the position and outlook of women dramatically changed. The Christian missionaries with their philanthropic zeal devoted much of their activities by paying special attention towards women. In addition to imparting reading and writing, the missionaries also introduced practically useful lessons like sewing, weaving, knitting, gardening, breeding and milking of cows and goats, singing, tonic solfa, and simple games etc.[36] such kind of philanthropic works was a real boon to the women folks as it brought about visible changes in the over all attitudes towards Lakher women.[37]

Women's organization called the 'Christian Women Fellowship' was established, and that women came to be included even in the church committee, which was a significant step towards women empowerment.[38] It would further seem that without women's participation, particularly in the church, progress would have been really difficult. In fact women played key roles even in matters of generating funds for the church through their various programmes, thus, they became virtually indispensable to the society.

Owing to the Lakher's adoption of the new faith, marriage system has also undergone a lot of changes in the form of compromise between the indigenous process and the Christian system of marriage. The Lakher converts would then follows the new system of Christian marriage, which virtually replaced numerous indigenous practices of marriage.[39] The Lakhers in their traditional form performed marriage with a series of rites and ceremonies along with offerings of sacrifices to both 'evil and good spirits'. All these have become redundant as a result of powerful forces unleashed by the new faith, Christianity. Accordingly, marriage is conducted in the church by the pastor and is, therefore, treated as a permanent, intrinsic bond between man and woman, which should not dissolve.[40]

In so far as marriage celebration is concerned, the church restricts the number of animals slaughtered on weddings. Preparation of wedding dress, exchange of wedding rings, certification, oath taking etc., are newly introduced elements. Regarding wedding dress, bridegrooms mostly wear suits, however, brides in some cases wear traditional dresses to preserve traditional culture but in general cases, they use western regalia. Besides, arrangement of service programmes, presiding over the ceremony by ordained ministers are new developments and marriage is regarded as ordained by God.[41]

Interestingly, presents and gifts are now an addition to the new marriage system. Presents may be both in kind and in cash. This has been solely attributed to the handiwork of the missionaries who started giving presents to the newly wedded couples.[42] Though modifications in terms of additions and replacement in some spheres have taken place, the Lakhers still retain some other traditional customs relating to marriage such as courting before marriage, intermediary activities in the process of marriage, marriage price etc.[43]

On the issue of divorce, the church maintained strict rules against it. Though the church does not allow divorce, such case was not uncommon among the Lakhers.[44] Traditionally, when divorce took place, there was nothing like excommunication as such from the society. But with Christianity firmly rooted by then, divorce of any nature was considered a serious case and persons concern would be excommunicated from the church. It is perceived that sanction in terms of excommunication reduces the cases of divorce among the Lakhers.[45] In other words, what seem to be evident is that, in actual practice, divorce has become rare among the active members of the church and even for the common people; it has not been as common as it had been in the past.

Medical work was another important factor that changed the notion of their beliefs and practices. Traditionally, sickness and misfortune has been attributed to malignant and hostile spirits.[46] In this connection, they resorted to sacrifices by killing a pig or a fowl. Practically, they had no knowledge of modern medicine, however, they had their own way of treating sickness and various ailments, and they used leaves, stems, roots, seeds and barks of certain plants for both oral and external applications.[47]

However, the missionary understands of the illness by making proper diagnosis and the consequent cure accelerated the breakdown of the traditional view thereby acting directly or indirectly as an effective agent of change in the society.[48] The missionaries were of the opinion that medical ministry was as important as spiritual healing and regarded as indispensable to their endeavour. Now that people became aware of the use of the new technique, and were cured and relieved of their sickness and pain which then created a strong sense of confidence towards the missionaries.

The impact of Christianity and the British rule were tremendous towards the political life of the Lakhers. The new wave of politics began to penetrate into the minds of the people. Laldenga has remarked, "Christian mission and colonialism was seen to assume both the roles of a 'politician' and a 'priest' and Christian missions appeared to be part and expression of western colonial expression."[49] The growth of the church and education had gradually brought about a lot of political awareness amongst the Lakhers. In fact, R.R. Lolly considered the advent of Christianity to the tribal society as a bright dawning day.[50] There has been an increasing political inclination of the chiefs and the people leading to the formation of regional and clan based political parties. The new awakening also brought about an end to the centuries old chieftainships.[51]

What was ironical was the fact that when political movement was intensified, the chiefs were one of the main targets of attacks because they had been considered as a stumbling block to the future political destination of the people. But the abolition of chieftainship was a great blunder for it was thought that in doing so, the long suffering of the people under the rule of the chiefs would ultimately come to an end. However, it appears that the abolition seem to have been a serious mistake on the part of both the Government and the people. The rule of the chiefs would have been far better in view of the local administration because the chiefs had a traditionally deeper sense of oneness with the people and the land than the newly elected body, the village council, through which the Government now runs its administration in the village level. The main defects of the councils were that it was unable to harbour any sense of personal involvement. This has resulted in administrative loopholes in the village level. It further enshrines corrupt practices among the general public.[52] In so far as the chiefs were concerned, it would have to take a lot of time to adapt themselves to order and discipline brought about by the new changes. This is shown very clearly by the songs of the Zyhno chief, "Government have taken over all our country, we shall always have to work for the Government, it were better had we never been born" or "Government has now hemmed us in, on the north, on the south, on the east, on the west. Henceforth, none of our young warriors will drink of the waters of the *Salyu* river, where we always used to raid."[53]

This evidently suggested that the Lakher life in the past was at times no doubt harsh and difficult. The dilemmas of superstitions and rituals, the constraining fear of the spirits, the cramping insistence on the privilege few of the traditional elites, the occasional tyranny of a chief, and the possible destruction of life and property through occasional warfare and irresistible famine did not always make for happiness.[54] But, however, to the average population, as long as things went well, life was far from unpleasant. Feasting with their companions or taking part in the many ceremonies and dances which lent so much colour to their life, listening with pride the glorification of their chiefs or sitting contentedly round the fire while nearby some old folks entertained with one of the many folk tales so abundant in the lore of the tribe, that they might well feel that it was good to be alive.

At heart they were peasant farmers, interested primarily on their domestic concerns and economic welfare, and to ignore this fundamental aspect of their life in favour of the many odd and picturesque customs and beliefs which separated the Lakhers culture from the Europeans is merely to arrive at a completely wrong impression of the tribes as they really were.

It has been quite true that Christianity and education have many positive contributions on the socio-cultural life of the Lakhers in general. For instance the Lakhers were not remarkable for their cleanliness[55]. They hardly maintained cleanliness in their homes and did not know much about personal hygiene. Lorrain and Savidge, when they arrived in the hills, observed that a baby was not washed since its birth until it became three years old, and a middle aged person after becoming forty often bade goodbye to water for the rest of his natural life.[56] They have no separate places for keeping their domesticated animals, therefore more or less, they dwell in the same arena. Regarding their dress, children below ten years hardly wear clothes.[57] However, with the introduction of education and Christian values steadily making in-road into the Lakher society, the people have become more hygienic in total contrasts to their old life. Now that their utensils, dresses, bodies, houses and their surrounding campuses are kept tidy and clean, and most of their animals are kept outside the house except cats and dogs.[58]

However, there were also another side of the picture, the idea of freedom, liberalism and 'equality in the eyes of God' has made people more individualistic. The unique principle of respect for the elders where younger people never smoke in their presence and not to speak of addressing their elders by name has gradually eroded. The reasons for this sharp decline seem to have been due to the forces unleashed by the new western culture and civilization.[59] The intrinsic principles of capitalism that have made an in-road into the society have gradually extinguished the Lakher's traditional practice of sharing meals, meat, vegetables and other things.

In the past, under the simple traditional economic system, people depended on agriculture and lives were hard with no other source of income. In the case of poor harvest, people struggle for survival. Barter was the system of exchange. People shared their products to meet their requirements, sharing and giving was the mode of practice amongst the Lakhers. But with the introduction of the new money economy, people started to experience a completely new orientation of buying and selling.[60]

In other words, the economy has become a market oriented economy with the scope for great change and profit making has become the main concern of the people and therefore, hitherto community based economy has turned into a selfish profit oriented economy. As was in the case of Tangkhul Nagas, who faced unprecedented ecological crisis,[61] as a result of their unsystematic management of resources, the Lakhers have also faced the same fate. Their forests resources were turned into semi-deserts, the thick forests which were once the source of life were being destroyed for the sake of money. It has completely altered their source of economy, as there has been sharp decline in production because of over-exhaustions of their natural resources.

The worst outcome was the fact that they became over dependent on others and imported commodities. The economic problem created many other related issues like land dispute, extortion, bribery, stealing and all sorts of adversities. Despite the fact that Christianity and colonialism had made significant contributions towards improving the cultural lives of the Lakhers, these few and unrealized negative impacts hinder the community's developments in many respects resulting in the erosion of their traditional cultures and practices giving way to alien and complex western values.

## NOTES

1. R.A. Lorrain, *The wonderful story of the Lakher Pioneer Mission*. London, 1913, p. 5.

2. *Ibid.*
3. *Ibid.*
4. Mangkhosat Kipgen, *Christianity and Mizo Culture,* Jorhat, 1996, p. 188.
5. *Ibid.*
6. N.E. Parry observed and remarked that, "Lakher and Lusei Christians were not allowed to drink wine, beer or spirits, and no one can become a Christian who ever touches alcohol. In this regard, the people had only few pleasures, and after strenuous work, most likely in torrents of rain, a stimulant is rather a good thing. It would therefore be better to encourage temperance than to insist on prohibition. Among more civilized people prohibition has led to deceit, its results are the same among these primitive hillmen. When they become more enlightened they will inquire deeper and naturally ask why their particular brand of Christianity prohibits all alcoholic drinks, and trouble will ensue. For this reason, to make abstinence from drink an essential tenet of Christianity is entirely wrong, and is bound to lead to trouble. Encourage temperance in every way possible, but teachings should not be based on false foundation."
7. J. Herbert Kane, *Understanding Christian Missions,* Baker Book House, 1974, p. 318.
8. It was due mainly to the aversion of the Administration to seriously involve itself in the education of the hill people that the subject was almost entirely left to the mission but subsidised by the Government. The Government grants at the beginning were not at all that generous and many schools were maintained entirely by the mission. For example, a sum of Rs. 450 was sanctioned by the Government of Bengal towards the education of the Garos in 1826, and Rs. 45 to the mission school in Naga hills in 1834 and in 1836 the Governor General granted Rs. 1000 to the American Baptist Mission in Assam for their educational institutions. The first Government grant for mission school in Mizoram was sanctioned in 1897-98 amounting to Rs. 333 only, and in 1899 it was increased to Rs. 902. For details see ASR, Proceedings of Foreign Department, October 1899, No. 35. ASR, letters issued to the Government, Vol. No. 13, January 1844—February 1846; Jenkins to officiating secretary, Government of Bengal, No. 104, dated 25.11.1845. See also William Gammell, *A History of American Baptist Missions,* Gould, Kendall & Lincoln, Boston; 1849, p. 42, cited by Pathak in *American Missionaries and Hinduism.*
9. Governor's Secretariat, Excluded B, Nos. 778-781, September, 1936.
10. *Ibid.*
11. *Ibid.*
12. Chapman & Clark, *The Mizo Miracle, op. cit.,* p. 85.
13. J.V. Hluna, *op cit.,* p. 225.
14. M. Kipgen, *Christianity and Mizo Culture,* Aizawl, 1997, p. 141.
15. G. McCall, *The Lushai Chrysalis,* Lusac & Co, London, 1949, p. 38.
16. Sangkima, *Mizos: Society and Social Change (1890-1947),* p. 134, Guwahati, 1992.

17. B. Foxall, *Sequel to Five years in unknown jungle,* Unpublished, Serkawr, 1962, p. 29.
18. G.M. Trevelyan, *A shortened history of England,* Reprint, 1960, p. 477.
19. Shakespear, *The Lushei Kuki Clans,* p. 46.
20. N.E. Parry, *op. cit.,* p. 227.
21. Shakespear, *op. cit.,* p. 50.
22. N.E. Parry, *op. cit.,* p. 228.
23. Lanuyanger Sangtam, *The Trans-Dikhu Mision,* Bangalore, 1992, p. 161.
24. Charles L. Allen, *Road to Radiant Living,* Fleming H. Revel Company, New Jersey, 1973, p. 80.
25. R.R. Shimray, *Origin and culture of the Nagas,* Aruna Press Publication, New Delhi, 1985, p. 234.
26. J.H. Thumra, '*The primal religious tradition*' in P.S. Daniel, ed., *Religious tradition of India,* Kottayam, Senate of Serampore, 1988, p. 45.
27. S. Mokia, *Mara Awnanopa Thati,* Serkawr, 1981, p. 41.
28. Sangkima, *op. cit.,* p. 117.
29. N.E. Parry, *A Monograph on Lushai Customs and Ceremonies,* TRI, Reprint, Aizawl, 1976, p. 4.
30. Sangkima, *op. cit.,* p. 118.
31. A.G. McCall, *Lushai Chrysalis,* p. 202.
32. Excerpts from an interview with S. Hrachu, saiha on the 23th December, 2005.
33. Chapman and Clark, *op. cit.,* p. 13.
34. Mylai Hlychho: *op. cit.,* p. 162.
35. *Ibid.,* p. 165.
36. S. Beizawzi, *The Lakher Pioneer Mission in Mara Land: A Historical Study,* Madras, 2002, p. 29.
37. Since education and Christianity was viewed as a passport to salaried jobs, and a relief from the wearisome toil of hard labour, more and more parents began to encourage and sent their children to mission school. p. 37.
38. Excerpts from an interview with Ithra Tluma Mision Field Director, Jagi Road, Assam, 30th August, 2004.
39. S. Mokia, *op. cit.,* p. 73.
40. *Ibid.*
41. Chawngkhuma Chawngthu, *A sociological study of Mara marriage system,* unpublished Ph.D. thesis, NEHU, 2002, p. 150.
42. V.L. Zaithanga, *A study of social and cultural changes among the people of Mizoram through the impact of the Gospel,* Unpublished B.D. Thesis, Bangalore, 1964, p. 33.
43. *Ibid.*
44. Chawngkhuma chawngthu, *op. cit.,* p. 152.
45. *Ibid.*
46. A.B. Foxall. *op. cit.,* p. 267.
47. S. Mokia, *op. cit.,* p. 194.

48. Laldena, *Christian Mission and Colonialism,* Vendrame Institute, Shillong, 1988, p. 106.
49. Laldena, *Ibid,* p. 1.
50. R.R. Lolly, *The Baptist Church in Manipur,* Modern Press, Imphal, 1985, p. 89.
51. L.C. Hlychho, *A brief history of M.A.D.C. and its developments,* published by Mara Autonomous District Council, Saiha, 1997, pp. 1-2.
52. Sangkima, *op. cit.,* p. 190.
53. N.E. Parry, *op. cit.,* p. 14.
54. Chaltuahkhuma, *op. cit.,* p. 35.
55. Majore Cole the Superintendent of the Lushai Hills (1906-1911) remarked the people of the Lushai hills as the filthiest on earth. In his meeting with Welsh Mission Executive Committee at Shillong in 1906, he was quoted to have said this, and is reproduced in the Welsh Calvinist Methodist Foreign Mission Report, 1906.
56. J.H. Lorrain and F.W. Savidge, *Among the Head-Hunters of Lushai,* Vol. IV, London, 1899, p. 380.
57. Excerpts from an interview with K. Heisa, Saiha, 13 January 2006.
58. Excerpts from ann interview with Rev.Thylua Hlychho, Finance Officer, ECM office, Saiha, 21 September, 2004.
59. S. Mokia, *op cit.,* p. 178.
60. Excerpts from an interview with C. Thalai, Chhaolo, 25th January, 2005.
61. R.R. Shimray, *op. cit.,* pp. 144-45.

# Chapter 15

## Women and Politics in Mizoram

IRENE COLBERT

### Introduction

In Mizoram, on the surface, women appear to enjoy more freedom than their female counterparts elsewhere in India, but on deeper scrutiny it is not so. The status of Mizo women in the past, especially in the pre-Christian days was very low both in the family as well as in the social life.[1] In the traditional Mizo society the fate of a woman seemed to have been determined and divided right from birth.[2] When the male child was born he was hailed and blessed by the Upa (elder) as "Mipa huaisen Sai kap tur" which means "a valiant, the would-be elephant killer." At the same time the birth of a female child was greeted with the words, "Se man tur" meaning "one who would cost a mithun."[3] She was indeed a burden while the opposite feelings went for their male counterpart. Even today, Mizo women are not liberated and they are regarded as subordinate to men and they are very much discriminated against in various aspects of life.[4]

### Mizo Women and Family/Society

In traditional Mizo family and society males alone decide and women do not have the power of making decision in the family.[5] One of the factors for the exclusion of women from decision making bodies and treatment of women as subordinate to men was due to practice of headhunting. In course of time, people became conscious of social status. Freedom of speech, rights, dignity and honour were won through success in headhunting. The villagers who brought the highest number of heads stood in the highest esteem. They were respected by all and received annual tributes such as daos, spears, clothes, cows, pigs and so on from the defeated village. This consciousness of social status brought subordination to women. For example, (i) Headhunting involved tremendous risks. It was not possible for women to participate in such a risky adventure as man. This led men to treat women as inferior physically. (ii) Since man alone can go and bring heads, people begun to think that men alone can bring honour, respect, dignity and magical power of blessing to the family and village. (iii) Headhunting involved many risks and thus requires proper planning, skill and sanctity.[6] The centre of headhunting activities became the zawlbuk. Women were not allowed entry in this house. Though the importance of zawlbuk could not be ignored, yet it can be said that it was from here that discussed many things which guided gender relations. It was also from here that men controlled women's character and decisions taken when a woman went against her wishes. So, women had to follow the norms and regulations which were laid down by men in the zawlbuk.[7] Some Mizo men used to show superiority over their wives so much to the extent of saying to them, "I chaw a liam e" (meaning "Your rice is overflowing") even though their wives may be very busy with other works while they were just sitting idle near the fire place and husbands who didn't beat their wives were considered Thaibawih (henpecked).[8] A well-known saying, "A crab's meat is not meat, so also a woman's word is no word" clearly indicates a woman's subordinate position in the family as well as in the society and is also devoid of voice in the same. This holds true even with regards to spending one's own income by the woman. All major decisions are taken by the man. Women are regarded as not having wisdom or intelligence.[9] Moreover, a woman has multiple roles to play and is overburdened with household chores and outside her home too. A Lushai (now called Mizo) woman is always very hard-working, has much hard work to do, and has all too little time available for any profitable leisure.[10] With the inclusion of Mizo women, "the vast majority of rural and urban women work more than 14 hours a day."[11]

The Assamese women do all kinds of domestic works of cleaning, washing, and cooking and of distribution of food items. But the participation of women in economic activities is higher. Male members are not expected to do some of the household works except in unavoidable circumstances. In fact men generally avoid some works assigned to women.[12] Mizo women, in addition to working outside the home, in the jhum or office, all the responsibilities of the home rest with the women—washing and ironing clothes, buying and preparing food, cleaning and beautifying of houses and campus, fetching water and wood, caring for domestic animals like pigs and poultry, kitchen gardening, rearing of children—feeding, clothing, studies, medicating, looking after husband and his belongings, giving instructions and so on and so forth which are never ending, right from early morning till late at night.[13] She has to bear and implement all these responsibilities without having authority. This holds true even in the traditional Mizo society. "Working the whole day at the jhum along with others she found no time for taking rest even when she reached home late in the evening. She had to spend the whole night with various engagements".[14] Even if women said, "We are not doing anything", they were busy throughout the day without having the time to rest at all. Their leisure time would be spent for spinning yarn.[15] When there were neighbours who could not pounce rice and carry water, it was their duty to help such people. Even to look after the pigs, poultry and other household works were told by their parents to help, which were willingly done by them.[16] "The extent of work they did with the little amount of food they consumed", said Challiana, "made one wonder how it was possible for the Mizo girls to remain healthy and strong".[17] Even in a Naga village a woman's life in the past was unbelievably arduous. With most of the menfolk organized for war, they fell on her the heavy burden of work in the jhums (clearings) on the steep slopes of hills often a long distance from the home.[18] In traditional Mizo society, women's place in the family in the sense was that they were under an autocratic dominance of their menfolk.[19] If parents of daughters' admirers are refused entry in their houses, then immediately males convened a meeting in zawlbuk (a boys' dormitory), they all agreed for a punishment to be meted out to them, they would dislocate their verandah and their outer walls and throw out their coop. Chiefs could not take action on such acts. For forgiveness, the father would give a small and a big pitcher full of liquor to the boys.[20] Since they would make them feel very discomfort to stay in the village, females would be most careful in every respect.[21] The qualifications looked for in a female for a partner by man were—

- Since they were workers, a female hard and fast worker used to score high marks.

- Since clothes and beddings were made by each family, a female with the knowledge of such things scored high marks.
- Since there was a lot of work to be done, men wanted to marry healthy females and therefore secretly studied their health.
- Family background was very much looked at. They were aware that bad character, theft, murder, alcoholic, laziness and other vices and also diseases like insanity, fits and deformity were hereditary. They tried to find out that such things happened to their ancestors.[22]

Despite their hard labour, Mizo women have no right of inheritance or ownership either in their parent's home or after their marriage. They have no right over their own income, over their children or over their properties.[23] In Mizo society, since linear and inheritance are through the males, property belongs to the father and to the mother in case of death of her husband, as long as she looks after their children and grandchildren. Inheritors are to be from the male siblings who reside in the ancestral home, and among them the youngest is given first preference as he is expected to look after the parents till death. In case he has left the house, he will be succeeded by the next youngest and so on. If at all there aren't any such person to do so, the daughter who looks after them will be the inheritor.[24] Some parents who are educated and have a broader outlook have on their own began to think about a share for their daughters. They divide their property among both sons and daughters share. But the majority, especially in rural areas, maintain the traditional practice."[25] Even among the matrilineal societies though the household property is inherited from mother to daughters and she is the owner of property, the management of property is always vested in the hands of a male. Among the Khasis, property is managed by the wife's brother, among the Garos, by the husband and his father-in-law, who usually is his paternal uncle also.[26] A Khasi woman is not the head of the family. This is left to her eldest brother and within the house it is he who ranks as the head, and not the house owning mother. The father has a definite role to play in the affairs of the family, but is limited by the final words of his brother-in-law.[27] Among both the Khasis and the Garos, although succession to important office is through females, it is always a male who succeeds a sister's son.[28] Among those interviewed by Caroline R. Marak, a few men regard their wives as equal partner and most men dominate over them and expect them to be at their service.[29] Regarding the Jaintia, the youngest daughter, although she inherits the ancestral property, is not free to deal with it as she pleases. Each and every move she makes should be within the knowledge and consent of her brothers or mother. She is merely the custodian of the property while real control over them is vested in the hands of her male matrikin.[30]

Many Mizo men mistreat their wives as helpers, subordinates or as servants and do not think of them as partners. In traditional society, peaceful conversation between husband and wife was considered degrading for the man and till today, if a man is found helping a wife in household chores, he is dubbed as a henpecked, not only by the males but also by the females themselves.

Mizo women suffer prejudice even with regards to divorce. Women, being purchased with a bride price of Rs.400—Rs. 500, can be divorced at husband's wish with no claims for anything except her own properties brought by her to the husband's house at the time of marriage, if the husband and the wife are still residing in the husband's house as everything belongs to the husband's father including those earned by both the husband and wife.[31] Earlier, the bride price consisted of Manpui, i.e. Rs.100 and Mantang consisting of Sumhmahruai (for the bride's father or brother) Rs.20, Sumfang (for the bride's father or brother) Rs.10, Pusum (for the bride's grandfather or maternal uncle) Rs.10, Palal (for a sought father and in turn such a person has to contribute a bucket of liquor) Rs.5, Niar (for the bride's aunty) Rs.5 and Naupuakpuan (for the bride's elder sister for carrying her when she was young) Rs.5. In addition to this, there is a bride price called Thian man, meant for the bride's friend, to be given by the groom, but this is not binding and is not to be returned even in times of divorce.[32] Since it is like purchasing a wife with money, when a daughter is married off, "Such and such a person sold his daughter" is often the saying. Moreover, some men would tell their wives, "Aren't you purchased by me with money?"[33] Such talks definitely portray a woman's position in the Mizo society.

The bride was to take with her to the husband's house Thuam (dowry) which consisted of a Thival (bead with three strings), Thifen (bead with one string) or an amber bead worth not less than Rs. 20 or cash not less than Rs. 20.[34] The bride had also to take with her Puanpui, Thul and Zawlpuan.[35] Today, the bride may take to her husband's house many valuable assets like steel/wooden wardrobes, dunlop mattresses, mosquito nets, blankets, quilts, bed sheets, bed covers, towels, dressing table, cars, etc. etc., depending on financial position. Even a poor bride may want to take with her many things beyond her means, as people put in high esteem those who can do so. Marriage has become a great burden for the bride's family.

In Mizo society, a woman may lose her reputation if she commits adultery and she is termed as Uire (adulteress). In such instances, if her husband does not forgive, she has to leave her house empty handed, with no claims of her own properties including her own children. In some cases, husband may even take away the wife's gold which entirely belongs to her. Moreover, she has to refund the bride price as well.[36] In the past the unfortunate husband had the right to kill his wife's lover.[37] After the death of her husband, the woman is still considered Uire if she sleeps with another man before performing a inkaihchhuah[38] ceremony. If such a thing happens, then her children or her husband's relatives may kick her out of the house. If her children want to continue staying with her, she may be allowed to do so, but she will not be permitted to sleep in the master bed.[39] On the other hand, if the husband commits adultery and if he divorces his wife, she will take out with her one-third of their earnings, except if they still live in a joint family and in such a situation she is entitled to take with her only her belongings.[40] Divorce was comparatively fewer in the traditional society as the partners were afraid that they will have to pay back the bride price by taking initiative in divorce. Since money was scarce, it controlled the divorce rate.[41] This is no longer the case as bride price is a very meager amount.

In the Mizo society, legitimate or illegitimate children belong to the father. Decision for their residing with their mother requires prior permission of the father. If a man has a child with a girl outside the wedlock, he has to pay a pittance of the bastards' price of Rs.40.[42] Such a small amount does not hinder a person to commit such act.

With the permission of the President of India, 'The Protection of Women from Domestic Violence Act, 2005 (Act 43 of 2005)' was published in *The Gazette of India* (*Extraordinary*) No. 49; 14th September, 2005/Bhadra 23, 1927.[43] Harassment of women has been rampant in Mizoram since earlier times. In the olden days Lushai believed that a man who had been unsuccessful in seducing his quota of young Lushai belles would be peppered by one, Pawla, near the entrance to the village of the dead men. The effect of these shots from Pawl's catapults would be to raise a sore in the man's ribs, which would give him acute discomfort for at least three years while in the dead men's village.[44] Moreover, those who already had sex were not expected to get a good match.[45] Today we can see that women are still sexually abused which is clear from the following table[46] :

**Table 15.1:** Showing Crimes Committed on Women

| *Sl. No.* | *Crimes/Offences* | *2001* | *2002* | *2003* | *2004* |
|---|---|---|---|---|---|
| 1. | Rape | 51 | 70 | 57 | 59 |
| 2. | Molestation | 64 | 66 | 80 | 78 |

*Source*: CID (Crime Branch), Aizawl, Mizoram.

Apart from family, young women also actively participate in social organizations like YMA (Young Mizo Association), which is the biggest non-government organization in Mizoram, VDP (Village Defence Party), Students Organisations, Youth Church Departments like Thalai Kristian Pawl (Baptists), Kristian Thalai Pawl (Presbyterians), Salvation Army Youth (Salvation), Pentecostal Youth Department (Pentecostals), etc. YMA assigns women the task of collecting rice and firewood (now money where gas is used) for the bereaved family. They also, along with the males, prepare food, tea and do the needful for social gatherings and yet, "at best, they are given membership in Executive Committee, but are seldom given the status of Office Bearers".[47] This is true especially at the Headquarters and Sub-headquarters, though there may be rare instances in the Units where females hold the post of Financial Secretary or Treasurer, but never the post of the President.

## Mizo Women and Economy

Mizo women, in spite of their being the main workforce of the family and without whose untiring labour cannot the family flourish, are often taken for granted by the family members. The unpaid services rendered by them throughout the day often go unnoticed. If she doesn't earn money, her husband may sometimes call her chawmhlawm (complete dependent, reliant) in times of quarrelling. She also considers herself as fully dependent on her husband and hesitates to ask for money to buy her smallest necessities. Even if she has monetary earnings, "there are many instances where a mother's income is misused and controlled by the husband".[48]

In pre-Christianity era, women were engaged in non-monetary occupations like jhum (shifting) cultivation, household works, preparing loin clothes from the loin looms, weaving, pottery, domesticating animals like pigs, poultry, goats, etc.[49] They played an essential role as food earners of the family. Hence when choosing a wife, a man would give priority to strength and skill at work.[50] Today women continue to engage in all kinds of business activities. Many educated women work in offices, schools, colleges, etc. while majority of villagers continue to work in the jhum. The result of the sample survey of women and men workers in offices, shops, etc. in Aizawl by Vanengliana, reveals that except for the meat shops, women are in the majority.[51] Women have also been doing quite well in running their petty business and small entrepreneurship—handloom and handicraft, floriculture, tailoring, beauty parlour, etc.[52] There are Mizo women, more in numbers than men going to Delhi, Calcutta, Bombay, Madras, Kathmandu and Thailand for business. Moreover within Mizoram itself, there are more females working and earning in offices, bazars, tea stalls, hotels and other business places.[53] Females who do not work hard are considered lazy and lethargic and if unmarried, such a person may find it difficult to get a good partner, hence, she will conceal her ill health as much as she can, unless absolutely unavoidable.[54] Till today, women are marginalized with regards to distribution of wages. For daily work which consists of around 7 hours of fieldwork from 9:00 A.M - 4:00 P.M women are paid Rs.80. For similar 7 hours daily work period men are paid Rs.100.[55] In 1976 the government promulgated an Equal Remuneration Act (ERA) No. 25 of 1976. As per this law it becomes "the duty of employer to pay equal remuneration to men and women workers for same work or work of similar nature". It also provides no discrimination on the ground of sex at the time of recruiting men and women workers. This act covers any employment carried on by or under the authority of the Central Government or a railway administration, or in relation to a banking company, a mine, oilfield or major part of any corporation established by or under government order.[56]

In Mizo society, women are very much marginalized and are put in subordination as far as their participation in the churches, politics and in the society are concerned, yet, they are given much freedom in the field of economics because in many of the families women have

**Table 15.2:** Showing a Comparison between Males and Females in Government Departments, Aizawl, Made between May and October 1991 and the Results[61]

| *Sl. No.* | *Name of Office* | *Occupation* | *Males* | *Females* | *Total* |
|---|---|---|---|---|---|
| 1. | Civil Secretariat | LDC (Lower Divisional Clerk) | 43 | 147 | 190 |
| | | UDC (Upper Divisional Clerk) | 54 | 80 | 134 |
| | | Asst. (Assistant) | 82 | 87 | 169 |
| 2. | D.C. Office, Aizawl | LDC (Lower Divisional Clerk) | 41 | 63 | 104 |
| | | UDC (Upper Divisional Clerk) | 23 | 25 | 48 |
| | | Asst. (Assistant) | 1 | 1 | 2 |
| 3. | Directorate of School Education | LDC (Lower Divisional Clerk) | 1 | 7 | 8 |
| | | UDC (Upper Divisional Clerk) | 6 | 4 | 10 |
| | | Asst. (Assistant) | 5 | 5 | 10 |
| | | Supdt. (Superintendent) | 1 | 1 | 2 |
| 4. | Directorate of Adult Education | LDC (Lower Divisional Clerk) | 1 | 7 | 8 |
| | | UDC (Upper Divisional Clerk) | 2 | 1 | 3 |
| | | Asst. (Assistant) | 1 | 2 | 3 |
| 5. | SDEO (E) | LDC (Lower Divisional Clerk) | 1 | 5 | 6 |
| | | UDC (Upper Divisional Clerk) | — | 1 | 1 |
| 6. | Directorate of AH & Vety. | LDC (Lower Divisional Clerk) | 1 | 8 | 9 |
| | | UDC (Upper Divisional Clerk) | 3 | 4 | 7 |
| | | Asst. (Assistant) | 5 | 1 | 6 |
| | | Supdt. (Superintendent) | 1 | 1 | 2 |
| 7. | Dist. Social Welfare Officer(E) | LDC (Lower Divisional Clerk) | — | 2 | 2 |
| | | UDC (Upper Divisional Clerk) | — | 2 | 2 |
| 8. | DSWO (W) | LDC (Lower Divisional Clerk) | — | 2 | 2 |
| | | UDC (Upper Divisional Clerk) | — | 1 | 1 |
| 9. | Directorate of Social Welfare | LDC (Lower Divisional Clerk) | — | 5 | 5 |
| | | UDC (Upper Divisional Clerk) | 2 | 6 | 8 |
| | | Asst. (Assistant) | 4 | 4 | 8 |
| | | Supdt. (Superintendent) | 2 | — | 2 |
| 10. | Controller of Accounts | LDC (Lower Divisional Clerk) | 1 | 8 | 9 |
| | | UDC (Upper Divisional Clerk) | 1 | 3 | 4 |
| | | Asst. (Assistant) | 1 | 2 | 3 |
| 11. | Directorate of Agriculture | LDC (Lower Divisional Clerk) | 3 | 31 | 34 |
| | | UDC (Upper Divisional Clerk) | 4 | 18 | 22 |
| | | Asst. (Assistant) | 5 | 4 | 9 |
| | | Supdt. (Superintendent) | 2 | — | 2 |
| 12. | Assembly Secretariat | LDC (Lower Divisional Clerk) | 6 | 9 | 15 |
| | | UDC (Upper Divisional Clerk) | 8 | 10 | 18 |
| | | Asst. (Assistant) | 5 | 7 | 12 |
| | | Supdt. (Superintendent) | 3 | 1 | 4 |
| | | Translator | — | 6 | 6 |
| | | Total | 319 | 570 | 889 |
| | | Per cent | 36% | 64% | |
| 13. | Primary teachers | Aizawl (E) | 468 | 570 | 889 |

*Source*: Upa Vanengliana, Khawiah nge Mizo Mipate?, in Khawtlang Nun Hruaina (Aizawl: Synod Social Front Committee, 2000).

to go out for daily bread as there are not anything to eat in the house. After they come home from jhum, they have to do all the household works and some of them have to go to their business places. Those owning shops go to their shops and some sell vegetables door to door.[57]

In Mizoram, there is an organization called UMGW (United Mizoram Grassroots Women), which consists of vegetable vendors, is fully focusing on economic right particularly claiming market-selling centre of their agricultural vegetables and their other kinds of harvested cereals in Aizawl city. Since they formed in April 2000 A.D. their voice has been listened and heard today and they know how to value their own economic contributions and actions.[58] The main Bazar (i.e. the New Market) in Aizawl Town looks like a women's market[59], as in other markets of Mizoram. "In New Market, most of the shopkeepers and hawkers are female. Hotels, Restaurants, Tea stalls, etc. are managed and run by female alone. But being a patriarchal society, the father is the head of the household and the shop is usually registered in his name. Besides running shops and other business one can see that women are also employed in large numbers in Departmental Stores. In most of the Government registered shops, societies and Government Fair Price Shops, majority of the employees are women. They engage themselves as agents and sub-dealers in supplying kerosene oil, gas, etc."[60]

In all parts of Mizoram, among the pure Mizo, there are more females than males to be seen in shops, restaurants and other variety stores.[62]

**Table 15.3:** Showing Shop-Keepers at Bazar, Bawngkawn, Aizawl (on 28.9.1991)[63]

| *Sl. No.* | *Name of food items sold* | *Males* | *Female* | *Total* |
|---|---|---|---|---|
| 1. | Beef | 7 | 3 | 10 |
| 2. | Fish | — | 8 | 8 |
| 3. | Pork | 8 | 1 | 9 |
| 4. | Chicken | 3 | 1 | 4 |
| 5. | Vegetables, etc. | 32 | 281 | 313 |
| | Total | 50 | 294 | 344 |

*Source*: Upa Vanengliana, Khawiah nge Mizo Mipate ?, in Khawtlang Nun Hruaina (Aizawl: Synod Social Front Committee, 2000).

**Table 15.4:** Showing Distribution of Main Workers as Cultivators, Agricultural Labourers, Household Industry Workers and Other Workers in Total Workers of Mizoram: 1971-2001[65]

| Census Years | Total Workers | | | Cultivators | | | Agricultural Labourers | | | Household Industry Workers | | | Other Workers | | |
|---|---|---|---|---|---|---|---|---|---|---|---|---|---|---|---|
| | P | M | F | P | M | F | P | M | F | P | M | F | P | M | F |
| 1971 | 151619 | 87858 | 63761 | 126652 | 65171 | 61481 | 558 | 385 | 173 | 488 | 375 | 113 | 23921 | 21927 | 1994 |
| 1981 | 206064 | 129011 | 76453 | 145545 | 75556 | 65989 | 5118 | 3465 | 1653 | 1758 | 959 | 799 | 53643 | 45628 | 8015 |
| 1991 | 290317 | 178011 | 112306 | 178101 | 94878 | 83223 | 9527 | 6181 | 3346 | 2958 | 1997 | 961 | 99731 | 74955 | 24776 |
| 2001 | 469597 | 264162 | 205435 | 253161 | 128829 | 124332 | 27494 | 13010 | 14484 | 6572 | 3164 | 3408 | 182370 | 119159 | 63211 |
| g | 3.84 | 3.74 | 3.98 | 2.34 | 2.3 | 2.4 | 13.9 | 6.86 | 11.59 | 9.05 | 7.4 | 12.04 | 7.01 | 5.8 | 12.21 |

P = Persons M = Males F = Females

Main Workers are those who have worked for 183 days or more in a year.

G = Annual Average Growth Rate (%)

*Source*: Lalthansangi, Situational Analysis of Women in the State of Mizoram (New Delhi: National Commission for Women, 2004).

**Table 15.5:** Showing Sex-wise Distribution of Employees in Mizoram, 1998—2003[66]

| Sl. No. | Statutory | Year | Group A | | | | Group B (G) | | | | Group B (NG) | | | |
|---|---|---|---|---|---|---|---|---|---|---|---|---|---|---|
| | | | M | F | Total | % of F | M | F | Total | % of F | M | F | Total | % of F |
| 1. | State Govt. | 1998 | 1884 | 470 | 2354 | 19.97 | 66 | 26 | 92 | 28.26 | 4916 | 1985 | 6901 | 28.76 |
| | | 1999 | 1972 | 518 | 2490 | 20.80 | 308 | 54 | 362 | 14.92 | 4915 | 2345 | 7260 | 32.30 |
| | | 2000 | 1928 | 483 | 2411 | 20.03 | 308 | 58 | 366 | 15.85 | 5027 | 2273 | 7300 | 31.13 |
| | | 2001 | 2047 | 428 | 2475 | 17.29 | 419 | 85 | 504 | 16.87 | 4870 | 2292 | 7162 | 32.00 |
| | | 2002 | 2203 | 446 | 2649 | 16.85 | 272 | 184 | 456 | 40.35 | 5168 | 2266 | 7434 | 30.48 |
| | | 2003 | 2252 | 558 | 2810 | 19.86 | 231 | 76 | 307 | 24.76 | 5202 | 2499 | 7701 | 32.45 |
| 2. | Central Govt. | 1998 | 56 | 13 | 79 | 16.46 | 34 | 01 | 35 | 02.86 | 71 | 11 | 82 | 13.41 |
| | | 1999 | 166 | 37 | 203 | 18.23 | 89 | 07 | 96 | 07.29 | 49 | 22 | 71 | 30.99 |
| | | 2000 | 157 | 36 | 193 | 18.65 | 84 | 07 | 91 | 07.69 | 42 | 16 | 58 | 27.59 |
| | | 2001 | 169 | 38 | 207 | 18.36 | 78 | 07 | 85 | 08.24 | 54 | 18 | 72 | 25.00 |
| | | 2002 | 164 | 42 | 206 | 20.39 | 68 | 05 | 73 | 06.85 | 67 | 18 | 85 | 21.18 |
| | | 2003 | 184 | 46 | 230 | 20.00 | 80 | 07 | 87 | 08.05 | 58 | 26 | 84 | 30.95 |
| 3. | Semi-Govt. | 1998 | 151 | 28 | 179 | 15.64 | 04 | 00 | 04 | 00.00 | 46 | 33 | 79 | 41.77 |
| | | 1999 | 63 | 08 | 71 | 11.27 | 02 | 00 | 02 | 00.00 | 40 | 31 | 71 | 43.66 |
| | | 2000 | 59 | 07 | 66 | 10.61 | 01 | 00 | 01 | 00.00 | 36 | 27 | 63 | 42.86 |
| | | 2001 | 61 | 09 | 70 | 12.86 | 11 | 02 | 13 | 15.38 | 36 | 26 | 62 | 41.93 |
| | | 2002 | 58 | 07 | 65 | 10.77 | 07 | 04 | 11 | 36.36 | 48 | 34 | 82 | 41.46 |
| | | 2003 | 59 | 09 | 68 | 13.24 | 06 | 05 | 11 | 45.45 | 49 | 36 | 85 | 42.35 |

*(Contd.)*

**Table 15.5:** (*Contd.*)

| Sl. No. | Statutory | Year | Group A | | | | Group B (G) | | | | Group B (NG) | | | |
|---|---|---|---|---|---|---|---|---|---|---|---|---|---|---|
| | | | M | F | Total | % of F | M | F | Total | % of F | M | F | Total | % of F |
| 4. | Banking & Insurance | 1998 | 151 | 29 | 173 | 16.76 | 04 | 01 | 05 | 20.00 | 133 | 78 | 211 | 36.97 |
| | | 1999 | 63 | 28 | 168 | 16.67 | 17 | 05 | 22 | 22.72 | 136 | 72 | 208 | 34.62 |
| | | 2000 | 59 | 27 | 168 | 16.07 | 18 | 04 | 22 | 18.18 | 133 | 69 | 202 | 34.16 |
| | | 2001 | 61 | 31 | 173 | 17.92 | 18 | 04 | 22 | 18.18 | 60 | 11 | 71 | 15.49 |
| | | 2002 | 58 | 45 | 243 | 18.52 | 20 | 04 | 24 | 16.67 | 57 | 28 | 85 | 32.94 |
| | | 2003 | 59 | 46 | 246 | 18.70 | 24 | 04 | 28 | 14.29 | 49 | 29 | 78 | 37.17 |
| 5. | Autonomous District Council | 1998 | 144 | 29 | 173 | 16.76 | 00 | 00 | 00 | 00.00 | 153 | 29 | 182 | 15.93 |
| | | 1999 | 140 | 28 | 168 | 16.67 | 15 | 02 | 17 | 11.76 | 165 | 34 | 199 | 17.09 |
| | | 2000 | 141 | 27 | 168 | 16.07 | 22 | 03 | 25 | 12.00 | 169 | 34 | 203 | 16.75 |
| | | 2001 | 142 | 31 | 173 | 17.92 | 102 | 10 | 112 | 08.93 | 108 | 24 | 132 | 18.18 |
| | | 2002 | 198 | 45 | 243 | 18.52 | 74 | 07 | 81 | 08.64 | 148 | 23 | 171 | 13.45 |
| | | 2003 | 200 | 46 | 246 | 18.70 | 107 | 11 | 118 | 09.32 | 123 | 25 | 148 | 16.89 |

*Source*: Lalthansangi, Situational Analysis of Women in the State of Mizoram (New Delhi: National Commission for Women, 2004).

Even in the remotest villages, workers and managers of hotels and restaurants are mostly women and while they are busy, working so hard and need extra helping hands, at the side those who play cards, eat quite a lot of food now and then, without any wages are mostly men who depend on their wives' income.[64]

In Mizoram, females concentrate in primary sectors as cultivators, household workers and agricultural labourers. Moreover, female annual growth rate is quite high and almost doubled males growth rate in agricultural labourers (11.58%: 6.86%); in household industry workers (12.04%: 7.4%) and other Workers (12.21%: 5.8%).

**Table 15.6:** Showing Sex-wise Comparison of Employees (groupwise) of Different Statutories in Mizoram for the Period 1998—2003[67]

| | | *1998* | *1999* | *2000* | *2001* | *2002* | *2003* |
|---|---|---|---|---|---|---|---|
| Group A | M | 2334 | 2429 | 2373 | 2511 | 2762 | 2791 |
| | F | 564 | 595 | 557 | 509 | 543 | 665 |
| | Total | 2880 | 3024 | 2930 | 3020 | 3269 | 3456 |
| | % F | 18.96 | 19.68 | 19.01 | 20.27 | 16.61 | 19.24 |
| Group B(G) | M | 108 | 431 | 433 | 628 | 441 | 448 |
| | F | 28 | 72 | 68 | 108 | 204 | 103 |
| | Total | 136 | 505 | 499 | 736 | 645 | 551 |
| | % F | 20.59 | 14.26 | 13.63 | 14.67 | 31.63 | 18.69 |
| Group B(NG) | M | 5319 | 5305 | 5407 | 5128 | 5488 | 5481 |
| | F | 2136 | 2504 | 2419 | 2371 | 2369 | 2615 |
| | Total | 7455 | 7809 | 7826 | 7499 | 7857 | 8096 |
| | % F | 28.65 | 32.07 | 30.91 | 31.62 | 30.15 | 32.30 |
| Group C | M | 19173 | 19470 | 20082 | 8281 | 20952 | 20615 |
| | F | 5840 | 6279 | 6603 | 6399 | 6391 | 6455 |
| | Total | 25013 | 25749 | 26685 | 24680 | 27343 | 27070 |
| | % F | 23.35 | 24.39 | 24.74 | 25.93 | 23.37 | 23.85 |
| Group D | M | 10068 | 10684 | 10531 | 9796 | 9848 | 9637 |
| | F | 1122 | 1279 | 1288 | 1634 | 1610 | 1612 |
| | Total | 11190 | 11963 | 11819 | 11430 | 11458 | 11249 |
| | % F | 10.03 | 10.69 | 10.90 | 14.30 | 14.05 | 14.33 |
| Over All Summary | M | 37002 | 38219 | 38826 | 38038 | 39455 | 38972 |
| | F | 9672 | 10725 | 10939 | 11021 | 11117 | 11450 |
| | Total | 46674 | 48944 | 49765 | 49059 | 50572 | 50422 |
| | % F | 20.72 | 21.91 | 21.98 | 22.46 | 21.98 | 22.71 |

*Source*: Lalthansangi, Situational Analysis of Women in the State of Mizoram (New Delhi: National Commission for Women, 2004).

Even after four decades of development and planning, majority of women in Mizoram are still concentrated in a narrow range of occupations characterized by low level of skill thereby low wages and income.[68] Adding to these, the unpaid strenuous works rendered by them clearly show that Mizo women are economically exploited, demoralized and oppressed. They are more or less treated as machines.

## Mizo Women and Religion

Mizo women are very much marginalized in the field of religion. The popular saying of the Mizos, "women and crabs do not have religion" clearly depicts the religious position of the Mizos. The primitive Mizos believed in the Supreme Spirit called *Pathian* meaning God.[69] They also believed that there were numerous other good spirits who belonged to the family of *Pathian* who dwelled in the high heaven with *Pathian*. They were *Pu Vana* (a male God of nature with power over thunder and lightning); *Khua Nu* (a female Goddess, considered to be the wife of Pathian); *Van Chung Nula* (damsel in the family of *Pathian* and was the Goddess of rain and water); *Khuavang* (He was believed to be the creator of all humanity, the spirit of kindness and greatness); *Vanhrika* (a male good spirit who was concerned with science and learning); *Sakhua* (ancestor spirit of the clan) and *Lasi* (a female spirit governing wild animals and hunting).[70] It is believed that *Lasi* is invisible good spirit, female with outstanding beauty dwelling in the rocky hill sides. They generally appeared in dreams offering themselves to hunters in marriage, and if one accepted the offer he was said to have been possessed by a Lasi and consequently would have success in hunting.[71] So primitive Mizos believed in Goddesses too, though the supreme God, *Pathian*, was considered a male. In the early years of Christianity in Mizoram, there were women preachers, evangelists and Bible women whose role was similar to those of men in the same positions. In the Baptist church women were ordained as elders from an early time. But as time passed, instead of seeing an increase in the number of women being as elders the trend has been in the opposite direction. Similarly, in the Presbyterian Church, the position of Bible woman has been completely abolished."[72] Presbyterians do not allow women to be ordained as elders though there is no such rule in their constitution. Salvation Army allot ranks as their husbands after training and their headquarters permits ordination of women as pastors. United Pentecostal Church gives licence to women evangelists and only in the absence of pastors, they can perform rituals like christening of children, baptism and marriage, but they do not have women elders and pastors as such.[73] In North East India including Mizoram, "in the churches, decision-making and administration are still dominated by men, be it Baptist, Presbyterian, or Catholic. Women are deprived of many privileges and responsibilities in the churches and this is due to the patriarchal system we have inherited from our own traditions as well as from the western culture."[74] Though the missionaries, both men and women, did much to improve the conditions of women in the hills of North East India, they brought with them the patriarchy of the nineteenth and early twentieth century western societies and churches. While the women missionaries worked among the local women, the churches established were entirely under the control of the men missionaries and, in due course, local men leaders. They did not bring the ideology of the Women's Movement with them.[75]

**Table 15.7:** Showing the Structure of the Presbyterian and Baptist Churches of Mizoram

| *Presbyterian Church Synod* | *Baptist Church Assembly* |
|---|---|
| Members: Moderator, Ministers and elders<br>Women Secretary as ex-officio<br>No women delegates | President, Ministers and elders<br>Women Secretary as ex-officio<br>No women delegates |
| (1) | (1) |
| Executive Committee<br>Members: 3 Executive secretaries<br>Ministers and elders<br>No women | Executive Committee<br>1 General Secretary and 2 Associate General Secretary.<br>Ministers & elders<br>No women |
| (1) | (1) |
| Pastoral Committee<br>Members: Ministers and elders<br>No women | Pastoral Committee<br>Ministers and elders<br>No women |
| (1) | (1) |
| Departmental Committees<br>Mission and Evangelism<br>Sunday School<br>Press and Bookroom<br>Board of Institutions<br>Theological Education Pension<br>Literature, etc.<br>No woman member in all these committees | Departmental Committees<br>Mission and Evangelism<br>Sunday School<br>Pastoral Committee<br>Board of institutions<br>Medical, Pension<br>Literature, etc.<br>No woman member in all these committees |

(*Contd.*)

**Table 15.7: (*Contd.*)**

| *Presbytery* | *Area baptist council* |
|---|---|
| It consists of 3 or more parishes<br>Members: Moderator, Pastors and elders<br>Generally no woman delegate<br>(once a woman delegate was sent for the first time in 1997 Presbytery) | It consists of 3 or more parishes<br>President, Pastors and elders<br>no woman delegate |
| (1) | (1) |
| Presbytery Committee<br>Members: Pastors and elders<br>No woman | Area Baptist Council Committee<br>Pastors and elders<br>No woman |
| *Parish* | *Parish* |
| Members: Chairman (Minister) and elders<br>No woman member | Chairman,(elder) Pastors and elders<br>No woman member |
| (1) | (1) |
| Departmental Committees<br>Sunday School<br>Mission and Evangelism<br>Youth Fellowship<br>Women Fellowship<br>No woman except in Women Fellowship | Departmental Committees<br>Sunday School<br>Mission and Evangelism<br>Youth Fellowship<br>Women Fellowship<br>No woman except in Women Fellowship |
| *Local Church* | *Local Church* |
| Committee members:<br>Chairman (Pastor)<br>Elders, no woman | Committee members:<br>Chairman (Pastor or elder)<br>elders, no woman |
| (1) | (1) |
| Departmental Committees | Departmental Committees |
| (1) | (1) |
| Sunday school<br>Mission and Evangelism<br>Building, etc.<br>No woman member | Sunday school<br>Mission and Evangelism<br>Building, etc.<br>No woman member |
| (1) | (1) |
| Youth fellowship<br>One or two women | Youth fellowship<br>One or two women |
| (1) | (1) |
| Women fellowship<br>Senior adviser: elder (man) | Women fellowship<br>Senior adviser: elder (man) |

*Source*: R.L. Hnuni, Role of Women in the Church.

The above structure shows that right from the highest level, the Synod/Assembly, on down to the level of the local church women have been excluded, except in their own Women's Fellowship. This type of exclusion has been called "structural sin". It is a sin because it excludes and ignores women who represent (or more than half in many churches) its members in all matters in which important decisions are made concerning its life. Women members are simply subject to the decisions of male members."[76] Till March 2005, among the women of different denominational churches in Mizoram, there were 20 Baptist Theologians and 19 ordained elders; 67 Presbyterian Theologians; 7 Theologians from Lairam Isua Krista Baptist Kohhran (Lairam Jesus Christ Baptist Church); 3 Theologians from Evangelical Church of Maraland[77] and 2 Theologians from Assembly of God. None of these have been given ordination. In USA, a Mizo woman Rev. Rothangliani was ordained in 1993 and soon after Rev. Lalhmingliani was also ordained. Rev. Rothangliani is now a Director in BWA Ecumenical Department.[78] These women are very much capable pastors and as no less competent than their male counterparts as far as Pastoral ministry is concerned. It is very sad that women in Mizoram are not given ordination (except by the Salvation Army). Among the Baptist Church of Mizoram, Assembly Executive Committee Members are the final authority for ordination of Ministers through secret ballots.[79] Since representatives of the Committee consist mainly of males, preference seemed to be given to males. Qualified and competent women theologians are given the posts which can be performed by untrained people. Moreover, they do not enjoy the same pay scale as ordained ministers. In many of the churches in Mizoram, women are not allowed to use pulpit for their ministry. Emphasizing the need for theological education for ecclesial and ministerial transformation, Connie Bickford said, "The church that refuses to accept the ministry of women, the church that marginalizes people based on caste or class is not the Body of Christ".[80] Looking at the 2005 statistical reports of seven Synods of Presbyterian Churches of India, there are 5,12,373 males and 5,37,170 females and females exceed men by 24,797. The PCI has 659 ordained Ministers, and 8,357 ordained Church Elders, plus 130 Probationary Pastors who are to be ordained soon. All these ordained and to-be-ordained soon are male in sex. Only ordained Ministers ansd Probationary Pastors can be permanent regular delegates and selection is made fro other delegates in every biennial assembly.[81] Quoting the words of the Senior Executive Secretary in-charge Theological Education Board (one that governs Aizawl Theological College) named Rev. C. Rosiama in answering the question of women ordination raised by Rev. Dr. and Mrs. Kavin Epting on 21st

November, 2005, that goes like the following, "Culturally we are not yet ready to accept women ordination. It is not that we have no qualified women to be ordained. Mizo culture is very patriarchal and ordination is something like cultural ordination. If people raise the question of women ordination please quote my word...."[82]

**Mizo Women and Education**

Prior to the coming of Christian missionaries in Mizoram, "Knowledge, traditions and customs were handed down from generation to generation in the family except for the family and Zawlbuk, a bachelor's dormitory where elders of a village would educate the young bachelors, there was no institution for formal education".[83] The history of education in Mizoram started with the coming of the two Christian Misssionaries, Rev. J.H. Lorrain and Rev. F.W. Savidge who arrived at Aizawl (the capital of Mizoram) on the 11th January, 1894. Immediately they erected a small hut on a suitable hillock, now called Mac Donald Hill at Aizawl. In this humble hut they began their first mission of imparting education to the Mizo.[84] Students consisted mainly of unmarried males and there were no females.[85] In the beginning of 1895 they ventured to prepare Mizo alphabets in Roman script. Few Mizos began to learn the preliminary lessons in this hut. The then Superintendent of Lushai Hills, Col. J. Shakespeare erected another hut for the hostel near Fort Aijal (Aizawl). The hostel accommodated only few learners mainly the chiefs and sons of the chiefs.[86] The two missionaries stayed for only four years and during this period they compiled a Grammar and Dictionary of the Lushai language which they took with them when they left. With the arrival at Aizawl of two other Presbyterian missionaries, Rev. D.E. Jones and Rev. Edwin Rowlands, towards the middle of 1897 and end of 1898 respectively, the two earlier missionaries yielded the place for them and left Lushai Hills for the Abors in upper Assam only to return to the South Lushai Hills in 1903 to establish there the Baptist Mission field with headquarters at Serkawn near Lunglei. They established a school there and resumed their unfinished work that they started while at Aizawl.[87] To celebrate his 28th birthday, Rev. D.E. Jones started school afresh on 15th February, 1898[88] on the hill behind the Synod Bookroom, Aizawl and it was co-educational. In 1904, a separate school for girls was established on the opposite hillock. At the beginning, it was looked after by Mrs. K.E. Jones (wife of D.E. Jones) and there were 12 pupils and in 1905, 17 and in 1906, 20.[89] [In 1919, a separate girl school was established by Mrs. Zirtiri (Mrs. Chapman) in Lunglei]. Every effort was made by the missionaries to provide girls with such education as would make them useful at home and society by incorporating in their curriculum weaving, knitting, sewing, embroidery, health-care, and nutrition and child-care with practical demonstration classes meant for such subjects. This made girls education very popular and their attendance in school increased so much that separate women teachers for girls school became necessary.[90] In 1909, Mizo females started helping her in teaching, the Mission and Government together constructed a hostel which could accommodate 20 students and apart from the 20 hostellers, there were 50 more student day scholars.[91] As reported by Zosaphluia (D.E. Jones) in 1899, there were 56 students, of which 6 were females[92] and in 1900, there were 11, in 1901, 20 and in 1902, 40 female students.[93] By 1900, there were six lower primary schools in different localities in Aizawl.[94] Till about 1950 there was comparatively smaller number of girls than boys in any educational institutions.[95] According to the yearly Report of the Lushai Hills, 1916-17 given by Rev. F.J. Sandy, "Special efforts have been directed towards increasing the attendance of girls at the village school, and it is gratifying to observe that their number has increased from 46 to 95. The people of Lushai have no ardent desire for their daughters to be educated. Here, woman is the drudge and burden-carrier. Our Christians are a long way from recognizing in practical life the dignity that belongs to every human soul. And in consequence there is a strong tendency to keep the girls ignorant and degraded".[96] The famous traditional sayings used to be, "Educating females is not good, it will be used for only writing love letters"; "Educating females is not useful, it will be taken away with marriage" and "Educating females makes them lazy".[97] These were the general beliefs throughout Mizoram and remained so among the parents till almost 1930.[98] Moreover, women and girl child were shouldered with the responsibilities of household chores and looking after younger siblings, so they had no time to go to school. The Report of the North Lushai Hills, 1928-29 by missionary Miss Morfydd Davies on the Girls' School, Aijal stated:

"I am convinced of one thing, that we must pay much closer attention to female education in this country, and that soon. There is a good proportion of boys attending the schools in every village but few girls, excepting little girls say under seven years of age. What is the explanation? Much work is expected of the girls immediately they become old enough to look after their younger brothers and sisters, or to carry water and firewood. The men, on the whole have an easy and lazy life. It is true that it is the father who goes out every year to select a place for the family rice field: it is he who clears the jungle. But it is the women who plant the rice, and it is they who do the weeding during the rainy months: and they gather the rice and winnow it in addition to carrying the water and firewood day by day, and preparing food and clothes for the family. The hardest work all falls on the women, and the girls are far too useful to be spared to attend school. The consequence is that most of the women are totally uneducated. Very few of them can read or write. Our first need is to educate the parents to believe in the education of their girls. It is to be feared that some send their girls to school simply in order that they may fetch a higher marriage price when they are asked for as wives".[99] One of the then female teachers, Ms. Lalchhawni said, "The main reason for less percentage of female enrolment in educational institution was work. They did all kinds of work. Moreover, people were too ignorant to be aware of the importance of education."[100]

**Table 15.8:** Showing Year of Passing Examinations[101]

| *Sl. No.* | *Name of Examination* | *Year of First Passing Males/Females* |
|---|---|---|
| 1. | Matriculation | 1910 (R.D. Leta)[103] 1927 (Nuteii)[104] |
| 2. | Bachelor of Arts | 1924 (Hrawva & Lianhnuna)[105] 1942 (Lalsangpuii)[106] |
| 3. | Master of Arts | 1939 (Khawtinkhuma)[107] 1952 (Neihpuii)[108] |
| 4. | Master of Science | 1958 (Lalnuntluanga)[109] 1959 (Rokimi)[110] |
| 5. | Bachelor of Divinity | 1945 1977 |
| 6. | MBBS | 1953 1965 |
| 7. | Bachelor of Engineering | 1960 1986 |
| 8. | LLB | 1954 1989 |

From the above table, it is clear that women were marginalized and lacked behind men in education. In 1903, 25th June, the first

Lower Primary examination was held at Aizawl, in which 27 appeared and 19 passed[110] and there were also 2 female students, acquiring 4th and 6th positions (Nu-i and Saii).[111] In 1904, 29 appeared and 23 passed, in which two females, Pawngi (the first nurse in Mizoram) and Thangi (a teacher in South Mizoram) passed.[112]

**Table 15.9:** Showing Names of Persons Who Passed First Lower Primary Examination, 1903[113]

| *Sl. No.* | *Name* | *Marks obtained out of 500* |
|---|---|---|
| 1. | Lala | 418 |
| 2. | Thanga | 415 |
| 3. | Dala | 410 |
| 4. | Nu-i | 398 |
| 5. | Thuama | 396 |
| 6. | Saii | 385 |
| 7. | Suaka | 366 |
| 8. | Kawhtea | 362 |
| 9. | Chawnga | 351 |
| 10. | Hmara | 327 |
| 11. | Chhunruma | 320 |
| 12. | Tawka | 304 |
| 13. | Chhinga | 290 |
| 14. | Chhuahkhama | 267 |
| 15. | Makthanga | 256 |
| 16. | Dohnuna | 237 |
| 17. | Sekaithanga | 193 |
| 18. | Challiana | 188 |
| 19. | Lalchhinga | 178 |

*Source*: Chaltuahkhuma, Political History of Mizoram.

The First ME Examination was held in 1909 in which 6 Passed. Mr. Saitawna (head clerk at Lunglei), Mr. Saptea (Doctor), Mr. Kawlkhuma (founder of Salvation Army in Mizoram), Mr. Lianhmingthanga (Pastor who used to stay in Lakhipur), Mr. Khianga and Mr. Ngaihthangvunga. Here, women were absent.[114] In 1918, 6 females passed their M.E examination, they were Darawti, Kulikawn; Kaithuami (w/o Daha); Chawngthuami (w/o Subedar Pakunga); Thangveli (w/o Rostosingh); Rosiami (w/o Lalzidinga) and Vailuti (one of the first teachers of the Girls school).[115]

**Table 15.10:** Showing Female Literacy in Mizoram[116]

| Year | Literate Persons | Female Literacy | Percentage |
|---|---|---|---|
| 1901 | 295 | 14 | 0.14 |
| 1911 | 472 | 34 | 0.34 |
| 1921 | 743 | 106 | 1.06 |
| 1931 | 1267 | 278 | 2.78 |
| 1941 | 2312 | 844 | 8.44 |
| 1951 | 3651 | 1947 | 19.47 |
| 1961 | 5124 | 4034 | 40.34 |

*Source*: Mizo Women Today.

The progress of female literacy during the seven decades (1901-1961) was tremendous. While literacy rate was below 3 per cent till 1931, in 1941, 1951 and 1961, it increased from 8.44 to 19.47 and 40.34 respectively. So, we can say that Christianity was the contributory factor to women's increased literacy rate in Mizoram.

**Table 15.11:** Showing break-up of Literacy Percentage-1961 on Tribal Population[117]

| Area | Male | Female | Average |
|---|---|---|---|
| Aijawl Sub-division | 57.69 | 40.16 | 48.79 |
| Lungleh Sub-division | 41.03 | 21.37 | 31.14 |
| District Total | 52.52 | 34.39 | 43.34 |

The marked difference between male and female (52.52 M and 34.39 F) indicates the need for further encouragement of female education.

The progress of women in literacy rate can be seen from the table below:

**Table 15.12:** Showing Literacy Rates (in percentages)[118]

| | Mizoram | | | | India | | | |
|---|---|---|---|---|---|---|---|---|
| Year | Total | Males | Females | Gender Gap | Total | Males | Females | Gender Gap |
| 1971 | 53.79 | 60.49 | 46.71 | 13.78 | 34.4 | 45.95 | 21.97 | 23.98 |
| 1981 | 59.88 | 64.46 | 54.91 | 9.55 | 43.56 | 56.37 | 29.75 | 26.62 |
| 1991 | 82.27 | 85.65 | 78.60 | 7.05 | 52.11 | 63.86 | 39.42 | 24.44 |
| 2001 | 88.49 | 90.69 | 86.13 | 4.56 | 65.38 | 75.85 | 54.16 | 21.69 |

The above table shows that though gender gap is more in India than in Mizoram and that there had been an increase in the female literacy rate in Mizoram, yet, it is still lower than the males.

## Mizo Women's Organisations

Various women oraganisations have been set in Mizoram for the uplift of their status, they are:

### Mizo Hmeichhe Tangrual Pawl (MHT)

This was the first organization of the Mizo women, set up on the 16th July, 1946 at Mizo High School, Aizawl. Its main objectives were:

- To step out of the very low status of women and to search for ways of becoming useful persons.
- To enable persons residing in and outside Mizoram to acquaint and develop themselves, to work cooperatively, to reflect on health and other topics.

In their first conference on 26-28 January, 1948, at Thakthing Veng Zawlbuk, Aizawl, they resolved the matters regarding bride price, divorce, inheritance, children, adultery and illegitimate offspring, to be discussed in their first General Assembly on 12th March, 1949. Besides, in their Assembly they resolved not to allow their children to play at night, not to be overprotective their children, to dress up according to one's own home, to clean up their houses including utensils, to be obedient to husbands and to be more careful about civic sense.[119]

The organization was a contemporary of the Mizo Union Party. Oraganised itself on the pattern and model of the party, the Tangrual resembled the Mizo Union Party in many ways. Thus the women leaders were boldly inspired to take active part in politics. In its meeting on 23rd August, 1947, it made a resolution that "This organization will take part in politics whenever it deems fit". The Mizo Hmeichhia Tangrual also met the Bardoloi Sub-Committee and discussed the would-be status of women in the society after Independence. It also repeatedly requested the authorities to include their representatives in the Advisory Council. In the election to the Advisory Council held on 15th April, 1948, its official candidate, Zami was challenged by its own President, Lalsangpuii and defeated her. The contests were very keen and interesting not mainly because the official candidate was challenged by its own President but because it was the election where women for the first time took part. The Constitution of the Mizo District Council on 26th April, 1952 was a dream come true to the women leaders. As a women's organization their main concern was the upliftment of their position in the society. They were also concerned with the participation in the District Council with a view to improving their position. Their third concern was to take part in the village level administration. They also talked among themselves about a "Greater Mizoram", they wanted the District Council to have certain provision for its future expansion in terms of membership so that the Mizos living in Cachar and Manipur areas might have a chance to send their representatives in the future. The women leaders also made it clear that they strongly opposed the the possible formation of the Regional Council in Mizoram. They also repeatedly passed resolution after resolution asking the authorities to give them seats in the Council for women. In its General Assembly held on 7-9 February, 1951, the members selected by secret vote three names as as possible candidates in the forthcoming District Council. The selected persons were Hmingliani, Thankimi and Varziki. This was done to give an impression to the people that the women members in the District Council were the real nominees of the women folk. After selecting Hmingliani and Thankimi, they conveyed their decision to the Government. With regard to the Village Council, in the special Assembly held in 1952, the members unanimously resolved to contest the election but reviewed in its General Assembly in 1953 that only candidates who would have a winning chance should contest the elections. In the first District Council, much to the amazement of the organization, Lalziki who was not its member was nominated. Buta new page in the history of Tangrual was opened when its President Hmingliani was nominated as member of the second District Council. When Hmingliani was nominated for the third District Council, she surrendered her seat to her colleague Malsawmi of Zarkawt, Aizawl. Since then women, a group of an organized fuctionary, gradually alienated themselves from active politics and as a result of disturbances following the outbreak of 1966, the whole political atmosphere was not normal. Hence, the organization completely divorced politics in its life and activities.[120] Now it is active only in Aizawl.[121]

**People's Conference Party's Women's Wing**

On 17th April, 1975, a new party known as People's Conference (PC) was formed with Brig. Thenphunga Sailo as its President. Apart from the General Secretary, there were six Secretaries. One of them was Ms. K. Thansiami.[122] It was the first organization to officially bring women into politics. A Women's Wing was created and its leaders were:

| | | |
|---|---|---|
| Chairman | : | Ms. Biakkungi |
| Vice Chairman | : | Ms. Vanbuki |
| General Secretary | : | Ms. K. Thansiami |
| Treasurer | : | Ms. Hlunpuii |

They were found to be of such help and importance that other political parties, too, started their respective Women's Wings.[123] In 1976, the People's Conference Party resolved to change its name to Mizo Democratic Front and elected a lady (Ms. Sanglianchhungi) to be its President. She is the first woman to head any party in Mizoram.[124] In 1975 a new political history was made in India. The Prime Minister Indira Gandhi declared emergency throughout India. In Mizoram too, the opposition leaders were put behind bars. Brig. T. Sailo, the then President of the P.C. Party and his colleagues were sent to Tezpur jail in Assam. Sanglianchhungi and some of her colleagues were also arrested and put in the District Jail in Aizawl. Sanglianchhungi may be the second Mizo woman who was interned for political reasons after Chieftain Ropuiliani who was arrested and imprisoned at Rangmati jail (now in Bangladesh) in 1894 by the British. Sanglianchhungi also made history in Mizoram. When she was in the prison cell the general elections to Parliament (Lok Sabha) were held on 11th March, 1977. Sanglianchhungi contested the elections from her internment on the MDF (Independent) ticket and used 'tiger' as her election symbol.[125] Unfortunately she forfeited her deposit.[126] After release, the MDP leaders drew up a new constitution for their party which *inter alia* declared that the MDF would strive for unification of all Mizo inhabited contiguous areas within the Indian Union under one single administrative unit. MDF had resigned its stand for 'total independence for Mizoram' and now stood for a 'Greater Mizoram' within the Indian Union.[127]

**Mizo Hmeichhe Insuihkhawm Pawl**

It is the biggest women organization in Mizoram. When Mizoram became a Union Territory (in 1972), State Social Welfare Advisory Board (SSWAB) was established in Mizoram. Through this, various activities were undertaken to promote the welfare of women and children. For facilitating the work of SSWAB and various government departments, MHIP (Mizoram Hmeiche Insuihkhawm Pawl), i.e. United Mizoram Women Organization, was established on 6th July, 1974, by the members of SSWAB and Office Bearers of the HTP and Mahila Mandal (established under Assam government in every Community Development Block), under the guidance of the then Social Welfare Officer Mr. Bonthanga Poonte(L).[128] The name Mizoram Hmeichhe Insuihkhawm Pawl was changed into Mizo Hmeichhe Insuihkhawm Pawl (United Mizo Women Organization) by the Special Assembly to include the Mizo women residing outside Mizoram. Through MHIP, Mizo women indirectly participate in the politics of Mizoram, influencing the government while making their policies. Its headquarters is in Treasury Square, Aizawl. According to MHIP 14th General Assembly Minute Book, 2003 it has 7 sub-headquarters and 702 branches and 10 Joint MHIP.[129] Its motto is service to others. The association also looks into the customs and traditions and suggests necessary amendments.[130] On the occasion of its 31st anniversary, B. Sangkhumi, the President came out with a public address saying,

> "Since we find our customary laws not safeguarding the rights of Mizo women, it is our greatest wish that a legislation is passed where these Rights would be safeguarded. It would be much beneficial to us if, 'The Indian Christian Marriage Act, 1872' is made applicable to Mizoram. However, it would even be more beneficial if a separate Mizo Christian Marriage Act is enacted."[131]

**Puitu Hmeichhe Pawl (PHP)**

It was set up in Mizoram as a branch of Mahila Imdad Committee in July 1976. The aims and objectives of the organization are:

- To render relief to people affected by natural calamities.
- To organize activities like rendering help to the needy and destitute children.

- To organize activities for the welfare of the women-folk.[132]
- The setting up of a Craft Centre is one noteworthy activity undertaken till date which trains the needy and handicapped women in sewing and knitting to help them earn a living.

**Young Women's Christian Association (YWCA), Aizawl**

It was started in Mizoram on the 30th December, 1985.[133] The aims and principles being to render help to the poor and needy in every possible way irrespective of age, race, etc.[134] Its main contributions are—renting a house for females since 20th June, 1986, opening a Family Counselling Centre since November 1996, to safeguard women's rights and help them in their suffering (organizing seminars), consoling and defending raped victims (also publishing steps to be taken by the raped victim in the newspaper), helping the poor women and children's (giving free clinic), maintaining relations with other YWCA of India.[135] It has worked hard for the uplift of women's status in Mizoram.

**Mizoram Hmeithai Association (Mizoram Widow Association)**

It was started on the 20th October, 1987 by Mrs. Lallianpuii, Aizawl, Khatla and her friends.[136] Widow is classified by the association into a person who lost her husband, a divorcee, who has an illegitimate child of 10 years or above and who is a spinster of 40 years or above.[137] Its main works include getting domesticating loans from Rashtriya Vikhas Nidhi (RVN) and distributing to 306 widows, opening a school for poor children, opening of a four storied Residential School of the Privileged Children at Chawlhhmun, Aizawl, the place donated by Mrs. Veronica and sponsored by a German Catholic Church called Miserior, taking girls to Court and hiring lawyers for them, orphanage, providing shelter to homeless mothers with small children, mobile clinic and helped ginger growers sell their products through Tribal Cooperative Marketing Development Federation Limited (Trifed).[138]

**Mizoram State Commission for Women (MSCW)**

The Indian government cares for the welfare of females and therefore, constituted the National Commission for Women on 31st January, 1992, under section 3 of the National Commission for Women Act, 1990 (Central Act 20 of 1990),[139] which looks after their welfare.

Since the Central Government considers it necessary to establish such a commission in every state, it was also established in Mizoram on the 11th August, 1998. Its main aims include[140]:

- To see if safeguards enshrined in the Constitution of India and other iegislations are carried out or not in accordance with the rules.
- To see and make necessary suggestions if there are loopholes in the Constitution of Indian concerning females.
- The Commission will report steps taken by it to the State government annually or when it feels it necessary.

  - To make suggestions for better utilization of standing rules for uplift of females.
  - If the constitution or rules concerning females are violated, then it will take the matter to the concerned authority.
  - In order to make suggestions for the needful in matters where they do not enjoy their rightful place, it will make research regarding housing, obstacles on the path to helping hands given in advanced studies, to minimize or remove ill health caused due to jobs held and to search for ways of using them in the best possible ways.
  - To search if there is any marginalization on grounds of being a fairer sex, organize studies and try to remove such discrepancies.
  - To take part in the meeting of the government regarding plans for their occupation and make suggestions.
  - To see if there is marginalization regarding violation of female's rights, usage of rules concerning safeguards, policies concerning females uplift and take the matter to the concerned authority, if necessary.
  - To visit Jails and Remand Homes for women and make suggestions for improvement to the authority, if necessary.
  - To check and study if there is progress among women in the state.

Mizoram State Commission for Women was established on executive order and needed to be legislated by the Assembly. As a result it was enacted by the Mizoram Legislative Assembly in the fifty fifth year of the Republic of India under the name the Mizoram State Commission for Women Act, 2004[141], on November 8, 2004.[142]

As reported by the Chairperson of the MSCW in the State level meeting with NGOs organized by MSCW, held at State Guest House, Aizawl, on 23rd September, 2004, "Normal and disabled children who are victims of rape, who reported themselves for help and assistance were provided help and assistance accordingly. The Commission also did a follow-up on the accused in rape cases to find out whether the guilty rapists received the punishment they deserved. It had also provided assistance to divorced ladies who sought assistance for alimony by means of getting for them lawyers, etc. The Commission members had also made a visit to Women's Cell in Central Jail and Police Station to have first hand information on the problems faced by women in Jails and Lock-ups and whether they can be solved."[143]

## Conclusion

In spite of the various attempts made by women's organizations to raise the status of women in Mizoram, it has failed to do so, particularly in the field of politics, as we see minimal participation of Mizo women in the administration of the State right from pre-Christianity era. From the above discussion, it is clear that patriarchy is the cause of women's subordinate position in the society, although to some extent Christian education contributed to the raising of the status of Mizo women.

## NOTES

1. Lalthansangi, *Situational Analysis of Women in the State of Mizoram* (New Delhi: National Commission for Women, 2004), p. 36.
2. Ms. B. Lalrinchhani, "Christianity and Women in Mizoram: A Study of the Impact of Christianity on Women in Lunglei District" (Unpublished M. Phil Dissertation, Department of History, North Eastern Hill University, Shillong, 1998), p. 21.
3. Sangkima, *Essays on the History of the Mizos* (Guwahati: Spectrum Publications, First Published 2004), p. 90, citing Pastor Challiana, *Pi Pu Nun* (The Trio Bookhouse, Aizawl, 1978) pp. 2-3. Right from her childhood days the tiny girl made herself available to the parents. She assisted her parents as much as she could. She had to take care of her younger brothers

and sisters, draw water, cook and do any other works whatever the family needed. Sometimes, accompanying her mother she fetched firewood. In this way, the girl helped her parents when she was still young. *Ibid.* p. 90. Girls of the traditional Zo (Mizo) society practically had no time to rest. At the same time a girl of *tlawmngaihna* (self-denial moral code of conduct possessed by Mizos) would see to it that she maintains a restrain in food habits, eating as little as possible, especially while eating in places other than her own home. "The extent of work they did with the little amount of food they consumed", said Challiana, "made one wonder how it was possible for the Mizo girls to remain healthy and strong." Mangkhosat Kipgen, *Christianity and Mizo Culture* (The Mizo Theological Conference, Mizoram c/o Eastern Theological College, Jorhat, 1996), p. 71.

4. Dr. R.L. Hnuni, *Women and Development*, a paper presented in the Seminar organized on Development organized by North East India Committee on Relief and Development on 15th November, 1988 in Dimapur, p. 2.
5. *Ibid.*, p. 4.
6. A. Wati Longchar, "Issues in Feminist Theory"' in R.L. Hnuni (ed), *Transforming Theology for Empowering Women* (Jorhat: Women's Studies, ETC, 1999) pp. 20, 21.
7. B. Lalrinchhani, "Mizo Migration and Gender Relations: A Historical Analysis", a Ph.D. Pre-submission seminar, Department of Hisdtory, North Eastern Hill University, 2006.
8. Rev. H.S. Luaia, *Mizo Nunphung* (Aizawl: Lalriliani, 1998), p. 12.
9. Dr. R.L. Hnuni, "The Impact of Christianity on the Hill Women of North East India", a paper presented in a Seminar on *In the North and North-East*, organized by Serampore College, 12th May, 1997, Jorhat. p. 3.
10. Major A.G. McCall, *Lushai Chrysalis* (Aizawl: Firma KLM Pvt. Calcutta for Tribal Research Institute, First Edition 1949, Reprint 1977) pp. 171-172. The *Lushai* mother will continue to work at her usual duties, even wood and water collection, upto the very day of delivery, there still being a sneaking belief that in this way the chances of a speedy delivery are greatly enhanced. *Ibid.*, p. 175. In the cultivation seasons the women will go off for the day to their fields, often taking their babies on their backs, if they have none with whom to leave them safely. *Ibid.*, p. 173.
11. Franklin J. Balasundaram, "Women Concern in Asia", (C.L.S., Madras, 1993), p. 7, cited by Shimreingam Shimray, *Women and Economy*, in R.L. Hnuni ed., *Transforming Theology for Empowering Women* (Jorhat: Women's Studies, Eastern Theological College, 1999), p. 46.
12. S.L. Baruah, *Status of Women in Assam* (New Delhi: R. Kumar Omsons Publications, 1992), p. 40.
13. Irene Colbert, *Women and economy*, an unpublished paper presented at Awareness Generation Programme organized by MHIP Salem Branch, Lunglei, on 8th-10th, July, 1999.
14. It was customary among married and unmarried women to engage

themselves with cotton works. Besides, the unmarried women had to perform a well-established social custom by receiving young men who came to spend time in amusing themselves after toiling the whole day at the *jhum*. This custom is called *Inleng* (courting). When the next day dawned she had to rise early to start life afresh for the whole day. In the early morning she proceeded to the spring (waterpoint) to fill bamboo tubes with water, finish unhusking the rice by pounding in a mortar and cook the breakfast. She should have finished all these tiring jobs before sunrise while the husband and the other male members were still asleep. Then after the meal the real work of the day began. All these pre-day engagements were performed by the young woman and the mother in the house. If the mother had no daughter she had to single out these duties. Sangkima, *op. cit.*, p. 90. When the weeding season was over, there Autumn set in. This was the season when the men engaged themselves with hunting. Those who did not go for hunting they roamed about helping the family. But for womenfolk it was the busiest season of the year. During this pleasant season sets her daily in two features. The first part of her work in a given day was to fetch firewood from the jungle. It was her duty to stock firewood for the next rainy season. The other part included making of clothes for the coming winter. *Ibid.*, pp. 90-91.

15. Selet Thanga, *Pi Pu Len Lai* (Aizawl: Lianchhungi Book Store, 1979), p. 16.
16. James Dokhuma, *Hmanlai Mizo Kalphung* (Aizawl: Padma Shri James Dokhuma at the J.D. Press, 1992), p. 205.
17. Mangkhosat Kipgen, *Christianity and Mizo Culture*, (Jorhat: The Mizo Theological Conference, Mizoram, c/o Eastern Theological College, 1996, p. 71, citing Challiana, Pi Pu Nun (1969, reprinted, 1979), p. 18.
18. Raj Kumar Pruthi, Ramesh Devi and Romila Pruthi, eds., *Indian Women: Present Status and Future Prospects*, (Jaipur; Mangal Deep Publications, 2003), p. 158. Her life was shadowed by anxiety for her husband, sons and brothers and by fear for herself and children who might at any time be attacked by raiders in search of human heads. When she returned in the evening she might have to climb down 500 to 1000 feet to the nearest water-point, for most Naga villages are perched on the tops of hills. There was the food to cook, the rice-beer to brew, the grain to husk, the children to nurse and a husband to console and cheer. She was always busy, and when there was no work in the fields, she busied herself with her loom, on which she wove beautiful and durable cloth.
19. Chitta Ranjan Nag, *The Mizo Society in Transition* (New Delhi: Vikas Publishing House Pvt. Ltd., 1993), p. 10.
20. Pastor Challiana, *Pi Pu Nun* (Aizawl: Lalrinliana and sons, 1986), p. 17.
21. C. Lianthanga, *Hmanlai Mizo Nun* (Aizawl: Mizoram Publication Board, 1999), p. 37.
22. Dr. Lathanliana, *Mizo Chanchin (Kum 1900 Hma Lam)* [Aizawl: Vanlalhmuaka and Mr. and Mrs. Vanlalhruaii (Hruaiteii), first edition 2000], pp. 185, 186.

23. Dr. R.L. Hnuni, *Empowerment of Women: Decision Making in the Society and Politics*, presented paper in Consultation on National Policy for Empowerment of Women, 24-25 March, 2004, (organized by Mizoram State Commission for Women), p. 2.
24. But if an only son is away from home due to holding of a job elsewhere, he is not to be considered ineligible. If offspring of another mother stay with the father, they can claim inheritance. But if they stay with their mother, they cannot be inheritors, as long as there are others staying with the father. In case of death of the rightful inheritor, the next rightful inheritor will be as above. If the father does not have any male offspring, then his daughter may be in the next line. Then, if the owner has parents still living, they may inherit, next will be the owner's brothers and their children, then his sisters and their children. If the owner does not have any brothers and sisters, his paternal grand parents' side may inherit and incase of shortage of males, from the females'side. The Mizoram Gazette Extraordinary, *Mizo Hnam Dan* (*Latest*) (*Mizo Customary Laws*), 2005, pp. 83-85.
25. Dr. R. Hnuni, Vision for Women in North East India, in R.L. Hnuni, ed., *Transforming Theology for Empowering Women* (Jorhat: Women's Studies, Eastern Theological College, 1999), p. 145.
26. S.P. Sharma & A.C. Mittal, eds., *Tribal Women in India: Tribal Women in Changing Society Volume I* (New Delhi: Radha Publications, first published 1998), p. 14.
27. Hasina Kharbhih, Gender and Matrilineal, a presented paper at Shillong Youth Hostel, organized by Vidyasagar School of Social Work and sponsored by Central Social Welfare Board, New Delhi, on 15th to 18th February, 2001.
28. S.P. Sharma & A.C. Mittal, eds., *Tribal Women in India: Tribal Women in Changing Society Volume I* (New Delhi: Radha Publications, first published 1998), p. 14.
29. Caroline R. Marak, Status of Women in Garo Culture, in Soumen Sen, ed., *Women in Meghalaya* (Delhi: Anil Mittal for Daya Publishing House, 1997), p. 70.
30. L.S. Gassah, Status of Women in Jaintia Culture, in Soumen Sen, ed., *Women in Meghalaya* (Delhi: Anil Mittal for Daya Publishing House, 1997), p. 43.
31. *Mizo Hnam Dan* (Mizo Customary Laws), (Aizawl: Mizo District Council, 1957), p. 35. It was N.E. Perry, I.C.S., the then Superintendent of the Lushai Hills District who first put these laws in black and white in 1927 in the form of a booklet named *Mizo Dan* (Brochure on the Mizo District Council). Chitta Ranjan Nag, *Post-Colonial Mizo Politics 1947-1998* (Vikas Publishing House Pvt. Ltd., New Delhi, 1999), p. 29. He revised in 1957 when the original Mizo Dan was renamed as Mizo Hnam Dan. *Ibid*, p. 54.
32. Rev. H.S. Luaia, *Mizo Nunphung* (Aizawl: Lalriliani, 1998), pp. 26-27.
33. Rev. Z.T. Khuma, in Hmeichhiate leh Mizo Hnam Dan, (Seminar papers on Women and and Mizo Customary Law on 6th May, 1999 at Co-operation

Conference Hall, Aizawl, organized by Volunteers for Community Mental Health, Sikulpui kawn, Aizawl), Zohmangaiha, IRS(Rtd.), Compiler, p. 27.
34. *Ibid.*, pp. 8-9.
35. *Puanpui* ia a cotton blanket and *thul* is a cane basket in which Mizo ladies keep all her valuables. These two items constitute an essential part of a Mizo women's possession and hence it is considered disgraceful if the bride does not bring these things to her husband's house. The *puandum* included in the women's possession when she gets married is called *zawlpuan*. This dark blue cloth is meant to cover the body of her husband when he dies. If she does not possess it at the time of her marriage, two ordinary cloth can be used to serve the purpose of *zawlpuan*. If a lady fails to bring this sort of cloth to her husband's home and in that case, her husband buys a *puanpui* and *thul*, her marriage price is subjected to a reduction of Rs. 20. E.J. Thomas. *Mizo Bamboo Hills Murmur Change: Mizo Society before and after Independence* (New Delhi: D.R. Chopra for M/S Intellectual Publishing House, 1993) p. 16, citing Parry, N.E, *Monograph on Lushai Customs and Ceremonies*, pp. 27-31.
36. *Mizo Hnam Dan, op. cit.*, p. 37.
37. *Mizo Women Today*, (Aizawl: Tribal Research Institute, Directorate of Art and Culture), p. 2.
38. *Inkaihchhuah* means a wife has to purify herself from her husband after three months of his death. Witnesses have to be there. If she does so before 90 days, she will be considered as divorcing her husband at her own will. In such cases, she has to return the bride price in full. She will leave the house with her belongings. *Mizo Hnam Dan, op. cit.*, pp. 31-32.
39. *Ibid.*, p. 37.
40. *Mizo Hnam Dan, op. cit.*, p. 37.
41. E.J. Thomas, *Mizo Bamboo Hills Murmur Change: Mizo Society before and after Independence* (New Delhi: D.R. Chopra for M/s Intellectual Publishing House, 1993), p. 42.
42. Lalhriatpuii, "Economic Empowerment in the Context of Mizo Women" presented paper in State Consultation Meeting on State Policy at State Guest House, Aizawl on 23-24 March, 2004 (organized by Mizoram State Commission for Women), p. 1.
43. H.T.C. Lalrinchhana, M.A., LL.B., "Domestic Violence with reference to the protection of women from domestic violence Act, 2005", presented paper for a State Level Seminar on 'The Promotion of Women's Rights in Mizoram', on 29th & 30th November, 2005, held at Lunglei (Centre for Peace and Development, Aizawl, Mizoram), p. 1.
44. Major A.G. McCall, *Lushai Chrysalis* (Aizawl: Firma KLM Pvt. Ltd., Calcutta, for Tribal Research institute, First Edition 1949, Reprint 1977, p. 111.
45. Zachhunga, *Tunhma Mizo Nunphung* (Mizoram: Tribal Research Institute, Directorate of Art and Culture, 1992), 72.

46. H.T.C. Lalrinchhana, "Violation of Women's Rights in Mizo Society (Some reflections and a Futuristic Approach)", Center for Peace and Development, Aizawl, presented paper for a State Level Seminar on 'The Promotion of Women's Rights in Mizoram', on 29th & 30th November, 2005, held at Art & Culture Auditorium, Lunglei (Centre for Peace and Development, Aizawl, Mizoram), p. 2.
47. Lalthansangi, *Situational Analysis of Women in the State of Mizoram* (New Delhi: Natioanal Commission for Women, 2004), p. 53.
48. Dr. R.L. Hnuni, *Women and Development*, a paper presented in the Seminar organized on Development organized by North East India Committee on Relief and Development on 15th November, 1988 in Dimapur.
49. *Mizo Women Today, op. cit.*, pp. 7-10.
50. Dr. R.L. Hnuni, "The Impact of Christianity on the Hill Women of North East India", a paper presented in a Seminar on *In the North and North-East*, organized by Serampore College, 12th May, 1997, Jorhat, p. 5.
51. Vanengliana, *Khawiahnge Mizo Mipate?* (Where are the Mizo men?), (Aizawl: Synod Social Front, 1991) pp. 3-6.
52. Lalhriatpuii, *op. cit.*, p. 3.
53. Upa Vanengliana, Khawiah nge Mizo Mipate ?, in *Khawtlang Nun Hruaina* (Aizawl: Synod Social Front Committee, 2000), p. 433.
54. Dr. T. Vanlaltlani, *Mizo Hmeichhiate Kawngzawh*, (Aizawl: Mizoram Publication Board, 2005) pp. 53-54.
55. *Ibid.*, p. 4.
56. Neera Desai and Vibhuti Patel, *Indian Women:Change and Challenge in the International Decade 1975-85* (Bombay: Ramdas G. Bhatkal Popular Prakashan Pvt. Ltd., first pulished 1985, second published 1990), p. 42.
57. F. Lawmzuali, Women Empowerment year 2001 (Hmeichhiate Tihchakna Hian Mizo Hmeichhiate tan kawng ro a su dawn em?, in *Zoram Kal Chhet Chhet* (Aizawl: Khamliana on behalf of Youth Club, 2002), pp. 54-55.
58. T. Vanlaltlani, "Economic Condition of Women Today" (presented paper in NEICCWA Workshop on Empowerment of Women, Lunglei, 2 April, 2004), p. 5.
59. *Mizo Women Today, op. cit.*, p. 14.
60. *Ibid.*, p. 16.
61. Upa Vanengliana, *op. cit.*, pp. 434-435.
62. *Ibid.*, p. 436.
63. *Ibid.*, pp. 436, 437.
64. *Ibid.*, pp. 437, 438.
65. Lalthansangi, *Situational Analysis of Women in The State of Mizoram* (New Delhi: National Commission for Women, 2004), p. 49.
66. *Ibid.* p. 50.
67. *Ibid.*, p. 51.
68. *Ibid.*, pp. 51-52.
69. Chitta Ranjan Nag, *The Mizo Society in Transition* (Vikas Publishing House Pvt. Ltd., 1993), p. 47., citing J. Shakespear, The Lushai Kuki Clans, p. 61.

70. *Ibid.*, pp. 47-49.
71. B. Poonte, Dip. SSA (Bombay), District Research Officer, Cachar and Mizo District, Compiler, *District Hand Book* (Mizo District Assam)(The Deputy Commissioner, Mizo District, Aizawl, 1965), p. 43.
72. R.L. Hnuni, The Role of Women in the Church, in R.L. Hnuni, ed., *Transforming Theology for Empowering Women* (Women's Studies, Eastern Theological College, Jorhat, 1999), p. 64.
73. P. Liandingi, Hmeichhiate Chanvo-Khawtlangah leh Kohhranah (Role of Women in the society and church), paper, Aizawl, Mizoram, p. 3.
74. Solmon Rongpi, Women Empowerment: A North East India Perspective, in *Transforming Theology for Empowering Women* (Jorhat: Women's Studies, Eastern Theological College, 1999), p. 122.
75. Dr. R. Hnuni, Vision for Women in North East India. In R.L. Hnuni, ed., *Transforming Theology for Empowering Women* (Women's Studies, Eastern Theological College, Jorhat, 1999), pp. 151-152. As F.S. Downs has observed, "by the time feminism became an important force (in the Western Churches), such developments in the west were no longer mediated to the churches and societies of North East India through missionaries, men and women." *Ibid.*, p. 152
76. R.L. Hnuni, The Role of Women in the Church, *op. cit.*, pp. 68-70.
77. Dr. T. Vanlatlani, *Mizo Hmeichhiate Kawngzawh* (Mizoram: Mizoram Publication Board,) pp. 83-180.
78. P. Liandingi, Mizo Hmeichhia leh Kristianna leh Zirna, paper presented on 8.2.2003 at MBKHP Inkhawmpui, Zotlang, Lunglei, Mizoram, p. 3.
79. Rev. C. Ngurhnema, Women Issue in the Church Ministry with special reference to the BCM, paper. p. 5.
80. Connie Bickford, Theological Education for Ecclesial and Ministerial Transformation, in R.L. Hnuni, ed., *Transforming Theology for Empowering Women* (Jorhat: Women's Studies, Eastern Theological College, 1999) p. 96.
81. Dr. T. Vanlaltlani, Women in Tribal Culture and their position in the Church, a paper presented in a consultation organized by Presbyterian Church of India on Theology and Culture at Shillong on May 23-26, 2006. pp. 10, 11.
82. *Ibid.*, p. 13. The quoted words are given in the text as remembered by the present paper writer nd if there are mistaken words, the writer asked for an apology to the Senior Executive secretary of MPC Synod.
83. Lalthansangi, *Situational Analysis of Women in The State of Mizoram* (National Commission for Women, New Delhi, 2004), p. 44.
84. *Mizo Women Today*, (Mizoram: Tribal Research Institute, Directorate of Art and Culture), p. 20.
85. Pu Lalbiakliana, Mizoram Zirna Chanchin, in Upa K.L. Rokhuma, *Mizoram Zirnaa Mission leh Kohhran Rawngbawlna* ( Aizawl: The Communications Department Baptist Church of Mizoram), p. 112.
86. *Mizo Women Today, op. cit.*, p. 20.
87. Laldinliani Hrahsel, An abstract of the Ph.D. Dissertation meant for Pre-Submission Seminar, a study of the educational Activities of various

Christian denominations in Mizoram and their impact on the Mizo Society. pp. 9, 10.

88. Upa K.L. Rokhuma, *Mizoram Zirnaa Mission leh Kohhran Rawngbawlna (Role of the Mission and Church ibn Mizoram Education)* (Aizawl: Communications Department, Baptist Church of Mizoram, 1988), p. 71.
89. *Ibid.*, citing Welsh Mission Reports of 1905-06, p. 113.
90. Laldinliani Hrahsel, *op. cit.*, p. 12.
91. Upa K.L. Rokhuma, citing a letter sent by Mrs. K.E. Jones to Lushai Hills Bawrhsap (Commissioner) on May 4th, 1916, p. 113.
92. *Ibid.*, p. 71.
93. *Ibid.*, p. 112 in Welsh Foreign Reports, 1899, 1900, 1901, 1902.
94. Lalthansangi, *op. cit.*, p. 44.
95. *Mizo Women Today, op. cit.*, p. 21.
96. K. Thanzauva, compiler, *Reports of the Foreign Mission of the Presbyterian Church of Wales on Mizoram 1894-1957* (Aizawl: The Synod Literature and Publication Boards, 1997), p. 61.
97. B. Sangkhumi, Mizo Hmeichhiate Thlenchin, in *Zoram Tang Fan Fan* (Aizawl: Khamliana on behalf of the Youth Club) p. 126.
98. Lalhmuaka, *Zoram Zirna lam chhinchhiahna (The records of Zoram Education*) (Mizoram: Tribal Research institute, Education Department, 1981), p. 5.
99. K. Thanzauva, *op. cit.,* pp. 89-90.
100. Interview with Lalchhawni, Shillong, 22 December, 2006.
101. B. Sangkhumi, *op. cit.,* pp. 125, 126.
102. Zatluanga, *Mizo Chanchin Bu I* (Aizawl: Zasanga, IPS, Secy, MLA, Ist published 1966, reprinted 1996, 1997), p. 279.
103. *Ibid*
104. *Ibid.*
105. *Ibid.*
106. *Ibid.*
107. *Ibid.*
108. *Ibid,* p. 280.
109. *Ibid.*
110. Lalhmuaka, *Zoram Zirna lam Chhinchhiahna (The Records of Zoram Education*), *op. cit.*, p. 6.
111. Upa K.L. Rokhuma, *op. cit.,* p. 135.
112. *Ibid.*, p. 19.
113. Chaltuahkhuma, *Political History of Mizoram* [Aizawl: Vanthangi w/o Chaltuahkhuma(L), 2001], p. 37.
114. Lalhmuaka, *Zoram Zirna lam Chhinchhiahna (The Records of Zoram Education*), *op. cit.*, p. 21.
115. Lalhmuaka, B.A & Upa T. Chawma, *Zoram Sikul Zirna Chanchin Mission leh Kohhran Hnathawh* (Aizawl: Lalhmuaka, B.A., First edition AD 2000), p. 77.

116. *Mizo Women Today*, *op. cit.*, p. 22.
117. B. Poonte, Dip. SSA (Bombay), District Research Officer, Cachar and Mizo District, Compiler, *District Hand Book* (Aijal: Mizo District Assam) (The Deputy Commissioner, Mizo District, 1965), p. 23.
118. Lalthansangi, *op. cit.*, p. 47.
119. In 1950, Mizoram Commissioner, S.N. Barkataki (Superintendent) gave them a big land at north of Khatla Bazar where they constructed buildings, imparting various trainings for upliftment of females in weaving, cleanliness, opened Dhai institution where candidates are selected by Civil Hospital Surgeon and leaders of MHT which were recruited by the government after training, set up maternity centre which was rented by government free of cost from 1956 till 17th July, 1975 (this is no longer in existence), helped famine victims in 1960 by supplying animal fat, ghee, vitamin, syringe, rubber cloth, water bag and eneme, opened loin loom centre in 1962 but closed down in 1966 due to insurgency, set up orphanage in 1969 till date, Working Women's Hostel. Dr. T. Vanlaltlani, *Mizo Hmeichhiate Kawngzawh* (Mizoram Publication Board, 2005), pp. 211-224.
120. Sangkima, *Essays on the History of the Mizos* (Guwahati: Delhi: Spectrum Publications, first published 2004), pp. 163-169.
121. *Mizo Hmeichhe Insuihkhawm Pawl Dan Bu* (Constitution) (Aizawl: MHIP General Headquarters, from introduction), p. 1.
122. Sangkima, *Essays on the History of the Mizos* (Guwahati: Delhi: Spectrum Publications, first published 2004), p. 170.
123. Dr. J.V. Hluna, Role of Women in the Politics of Mizoram through the ages, presented paper on 27th September, 2001, p. 3.
124. V. Venkata Rao, H. Thansanga & Niru Hazarika, *A Century of Government and Politics in North-East India Volume III-Mizoram* [New Delhi: S. Chand & Company (Pvt.) Ltd., First Published 1987], p. 153.
125. Sangkima, *Essays on the History of the Mizos* (Guwahati: Delhi: Spectrum Publications, first published 2004), p. 170.
126. V. Venkata Rao, H. Thansanga & Niru Hazarika, *op. cit.*, p. 153.
127. H.M. Bareh, ed., *Encyclopaedia of North-East India: Volume V: Mizoram* (New Delhi: Naurang Rai for Mittal Publications, 2001), p. 23.
128. *Mizo Hmeichhe Insuihkhawm Pawl Dan Bu* (Constitution)(Aizawl: MHIP General Headquarters), from introduction, p. 1.
129. Dr. T. Vanlaltlani, *op. cit.*, p. 240.
130. *Mizo Women Today* (Aizawl: Tribal Research Institute, 1991), p. 4.
131. Editorial, "MHIP demands legislation for women's rights", *Newslink* (Aizawl), 7 July 2005, p. 1.
132. *Mizo Women Today*, *op. cit.*, p. 5.
133. Dr. Vanlaltlani, *op. cit.*, p. 264.
134. *Mizo Women Today*, *op. cit.*, p. 5.
135. Dr. Vanlaltlani, *op. cit.*, pp. 270-275.
136. *Ibid.*, p. 277.

137. *Ibid.*, p. 121.
138. *Ibid*, pp. 280-284.
139. The Mizoram State Commission for Women Bill, 2004, p. 1.
140. Report of Mizoram State Commission for Women, Aizawl, Mizoram, p. 1.
141. The Mizoram State Commission for Women Bill, 2004, p. 1.
142. Editorial, "Dan Tha awm loh vanga Hmeichhiate tawrhna zirho", *Vanglaini*, Mizo Daily, on June 2, 2005, p. 1.
143. Lalthansangi, *Situational Analysis in the State of Mizoram* (New Delhi: National Commission for Women, 2004) p. 63. Moreover, it organized State Level Awareness Campaign in all the district headquarters and some other interior village, gave gifts to women prisoners, organized Women Commission Week at Vanapa Hall, organized various seminars, workshops, helped raped victims by giving money, making press release at Local Newspapers and Local TV Channels, organized State level consultation meetings. *Ibid.*, pp. 74-78.

# Chapter 16

## Status of Mizo Women
### *Some Reflections*

PADMALAYA MAHAPATRA

### Introduction

Women are coordinate, not just the subordinate half of the human race. The twentieth century has developed the cause of gender justice by internationalizing the struggle for equality. Women's struggle against their subordination and subjugation were intertwined in varying degrees with ideologies and movements based on the values of freedom, self-determination, equality, democracy and justice.

Mizo society is basically patriarchal in nature which is responsible for hyper-masculine bias thereby tending to push the woman to traditional familial roles. As a result patriarchal elites in Mizo society continue to dominate the society and politics till today. Rose J. Lee and Clark emphatically contend that "in almost all societies, women as a whole are forced into subordinate roles and status which is reinforced by a wide array of patriarchal cultures."

### Historical Resume

In the traditional Mizo Society, the father was the head of the family. The power and authority of the patriarch over his children, young or adult was often almost unlimited. In most of the developed communities in which patriarchy flourished, occasionally an individual woman would achieve great fame and even became a ruler. A case in point was the emergence of Ropuiliani who became the

Chief of Denlung after the death of her husband. Vandula had established her hegemony over other surrounding nine villages in South Mizoram in 1995. In a Mizo family in the past a woman enjoyed no right either in the family or in the community.

The following sayings clearly testify the inferior status of mizo women in the traditional society in the past (1) the wisdom of women does not extend beyond the bank of river. (2) Woman (wife) and old fencing can be replaced beyond the bank of the river. (3) Let a women and a dog bark as they like. (4) Women and crab have no religion. Performing religious rites was considered to be the exclusive preserve of the males.

Some of the important traditional social institutions relating to women and Mizo society have been briefly discussed:

### *Nularim vis-à-vis Zawlbuk*

Birth of a female child in a Mizo family is hailed with the same joy as that of a male one. And in her upbringing she was not treated differently from a male child. It was customarily compulsory that a male child on his attaining the age of five or six years was christened to join the 'Zawlbuk', the 'Bachelor's House' (or Dormitory) a social institution at which young boys were placed under discipline till they become grown up boys. On the otherhand a female child who always stays at home helping her parents so that she could make herself more attracted towards her parents and *vice versa*. She is also obliged to sit around the hearth to attend the visiting young boys who turn up almost every evening to spend the time in frolic, chit-chatting reviewing the day's tales, incidents as normal courses of courtship, practice of which still exist as an indispensable institution and is known as 'Nularim' or 'Sawmleng' in Thadou. As a matter of fact it is through the institution of Nularim (Courting of girl), most marriages take place. 'Zawlbuk' is used as an 'intermediary' on 'matchmaker' known as 'Puarak.'

Such social life is no longer popular and is being gradually abandoned due to the acceptance of Christianity and pursuit of knowledge through modern education system. In ancient time in the context of inter-tribal feud this institution was considered indispensable for prompt mobilization on deployment of able young boys for defence.

### *Bride-Price*

In Mizo marriage system payment of bride-price forms an important aspect of the traditional life of the people. In the past glorious days when the traditions of bravery and spirit of adventure were the order of the day, the bride "to be" usually asked for bringing back heads of the enemies as bride-price in addition to the price of 'Mithuns' which he had to pay. Bride-price also constitutes significant factor in Mizo marriage, no marriage can be performed unless part of the bride-price is paid before actual marriage takes place. It is a sacred institution prevalent in Mizo society. Bride-price is not a commercial transaction and it is sometimes used as a weapon for a clever parent to reject a suitor.

Another biasness of Mizo customary law was that a woman could commit adultery either while her husband was alive or even after the death of her husband. If she committed adultery while her husband was alive, the whole of the bride-price paid must be returned to her husband who was also entitled to retain his wife's dowry. If she committed adultery after her husband's death while living in her husband's house, she had to perform compulsorily three ceremonies such as *thlaichhiah, thlahual, mithi chaw pek.*

Thlaichhiah is a sacrificial ceremony for a dead husband. Because it was once believed that the spirit of the slain animal on the occasion might accompany the departed soul to the other world. Another inseparable ceremony is the thlahual which was performed in general for those who grieved too much over their beloved ones in order to prevent their *thla* (soul) from following the spirit of the deceased. But in this particular context, the women's unfaithful behaviour was believed to have disturbed her husband's spirit and the ceremony was usually performed in order to quieten her husband's spirit. It was a kind of expression of deep anguish over her immoral act. When this ceremony was performed, the woman had to remain at her father's house at least three months.

During this period, she was to perform everyday another sacrifice called *mithi chaw pek*—a ceremony of putting aside a portion of the food the woman was to eat at each meal for her dead husband.

### *Marriage*

Before the advent of Christianity, Lushai customs, marriage and divorce were easily contracted without any religious sanction. In the selection of life partner for their children mizo parents exercise utmost care and solemnity. The parents carefully enquire not only into the character and accomplishments of the prospective bridegroom of the bride to-be but also into his or her pedigree, reputation of the parents, grandparents and the earlier ancestors. Marriage takes place on the basis of payment of bride-price and a man may marry any girl who is no too closely related to him. The exogamous group in mizo society is limited to a small group of relatives.

Marriage between first cousins is not encouraged though in the case of Sailo clan/family, such type of marriage is allowed for the advantages secured during the days of inter-village feuds.

There were several ways of divorce leading to termination of marriage in traditional Mizo society (by simply returning the bride-price, by mutual agreement etc.) or one had to simply say to his wife "ka ma che" meaning "I divorce you". When divorced a woman could not claim ownership of the children. She had no rightful claim over the properties in the family except the thuam (dowry) she had brought at the time of her marriage.

### *Law of Inheritance*

A daughter has no share in the property of her father. Her responsibility is to become a true housewife. On the contrary, a boy is taught his duties and responsibilities towards his village and community from childhood. His life in youth is mostly regulated by the discipline of "Zawlbuk" and within a year of his marriage if he has his first baby he is allowed to stay in a separate house. Similarly, the second, third, fourth and all other sons except the youngest settles down in the same manner after marriage. The youngest son is left to look after the parents and is also the inheritor of his father's property including the ancestral home. But this custom has changed when the British Government considered the traditional law of inheritance as inconsistent with British and Christian doctrines. As a result the eldest son is made the heir of the parents' property. In more recent times the District Council has introduced a far reaching change whereby a daughter may now be said to enjoy equal rights and privileges with the brother (Lalbiakthanga, 1978). As per Mizo society Law of Inheritance, property cannot descend to a woman except in trust of her children. But if there were no male with a better claim a woman may inherit and she would do so before people belonging to the same clan as the deceased, unless they had some other claimant to the estate beyond their clan relationship.

**Changes in the Status of Mizo Women**

During 1902-03, three temporary Girls' School were opened one at Hriangmual, another at Thakthing and third at Rahsi Veng. These Schools were run by Nui, Saii and Pawngi had 6 girls on the rolls. The three attended the Aizawl Mission School during the day time, and took their own classes after their return to the village.

Soon after her marriage, in December 1903 with the Rev. D.E. Jones, Mrs. K.E. Jones who had already been working at Sylhet for 7 years, started her work among the Mizo women and in 1904 she opened the first regular Girls' School with 12 girls at Aizawl. The existing mission school was then converted to a Boys' School. Besides the usual course in the school, she convened women's meetings where she taught sewing, knitting, simple medication, sanitation and child care. She ran the mission girls' school alone until 2 Mizo girls joined in 1909.

Rev. D.E. Jones, Honorary Inspector of Schools in the North took personal interest in giving education to more chief's daughters, as they were allowed to rule over their villages when they become widows or separated from their husbands.

The prejudice existing among the Mizos against female education had to a great extent declined by this time and the Mission Girls' School had been put on a sound footing. Knowing her limit, and also having an extra duty of a house-wife, Mrs. Jones in 1912, applied to the Welsh Mission authorities for a lady teacher from whom to take charge of the girls' education. Accordingly, the Directors in Liverpool appointed Miss. Francis, B.A. for this purpose in 1913. But before she sailed, word reached the Directors that the Government did not approve of the fast growth of education of girls in Mizoram and consequently Miss. Francis did not come.

Mr. J. Hezlett, who was the Superintendent of Lushai Hills from 1913-1917 was highly pleased at the work of Mrs. Jones and felt pity at the decision of the Government. To him female Education was the urgent need of the Mizos. In his letter to the Commissioner, Surma Valley and the Hill Districts, in 1916, he pointed out emphatically the importance of starting female education on the right lines. He further stated that female education in Mizoram was not yet seriously taken into consideration.

Supporting the application of Mrs. Jones for a lady missionary, the Inspector of Schools, Surma Valley and Hills District, Mr. F.B. Wilkins, wrote to the DPI Assam, in 1915, thus: "the Authorities of the Welsh Missionary might be given to understand that the sending of a lady to Aizawl for this school would be welcomed". In his inspection report Wilkins noted that he was very impressed by the performance of the Mission Girls' School, Aizawl, and remarked that the school did an excellent work. As a result of these exertions the government finally granted, in 1916, the permission for entry of lady missionary into Mizoram.

The first batch came to Mizoram in 1919. They were Miss. Edith M. Chapman of Catford, a trained teacher, and Miss Oliver E. Dicks of Chaltenham, a trained Nurse and Midwife. Three years later Miss. A. Catherine Mostoyn Lewis came to Aizawl in November 1922. These were the people that brought a real change with women in the Mizo society.

The first experience of the lady missionaries was that the menfolk did not want to have their girls educated for, they said, the women and the girls were destined to do the household work. "Who would do it if they were educated?" was the argument of menfolk. They also argued that women had no mind and they could not learn anything, so it was no use trying to bother for their education. Besides, no young man would marry an educated girl. The educated women and the girls should be left alone. Some of the menfolk boldly told the lady missionaries that no one had asked for women missionaries, and no one wanted them. There would never be a girls' school in their country.

To the Missionaries and the Government the object of female education should be to enable them to perform their domestic duties more efficiently, with greater comfort to their families and to themselves, and at the same time to give them a broader outlook in life so that they might lead a happier and more useful life. To them education which would make the girls unfit for their domestic duties or give them a distaste for such duties must be avoided at all costs. Therefore, the missionaries introduced cooking, embroidery, sewing, spinning, knitting, child care, needle-work, simple hygiene and sanitation, in addition to learning to read and write. With the introduction of the new education system there were sweeping changes in the value system in the Mizo society.

The educated women formed Mizo Hmeichhia Insuihkhawm Pawl (MHIP), a popular women's non-religious and non-political organization committed to work for the welfare and emancipation of women folk in Mizo society as well as combating the social evils like drinking and drug addiction. MHIP is also keen on eradicating commercialization of bride-price, the dowry system, sexual exploitation of women and inequality between men and women.

As the Salvation Army became established so women were given leadership responsibilities. Some were sent to open new corps, others started social work among the women of the streets. Emma Booth was responsible for training women cadets. By 1878 there were nearly an equal number of women officers (41) and there were men officers (49).

Within a few years of establishing work in India the Army's leaders in India recognized the necessity of training to Indian women for the responsibilities of officership. The project was considered impossible by most Indians and westerners. Indian women would not think of engaging in public work, nor would their families allow them to do so. Only two or three exceptional women had become officers. But despite the difficulties it was decided to make the experiment in South India, and, Captain Clara Case was chosen to open a training college in Madras. In 1890 the first session was started with twelve women cadets and Nurani (Captain Case) as their principal. The cadets spent time in study and in visitation, prayer and open-air meetings. Once some of the women were put to prison for playing their tambourines in public. But these women were commissioned as Salvation Army Officers. The impossible had become a splendid experience, and since then thousands of women have followed their example, many as wives and some occupying positions of responsibility them. Nurani later appealed for more women candidates.

The mizo society being patriarchal, patrilocal and patrilineal, domestic violence is a silent crime which many suffer throughout their life. The society itself refrains from interfering when it comes to family matters. "There are a number of incidents where a husband killed his wife but the neighbours refused to intervene and prevent it" (*Source*: Local Records of NGO working for Human Rights).

MHIP in its 6th special assembly held at on 11-11-2006 demanded the Mizoram Government to introduce the "Protection of Women from Domestic Violence Act, 2005" in Mizoram. It has also voiced concern over the "prevalent" rape cases in Mizoram.

Socially and economically, Mizo women are now enjoying an honoured place. But in terms of their political participation they are still lagging behind their male counterparts. On the whole women representation in political decision-making process is abysmally low in the whole of Asia. In a state which boasts of nearly 87 per cent female literacy there are only four women among the 192 candidates contesting the assembly poll on November 20, 2003. The ruling Mizo National Front had no woman candidate. The Congress had one candidate while Zoram Nationalist Party has fielded two. There were as many as eight women contestants in the 1998 assembly elections. In the opinion of a former Chief Minister and Congress leader Lalthanhawla, "the state's history has shown that they have failed to get any response from the electorate although every party would ideally like to give some tickets to women." This is a state in which women outnumber men in 26 of the 40 constituencies. Since Mizoram attained statehood in 1987 only one woman has been elected. Lalhlimpuii was made a minister in the Laldenga ministry during 1987-88 when the MNF had formed the government.

Mizo Women's federation has urged the church leaders to accommodate qualified women theologians as pastors and elect women as elders. Till today the churches including the Presbyterian Church do not accommodate women as pastors on church elders.

## Conclusion

In the final analysis overall democratization of Mizo's socio-economic and political structures can be expected to promote women's empowerment and emancipation. A key instrument to promote women's participation in the development process not just as beneficiaries but as active agents of change is what is normally referred to as grassroots level organizations of women. In India two strategies had been articulated in the early years after independence to achieve women's involvement in public life. The first process was as voters and candidates. The case of rural areas and the Panchayats which were established as grassroots bodies to develop democratic decentralization, it was presumed that women may not be returned through normal electoral process a provision was made for co-opting or nominating one or two women into these bodies in case they failed to come through normal election. The second model of Mahila Mandals or village level women's organizations those developed under the Community Development Programme in the 1950s had declined its credibility over the years. The implementation policy of reservation of women in legislative bodies of Mizoram is the need of the hour. The enhanced political representation will enable Mizo women to increase their political power so that they can have more equitable share in the decision-making process of society.

Only democratization and empowerment can provide a Mizo women an avenue through which she can continue her long journey towards her total emancipation. To be more specific, two political mechanisms may be considered in this regard: increased proportional representation of women in all elected bodies and fixation of a certain quota of "offices therein and increased political activities by autonomous women's bodies. So that a Mizo women can play a very effective role as a decision-maker and can be successful to bring about a revolutionary change in the social, political, economic, psychological, moral and cultural angles of the Mizo society.

## REFERENCES

K.P. Nath, Education and Change with the Women in Mizo Society, *Journal of Social Sciences and Humanities*, North Eastern Hill University, Vol. IX, No.2, April-June, 1991.

Lal Dena, States of Mizo Women, *The Sangai Express*, February 8, 2003.

P.K. Bandyopadhyay, *Leadership among the Mizos,* Delhi, B.R. Publishing Corporation, 1985.

Priyadarshini M. Gangte, *Impact of Christianity on Mizo Society*, www.manipuronline.com

S.N. Singh, *Mizoram: Historical, Geographical, Social, Economic, Political and Administrative,* New Delhi, Mittal, 1994.

Sangkima, "Women and Politics in Mizoram Through the Ages" published in *Essays on the History of the Mizos*, Guwahati, Spectrum Publications, 2004.

# Chapter 17

## Gender and Economic Development in Mizoram
### *A Study of Female Work Participation*

LALHRIATPUII

### Introduction

A country can achieve a high rate of economic development through the best and the fullest use of its resources. In a developing country like India, burdened with a huge population, an ideal strategy would be to utilize its human resources to the maximum for rapid economic growth of the nation. This would necessitate optimum participation of women in the various sectors of economic activity[1]. The development of an economy cannot only be measured in terms of GDP, per capita income and wage but it needs to be seen also in terms of effective participation and utilization of the capabilities of both men and women as an effective human resource potential[2]. In this context, the economic role of women cannot be isolated from the total framework of development. Equal participation of women is a pre-condition for the development of not only the women but also the country as a whole.

### Female Work Participation Rate (FWPR) in Mizoram

Women in Mizoram constitute almost 49 per cent of the total population with almost 43.7 per cent of the total female population working according to 2001 census. Majority of the population are engaged in the informal sector and therefore are subjected to the discrepancies, which exists in the labour market. Traditional handicrafts, like weaving and bamboo works occupy a prominent place next to agriculture. In Mizoram the impact of the developmental activities on women during the post-independence period is significant. The role and status of women in Mizoram have undergone notable changes with improvement in literacy and awareness that comes along with development and change in the social and economic life. Yet inequality of status persists in different aspects of economic, social and family life. Inadequate employment opportunities compel women to concentrate in the unorganized sector and women lag behind men in employment in salaried jobs and in sectors, which involves decision-making and exercising power.

**Table 17.1:** Work Participation Rate

| Year | Detail | India | | | Mizoram | | |
|---|---|---|---|---|---|---|---|
| | | Number | %WPR | AG% | Number | %WPR | AG% |
| | TW | 186405113 | 32.91 | — | 149576 | 45.61 | — |
| 1971 | FW | 36711290 | 19.69 | — | 65843 | 44.02 | — |
| | MW | 149693823 | 52.50 | — | 83733 | 55.98 | — |
| | TW | 251455499 | 36.8 | 3.49 | 224364 | 45.44 | 5.0 |
| 1981 | FW | 49788188 | 19.8 | 3.56 | 97823 | 43.6 | 4.86 |
| | MW | 201667311 | 51.09 | 3.47 | 126541 | 56.4 | 5.11 |
| | TW | 314121370 | 37.6 | 2.49 | 337360 | 48.91 | 5.04 |
| 1991 | FW | 89767563 | 22.05 | 8.03 | 151205 | 44.82 | 5.46 |
| | MW | 224363807 | 51.08 | 1.13 | 186155 | 55.18 | 4.71 |
| | TW | 401289511 | 39.1 | 2.77 | 467159 | 52.6 | 3.85 |
| 2001 | FW | 126802251 | 31.59 | 4.13 | 204151 | 43.70 | 3.50 |
| | MW | 274487260 | 68.40 | 2.23 | 263008 | 56.29 | 4.13 |

*WPR* : Work Participation Rate
*AG %* : Annual Growth with reference to last available record
*TW* : Total Worker,
FW : Female Worker.
*MW* : Male Worker: Not Available.
*Note* : Saiha District 1981 and 1991 are undivided, i.e. Chhimtuipui district record. 2001 is Saiha District record.
*Source*: Census Reports 1971, 1981, 1991 and 2001 (India and Mizoram), Statistical Hand Book 1981 (Chhhimtuipui District).

Female population constitutes a strong force in Mizoram and the proportion of female workers in work participation show an improving trend like the rest of India. The latest census reveals that work participation in Mizoram is much higher than India. The total work participation in Mizoram is 52.6 per cent as against 39.1 per cent in India. The FWPR, according to the 2001 census is 43.7 per cent as against 31.59 per cent in India for the same period. MWPR in Mizoram during 2001 census was 56.29 per cent as against 68.4 per cent in India.

There has been an increase in the proportion of total workers through India and Mizoram this could be due to an absolute increase in the number of male and female workers in all the areas respectively. Increase in female workers during this period may be counted for a growth in the literacy rate between the period 1971 to 2001 and also due to a greater social awareness among the people to seek monetary value for the services rendered.

**FWPR: A Prognostication to Determine the Factors**

An attempt has been made in this study to introduce the variables, identify their importance and examine their effect on the work participation of women in Mizoram. Consequently, the combined effect of the variables has been examined to determine their overall effect and influence on the work participation of females.

One major part of the work has been the collection and treatment of the primary data, which have been obtained from the districts of Aizawl, Lunglei and Saiha. The districts have been divided into rural and urban areas. For the rural areas, three villages have been selected on the basis of random sampling. For the urban areas, three localities have been taken into consideration.

Total sample size happens to be 390, Aizawl district contributing a major share of 159 samples followed by Lunglei district and Saiha district with 126 samples and 105 samples respectively. Questionnaires have been sent to the respondents to obtain the required information necessary for our study. Information has also been obtained through the method of personal enquiry by the researcher. The information obtained has been collected using multi-staged stratified random sampling. And has been classified, tabulated and analysed and fitted into regression models.

These models attempt to examine the relationship between the Work Participation and female literacy, sex ratio, male literacy and two forms of individual behaviour, i.e. freedom of decision making of females and attitude of male towards Female Work, which are assumed to affect the participation rate.

Let us first introduce the model represented by the equation—
Model: WF = $a + b1$LitF ...(1)

where WF represents FWPR and LitF represents female literacy rate.

Testing the model with the help of the primary data reveals that there exists a positive relationship between female literacy and work participation. Higher the level of literacy, higher is also the rate of participation. This supports the Human Capital theory, which confirms that schooling leads to acquisition of productivity related skills, which increase productivity and therefore wages. In other words, Human Capital and screening theories both predict significantly higher earnings for the better educated. The degree of literacy among women is an important factor in their appreciation of their legal rights and in widening the range of possibilities for employment.[3] But the radical Marxism theorists confirm that there are significant differences in rates of return to education both for individual and between the sexes and racial groups.[4]

The results based on the model 1 are indicated in the table below:

**Table 17.2:** Model: WF = $a + b1$LitF

| *Sl. No.* | *Areas* | *a1* | *b1* | *F* | *R2* |
|---|---|---|---|---|---|
| 1. | Mizoram | -14.68 (14.90) | 0.613 (0.163) | 14.18 | 0.47 |
| 2. | Aizawl District | -250.01 (78.58) | 3.014 (0.81) | 13.84 | 0.776 |
| 3. | Lunglei District | -135.28 (74.69) | 1.97 (0.84) | 5.56 | 0.58 |
| 4. | Saiha District | -81.82 (43.28) | 1.46 (0.52) | 8.05 | 0.67 |

Figures in the parentheses indicate the Standard errors.

(i) $F_{1, 16}(0.05) = 4.49$, (ii) $F_{1, 4}(0.05) = 7.71$.

*Source*: Field Survey.

The model is acceptable both on theoretical and statistical accounts. The coefficient of determination between WPR and female literacy rate is 47 per cent for Mizoram and ranges from 58 per cent to 77 per cent for the other three districts as revealed by R2. The regression coefficients are statistically significant and have the required signs. Higher the literacy rate higher is the FWPR in Aizawl and Saiha districts as well as for Mizoram as a whole.

The correlation between LitF and FWPR emerges to be highest in case of Aizawl district which is 77.6 per cent. This relationship is further supported by primary data analysis where Aizawl records the highest percentage of female literacy (96.4%). This is possible due to high growth of literacy in the town and the various villages in the districts. With the increase in literacy women in this area are more aware to pursue a better chance in the labour market. Though this reflects a positive trend, yet a larger share of women participation remains in the unorganised sector of the labour market. Therefore, the increase in participation is mostly concentrated in the rural sector, which presents a slightly gloomy picture of gender discrimination and inequalities. However, taking an overall picture of the area and its constituent units, it is revealed that all the three districts show almost similar pattern of relationship between female literacy and their participation rates.

The statistical validity of the model prompts us to conclude that the growth of literacy among females has a strong influence in determining their effective participation in the wage market. With regard to education, women certainly are at a disadvantageous position than men. The low rate of female literacy in India is due to the low rates of females' involvement in education and high incidence of retention.[5] It thus emerges that education can be an important factor in promoting individual participation as it may be mentioned further that along with literacy, awareness, aspiration and desire to earn also develop, creating a window to the outside world.

Sex ratio or the number of females per thousand males is an important factor to determine the growth of female population over the years. Various academic discussions have given credence to the fact that in cultures where woman was allowed to work outside home either in own farm or as paid labour, the female neglect and discard was relatively low. As a result the next model we have tested is as follows:

Model: $WF = a + b2SR$ ...(2)

where, SR represents Sex Ratio.

Sex ratio determines WF in Mizoram and the results as indicated in Table 17.3 reveals that the model is acceptable on statistical grounds. R2 is 46 per cent in Mizoram as a whole. In Lunglei and Saiha districts the model is acceptable and significant. Even in Aizawl district though F is 6.901, R2 is 63 per cent, i.e. to a great extent variability of WF is also determine by sex ratio. The sign of the coefficient is also negative in case of Aizawl district. This could be indicative of the fact that in absence of sufficient growth of employment opportunities in the district, a higher growth of female population lowers the chances of additional females being employed; hence participation rate does not increase proportionately. In Lunglei and Saiha district, the lack of diversification of the economy of the district and over concentration of female population in agriculture are the two basic reasons which could explain a positive correlation between sex ratio and FWPR.

**Table 17.3:** Model: WF = a + b2SR

| *Sl. No.* | *Areas* | *a* | *b2* | *F* | *R2* |
|---|---|---|---|---|---|
| 1. | Mizoram | -157.31 (54.27) | 0.205 (0.056) | 13.41 | 0.46 |
| 2. | Aizawl District | -504.67 (208.25) | 0.562 (0.214) | 6.901 | 0.63 |
| 3. | Lunglei District | -94.3 (38.17) | 0.14 (0.04) | 12.56 | 0.76 |
| 4. | Saiha District | -216.46 (96.18) | 0.27 (0.1) | 7.17 | 0.64 |

Figures in the parentheses indicate the Standard errors.

(i) F1, 16(0.05) = 4.49, (ii) F1, 4(0.05) = 7.71.

*Source*: Field Survey.

Combining the two independent variables LitF and SR we have tried to examine whether these two variables taken jointly increase the explanatory power of the independent variables. We, therefore, test the next model, which is as follows:

Model: WF = $a + b1$LitF + $b2$SR ...(3)

**Table 17.4:** Model: WF = $a + b1$LitF + $b2$SR

| *Sl. No.* | *Areas* | *a* | *b1* | *b2* | *F* | *R2* |
|---|---|---|---|---|---|---|
| 1. | Mizoram | -152.89 (57.08) | 0.056 (0.152) | 0.196 (0.064) | 6.41 | 0.46 |
| 2. | Aizawl District | -533.91 (148.188) | 1.448 (0.650) | 0.45 (0.16) | 9.345 | 0.86 |
| 3. | Lunglei District | -181.7 (20.17) | 1.31 (0.24) | 0.11 (0.15) | 65.4 | 0.99 |
| 4. | Saiha District | -211.35 65.45) | 0.997 (0.42) | 0.18 (0.08) | 10.56 | 0.88 |

Figures in the parentheses indicate the Standard errors.

(i) F2, 15(0.05) = 3.29, (ii) F2, 3(0.05) = 9.55.

*Source*: Field Survey.

The results as revealed in Table 17.4 indicate that this model can also be accepted.

R2 has increased in this model with respect to model 1. The relationship is highly significant in Lunglei and Saiha districts and also in Mizoram as a whole. In Aizawl district the relationship is not significant but R2 is quite high indicating the presence of multi co-linearity between LitF and SR in the district.

Freedom to take decision in family matters automatically entrusts some degree of authority to the person who takes decision. Some sociologists point out that it is poverty or dire economic necessity, and not the social patriarchal order, which confers power and entrusts women to take decisions to work. In other words, it is poverty and economic necessity, which affords freedom to a woman to decide her entry into wage market. The ability to take independent decision appears to be more common in urban than in the rural areas. On the other hand, feminists argue that patriarchal society demands that women are expected to obey rather than discuss. Regardless of the extent to which society tolerates the making or influencing of decision by women, their overt role in community village or other unit is usually minimal. Consequently, we specify the next model as follows:

$$\text{Model:WF} = a + b3\text{DF} \qquad \text{....(4)}$$

where DF represents freedom of decision making of females.

**Table 17.5:** Model: WF = a + b3DF

| *Sl. No.* | *Areas* | *a* | *b3* | *F* | *R2* |
|---|---|---|---|---|---|
| 1. | Mizoram | -14.68 (14.90) | 0.613 (0.163) | 14.18 | 0.47 |
| 2. | Aizawl District | -18.51 (19.25) | 0.663 (0.21) | 10.02 | 0.72 |
| 3. | Lunglei District | 29.57 (59.54) | 0.12 (0.65) | 0.036 | 0.009 |
| 4. | Saiha District | 0.844 (68.28) | 0.44 (0.74) | 0.34 | 0.08 |

Figures in the parentheses indicate the Standard errors.

(i) F1, 16(0.05) = 4.49, (ii) F1, 4(0.05) = 7.71

*Source*: Field Survey.

In this model it has been observed that in Mizoram 47 per cent of FWPR can be explained by the autonomy of taking decision by women. The coefficients relating to decision making for Mizoram as well as Aizawl district are statistically significant, and also possess their required signs. But the relationship of the model is not acceptable in Lunglei and Saiha districts. The position seems to be the best in Aizawl district where decision making of females has influenced 72 per cent of the FWPR.

Since female literacy and freedom of decision making of females seems to have a significant impact on FWPR, and in view of the acceptable of both the functions, we have included LitF and DF in the next model, which is as follows:

Model: WF = $a$ + $b$1LitF + $b$3DF ...(5)

**Table 17.6:** Model: WF = $a$ + $b$1LitF + $b$3DF

| *Sl. No.* | *Areas* | *a* | *b1* | *b3* | *F* | *R2* |
|---|---|---|---|---|---|---|
| 1. | Mizoram | -33<br>(17.39) | 0.22<br>(0.125) | 0.596<br>(0.153) | 9.62 | 0.56 |
| 2. | Aizawl District | -157.95<br>(15.02) | 1.55<br>(0.16) | 0.57<br>(0.044) | 166.05 | 0.99 |
| 3. | Lunglei District | -144.55<br>(95.63) | 1.97<br>(0.96) | 0.11<br>(0.49) | 2.144 | 0.59 |
| 4. | Saiha District | -81.52<br>(59.31) | 1.46<br>(0.64 | -0.005<br>(0.551) | 3.02 | 0.67 |

Figures in the parentheses indicate the Standard errors.
(i) F2, 15(0.05) = 3.29, (ii) F2, 3(0.05) = 9.55.
*Source*: Field Survey.

Examining jointly the effect of the variables, in the model we find that predictive value of the function now ranges from 56 per cent in Mizoram and 99 per cent in case of Aizawl district. This is indicated in Table 17.6. The F test as also found to be significant. Though the value of the partial regression co-efficient has gone down, in comparison to their individual function, yet they are all statistically significant and possess the necessary signs as well, hence the model can be accepted for Mizoram and Aizawl district. In Aizawl district the combined effect of the variables literacy and decision of the females to work stand out as a strong explanatory variable in determining the participation of women in the labour market. The high literacy rate could be a strong casual factor explaining this behaviour.

The attitude of males towards women's work play a significant role in deciding a women's entry or exit from the labour market, particularly in a patriarchal society. In most societies, men express their positive attitude towards women's work provided the façade of male dominance is maintained. In recent years, in urban societies, with the necessity of dual earners, men display a positive attitude towards women's work unlike in more rural and/or conservative societies where tradition, social custom, and/or religious beliefs dictate males' expression of resentment towards allowing women to work outside the household.

Taking these entire factors into account we tried the following model:

Model: WF = $a$ + $b$4MA ....(6)

where, MA represents male attitude towards female work participation.

**Table 17.7:** Model: WF = a + b4MA

| *Sl. No.* | *Areas* | *a* | *b4* | *F* | *R2* |
|---|---|---|---|---|---|
| 1. | Mizoram | -13.92 (18.28) | 0.618 (0.204) | 9.17 | 0.36 |
| 2. | Aizawl District | -51.73 (2.84) | 1.072 (0.032) | 1099.38 | 0.996 |
| 3. | Lunglei District | -94.3 (38.17) | 0.14 (0.04) | 12.56 | 0.76 |
| 4. | Saiha District | 29.446 (34.57) | 0.13 (0.38) | 0.11 | 0.03 |

*Source*: Field Survey.

The results of the model reveals (Table 17.7) that since the explanatory power of the variable now ranges from 36 per cent in case of Mizoram, 99 per cent in case of Aizawl district and 76 per cent in case of Lunglei District and the regression coefficient too has got necessary signs and is also statistically significant, the function is acceptable on all accounts and therefore, we may conclude that male attitude plays a typical behavioural attitude of a patriarchal society.

The next regression model tested is as follow:

Model: WF = $a$ + $b$1LitF + $b$3DF + $b$4MA ....(7)

In this model we have introduced the three independent variables LitF, DF and MA jointly into the function to examine their total impact on FWPR.

**Table 17.8:** Model: WF = a + b1LitF + b3DF + b4 MA

| *Sl. No.* | *Areas* | *a* | *b1* | *b3* | *b4* | *F* | *R2* |
|---|---|---|---|---|---|---|---|
| 1. | Mizoram | -48.97<br>(19.596) | 0.263<br>(0.123) | 0.372<br>(0.2060 | 0.366<br>(0.237) | 7.796 | 0.63 |
| 2. | Aizawl District | -68.94<br>(17.63) | 0.235<br>(0.256) | 0.0103<br>(0.11) | 0.001<br>(0.19) | 1098.32 | 0.999 |
| 3. | Lunglei District | -85.13<br>(58.08) | 3.09<br>(0.68) | 0.38<br>(0.29) | -2.03<br>(0.74) | 6.99 | 0.91 |
| 4. | Saiha District | -79.39<br>(71.97) | 1.5<br>(0.78) | -0.17<br>(0.94) | 0.11<br>(0.44) | 1.4 | 0.68 |

Figures in the parentheses indicate the Standard errors.

(i) F3, 14(0.05) = 3.29, (ii) F3, 2(0.05) = 19.2.

*Source*: Field Survey.

The results are shown in Table 17.8. The predictive value of the function has increased, as is evident from the increase in the value of R2 in all the cases of Mizoram as well as the three districts. The explanatory power now ranges from 99 per cent in case of Aizawl, 91 per cent for Lunglei, 68 per cent for Saiha and 63 per cent for Mizoram as a whole. Though the value of the coefficients of LitF, DF and MA is reduced, their statistical significance is maintained. The model, therefore, is significant for Mizoram as a whole and Aizawl district but is not significant for Lunglei and Saiha districts. But as mentioned above, R2 is high for the two districts indicating the presence of multi-colinearity. Though multi co-linearity is not unusual in case of such economic variables yet the seriousness of the problem in this model induce us to reject this function for the districts of Saiha and Lunglei.

In a typically patriarchal society, male literacy rate moulds the male attitude and hence this in turn may affect FWPR. We have, therefore, tried the next model incorporating the literacy of males as an independent variable as follows:

Model: WF = a + b5LitM ....(8)

where, LitM represents the male literacy.

The estimated results (Table 17.9) reveal that the explanatory power of the variable goes down as R2 is now only 0.156 for Mizoram and extremely low for Saiha district as well. The function, therefore, is unacceptable for Mizoram as a whole and for the individual district of Saiha, indicating that male literacy plays an insignificant role in determining FWPR. But the function is significant in Aizawl and Lunglei districts, where R2 is as high as 78 per cent in Aizawl and 71 per cent in Lunglei. This shows that male literacy do have a strong influence on FWPR in the two districts. Perhaps males in these two districts are liberal in their views and open to the ideas of female involvement in work outside the household.

**Table 17.9:** Model: WF = *a* + *b*5LitM

| *Sl. No.* | *Areas* | *a* | *b5* | *F* | *R2* |
|---|---|---|---|---|---|
| 1. | Mizoram | 9.52 (18.54) | 0.346 (0.201) | 2.963 | 0.156 |
| 2. | Aizawl District | -250.01 (78.58) | 3.014 (0.81) | 13.84 | 0.776 |
| 3. | Lunglei District | -129.72 (55.19) | 1.86 (0.6) | 9.56 | 0.71 |
| 4. | Saiha District | -92.21 (61.48) | 1.5 (0.77) | 4.69 | 0.54 |

Figures in the parentheses indicate the Standard errors.

(i) F1, 16(0.05) = 4.49, (ii) F1,4(0.05) = 7.71.

*Source*: Field Survey.

However, to test whether introduction of this independent variable of LitM along with other independent variables discussed above, increases the explanatory power of the function, we then present the final model as follows:

$$\text{Model: WF} = a + b1\text{LitF} + b3\text{DF} + b4\text{ MA} + b5\text{LitM} \quad \ldots(9)$$

In comparison to model 7, where we had introduced LitF, DF and MA jointly; we have now introduced LitM as another additional variable to assess the explanatory power of the function. The results are provided in Table 17.10.

The explanatory power of the variable has not improved in comparison to previous model. The function is significant for Mizoram as a whole and Aizawl district alone. R2 also improves for Mizoram and Aizawl district. In case of Lunglei district R2 also improves to 92 per cent yet the negative sign of the coefficient compels us to reject the function. In case of Saiha district R2 also improves to 77 per cent but the coefficient is insignificant, though the sign do not change. Hence the function cannot be accepted as satisfactory model of determination of FWPR in Lunglei and Saiha districts.

**Table 17.10:** Model: WF = $a + b1$LitF + $b3$DF + $b4$ MA + $b5$LitM

| *Sl. No.* | *Areas* | *a* | *b1* | *b3* | *b4* | *b5* | *F* | *R2* |
|---|---|---|---|---|---|---|---|---|
| 1. | Mizoram | -50.38<br>(22.99) | 0.159<br>(0.801) | 0.364<br>(0.222) | 0.363<br>(0.247) | 0.126<br>(0.965) | 5.44 | 0.626 |
| 2. | Aizawl District | -103.39<br>(37.56) | 0.449<br>(0.326) | 0.153<br>(0.173) | 0.702<br>(0.345) | 0.280<br>(0.27) | 852.39 | 0.99 |
| 3. | Lunglei District | -73.87<br>(85.53) | 4.61<br>(4.79) | 0.38<br>(0.39) | -2.48<br>(1.7) | -1.15<br>(3.55) | 2.92 | 0.92 |
| 4. | Saiha District | -102.42<br>(93.82) | 0.47<br>(1.89) | -0.57<br>(1.3) | -0.16<br>(0.69) | 1.95<br>(3.12) | 0.83 | 0.77 |

Figures in the parentheses indicate the Standard errors.

(i) $F4, 13(0.05) = 3.01$, (ii) $F4,1(0.05) = 225$.

*Source*: Field Survey.

The overall conclusion that may be derived is that the best fit of the function is represented by model 7 (involving female literacy, decision making of women and attitude of males towards female work) in case of Aizawl district as well as Mizoram as a whole. In case of Lunglei and Saiha districts, however, among all the models, model 3 (involving female literacy and sex ratio) seems to be the most acceptable function determining the FWPR in these districts.

## Conclusion

In the overall analysis it could be said that the best predictors of female labour force participation in Mizoram as a whole are female literacy, freedom to work for women, sex ratio and attitude of males towards female work. Male literacy does not hold any significant role in predicting the behaviour of women work participation.

In the case of Saiha and Lunglei districts, the best predictors of female labour force participation are female literacy and sex ratio. The attitude of males towards female work and male literacy does not play any significant role in predicting the behaviour of women participation in the labour market.

In Aizawl district, the best predictors of Female Work Participation are female literacy, decision making of women, male attitude towards females work and male literacy. Sex ratio does not hold any significant role in predicting the behaviour of women work participation in the district.

Literacy has a strong influence on work participation and this is evident from our primary field data, which shows that in all the three districts and Mizoram as a whole there exists a high literacy rate, which is followed by high participation rate. Feminists, however, argue that even with growing literacy women's subordinate status is rooted in private property and a society smeared with sexist ideology structure.[6] Consequently, the predominant role of the patriarchal society can still be not ruled out altogether.

The pattern of low female work participation as compared to male as examined in Mizoram is consistent with the character of gender relations in different parts of the country. The north western states are distinguished for their highly unregulated gender relations and distribution of work patters between males and females. High literacy rate, which is a characteristic feature of the state of Kerela, also has distinguishing history of a liberated society. This has in return enhanced the social standing of women in the state and has brought about significant changes in terms of social achievements, less unequal gender relations, less patriarchal kinship systems, less male dominated property rights and greater prominence of women in influential social, political and economic activities. Similarly, the rapid transformation of the women of South Korea and China brought about by enhancing the educational status of women and equipping them with necessary training skill has created a transformation in the participation of women in the economic sphere. The success of these states and countries could be taken as an example to illuminate the social standing and position of the women of Mizoram, which also dominates in aspects of literacy among females and high sex ratio. These regional contrasts provide a useful means of investigation in different aspects of women's participation in the area and these experiences are but important lessons to emulate and adopt them in practice.

## NOTES

1. Bagchi, J. (1995). *Indian Women Myth and Reality*, Sangam Books, Hyderabad.
2. John E. Mary (1996). Gender and Development in India, 1970-1990s some reflections on the constitutive role of contents, *EPW*.
3. Dixit, Maitreya (1998). *Women and Achievement Dynamics of Participation and Partnership*, Kanishka Publishers, New Delhi.
4. King, K.E. (1972, 1990). *Labour Economics*, McMillan Press Ltd.

5. Thappar, Meenakshi (1997). "Linkages between Cultures, Education and Women's Health in Urban Status", *EPW*, Oct. 25,1997, Vol. XXXII, No. 43.
6. Desai, Neera and Krishnaraj, Maithreyi (1987). *Women and Society in India*, Ajanta, New Delhi.

## REFERENCES

Acharya, N. (1981). 'Women Workers in the Organised and Unorgainsed Sectors in India', *Indian Worker*, Vol. 29. No. 23.

Anthuvan, V.L. (1981). Discrimination agains Women Workers, *Southern Economist*, Vol. 20 (2).

Bagchi, J. (1995). *Indian Women Myth and Reality*, Sangam Books, Hyderabad.

Banu, Zenab (2001). *Tribal Women Empowerment and Gender Issues*, Kaniska Publication, New Delhi.

Bose, A. (1971). Census Figures Reveals Discrimination against Women's Organiser, *The Indian Labour Journal*, Vol. 24, No. 39.

Desai, Neera and Krishnaraj, Maithreyi (1987). *Women and Society in India*, Ajanta, New Delhi.

Dholakia, B.H. and Dholakia, R.H. (1978). Inter State Variation in Female Labour Force Participation Rates, *Indian Journal of Labour Economics*, Vol. XX, No. 4.

Dixit, Maitreya (1998). *Women and Achievement Dynamics of Participation and Partnership*, Kanishka Publishers, New Delhi.

Encyclopaedia of Social Change (2000). *Women's Participation at the Grassroots Level*, vol. 5, Anmol Publications Pvt. Ltd., New Delhi.

Fong M.S. (1982). 'Measuring Women's Work in Agriculture', Seminar Paper, Institute of Social Studies, New Delhi.

Frances I. Jeanne (1994). Working and Living for the Family, Gender, Work and Education, *Indian Journal of Gender Studies*. Vol. 1, No. 1.

Gulati, Leela (1975). Female Work Participation: A Study of Inter-State Differences, *Economics and Political Weekly*, Vol. X, Nos. 1&2 January.

Guy Standing (1981). *Labour Force Participation and Development*, ILO, Geneva.

Hill, A.M., (1983). Female Labour Participation in Japan: An Aggregate Model, *The Journal of Human Resources*, Vol. 19, No. 2.

John E. Mary (1996). Gender and Development in India, 1970-1990s some reflections on the constitutive role of contents, *Economica and Political Weekly*.

King, K.E. (1972, 1990). *Labour Economics*, McMillan Press Ltd.

Lalhriatpuii, (2006). Status of Women: Focus Mizoram-Past Trends and Desirable Perspective, Seminar Paper on Emancipation of Women' NE-ICSSR, Shillong.

Nath, Kamal (1968). Women in the Working Force in India, *Economica and Political Weekly*, Vol. 3. No. 31.

Parthasarthy, G. and Dasaradharma, Rao (1981). *Women in the Labour Force in India*, ILO-ARTEP.

Paul, Ruma (1999). Economic Participation of Women: The Scenario in India, Assam and Barak Valley. Unpublished Thesis, University of Assam.

Rothschild, K.W. (1980). A Note on Female Labour Supply, *KYKLOS*, Vol. 33, No. 2.

Sunderam, K. (1996). *Inter State Variations in Workforce Participation Rate of Women in India: An Analysis*, ILO.

Thappar, Meenakshi (1997). Linkages between Cultures, Education and Women's Health in Urban Status, *Economica and Political Weekly*, Oct. 25,1997, Vol. XXXII, No. 43.

Tilak, Jandhyala B.G. (1980). Education and Labour Market Discrimination, *Indian Journal of Industrial Relations*, Vol. XVI, 1 July 1980.

Verrier, Elwin (1976). *Tribal Women in Indian Women*, edited by Jain, Devaki, Delhi: Publications Division, Ministry of Information and Broadcasting, Govt. of India, 1976 (reprint).

# Chapter 18

## Human Rights and Judicial Administration in Mizoram

### *Problems and Prospects*

LALLIANCHHUNGA

---

A hot debate has been triggered in the Mizo Society regarding the promotion of human rights in Mizoram. This has happened at a time when the watchdogs of human rights and defenders of Mizo society seem to cross their path. The issue of the relationship between human right and judicial administration has now assumed great significance in the context of the transition of the civil society from tradition to modernity. In fact, the link between human rights and judicial administration is questioned when one group accused the other of unleashing a 'reign of terror' unmindful of human rights and dignity in the name of cleansing the Mizo society by unnecessarily interfering in the administration of justice.

Human rights, which every human being is entitled to enjoy and to have protected, have assumed a global importance during the past few decades. The Universal Declaration of Human Rights, which was adopted by the UN General assembly on 10th December, 1948, is a great effort on the part of mankind to evolve a code for defining and maintaining human rights. Since then, it is trying in right earnest to spread the message of hope, equality, liberation, and empowerment for all those who are committed to freedom, justice, and peace. India has also established National Human Rights Commission in December 1993 and acceded to several international treaties on human right, including UNDHR, 1948.

Mizoram has also come under the watchful eyes of global and regional organizations concerning human rights. In fact, the insensitivity and the negligence of the government towards alleged violation of human rights by some NGOs have increasingly (and rather controversially) sensitized the issue of human rights in Mizoram.[1] Added to that, the emergence of civil society and the formation of NGOs such as Human Rights & Law Network (HR&LN) dedicated to the promotion of human rights further encouraged the debate about the role of judiciary in guaranting human rights in the state, which needs a conceptual attention of the intellectuals in the Mizo society.

## I. HUMAN RIGHTS AND JUDICIAL SYSTEM IN MIZORAM DURING THE BRITISH RAJ

During the reign of chieftainship, the village chief enjoyed full control over the village administration, including administration of justice according to customary laws. The chief's jurisdiction, however, was his village. While discharging the village administration he was always assisted by his Council of Elders (Lal Upa) who were men of his personal choice. The Chief was the only court of justice in the village and hence his decisions were final, against which there was no appeal system, although there may be some exceptional case wherein an unsuccessful litigant found a way of getting his case reheard.[2] The system of village administration, including judicial administration were, however, modified by the British administrators when they annexed the then Lushai Hills in 1890s to suit their administrative convenience.

The first modification was regarding the introduction of appealing system against the decision of the chief. Any person who was not satisfied with the decision of the chief was allowed to appeal their case to the Superintendent who was administrative head of the Lushai hills. The second modification was regarding limitations imposed on the chief's power to decide cases of importance. The chief's power to try major cases such as murder, rape, suicide, offences regarding government property and other major crimes was passed on to the district Superintendent. Since the powers of the Superintendent were almost undefined, some of the Superintendent acted as if they enjoyed unlimited powers, although the approval of the Governor of Assam was necessary for judicial decisions in capital punishments.[3]

In 1937, an important landmark was affected in the judicial administrative system in the Lushai Hills. By virtue of the powers conferred by Section 6 of the Scheduled District Act, 1874 (Act XIV of 1874), a body of rules popularly known as Administration of Justice Rules, 1937 was promulgated by the then Governor of Assam. It resulted in the creation of the court of Deputy Commissioner and his Assistants for criminal justice. In other words, magisterial powers were vested in the Deputy Commissioner and his Assistants. Under this rule, criminal justice system was organized in such a way that the Deputy Commissioner enjoyed the right to hear an appeal against the decision of his Assistants and to the Assam High Court in the case of Deputy Commissioner.[4] Nevertheless, the British administrators adopted a policy of non-interference in cases of petty nature, and they hardly entertained litigations and appeals against the decision of the chief in minor cases.[5] This policy of patronize continued till Indian independence in 1947 which in turn became a major reason for the campaign against the institution of chieftainship which eventually succeeded in abolishing chieftainship in Mizo Hills District after the passing of Lushai Hills District (Acquisition of Chiefs' Rights) Act in 1954.

When the Lushai Hills District Council was inaugurated on 25th April, 1952, important changes were again witnessed in the system of judicial administration. By making the Lushai Hills District (Administration of Justice) Rules, 1953, various courts such as Village Council Courts, Subordinate District Council Courts and the District Council Courts were set up by the District Council on the 16th August, 1954. These three-tier courts were functioning side by side with the court of Deputy Commissioner and his Assistants. The District Council thus becomes a miniature state government entrusting in itself legislative, executive and judicial functions within the framework of Sixth Scheduled to the Constitution of India. The judicial powers that were once vested in the Chief have now been administered by these courts according to Indian Penal Codes and Mizo customary laws in the case of Village Council Courts after the abolition of Mizo Chiefs. This judicial administrative system continued even after the elevation of Mizo District into the status of Union Territory in 1972 and statehood in 1987, though minor changes were made regarding the introduction of court fees, which only make getting justice expensive.[6]

From the above account of the system of judicial administration in Mizoram, it has been clear that there could be enough opportunities for abrogating the rights of others. The starting point could be made from the privileges and position of the chief *vis-à-vis* his subjects. The village chief was supreme, in whose hand there was concentration of powers. He assumed legislative, executive, and judicial responsibilities. The chief, as some authors put, was 'the fountainhead of justice'. He was all in all within his jurisdiction, and as such, challenging the decisions of the chief by the subjects would be suicidal and uncalled for. In other words, since his words were law, no laymen, or even his 'council of elders' would dare to cross his path. The subjects, therefore, felt suppress under their autocratic chiefs. All this was due to the absence of accountability on the part of the chief towards none.

Moreover, the subjects enjoyed limited human rights. First of all, they had the right to freedom of speech as long as they avoid criticizing their chief and his council of elders. Secondly, they also enjoyed a very limited right to property since their chief had the rights over land within his jurisdiction. Thirdly, the chief could forcibly take the property of the villagers; though the villagers had the practice of leaving any autocratic chief and migrating to another village which acted as a check on the authority of the chief. Yet on the pretext of transferring their allegiance to another chief, the chief still enjoyed the right to seize the property of their villagers. Fourthly, The way of punishment given to girls of loose character popularly known as 'Zawn' would in no way be acceptable to modern civil society, as it is blatant violation of Art 5 of Universal declaration of Human Rights, 1948 which reads, *No one shall be subjected to torture or to cruel inhuman or degrading treatment of punishment*. Fifthly, their system of dealing with a murderer was what we call 'retributive justice', in which the family members of the victim were permitted to take revenge unless the murderer took the chief's protection thereby submitting himself to the status of a slave (Chemsen Bawih). Herein also, neither the family of the victim gets justice from the chief nor does the murderer, his family and descendents who thus becomes slaves of the chief until they paid redemption price. Since the chief was the centre of power, there were certain cases of human rights violation during those periods. This was foretold by French philosopher, Montesquieu long ago. He wrote, "When the legislative and executive powers are united in the same person, or in the same body of magistrates, there can be no liberty......Again, there is no liberty if the judiciary power be not separate from the legislative and executive. Were it joined with the legislative, the life and liberty of the subjects would be exposed to arbitrary control, for the judge would then be the legislator. Were it joined to the executive power, the judge might behave with violence and oppression. There would be an end of everything, were the same men or the same boby...to exercise those three powers, that of enacting laws, that of executing...and of trying the cases of the individuals."[7]

Even after the introduction of British administration in the Lushai Hills, only few changes were made in the judicial administration of the village, by taking away some powers of the chief with regard to the chief's power to try major cases. The British authorities thus ruled over the entire Hills through their village chiefs. Their policy of 'non-interference' in the day-to-day life of the villagers and in the chief's administration was not governed by their 'respect' to the local customs and traditions but of administrative convenience.[8] Moreover, the British authorities continued to hold administrative and judicial powers, which made them look like autocrats in several cases. As has been pointed earlier, the British Superintendent of the Lushai Hills usually discouraged litigations and appeals, especially against the decisions of the village chiefs. Not only that, forced labour was rampant and the villagers who were compelled to carry the belongings of the authorities from villages to villages were often paid meagre wages, which is a clear violation of human rights.

## II. THE STATE OF JUDICIARY IN MIZORAM

After the democratically elected institution called District Council was set up under the purview of Sixth Scheduled to the Constitution of India, which eventually established Court of Deputy Commissioner and his assistants, Subordinate District Council Courts and Village Council Courts, the system of judicial administration in Mizoram remained almost the same. Powers were still not distributed, much against the paraphernalia of democratic institutions, which derive its inspiration from the Constitution of India. In fact, the authorities who administered justice in these courts were neither legal experts nor trained judicial officers to try disputes effectively. For instance, the educational qualification of Shri Sainghinga, the first president of the District Council Court was only upper primary.[9] In the words of

V.V. Rao, an eminent authority on North-East politics, "Qualified persons are not appointed".[10] Under this scenario, one cannot hope to promote and protect individual human rights in a rational method. In short, what the founding fathers of the Constitution of India had visualized to achieve regarding the deliberation of justice for the protection of individual rights in an efficient and effective manner remained unfulfilled.

Part III of the Constitution of India contains a long list of fundamental rights. These rights are regarded as fundamental because they are most essential for the individual to attain his full intellectual, moral and spiritual status. In the words of Harold J. Laski, an eminent English political philosopher, "Rights are those conditions of social life without which no man can seek, in general, to be himself his best".[11] The object behind the inclusion of these rights in the Constitution of India is to establish 'a government of law and not of men', a governmental system where the tyranny of the majority does not oppress the minority. However, mere incorporation of these rights in the written constitution without any provision for their proper safeguard will not serve any useful purpose. Indeed, the very existence of rights depends upon the remedy for its violation at the hands of individual, group of individuals or the excessive authorities of the state. For this purpose an independent and impartial judiciary coupled with a provision for the separation of judiciary from the executive has been provided under several provisions of the Constitution of India. Art. 50 also reads, "The state shall take steps to separate judiciary from the executive in the public services of the state". The independence of the judiciary is the live wire of judicial system and if that wire is snapped, the doomsday of judiciary will not be far off.[12] Added to this, BASIC PRINCIPLES ON THE INDEPENDENCE OF THE JUDICIARY adopted by the Seventh United Nations Congress on the *Prevention of Crime and the Treatment of Offenders* held at Milan from 26 August to 6 September, which was subsequently endorsed by UN General Assembly resolution 40/32 of 29th November 1985 and 40/146 of 13th December 1985 has been an important endorsement in this regard. Apart from calling the member states to uphold independence of judiciary, it said: (1) The judiciary shall have jurisdiction over all issues of a judicial nature and shall have exclusive authority to decide whether an issue submitted for its decisions is within the competence as defined by law; (2) There shall not be any inappropriate or unwarranted interference with the judicial process, nor shall judicial decisions by the courts be subject to revision. This principle is without prejudice to judicial review or to mitigation or commutation by competent authorities of sentences imposed by the judiciary, in accordance with the law; (3) The principle of the independence of the judiciary entitles and requires the judiciary to ensure that judicial proceedings are conducted fairly and that the rights of the parties are respected. The very spirit of this proviso has yet to find a place in the judicial administration in Mizoram, even after 56 years of the Constitution of India coming into operation.

However, the first direction given to the Government of Mizoram for the separation of the judiciary from the executive was issued by the Guwahati High Court on 5th August, 1985.[13] It reads, "Call for a report from the Secretary (Law), Government of Mizoram as to why the judiciary should not be separated from the Executive and what prevents the Government to separate Judiciary. It is the constitutional obligations of the Union Territory of Mizoram to implement the Directive Principles of State Policy...." Following this direction, the Mizoram Government had informed the Guwahati High Court that *the question of separation of judiciary from the executive is under active consideration.* In spite of this, the Government of Mizoram did little for the separation of judiciary from the executive. Then, the High Court again issued a directive to the state government to comply with the constitutional mandate following a Public Interest Litigation (PIL) file by the People's Union for Civil Liberties (PUCL), Mizoram.[14]

In 2002, an important landmark was achieved with regard to separation of judiciary from the executive. The Council of Ministers' meeting on 15th January 2002 had passed a resolution for the separation of judiciary from the executive which would be effective in the district of Aizawl only, and official notification to this effect was published in the Mizoram Official Gazette on the 22nd January 2002.[15] But this attempt to separate judiciary from the executive had to be repealed by the Government of Mizoram on 1st April, 2002[16] when some NGOs, notably Central Young Men's Association in support of Mizo Zirlai Pawl put a strong pressure on the government. Although short-lived, yet it started a debate amongst the intellectuals and lawyers in the Mizo society on the need to have impartial judiciary which will be independent from the clutches of the state executive for the protection of individual human rights in the state. So far, the

Mizo community has never witnessed such lively debate on the role of an independent judiciary in protecting human rights which is still continuing till date. Some people even go further in criticizing the CYMA for their opposition to separate the judiciary from the executive.

Again, as per the resolution of the meeting of the Council of Ministers on 21st February, 2005, an official notification for the separation of judiciary from the executive was published in the Official Gazette on 16th June, 2005 [*vide* No. A. 36016/5/2001-P & AR (CSW)]. It may be noted that this notification for the separation of the same will cover the whole of Mizoram. This notification, however, had to be kept in abeyance by order of the Governor of Mizoram on 10th November, 2005 [*vide* No. A. 36016/5/2001-P & AR (CSW)] since a misunderstanding had arisen over Mizoram Judicial Services Rules between the Government of Mizoram and the Guwahati High Court. Nevertheless, the public demand for the separation of judiciary from the executive in Mizoram could not be cowed down by the stiff opposition of some NGOs. In their Press Statement on 29th November 2006, the Mizoram Bar Association accused the state government of not acting logically and said the repeal of the notification which handed over the control of the Mizoram judicial officers to the Guwahati High Court was nothing but a *pre-conceived plan to transfer MJS officers*,[17] which the state government actually did on 13th November 2006, three days after the repealing of the said notification. On 22 November, 2006 Shri K.N. Madhusoodhanan, Counsel for the State of Mizoram sent a letter to the Government of Mizoram saying that the Supreme Court had directed the government to expedite the separation process and that it expected to receive affidavit of compliance from both the state government and the Guwahati High Court by December 15, 2006, which eventually compelled the state government to take necessary actions.

Therefore, a compromise between the Government of Mizoram and Guwahati High Court was made between Hon'ble Chief Justice Shri Sudarshan Reddy on the one hand and Shri Zoramthanga, Chief Minister with Shri H. Rammawi, Law Minister on the other on 5th December 2006 over the Mizoram Judicial Services Rule, 2006. Therefore, with the approval of the Mizoram Judicial Services Rules, 2006 by the Hon'ble Guwahati High Court, the judicial officers under the Government of Mizoram are to be functioning automatically under the purview of Guwahati High Court[18]; the functioning of the Law

Secretariat under the Government of Mizoram: recruitment of judicial services through Mizoram Public Services Commission (MPSC); and recruitment rules with qualification for the knowledge of Mizo language up to middle school standards for judicial services.[19] But an official notification to this effect has not yet been made by the Guwahati High Court.

From the above accounts of judicial administration in the state of Mizoram, it is a fact that Mizoram has been behind other states of the Indian Union in granting the rights of the citizens through the judicial system. In the absence of an independent judicial administrative system in Mizoram, people are easily deprived of their right to get impartial justice from the judiciary as the judicial administration is still under the control of the state executives. This has eroded the public faith in the judiciary, and due to this, there have been several cases of NGOs taking the law into their own hands. Rather than trying to get justice from the judiciary, these NGOs usually prefer to take on quicker method which naturally involves human rights violation in the name of cleansing the society. Therefore, in order to restore public faith, the legal system and the judicial administrative system should be reformed keeping in view the socio-political situations of the state. Meanwhile, the mandatory obligations imposed by the Protection of Human Rights Act, 1993 should be taken into account.

## III. THE STATUS OF HUMAN RIGHTS IN MIZORAM

In 1993, the Central Government thought it expedient in the national interest to set up a commission through the Presidential Ordinance on 29 September, 1993, which became an Act in 1994. The National Human Rights Commission, as officially declared, has its own nucleus of investigating staff to inquire into specific complaints of the violation of human rights relating to life, liberty, equality and dignity of an individual as guaranteed in the Constitution or embodied in International Covenants and enforceable by the Courts in India. One important feature of this law is that it has empowered the state governments to set up their own Commission for such purpose. In spite of this clarion call, the Government of Mizoram has neither constituted a Commission nor has any attempt been made so far in this direction. This is despite the Supreme Court ruling on 8th December, 1986 that all those states which do not have their own

Human Right Commission shall constitute Human Rights Committee.[20] In its order, '*Supreme Court has requested the Chief Justices of High Courts of the States and Union Territories where Human Rights Commissions are not constituted a Committee to oversee whether the requirements said by Supreme Court (*Vide its *order dated 8.12.1996 in the case of D.K. Basu* Vs *Government of West Bengal and others) to eliminate custodial violence, are being carried out or not and to take all such further necessary steps as required to ensure that those requirements are carried out and make surprise checks with a view to see actual implementation of these requirements. Supreme Court has further directed that a report of the action taken by the Committee constituted by Chief Justices of High Courts as per the above order is to be sent to the Supreme Court directly, within three months from the date of passing this order*'.[21] Accordingly, Mizoram Human Rights Committee (MHRC) has been set up under Aizawl Bench of Guwahati High Court on 7th February, 2002 at the instance of this Supreme Court ruling under the Chairmanship of the Registrar, Guwahati High Court (Aizawl Bench) with other members such as IG (Prison), DC (Aizawl District), SP (CID-Crime Branch) and ADM (J). But only few cases, if none, have come to this Committee for redressal till date. This is established by the information given by the Chairman of this Committee to the unstarred question No.32 for the Assembly Monsoon Session in 2004. It reads, "The activities of the Committee till date are as follows: (A) Translation and circulation of the directions of the Hon'ble Supreme Court in D.K. Basu's case and Common Causes Case to all district authorities for compliance. (B) The Chairman made inspections of the district jails in Champhai, Saiha, and Lunglei. (C) Inspection of the Police Stations and conditions of the Lock-up were carried out in Champhai, Saiha, and Lunglei. (D) Inspection of Excise Offices and Lock-up in the Champhai, Saiha, and Lunglei. (E) Inspections of Courts in the above mentioned districts were also carried out. (F) Inspection reports and tour notes were given to the Government of Mizoram for further necessary action. (G) Regular reports have been submitted to the Hon'ble Guwahati High Court on the activities of the Committee."[22] It is not that there is no human rights violation in the state, but lack of public faith and ignorance of the very existence of this Committee have become a major factor for not approaching this Committee in this case.

Therefore, the slow process in the implementation of separation of the Judiciary from the executive and the lack of cases of human rights violation before the Mizoram Human Rights Committee have only worsen the situation of human rights in the state. But, the judicial process is still an obvious area for the notion of human rights to play a fundamental role. In the words of Justice S.B. Sinha, "Human right is a universal entitlement necessitating its fullest implementation. However, despite our enormous concern, the actual application of human rights at the ground level has been rather dismal....It is here where the judiciary has to play the role of a central player and ensure the prevalence of the rule of law".[23] In the sphere of judicial process it has been established that it is the state which possess the biggest threat to human rights, since by using its judicial process the state authorities can deprive its citizens of their liberty and argue for the title to punish them. It is thus no wonder that in many cases, it is the judicial process which is the area of law in which human rights have found their most long-standing and traditional applications. It is, however, the NGOs interpretation that has, in the Mizoram context, progressively expanded the human rights content of the law. In the field of human rights, whatever we have owed more to the NGOs than to the Courts and the legislature of the state.

## IV. CONCLUSION

It may be said that along with the genuine human rights agencies, official or non-governmental organizations, the human rights movement in Mizoram is moving in the right direction. One should not forget that the road towards reaching the destination of human rights is very long, full of detours and potholes. Yet, we have to reach that destination. The fundamental challenges in this 21st Century before the human rights movement in Mizoram are sensitizing the people, police and armed forces about human rights, updating the state arms of judiciary and legislations, increasing role of the NGOs and infusing credibility into their actions and reports. The first challenge before the Mizo civil society is to sensitizing the people about human rights in a more effective manner, though educating and sensitizing the people on human right is in full swing. Human rights have no meaning to persons who are ignorant of human rights. Evolution of human right awareness from the common people can only help us to achieve what Former Chief Justice of India, Shri Misra calls 'human rights culture' in the state.

Secondly, Police personnel should be trained in matters of human right. In Mizoram and elsewhere, third degree methods and torture have been employed to extract confession from the detenues as it is believed that they are a quicker way to success, although custodial death may be rare in Mizoram. These are due to lack of training in investigation and lack of facilities and equipments. According to Former Chief Justice of India, M.N. Venkatachaliah, investigating officers should less rely on human elements and, instead modern scientific methods like DNA tests should be used during investigation. This has called for the setting up of State Forensic Science Directorate equipped with latest technology in crime investigation in the state. Third degree method and custodial deaths could be properly investigated only with the help of forensic science laboratory having modern equipments; and we must not forget that there can be no justice without complete and impartial investigation. Human rights should also be a part of the curricula in all police and armed forces trainings. Further, the Mizoram State Security Commission which is established on 9th November, 2006 under the chairmanship of Home Minister, Government of Mizoram should be effective in evaluating the performances of the state police by maintaining its independence and extensive participation of civil society members, and the constitution of Police Complaints Authority at the state and district levels is also essential in this regard.[24]

Thirdly, the state should be a central pillar in guarantying various human rights of its citizens. This, however, is possible only when the state administration assumes utmost responsibilities by equipping the judicial machineries with necessary powers and facilities. Establishment of Human Rights Commission in the state, providing necessary equipments to the State Forensic Science Laboratory and establishment of District Mobile Forensic Science Unit thereof, making important changes in the existing redundant laws and rules, training of judicial officers and District Magistrates with state of the art facilities and improvement of judicial man-power infrastructures in all districts are the exclusive responsibilities of the state government in matters of human rights protection.

Fourthly, the NGOs which are working in the state can play a major role in disseminating information on the cases of human rights violations and the role of the judiciary in protecting human rights through their reports. The credibility of their reports/information should be above personal whims and favour, otherwise their credibility will be questioned and the shadow will be cast over their good works.

Lastly, the importance of the media in focusing and attracting the attention of the public on human rights situation and its violation cannot be overlooked. Print media and electronic media in Mizoram are known for their ability to move the opinion of the public. It is only through their efforts that political and public pressure can be established on the state government to make human rights as an agenda of governance. The NGOs and the media can pressurize the state government for establishing State Human Rights Commission or providing the existing Mizoram Human Rights Committee with at least basic infrastructures such as funds for basic stationery, separate staff, accommodation etc. All this will help us in achieving the cherished goals of human rights advocacy to a great extent.

## NOTES

1. Lallianchhunga, (2005). "Human Rights in Mizoram" Borderlines, Vol. I No. 3 Spring Summer, 2005.
2. Prasad, R.N. (1995). "Administration of Justice in Mizoram" in R.N. Prasad & A.K. Agarwal (Eds) *Landmarks: A Study of Public Administration in Mizoram,* Aizawl: Lengchhawn Press, p. 244.
3. Thanga, L.B. (1995). "Office of the District Magistrate in India and Mizoram" in R.N. Prasad & A.K. Agarwal (Eds) *Landmarks: A Study of Public Administration in Mizoram*, Aizawl: Lengchhawn Press, p. 276.
4. Michael, Lalrinsanga Sailo, (2006). "The Legal System in Mizoram—Before and After the Advent of the British" in R.N. Prasad & P. Chakraborty (Ed) *Administration of Justice in Mizoram*, New Delhi: Mittal Publications, pp. 24-25.
5. Prasad, R.N. (1995). *op. cit.* p. 246.
6. Michael, Lalrinsanga Sailo, (2006), *op. cit.* p. 29.
7. Montesquieu: *Spirit of the Law*, Book VI.
8. Lalchungnunga, (1994). *Mizoram: Politics of Regionalism and National Integration*, New Delhi: Reliance Publishing House, pp. 33-34.
9. Thanhranga, H.C. (1986). *District Council Courts in Mizoram* Unpublished Ph.D. thesis of Guwahati University, pp. 309-310.
10. Rao, V.V. (1987). *et al. A Century of Government and Politics in North East India*, Vol. III (Mizoram) New Delhi: S. Chand & Company, p. 234.
11. Laski, H.J. (1973). A *Grammar of Politics*. London: George Allen & Unwin, p. 91.
12. Gupta, S.P.V. (1994). *Union of India*, AIR 1994 SC 268.

13. Lalramzauva, C. (2006). *Separation of Judiciary in Mizoram* in, R.N. Prasad & P. Chakraborty (Eds) *Administration of Justice in Mizoram*, (New Delhi: Mittal Publications, p. 70.
14. PUCL, Mizoram *Vs* State of Mizoram and Others (Civil Rules No. 4/91(MB)/Civil Rules No. 3626 of 1991.
15. *Vide* No. A. 48011/2/92-LJD/290.
16. *Vide* No. A. 48011/2/92-LJD/294.
17. *Newslink* Vol. VIII No. 269 November 30, 2006, Aizawl.
18. *Vide* the Mizoram Gazette Vol. XXXV, 12.12.2006, Issued No. 321.
19. Press Release made by MNF Gen. Hqrs, Aizawl on 13th December 2006, published in *The Aizawl Post* (daily) Vol. IV No. 280 December 14, 2006, Aizawl.
20. Dilip, K. Basu v. Govt. of West Bengal and Others (AIR 1997 SC 3017).
21. Text of the letter of Joint Secretary, Govt. of India, Ministry of Home Affairs (12/13 February, 2002) forwarded by Shri S.R. Sarma, Registrar (I & E), Guwahati High Court, Guwahati to the Registrar, Guwahati High Court, Aizawl Bench (No. HC. III-25/2000/2515/G Dated Guwahati), the 19 July, 2002.
22. Text of the letter sent to the Secretary, L & J Deptt, Govt. of Mizoram by Chairman of the MHRC on 8th July, 2004. [No. P. 16015/1/2002-HC (AB)/69].
23. Text of the Speech delivered by Hon'ble Justice S.B. Sinha, Judge, Supreme Court of India on the theme entitled 'Human Rights and Judicial Officers' at Bilaspur on 17th June, 2006, published in *Nyaya Deep*, Vol. VII Issue 3, July 2006. (The Official Journal of National Legal Services Authority).
24. The Supreme Court has directed all the states to establish State Security Commission and Police Complaints Authority, which are non-negotiable and binding and that all states across the country must file affidavit of compliance by April 10, 2007 or face contempt of court. Accordingly, MSSC is established on 9th November 2006 and the first meeting was convened on 23rd February, 2007 without civil society groups.

## REFERENCES

Bhargava, Gopal, (2001). *Human Rights: Concern of the Future*, Kalpaz Publications, Delhi.

McCorquodale, Robert (Ed.) (2003). *The International Library of Essays in Law & Legal Theory: Human Rights*, Second Series, Trowbridge: Wiltshire. The Cromwell Press, Great Britain.

*Newslink*, Vol VIII No. 263 November 23, 2006, Aizawl.

*Newslink*, Vol VIII No. 282 December 14, 2006, Aizawl.

Paradhar, Parmanand (2001). *Enforcement of Human Rights*, Book Enclave, Jaipur.

Sahu, Asima (1999). *Human Rights Violations and the Law,* Pointer Publishers, Jaipur.

Saibaba, G. & Rao, Sreenivasa (Eds) (2003). *Structural Adjusment and Implications of Human Rights,* Serials Publications, New Delhi.

Sinha, P.C. (2000). *Global Sourcebook on Human Rights*, Part II, Kanishka Publishers & Distributors, New Delhi.

Subramanian IPS, Dr. S. (Ed) (2000). *Human Rights Training*, Vol. I, Manas Publications, New Delhi.

Thanhranga, H.C. (1994) *Administration of Justice in Mizoram* (Aizawl: Lengchhawn Press) 4th Impression.

Vadkar, Praveen, (2000). *Concepts, Theories and Practices of Human Rights*, Rawat Publications, New Delhi.

Yasin, Adil-Ul & Upadhyay, Archana, (2003). *Human Rights*, Akansha Publishing House, New Delhi.

# Chapter 19

# Human Rights and Community Based Organizations in Mizoram

C. LALHMANMAWIA

## Introduction

The fabric of Mizo society has undergone tremendous changes over the years. Before the British moved into the Lushai Hills, for all practical purposes the village and the clan formed units of Mizo society. However, with the advent of the British and the consequent introduction of Christianity and education on the western pattern, the society in no time got radical transformation. Education has successfully flourished in the state and Mizoram ranks second highest literate state among the Indian states with 88.49 per cent after Kerala with 90.92 per cent. Mizoram also has another distinction of being the most urbanized state in India with as much as 49.50 per cent of its population living in urban areas.

The whole public life in the early period was guided by the Mizo social code of ethic known as 'Tlawmngaihna' an untranslatable term meaning on the part of everyone to be hospitable, kind, unselfish, and helpful to others. It also stands for self-sacrifice for the service of others. The Mizo people under this useful custom render all voluntary services. With the advent of the Christian missionaries in the area, majority of population embraced Christianity with so much dedication and submission that the Christian Church Organization guides the entire social life and thought process. Again, when the area was engulfed with political strife and insurgency problem as a result of Mizo National Front (MNF) independence movement since

1966, Mizo society experienced drastic changes that affected sense of values and hence materialism started to gain a ground in the minds of the people. Egalitarian nature of the Mizo society has been fading away in the event of the ever-growing multiple economic activities. More importantly, the Mizo society experienced new development during the last few decades, the trend being that present Mizo society is now under the dictum of non-Governmental organizations. In spite of its small size in terms of population and economic backwardness, Mizoram has quite a number of voluntary organizations. Some of them are Young Mizo Association (YMA), Mizo Zirlai Pawl (MZP), Mizo Students Association (MSA), Mizo Students Union (MSU), Mizoram Hmeichhe Insuihkhawm Pawl (MHIP), Mizoram Women Federation (MWF), Mizoram Upa Pawl (MUP), Mizoram Aged Persons Association (MAPA), etc. These NGOs/CBOs exert enormous influence upon the lives of the Mizo. Amongst them YMA is the most prominent one.

These voluntary organizations are organized with the aim to meet their respective needs and objectives. All of them mentioned above are confined within the state and have no connection with NGOs of the outside states; and hence the nature and operations of these organizations are basically local in nature. However, despite their limitations in terms of geographical area, they are found to have been making positive efforts especially for the welfare of the people. It is natural that in a country like India, the state alone could not fulfil it constitutional obligations for making the country a true 'Welfare State,' as a result of which these NGOs are essential for welfare activities. In Mizoram also the state and the voluntary organizations supplement to each other to meet the requirements of social administration and for all-round development of the people.

However, the role of these NGOs in the promotion and protection of human rights is very much debatable in the state. The issue becomes more sensitive during the last few years when many instances of human rights violations occurred as a result of efforts made by the most powerful NGO in the state, i.e. YMA. Consequently the question of the role of the NGOs *vis-à-vis* human rights in the state involves many complications and its sensitivity makes the issue more interesting and challenging. In other words, human rights is seriously challenged in recent time when the most forceful community based organization in Mizoram, Young Mizo Association (YMA) declared war against drugs and took steps to contain drug trafficking. The campaign launched by YMA brought both positive and negative results having a serious impact on the human rights situation in the state. It is in this background that the study of human rights situation in the state and the role of Non-Governmental Organization in the promotion and protection of human rights shall be mainly dealt with in this chapter. The reasons responsible for human rights violation in the state shall be highlighted and some suggestions will be made for the improvement of human rights situation in the state as well.

## What is "Human Rights"?

According to UN's 'Center for Human Rights', it refers to "those rights which are inherent in our nature and without which we cannot live as human beings." The Protection of Human Rights Act, 1993, Section 2(d) defines the term that "Human Rights means the right relating to life, liberty, equality, and dignity of the individual guaranteed by the Constitution or embodied in International Covenants and enforced by courts in India." Therefore, human rights are those minimum set of rights of mankind available in all spheres of life to all individuals or groups of societies individually or collectively which is expected to be permanently unalienable since birth up to the last of man or society for the purposes of survival or benefit of mankind, individual or society. As per these rights, everyone must have it by virtue of being human, and without which no man can seek to be himself at his best. Human Rights are essential for making life more meaningful and enjoyable. From the human rights point of view, there must not be any kind of discrimination on ground of religion, social status, and sex or on the ground of being member of any organization.

## Human Rights Situation in Mizoram

The term, human rights itself is very much unknown to the general public in Mizoram. Only way back in 1966, the Mizo began to recognize the term Human Rights for practical purposes as a result of various atrocities and excesses committed by the Indian Army countering the Mizo insurgency movement. The Declaration of Independence by the Mizo National Front (MNF) was condemned by the Government of India as secessionism and then launched counter insurgency operations committing serious violations of human rights of the Mizo.

The Area was declared 'Disturbed Area' on 2 March 1966 under the Assam Disturbed Areas Act, 1958 by the Government of Assam.

The Assam Government adopted tit for tat policy, to subdue the movement. The Government of India also declared the MNF as an unlawful organization and banned it on 6.3.1966.[1] The Armed Forces Special Power Act, 1958 was promulgated in the area bringing rampant violations of human rights of Mizo in the form of committing atrocities like unauthorized trespassing into private houses and looting of properties or forcible burning of houses by the members of the security forces. Rape and other deplorable activities became common throughout Mizoram.[2]

The trauma caused to the Mizo by the Indian army during the insurgency period resulted in the death of 2116 innocent people. Due to army atrocities countless number of men became handicapped or physically disabled. Moreover, around 600 villages, more than 30000 houses were burnt to ashes and even the Church buildings were not spared in many villages. The army with no compensation arbitrarily confiscated around 4000 guns; the Mizo valued most among their possessions.[3] In all such incidents, the Mizo suffered silently as there was no institution or agent to which the victims can resort to for the relief or seeking redress for their grievances. The whole population of Mizoram was made subservient to the power and authority of the Security Forces.

In such a situation Brig. Thenphunga Sailo (Retd.) formed the Human Rights Committee (HRC) in the month of June 1974.[4] In an effort to realize its objectives, members of the Committee toured throughout the state launching campaign against rampant human rights violations. The public was enlightened about the rights and showed great appreciation of the venture of the Committee and at the same time the Indian Army also showed some sign of positive response. The establishment of Human Rights Committee was the first and foremost step in human rights movement in the state. The Committee achieved successes in its pursuit and the public were made aware about their basic freedom and fundamental rights guaranteed under the Constitution. The Committee, in fact had made the terminology of human rights well known to the people and people began to realize the importance of the term for practical purposes. People were encouraged to fight for their inalienable rights even against military might. Though very successful in its endeavours, the HRC was very short lived. By 1975, the Chairman of the HRC along with some of his friends formed a new political party called, Peoples Conference.

This led to the decline of HRC and since then the HRC became almost defunct.

## Human Rights in the Post-Accord Mizoram

When the Memorandum of Understanding popularly known as Peace Accord was signed between the underground MNF and the Government of India in 1986, the situation has improved to a great extent and consequent upon this Mizoram happened to be one of the most peaceful states in India. However, looking at the real situation and viewed from the human rights angle, the actual picture proved ironical. Promotion and protection of human rights and more particularly recognition of individual liberty do not get due place in the state.

There have been incidents of human rights violation in the form of torturing, destruction of private buildings and property, even loss of lives. The practice of mob rule still prevails resulting in sheer violations of basic human rights. In many incidents some NGOs operating in the name of public interest are found to have been directly or openly involved. The practices of harassment or cruel treatment on some people on the ground of mere suspicion are still rampant in the state. It is a fact that in most of the incidents of violation of individual freedom and dignity, the CBOs had direct bearing or responsibilities. The reason for this is nothing but the NGOs operating in the state are permitted by the society to behave unbounded.

The YMA, born in 1935, is now having more than 340,000 members and 747 branches.[5] By virtue of its enormous membership it has now emerged as one of the strongest voluntary organization in the region. It has now assumed a status of a vigilant group, who together with the Church, showed with no hesitation their authoritative control of the state decision-making apparatus on some issues. In fact, YMA today seems to be the repository of power. This is even accepted by the elected representatives in the government. The MLAs, ministers and other political wannabes desirous of contesting the next elections have to work in collaboration with the YMA's objectives. While a constitutionally elected government is running the state, the most powerful NGO in the state, the Young Mizo Association (YMA), a non-state body, assumes an authoritative role.

It is no doubt that the YMA since its birth has been doing good to the general public, yet recent trend has shown authoritative behaviour when it launched a campaign called "war on drugs". To achieve this end, it has adopted the most brutal methods and adopted even violence as a means, and for putting a check on drug peddlers and bootleggers. Surprisingly, the state government is looking the other way even as atrocities are committed by the militant wing of the YMA, namely the Supply Reduction Service (SRS) formed to contain drugs trafficking from the neighbouring areas, MTV or Mizo Tlangval. To one estimate, due to militant activities of the YMA's campaign during 2005, six people lost their lives.[6] Launching of campaign against drugs or any other intoxicating substance itself is not challengeable. Further, social reformation and the prevention of uncountable numbers of Mizo youth from addiction or for that matter preventing untimely death is needed beyond doubt. However, various atrocities committed on many people on the ground of mere suspicion and adoption of such brutal forms leading to the death of as many as six people can never be justified. The fundamental law of the land guaranteed rights for equal protection of law or right to equality. And human rights are violated by this movement. It is now beyond doubt that the CBO like YMA and its militant groups are permitted to exercise their power unchecked. This trend gives the impression that these NGOs are above the laws. It creates such an unfortunate situation that even the elected Government turned out to be a silent spectator to different incidents of violations of basic human rights. This is, in fact, a matter of negative step for the promotion and protection of human rights in the state. The state government is becoming weak in reining in such acts of the non-state actors.

In a memorandum dated 24 May 2005 submitted to the state Chief Minister of Mizoram signed by H. Zosangliana, President, Forum for the Implementation of Constitutional Rights in Mizoram (FICORM) and Vanramchhuangi, Director, Human Rights and Law Network, Aizawl, Mizoram, they cited as many as ten cases of excesses and atrocities reported by various local newspapers. All these incidences were cases of human rights violations. In these incidents local NGOs are alleged to have taken law into their hands or have committed human rights violations in the course of launching campaign against drugs in Mizoram.[7]

These are in fact only few instances of excesses or rude behaviours of NGOs that took place during the year 2005. There is no denying the fact that effort to contain drug trafficking and other substances is an urgent need in the state, but at the same time there can be no just ground for the NGOs to continue excesses which might cause violation of basic human rights as it was experienced in recent times. Surely, the moment when untrained or human rights unfriendly NGOs other than appropriate state agencies are taking the responsibilities of maintenance of law and order or taking law into their hands, basic human rights as well as fundamental human rights guaranteed by the Constitution have been violated. In such a situation a State Government has to assume its authoritative role. But unfortunately, in almost all incidences mentioned above, the State Government or its agencies turned rather indifferent, giving more chances of human rights violations or breach of fundamental law.

## The Society is in a Dilemma

The main cause of human rights violations that occurred in recent times in Mizoram is the so called campaign launched against Drugs Abuse/Addiction and Drug trafficking in the state by the YMA. It is an undeniable fact that declaration of war against drugs is a must. Thousands of young men are now victims of drug addiction. Thousands of them became handicapped in someway or the other debarring human dignity and value. Countless lives were lost due to drug abuse. It is thus an urgent and inevitable task for the whole community to work for the liberation of thousands of young men from drug addiction. In such a situation organization like Central YMA, concerned for the welfare and good of the community has to come forward for the safety of the society. Under such circumstance, strong contentions prevail: 'Drug traffickers or peddlers are the one who violated the law and there is no question of containing them as per the law', or 'harsh measures are needed for the reformations of anti-social elements', or 'more importance must be given to collective rights over the individual rights' and 'we must not be very mindful about the means but to the results and hence means to realize the objectives does not matter much' etc. This in turn however makes the NGOs and private organizations not careful about their limitations. People are loosing their confidence upon the elected government and giving more and more trust to the NGOs. This, however, opens chances of violations of law and the individual rights guaranteed by the Constitution and various other human rights instruments.

**Causes of Human Rights Violations in Mizoram**

1. *Lack of Legal Awareness*: The society is still very much lacking legal awareness. Rights and ideals enshrined in the Constitution and other human rights instruments; like equality before law, due process of Law etc. do not get proper recognition among the Mizo. Instead of following legal procedure majority is still inclined to make judgement according to their traditional or custom-like mob rule, which make the whole society an easy prey for breach of fundamental law. Wrong contentions about lawyers and law experts that they are friends of culprits but not the custodian of the rights of ideal citizens still prevail in the state. The social attitude towards the legal/judicial institutions is still not conducive for human rights culture.
2. *Government Inefficiency*: There are every sign of the weaknesses in the maintenance of law and order in the state. Due to lack of efficiency in maintaining law and order in the state, people lose their trust towards the state government. The state government as the legal and constitutional authority is losing its control over some non-government organizations. The government rather silently approves the activities of the group, as the police and enforcement wings have failed to do. People now appear to have more confidence upon the NGOs other than the state government. As a reward for its vigilantism, the YMA is even sanctioned funds by the government to meet its objectives. This in turn brings the NGOs to the position, which many people think that they are above the law. This misconception in many occasions brought human rights violations in the state.
3. *Ignorance about the Concept*: Lack of understanding about the concept of human rights and its implications. It appears that the people do not properly understand the term human rights. There is a strong contention among the people that human rights itself is a matter of protecting the rights and interest of the few people only. Even certain sections of the leaders of the Churches and most influential public leaders do not welcome the human rights movement. Certain people

who launched legal awareness campaign do not get public cooperation and even human rights activists are condemned as anti-social elements.

4. *Lack of Human Rights Institutions*: The Protection of Human Rights Act, 1993, Section 21 desires every state to form state human rights commission but sadly enough, till today the state government never took concrete step to realize this obligation. At present there is a private organization working for the promotion and protection of human rights in the state, Human Rights and Law Network operating since 2003, yet even this organization never received full cooperation from the general public. Even the Human Rights Committee formed under the Guwahati High Court, Mizoram Bench (*Vide* memo. No. HC.VII.126/2001/... Dated 7th February, 2002), do not produce desired result and rather very less unknown to the public.
5. *No Human Rights Education in the State*: Despite effort of the UN to disseminate human rights information and the adoption of the last decade as Decade of Human Rights Education, (1994-2004) the state has not yet introduced human rights education as a subject till today. Though included human rights paper as optional subjects in the college and university level, none of the colleges in Mizoram has paid any importance to the subject and it is still one of the most neglected paper today.

In Mizoram it is noticeable that the fundamental freedom and individual dignity enshrined in the Constitution of India are prominently in place. However, in recent years, human rights violations become almost everyday phenomena. The commutative effects of the capitalist path of development brought the decay of egalitarian society that opened chances of social stratification on the basis of income, land possession, social status. This, in turn, paved the way for the decline of close-knit homogeneous Mizo society. In such a situation problems like unemployment, lack of proper development of rural areas, lack of medical facilities, denial of gender equality, and a growing gap between the rich and the poor etc., is obvious in Mizoram. Thus enjoyment of human rights enshrined in various international human rights instruments in general and the rights enshrined in the Constitution in particular is still a distant dream. Keeping in mind, all these harsh realities, it is now imperative to make some remarks/suggestions which are as follows:

1. It is very important to ensure human rights on the basis on 'cultural relativism' or 'cultural specificity'. This implies that human rights must be applied and interpreted according to different cultural values. The question of cultural specificity appears to be more relevant in the Mizoram context. Contemporary Mizo society presents a contrasting picture of various hues and colours in its structure. Although such concepts as class and caste are unknown, nevertheless, there is a sharp division between the 'haves' and 'have-nots'. Standards of living now vary widely not only in the urban areas but also in the less-urban areas. In spite of these, yet, there exist several mechanisms responsible for uniting almost all of the Mizos into a single homogenous order where status, wealth, or official positions do not seem to matter. Such all-embracing institutions as the Churches and the Young Mizo Association (YMA) practically permeate every aspect of the life of a Mizo.

   One feels that concepts such as human rights do not find much favour among the Mizo people is due to ignorance. It is the general opinion that the concept of human rights carries with it 'individualism' in the Western sense of the term. This ultimately creates a fear psychosis in the minds of the people that the practical application of the principles of human rights would violate the general norms and values of the society. That is, if every individual is made aware of his/her rights, and these be exercised, then, it is felt that the communitarian ethos of the society would be badly damaged (for instance, throughout the state, every locality has its own set of rules and regulations laid down by leaders of different NGOs, and every member of the locality is supposed to abide by these). This in itself puts into question whether the state government's law and order machinery has the ultimate authority or not. And the controversial role that civil society is playing in Mizoram. It is in this context that efforts for human rights movement in Mizoram area needed with slight change to adopt Mizo ethos or cultural specificity.

2. Dissemination of human rights knowledge through systematic education is an urgent need. Education on human rights in making individual conscious of the basic and inalienable rights of others, regardless of sex, language, religion and other social and economic condition need to be disseminated to make a person more responsible citizen not only for his own country but of the world. Therefore, education aiming at better understanding of the whole concept with its implications and ramifications need to be introduced in educations at all stages. It is imperative that Government decision makers and public officials need to have a fresh look in framing the educational system in the state. Programmes and educational curriculum need to be changed to inculcate human rights awareness to the new generations. Hence, introduction of the human rights studies from the bottom to the top of the educational system is an urgent need.
3. Formation of State Human Rights Commission in Mizoram is an urgent need as desired by Section 21 of the Protection of Human Rights Act, 1993. Establishment of State Human Rights Commission would strongly indicate the degree of the State Government's commitment to human rights cause. It is in fact quite essential to have an institution to which citizens may seek redress of violation of their rights and at the same time will relieve the arduous work of the state judicial administration. While fifteen states have so far established State Human Rights Commissions, there is no positive effort for the formation of Human Rights Commission in the state. It is thus much needed to form statutory institution to entertain complaints out of human rights violation. The well-being of every individual is greatest importance and beneficial for the whole country. The Commission would surely serve as an advisory or recommending body for the redressal of grievances. It is thus in the greater interest for the state to establish Human Rights Commission at the earliest possible extent for the creation

of better governance and a more humane society. Obstacle in the establishment of State Human Rights Commission like financial constraint or administrative reasons should be set aside keeping in mind how best the people could have access to the institution for redress for violations of their basic human rights.

In the absence of State Human Rights Commission in Mizoram, the Gauhati High Court set up Human Rights Committee under the chairmanship of the Registrar, Gauhati High Court, and Mizoram Bench at Aizawl since 2002. However, the Committee's performance in its venture is quite unknown to the public. Therefore, it is important that the Human Rights Committee must be made more effective and operative until and unless state Human Rights Commission is formed in the state.

4. Human Rights friendly behaviour of the police personnel is one of the most important foundations of human rights culture. There is no doubt that maintenance of law and order, detection of crime, booking of criminals, prevention of anti-social and criminal etc., are the very corner stones of police functioning. Nevertheless, the police personnel from the highest to the lowest ranks are inclined to think that they can behave in any manner they like, and the human rights of the public hardly matters because they are the custodians of the law. Mizoram is not an exception in this regard.

   In order to create human rights culture among the police personnel, it is now emphasized that police personnel must be better equipped with modern techniques including proper training on human rights. In this connection, it is further suggested that the Women Cell (Estbilished 1998) at Aizawl Police Station needs to be properly equipped with more staffs and other facilities.

5. Fair and impartial judicial administration based on the principles of equality and judicial independence is the main foundation of human rights culture. The administration of justice in Mizoram is being carried on in a very simple and rude form since the Indian independence. Justice is maintained on the basis of well established Mizo Custom

and modern legal system. Only the well-to-do persons in the Mizo society have been beneficiaries of this confused state of judicial administration. This trend is in fact a matter of denial of justice to the poor people.

Another most serious complication in the judicial administration of Mizoram is absence of separation of judiciary from the executive control. Despite strong pressure for the separation of judiciary from the executive control, separation of judiciary has not yet been practiced in Mizoram till today. It is thus an inevitable duty for the state government to take concrete measures for the realization of this requirement. There is no valid reason for not separating judiciary from executive in Mizoram having the most literate population among the Indian Union.

6. Development targeting general welfare of the people must be the main objective of the State Government. All the developmental schemes and projects must be made people oriented. Public officials engaging in this field need to have a fresh look at discharging their duties. More emphasis must be given to realize human development to ensure right to life in all its ramifications. Right to life mentioned in Article 21 of the Constitution of India does not mean a mere existence but to live with dignity and freedom from starvation. Therefore, a mere physical existence without availability of basic human needs like food, shelter, and medical facilities are not enough conditions for living. The development schemes and programmes are not bearing desired result. The capitalistic pattern of development needs to be readjusted to realize the welfare interests/needs of the rural people/masses comprising around 80 per cent of the total population of Mizoram. Otherwise the growing frustration among the youth would surely have negative impact.
7. Education system in the state must strive for the fullest development of human potential of every person through enlarging the coverage and improving the quality of education. Hence standard education system ensuring equity and social justice is an urgent need. In this regard responsible

public officials must take concerted effort by framing state education system to meet requirements of the present society.

8. The prevalence of rampant corruption is another serious matter. Administrative functionaries at all levels seem to be more interested in making money by wrongful means rather than delivering the goods to the public. Corruption denies the public of the benefits of development. Corruption is, in reality, a serious violation of human rights for it has deprived the people of means (purchasing power or money) to realizing human right ideals such as basic necessities like food, water, and shelter. It is a pity that the state administration has chosen to remain more or less a mere spectator of this malaise that is now seriously affecting both efficiency of the administration and societal peace and tranquillity. The insensitivity of the administration to corruption, and hence human rights violations, can be gauged from the fact that the State's Anti-Corruption Branch (ACB)—the agency established specifically to check corruption of 'public servants' is manned mostly by people largely considered mediocre in official circles. The ACB is not granted autonomy as it is directly controlled by the state government and recruitments, promotion, and transfer of all the officials in the ACB are done by the state government. Therefore, it is an urgent need for the state administration to take stern action to equip the ACB with more powers and autonomy for realization of the purpose for which it had been established. Corruption endangering the whole social life must be fought with strong determination.
9. For the proper realization of the main objective of development, as opined by Amartya Sen, enhancement of human freedom should be the main target of the administration. In this regard, it is emphasized that the majority share of the total budget should be earmarked for developmental activities. It is learned that more than half of the total budget is spent on salaries and wages in Mizoram, leaving no room for developmental activities. In this regard down-sizing of administrative structure of government may be continued with sincerity so as to avoid

unnecessary expenditure on the salaries and establishments due to overstaffing.

## Conclusion

This chapter is mainly concerned with the role of CBOs *vis-à-vis* the human rights situation in Mizoram. It is to be read and interpreted with due care keeping in mind the complications and sensitivities involved in it. It is not the intention to give the impressions that state NGOs are mainly responsible for the incidence of human rights violations in the state. It is rather beyond doubt that state NGOs are working for the interest of the whole society and, in fact, only because of the positive contribution of these NGOs that the Mizo society is comparatively much better than other states in the North East in terms of promotion and protection of the welfare of the downtrodden as well as the vulnerable sections of the society.

With the change of time and growing complexity of the Mizo society, many instances of law and order problems are now coming up in Mizoram. Apart from the anti-social elements, some NGOs in some circumstances are posing problems. The law and order situation had some negative impact on the life and liberty or basic rights of the citizens. The need in the case is that leaders of these NGOs need to be properly equipped with human rights awareness. Only a slight change in the attitude of the leaders of NGOs towards rights of every citizen irrespective of membership to any organizations, social status, political affiliation, faith, sex, caste, or identity would serve the purpose. This will make the Mizo more human rights conscious and friendly community.

## NOTES

1. Extraordinary Gazette of India (Part-II Section 3, Sub-section 1 dated 6.3.1966, published by the Government of India.
2. C. Nunthara, (1996). *Mizoram, Society and Polity.* Indus Publishing Company, New Delhi, p. 201.
3. C. Thangmura, (2000-01). *Human Rights leh Kan Khawtlang Nun (Mizo)* (Human Rights and Mizo Social life) vol.xii, Bangalore Mizo Association, Annual Magaizine, p. 69.
4. See Brig. Thenphunga Sailo, *A Soldier Story* (Cambridge Laser Print, Calcutta, 2000) p. 101.

5. As recorded by the Zonet Cable News Services telecast on 24.10.06.
6. *Zozam Magazine* (Mizo) vol. II, issue no.9, October 11-17, 2005.
7. The memorandum contained following newspaper reports such as—

   (i) *Bawngkawn, Aizawl locality Joint Action Committee (JAC) and Village Council jointly drove 40 families out of their homes said to be peddling in drugs and intoxicating substances (*Aizawl Post, *12th October 2004).*

   (ii) *Alleged drug peddler, Mr. Lalliana s/o Zorama had his ankle broken by members of a group calling itself Mizo Tlangvalte (MTV) (*Vanglaini *28th February 2005).*

   (iii) *Mr. Zokhuma of Thuampui locality was beaten up by a mob and his Maruti car burned because of allegations in involvement in drug dealings on January 22, 2005. Many local papers reported the incidence on 22 January 2005).*

   (iv) *A vehicle belongings to Ms Kawlchhungi and a house belonging to Mrs Remchhungi were destroyed by a mob from Bawngkawn locality on 26 January 2005 (*Vanglaini *Daily, dated 28 January 2005).*

   (v) *Mr. Zothanbuanga's house was vandalized by a mob from Republic locality on 25th February 2005 (*Tawrhbawm *Daily dated 28th January 2005).*

   (vi) *Mr. Vanlalzuia, Commander of Mizo Tlangvalte (MTV) issued a Press Release on 23rd February where he owned up a barbarous action taken against alleged 5 drug peddlers (a verbatim reproduction of the Press Release in* Vanglaini *Daily dated 28th February 2005).*

   (vii) *A house belonging to one Mr. Famkima, an alleged alcohol peddler, located at Airfield locality, Tuirial Village was destroyed by the local residents on 25th March 2005 (A news report in the* Aizawl Post *Daily dated 26th March 2005).*

   (viii) *May 5, 2005; Mr. Islam Laskar-44 of Sonai Road, Silchar jump from a fourth storey floor while in the custody of the Khatla YMA Branch on drug peddling charge and suffered serious injuries (a news report in the* Aizawl Post *dated 9 May 2005).*

   (ix) *Two young men were ankle-cuffed and displayed in public (at roadside) at Rangvamual locality on March 13, 2005 for allegedly carrying alcohol (a news report in* Vanglaini *14th March 2005). The same newspapers report said Rangvamual Village Defence Party (VDP) members collected money from persons found possessing alcohol and drugs which was used by the VDP towards "administrative costs".*

   (x) *An alleged drug dealer Mr. N. Rajen Singh, a Manipuri was beaten up by members of the Central Young Mizo Association (CYMA)'s Supply Reduction Service, (a special body formed by CYMA to succumbing to his injuries (a news report in the* Aizawl Post *dated March 18, 2005*).

**REFERENCES**

*Annual Report, (2004-2005).* National Human Rights Commission, New Delhi.

*Chhinlung, (Mizo) (2000-2001).* Vol. XII. Publiished by Bangalore Mizo Association.

Dr. V.K. Anand and RK Singh, (2003). *Human Rights*, Allahabad Law Agency.

K.P. Saksena, (1995). Human Rights, Lancers Book, New Delhi.

Prasad, R.N. and P. Chakraborty (ed), (2006). *Administration of Justice in Mizoram.* Mittal Publications, New Delhi.

Thenphunga Sailo, Brig., AVSM (Rtd.) (2000). *A Soldier's Story*, Cambridge Laser Print, Calcutta.

# Chapter 20

## High Court in Mizoram: The Structure and Function of Aizawl Bench

S. NONGPOKNGANBA MEITEI

### Introduction

Mizoram has transformed itself from being an illusive land before the advent of British to a province of Assam and then a Union territory and now a full-fledged state of the Indian republic. The justice system in Mizoram has also changed through the tides of times. The tribes of Mizoram remained unaffected by foreign political influence until the British annexed Assam in 1826 under the Treaty of Yandabo. During the next decades, Mizo raids into British territory led to occasional punitive expeditions by the British. Although not formally annexed until the early 1890s, the region had come under British control two decades earlier. For the first few years after the British annexation, Lushai Hills in the north remained under Assam while the southern half remained under Bengal. Both these parts were amalgamated in 1898 into one district called Lushai Hills District under the Chief Commissioner of Assam. With the implementation of the North-Eastern Reorganization Act in 1972, Mizoram became a Union Territory and as a sequel to the signing of the historic memorandum of settlement between Government of India and the Mizo National Front in 1986, it was granted statehood on 20 February 1987[1] with the enactment of the Mizoram State Act of 1986.

**The Justice System in the Lushai Hills**

In the Lushai Hills (the present Mizoram) before its annexation by the British, the Chief was the head of the village and the sovereign master of the villagers. He was the source of law, the fountain of justice and he must administer justice according to the customary law. His decision was final and there was no appeal against his decision though aggrieved person could get his case retried.[2] This was the state of affairs then and there was not much change in the administration of justice even after the advent of British in this part of the country. But with the independence of the country, changes started to take place for the better.

The officers entrusted with the administration of justice in the Lushai Hills during the British Raj were the Head of the Province, the Chief Commissioner of Assam till 1921 and the Governor till 1958, and the superintendents and his assistants, the Chiefs and the head men.[3] But the High Court of Fort William (Calcutta) had no jurisdiction over the Lushai Hills,[4] even though the said High Court was exercising jurisdiction over Assam and the Lushai Hills was a part of it at that time. During 1874 to 1952, the Superintendent was competent to try any case and to pass sentence of death, transportation or imprisonment up to the maximum amount awardable under the Indian Penal Code, whipping, and fine up to any amount subject to the condition that the sentence of death or transportation were subject to confirmation of the head of the province. Further all sentences of imprisonment of seven years and upwards were subject to the confirmation of the Commissioner of the Assam Division.[5] This situation continued till the establishment of the Assam High Court (now the Gauhati High Court). Till this time the Assam Governor used to exercise the powers of an appellate as well as revision court except in cases where sentence of death had been passed by the deputy commissioner. The Governor in exercise of such powers could call for the proceedings of any officers subordinate to him and reduce, enhance or cancel any sentence passed or remand the case for retrial. But as soon as the Assam High Court was established, this High Court started exercising such original, appellate, or other jurisdiction exercisable by the Governor immediately before the prescribed day that is 5.4.1948.[6] However, it may be stated that the first Rule to administer justice in the Lushai Hills which was promulgated by the British was the Rules for the Regulation of the procedure of officers appointed to administer justice in the Lushai Hills, 1906. But with a view to regulate the cases of awarding of death sentences, a separate rule, namely "Rules regarding Sentences of Death in the Lushai Hills was promulgated on 1915. The said two Rules, however, ceased to continue with the promulgation of the Rules for the regulation of the procedure by officers appointed to administer justice in the Lushai Hills, 937 which came into effect from 25.3.1937[7] and this Rules of 1937 continued to have effect in its application to all classes of persons without any differences till 1953 when the Lushai Hills District Council promulgated the Lushai Hills Autonomous District (Administration of Justice) Rules, 1953. These Rules specifically provide that the three classes of courts, namely District Council Courts, Sub District Council Courts, and the Village Council Courts shall try suits and cases between the parties all of whom belong to a schedule tribe or tribes. But these courts cannot try cases involving offences punishable with death, transportation for life or imprisonment for a term of not less than five years unless specifically empowered so by the Governor. From this follows that now there are two systems of courts functioning in Mizoram; the courts of the Deputy Commissioner and his assistants and the District Council Courts.

### *The Judiciary in Mizoram*

The historic signing of the Mizoram Peace Accord between the Mizo National Front under the leadership of Laldenga and the Government of India on 30th June 1986 marked a new and great beginning for Mizoram. This event has as well represented too another big milestone in the judicial and legal history of Mizoram. Para 12 (iii) of the said Memorandum of Settlement clearly provides, "In the light of the Prime Minister's statement at the joint Conference of the Chief Justices, Chief Ministers and Law Ministers held at New Delhi on 31st August, 1985, Mizoram will be entitled to have a High Court of its own, if it so wishes." Accordingly, the President of India promulgated on June 21, 1990 the Gauhati High Court (Establishment of a Permanent Bench at Aizawl) Order, 1990 by invoking the provisions of Section 31(2) of the North Eastern Areas (Reorganization) Act of 1971 thereby providing for establishment of a Permanent Bench of Gauhati High Court at Aizawl. The order further envisaged that not less than two judges shall sit at Aizawl. Here mentioned also can be made that the North Eastern Areas (Reorganization) Act of 1971 has provided for creation of the Union territory of Mizoram. At the same time this Act has also provided for establishment of a common High Court of Assam, Nagaland, Meghalaya, Manipur and Tripura by abolishing the then existing Assam (and Nagaland) High Court to be known as the Gauhati High Court (the High Court of Assam, Nagaland, Meghalaya, Manipur and Tripura) and has further extended the jurisdiction of the said High Court over the Union territory of Mizoram. Though the extension of jurisdiction of the said common High Court has been made over the Union territory of Mizoram, no provision was made for establishment of a separate bench of the High Court for Mizoram though the President of India is authorized to establish permanent bench of the said High Court at one or more places within the territories over which the said court exercise jurisdiction which include the Union territory of Mizoram.

The Aizawl Permanent Bench of the Gauhati High Court was established on the 5th July 1990 and was inaugurated by the then Chief Justice of India, Mr. Justice S. B. Mukherjee (L), in the presence of the then Chief Justice of the Gauhati High Court, Hon'ble Mr. Justice A. Raghuvir, the then Governor of Mizoram, Mr. Swaraj Kaushal and Chief Minister Mr. Lal Thanhawla. The said Bench is situated at a distance of about 5 kms from the heart of Aizawl City. The majority of the cases are of civil nature mainly concerning service matters. The Mizo as such are peace loving in nature, and there are very few major criminal cases. Many disputes are being settled in the village and District Council Courts. About 60 Officers and Staff headed by the Registrar man the Registry of the Aizawl Permanent Bench of the Gauhati High Court.[8] The first bench was constituted by the late Hon'ble Justice Y.I. Singh and Hon'ble Justice W.A. Shishak and it started initially with about 85 cases which were earlier registered at the principle seat at Guwahati. Till early November 2000, about 1800 cases have been registered at the Aizawl Bench of the Gauhati High Court and about 1550 cases have been disposed.[9] The statistics of the year 2006 show that 360 numbers of civil cases was the balance of cases to be disposed as on 1.1.2006 and 373 new civil cases were instituted from 1.1.2006 to 31.12.2006 whereas only 299 of such cases could be disposed of in the said year leaving a balance of 434 civil cases to be disposed as on 31.12.06. On the other hand 23 criminal cases were pending as on 1.1.2006 and 43 criminal cases were instituted during the whole of the said year out of which a total of 37 criminal cases were disposed leaving 29 criminal cases pending as on 31-12-06 thereby leaving a total number of 463 cases pending as on 31-12-06.[10]

Needless to say, the Aizawl Bench of the Gauhati High Court exercises its territorial jurisdiction over the entire state of Mizoram. Any case that arises within Mizoram which can be filed before the High Court under its original or appellate or other jurisdiction shall be filed in the Aizawl Bench. However, in exceptional and exigent circumstances, a case which arises within Mizoram may be filed in the principal seat in Guwahati after taking prior permission from the Chief Justice. Article 215 of the Constitution of India provides that every High Court shall be a court of record and shall have all the powers of such a court including the power to punish for contempt of itself. Article 225 further provides that the High Court shall exercise jurisdiction as per the relevant laws which was existing immediately before the commencement of the Constitution and therefore, in case of the Gauhati High Court, it shall primarily mean the Assam High Court Order, 1948 among others. From this Order of 1948, the Constitution of India, the Assam High Court (Jurisdiction over District Council Courts) Order, 1954, the Rules for the Regulation of the Procedure of Officers Appointed to Administer Justice in the Lushai Hills, 1937 popularly known as Administration of Justice Rules, 1937 and the Lushai Hills Autonomous District (Administration of Justice) Rules, 1953 popularly known as Administration of Justice Rules, 1953 and of course, the Gauhati High Court Rules, 1954 amongst others, it can issue writs or any other directions as per the provisions of Art 226 of the Constitution of India in matters that arise in Mizoram and in respect of which it can issue such writ or direction. It can also exercise supervisory jurisdiction over all the subordinate courts and tribunals existing in the state. It also can entertain election petition under its original jurisdiction. It can also exercise appellate and revisional jurisdiction from the judgements and orders passed by the District Council Courts or the Deputy Commissioner.

It goes without saying that the establishment of the Aizawl Permanent Bench has benefited the people of Mizoram to a very great extent. Before its establishment people had to go up to Guwahati to file their cases for the enforcement of their rights thereby forcing the litigant to travel a very long distance and also incurring heavy expenses. So it was one of the greatest hurdles for the people in their tryst for justice. Another strongly felt benefit is that there has been a greater awareness of the rights among the people as more and more people comes forward for the enforcement of their right. The increase in the amount of litigation clearly indicates that a legal awakening has been commenced. His Lordship B.S. Reddy, the former Chief Justice of the Gauhati High Court who is now elevated to judge of the Supreme Court of India in an informal chit-chat have said to a remark from the bar that there has been an increase in the number of litigation in Mizoram in the Gauhati High Court after the Aizawl Permanent Bench has been established that it is a good sign, let more people come forward to enforce their rights. His Lordship was quite right in his view. In fact an increase in the litigation in other parts of the country may not have been a bad sign in view of the fact that alternative dispute resolution has been considered as a better solution than litigation in settling disputes. But in Mizoram where legal awareness and rights consciousness is still in its infancy, an increase in the number of litigation is a good sign indicating the increased awareness of law and rights. This awareness to a great extent is the result of the establishment of the permanent bench at Aizawl where the people in general are seeing rights being enforced with their own eyes. Certainly legal awareness and rights consciousness is contagious. This sense traverses from one to another after the rights of the one is being enforced in front of the very eyes of the other. In fact the permanent bench of Aizawl in the last sixteen seventeen years from its inception, has played its role of sensitizing the people about their rights and bringing legal awareness to the masses. Some of the activities which have been taken up by this bench can be summed up as follows:[11]

- The first Lok Adalat in the state of Mizoram was held in the year 1993 under the chairmanship of Justice S.N. Phukan.
- On the occasion of the Golden Jubilee Celebration of the Gauhati High Court, the first official function was held in Aizawl where a seminar on the "Administration of Justice in pre- and post-independence in the state of Mizoram" was held on 17th July, 1998 under the chairmanship of Justice V.D. Gyani, Chief Justice (Acting) of the Gauhati High Court. This seminar was jointly organized by the Aizawl Permanent Bench and the Law Research Institute of Gauhati.
- The Mizoram State Legal Service Authority under the Chairmanship of the Justice H.K.K. Singh has been

constituted for providing legal aid and awareness to the people of Mizoram.

- The High Court Legal Services Committee has also been established under the chairmanship of Justice D. Biswas.[12]
- The Mizoram State Human Rights Committee under the chairmanship of Shri R. Thanga, Registrar of the Aizawl Permanent Bench has been constituted with effect from February 7, 2002 by order of the Chief Justice of the Gauhati High Court. The Committee members are Inspector General of Prisons, Deputy Commissioner, Aizawl, Superintendent of Police (CID), and Additional District Magistrate (Judicial), Aizawl and this Committee had visited jails, district courts, police stations, etc. at Lunglei, Saiha and Champhai.[13]

Another very remarkable benefit that has been reaped by Mizoram after the establishment of the Aizawl Bench is the elevation of Shri Tinlianthang Vaiphei as Additional Judge, Gauhati High Court on 17-7-2003 from Mizoram. This event in the History of Mizoram has come sooner than latter due to the establishment of the said Aizawl Bench which has and is polishing the young entrants into intelligent wizard for a better Mizoram. In fact the establishment of the said bench has made the legal profession greener in Mizoram attracting more people into the profession of law. I would also like to mention lastly but not the least that the establishment of the Aizawl Permanent Bench has not only created jobs for Mizoram but also has developed Luangmual physically where the bench is situated into a hub. The High Court is employing a number of persons starting from the Registrar to the librarian to the peon and these employment should not have been there if the Bench had not come to Aizawl. Thus the Aizawl Permanent Bench has also helped in solving employment problem in the state to a certain extent. On the other hand the coming of this Bench has led to enhancing the importance of the place thereby requiring better road connectivity and availability of other things. Now this place has seen a tremendous improvement on road conditions. A local lady who is a small vendor in Luangmual whom I happened to talk to told me that the roads in Luangmual and from Aizawl to Lungmual has become better because of Justice N.S. Singh. In fact this Justice N.S. Singh who is now transferred to the High Court of Sikkim had pulled up the state administration to make the roads much better and his act has really born fruit also. Now Luangmual is no more a sleepy village at the outskirt of Aizawl City.

However, everything is not rosy. The present court complex is without adequate facilities apart from its distance from the city. There is no proper bar room, no bar library, no staff quarter, etc. Even the Judge's library which is maintained by the court now is not just well equipped with sufficient number and varieties of books and with modern facilities. Even today two Public Interest Litigation cases are pending before the Aizawl Bench itself being filed by the Mizoram Bar Association: one for allotting a plot of land in or around the city of Aizawl for location of the high court building and the other for issuance of a direction for separation of judiciary from executive in the state of Mizoram.

The present temporary location of the Aizawl Bench where it has been situated since its inception in 1990 till date is at least about 5-6 km from the city of Aizawl and this is creating a lot of practical problem. Aizawl being hilly, and the roads though has improved tremendously in recent times, being meandering, it is not so easy to come to the High Court. Though the conditions of the roads have considerably improved in recent times, for the common man who relies on public transport, it is still not a small problem to come to this court. The bus service that is available between Aizawl City and Luangmual (government complex to be specific) where the court is situated is only in hourly interval and the taxi service is available only at a high fare. Also one has to spend his whole day once he has come to this court due to the practical problems that he faces in coming over to this court. As a matter of fact the problem is also very felt even by the advocates and other staffs of the High Court though luckily, for the staff, there is a staff bus plying for them. Here it shall not be wrong to say that to a great extent the location of the High Court Aizawl Bench is denying the people a very easy access to justice though it may be equally true for a town planner to say that everything cannot be inside the present city area of Aizawl and this small city needs expansion.

As said just hereinabove the present location is only a temporary location but so far even after 17 years, there seems to be no concrete and effective plan to shift the bench to a permanent place. The Aizawl bench was initially offered for consideration and acceptance at Berampu Tlang within Luanmual. However this site was found inadequate and in June 1991, Hon'ble Mr. Justice W.A. Shishak, one of the then station judge of Aizawl Bench, was shown a site at Khatla

(Assam Rifles Complex for vacation of which the government is taking steps since quite long) which was supposedly earmarked for the Aizawl bench by the then Law Secretary, Shri K.N. Srivastava. Even when a plan of capital expansion project was made in 1998, a plot of land in the said Assam Rifles complex was actually earmarked for High Court complex. However quite unfortunately, when the master-plan and estimate for the proposed facilities at Assam Rifles areas has been made in the year 2000 no site for the High Court has been included either in the said area. And now the Government is offering land in the capital complex area which land is also quite inadequate.[14]

However, after a lapse of even seventeen years of its existence, the Aizawl Bench of the Gauhati High Court and despite the fact that so many communications not only from the registry of the court but also from the judges has been made to the state government, the court is not still having a permanent land and complex of its own and it is still running in the present temporary complex with inadequate facilities. The present government also has remained not benign enough to look into the matter and actively pursue the matter and work towards better legal and judicial development in the state.

Another worry that is eating the legal and judicial mind of the people is the nonchalant attitude of the present government towards separation of the judiciary from the executive. Though the existence or non-existence of the Aizawl bench does not directly relate with the separation of judiciary from the executive, the establishment of the Aizawl Bench has given a large fillip in the movement for separation of judiciary from the executive inasmuch as the coming of this bench has enlightened the people about their rights and the judges also it seems when they meet the state government officials, they impressed upon the government about the need of separation, though. In fact the movement for separation of judiciary from the executive in the state of Mizoram may be said to have actively commenced with the filing of Civil Rule (HC) No. 30 of 1985 (Dingliana *Vs* U.T. of Mizoram and others) in which case the government has submitted that the question of separation of Judiciary from the executive is under active consideration of the government but this "active consideration" of the government has not resulted into the separation till date even after more than 22 years from the date of making this statement, though of course the government at certain times makes some splashes. It may be mentioned here that separation of judiciary from the executive is the mandate of the

Constitution of India and it is in line with the spirit of the legal and judicial system of the country. Even the Supreme Court of the country in *All India Judges' Association and others* Vs. *Union of India and others*[15] has professed the need of separation of judiciary from the executive. But till date nothing has happened. Now what is to be seen is that the Gauhati High Court Aizawl Bench before which the present public interest litigation being filed by the Mizoram Bar Association for separation is pending can really do the job.

It also remains a hard fact that even though the Aizawl Bench has been called a permanent bench, it is now practically functioning like a circuit bench to the discontentment of all concerned. Though there is a station judge for name's sake, (the sanctioned number is two judges) there is no judge actually stationing in Aizawl throughout. The judge comes generally for two weeks in a month and for the rest of the month the court rooms remain vacant. Sometimes though programme for holding court has been made, the court cannot be hold due to non-arrival of the designated judge because of certain reason, the most frequently cited reason being cancellation of flight to Aizawl or otherwise the holding of court is delayed for one or two days. In fact administrative difficulties have also been cited for the present pathetic situation. However, one may feel tempted to ask as to why such a situation is prevailing when the sanctioned number of twenty-two judges and one Chief Justice of the Gauhati High Court are well in place. It may be bitter to be swallowed but it is true that, Aizawl Bench is at the bottom of the priority list of all six outlying benches of the Gauhati High Court. This may be because, there are less cases filed and pending in this bench in comparison to other benches and the bar here is very small. As of now the total number of advocates practicing in the whole of Mizoram is less than one hundred and those who are practicing in the High Court is only a handful ten/fifteen advocates. And also perhaps the standard of the bar is not up to the mark. On the other hand the Principal Seat at Guwahati as it undoubtedly should be and the Imphal and Agartala Benches remain always busy with pending cases pilling up day by day and hence more priorities are given to these benches. These may be some of the reasons why the Aizawl bench has not been put on upper priority. Be that as it may, the same age old problem of requiring to travel up to Guwahati to file cases still remains if the case to be filed is of urgent nature and if it is "off days" of the court in Aizawl Bench.

## Conclusion

Though there are some dark sides, the establishment of the permanent bench has really solved a great deal of problems which Mizoram faced earlier. There cannot be any denial that the establishment of the Aizawl Bench had benefited the people and the state. However, it also goes without saying that there is also room for improvement and further development of the bench. For this not only the state government but also the bench and the bar and of course the public in general, need to work towards it as an avowed mission. To this end the first step must be the separation of judiciary which hopefully shall come through in the next few months. This will enhance the importance of the said bench to a much higher level. Needless to say the increase in importance and ultimately the inevitableness of the Bench in the society shall, finally, bestow the place which Aizawl bench of the Gauhati High Court deserves. This shall enable the court to protect the rights of the people from arbitrariness and violation.

### NOTES

1. http://www.economywatch.com/stateprofiles/mizoram/profile-oldversion.htm.
2. Rao, V. Venkata, Thansanga, H. and Hazarika Niru (1987). *A Century of Government and Politics in North-East India*, Vol. III, Mizoram, p. 225.
3. *Supra* 2 page 226.
4. *Supra* 2 Page 225.
5. *Supra* 2 page 226.
6. Chakraborty, P., (1995). *Mizoram Compendium of laws,* Vol. II., pp. 41-42.
7. *Supra* 6 page 18-19.
8. http://ghconline.gov.in/mizoram.html.
9. "Brief History of the Aizawl Permanent Bench: Gauhati High Court by Sh. Lalhuamliana published in the Souvenir published at the occasion of the North East High Court Employees' Conference held from 10-12 November, 2000 held at Guwahati. p. 10.
10. http://ghconline.gov.in/stats.html.
11. *Supra* 9, page 10-11.
12. *North East* (Sunday, September, 14, 2003)
13. *Ibid.*
14. The Registrar of this Bench has forwarded the requirement of the proposed High Court complex in a letter dt. 5-8-91 to the Government of Mizoram.
15. AIR 1993 SC 2493.

# Chapter 21

## Information and Communication Technologies (ICT) Application in Higher Education with Special Reference to Mizoram

PRAVAKAR RATH

### Introduction

Universities in the country form the pillar of success of higher education and are aimed at advancement of knowledge and learning through teaching and research. These institutions of higher learning require constant support from the government, teachers, and students. Besides application of Information and Communication Technologies (ICT) is deployed for ensuring quality higher education for all and promote excellence in the changing information scenario. This new technology is used by the people and supposed to help especially in the areas of education, efficient government administration, economic development etc. The major advantages of such new technology are:

- New technologies have potential to change the teaching-learning paradigm in a way that has not been possible before.
- New technologies have a profound impact on the way the research is conducted. Building new knowledge on the basis of existing knowledge and collaboration with peers—both essential part of research are possible with a maze of interconnected computers and huge distributed knowledge repositories sitting in different parts of the world in a manner that was even difficult to think before.

- New technologies have also significantly impacted the governance both at the institutional and the systemic level in the higher education system.

As on date there are 310 universities (Central, State, Deemed) in India out of which 15 universities and more than 300 colleges are located in North-Eastern states. North Eastern states consist of Arunachal Pradesh, Assam, Manipur, Meghalaya, Mizoram, Nagaland, Tripura and Sikkim. Although Department of North Eastern Region (DONER) and North Eastern Council (NEC) have taken a number of initiatives for the development of the region, still development of higher education needs top most priority at par with other developed states of the country. The present paper discusses about the essential resources required by the institutions of higher learning in Mizoram as well as the national level for qualitative delivery of teaching and research and to achieve learning outcomes with special emphasis on ICT applications. These resources/ components include:

**Resources for Higher Education**

- *Physical Resources*: Physical resources not only include building, furniture and equipment, laboratories and libraries but in today's age of information, computer, and communication infrastructure (Information and Communication Technologies) are very much essential in the present global scenario for socio-economic and educational development and creation of manpower and fast communication and competition in the global market as well. The successful delivery of the courses offered by colleges and universities could only be possible with the help of state-of-the-art technology and infrastructure. Libraries and Laboratories also form part of the infrastructure in strengthening the pillar of higher education of this region. This will go a long way in generating ethos to attract students of all India basis and foster national integration sand requires a provision of specially tailored development grants for the universities of hill regions by University Grants Commission.
- *Human Resources:* Human Resources constitute both

teaching and non-teaching community, their recruitment and training. Teaching community plays an important role to achieve academic standards of the university. Therefore, teachers need to be up-to-date and revise the curriculum and syllabus at periodic interval in imparting knowledge and skills to the learners. Equally important is to retain the talented teachers in order to realize the vision of all India character particularly in the distant hill regions. Schemes of financial incentives will help to fight the prejudice among the highly accomplished professionals. This will further brighten up the prospect of quality education, on par with the best of the universities in the country and for students of the far-flung areas.

- *Financial Resources:* Regular flow of finance not only maintains standards of higher education but build up a sound university and higher education system to support physical and telecommunication infrastructure.

**Teaching and Learning in Changing Scenario**

The best teaching and learning outcome could be achieved when the universities in this region adopt need based courses (both conventional and non-conventional) with up-to-date Syllabus and Curriculum which is competitive in the global market. This requires selection and timely recruitment of good teachers, training and development, adequate teaching aids, technological support etc. Besides the conventional and emerging disciplines, emphasis on professional subjects with appropriate learning environment could give rise to unique institution of higher learning. In the changing scenario of teaching and learning, faculty members play an important role in capacity building (creativity, innovations and transfer of knowledge, capacity to use high technology). Success of the students determine the testimony of faculty members. The role of faculty members in 21st century higher education is to create competition in the global market. Education through technology-based learning making full use of developments in Information and Communication Technologies such as video conferencing, web-based education will accelerate the pace of learning. Distance education through invoking IT should eventually lead to the establishment of cyber universities imparting anytime, anywhere and anyone education.

## University Library and Information System

In order to supplement the teaching and learning activities, universities and higher education institutions in the country require an effective and efficient library and information system with up to date multi-media educational resources. University Libraries should develop digital collections, which could be easily accessible by students and teaches, there by providing more contents with less cost. Design and development of library website can upload vast amount of information resources like e-books, e-journals, reference collections and provide the opportunity to teachers and learners to access these resources anytime, anywhere, any medium and eliminate the duplication of money, manpower and material. The computerized and networked based services like alerting, document delivery, database, CAS and SDI could supplement the teaching and learning in effective and efficient manner.

## Creation and Maintenance of University Website

Each and every university should have its own website which not only provides an opportunity to that university fraternity but all others who are interested to know the courses offered by that university, admission policy and it forms an appropriate means of communication among the universities at national and international level. The website can also provide a link for library website. Regular maintenance (addition, deletion and updation) of both university and library website can be accessible from distant location not only by the all university fraternity but anybody from outside the university interested to know more about the universities and its resources. This will further facilitate to develop and strengthen university management system in the decision making process.

## UGC Mandate on Higher Education

Higher Education system in the country is a loose configuration of heterogeneous organizational units—universities, colleges, professional councils etc. This diversity is a source of excellence and makes it vibrant. Coordination of such a diverse system of education is tricky yet necessary to ensure its credibility. UGC is mandated to ensure coordinated development of higher education system in the Country—Ensuring Quality Higher Education for All. More specifically, UGC would like to:

- Leverage its funding to bring about change in the higher education in the country in a systematic manner.
- Adopt objective based criteria for funding of universities and colleges maintained by it that promotes greater accountability and would like the other funding agencies to adopt similar mechanism.
- Provide an efficient mechanism for data collection, compilation and dissemination on higher education with more comprehensive coverage.
- Better targeting and monitoring of research funding both by it and through other funding agencies.
- Promote greater collaboration between higher education institutions themselves and with industry and society through sharing of expertise and facilities.
- Provide credible information about higher education institutions and programmes—including their recognition status and accreditation details in partnership with Professional Councils.
- Ensure a grievance redressal mechanism for students and parents linking it with processes of inspections etc.
- Create a labour market information system for graduates by evolving a mechanism for tracking them and build up confidence in education loans.
- Create a Knowledge Repository for communities of teachers and researchers in the country.

With such an ambitious mandate and huge system of higher education, adoption of an IT strategy is a must. A properly implemented information system project in the higher education sector would not only enhance its efficiency and effectiveness at the operational level, but also bring about a paradigm shift in the management of the higher education system.

**Higher Education in Mizoram: Some Suggestions**

Government should give special attention to the universities located in north-eastern, remote/inaccessible areas specially the young universities like Mizoram University in strengthening the higher education system. The Ministry of HRD, University Grants

Commission, UGC-Infonet, Information and Library Network, Education and Research Network should make all efforts to strengthen ICT resources and its application in eliminating remoteness and providing access to vast amount on information resources to students, teachers, and research scholars. Effective coordination among these three networks will provide opportunities to the learners, teachers, and researcher for easy access to the huge electronic recourses, which will save an unnecessary duplication of funds being spent by the universities for the same journals and other electronic educational resources. Some of the existing opportunities that may be availed by all the universities located in the north-eastern region in general and Mizoram in particular for the greater interest of the teachers and learners are explained below.

### *EDUSAT*

Launching of Educational Satellite (EDUSAT) is a revolution in India. EDUSAT is the first Indian satellite built exclusively for serving the educational sector. It is mainly intended to meet the demand for an interactive satellite based distance education system for the country. It strongly reflects India's commitment to use space technology for national development, especially for the development of the population in remote and rural locations.

ISRO Chairman G. Madhavan Nair, one of the main forces behind the project's launch, says, "Satellites can establish the connectivity between urban educational institutions with adequate infrastructure imparting quality education and the large number of rural and semi-urban educational institutions that lack the necessary infrastructure." "The universalisation of education is a top priority for the government all these years. But some 35 per cent of India's billion-plus population is illiterate. To make all of them literate, India will have to set up 10,000 new schools every year. EDUSAT is going to bring about a revolution in the field of education in the country in the coming year," as opined by ISRO chairman.

### *INFLIBNET*

Information and Library Network (INFLIBNET) Centre is an Autonomous Inter-University Centre (IUC) of University Grants Commission (UGC) involved in creating infrastructure for sharing of library and information resources and services among Academic and Research Institutions. INFLIBNET works collaboratively with Indian university libraries to shape the future of the academic libraries in evolving information environment.

The new E-Resource culture on UGC-Infonet which is a scaleable architecture will usher in a new era in academic ambiance thereby increasing productivity, opening new vistas of research, collaborative ventures and reduce turnaround time and contribute to the education growth enabler. Successful implementation of UGC-Infonet has created many avenues and new challenges for INFLIBNET to take up. Academic community has immensely benefited out of the UGC-Infonet E-Journal Consortia and it is felt that the facility should be extended to the colleges in a phased manner.

### *Education and Research Network (ERNET)*

ERNET was initiated in 1986 by the Department of Electronics (DoE), with funding support from the Government of India and United Nations Development Program (UNDP), involving eight premier institutions as participating agencies—NCST (National Centre for Software Technology), Bombay, IISc (Indian Institute of Science), Bangalore, five IITs (Indian Institutes of Technology) at Delhi, Bombay, Kanpur, Kharagpur and Madras, and the DoE, New Delhi. ERNET began as a multi-protocol network with both the TCP/IP and the OSI-IP protocol stacks running over the leased-line portion of the backbone. Since 1995, however, almost all traffic is carried over TCP/IP. ERNET has made a significant contribution to the emergence of networking in the country. It practically brought the Internet to India and has built up national capabilities in the area of networking, especially in protocol software engineering. It has not only succeeded in building a large network that provides various facilities to the intellectual segment of Indian society—the research and education community, it has over the years become a trendsetter in the field of networking. UNDP has lauded ERNET as one of the most successful programmes it has funded. The Government of India has committed itself to further strengthen the project by including it in the Ninth Plan with the allocation of funds and by creation of a new organisational set-up in the form of a Society. The Science community of the country has also recognized ERNET's contribution—both for infrastructure services as well as for R&D. The Scientific Advisory

Committee to the Cabinet has adopted ERNET as the platform for launching an S&T network in the country.

### *Objectives of ERNET*

- ERNET operations, i.e. providing state-of-the-art communication infrastructure and services to Academic and Research institutions, Government organisations, NGOs, private sector R&D organisations, and various other non-commercial organisations;
- Research and Development;
- Training and Consultancy; and
- Content Development.

### *UGC-Infonet*

UGC is modernizing the university campuses with state-of-the-art campuswide networks and setting up its own nationwide communication network named UGC-INFONET.

The UGC-INFONET will be overlaid on ERNET infrastructure to provide assured quality of service and optimal utilization of bandwidth resources. The project is being funded by the UGC with 90 per cent capital investment and 100 per cent recurring cost during the Tenth Plan period. A Joint Technical and Tariff Committee (JTTC), consisting of leading experts in the country has been set up to guide and monitor the entire project. INFLIBNET Centre, an autonomous IUC of the UGC, is the nodal agency for coordination of the UGC-INFONET and facilitates linkage between ERNET and the universities. UGC-INFONET will be a boon to the higher education system in several ways.

- Vehicle for distance learning.
- Tool to distribution of education material and journals to remotest of areas.
- Resource for researchers and scholars for tapping most up-to-date information.
- Medium for collaboration among teachers and students, not only within the country but all over the world.
- On Intranet for university automation.
- Establish a channel for globalization of education.

- Use of ICT and Internet for virtual enhancement of Academic Infrastructure.

UGC-INFONET was formally inaugurated by the Hon'ble Prime Minister on 28th December, 2002.

### *UGC-Infonet Training*

Training manpower is one of the most critical resources for successful implementation of high-tech programmes like UGC-INFONET. INFLIBNET/ERNET is giving training to network managers and library professionals for managing the WAN connectivity, network security, Mail Server, Web Server configuration, and e-journal access management at their premises. More than 108 network managers from around 99 universities have been trained at ERNET India, New Delhi. Around 63 Library professionals from more than 63 universities have been trained at ERNET India, New Delhi. Above 63 Library professionals from 63 universities have been trained for e-resources management at INFLIBNET Centre, Ahmedabad.

Main Features of the UGC-INFONET are:

- Scaleable Architecture to grow from Universities to affiliated colleges.
- Nation-wide Terrestrial Backbone using Fiber Optic links.
- Integrated Satellite WAN supporting broadband and SCPCV.SAT technology.
- Comprehensive Network Management Systems.
- Linkage with Academic and Research Networks all over the world.
- Data security and virus protection using firewalls and Intrusion Detection Systems.
- Data Centres and Mirror Sites Content Hosting.

### *UGC Infonet E-Journal Consortium*

University Grants Commission (UGC) has initiated a programme called "The UGC-Infonet E-Journals Consortium" to provide online access to electronic journals and databases in all disciplines to the universities in India. All universities which come under the purview of UGC will be beneficiary members of the programme. The scheme would be gradually extended to colleges as well. The programme is being executed by Information and Library Network (INFLIBNET) Centre, Ahmedabad, an autonomous institution under the UGC. Access to various electronic resources have formally commenced from January 1, 2004, initially for 30 universities.

The programme aims at increasing accessibility of electronic resources to the universities. It will go a long way in mitigating the severe shortage of periodicals faced by university libraries for several years. The E-Journals programme is a cornerstone of the UGC-INFONET effort, which aims at addressing the teaching, learning, research, connectivity and governance requirements of the universities. The E-Journals programme demonstrates how communication networks and computers can be used to stretch and leverage available funds in furthering these aims. The programme has been made possible due to the close and understanding cooperation between the UGC, ERNET, the Inter-University Centres IUCAA, INFLIBNET and CEC, and national and international publishers. A bouquet of e-journals was presented to the nation by His Excellency the President of India Dr. A.P.J. Abdul Kalam on 28th December 2003 during the concluding day of UGC's Golden Jubilee Celebrations.

## Conclusion

An effective and efficient higher education system supported by ICT applications can facilitate the interface with the internal and external stakeholders of the higher education system. Incremental computerization effort would involve effective utilization of existing hardware/software infrastructure including training of the staff. It also involves procurement/upgradation of additional PCs/printers, other hardware/software, and appropriate maintenance of the infrastructure. Certain standards need to be developed for computerization for institutional functions in educational set up, so that independently evolved computerization initiatives of different higher education institutions.

Higher education institutions particularly universities located in the north eastern states with the special financial support of UGC can develop ICT infrastructure as enabling technologies. These technologies can only bridge the "Digital Divide" between the states and nations. All government initiatives for promoting higher education in the country must reach its destinations irrespective of remote and inaccessible locations to derive maximum learning outcome and contribute to an emerging knowledge society. An ICT based effective higher education system in India in general and Mizoram in particular, could only lead to societal transformation in the shape of knowledge generation, exchange, and utilization that will transform itself into a knowledge superpower.

## REFERENCES

Center for the Advanced Study of India (University of Pennsylvania, USA). India in Transition: Economics and Politics of Change, India's Strategy of IT Led Growth: Challenges of Asymmetric Dependence. Philadelphia: 2005.

Department of North Eastern website (http://northeast.nic.in).

India, Planning Commission (2001). India as a Knowledge Superpower: Strategy for Transformation. New Delhi: Planning Commission. 2001.

Information and Library Network website (www.inflibnet.ac.in).

Mizoram University. Issues before the University. *A Note prepared for the Committee for Development of Central Universities in the North-East* constituted by UGC. (Ref. Chairman, UGC addressed to Vice Chancellor, Mizoram University) 21st April, 2004.

Ministry of Communication and Information Technology website (http://www.mit.gov.in/).

North Eastern Council website (www.necouncil.nic.in).

University Grants Commission website (www.ugc.ac.in).

# Appendices

## APPENDIX-1

## Agreement between the Indian National Congress (I) and the Mizo National Front, Mizoram

The Government of India under the leadership of Shri Rajiv Gandhi has brought about a situation wherein the long years of disturbed conditions in Mizoram are being brought to an end. The Memorandum of Settlement is being signed between the Government of India and Shri Laldenga, President of Mizo National Front, to give shape to this effort to usher peace and prosperity in Mizoram within the framework of the Indian Constitution. Shri Laldenga has pledged to bring the MNF into the mainstream of the Indian polity and irrevocably commit it to strive for a strong and united India.

In order to further strengthen this resolve and to enable a smooth and orderly transition the Indian National Congress (I) and the MNF headed by Shri Laldenga agree to form the coalition Government. This decision shall be implemented soon after the members of the MNF, who are underground, lay down their arms and join the national mainstream.

1. On a date agreed to between Shri Laldenga and the Government of India, Shri Lal Thanhawla, the present Congress (I) Chief Minister will submit his resignation and Sri Laldenga will be elected the leader of the Government of Mizoram and be sworn in as the Chief Minister there.
2. Shri Lal Thanhawla, the present Chief Minister, shall be sworn in as the Deputy Chief Minister.
3. In addition to the Deputy Chief Minister, four members of the Congress (I) Party shall be made Minister of the new Government.

4. In addition to the Chief Minister, three members of the MNF Party will be made Ministers.
5. The names of the Ministers will be nominated by the representative Political Parties and the Chief Minister will propose them to the Lieutenant Governor.
6. All issues concerning the formation and induction of this new Government will be decided mutually by the Chief Minister and the Deputy Chief Minister.
7. In order to smoothen the function of the coalition Government, a coordination committee will be constituted consisting of the following:

    a. Shri Laldenga, Chairman,
    b. Shri Lal Thanhawla, Vice-Chairman,
    c. Two members of the Congress Party, and
    d. Two members of the MNF Party.

    This committee will take into consideration all matters concerning the Party and the Government, which either of the Political Parties may deem necessary to bring for its consideration in order to help smooth functioning of the Government and to bring better coordination between Congress (I) and MNF.
8. This coalition Government will continue to function till such date when the President is satisfied that normalcy has returned and the holding of elections has become feasible.
9. In the event any difference arising between the two parties, they would seek the help of the Hon'ble Prime Minister.

*Sd/-*
Laldenga
President
Mizo National Front
2nd June, 1986

*Sd/-*
Arjun Singh
Vice-President
Indian National Front

# APPENDIX-2

# Mizoram Accord, 1986

## MEMORANDUM OF SETTLEMENT

### Preamble

1. Government of India have all along been making earnest effort to bring about an end to the disturbed condition in Mizoram and to restore peace and harmony.

Toward this end, initiative was taken by the late Prime Minister Smt. Indira Gandhi on the acceptance by Shri Laldenga on behalf of the Mizo National Front (MNF) of the two conditions, namely, cessation of violence by MNF and to hold talks within the framework of the Constitution. A series of discussions were held with Shri Laldenga. Settlement on various issues reached during the course of talks is incorporated in the following paragraphs.

### Restoration of Normalcy

1. With a view to restoring peace and normalcy in Mizoram, the MNF Party, in their part undertake within the agreed time-frame, to bring out all underground personnel of the MNF with their arms, ammunitions, and equipments, to ensure their return to civil life, to abjure violence and generally to help in the process of restoration of normalcy. The modalities of bringing out all underground personnel and the deposit of arms, ammunitions and equipments will be as worked out.

The implementation of the foregoing will be under the supervision of the Central Government.

2. The MNF party will take immediate steps to amend its articles of Association so as to make them conform to the provision of Law.
3. The Central Government will take steps for the settlement and rehabilitation of underground after considering the scheme proposed in this regard by the Government of Mizoram.
4. The MNF will not undertake to extend any support to the Tripura National Volunteer (TNV), Peoples' Liberation Army of Manipur (PLA) and any other such group by way of training, supply of arms of providing protection or in any other matters.

**Legal Administrative and Other Steps**

1. With a view to satisfying the desires and aspirations of all sections of the people of Mizoram, the Government will initiate measures to confer Statehood on the Union Territory of Mizoram subject to the other stipulation contained in this Memorandum of Settlement.
2. To give effect to the above, the necessary legislative and administrative measures will be undertaken, including those for the enactment of Bills for the amendment of the Constitution and other laws for the conferment of Statehood as aforesaid, to come into effect on a date to be notified by the Central Government.
3. The amendment aforesaid shall provide, among other things, for the following:

   I. The territory of Mizoram shall consist of the territory specified in Section 6 of the North Eastern Areas (Reorganization) Act, 1971.

   II. Notwithstanding anything contained in the Constitution, no act of Parliament in respect of (a) Religion or Social practices of the Mizos, (b) Mizo Customary Law or procedure, (c) Administration of Civil and Criminal Justice involving decisions according to Mizo Customary Law, (d) Ownership and transfer of land, shall apply to the State of Mizoram unless the Legislative Assembly of Mizoram by a resolution so decides:

Provided that nothing in this Clause shall apply to any Central Act in force in Mizoram immediately before the appointed day.

III. Article 170 Clause (1) shall, in relation to Legislative Assembly of Mizoram, have effect as if for the word sixty the word *forty* has been substituted.

1. Soon after the Bill of Conferment of Statehood becomes law, and when the President is satisfied that normalcy has returned and that conditions are conducive to the holding of free and fair elections, elections to the Legislative Assembly will be initiated.
2. (a) The Centre will transfer resource to the new Government keeping in view the change in Status from a Union Territory to a State and will include resources to cover the revenue gap for the year.

   (b) Central assistance for Plan will be fixed taking note of any residuary gap in resources so as to sustain the approved plan outlay and the pattern of assistance will be as in the case of Special Category State.
3. Border trade in local produced or grown agriculture commodities could be allowed under a scheme to be formulated by the Central Government, subject to International arrangement with neighbouring countries.
4. The innerline Regulation, as now in force in Mizoram, will not be amended or repealed without consulting the State Government.

**Other Matters**

5. The rights and privileges of the minorities in Mizoram as envisaged in the Constitution, shall continue to be preserved and protected and their social and economic advancement shall be ensured.

6. Steps will be taken by the Government of Mizoram at the earliest to review and codify the existing customs, practices, law or other usages relating to the matters specified in Clauses (a) to (b) of para 4.3 (II) of the memorandum, keeping in view that an individual Mizo may prefer to be governed by Acts of Parliament dealing with such matters and which are of general application.
7. The question of Unification of Mizo inhabited areas of other States to form one administrative unit was raised by the MNF delegation. It was pointed out to them, on behalf of the Government of India, that Article 3 of the Constitution of India describes the procedure in this regard but that the Government cannot make any commitment in this respect.
8. It was also pointed out on behalf of the Government that as soon as Mizoram becomes a State:

    I. The Provisions of Part XVII of the Provision of the Constitution will apply and the State will be at liberty to adopt any one or more languages to be used for all or any of the official purposes of the State.
    II. It is open to the State to move the establishment of the separate University in the State in accordance with the prescribed procedure.
    III. In the light of the Prime Minister's Statement at the Joint Conference of the Chief Justices, Chief Minister and Law Ministers held at New Delhi on 31st August, 1985 Mizoram will be entitled to have a High Court of its own if it so wishes.

1. (a) It was noted that there is already a scheme in force for payment of ex gratia amount to heirs/dependants of persons who were killed during disturbances in 1966 and thereafter in the Union Territory of Mizoram. Arrangement will be made to expeditiously disburse payment to those eligible persons who have already applied but who had not been made such payment so far.

    a. It was noted that consequence on verification done by a joint team of officers, the Government of India had already made arrangement for payment of compensation in respect of damage to crop, building destroyed/damaged during the action in Mizoram, and rented charges of building and land occupied by security force. There may, however, be some claim which were referred and verified by the above team but is not yet settled expeditiously. Arrangement will also be made for payment of pending claim of rented charges or land/building occupied by the security forces.

*Sd/-*
LALDENGA
On behalf of Mizo National Front

*Sd/-*
LALKHAMA
Chief Secretary,
Government of Mizoram

*Sd/-*
R.D. PRADHAN
Home Secretary
Government of India.

Dated: 30th June, 1986.
Place: New Delhi

---

*Note*: For more documents related to North East, kindly refer to www.satp.org.

# Index